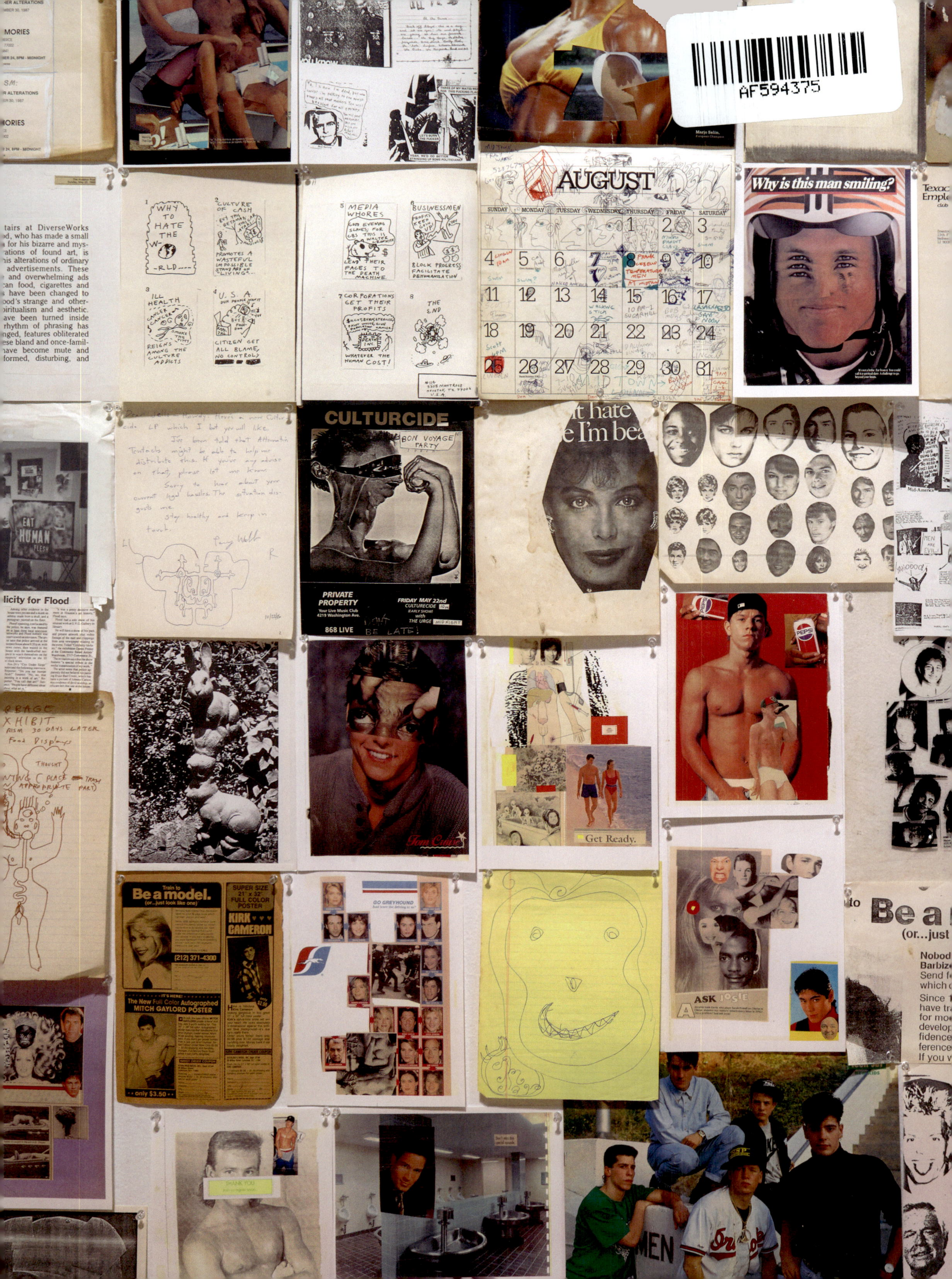

AF594375
AUGUST
SUNDAY
MONDAY
TUESDAY
WEDNESDAY
THURSDAY
FRIDAY
SATURDAY
Why is this man smiling?
WHY TO HATE THE W-RLD
CULTURE OF CASH
PROMOTES A WASTEFUL IMPOSSIBLE STANDARD OF LIVING
ILL HEALTH
REIGNS AMONG THE CULTURE ADDICTS
U.S.A.
CITIZEN GET ALL BLAME, NO CONTROL
MEDIA WHORES
LEND THEIR FACES TO THE DEATH MACHINE
BUSINESSMEN
BLOCK PROGRESS FACILITATE DEHUMANIZATION
CORPORATIONS GET THEIR PROFITS
WHATEVER THE HUMAN COST!
THE END
tairs at DiverseWorks
licity for Flood
CULTURCIDE
BON VOYAGE PARTY
PRIVATE PROPERTY
FRIDAY MAY 22nd
CULTURCIDE
868 LIVE
BE LATE!
EAT HUMAN FLESH
PEPSI
Get Ready.
Be a model.
(or...just look like one)
KIRK CAMERON
MITCH GAYLORD POSTER
only $3.50
GO GREYHOUND
ASK JOSIE
Be a
(or...just
MEN

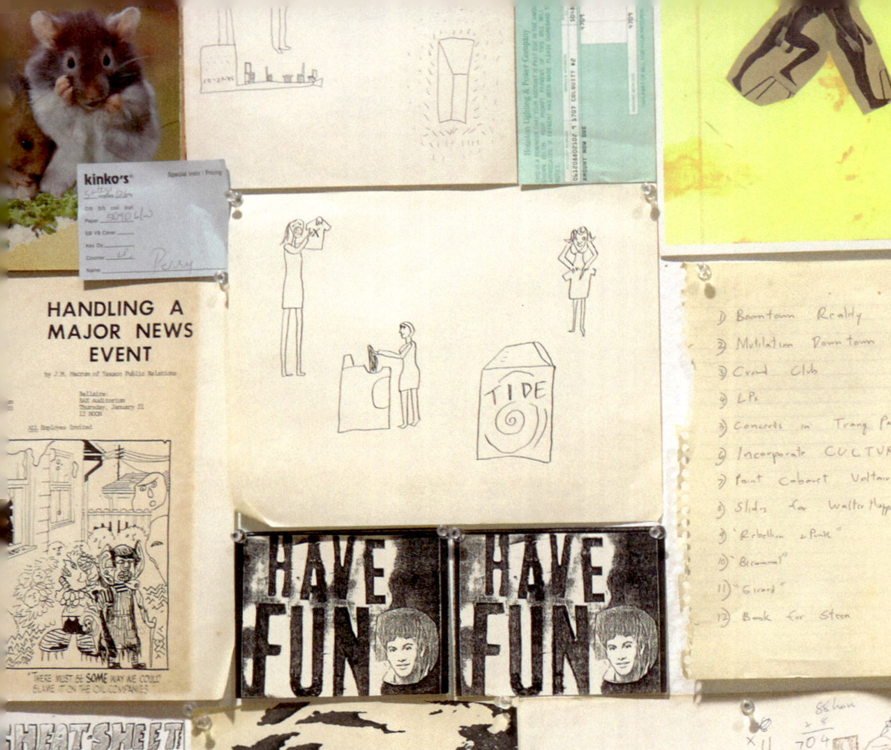

5. HOME WORK IN CAR
6. PARTY IN PARKING LOT
HOW I GOT READY FOR SCHOOL 12/28/81

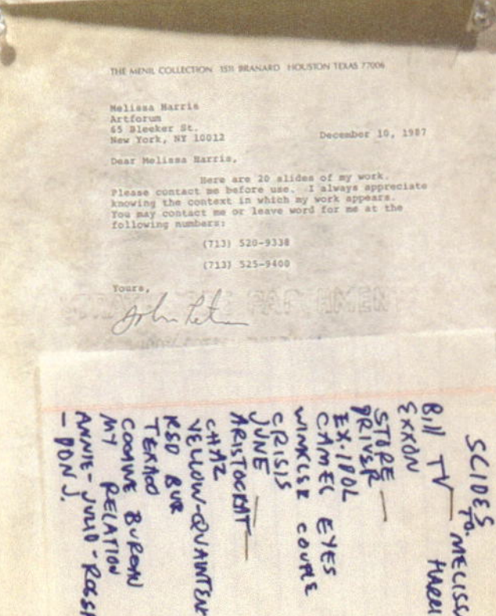

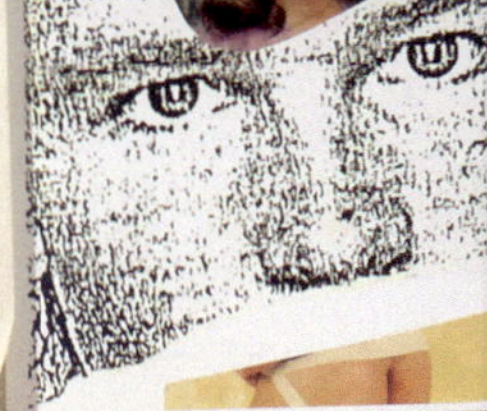

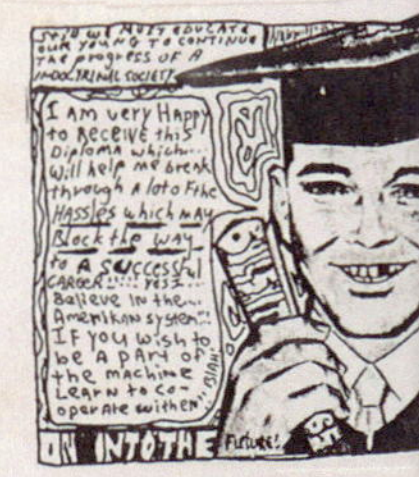

SCREEN MEMORIE
2315 COMMERCE
HOUSTON, TX 77002
(713) 526-5841
OPENING: SATURDAY, OCTOBER 24, 8PM

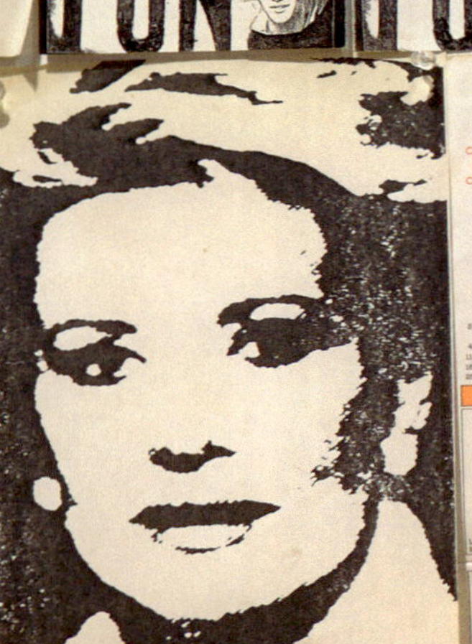

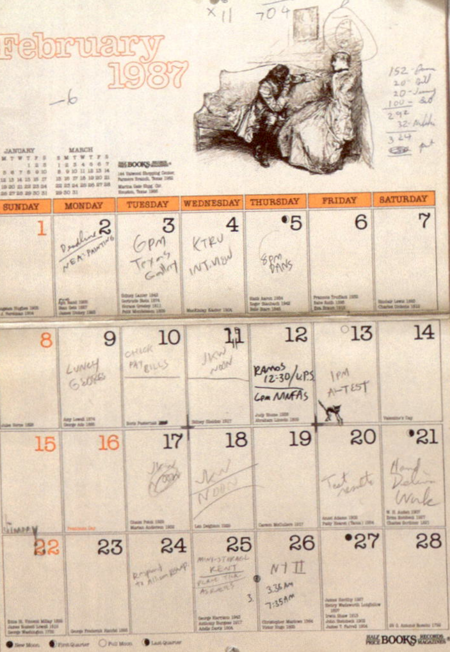

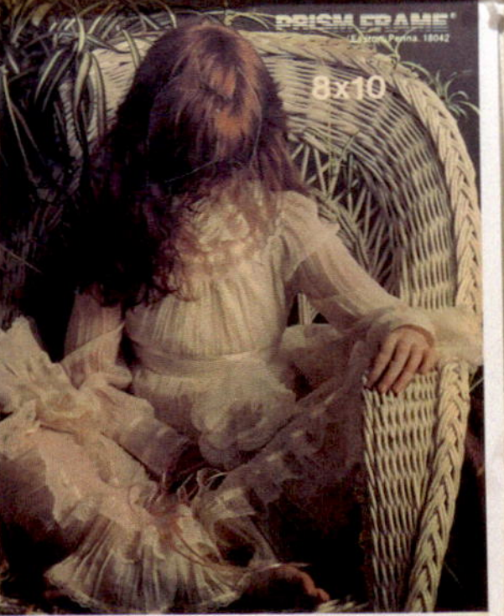

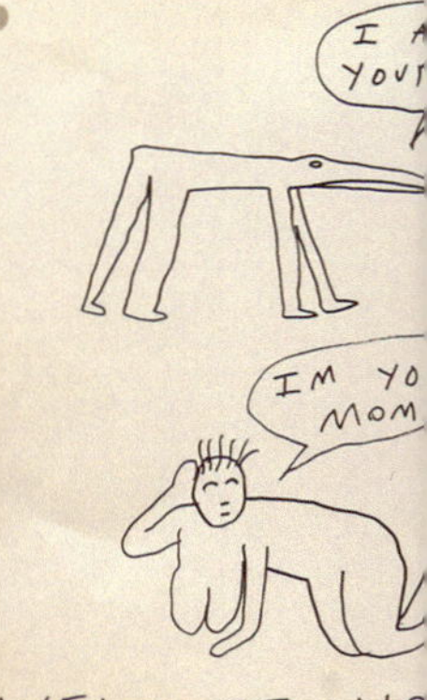

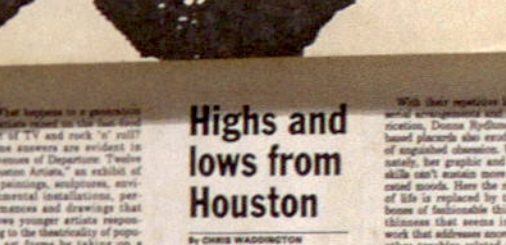

Mark Flood's acrylic paintings are equally hollow. Mimicking the scale and language of billboards, they grab a viewer's attention, but cannot hold it — a common problem in today's art world, where would-be painters compete for the distracted, image-glutted audience created by the mass media.

Ultimately, it's hard to rate an exhibit that so expressly avoids themes or local trends. To do so would be a disservice to the half-dozen fine artists who find their work stranded in a hodge-podge of mediocrity.

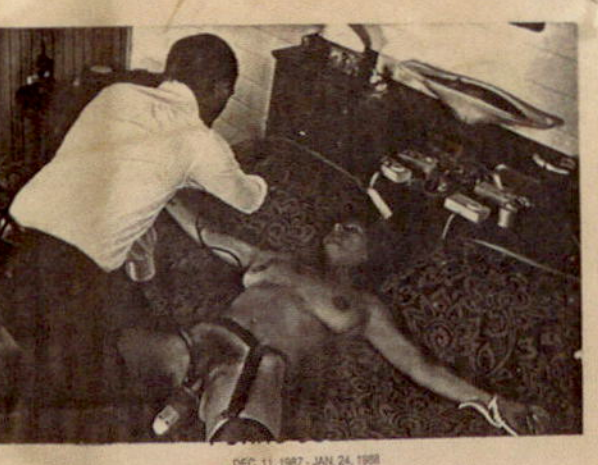

SCREEN MEMORIES
2315 COMMERCE
HOUSTON, TX 77003
OPENING: FRIDAY, DECEMBER 11, 8PM - MIDNIGHT

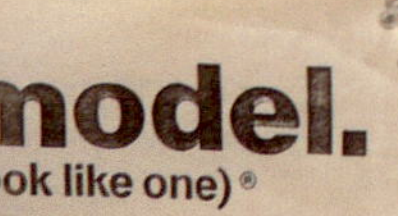

model.
ok like one)®
does it better than
your 32 page book
n start you on your way!
39, Barbizon Schools
ned thousands, either
eling careers or to
he "look," poise and con-
hat could make the dif-
n any career you choose.

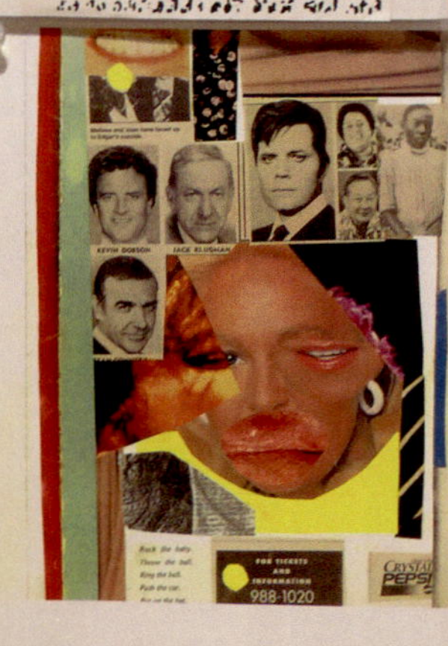

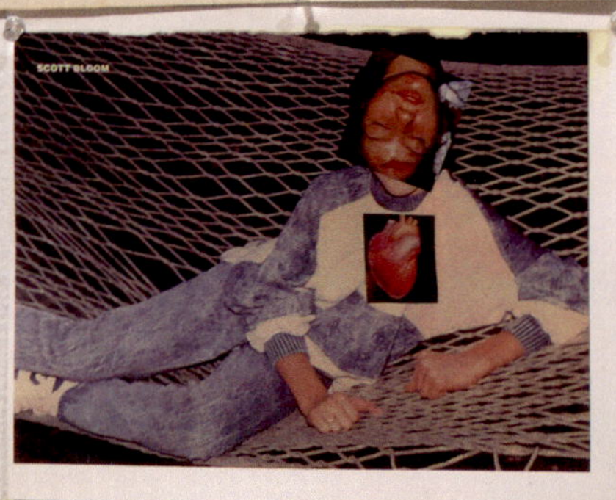

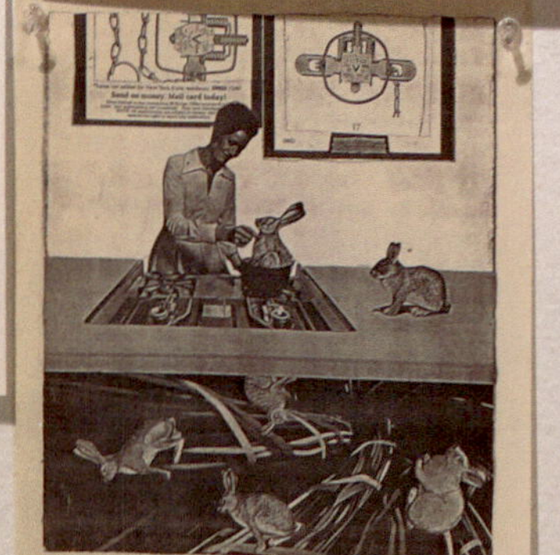

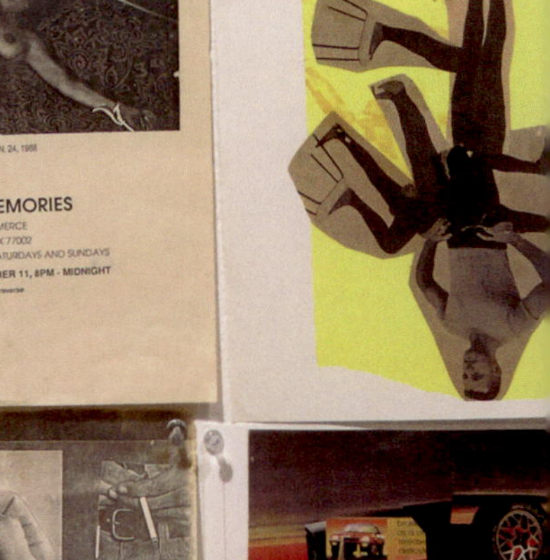

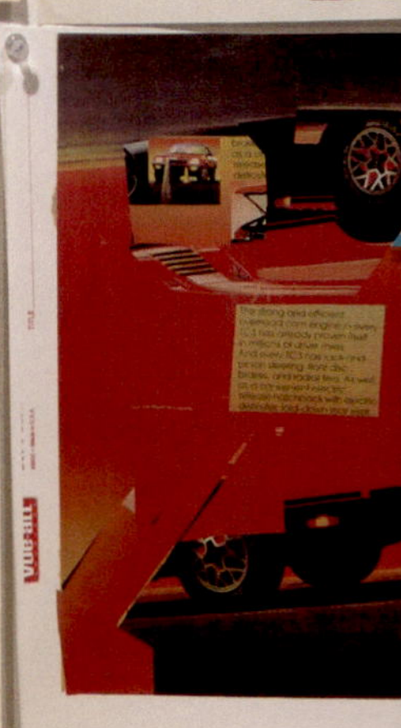

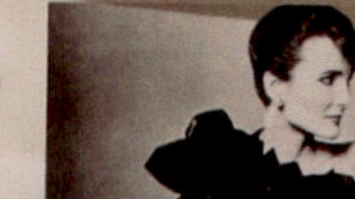

• LYNN GOODE GALLERY •

1805 W. Gray • Houston, Texas 77019 • (713) 526-5966

May 14, 1991

Dear

Thank you for considering the Lynn Goode Gallery.

We enjoyed looking at your slides very much, however at the present time the gallery schedule is complete until the end of 1992.

Should you ever be in the area please come by to visit, and feel free to bring some current slides with you.

We wish you every success.

Sincerely,

Lynn Goode

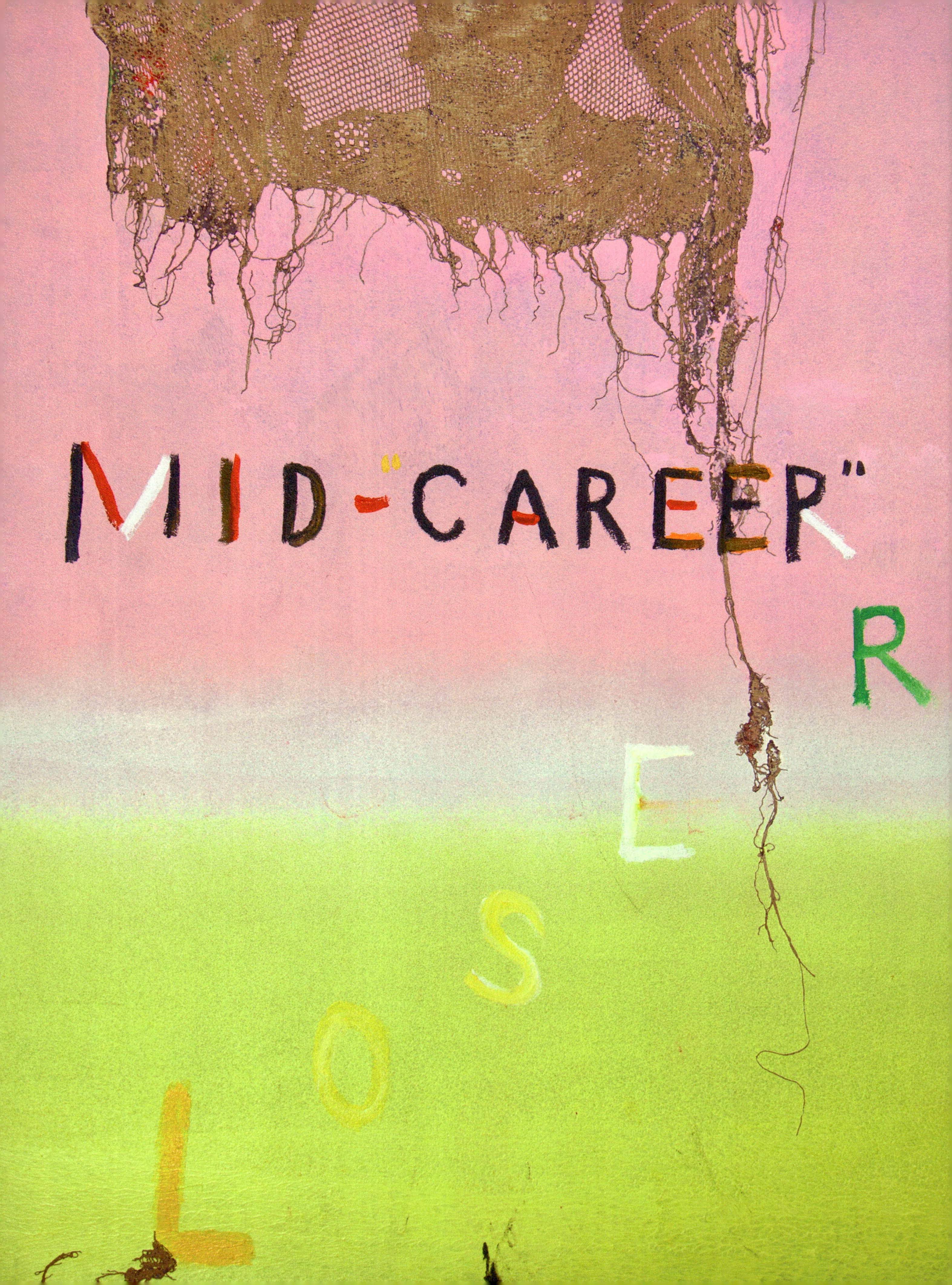
MID-"CAREER"
R
E
S
O
L

Mark Flood

Gratest Hits

Contemporary Arts Museum Houston

April 30–August 7, 2016

Bill Arning
Alison M. Gingeras
Carlo McCormick
El Topito
Scott Indrisek

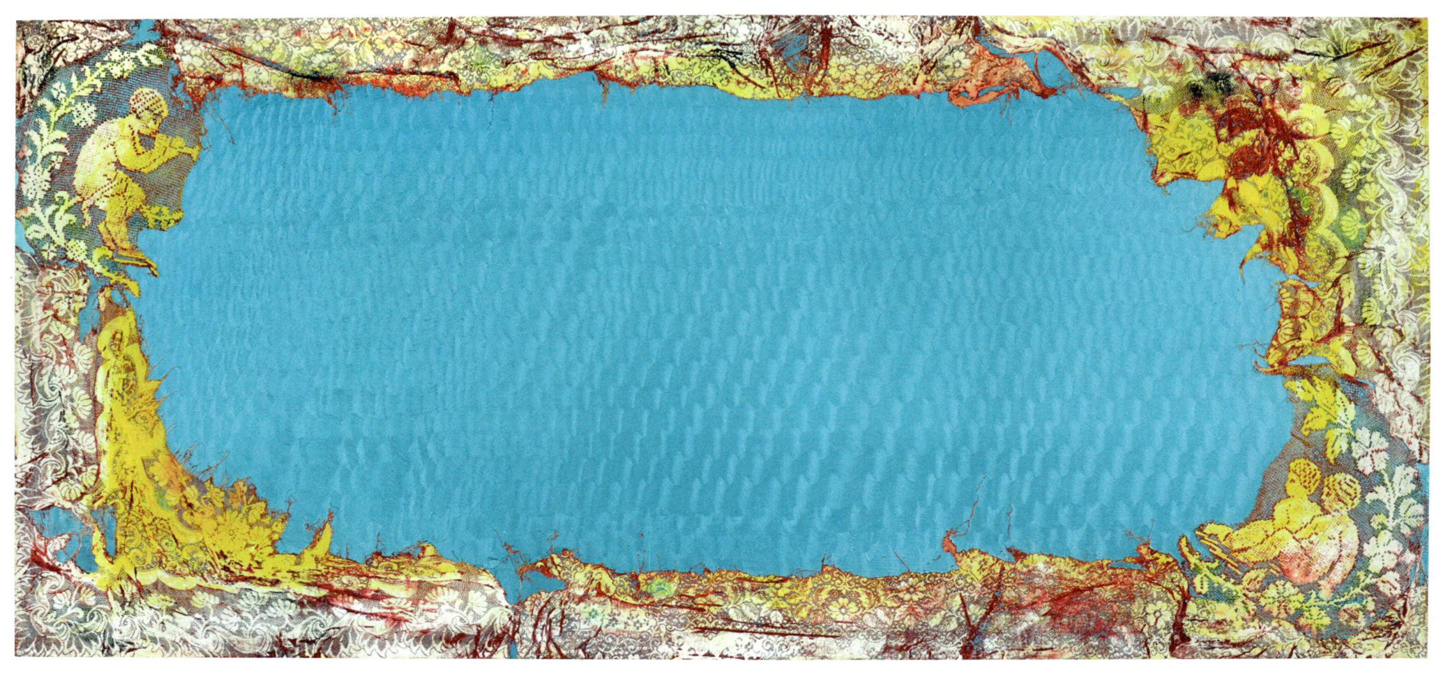

First Song 2014 acrylic on canvas 84 x 198 inches

Contents

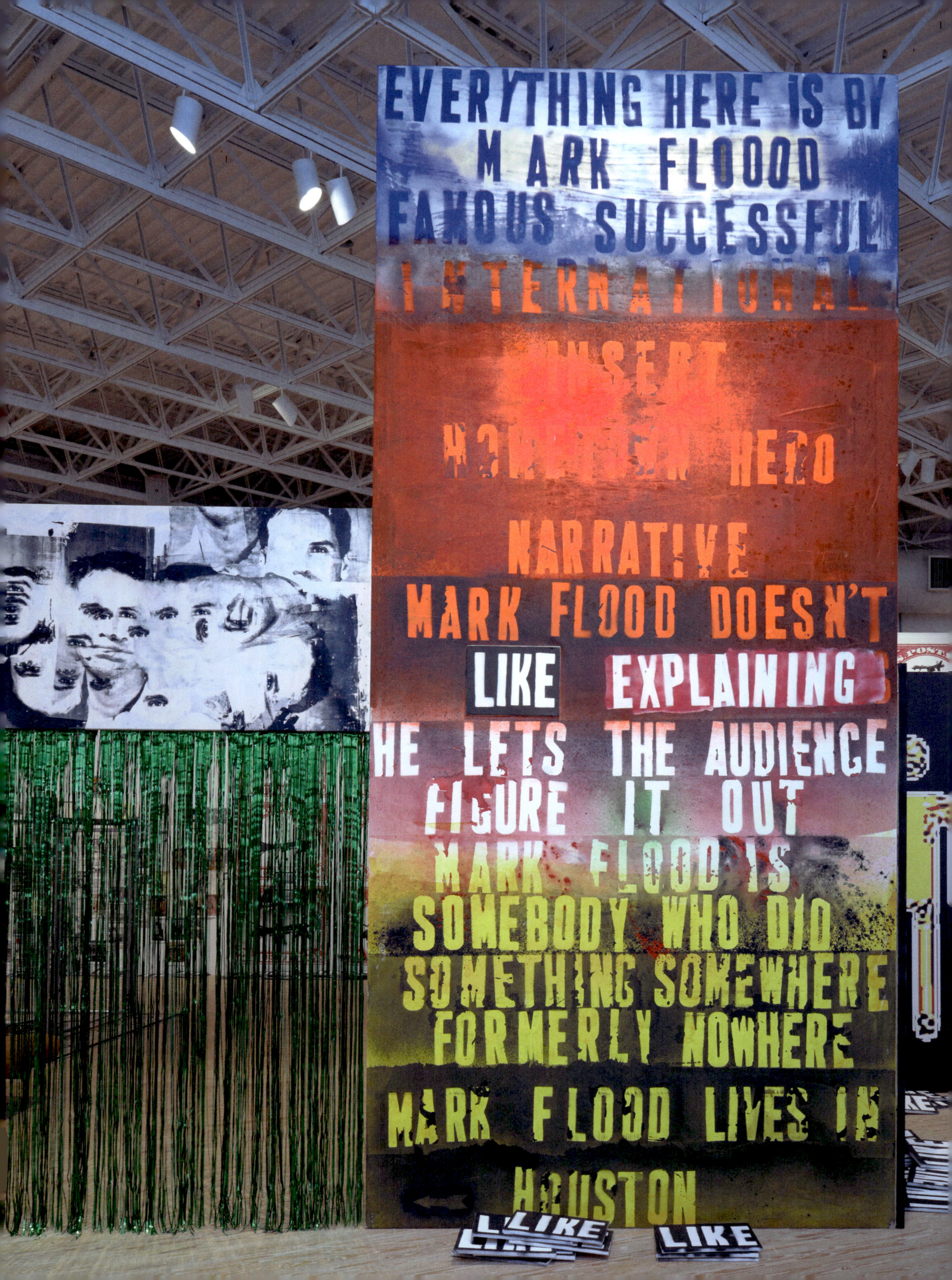
EVERYTHING HERE IS BY
MARK FLOOOD
FAMOUS SUCCESSFUL
INTERNATIONAL
HERO
NARRATIVE
MARK FLOOD DOESN'T
LIKE
EXPLAINING
HE LETS THE AUDIENCE
FIGURE IT OUT
MARK FLOOD IS
SOMEBODY WHO DID
SOMETHING SOMEWHERE
FORMERLY NOWHERE
MARK FLOOD LIVES IN
HOUSTON
LIKE
LIKE

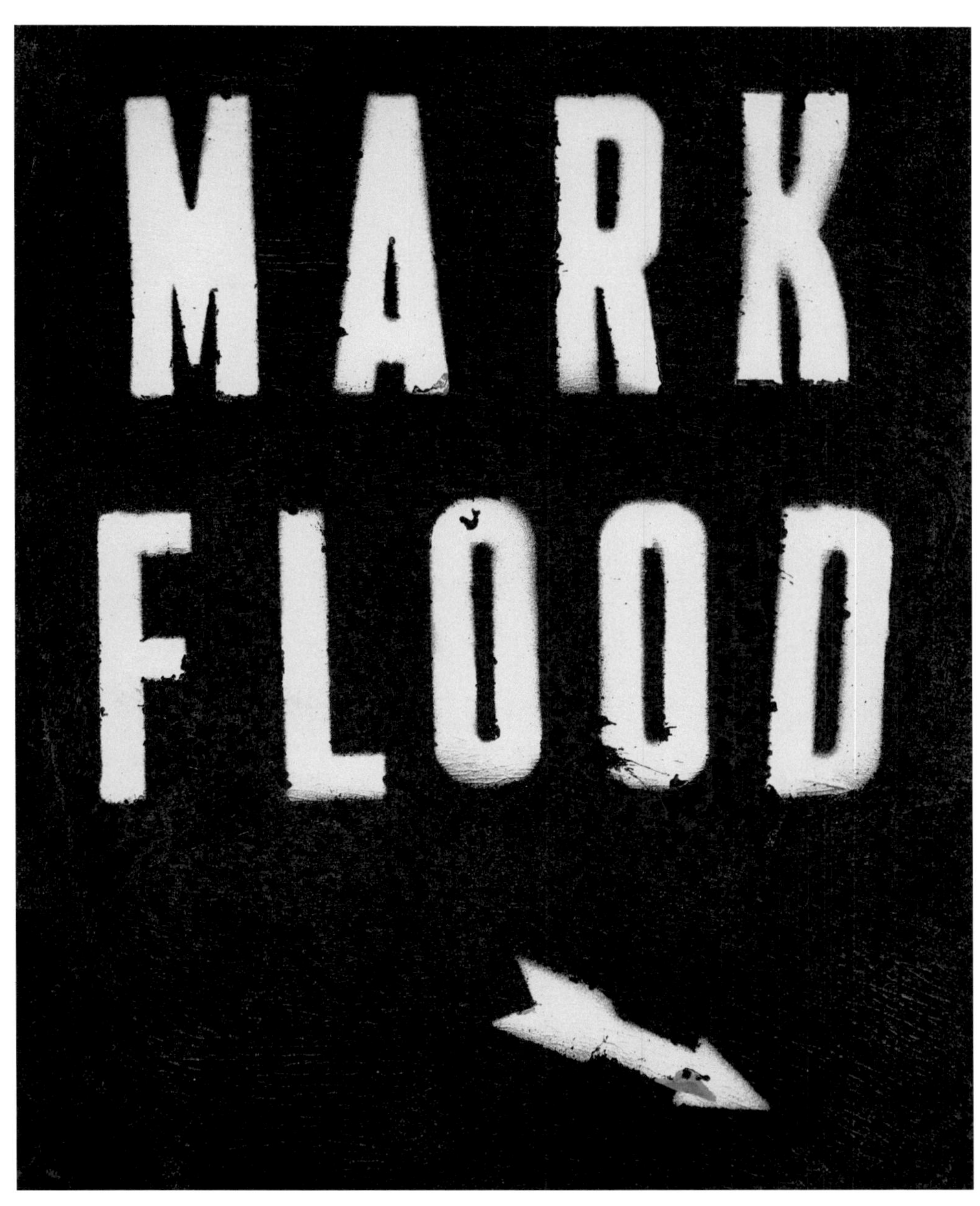

Indicator 2015 acrylic on canvas 36 x 30 inches

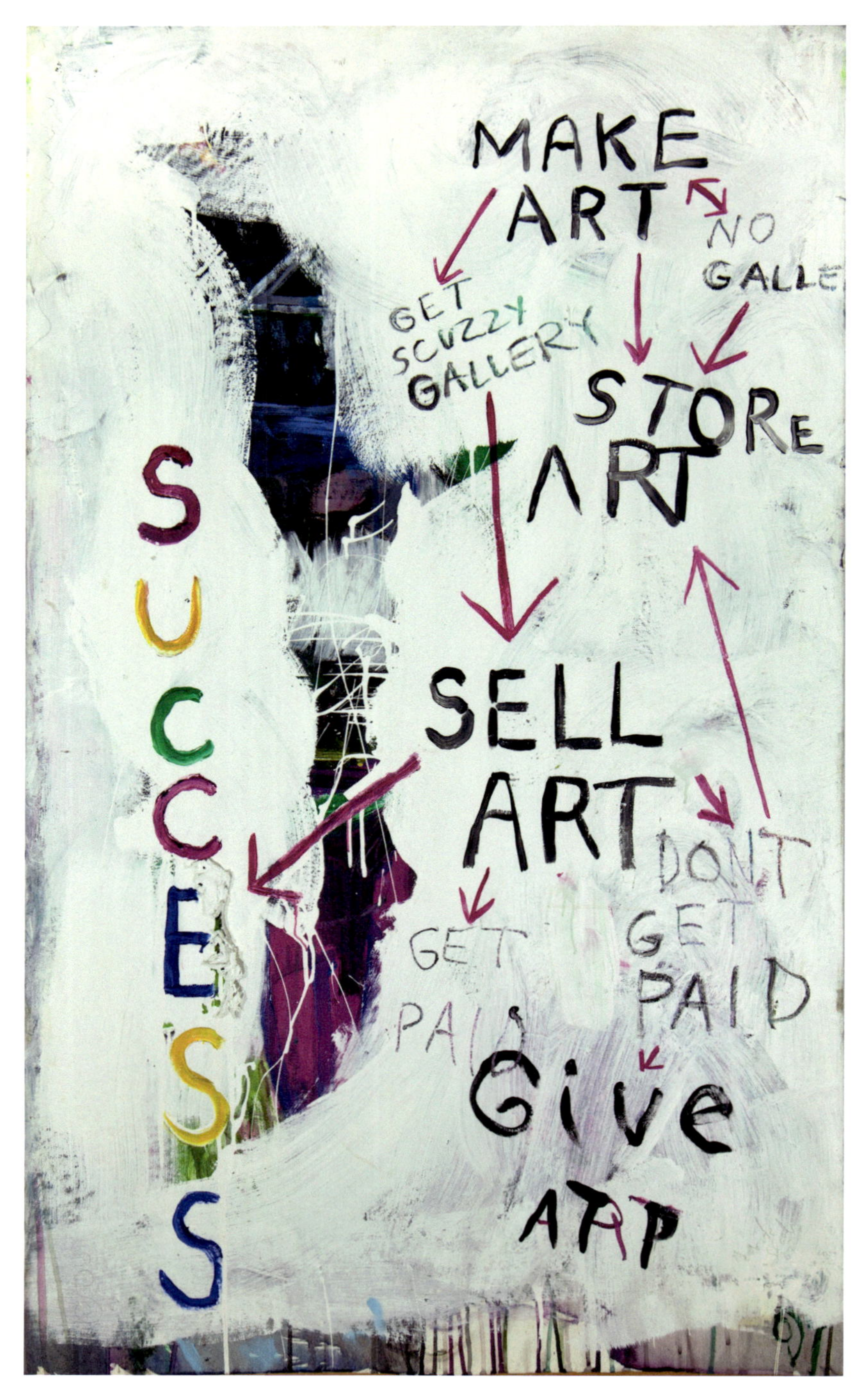

The Deep 1997 acrylic on canvas 52 x 36 inches

Foreword Bill Arning

Director Contemporary Arts Museum Houston

MARK FLOOD: GRATEST HITS is the culmination of more than two years of preparation by the Contemporary Arts Museum Houston, but it represents forty years of hard work on the part of the artist. I am tremendously grateful to him for letting me put together an exhibition of this scale. *Gratest Hits* speaks to a moment in time when artists no longer feel the need to apologize for making Houston their home. Flood is one of the small cadres of internationally recognized and respected artists who, while spending an inordinate amount of time on planes, keep their main studios here. They see little reason to leave.

No artist should be pressured to be a spokesmodel for his city. As demonstrated by Flood's art and associated writings, he clearly has a love/hate relationship with the city he grew up in. Yet although Flood is worldly and his practice is such that he could work anywhere, he chooses to stay in Houston. He is also famous for sharing his unusual vision of the city's charms with various art-world visitors, who will see the shipping channel and San Jacinto Monument but might miss the Rothko Chapel. I promised to spare Mark many of the normal demands a large-scale museum show puts on its subject. But I can't avoid framing him as a hometown hero. Nor can I avoid publicly praising both the man and his work (which also makes his skin crawl), and my effort starts most emphatically in this foreword.

So taking this back to an overly revealing personal statement (masquerading as a foreword), Flood's show has a great deal of meaning for me. As a director I allow myself relatively few curatorial slots, and inviting Flood to exhibit here was a significant choice. I am a native New Yorker whose formative years in the art world took place in Manhattan below 14th Street. That my worldview was formed without the entire middle of the country is still a shock, and I have found myself falling increasingly in love with Houston, its culture, and its attitude. Flood and Houston are totally interwoven in my mind as well as in the collective imaginary of the art world, as every profile at some point feigns surprise that he has chosen to stay.

Houston is a city that loves eccentrics, has a great arts and cultural life, and is incredibly welcoming to newcomers who show the slightest openness to it. My own experience—coming here in 2009 after a decade in Cambridge, Massachusetts, and my past life in bands—gives me a natural way into Flood's work. Hell, I find all the jokes in *Art Fair Fever* and *Clerk Fluid* so funny that I repeat them at parties as my own witticisms.

I speak for all of us here at the Contemporary Arts Museum Houston when I declare that making *Gratest Hits* has been a startlingly enjoyable and stimulating project from start to finish. There are many people I must thank for their dedication to this project and their help in making it such an enriching experience.

We are all aware that the artist's reputation as a badass will be permanently damaged if it becomes too widely known that he is in fact a nice guy, and, while Flood is clear and uncompromising about what he will and won't do, the CAMH staff would like to express our gratitude to him as a marvelous friend and colleague in making *Gratest Hits* a killer exhibition.

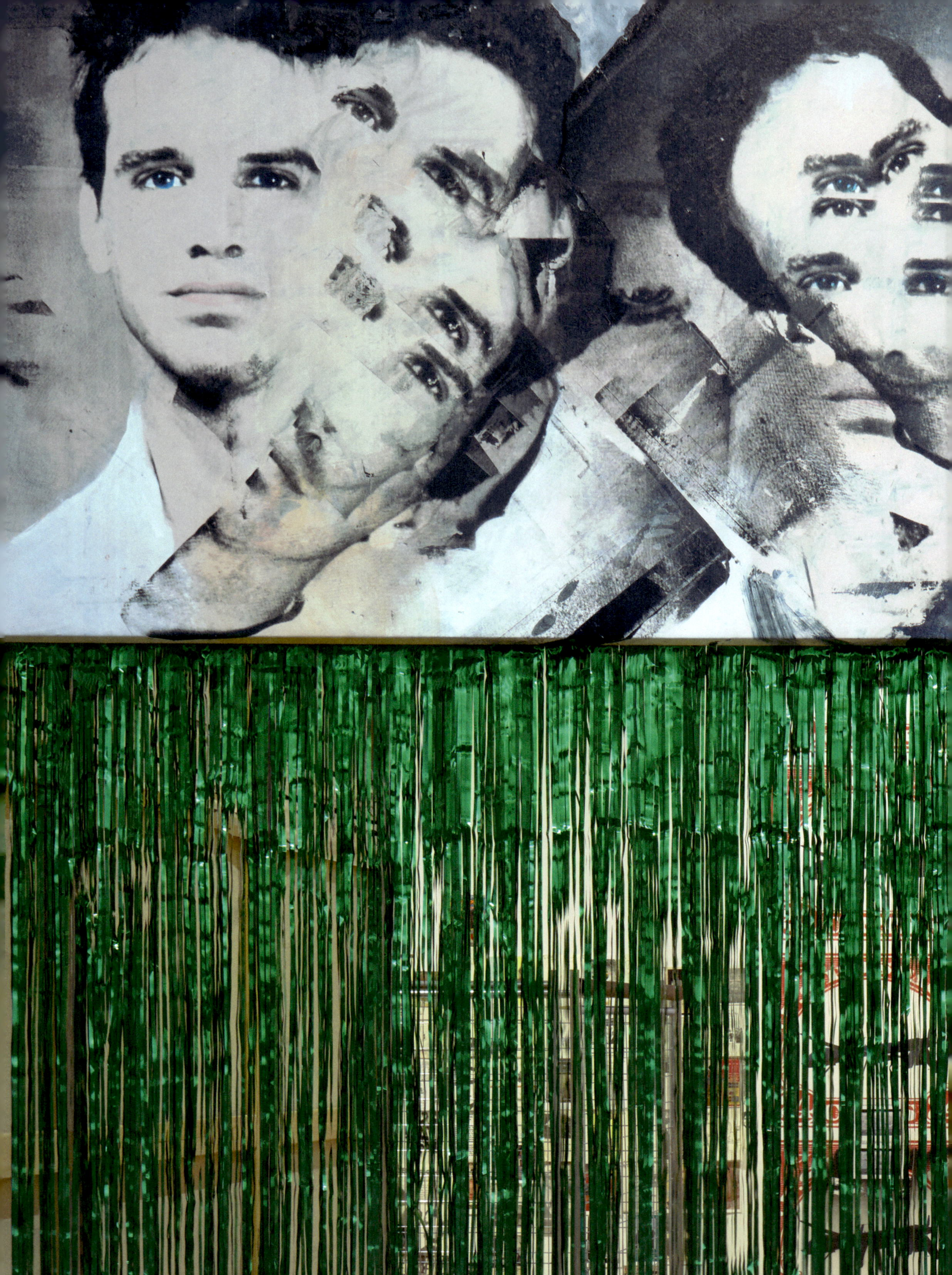

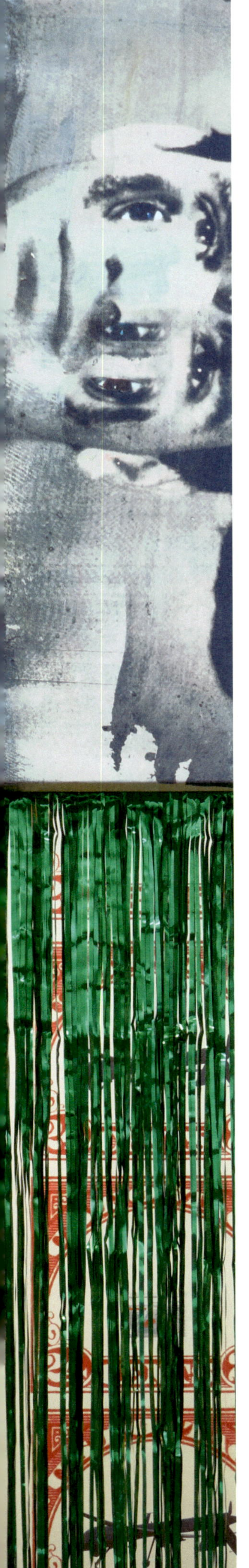

Foreword 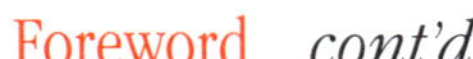

Russell Etchen, who has worked with Flood for several years on his books, balanced the need to make *Gratest Hits* a Flood book while also a proper CAMH publication. Russell and I have been friends for several years but in the course of working on this project we have grown much closer and are now able to complete each other's sentences, which has been a great pleasure. At CAMH, Patricia Restrepo organized every detail of the exhibition and publication. She and my assistant Shane Platt also fielded the majority of the unpredictable questions and queries a huge and conspicuously chaotic *Gratest Hits* package such as this demands. Connie MacAllister, Amanda Thomas, Max Fields, Jeff Shore, Felice Cleveland, and Tim Barkley all joined Team Flood, and I am truly grateful that via their enthusiasm and interest this has morphed into such a celebratory team effort.

Mark Flood's studio, a.k.a. Party-Tyme, feels like a type of playground. The artists and musicians who work there are all heavily involved with and inspired by Flood's philosophy and way of working, and by and large they share his uncompromising vision. Flood's crew built the largest scale model of CAMH's Brown Foundation Gallery that I have ever seen in order to clearly articulate his vision for this presentation of forty years of his work. His studio and management family, Barry Elkanick, Alika Herreshoff, Lane Hagood, Edgar Meza, Dylan Roberts, Alex Sterling, Ryan Storm, Dan Workman, and Chris Bexar Olivier are all swell, talented folks. I am grateful to have made their acquaintance and several have become buddies through this process.

Mark Flood would like to send special tributes to his longtime friends and supporters Adam Kimmel, Harmony Korine, and the legendary Mickey Rosmarin. Mark would also like to thank the galleries that have helped make this book and exhibition possible: Blum and Poe in Los Angeles; Feuer/Mesler, Marlborough Chelsea, Maccarone, and Luxembourg and Dayan in New York; Peres Projects in Berlin; Stuart Shave/Modern Art in London; and Cardoza Fine Art here in Houston. Stuart Shave, Javier Perés, Nick Koenigsknecht, Ellen Langan, Pablo Cardoza, and Zach Feuer have been especially helpful to me and I consider them all friends.

The Contemporary Arts Museum Houston Major Exhibition Fund supports all CAMH-generated curatorial projects, and the faith and enthusiasm of these donors help us be brave curators, going where more timid institutions fear to tread. For *Mark Flood: Gratest Hits*, we have also received direct project support from friends of the museum—the enthusiasm shown by Melissa and Albert J. Grobmyer IV, Susanne and William E. Pritchard III, Cynthia Toles, Margaret Vaughan, and the Union Pacific Foundation for this project assured me that I was working in the right direction. CAMH's leadership team, J. B. and Marita Fairbanks and Jereann Chaney, likewise cheered me on in making the exhibition a reality.

My greatest thanks goes to Mark Flood himself—visionary, philosopher, friend—whose wicked sense of humor keeps me cracking up every day. It is a pleasure to know you.

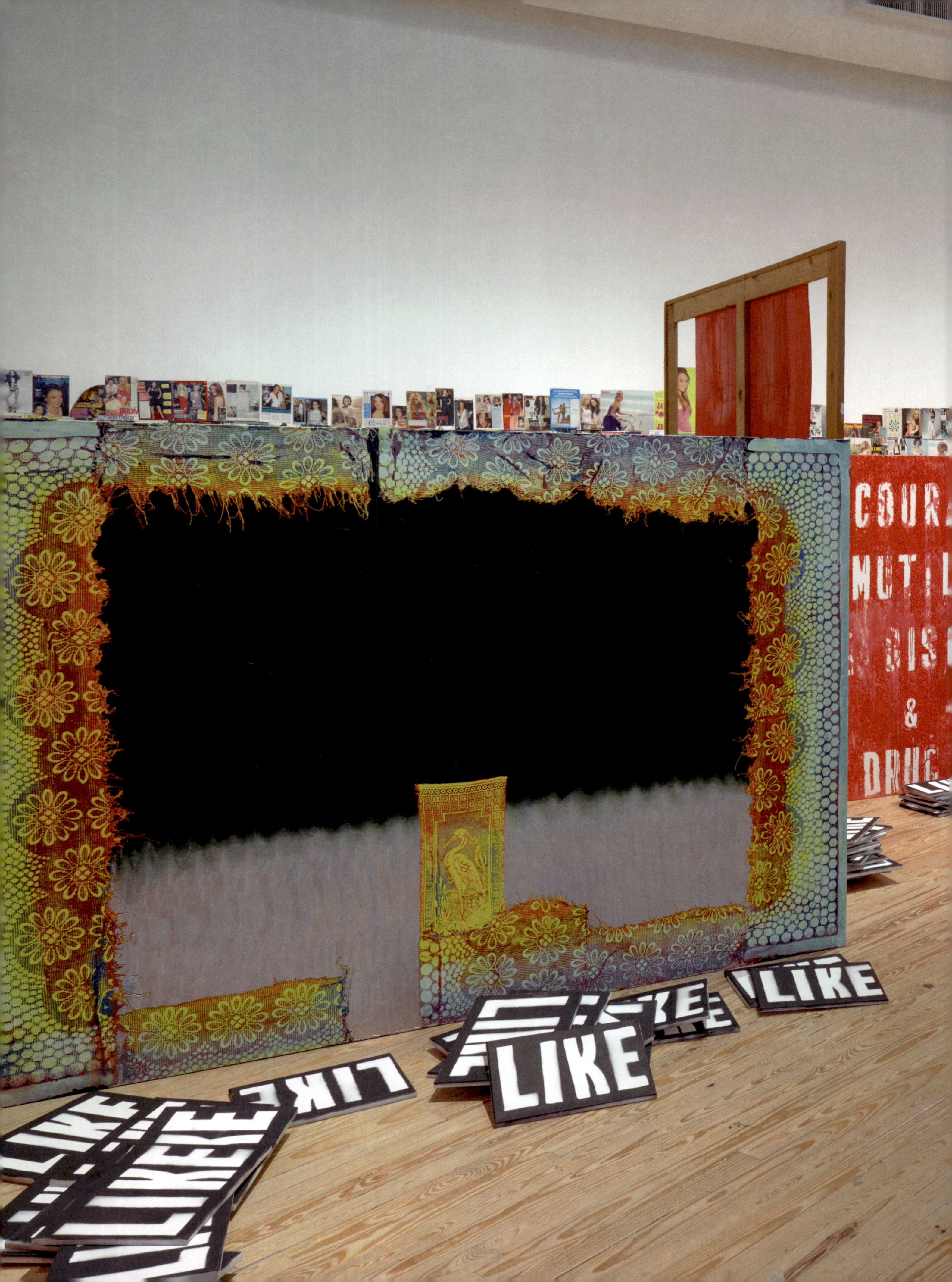
LIKE

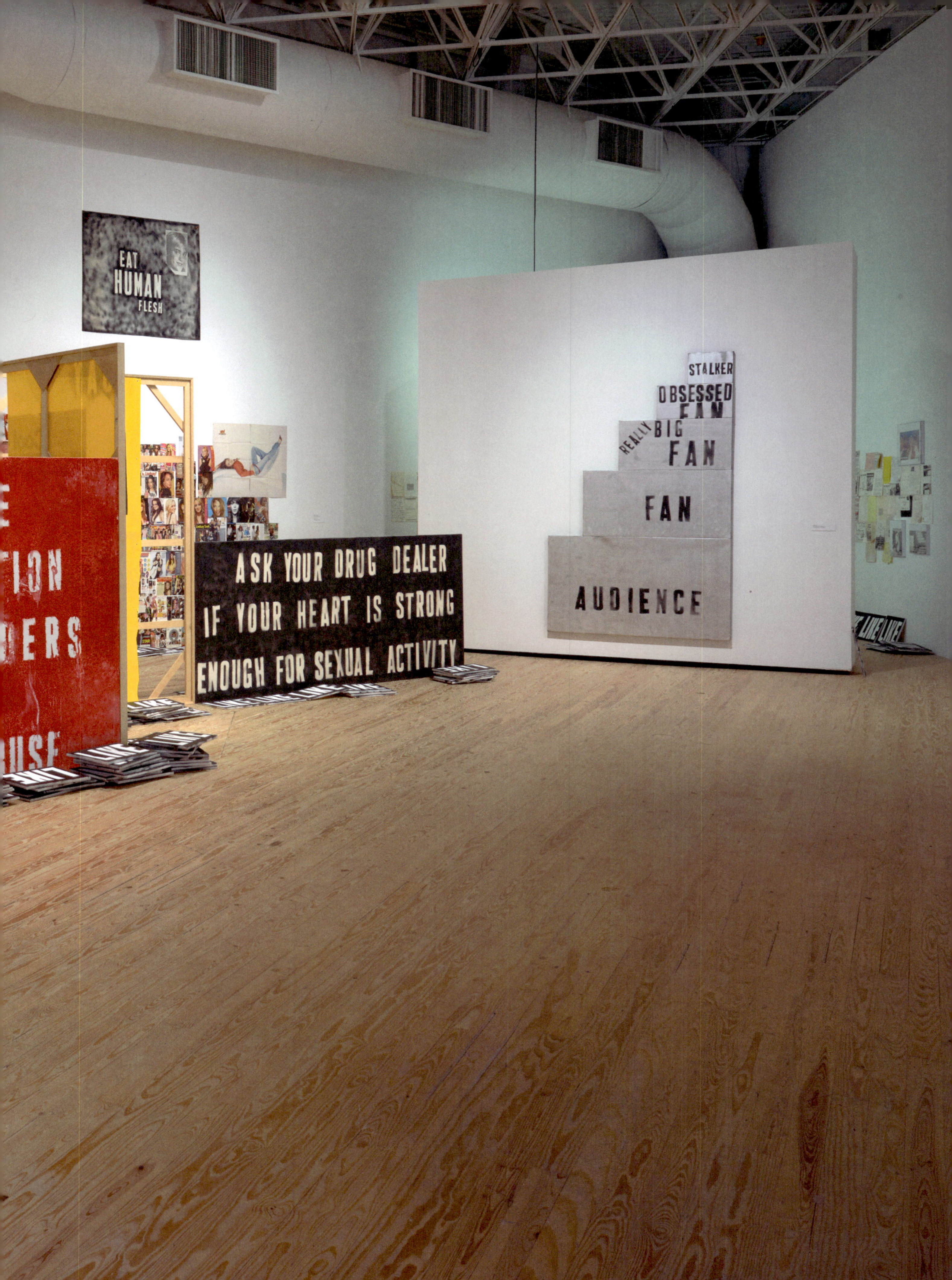
EAT
HUMAN
FLESH
ASK YOUR DRUG DEALER
IF YOUR HEART IS STRONG
ENOUGH FOR SEXUAL ACTIVITY
STALKER
OBSESSED
REALLY BIG FAN
FAN
AUDIENCE

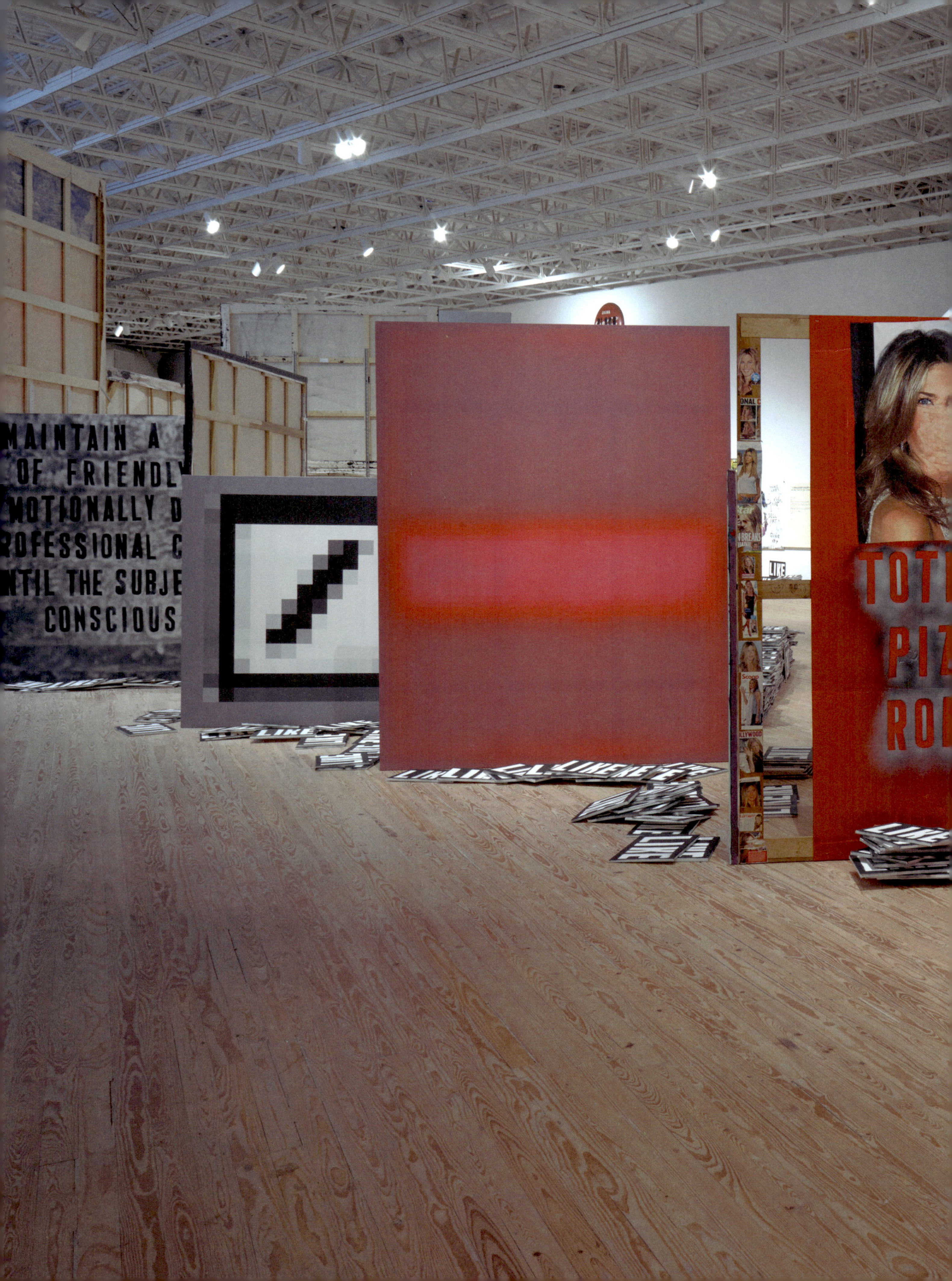
MAINTAIN A
OF FRIENDLY
MOTIONALLY D
ROFESSIONAL C
NTIL THE SUBJE
CONSCIOUS
LIKE
TOT
PIZ
RO

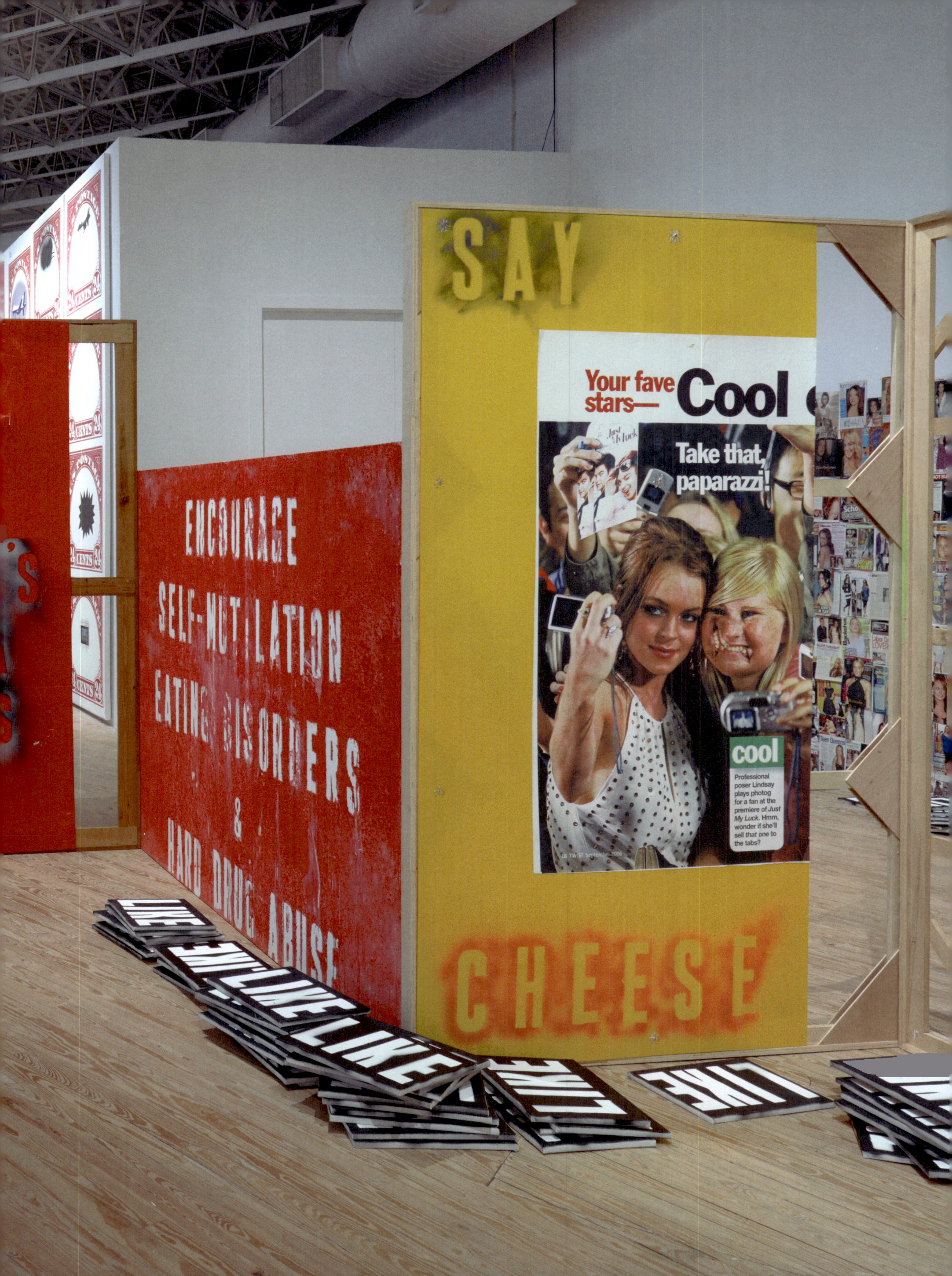

SAY
Your fave stars—
Cool
Take that, paparazzi!
cool
Professional poser Lindsay plays photog for a fan at the premiere of Just My Luck. Hmm, wonder if she'll sell that one to the tabs?
CHEESE
ENCOURAGE
SELF-MUTILATION
EATING DISORDERS
&
HARD DRUG ABUSE
LIKE
LIKE
LIKE
LIKE
LIKE

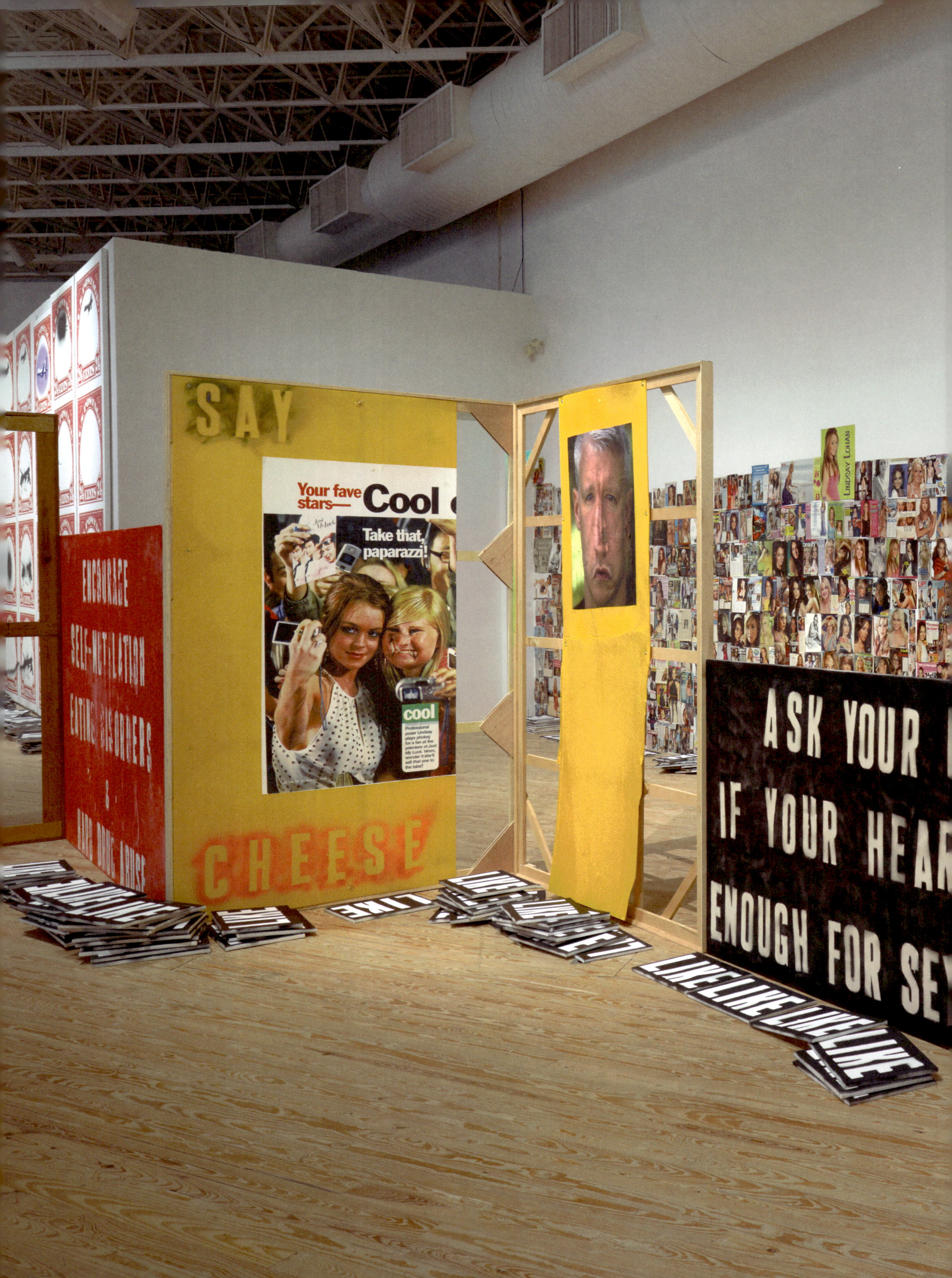

SAY
Your fave stars—
Cool
Take that, paparazzi!
cool
CHEESE
ENCOURAGE
SELF-MUTILATION
HARD DRUG ABUSE
LINDSAY LOHAN
ASK YOUR
IF YOUR HEA
ENOUGH FOR SE
LIKE

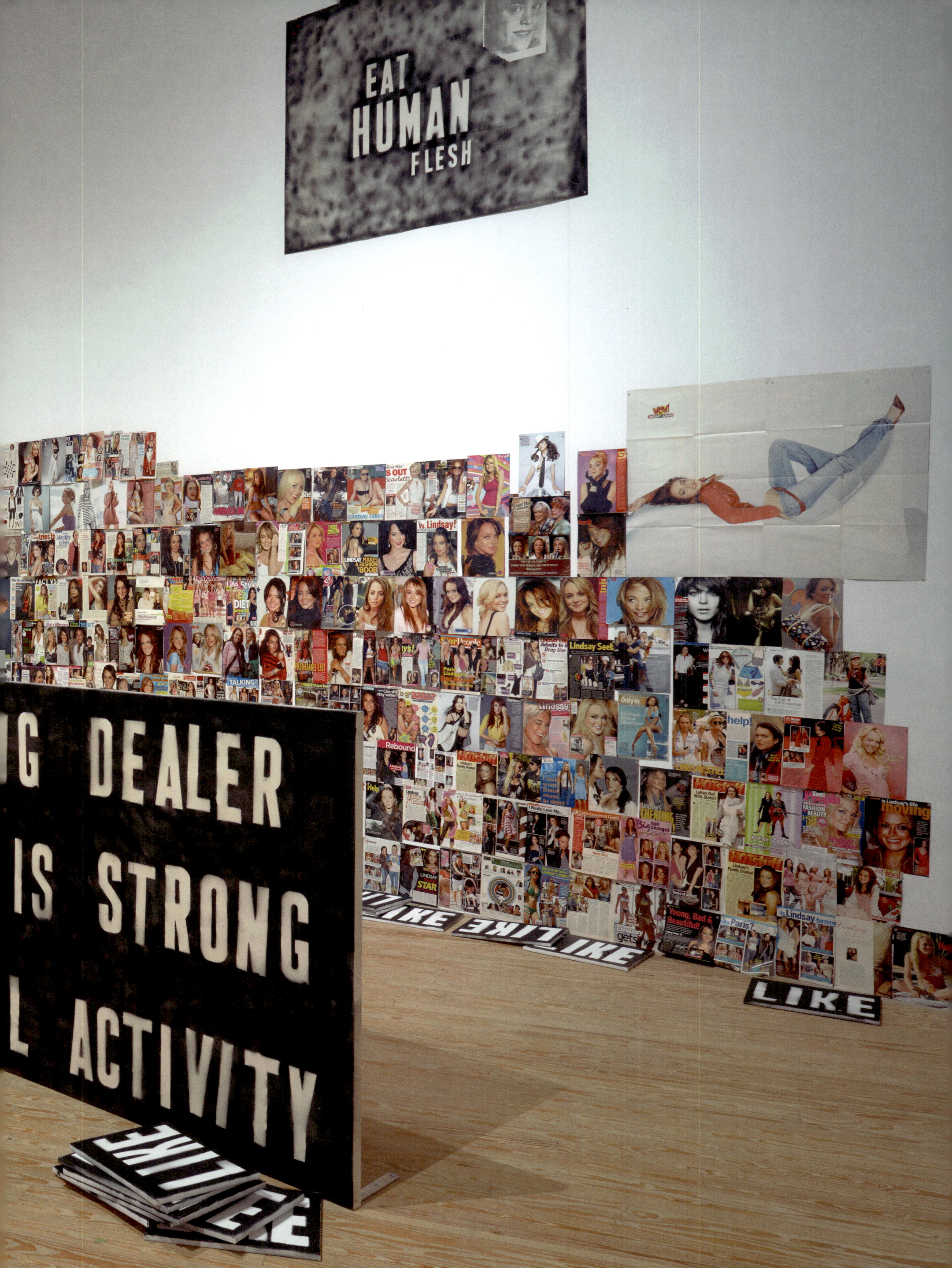
EAT
HUMAN
FLESH
G DEALER
IS STRONG
L ACTIVITY
LIKE
LIKE
LIKE
LIKE

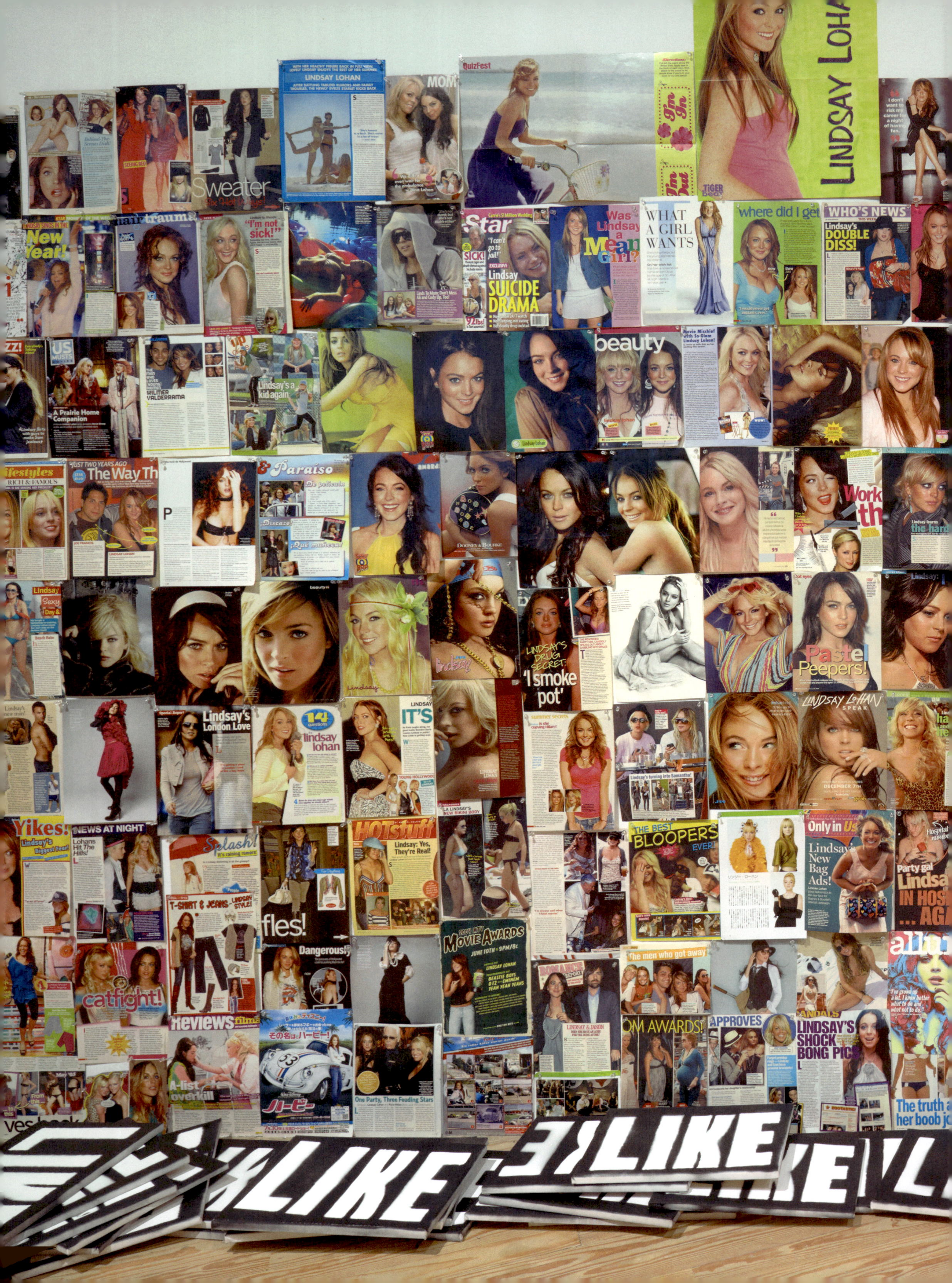

LINDSAY LOHAN
QuizFest
Sweater
"I'm not sick!"
Star
Lindsay SUICIDE DRAMA
Was Lindsay a Mean Girl?
WHAT A GIRL WANTS
where did I get
WHO'S NEWS
Lindsay's DOUBLE DISS!
New Year!
US
A Prairie Home Companion
WILMER VALDERRAMA
Lindsay's a kid again
beauty
lifestyles
RICH & FAMOUS
JUST TWO YEARS AGO
The Way Th
& Paraíso
DOONEY & BOURKE
Sexy
LINDSAY'S DRUG SECRET: 'I smoke pot'
Pastel Peepers!
Lindsay's London Love
14 questions lindsay lohan
IT'S
LINDSAY LOHAN SPEAK
Yikes!
NEWS AT NIGHT
Splash!
T-SHIRT & JEANS
HOTstuff
Lindsay: Yes, They're Real!
THE BEST BLOOPERS EVER!
Only in Us
Lindsay's New Bag Ads!
Party gal
catfight!
Dangerously
MOVIE AWARDS
The men who got away
Reviews
その名は、ハービー！
ハービー
One Party, Three Feuding Stars
LINDSAY & JASON
APPROVES
LINDSAY'S SHOCK BONG PIC
The truth a
her boob jo
A-list overkill
LIKE

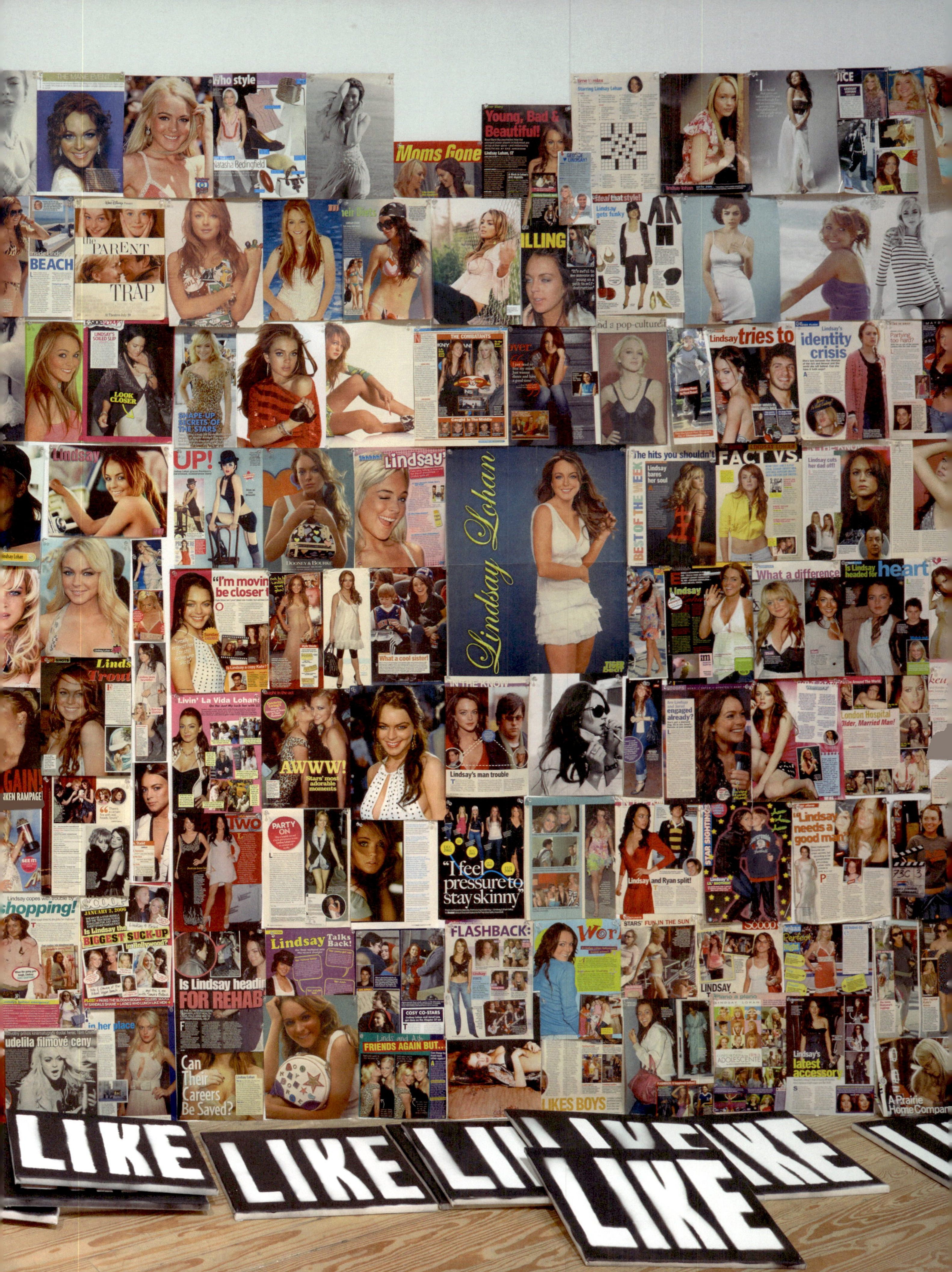
THE MANE EVENT
Who style
Natasha Bedingfield
Moms Gone
Young, Bad & Beautiful!
Starring Lindsay Lohan
BEACH
The PARENT TRAP
Steal that style!
Lindsay gets funky
ILLING
LOOK CLOSER
SHAPE-UP SECRETS OF THE STARS
THE COMBATANTS
Caught In The Middle
a pop-culture
Lindsay tries to
identity crisis
Lindsay
UP!
Lindsay
Lindsay Lohan
The hits you shouldn't
Lindsay bares her soul
BEST OF THE WEEK
FACT VS.
Lindsay cuts her dad off!
"I'm movin be closer t
What a cool sister!
What a difference
Is Lindsay headed for heart
Lindsay Lohan
Livin' La Vida Lohan
AWWW! Stars' most adorable moments
IN THE KNOW
Lindsay's man trouble
London Hospital Older, Married Man!
AGAIN!
KEN RAMPAGE
PARTY ON
"I feel pressure to stay skinny"
Lindsay and Ryan split!
STAR SIGHTING
"Lindsay needs a good man"
shopping!
Is Lindsay the BIGGEST SUCK-UP in Hollywood?
Lindsay Talks Back!
Is Lindsay heading FOR REHAB
FLASHBACK:
STARS' FUN IN THE SUN
LINDSAY
Lindsay's latest accessory
in her place
udelila filmové ceny
Can Their Careers Be Saved?
COSY CO-STARS
FRIENDS AGAIN BUT...
LIKES BOYS
A Prairie Home Compan
LIKE
LIKE
LIKE
LIKE

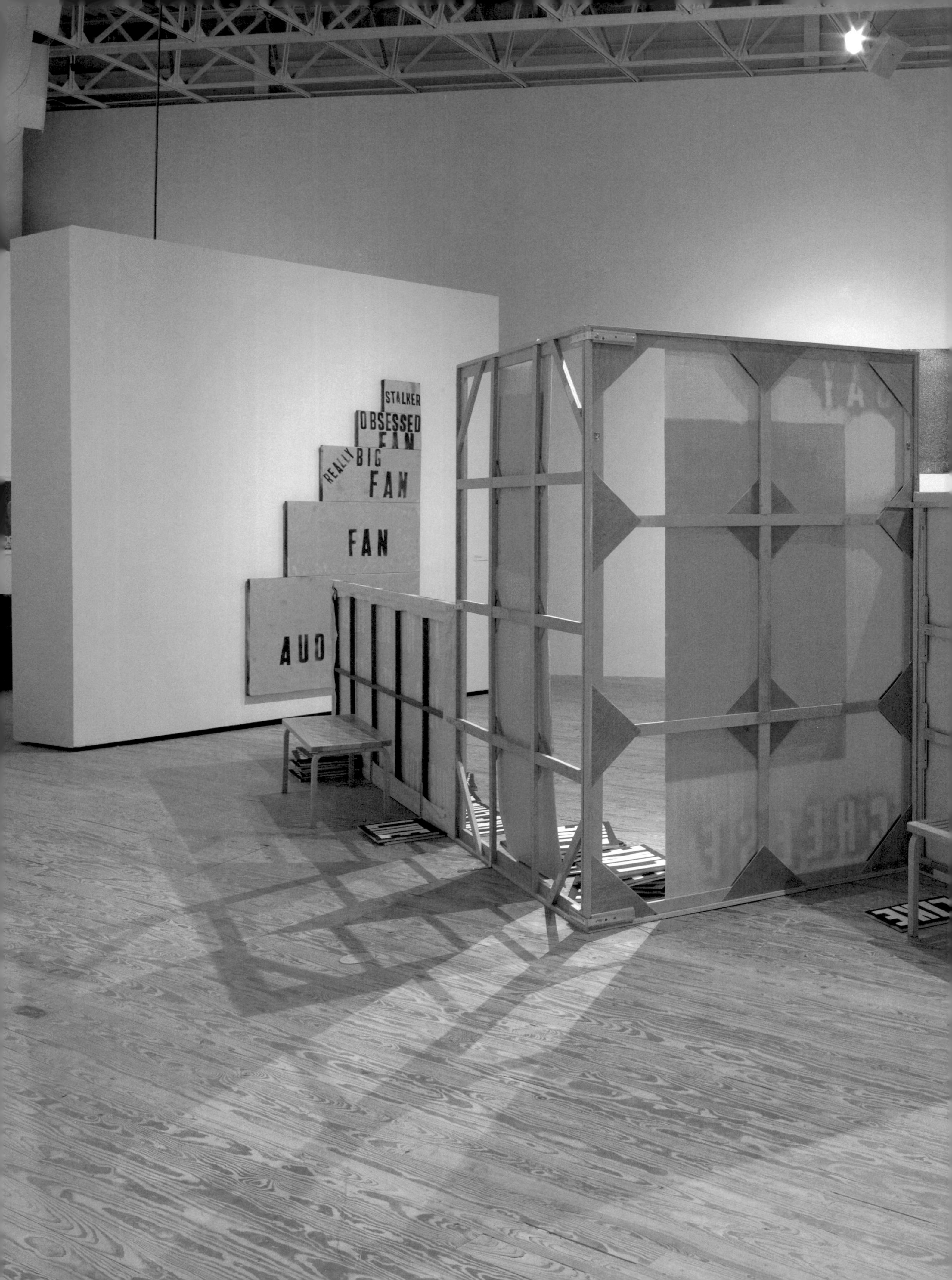
STALKER
OBSESSED
FAN
REALLY BIG
FAN
FAN
AUD

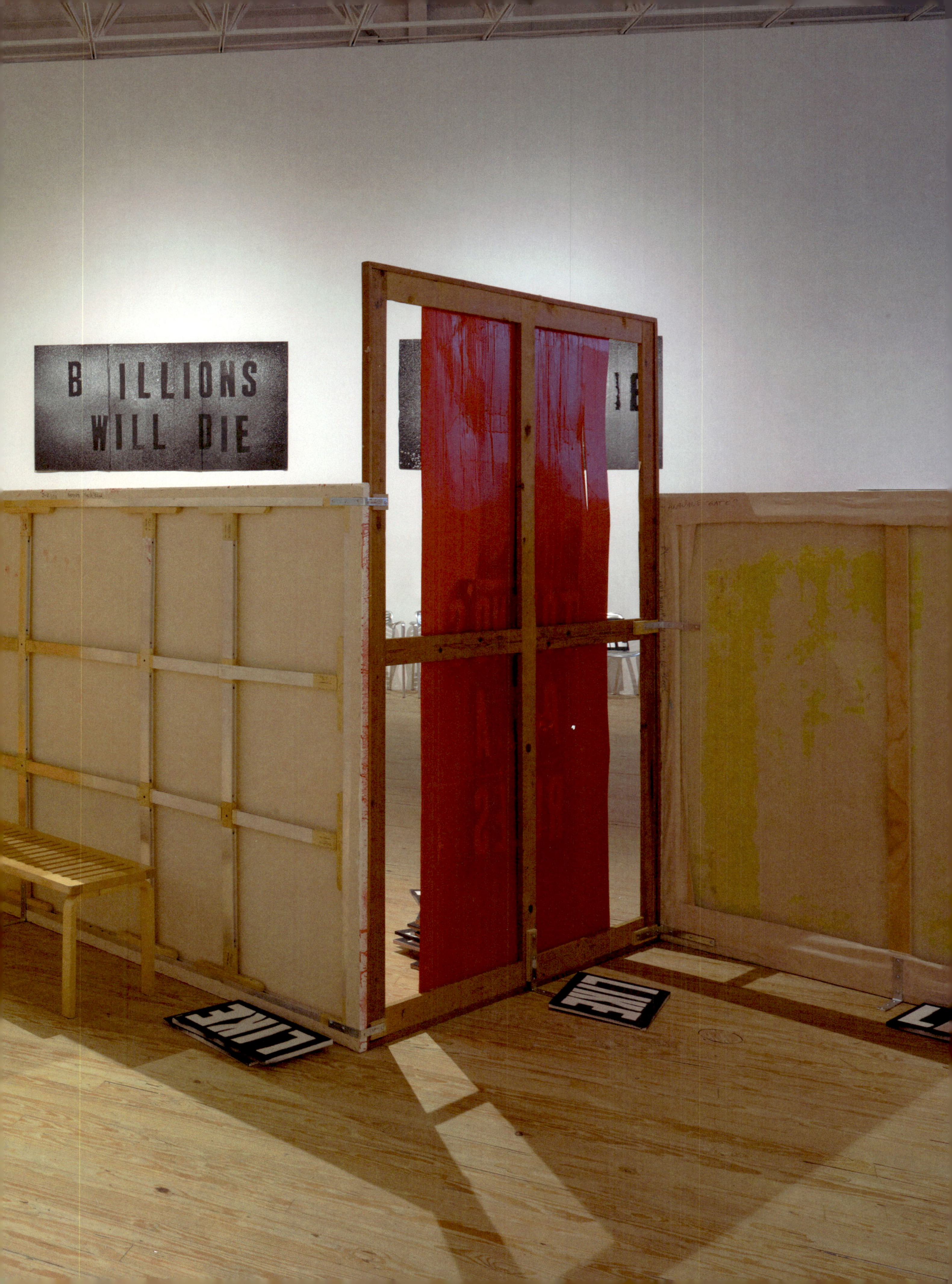
B ILLIONS
WILL DIE

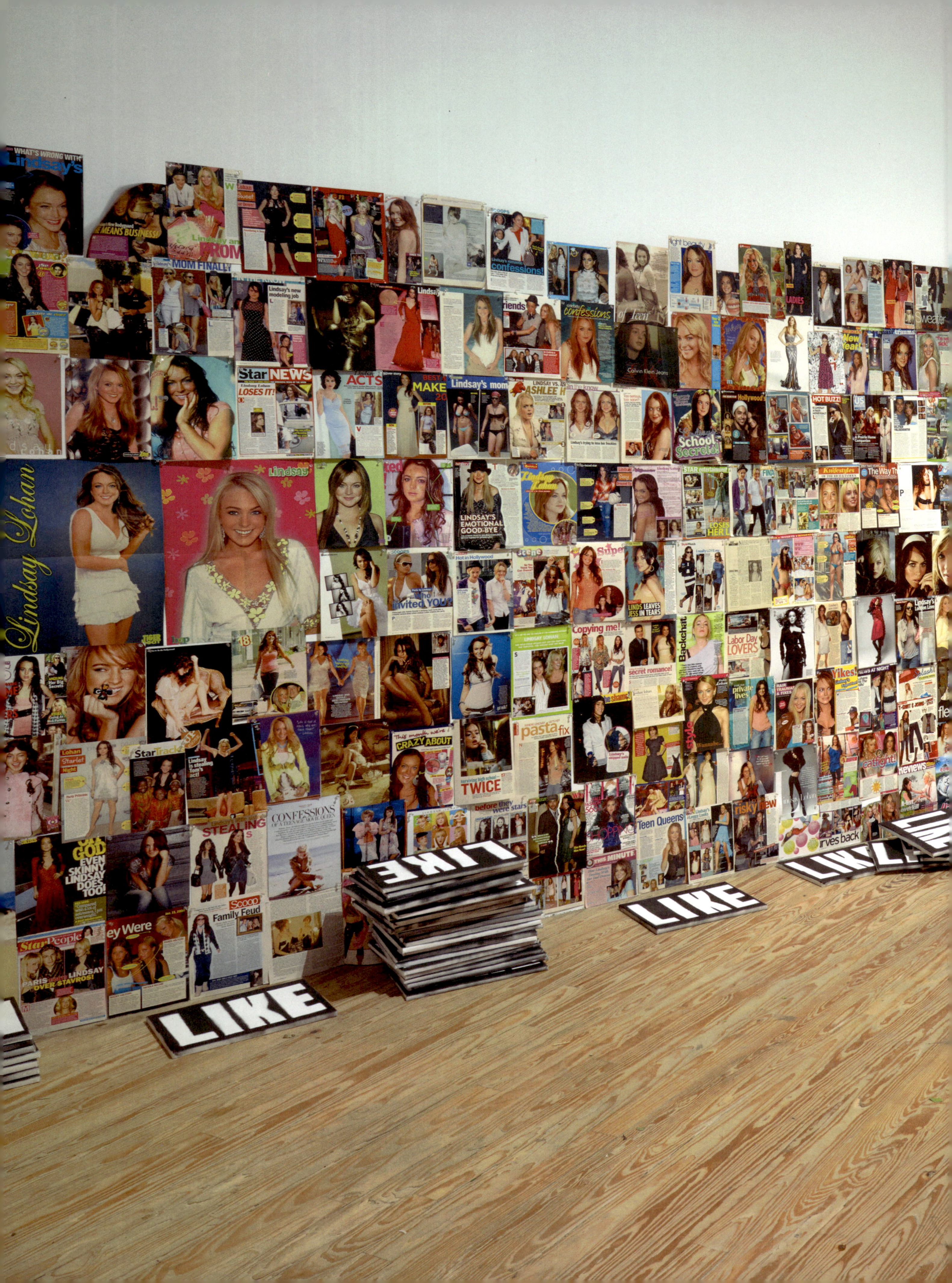

WHAT'S WRONG WITH Lindsay's
MOM FINALLY
confessions!
Lindsay's new modeling job
Star NEWS
LOSES IT!
ACTS
Lindsay's mom
School Secrets!
Lindsay Lohan
Lindsay
LINDSAY'S EMOTIONAL GOOD-BYE
Hot in Hollywood
invited YOU!
LINDS LEAVES JESS IN TEARS
Copying me!
secret romance!
Backchat
Labor Day LOVERS
Yikes!
private lives
pasta fix
CRAZY ABOUT
TWICE
Lohan Starlet
StarTracks
STEALING
CONFESSIONS OF A TEENAGE MOVIE QUEEN
Teen Queens
risky new
OH GOD! EVEN SKINNY LINDSAY DOES, TOO!
Scoop
Family Feud
ey Were
PARIS LINDSAY OVER STAVROS!
Reviews
catfight!
LIKE
LIKE
LIKE
LIKE
LIKE

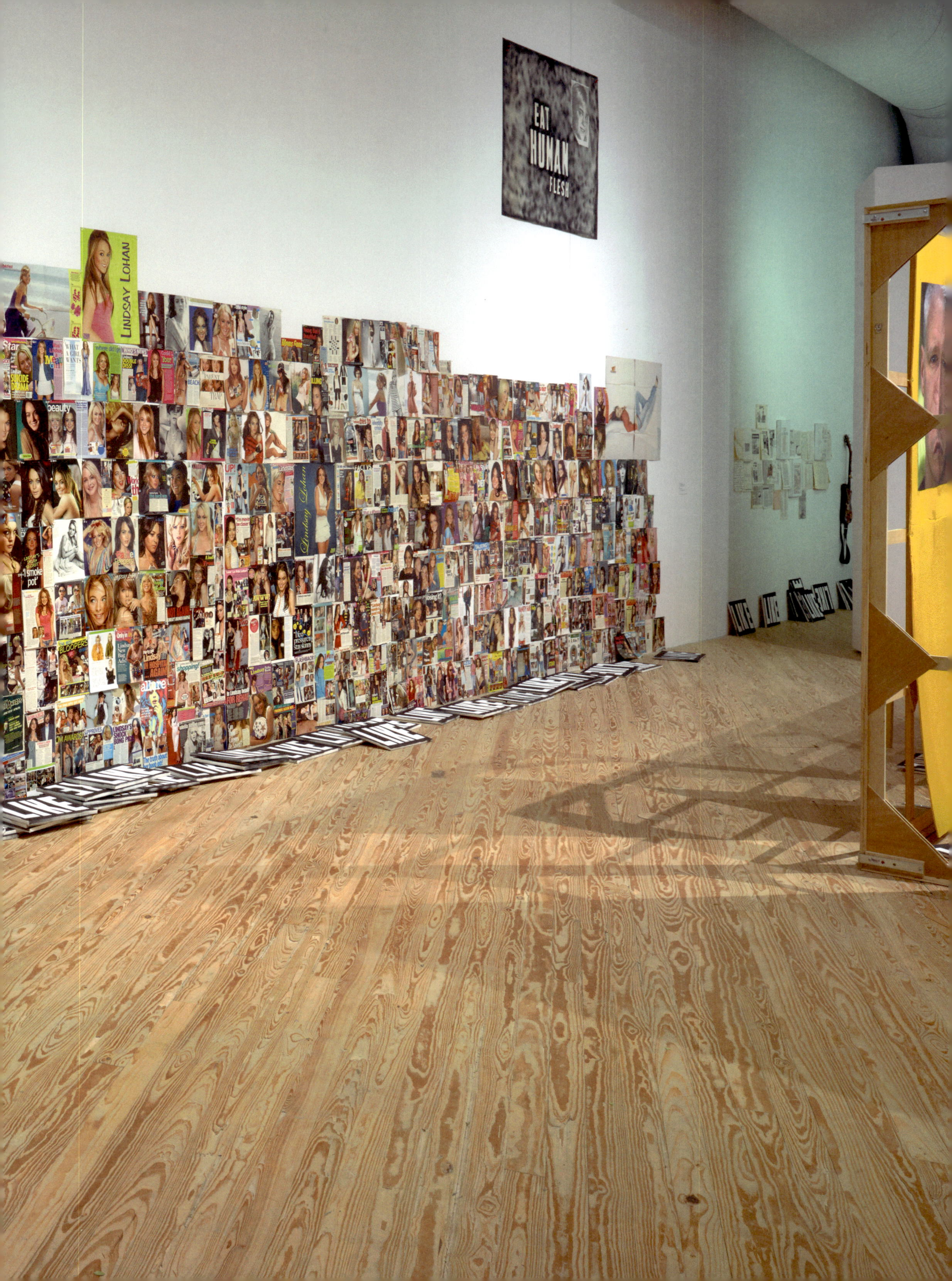

EAT
HUMAN
FLESH
LINDSAY LOHAN

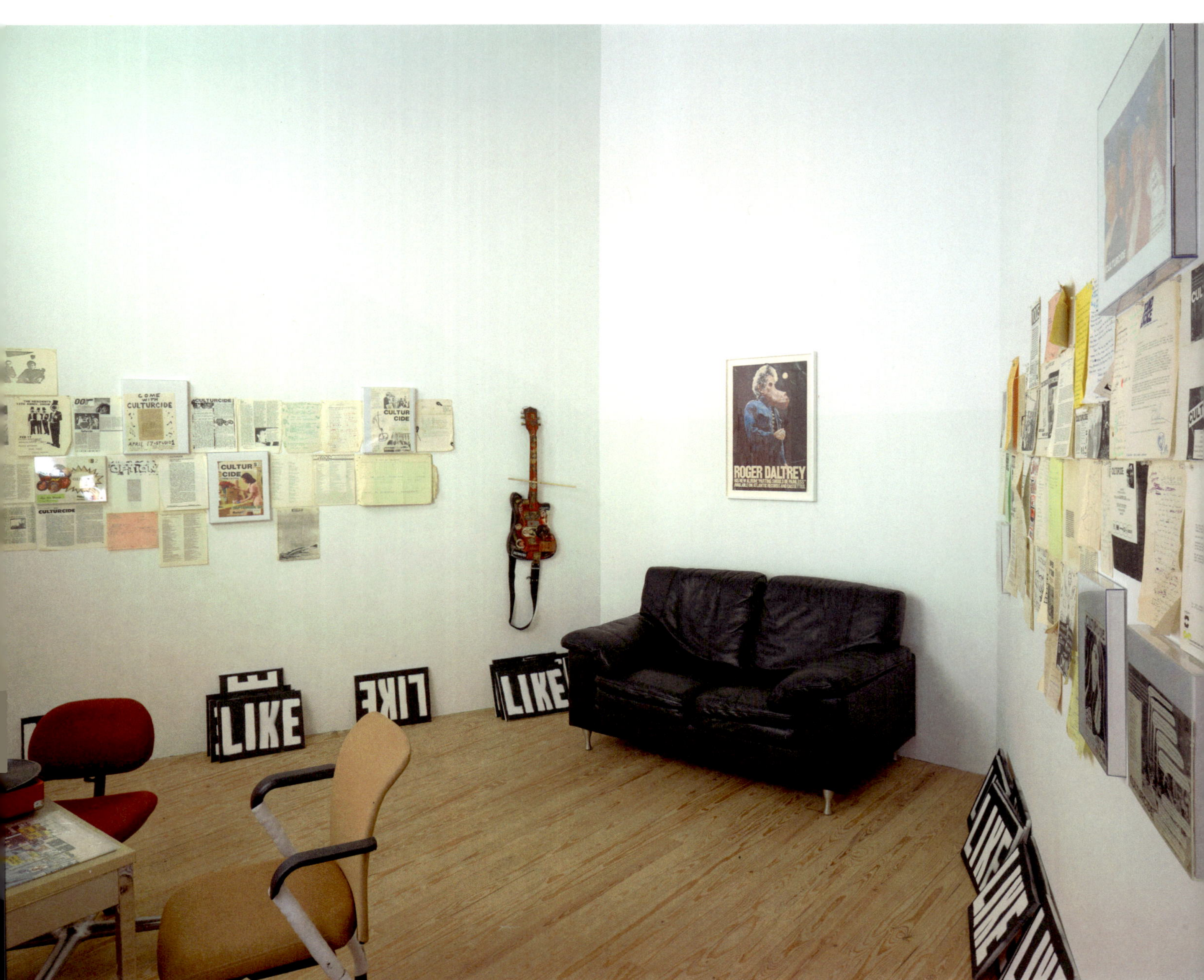
COME WITH CULTURCIDE
CULTURCIDE
CULTUR CIDE
CULTUR CIDE
ROGER DALTREY
LIKE
LIKE
LIKE

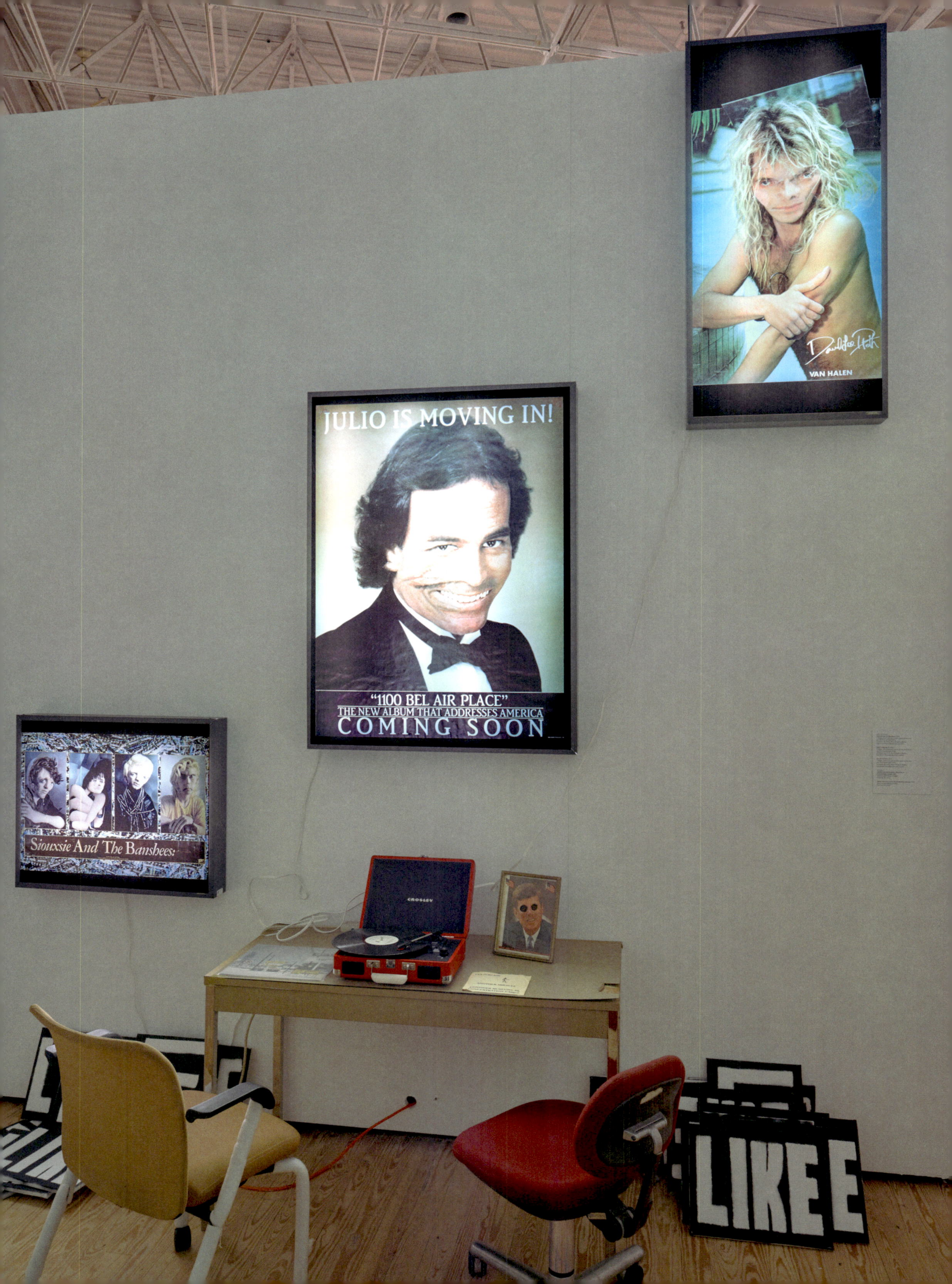
VAN HALEN
JULIO IS MOVING IN!
"1100 BEL AIR PLACE"
THE NEW ALBUM THAT ADDRESSES AMERICA
COMING SOON
Siouxsie And The Banshees:
CROSLEY
LIKE E

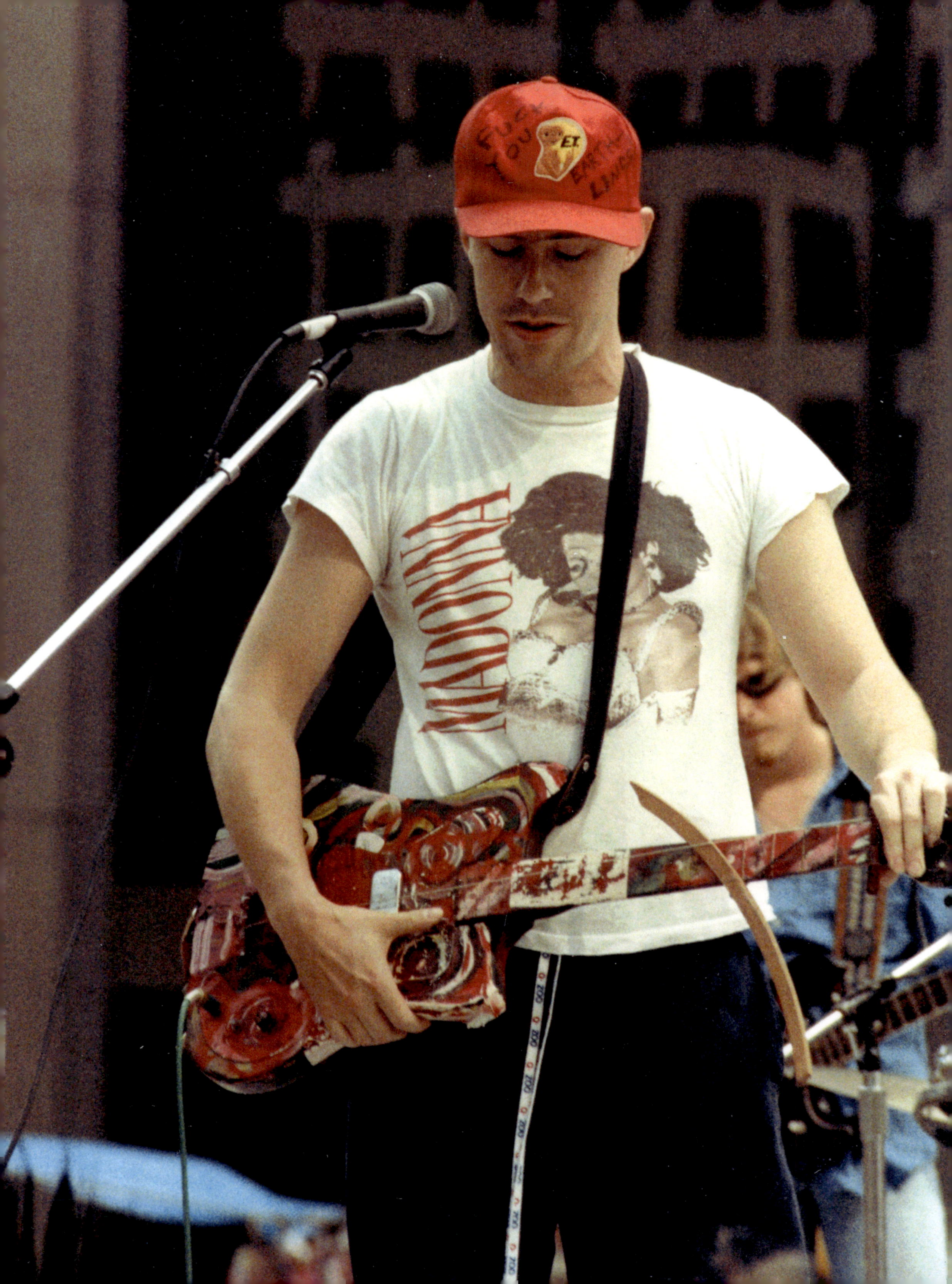
FUCK YOU
E.T.
MADONNA

Asger Jorn Meets Mark Flood:
From Denmark's "Intimate Banalities" to Houston's Culturcide

Alison M. Gingeras

Those who seek to curtail the production of banal art are enemies of the best of today's art.
—Asger Jorn, "Intimate Banalities," 1941[1]

DECADES BEFORE JEFF KOONS trafficked in low-class tchotchkes and proclaimed "Banality as Saviour" in his infamous *Artforum* ads, the Danish artist Asger Jorn offered this astonishingly prophetic vision in an essay entitled "Intimate Banalities." Published in the journal *Helhesten* during the Nazi occupation of Denmark, this incendiary manifesto—illustrated with images of clichéd designs by a local "Tattoo Jack," a tacky postcard reproduction of Raphael's angels, a pulpy horror novel graphic, and other examples of beloved trifles—effectively waged war on the tyranny of bourgeois taste and the sanctity of high culture. Opening his text with a lambasting tone, Jorn contends:

> One typically sees that he who has lost touch with the fundamentals of art also lacks a sense of the banal... I speak of the ability to understand the artistic value of banality. Indeed, its fundamental importance for the arts. There are countless examples of anonymous banalities whose validity and power span centuries and far surpass any brilliant performance by our so-called great figures.[2]

Jorn's tirade foretold many of the central tenants of the Cobra group, which he helped found in 1948 in Paris. Such principles include the non-hierarchical embrace of kitsch, amateur, populist, and folk forms, an antibourgeois rejection of good taste, and a fully politicized conception of aesthetics. His oracular call for a "new popular art" was grounded in an emotional *and* intellectual investment in the collective humanity enshrined within these banal cultural relics. Jorn would argue that a crummy painting by an unknown Sunday painter has greater pictorial and affective power than a rarefied masterpiece by an acknowledged genius. To contemporary ears, such statements are hardly shocking. Grandfather to the generation of Mike Kelley and Jeff Koons, Jorn paved the way for a critical recuperation of low culture for its poetic, political, and mnemonic value.

During the Cobra period (1948–51), Jorn first translated the subversive ideas of "Intimate Banalities" into his own art practice. In 1949 he made a series of ink drawings on top of several commercial reproductions of well-known works—the same image of Raphael's angels that he had used in *Helbesten*, as well as compositions by Salvador Dalí, Édouard Manet, and Pierre-Auguste Renoir. Overlaid on these masterworks, Jorn's humorous scrawls have been often mistaken as a mere reapplication of Marcel Duchamp's Dadaist defacement of the Mona Lisa, *L.H.O.O.Q* (1919). Yet as Jorn scholar Karen Kurczynski argues:

> Where Duchamp was more interested in the outmoded status of painting as personal expression, however, Jorn celebrates an oppositional form of outsider expression.... In 1950, Jorn wrote to Constant of his idea to create what he called "La section d'amélioration des anciennes toiles" (The Section for the Improvement of Old Canvases), for which these

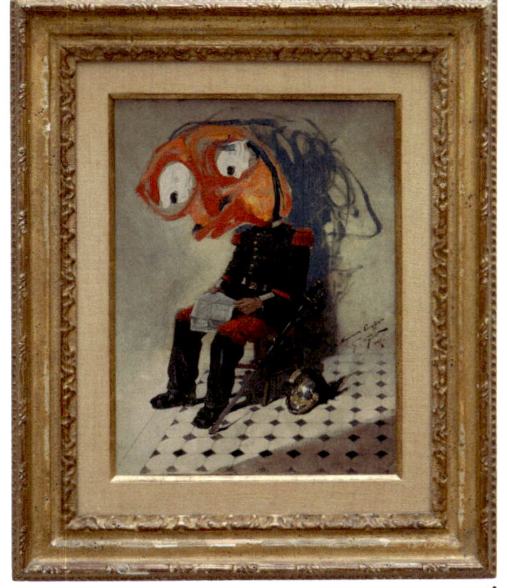

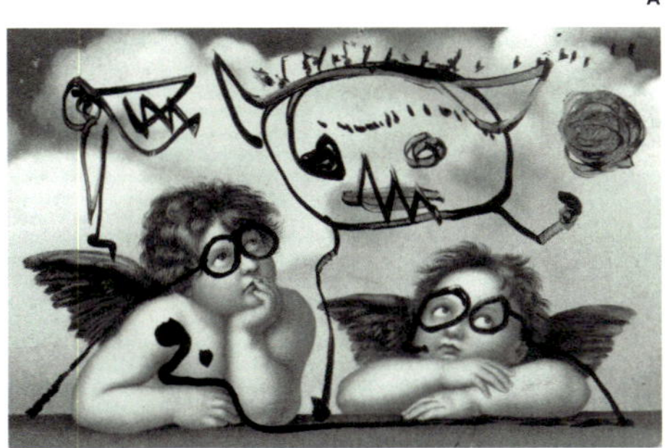

LEFT
Mark Flood performing with Culturcide on April 13, 1986, at New Music America, Houston, on the Houston Town Square Stage

A
Asger Jorn
Une tête comme ça, 1962
Modification of a found oil painting on canvas
Image: 12⅜ x 9¼ inches
Framed: 19⅜ x 16 x 2 inches
Private collection

B
Asger Jorn
Untitled (Raphael's Angels), c. 1949
Ink on commercial postcard
3½ x 5½ inches
Collection Troels Jorn, Copenhagen

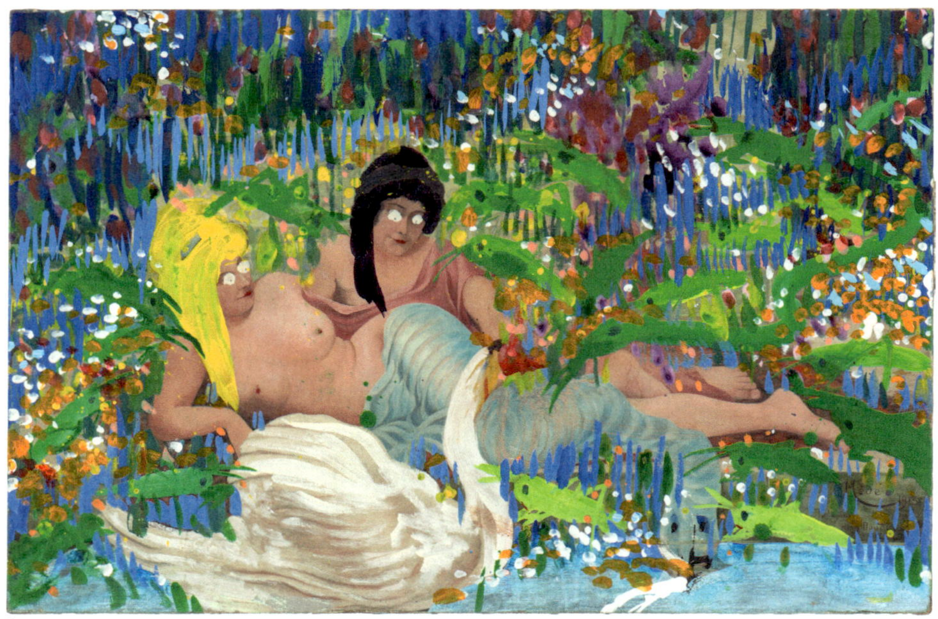

C

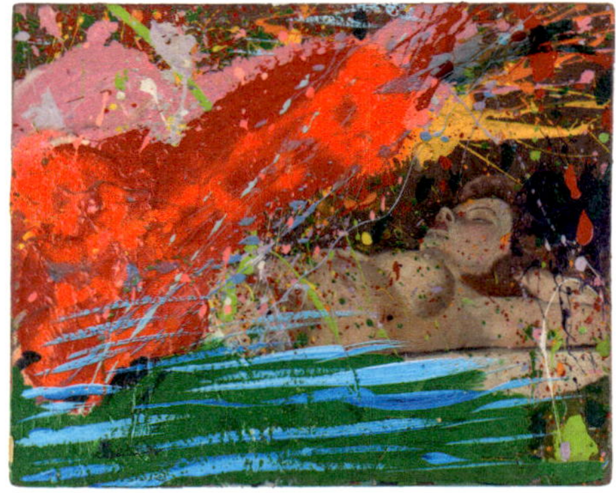

D

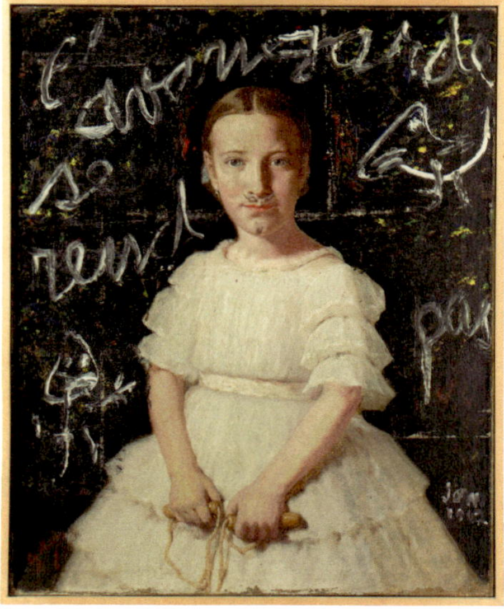

E

> works were experimental prototypes. He specified then that their function would be positive, in order to preserve the "*actualité*" of old pictures and save them from oblivion.[3]

These early gestures thus foreshadow one of Jorn's most famous and resonant series: the Modification paintings, which he began while active in the political avant-garde group the Situationist International during the late 1950s and early 1960s.

Jorn first met Guy Debord and Michèle Bernstein in Paris in 1954. Prompted by Enrico Baj (one of his main post-Cobra collaborators) to delve into the journal *Potlatch*, Jorn sought out these kindred spirits, to which Debord replied, "We are happy to learn of your actions in a struggle that is also ours."[4] After the First World Congress of Free Artists in Alba, Italy, in 1956, Jorn was able to build an official alliance between key members of his post-Cobra group—the International Movement for an Imaginist Bauhaus—and Debord's politicized intellectual circle to eventually form the Situationist International (SI), one of the most mythologized leftist groups of the postwar era. While Jorn was active within the SI for just a few years (from 1957 to 1961, though the movement endured until 1972), many of his experiments begun with Cobra came to fruition during this period. As Kurczynski suggests, "The significance of the Situationist International for contemporary art, architecture, film and critical theory is undeniable.... Jorn's role in the movement, however, has been overlooked; it was he who most strongly related the early practices of the SI to visual art and he financed Situationist activities with the sale of his paintings."[5] It was Jorn's particular embrace of the theory and practice of *détournement*—a term the Situationists coined to mean "the re-employment in a new unity of preexisting artistic elements"—that served as the artistic motor of the group.[6] Early examples of *détournement* include Jorn's collaboration with Debord on two artists' books: *Fin de Copenhague* (1957) and *Mémoires* (1958). Both publications bring together a pastiche of found texts, cartoons, advertisements, maps, and photographs from commercial or mainstream sources to create an experimental narrative stream. Jorn contributed painterly interventions on the pages—colorful drips that mock the style of Jackson Pollock and other gestural marks that quote *informel* abstraction popular at that time. These seminal early collaborations between Jorn and Debord, which the group described as "transforming kitsch into

C
Asger Jorn and Walasse Ting
Spring Garden for Asger, 1963
Acrylic on found oil painting on canvas
25½ x 39½ inches
Collection Mia and Jesse Ting

D
Asger Jorn and Walasse Ting
Think of You Every Morning, Dream of You Every Nite Darling, c. 1969
Acrylic on found oil painting on canvas
16 x 20 inches
Collection Mia and Jesse Ting

E
Asger Jorn
L'avant-garde se rend pas, 1962
Oil on found painting on canvas
28¾ x 23⅝ inches
Collection Micky and Pierre Alechinsky

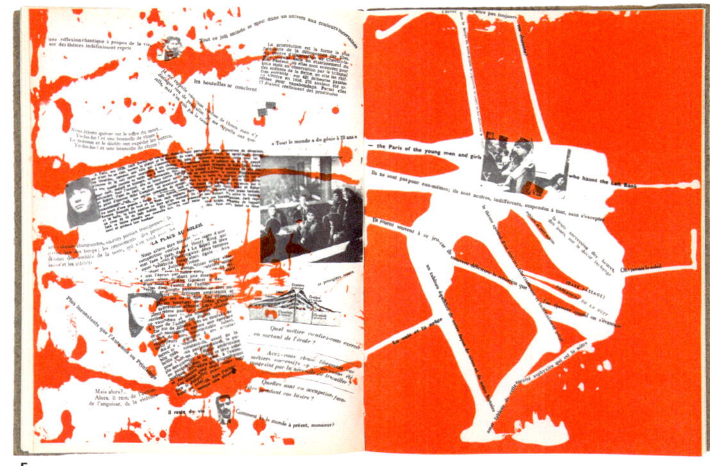

F

agitation and high art forms into kitsch,"[7] laid the foundation for further critical deployments of appropriation, fragmentation, and the recuperation of historical memory in Jorn's Modification series.

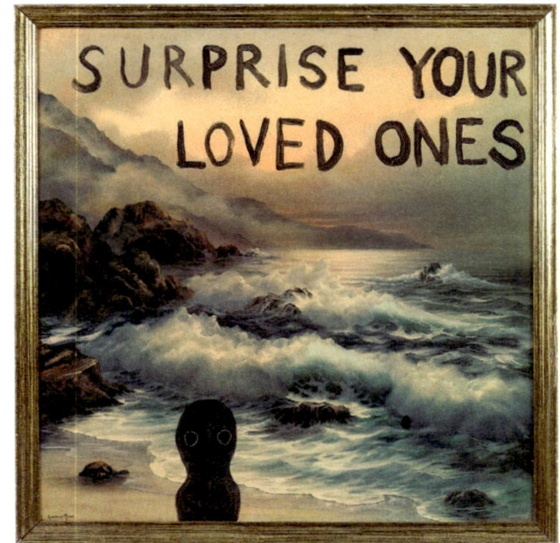

G

What might be more plainly described today as a form of radically politicized appropriation, Jorn called Modifications, New Disfigurations, or Détourned paintings (he used these three different terms for the three exhibitions of his work made on "found" paintings executed between 1959 and 1962). Most of Jorn's overpainted canvases are humdrum or kitschy examples of nineteenth- and early-twentieth-century genres that he bought in flea markets while traveling through Italy, France, Holland, Germany, and England in the mid-to-late 1950s.[8] In 1959 Jorn revisited his original theorizations from "Intimate Banalities" while writing a text for his first exhibition of Modifications, held at the Galerie Rive Gauche in Paris: "I have expressed my love for sofa painting and for the last twenty years I have been preoccupied with the idea of rendering homage to it. In this exhibition, I erect a monument in honor of bad painting.... It is painting sacrificed."[9]

From the perspective of the Situationists, the object of "sacrifice" in Jorn's Modifications was the sanctity of high art or modernism itself—Debord and his colleagues rejoiced in what they saw as Jorn's frontal attack or critical devaluation of painting as such. Yet Jorn's *détournement* was far more complex and ambivalent than the negation or oppositional intent that the Situationists projected upon this body of work. As much as they are emblems of vociferous critique, the Modifications are concurrently imbued with reverence and humor. They are in fact most subversive when understood as lamentations for the traces of humanity that survive on the lowly canvases, or emblems of veneration of the forgotten authors that created the scavenged pictures. Jorn saw the source material for his painting *L'avant-garde se rend pas* (1962)—a portrait of a conservative young girl in a white confirmation dress that he playfully defaced—as "a form of folk creativity unfairly marginalized from the discourse of both modernism and the avant-garde, now both equally aligned with social elitism and outmoded conceptions of artistic progress."[10] And he unrepentantly loved the humanity encapsulated in his appropriated works—a romance roguishly suggested in the erotic series of Modifications he made in collaboration with Walasse Ting during the late 1960s, including *Think of You Every Morning, Dream of You Every Nite Darling* (c. 1969). This display of transgressive affection for kitsch, popular art was as subversive as any act of recuperation or defacement.

Not all intimate banalities are quite so romantic. Fast forward to the early 1980s: almost any of Mark Flood's early works could be seen as an angry update of "The Section for the Improvement of Old Canvases." Flood is one of the most compelling of the contemporary heirs of Jorn's use of *détournement*. "SURPRISE YOUR LOVED ONES"—a command shouted in angry black lettering on a ghastly, tacky seascape—is just one of Flood's garage-sale tableaux created in early 1980s Houston. "DEATH CAREER PISS" screams another condemnation, painted atop an anodyne autumnal panorama in shades of orange, abruptly turned vertically. Both works were made during a period that Flood has dubbed his "Hateful Years," during which he forged a quasi–outsider art practice that mediated upon the dire nature of the American condition under President Reagan. The decade spawned several different series of paintings—Directives, Idols, Monsters, and

F
Asger Jorn and Guy Debord
Mémoires: Structures portantes d'Asger Jorn
Artist's book (drawings with sandpaper cover), 1958
10 13/16 x 16 13/16 inches

G
Mark Flood
SURPRISE YOUR LOVED ONES, c. 1980s
Mixed media
39 x 39 inches

Stick Figures—all of which feature amateur thrift store art as background supports. As of 1982, when Flood began this work, he was unaware of the precedent of Jorn's Modifications (and only after 1984 did he begin to immerse himself in the writings of the Situationists).[11] Coming from an intuitive perspective, Flood found that old canvases provided a cheap, nasty materiality that mirrored the punk attitude and aesthetic of his band, Culturcide. Like Jorn, Flood sought to address issues surrounding class and taste while also rescuing cultural relics from the "abyss of the average."[12] This is the subject of Flood's *WHORE* (1983), another painting from the Hateful Years that depicts a lone stick figure rendered in thick black paint in the foreground of a beach landscape complete with a blazing sunset. If this scene is the illustration of the anonymous Sunday painter's utopic hopes and dreams, Flood seized upon such aspirational expression to comment on the more pessimistic reality of our collective situation. Here the whore is an Everyman: an emaciated member of the masses, enslaved to consumerist debt and media-generated desire. Flood deployed the Jornian-paradigm of modification to transform a banal folk art relic into a dystopian icon that reflects the darkest corners of the American condition. As the artist recently confirmed, "My theory was that capitalism permeated everything cultural so any cultural object could be made into some significant counter-statement. Putting my figures into empty unpopulated product-paintings was about colonizing the anti-human with the human."[13]

With this added layer of political darkness, Flood's scavenging of populist forms took Jorn's legacy to an even gloomier place under the guise of the band Culturcide. Just as Jorn's precocious texts and politicized uses of *détournement* initiated a call for a radical new popular art—directly attacking the sanctity of classical, high culture and replacing it with more lowly counterparts—so too did Flood's band. Offering the musical equivalent of the modification, Culturcide did not appropriate, sample, or cover pre-existing popular songs. Instead Flood and his bandmates wrote their own lyrics for about a dozen well-known songs and then sang directly on top of the original recordings, resulting in an anarchic transformation. The black humor of the band's 1980 single "Consider Museums as Concentration Camps" leaves no doubt as to the object of Flood's rage. No form of cultural production is sacred in his eyes—had Jorn lived to see the birth of punk, he could have only been a Culturcide fan.

More than just a juvenile punk band, Culturcide takes on a greater symbolic importance. It becomes a banner term to summarize how Jorn's legacy has been translated and adopted by a contemporary American context. While there is a zigzagging genealogical line that connects artists such as Flood, Friedrich Kunath, Per Kirkeby, Jim Shaw, and other contemporaries to their Cobra forebears, each of these artists shares in the spirit of Culturcide—carrying out Jorn's revolutionary investment in anticlassicism, collective, transgenerational authorship, and celebrating the continuity of human culture from the bottom up. To quote the critic and early defender of Flood's work Bob Nickas, Culturcide is more than just "the killing of culture." It's also an alternative response to the state of culture, "homicide, patricide, suicide... culturcide."[14]

Echoing this mix of black humor and rage is Flood's own stream-of-consciousness writing in *Clerk Fluid* (2009), an expansive tome that collects the artist's critical musings on the art world's hypocrisies, the bankruptcy of academia, and the wasteland of corporate culture. The whole book could be summed up as Flood's "corrosive hostility to the social order."[15] On his embrace of his outsider position and its correlation to his own recuperative plundering of low culture, Flood comments, "All my artist idols had been renegades and transgressors, and the history of Modernism, as I understood it, was a story of rule-breakers who ended up being heroes. I was hateful and I made hateful art, so I thought I should fit right in.... The Dadaist Tzara had said, 'There is a great negative work of destruction to be done,' and as of the nineteen eighties, I didn't think the chore had been satisfactorily completed."[16] Flood's invention of Culturcide

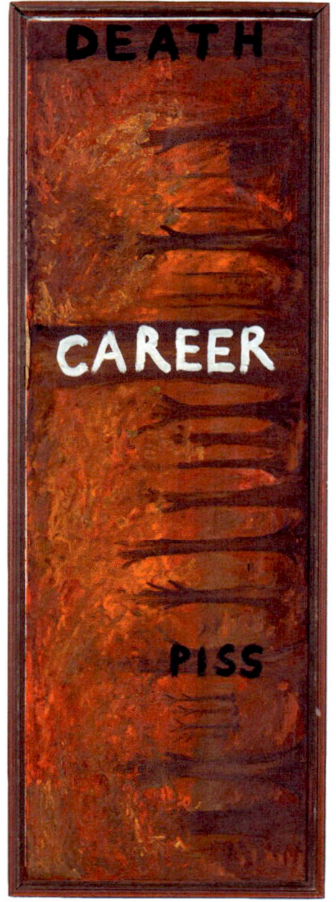

H

H
Mark Flood
DEATH CAREER PISS, c. 1980s
Mixed media
50 x 17½ inches

and his Hateful Years were his response to this multisided sense of alienation.

The parallels between Flood's own critical musings as a young outsider in Houston in the early 1980s and those of Jorn in Denmark in the 1940s (and later in Paris in the 1960s) are uncanny. Culturcide should be understood as part of this long lineage whose seeds were sown on the pages of *Helhesten* and whose fruit was borne from the network of Jorn's influences in Cobra, Situationism, and a host of contemporary practices that carry this contestatory DNA. Culturcide is shorthand for the failure of high modernism. It's a catchy and angry American update of "Intimate Banalities"—a raging anthem of radical populism entwined with blasphemous political critique. As the American cultural critic Greil Marcus noted in 1989, a direct parallel can be seen between the Situationist International and the punk movement of the 1970s, both of which "tried to banish sorrow for fury" in their shared rejection of bourgeois taste and sociopolitical complacency.[17] This rage-filled family tree reaching back to Asger Jorn provides the necessary art-historical context to understand the works of the Hateful Years, but this ferocity also informs the entire forty-year span of Flood's diverse oeuvre.

Notes

1 Asger Jørgensen, "Intimate Banalities," trans. by René Lauritesen in *Hvad skovsøen gemte: Jorns modifikationer og Kirkebys overmalinger* (Silkeborg: Museum Jorn, 2011), p. 130. Originally published in *Helhesten: Tidsrift for Kunst* (Copenhagen) 1, no. 2 (1941), pp. 33–38.

2 Ibid, p. 129.

3 Karen Kurczynski, *The Art and Politics of Asger Jorn: The Avant-Garde Won't Give Up* (Burlington, Vt.: Ashgate, 2014), p. 178.

4 Ibid., p. 147.

5 Ibid., p. 148.

6 "Le détournement comme négation et prélude," *Internationale Situationniste* 3 (December 1959), p. 78.

7 Ibid., p. 161.

8 Kurczynski, *Art and Politics*, p. 176.

9 Asger Jorn, "Detourned Painting," trans. by Thomas Y. Levin in *Hvad skovsøen gemte: Jorns modifikationer og Kirkebys overmalinger* (Silkeborg: Museum Jorn, 2011), p. 133. Originally published as "Peinture détournée,' in *Modifications: Vingt peintures modifiees par Asger Jorn*, exh. cat. (Paris: Galerie Rive Gauche, 1959).

10 Kurczynski, *Art and Politics*, p. 174.

11 Mark Flood, correspondence with the author, March 2016.

12 See Alison M. Gingeras, "Resist Much, Obey Little," in *Pressed Release: Notes on Mark Flood's Hateful Years, 1979–1989*, exh. cat. (New York: Luxembourg and Dayan, 2012) pp. 15–17.

13 Mark Flood, correspondence with the author, March 2016.

14 Bob Nickas, "Assisted Culturcide: Bob Nickas and Crack Foyer on the Art of Mark Flood," in *Pressed Release*, p. 43.

15 Clark Flood, *Clerk Fluid* (2009), p. 139.

16 Ibid., p. 138.

17 Greil Marcus, *Lipstick Traces: A Secret History of the Twentieth Century* (Cambridge, Mass.: Harvard University Press, 1989), p. 123.

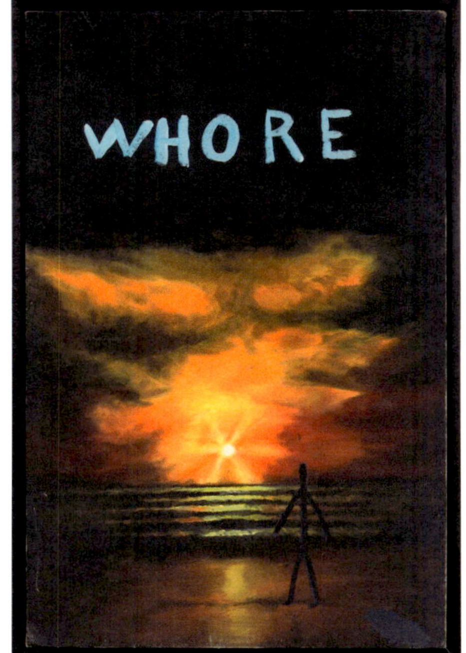

I
Mark Flood
Whore, 1983
Mixed media
36 x 20 inches

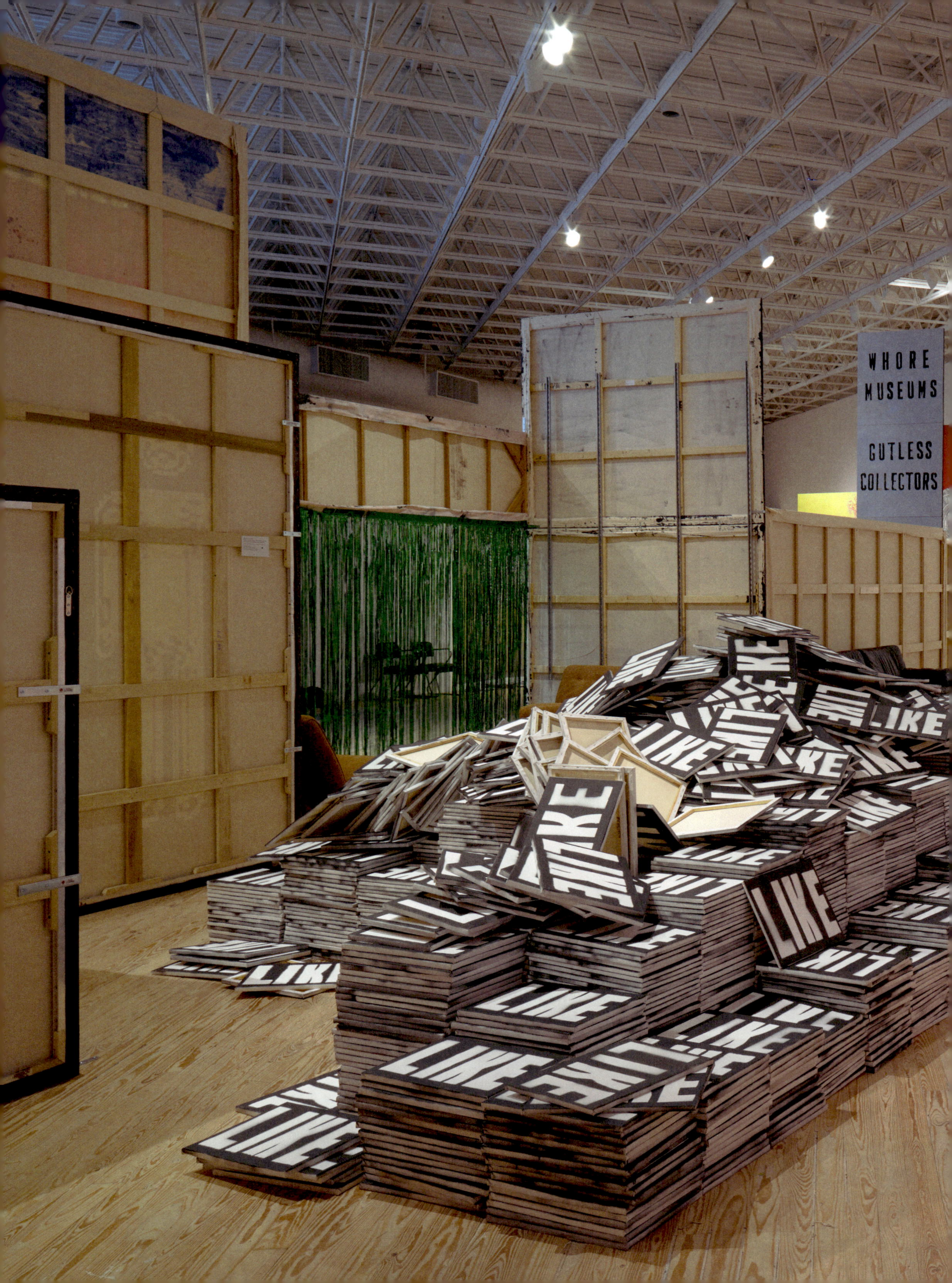
WHORE
MUSEUMS
GUTLESS
COLLECTORS
LIKE

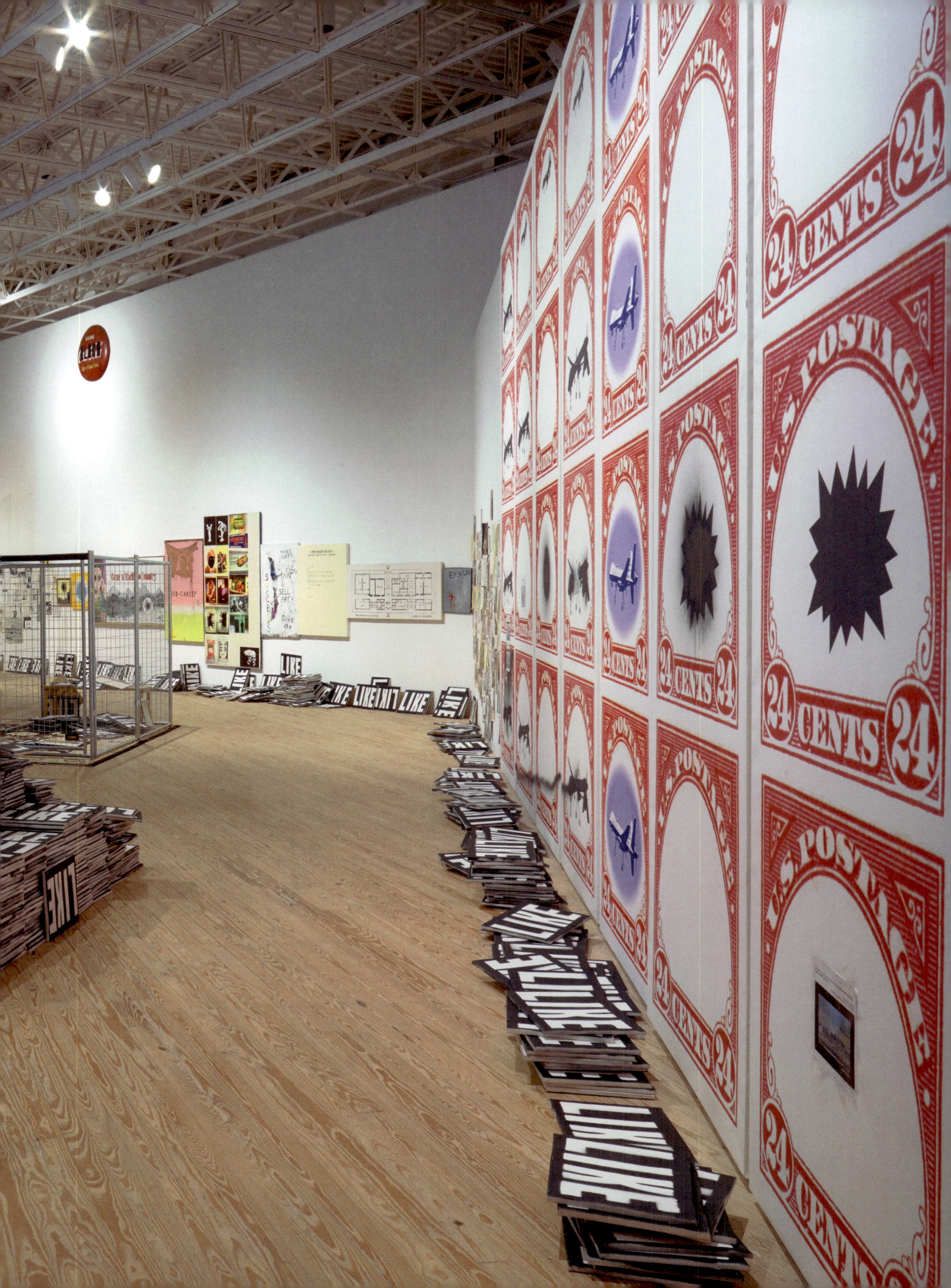
U.S. POSTAGE
24 CENTS 24
LIKE

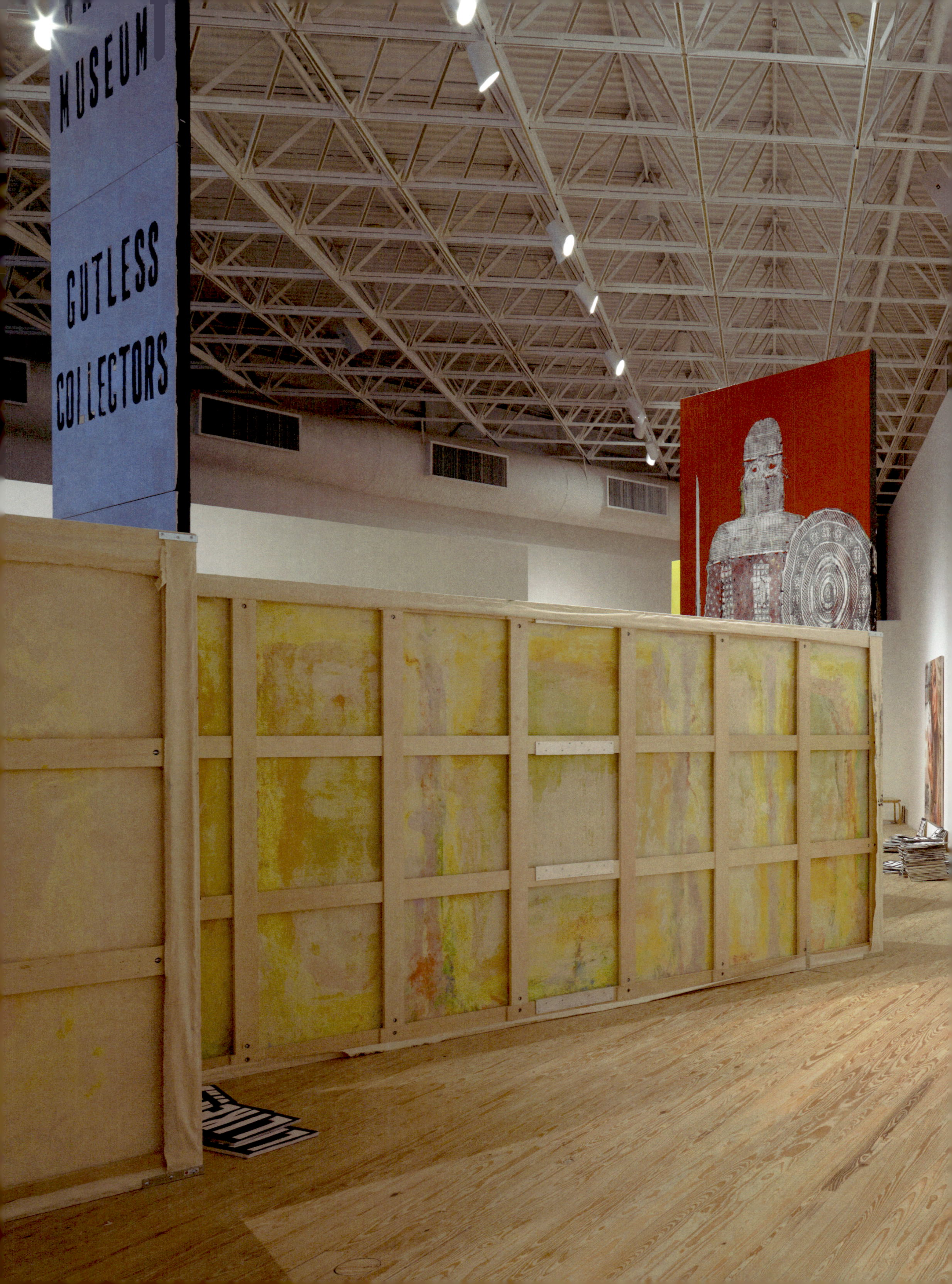
MUSEUM
GUTLESS
COLLECTORS

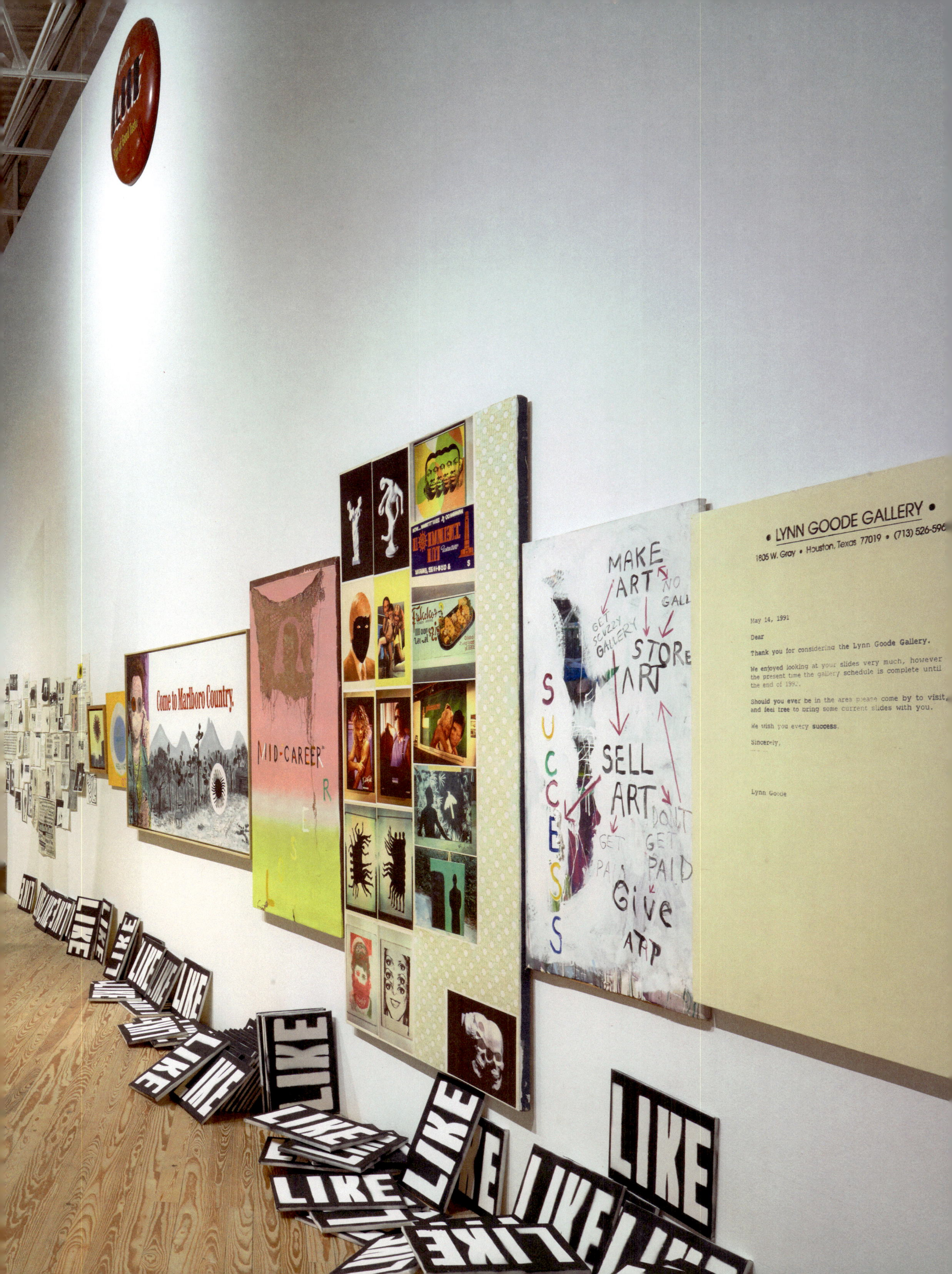
Come to Marlboro Country.
MID-CAREER
MAKE ART
NO GALL
GET SCUZZY GALLERY
STORE ART
SUCCESS
SELL ART
GET PAID
DON'T GET PAID
Give
• LYNN GOODE GALLERY •
1805 W. Gray • Houston, Texas 77019 • (713) 526-596
May 14, 1991
Dear
Thank you for considering the Lynn Goode Gallery.
We enjoyed looking at your slides very much, however the present time the gallery schedule is complete until the end of 199
Should you ever be in the area please come by to visit, and feel free to bring some current slides with you.
We wish you every success.
Sincerely,
Lynn Goode
LIKE

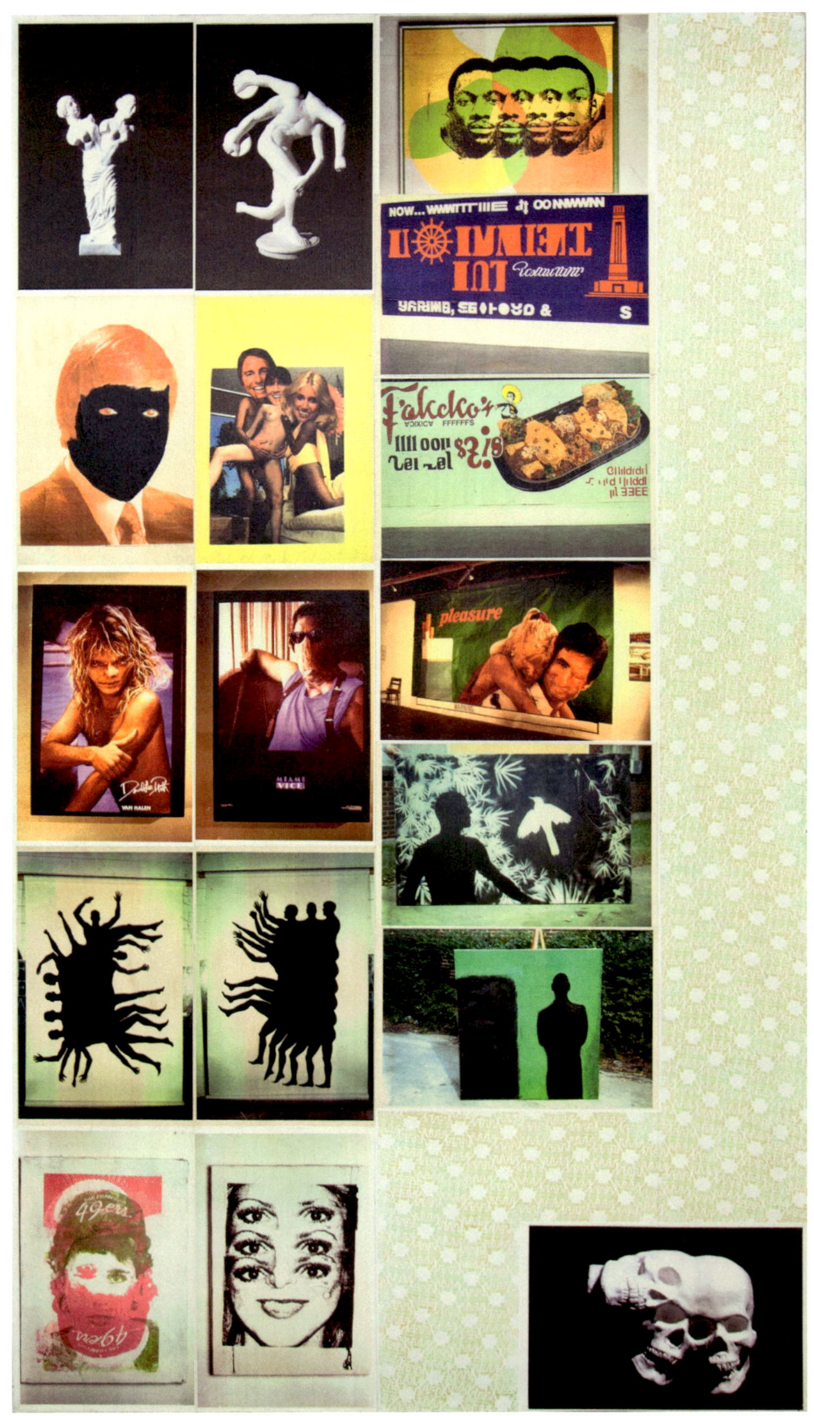

Retrospektro 1998 collage and acrylic on canvas 82 x 48 inches

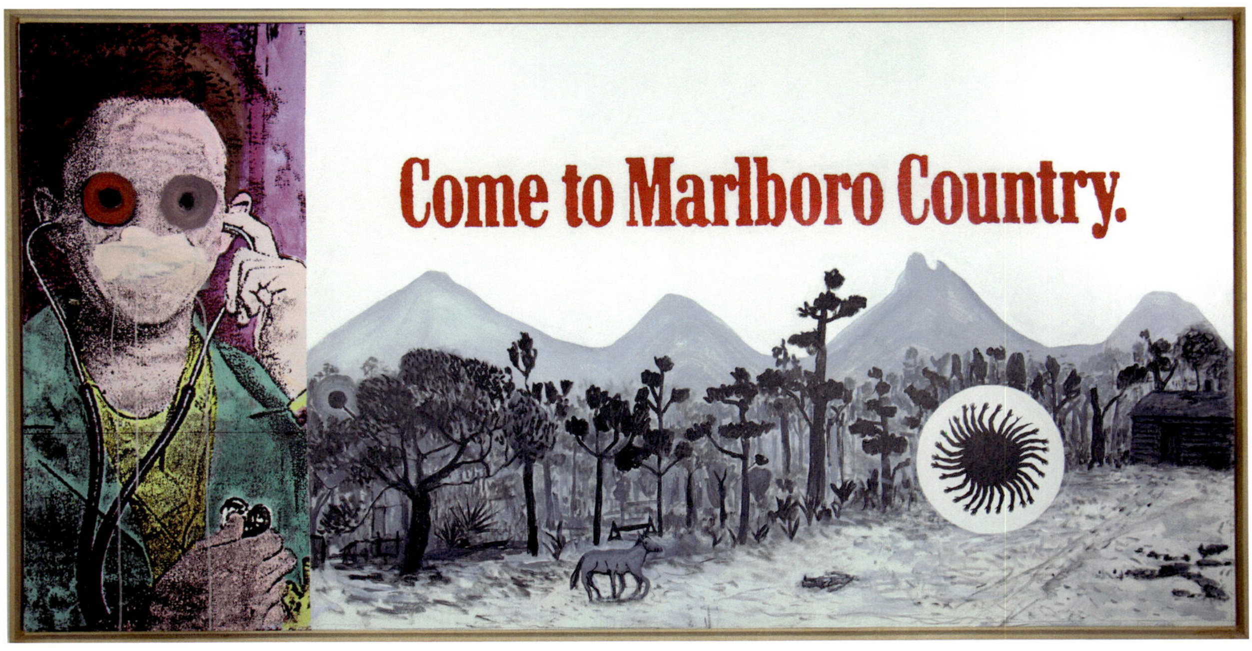

Bonanza 1995 acrylic on canvas 40 x 80 inches

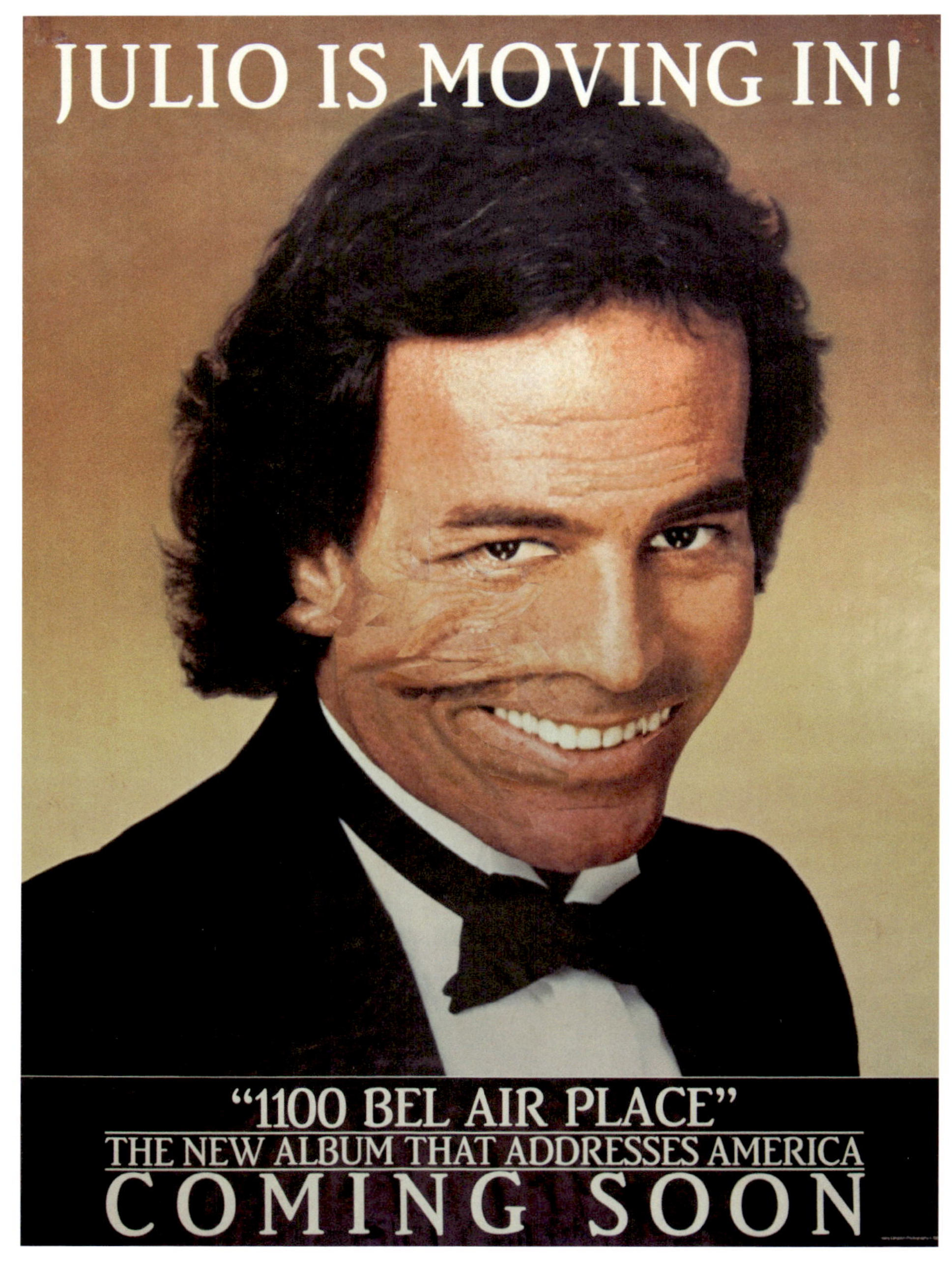

Julio Is Moving In 1984 collage, ultraviolet ink, acrylic panel, aluminum, and florescent light bulbs 48 x 36 inches

Après moi le déluge: Mark Flood at a High-Water Mark

Carlo McCormick

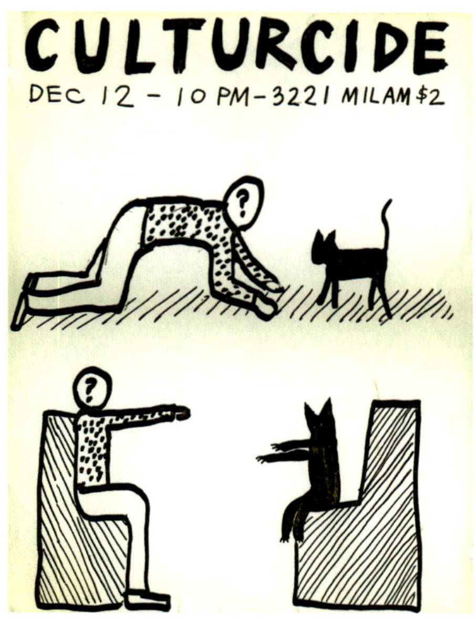

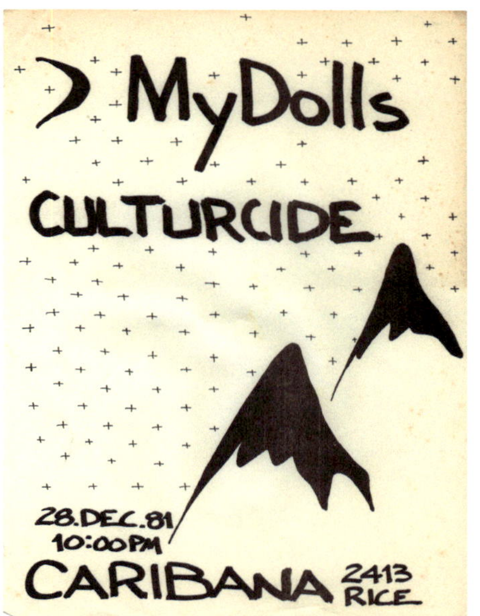

A

THE NERVOUS LAUGHTER THAT shatters an uncomfortable silence, the ugly truth so seldom spoken, the shrill voice that just won't shut up, the funny money fobbed off on fools by disreputable agents, the passing gas from the bloated corpse of late capitalism; Mark Flood is the face of our disgrace. Having been convinced of his genius long before most anyone else would give him the time of day, I must admit that his remarkable success now seems less a matter of his own brutal intelligence than the unmitigated stupidity of our culture at large. He's the kindest man I know making the most hateful art possible, drenched in beauty and dripping with resentment, the oversweetened taste of a shit pie thrown right in our kisser. The only reason that we're all finally paying attention now is because he has managed to come up with a version of the facts that's actually more entertaining than all the lies we normally tell ourselves.

I suspect it takes a particular kind of idiocy to decipher such an enigma, and that my abiding folly allows me certain insights into the checkered past that has brought Mr. Flood to public attention. We know things…

And what we cannot say for certain, we conjure in the imagination, where the black and white of a dog's vision is made lurid and you can smell the cloying lust of some secret sex through the lace curtains of our social politesse. Yes, though he swore me to silence long ago, I want to tell you about this man. And to do so, the worst crime of a writer, far more vulgar than whatever graphic details we may have to share, is the self-incrimination of having to use the first person. How patently inept to use the word "I" in any text, and Mark taught me ages ago that it was never so much a matter of self as the prevailing conflict of us versus them, but to bear witness it demands that we dot every jaundiced eye. His art allows an infinitely expansive space for personal sins and collective transgressions, but whatever pleasure you may take or shame you may earn from it depends wholly on the investment of your own culpability. Anyone who thinks his art is making fun of someone else just needs to take a good long look in the mirror.

In the end, all that we know is simply that which we cannot forget. This, then, is how I remember Mark Flood, though to be entirely honest for many years I did not know him by that name. Mark gave me my first copy of *The Society of the Spectacle* and my very first Culturcide record. Surely you must know of these things? If not there can be absolutely no hope of understanding Mark Flood, so let's do a little recap just in case. Both the book and the band changed my life—and forever altered a whole lot of our culture without most people realizing it—and not necessarily in a good way, more like what happens when you take the red pill in *The Matrix*. Written in 1967, just in time to be the philosophical rallying cry for the student revolts of 1968, *The Society of the Spectacle* was the most damning testament to the ways in which authentic experience is supplanted by ersatz simulacra in the materialist modern world. Its author, Guy Debord, was certainly already one of capitalism's harshest and most astute critics, but what he lays out in his description of a society in which "life is presented as an immense accumulation of spectacles," and "everything that was directly lived has receded into a representation," is like the child's voice that calls out the bald-ass lies of the Emperor's New Clothes bottled up in a Molotov cocktail thrown to burn down the whole house of fashion. To fathom the deeper antagonism lurking in Flood's highly dysfunctional love/hate relationship with the art world, consider

A
Culturcide
Flyers, c. 1980s
Courtesy Dan Workman

Like an ugly child or a bad joke, Culturcide would not go away and only became more hideous with the passing years.

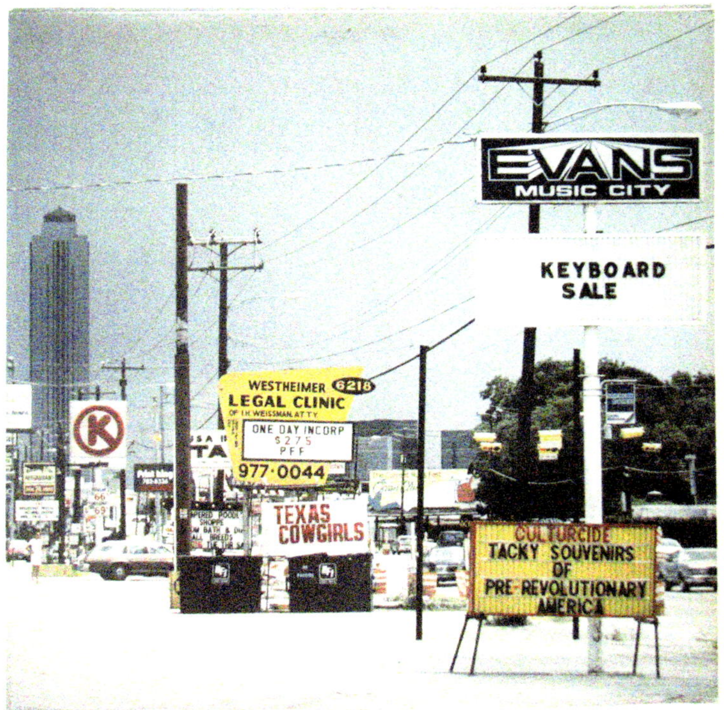

B

Debord's parsing of visual culture. "The Spectacle is not a collection of images," he tells us, "it is a social relationship between people that is mediated by images." And while we might think that such sentiments would turn Mark into a Marxist, it's more like when he heard the laughter of the crowd realizing their king was indeed nude: he appreciated the joke as much as the lie and would forever take perverse pleasure in the orgy of mortified flesh.

As the urtext of the Situationist International, *The Society of the Spectacle* can easily be seen as the first cobblestone lobbed at a window with the missive "beauty is in the streets," just as one can connive a political meaning for punk. The wrath and the poetics unleashed in the uprisings of 1968 can be heard like the grating noise of appropriated atrocities that make up Culturcide's first single, "Another Miracle" (with its prescient flipside, "Consider Museums as Concentration Camps"), although it was released a dozen years later. What Culturcide brought to the revolution, thankfully, was a sense of humor. That mordant and morbid wit, its most lethal weapon, was from the outset anthemic to the times with its terminal interment of any hope—not just a rejection of the optimism invested in sixties idealism but an embrace of pessimism so utterly violent it was as if the singer was trying to drag us to the back room necrophilia where the history of humanism gets fisted by the warty hand of the no-future generation. It wasn't pretty and it wasn't meant to be. Like an ugly child or a bad joke, Culturcide would not go away and only became more hideous with the passing years.

Because of an unfortunate chronological and geographical proximity—both hailing from that fetid armpit of disreputable industries called Houston at that moment when punk would take a nasty turn toward experimental noise—and a disturbing resemblance between Culturcide's lyricist/vocalist Perry Webb and the artist who now goes by the name Mark Flood, there has been ample speculation that they are one and the same. No more verifiable or deniable than most of the other rumors that seem to circulate freely about these mysterious personas, the linkage between Webb and Flood is complicated by their penchant for avoiding recognition.

B
Culturcide
Tacky Souvenirs of Pre-Revolutionary America, 1986
Vinyl record, edition of 3000
12 x 12 inches

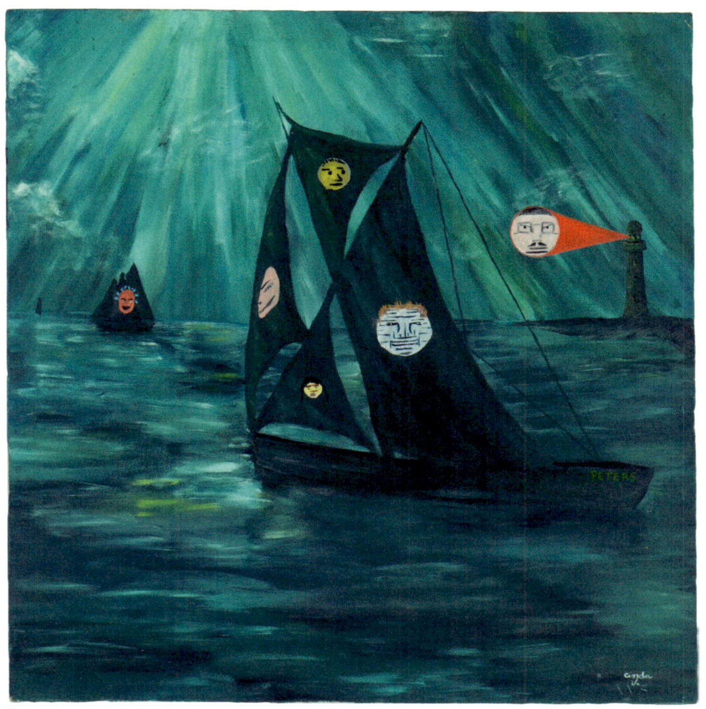
C

How esoteric has our culture become that we must name-drop the unknown?

Both were more known for their habit of hiring surrogates and impersonators than for what they might actually look like, and, just as tellingly, both careers languished in indifferent obscurity for decades before a belated, almost cultish, celebrity redefined their work for younger generations. Honestly, I should have seen it coming when famous "hot" young artists and musicians started telling me that they were "friends" of Perry or knew Mark personally, but it all seemed like such a joke. How esoteric has our culture become that we must name-drop the unknown? It would seem in the end to be just another elaborate hoax perpetrated by this aesthetic fiction of a man who's long been teasing us for our fascination with fame. And now, when the punch line of this shaggy dog joke finally occurs to me, I can hear him laughing all the way to the bank.

Mark's anonymity served him well, like a Duchampian silence, the unmistakable presence of an absence as one might feel the gravity on a day fecund with ominous rains. I think quite surely that he actually did want success and recognition in those early years, was positively hungry for it, but his skills of avoidance and denial—and, when absolutely necessary, deliberate self-sabotage—were so deft that his art danced on the overcrowded floor of contemporary practice alone, forlorn of any partner, as if it was hearing an entirely different song than the rest. Flood was truly postmodern in the very epitome of what that means, and not because he read the right books (which he did, though thankfully he was never one of those assholes who used the absurd art speak of that time), but because he had the heart of a thief and the soul of a saboteur. Mark kept a critical distance from and modest engagement with the art world, the witness who must by nature blend into the shadows, never so much trying to strike up a conversation as working to case the joint—perhaps a cat burglar waiting to break in and steal the beauty there, or just as likely an arsonist ready to torch the whole damn thing to the ground. Always funny simply because he had a wicked wit and the most perverse sense of humor, he was nonetheless hard to read. As anyone who has shared his confidences can tell you, what's actually whirling in his head is so outré

C
John Peters
Boat Trip, c. 1980s
Mixed media
36 x 36 inches

When you're plagiarizing Michael Jackson, maybe it's a good idea to not leave a return address.

that it makes his art seem almost tame in comparison. Don't let his immense kindness fool you—for surely he is one of the sweetest gents around—behind that rictus his brain churns with a veritable Tourette syndrome of blasphemy and invective.

This, then, would be all the secrets about Mark Flood I feel comfortable enough to share at the moment, but in closing it seems important that we address this curious turn toward beauty in Mr. Flood's work. Much has been made, and quite rightly so, of the gorgeous swirling abstractions that play with such diaphanous grace in his lace paintings. To be sure they are impossibly seductive, but these are the predator's laws of attraction, like some gorgeous flower in the jungle weeping the ineffable smell of pure joy waiting for your gentle caress just so it can bite your fucking hand off. The lace paintings were from the outset Flood's address to the conundrum of beauty as a valid aesthetic term as proposed by the critic Dave Hickey, a fellow misanthrope well deserving of Mark's attentions. Love them as we do, they are less about being beautiful than they are about beauty itself. The artist here is only indulging in the sly tricks by which objects (and people) make themselves desirable so he can explore the phenomenology of beauty as a dialectics of perception. And if this seems doubtful, rest assured he is totally sincere in his skepticism. You see, even though he has been making paintings for at least some forty years now, Mark Flood is not so much a painter as a conceptual artist who happens to use paint frequently to get his ideas across.

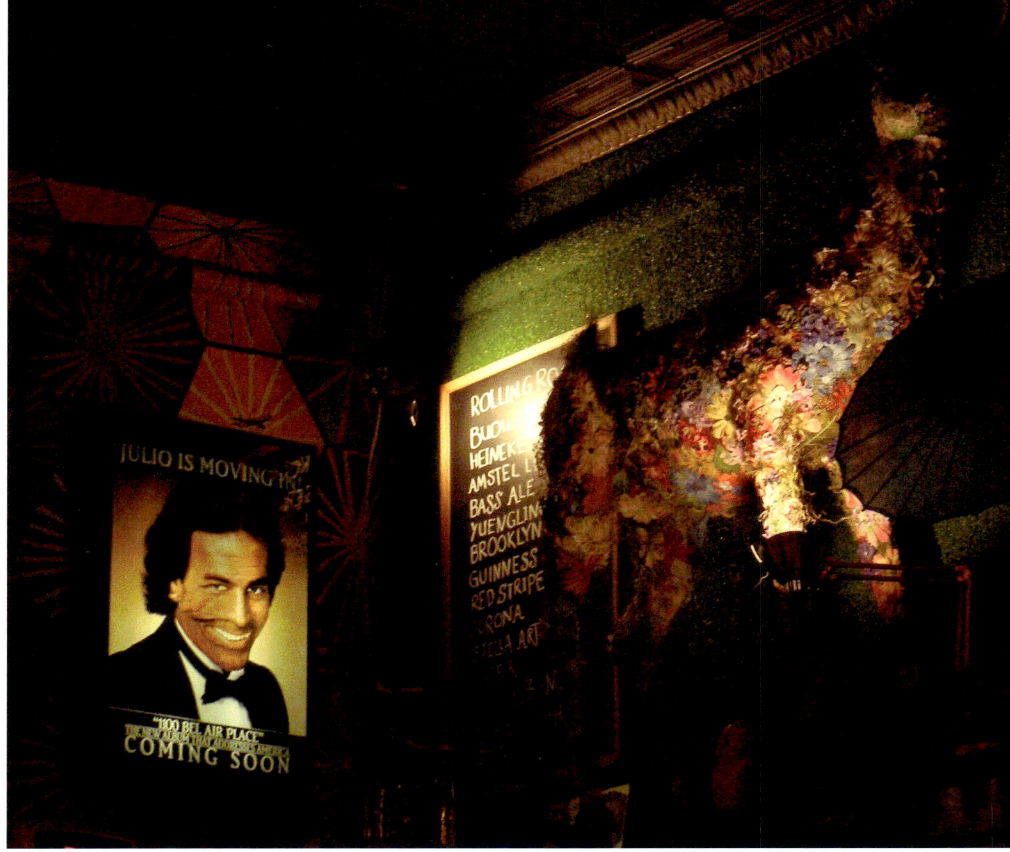

D

Some of the earliest paintings we might attribute to Mark Flood, though they were apparently produced by someone named John Peters, are ransacked defacements, desecrations of the ugly in search of truth. Likely found objects, they have an air of abandonment and promiscuous availability redolent of thrift shop and junk store display. Flood's modifications are violations of form in the name of content. Faces corrupted to map the corruption of our body politic, they are what might be expected if you asked Vincent Price to do plastic surgery on Frankenstein: portraits of our sociopolitical malignancy as mutant aberrations of that terminal mundane we call normal. Freaks that speak to the weirdness of our world, as much as to our collective alienation within it, their myriad anatomical dislocations are a manner of cartography, a psychogeography by which corporate architectures, market globalism, bottom-line economics, and heedless profiteering are reconfiguring the human condition. In terms of subject they are about something quite repulsive, and I suppose as pictures they aren't as pretty as some nice paintings might look, but the authenticity and honesty Flood invested in them, and in every damn piece of art he has made since, is in some measure a fathoming of the sublime.

D
Installation view of *Julio Is Moving In* (1984) in Max Fish, New York, from 2006
Courtesy Jill Robidoux

This, then, is how Mark Flood found his own way out of that suffocating body bag the corpse of culture got stuffed into. Yes, he's a mad inventor (producing much more novelty than all the tripe ruminated as something fresh in contemporary art) and a wily commentator of satirical sophistication, but his greatness is less about what he creates than how he perverts. Before all the attention he got from those galleries, museums, collectors, and critics, Mark Flood was known mostly for a single work of art he made that hung behind the bar of Max Fish, the legendary artist's haunt on New York's Lower East Side. The piece was a light box illuminating a transparency image of that most insipid of Latin Music stars, Julio Iglesias. Nothing could be more quotidian or banal, no airbrushed invocation of ideal perfection more like an imprecation of the flawed and shoddy, nothing more out of place for one of those few sanctuaries where the intellectually and creatively daring might gather. Beauty exaggerate, celebrity magnified, is an atrocity of immeasurable proportions, and one we accept with prurient bliss unaware of just how toxic and virulent it truly is. Flood's Julio was just such a star bared in all his invasive unsightly beauty—that winning smile with those impossibly white and perfect teeth just wouldn't quit. Yes, the smile that was meant to win our hearts just kept going, altered by endless discrete compulsive collage to extend into so broad a grin that it contained an impossible multitude of teeth. The essence of the beauty remains, but yields the deformity by which such perfections are perpetrated.

Mark Flood is far too prolific and popular an artist for a casual bystander like me to iterate all his mad gestures these days. I can say for sure that they are just as hilarious, irreverent, and subversive as ever: text pieces like invectives we adopt as blessings, pictures torn from the shabby dark side of our most unhealthy obsessions, renderings out of register, compositions off the wall, all together a memento mori for the slow death of civilization. But as the worst loose cannon left in his self-abnegating arsenal, as the fool Mark has personally chosen to tell his darkest secrets, let me just impart this shadow of a past to foreground his brilliant present. The Julio light box was not alone; there were many abominations in his epic art of cruelty, mutant portraits of myriad celebrities too disgusting to iterate. And then, that music we were talking about earlier. Oh what an assault, but it wasn't just unpleasant the way noisy things happen to be; it was offensive with direct consequence. The real trip of Culturcide, especially by the time they achieved their unquestionable masterpiece, *Tacky Souvenirs of Pre-Revolutionary America*, was that they weren't writing pop tunes but ripping out the vocals of the most recognizable hits so that deranged singer might supply his own lyrics. In all the years of my avid record collecting, I had never before come across an album that had no record company, address, or contact information on it. Well, when you're plagiarizing Michael Jackson, maybe it's a good idea to not leave a return address.

We say all this not simply because it might be worth your knowing that Flood was practicing the seditious forms of appropriation long before they became de rigueur for smart art and certain artists got awfully rich on the trope, but to remind you what a wicked little scoundrel still lurks within his infinitely kind heart. Some time recently a gallery mounted a big show of Flood's early work, those various disruptive renegade revolutions before everyone fell in love with his purloined forgery of beauty, and when asked how someone who had done such hateful work could now make art of such unmitigated beauty, he corrected them: he wants us all to know that he carries just as much angst and animosity in his heart as ever, he's simply changed the mode of address. Personally when I see those gorgeous paintings he makes now I feel the full frisson of the artist's immense perversity. Here the dainty and frail is violated in the worst possible ways, twisted and torn asunder, blasted with the effluvium of orgasmic creation, the beauty left but a pasted shadow of the artist's ego. Yes, we all love Mark Flood, we can agree on that, but please let's not fool ourselves into thinking these affections are reciprocal.

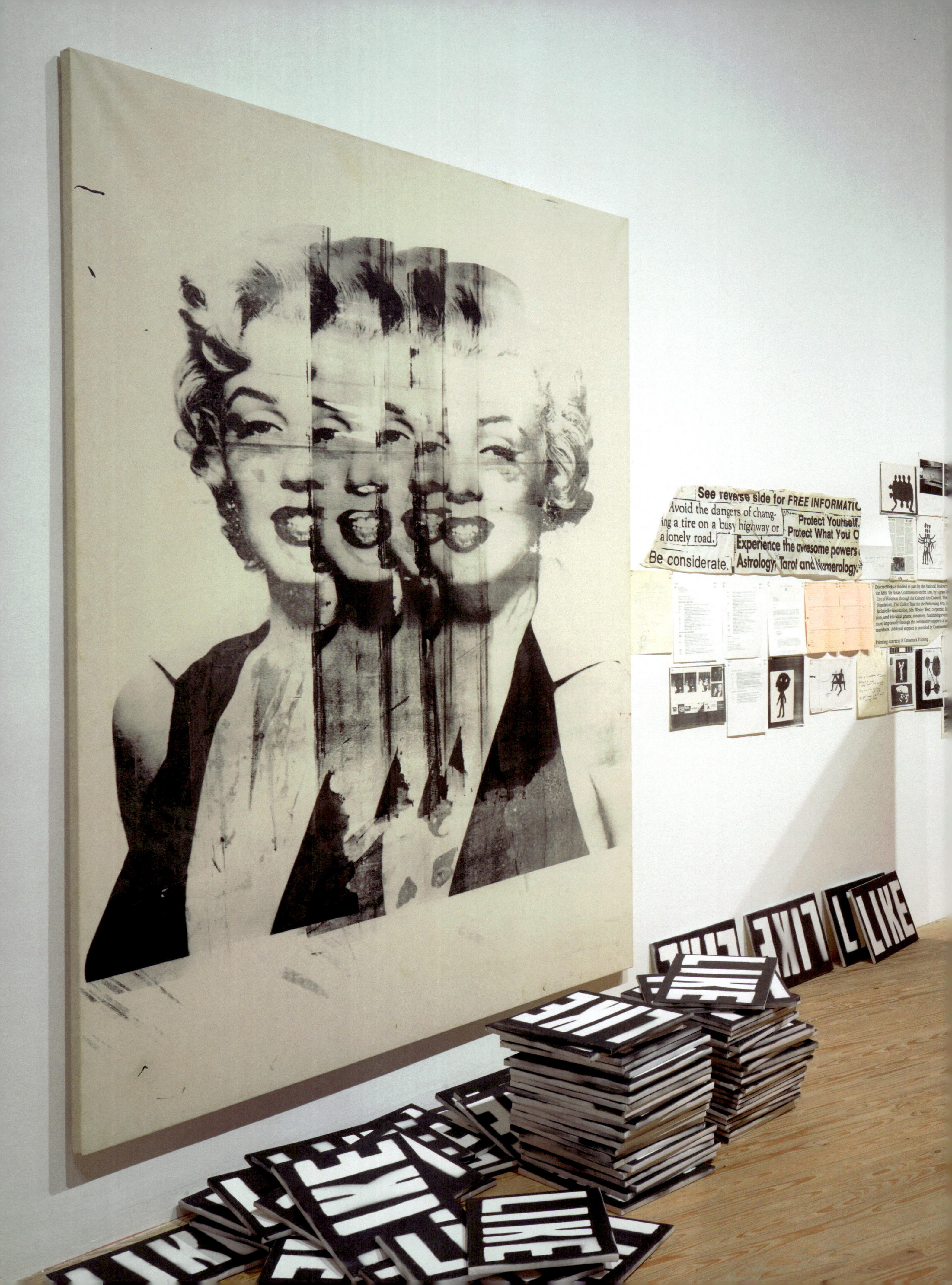

See reverse side for FREE INFORMATIO
Avoid the dangers of chang-
ing a tire on a busy highway or
a lonely road.
Be considerate.
Protect Yourself.
Protect What You O
Experience the awesome powers
Astrology, Tarot and Numerology.
LIKE

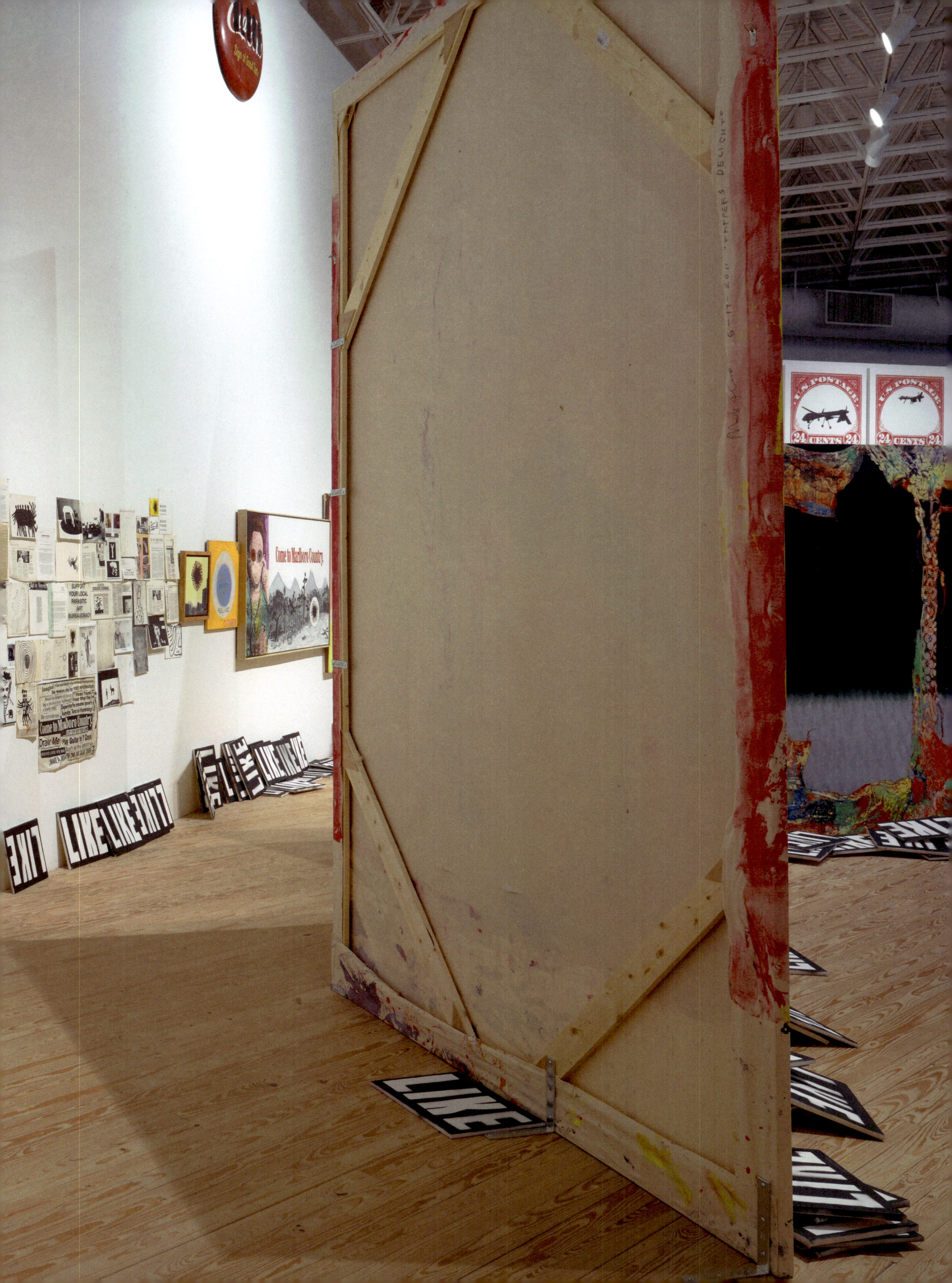

SUPPORT
YOUR LOCAL
PARASITIC
ART
BUREAUCRACY
Come to Marlboro Country
LIKE
U.S. POSTAGE
24 CENTS 24

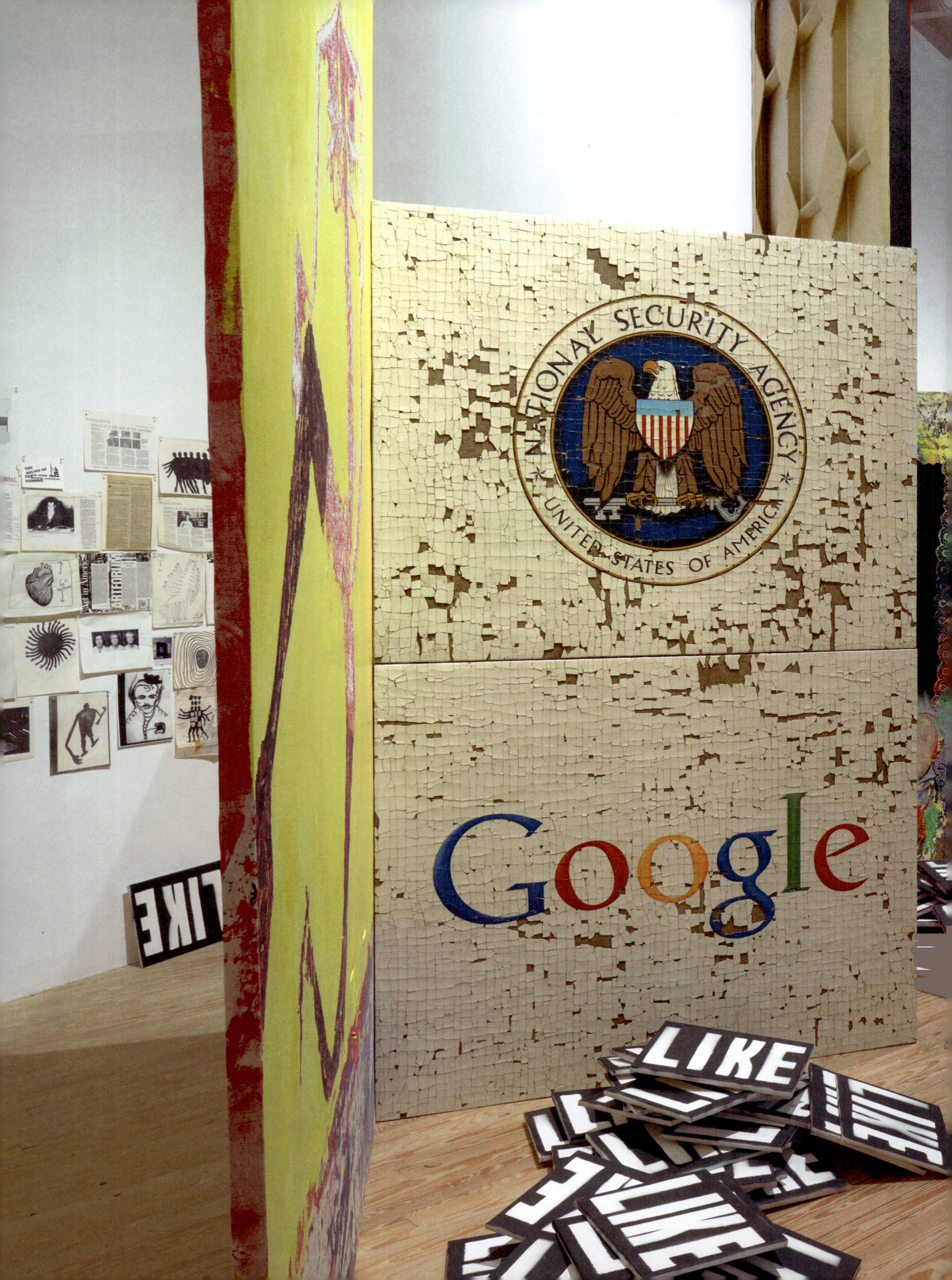

NATIONAL SECURITY AGENCY
UNITED STATES OF AMERICA
Google
LIKE
LIKE

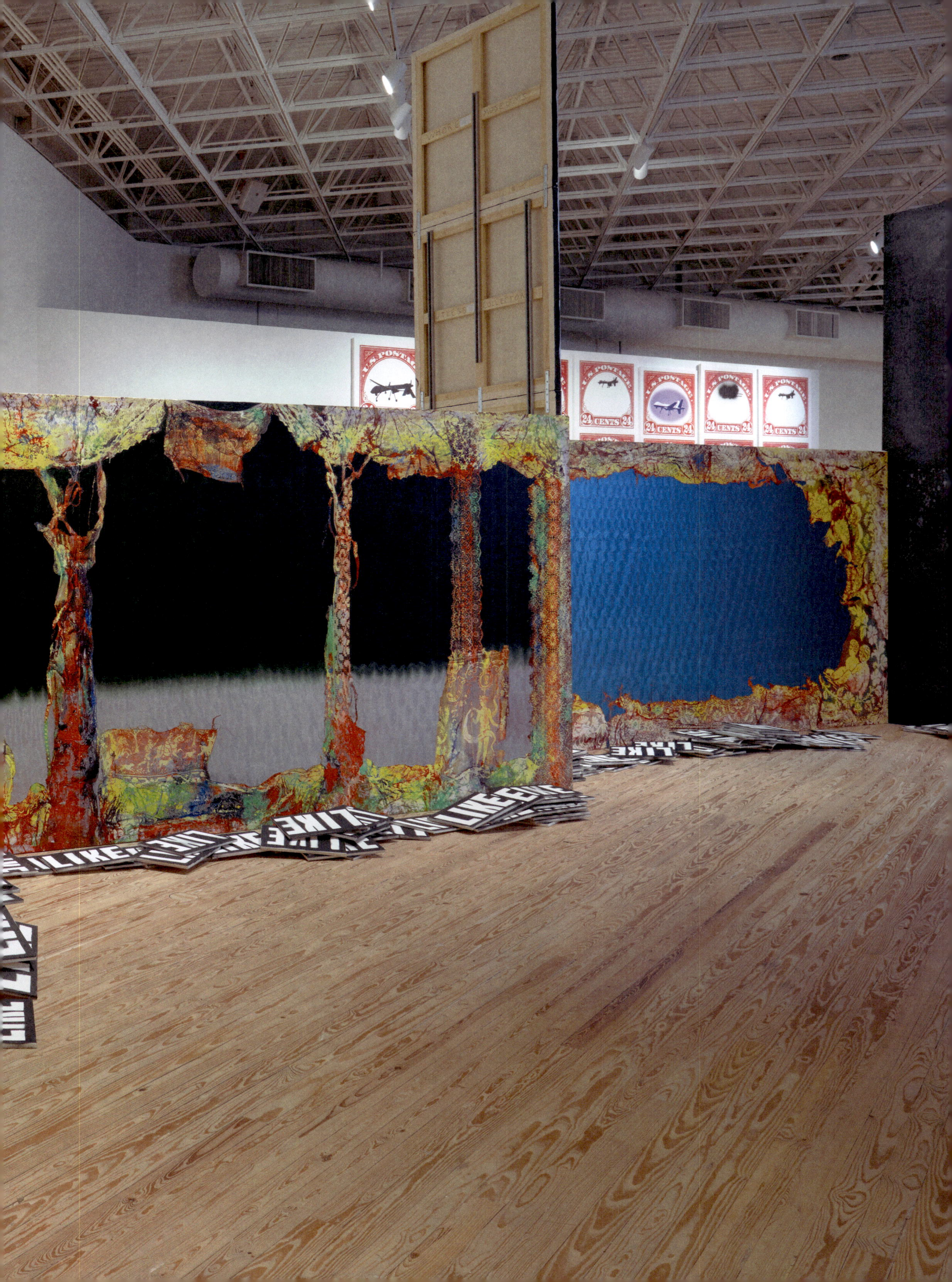
24 CENTS 24
LIKE

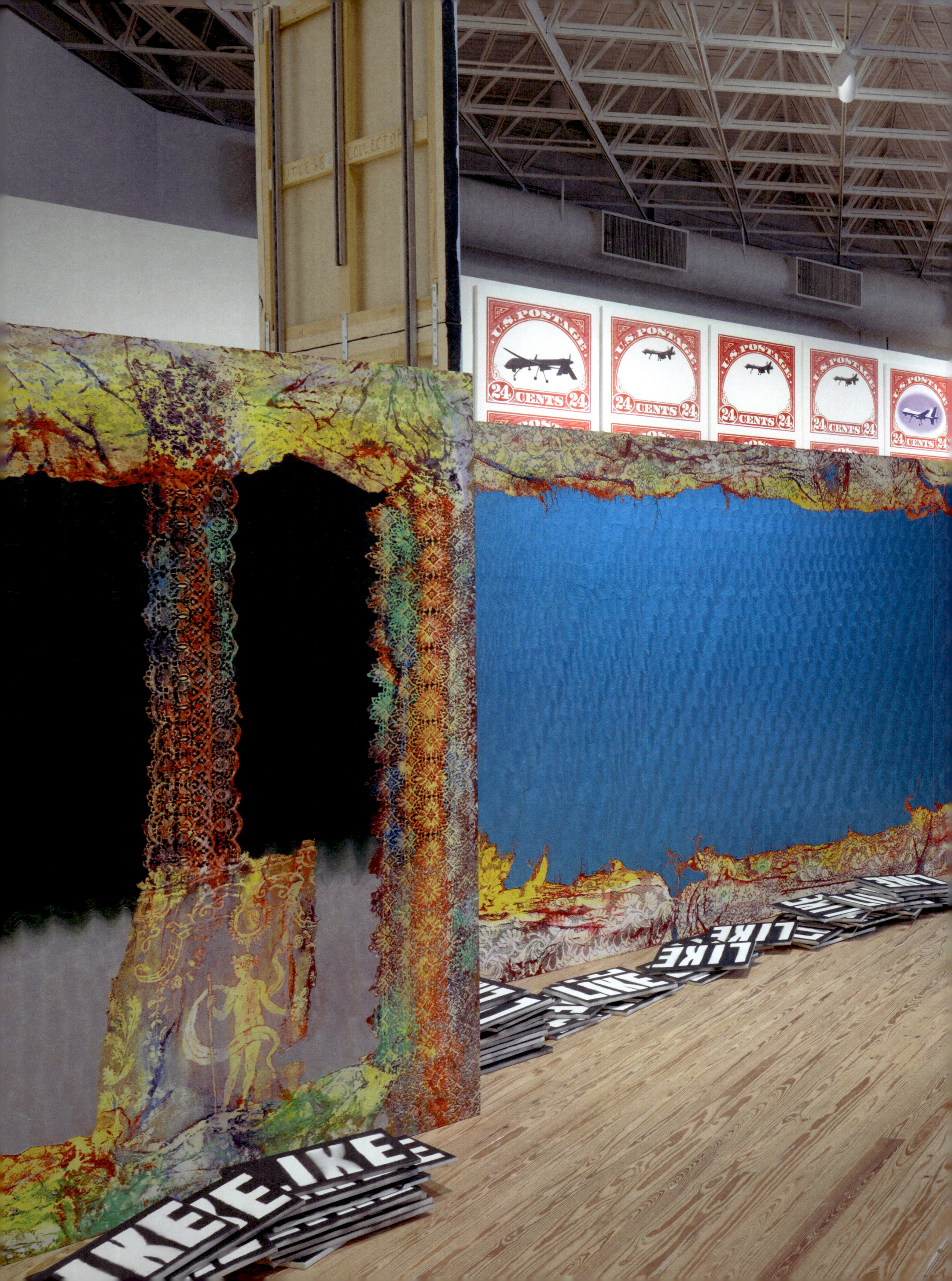
U.S.POSTAGE
24 CENTS 24
LIKE

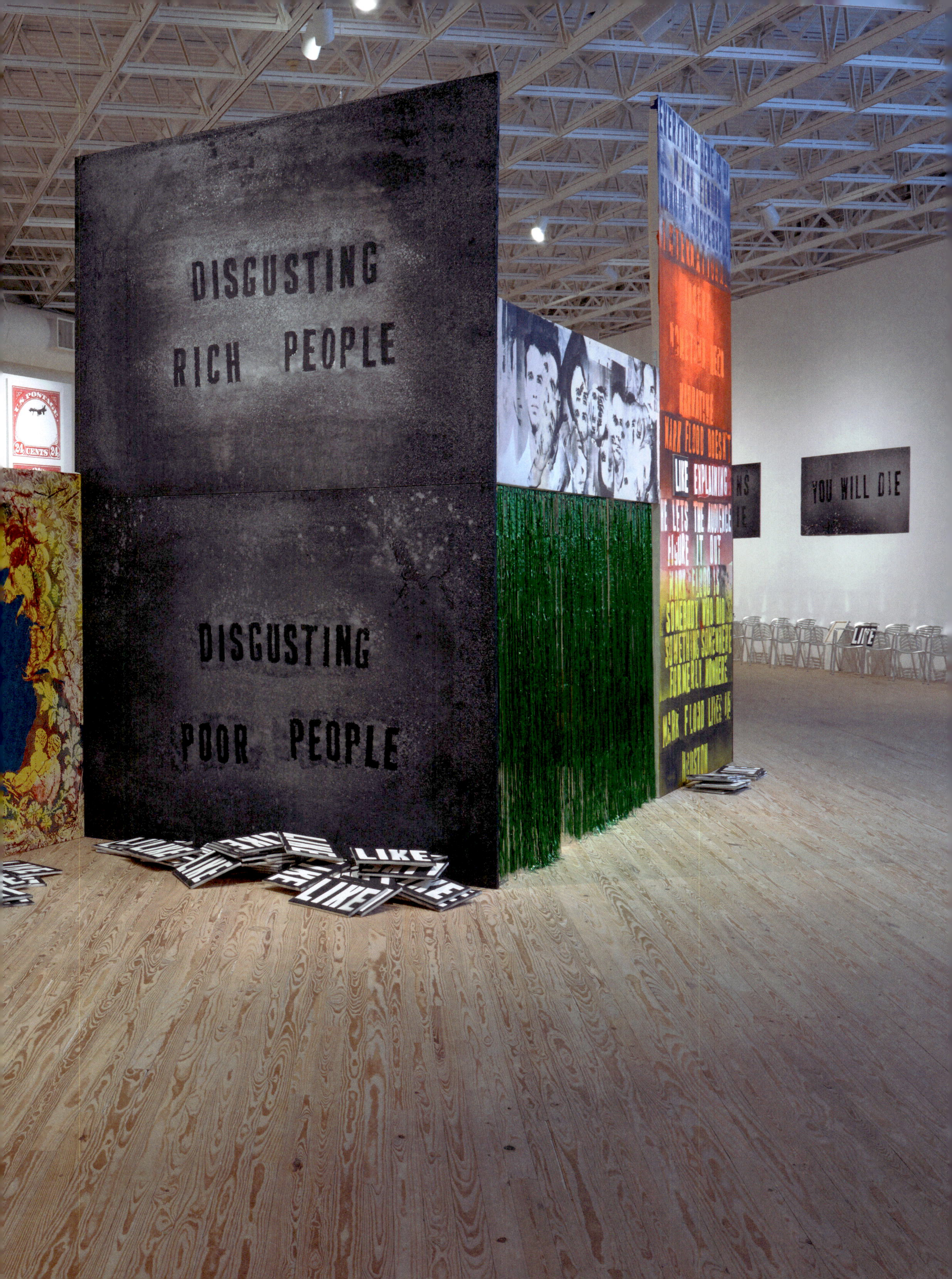
DISGUSTING
RICH PEOPLE
DISGUSTING
POOR PEOPLE
MARK FLOOD DOESN'T
LIKE EXPLAINING
FIGURE IT OUT
SOMEBODY WHO DID
SOMETHING SOMEWHERE
FORMERLY NOWHERE
YOU WILL DIE
LIKE

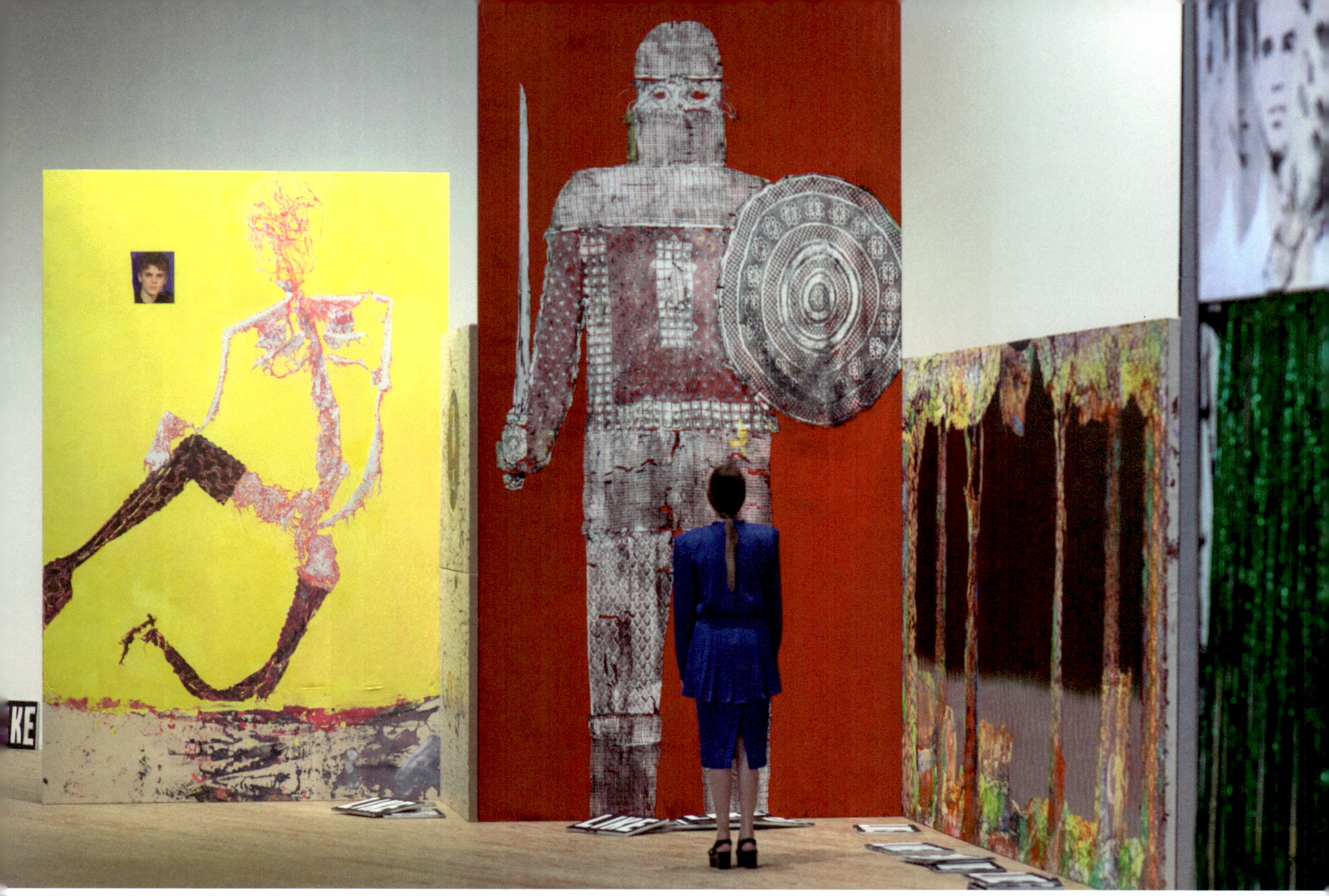

LIKE
U.S. POSTAGE 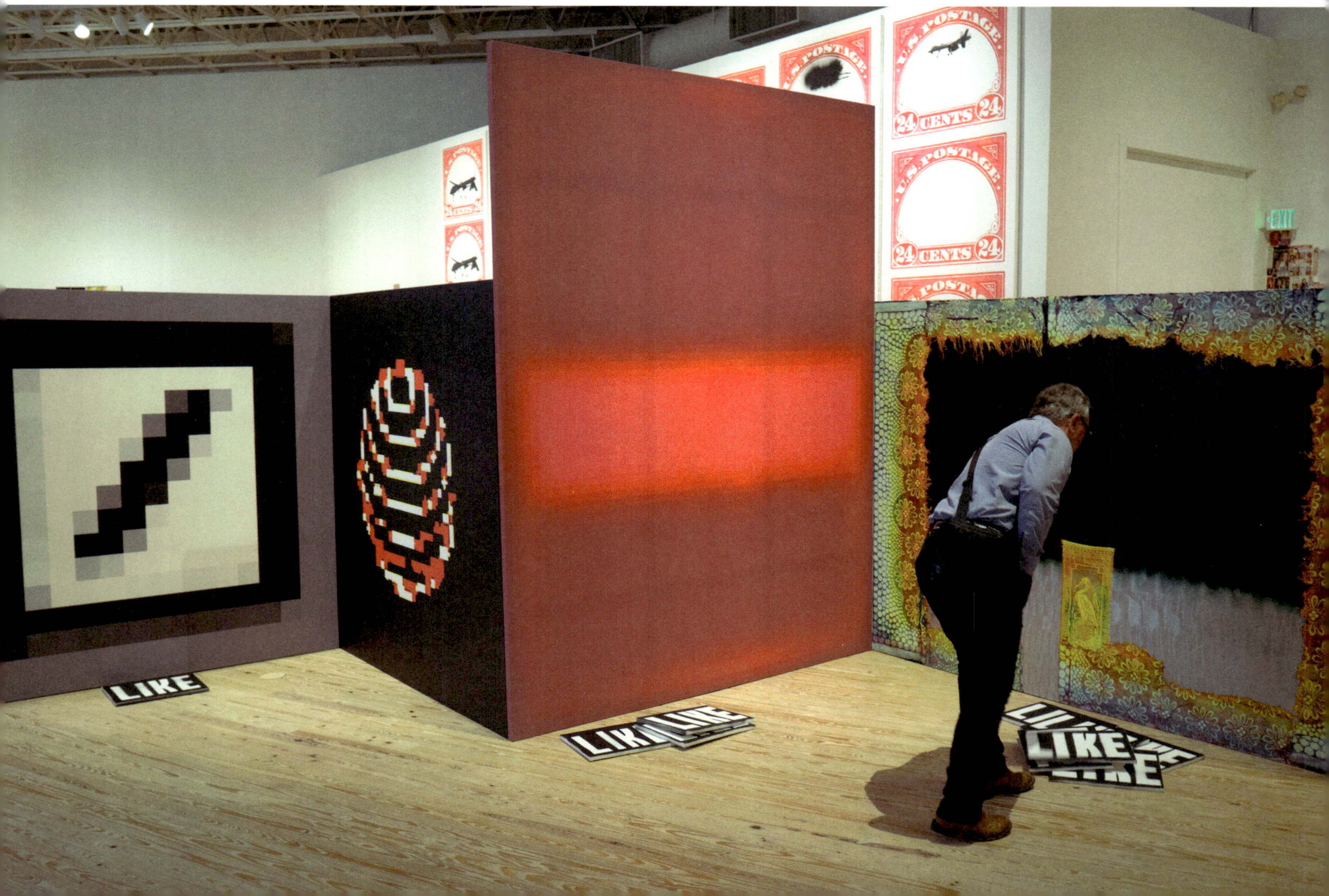
24 CENTS 24
EXIT

Mark Flood: Gratest Hits

Bill Arning

A Greater God than Outrage

OVER THE PAST FOUR DECADES, Mark Flood has defined his own unique position in the cultural landscape. Creating art that makes even the most seemingly edgy work appear conservative, he has turned celebrities into monsters and berated the institutions of the art world (while admitting his place in that world). At the same time, he produces some of the most seductive art visual pleasure seekers have ever experienced. Employing a wide range of media—painting, collage, film, video, music, writing, and installation—Flood has kept his distance from the artistic trends of his time, choosing instead to chart a course that few could have predicted would lead him to the international success he enjoys today.

> The dealers used to think they controlled it, then the curators tried controlling it, now the collectors think they control it... the mechanism of the art world. But only the artists control it and only the good ones.

"It" is the hyperinflated, professionalized art world that came into focus after 2001 with the explosion of big art fairs—the Armory Show in New York and Art Basel Miami Beach—which converted a cottage industry into a grand public orgy. By so single-mindedly determining and stating what is important to him in art and the world at large, Flood constructs a system to better make his philosophical case for what truly matters. He leads his fellow believers out of the morass of bad-faith situations that even art students today are told they must accept. Flood proves that such widespread acquiescing to value systems relegating art to mere entertainment, decoration, or investment can and must be called out and thereby tamed; not changed necessarily, but kept from ruining the pleasure—and souls—of both makers and viewers of art.

To many casual observers, Flood appears to be a quintessential "bad boy" artist who enjoys offending tender sensibilities and ignoring the rules of politeness for the sheer joy of seeing the looks of horror on the faces of gallerists, collectors, and critics. One example of his rebellious ways occurred when he wallpapered the entrance of a recent gallery show with his auction results. The installation was intended to discomfort potential collectors, who knew perfectly well how to get such sales information on their smart phones, but perhaps didn't want a blatant reminder that the talented artist they were there to appreciate was so aware of the role that money played in their decision-making processes.

While these confrontational joys are not insubstantial (or trivial), I will argue here that Flood serves a greater god than outrage. For his exhibition at the Contemporary Arts Museum Houston, the artist has pulled together his *Gratest Hits* mainly from works that remain in his possession. The artist-driven selection of paintings and collages will, we hope, make clear that the position he enjoys is less an agent provocateur than a moral compass. The auction results, for instance, were not intended to point a finger at "bad" collectors or gallerists, but rather to call to attention to the fact that art and commerce are always grossly entangled in the grand theater that is the New York art scene. Galleries can enlist professional guards and publish scholarly books, but that doesn't make them museums.

The fact that galleries aspire to appear museum-like is already a mistake in Flood's program; a gallery's purpose, selling art and satisfying desires, is purer than the conflicted agenda of non-profit institutions, which must disguise the profound, subversive pleasures of art behind education and a program of public betterment. And no one, including those of us on the museum side, gets to wander through the cultural landscape without regularly compromising our ideals about the value of art. We want our artists to be outlaws of modernist mythologies, but we get annoyed when they don't mix well with donors.

Any conscientious art-loving person lives with a fair amount of cognitive dissonance—there are realities of today's art world that we know are not right, yet we live with them, going about business as usual. Flood is unique among significant makers of contemporary culture because in his work nothing is sublimated or unspoken, and he has found a way to bring all the icky points to the surface. He reminds us that young people aspiring to become artists don't imagine the path to success involves mindless self-promotion at Art Basel parties, decorating homes they will never be able to afford, or selling work to and dining with arms dealers and slumlords. Yet with each small concession such moral degradations become normalized.

Artists used to be dangerous company. As a society we fetishize the image of a drunken Jackson Pollock (as played by Ed Harris) pissing into Peggy Guggenheim's fireplace, because it contrasts so sharply with the domesticated careerist model that artists are socialized into today. While I hesitate to seem like a champion of great artists self-destructing as Pollock did, I still miss the days when bringing a visiting artist to a museum patron's home required extra security and sending the kids to the grandparents for the night. Flood, too, seems to acknowledge as much; in his 2012 music video *Bushwick Basement*, the lyrics pessimistically state that "everybody has the art dream but most people get it beaten out of them before they turn thirteen." Flood raps these words while dressed as Batman, and in the next line he charges the art-school system with turning artists into the equivalent of Burger King, churning out endless amounts of crap. This is only one of many moments throughout his work where it's clear that, uniquely among his contemporaries, Flood believes we must reclaim the importance and power of good art most intensely.

Flood has a reputation for being reclusive, changing his name, avoiding photographs, and not attending his openings. Public praise, even in press releases, makes him very uncomfortable. While aspects of this aversion are very real, I interpret it as a deconstructive strategy inverting the less-than-noble motivator for so many artists: attention and fame. The hyperbolic rhetoric museums, galleries, and collectors employ freely is in fact cringeworthy, and phrases such as "Mark Flood is among the most important painters of his generation" should make anyone who cares about clarity and meaning demand revision.

It is true, however, that Flood wants his work to be seen, discussed, and to have an effect on art discourse. Between releasing music videos on YouTube as exhibition announcements, planning his *Artforum* ads with the tactical precision of a twenty-first-century military strike, and writing critical columns, he is far from reticent. Listen carefully to the lyrics of his exhibition promos and we hear his incendiary call to arms for the next generation of artists to be stubborn and impolite, to avoid capitulating to tired art systems or making work to appeal to the official gatekeepers of cultural heritage. In the history of revolutionary art manifestos—the multiple salvos to burn down museums and all other

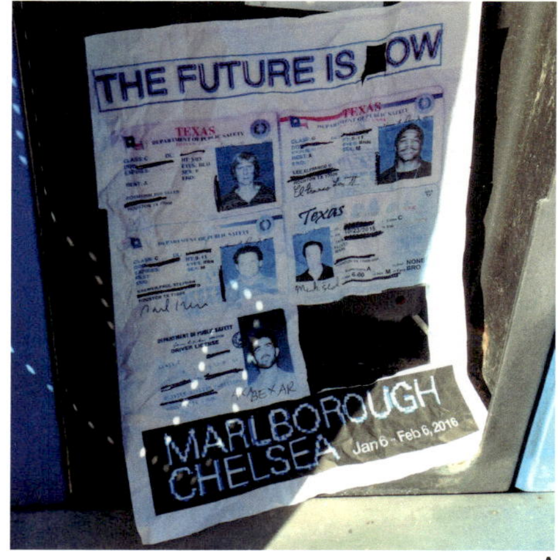

A

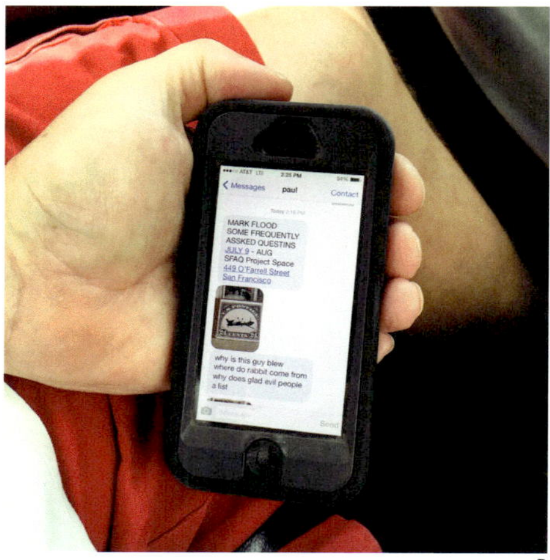

B

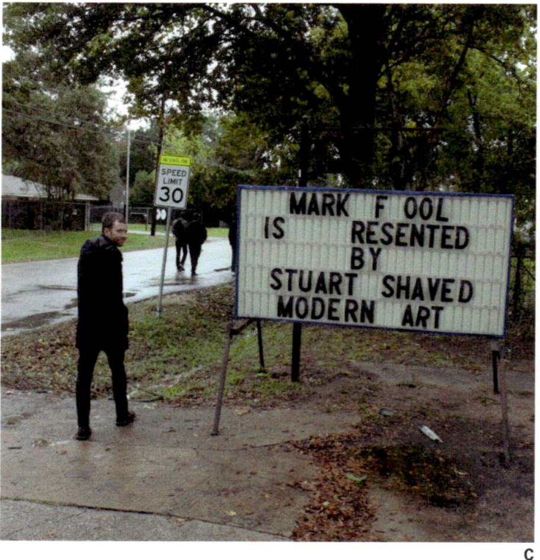

C

A
"The Future Is Ow: Susie Rosmarin, El Franco Lee II, Paul Kremer, Mark Flood, Chris Bexar," exhibition advertisement, *Artforum*, January 2016

B
"SOME FREQUENTLY ASKED QUESTINS," exhibition advertisement, *Artforum*, July 2015

C
"MARK FOOL IS RESENTED BY STUART SHAVED MODERN ART," representation advertisement, *Artforum*, December 2013

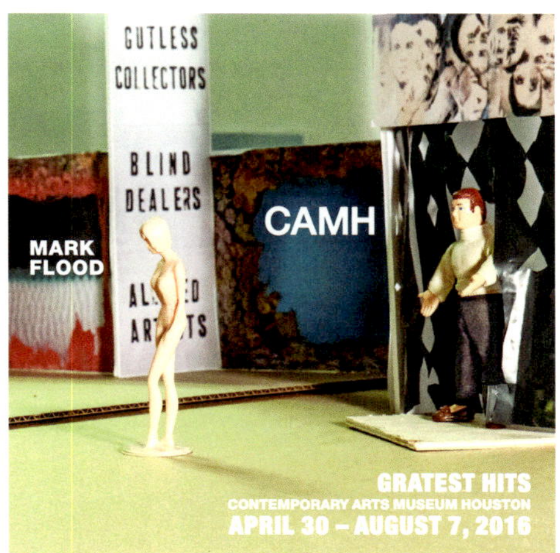

D

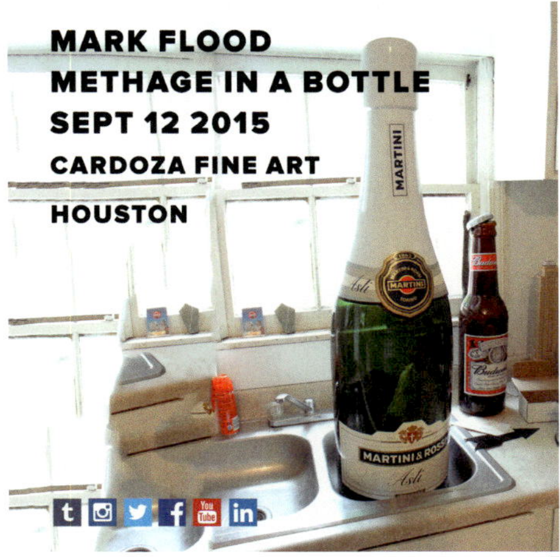

E

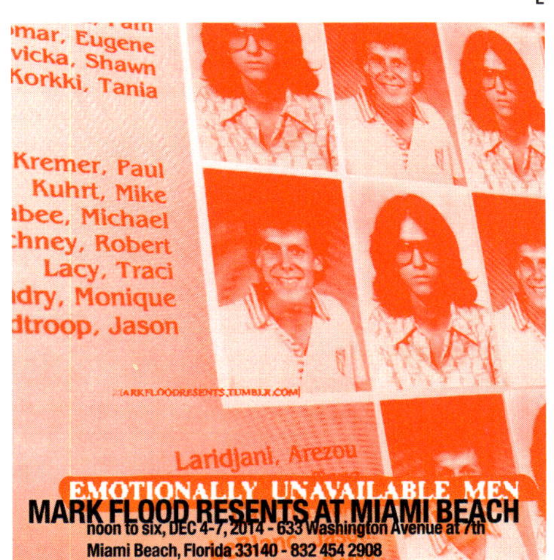

F

restrictive institutions—Flood's is perhaps one of the most engaging of our time.

We are attempting here to frame Flood's work in a museum context without denaturing it and making it safe. We must acknowledge the possible futility of our effort, but working through these inherent contradictions is the job before us.

Lace and Liberation

Flood's own moments of revelation in becoming the artist we know today have been documented in a relatively scant body of scholarship. Born and raised in Houston, he worked at the Menil Collection during the early days of its existence. There, under the tutelage of Walter Hopps, Flood clearly learned the rules of museum behavior and professional conduct. He knows how art and the public are "supposed" to be treated. (Now, when he posts a video of one of his assistants dragging a painting face down through a grassy field, the provocative humor becomes even funnier once you realize he spent years wearing white gloves to handle the most delicate Joseph Cornell boxes.)

Hopps, who died in 2005, was one of the most robustly influential curators, gallerists, and museum directors who still holds a huge presence in the minds of those earnestly aspiring to attain any or all these professions. A thirty-second vita brevis on Hopps usually begins in 1963 with the game-changing Marcel Duchamp retrospective he organized at the Pasadena Art Museum, where he soon became the youngest museum director in America, though he was fired in 1967 for his unusual managerial style. Even during his time at the Menil, he was reassigned from director to curator so that he could exercise his genius for the good of the art-viewing public.

In an appreciation of the curatorial vision that motivated Hopps, along with the Swiss curator Harald Szeeman, the poet and critic David Levi Strauss claimed that both men "felt most at home with artists, sometimes literally.... Szeemann and Hopps reserved their harshest criticism for the various bureaucracies that got between them and the artists. Hopps once described working for bureaucrats when he was a senior curator at the National Collection of Fine Arts as 'like moving through an atmosphere of Seconal.'" The idea that bureaucracies get between not only artists and curators but also artists and the public ran throughout Hopps's practice. Mitigating these structures required unusually visionary arts patrons, two of whom Hopps found in John and Dominique de Menil. This deeply passionate—and deeply pocketed—couple worked together with Hopps to create something magical; the same could be said of Flood's desire to find supporters who have both the means and the guts to think outside the box.

The other narrative twist in Flood's artistic development was the publication of Dave Hickey's *Invisible Dragon: Four Essays on Beauty* (1993). Hickey's manifesto was widely read by artists at the time and was especially popular with graduate students seeking a way out of a puritan cultural regime that distrusted and despised visual pleasure. Numerous discussion panels and exhibitions on beauty followed in the wake of the book's publication. Hickey proposed that artists could get viewers to accept and absorb dangerous ideas if they made seductive and alluring formal decisions to render their work alarmingly gorgeous. Robert Mapplethorpe was Hickey's prime exemplar, as the photographer was able to entice straight, upper-class couples into buying art that depicts such provocative images as gay sadomasochist sex acts because the work was so damn beautiful. The conventional wisdom is that Flood found in Hickey's text a license to make his own work as beautiful as he wanted, realizing that such a strategy might free him from depending on more bureaucratic sources of funding such as grants and curatorial favor.

Flood found that magic ticket with his lace paintings, his most ambitious—and perhaps most surprising—series to date. These unabashedly beautiful, lush, vibrant canvases, which I'll describe in more detail later, represent a sea change in the artist's practice. As Flood told the *New York Times* journalist Randy Kennedy, upping the ante with the seductiveness of these works had unexpected

D
"Mark Flood: Gratest Hits," exhibition advertisement, *Artforum*, May 2016

E
"METHAGE IN A BOTTLE," exhibition advertisement, *Artforum*, September 2015

F
"Mark Flood Resents," exhibition advertisement, *Artforum*, December 2014

consequences. The paintings seemed to compel collectors to buy them. At Art Basel Miami Beach in 2013, I watched as his galleries sold lace paintings moments after hanging them, and I made a sport of returning to the booths to see how many new ones were hung and sold in the course of a day. Only Flood can frame this relationship to the art market—which the puritan regime finds inherently distasteful—as a liberation strategy:

> I didn't know that they would be popular, though people sometimes assume that it was some calculated sellout on my part. Because if I could calculate how to sell out, I wanted to wait until 2000. [Laughs.] My life changed dramatically. I no longer needed some art professional standing there saying, "This is good because of Jasper Johns, because of Duchamp," because someone was coming up to me saying: "That's the most beautiful thing I've ever seen. Here's $5,000." And then I quit my job.

For, like an art world Ayn Rand, Flood has developed a belief in the beauty of the art collector's uncontrollable passion, the "crazy rich people" who give anything to own a coveted piece. Unlike the "art professionals" discourse in which the irrational desire to be the owner of a great work is legitimized by said work's historical or educational value, Flood's view upholds compulsion itself as a beautiful thing.

Clerk Fluid

Flood's self-assessment usually involves some admission of befuddlement as to why his art has been met with such success. Take, for example, a line from his music video *MURK FLUID* (2010):

> My ART's ridin high I couldn't tell ya why
> since every move I'm makin is career suicide

As a longtime observer of and cheerleader for bad boy and bad girl behavior in art, I await the statistical study of which gestures that seem designed to merely outrage viewers and annoy art-world guardians prove to have greater resonance, meaning that not only do new impacts occur over time, but also that young artists find in these events new grounds for creating the work of the future. My theory is that, in order to continue reverberating, the gesture needs a clear purpose that reveals a coherent ethical system. Flood delivers in several ways, but most consistently and approachably through the wide-ranging screed *Clerk Fluid* (2009).

The book is one of Flood's great achievements, a compendium of his semi-anonymous writings that, while never officially acknowledged as having been authored by Flood, nonetheless read as a direct proclamation of the artist's position. Originally published on the Texas art website *Glasstire*, the texts are told though the voice of a critic—aptly named "Clark Flood"—who says the types of things many of us think, but have learned to keep to ourselves, when hitting the galleries. Clark Flood cares deeply about art yet is still clearly not a romantic in the traditional sense. He despises those who use "art" as a one-word license to annoy others with self-involved musings. He is unmoved by the mushier values of unfettered creativity. He can be a harsh critic and is offended when he is let down by institutions or fellow artists. Yet overall, in Flood's worldview, art matters greatly; it has a moral weight, contains ethical imperatives, and can redeem and transform us. In all his images of horror and deformity, his gruff persona, and his rough critiques of celebrity and commerce, Flood is ultimately a devotee of art's ability to make the universe better, even if just by crashing through learned complacency.

One thing Flood is not shy about is loving the company of artists and gathering them around him, essentially creating a society in which his values find followers. He uses his success and celebrity to create a better world in which artists—and the things that matter to them—rule. Case in point, Flood brought dozens of young artists with him to Art Basel Miami Beach in 2013, as he said to me, "because they should see this." He knew that after doing what young artists do at their first fair (sucking up open-bar booze, adding tattoos, and getting laid) they, as smart observant sponges, would be able to see the irresistible power systems of the art world and make conscious decisions about their places in it.

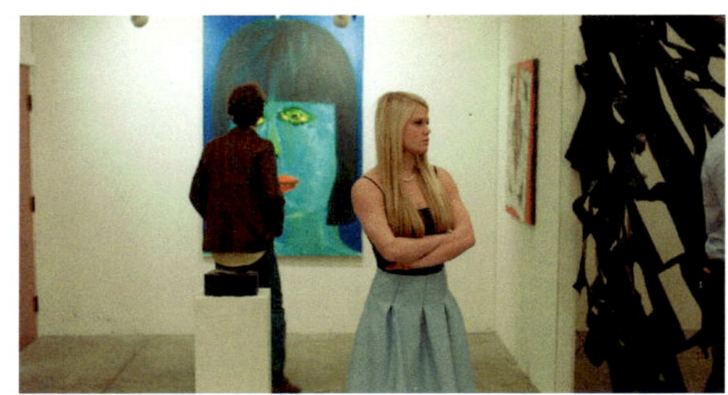

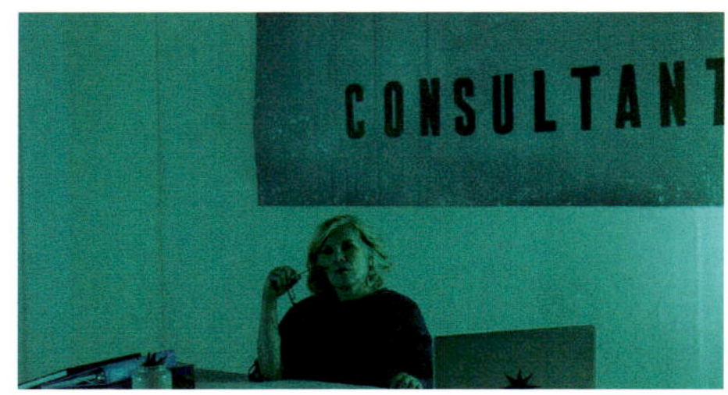

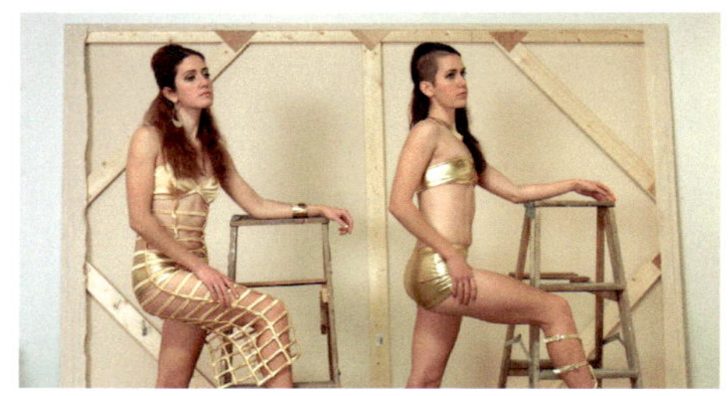

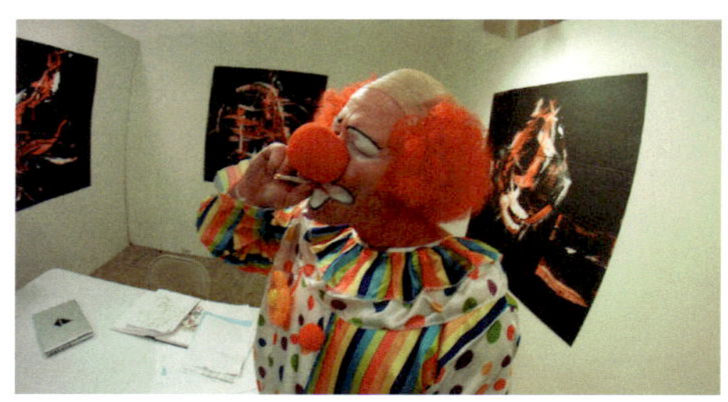

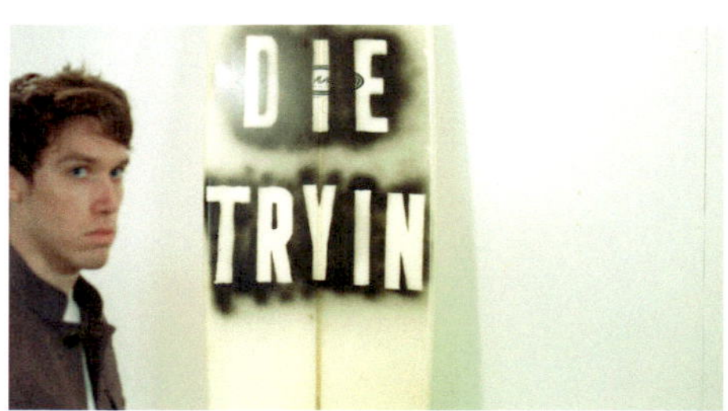

G

G
Film stills from *Art Fair Fever*, 2016
Digital video: color, sound, 79 minutes
Courtesy David Bartner

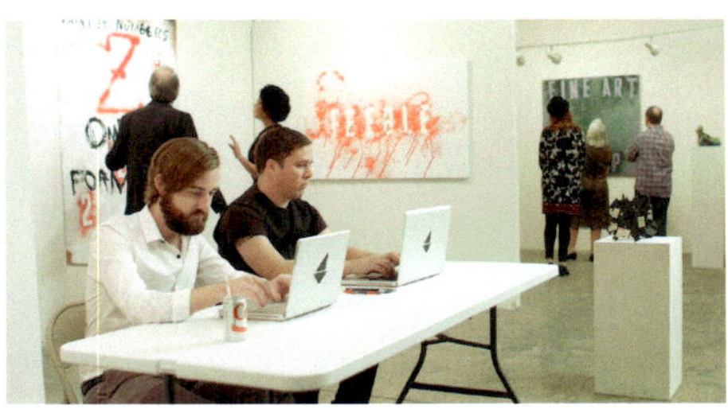

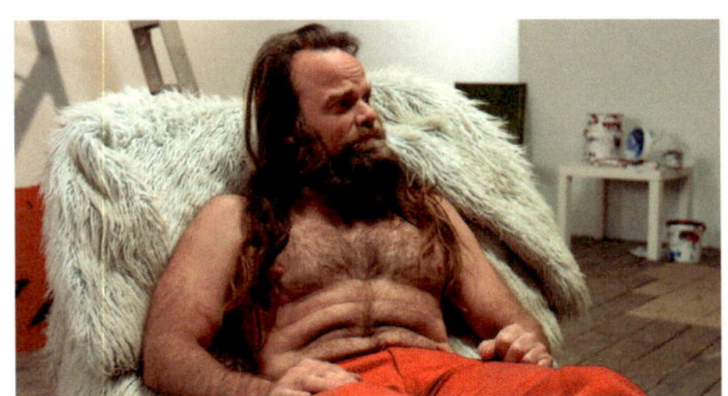

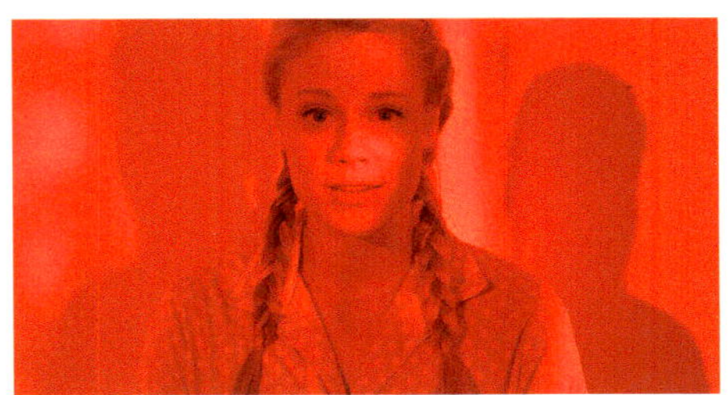

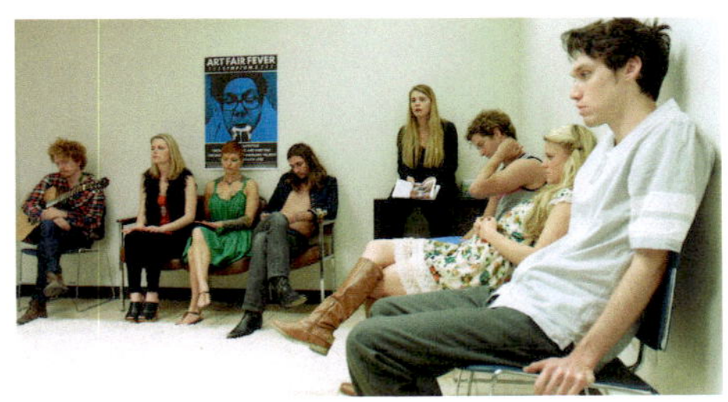

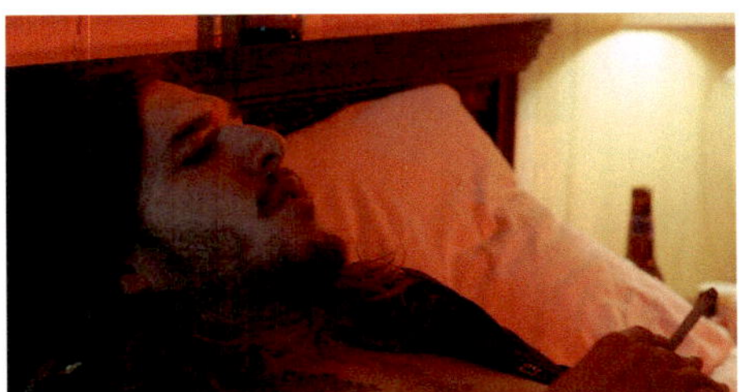

In the latter half of 2014, Flood opened *Mark Flood Resents*—a gallery with outposts in Miami Beach and New York—to display work by artists that he loves and has felt the passion to own. The space was designed as a great model of how NOT to run a gallery, as Flood bought all the best work himself. It felt more like a squat or a club, including sofas and mattresses to sit on and a live webcam feed so that anyone could watch visitors (primarily friends and attractive young artists) chatting, hanging out, and napping in real time. Similarly, in January 2016, Flood curated a show at Marlborough Chelsea Gallery in New York that featured the work of four Houston artists: Chris Bexar, Paul Kremer, El Franco Lee II, and Susie Rosmarin. Flood's hometown boosterism not only made all the New York papers (a fact that seems to embarrass him somewhat) but also outed him as an unashamed enthusiast for artists he loves. Any worries that cynicism and naysaying were the basis of his worldview promptly disappeared, and his prime motivation was instead revealed as the wonderment that we live in a time where people make art and find others to care about it. The amount of strangers who care passionately about his art might be even more miraculous to him.

In 2013 Flood sent a few dozen friends to Art Basel Miami Beach armed with lightweight video cameras to record the goings-on, including the atrocious self-aggrandizing behavior that appears unavoidable when art-world players compete for power, artworks, and money. That footage—as well as other scenes shot at various events over the next few years—became the source material for Flood's first feature film, *Art Fair Fever* (2016), which will be screened at CAMH during the exhibition. The movie's central fictional narrative concerns a group of students who arrive at the fair to learn the mechanics of the art world; instead, they contract a disease, foaming at the mouth and ruminating on the futility of their aspirations to become real artists. The film also depicts collectors manically trying to get the best works by whatever means necessary, be it financial, sexual, or unrestrained braggadocio. Successful artists are portrayed as crippled by too much undeserved attention, fussed over and thereby infantilized by fawning studio assistants.

Art fairs only exist because as a culture we care about what artists make, yet few works are well served by the conspicuous overproduction the fairs make all too visible. The issue of artists seeing their work reduced to one price tag among thousands has been the cause of limitless anxiety. Famous artists complain that their work tends to disappear from the dialogue when displayed and dispersed at a four-day fair (rather than at a proper six-week gallery exhibition). These same artists then grow resentful that their galleries, ever more dependent on these events as labor-intensive cash machines, demand more work to feed the Basel beast. Yet many artists—Flood included—have found ways to expose the beast and reach curious publics amid the chaos of the massive, convention-center locales.

Art fairs are a surprising source of shame in the art world; I have been chastised for writing a critical essay that analyzes the way an artist's work conveys meaning in the particular and highly visible context of Art Basel Miami Beach. The message is that what happens at a fair is some sort of dirty secret, best never mentioned in polite society. What happens at Art Basel stays at Art Basel. Within the complex conversations needed to reach consensus about the cultural importance of an artwork, fairs (like auction houses) have undeniable power; to ignore them would be like trying to understand nineteenth-century art without considering the salons. Flood's depiction of this comedy of fairs is both critical and oddly loving, effectively turning the art-fair dragon into a house cat.

Gratest Hits

When Flood first began to conceive installing *Gratest Hits* at CAMH, he imagined how great the lace paintings would look in the museum's most open, wall-less configuration. Rivaling in scale the largest works of abstract expressionism, the lace paintings are serious artworks writ big. To create the immense compositions, the artist developed a technique in which he applies pieces of lace to a surface, paints over them, and then removes them. The patterned imprints that are left behind encroach on all edges of the canvas, forming thick, densely woven frames for brightly colored, window-like expanses. Using a custom-made oversize brush, Flood adds textured, wavy strokes to these hollow centers, often pushing his palette into insanely beautiful optic ecstasies. The hallucinogenic quality is heightened by the vacillating images that emerge from the lacy webs, from small figures and animals to horrific growths resembling hairballs that could choke us.

Flood's technical invention has art-historical precedents, for example, we could compare it to the moment Picasso started imprinting corrugated cardboard onto wet plaster to create textured and illusionistic effects (as recently examined in the Museum of Modern Art's exhibition *Picasso Sculpture*). Similarly, Flood's method can achieve a very broad range of effects, leaving what appears to be quasi-photographic records of the material's vanished presence. Many casual viewers remember there being actual lace swatches embedded in the woozy surfaces. While the effect is often spectacular, the paintings also betray their own slickness, showing off the ease and mechanical nature of their manufacture. Like an Andy Warhol silkscreen, the fact that the lace paintings look so good despite their factory assembly line production is part of their meaning.

For those of us trained to figuratively hammer off the corners of an artwork to make it fit into grander narratives, the lace paintings present a complicated challenge. Lace as a material is fussy, and in terms of art criticism it is seen as the antithesis of all that is robust and masculine. Lace is seductive and grotesque in equal measure; it is the turf of elderly widows covering mantels with dust-collecting decoration redolent of necropsy. It also fulfills a sexual fetish, transporting a dowdy housewife to the erotic field of a seasoned Vegas hooker. Its magic extends to men as well, since nothing says "find the women in me" quite as effectively as a hirsute businessman crammed into lace panties.

The earliest lace paintings that have earned their way into Flood's Gratest Hits lineup are *The Warrior* (2006) and *The Fapper* (2010). Taken together, these two figures—the dominating male and the masturbating female—constitute a fecund moment in which the future potential of the lace-based works is manifest. The warrior embodies a classic Jungian archetype, a period in a young virile man's life when conquering the world and proving oneself is all that matters, a period that is supposed to end as one matures. This model—which became popularized via the men's movement, a mirror to the essentializing transhistorical feminine of the women's movement—tried to find ways to adopt classic masculine traits that were positive and celebrated the small heroisms of everyday life. (It was soon perverted into hateful Christian groups that tried to shame any life choices outside of traditional marriage.) Flood's warrior is a lovable cartoon, with the humanity of an emoticon, his arms and legs made from the imprints of lace panels. He is as frozen as an Assyrian soldier carved in stone, too unthreatening to be fierce.

Although Flood inhabits a very male world, women's sexuality comes into play. For his Insider Art Fair—held from May 14 to May 17, 2014, in a rental space in the former Dia Art Foundation building in Chelsea (above Zach Feuer's old location)—the artist invited strippers to participate in the making of several works. The dancers, with an infectious spirit, created paintings as live theater while rolling about with their oversize boobs, big-ass butts, push-up bras, and crotchless panties. Two waiflike young males also made text paintings while stripping (I witnessed a bunch of Another Paintings being cranked out on the nearly naked bodies, the world's endless desire for sex in perfect alignment with its endless desire for art). The result was a cacophony of bumping, grinding, and a splattering of liquids; the paintings were sometimes even dragged along the floor, with Flood's gallerists running after him trying to get him to sign the canvases so they could be sold while still intact.

Similarly, the female figure in *The Fapper* is all wriggly motion, uncontrollable and

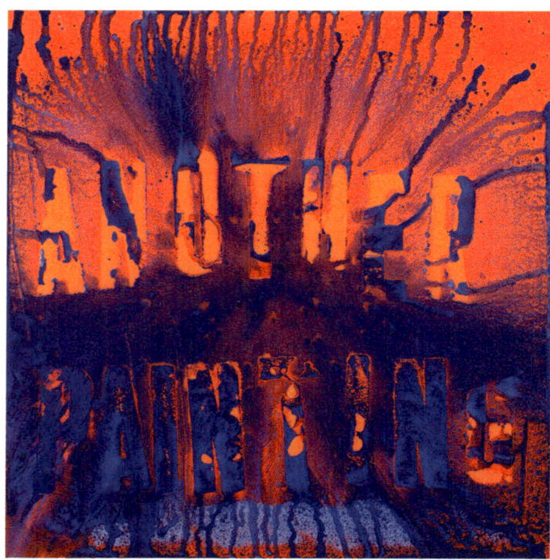

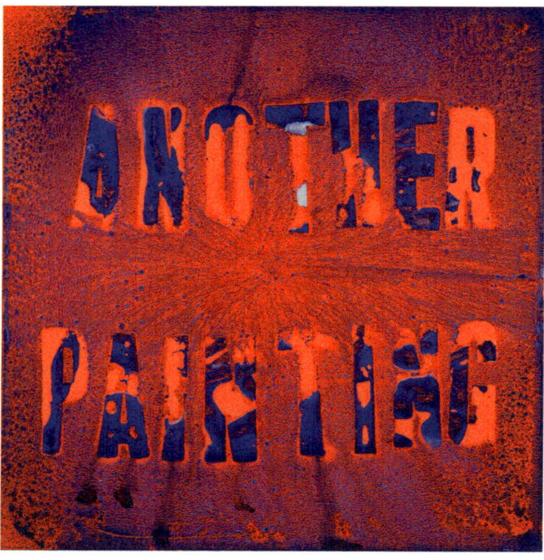

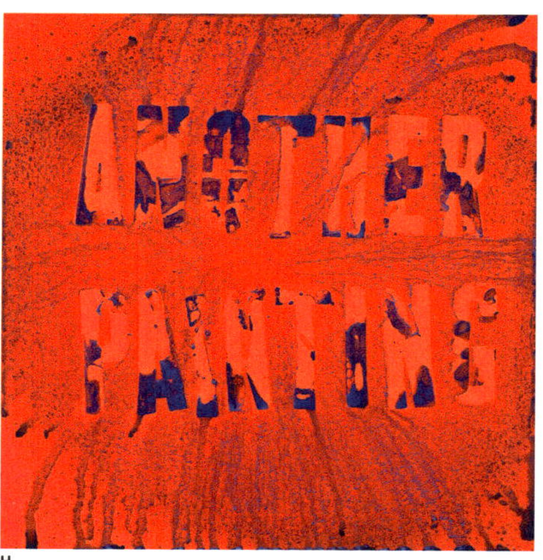

H

H
ANOTHER PAINTING (CAMH SUITE) (detail), 2016
Florescent and spray paint on canvas (7 parts)
40 x 40 inches each

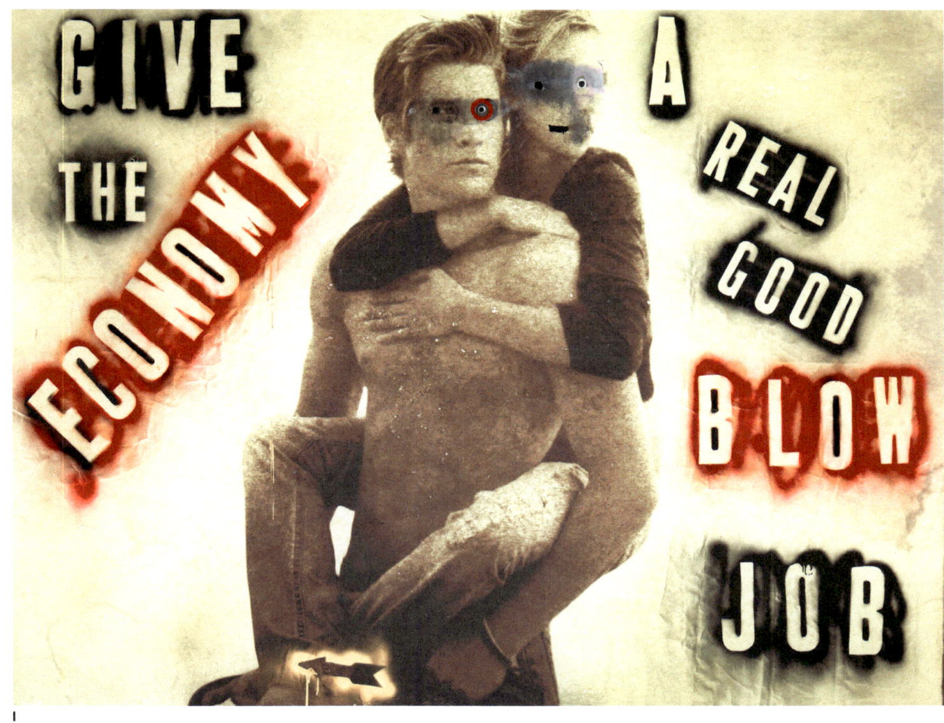

I

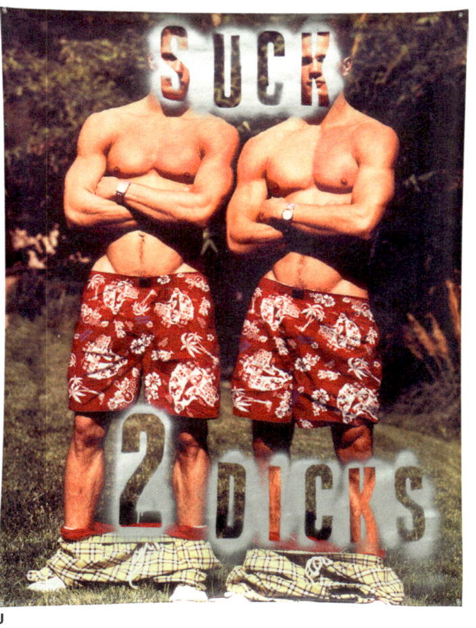

J

Flood consistently describes the art world as a libidinal economy in which the reasonable quality assessment that museum professionals and funding panels enforce is already dead and toxic. Art collecting should be engaged in scandalous misnomers such as a right-wing politician hiring a callboy, acts that are logically indefensible and therefore extra pleasurable. Large-scale advertisements featuring unassailably beautiful people defaced with texts like "SUCK 2 DICKS" or "GIVE THE ECONOMY A REAL GOOD BLOW JOB" uphold the larger philosophical statement that sex and art are at their most sublime when serving no other purpose, be that stable, long-term relationships and family planning (sex) or investment and public edification (art).

The lace paintings manifest an indefensible beauty, one whose utility to society would be hard to defend. Therefore when Flood follows them in the exhibition with corporate paintings and nearly identical text works that read "ANOTHER PAINTING," the realities of art today as a cog in a huge financial machine become unbearable. As a culture we celebrate Warhol's transformation of the traditional artist's studio into a factory, hence de-romanticizing and deskilling the troublesome genius-model of art value, but Flood throws that critique back in our overtheorized faces. These paintings seem to ask, "Who the hell becomes an artist to run a factory?"

terrifying. She is equally archetypal, but probably more linked to the primal fear straight men might experience when a woman takes sexual pleasure into her own hands. But, for Flood, sexuality is deliberately presented in what progressive psychologists would call infantile mode. He upholds a firm belief in deep, instinctual urges and rhymes lust with the desire to buy art, finding in each something uniquely affirmative. In his self-published guidebook to the Insider Art Fair he even willfully considers sex an essential act in obtaining coveted art, both of which are expressions of a pure overwhelming desire worthy of our utmost respect:

> In order to buy art intelligently you have to master three basic skills. The first is being able to effectively research and evaluate and buy any single work of art that attracts you, The second is being able to choose each individual work in such as way as to form a meaningful grouping, a practice more commonalty known as collecting. The third is performing expert sex on both males and females in order to make them like you enough to sell you the art you need.

Creativity-on-demand is always problematic, and the very idea of art-making as a "career" that can be strategized and managed—a new idea in the art world—should still give us pause. Any artist struggling to make it dreams of the day when demand outpaces production and dealers nag them to skip vacation, but soon the ability to enjoy overproduction becomes more of a burden. At that point, you might as well hire strippers as naked studio assistants to make you WANT to return to the studio. Flood's Another Paintings are each gorgeous, but they are not unlike Winnie saying "another happy day" in the Samuel Beckett play *Happy Days*.

Hometown Hero

Young painters, educated at Yale or Columbia

I
GIVE THE ECONOMY A REAL GOOD BLOW JOB, 2014
Spray paint on found printed advertisement
73 x 98 x 1½ inches

J
SUCK 2 DICKS, 2014
Spray paint on printed canvas
48 x 38 inches

and shipped directly to their perfect Bushwick studios, are unlikely to have the perspective to see the "bad faith" in the art world's standard practice revealed at events such as the Insider Art Fair. Here we see the value of Flood's alternative Texas trajectory at its most revelatory.

Flood has been based for most of his life in Houston, a peculiarly American melting pot of unplanned juxtapositions and radical individuality that combines extreme crudity with exquisite taste, a combination that is also true of his work on the whole. He came out of the eighties punk music scene, yet he always made visual artworks even when more in support of his anarchistic anti-band Culturcide than intended for the gallery/museum system. Today Culturcide is legendary for anticipating the pressures that the endless reproducibility of recorded music would put on both business norms and concepts of originality. Even during his music-making and performing period, Flood held a mirror up to the world of art, titling the B-side of Culturcide's first single "Consider Museums as Concentration Camps" (1980). Dedicated to the Museum of Fine Arts Houston, it calls out the basic contradiction that conservative folks who could never stand to be around someone as untamed as Vincent van Gogh would happily pay twenty bucks to see his relics.

Punk was nothing if not judgmental of the world and its compromises, and in Culturcide's version of the "Star-Spangled Banner" the spewing forth of outrage is infective, intoxicating, and so pure it's beautiful:

> Oh, say can you see in the blinkless electron-gun eye of the mainstream media mirage that what we hail are the hallucinations of authority and progress and righteousness whose sweet and stern voices have captivated and conditioned millions of human creatures, stimulating in them a passive acceptance of technological disruption and destruction of environment, of history, of possibility of alternative ways of being?
>
> Whose seven stripes are broken swastikas, whose fifty stars are black holes sucking 200 million atomized existences into the daily routine of the human herd, of hamsters rolling the great wheels of death machine, squeaking at the shocks and nibbling the cheese and reciting and discussing and delighting in their shared programming history, in their stupid lives, in their cancers, their deaths, their TV shows, their jobs, their ignorance, their endless, pointless, forward creeping, their glorious, blithe nose-dive into their pay-check's pleasures, into an ecstatic emptiness: a glowing incinerator: a parking-lot full of business-men conspiring and colluding on the big lie, the big dream, the big nauseating screaming sweating nightmare of Business America / Consumer America / Corporate America / Media America / FASCIST AMERICA... "

Throughout the song, Flood's voice never pauses or slows.... What is often forgotten in writing the history of this musical revolution is the theoretical base of punk's politics, when bands would read Guy Debord's *Society of the Spectacle* on broken-down tour buses. (Flood is notorious for constantly recommending books to all in his orbit.) For every moment of unnuanced rage about hating his father, there are twenty in the recorded work that reflect a deep theoretical relationship to the problems of commodity, celebrity, entertainment, and art. On Culturcide's famously illegal record, *Tacky Souvenirs of Pre-Revolutionary America* (1986), the artist sings over banal pop hits of the time, adding layers of commentary and humor to insipid hits by Michael Jackson and Huey Lewis. Like Houston cultural hero DJ Screw—who could even make the Dixie Chicks sound psychedelic by slowing them down, adding a sultry beat, and rapping—Flood made MTV's most mainstream pabulum into a manifesto of uncreative authorship nearly simultaneously with the art-theory crowd, who took on the idea via appropriation (which I date to Sturtevant's first American retrospective at White Columns, also in 1986.) Before punk, pop music was ruthlessly manufactured and groomed to create the next hit. Punk singles were seen as the wrench in the system. In this genre, real kids indulged their real desires for songs that

…the B-side of Culturcide's first single… calls out the basic contradiction that conservative folks who could never stand to be around someone as untamed as Vincent van Gogh would happily pay twenty bucks to see his relics.

would speak to their deepest feelings, scare their parents, and reveal the shallowness of manufactured pop music. Songs such as "EMI" by the Sex Pistols—which critiques the unlimited supply of money-making records for labels like EMI—were masterpieces of the genre. So too, Flood's act of hiring strippers to make "another painting" after "another painting" in a pseudo-art fair context reflects this sensibility and demonstrates a clear translation from the playing field of music to that of art.

The city of Houston facilitates this kind of dialogue, due in large part to the abundance of progressive cultural institutions that provide paying jobs to both artists and musicians. Much of our city's artistic experimentation was brought about by John and Dominique de Menil's incredible largesse, which Flood experienced firsthand at the Menil Collection. It also gave him a close view of the art-market machinery as it grew in size and power during the eighties and nineties. And though Flood spent enough years in New York's freewheeling East Village to count as a participant in that scene, he stayed connected to Houston. To this day, he will set up shop in Miami, New York, and other cities to produce certain bodies of work, but he always comes back to Houston, the city that gives him the distance to really see the capitals of the art world clearly. (When in New York, where the mechanisms of the art world are ubiquitous and it seems every third person self-describes as an artist, the weirdness of it all disappears. In Houston, self-describing as an artist is still worthy of comment.)

Mark Flood: Gratest Hits is not a retrospective, or even a survey; the selection of work from the artist's own horde celebrates this stimulating and revolutionary local treasure trove. His passion for his own vision is such that he will gleefully keep these works unless his gallerists forcibly remove them. Mark Flood, poster boy for the weird cultural swamp that is Houston, has established such a morally coherent, intelligently disciplined position that his work deserves to be the focus of and help redefine museum scholarship, of which this essay is just a start.

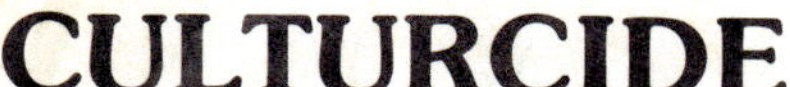

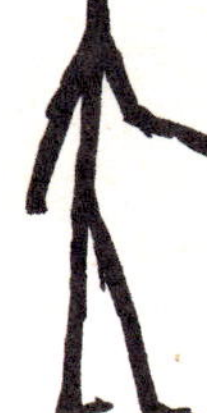

K

K
Culturcide
Another Miracle/Consider Museums as Concentration Camps, 1980
Vinyl record, edition of 1000
7 x 7 inches

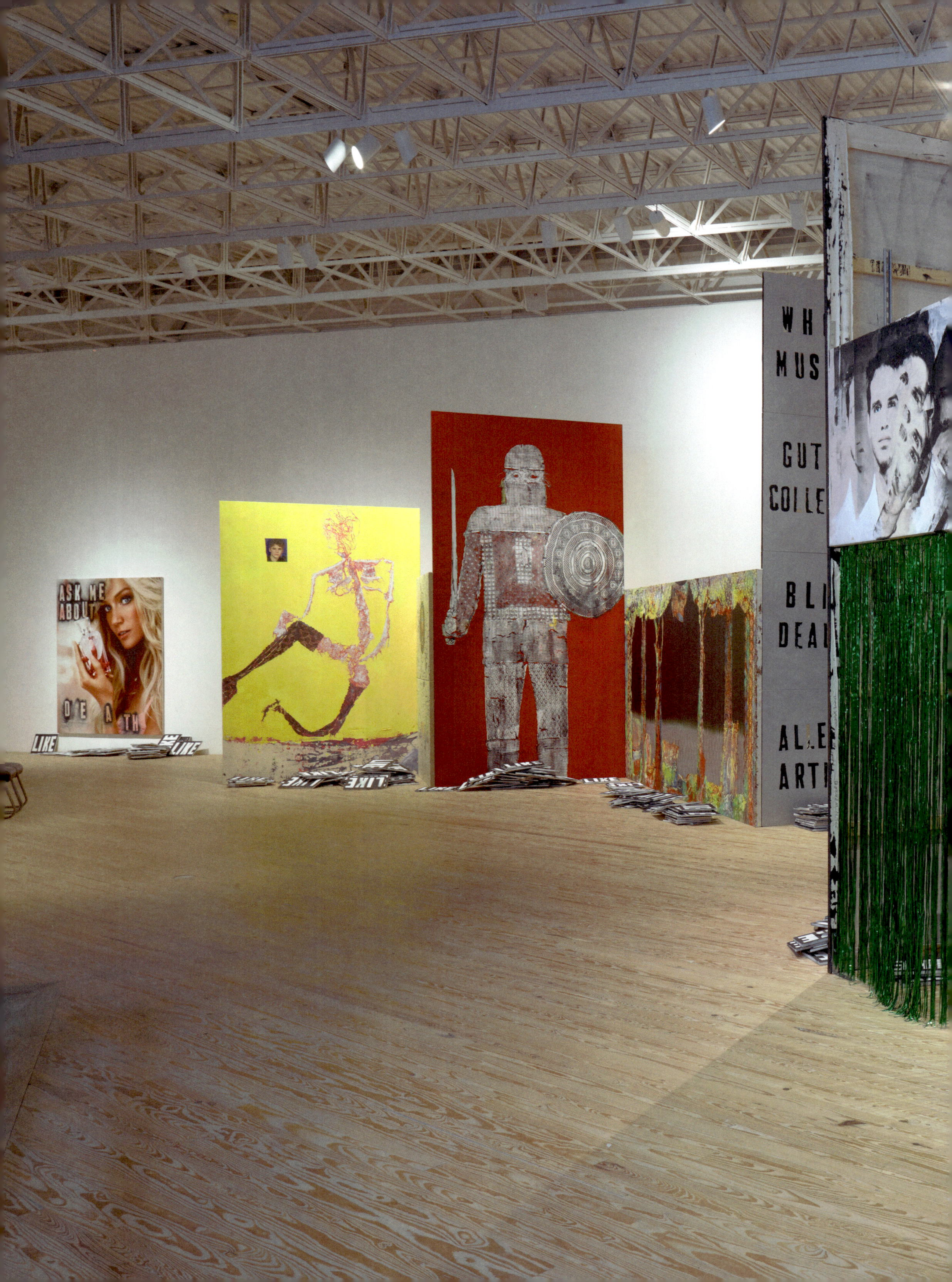
ASK ME
ABOUT
DE A TH
LIKE
LIKE
LIKE

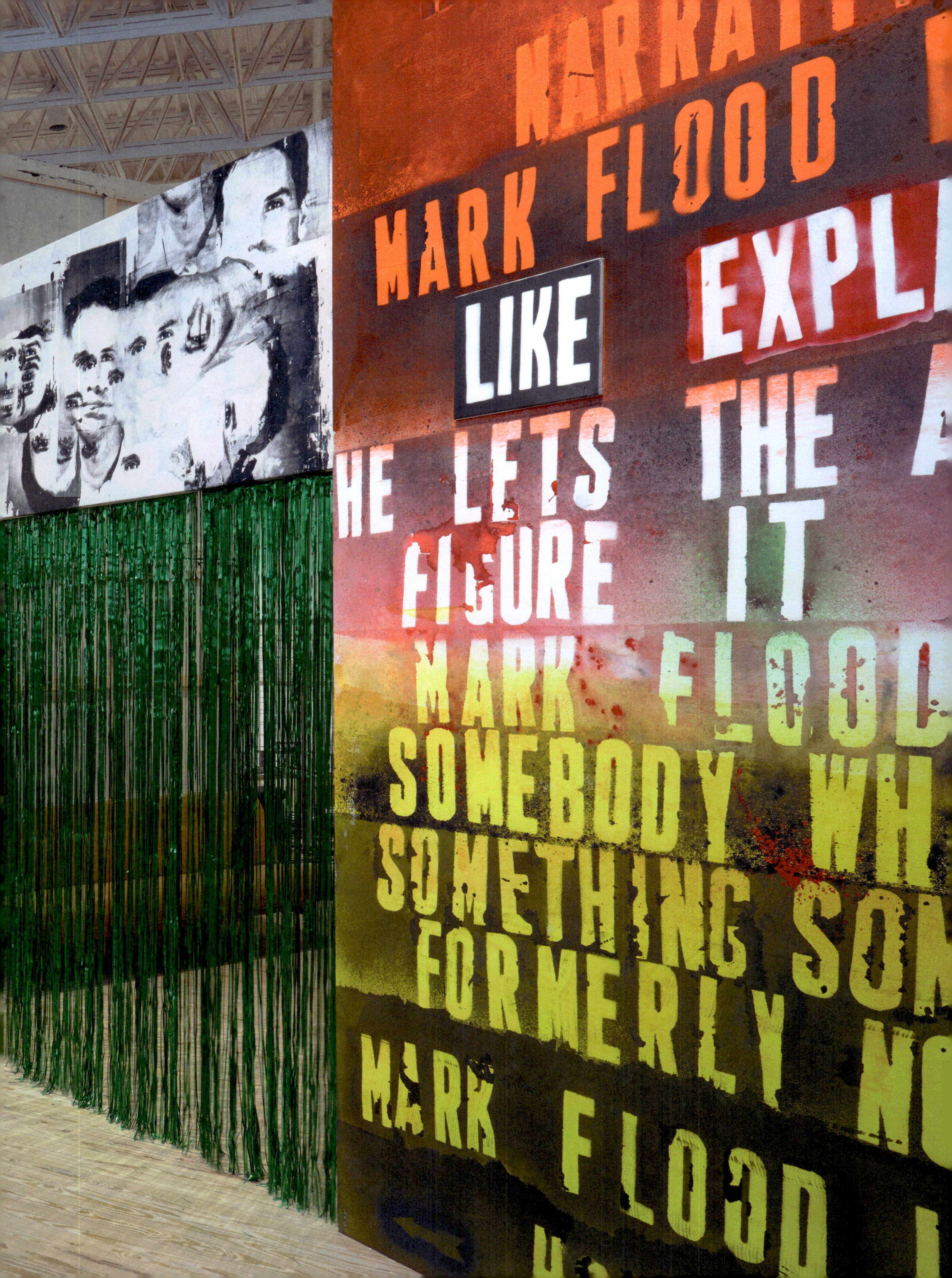
MARK FLOOD
MARK FLOOD
LIKE
HE LETS THE
FIGURE IT
MARK FLOOD
SOMEBODY
SOMETHING
FORMERLY
MARK FLOOD

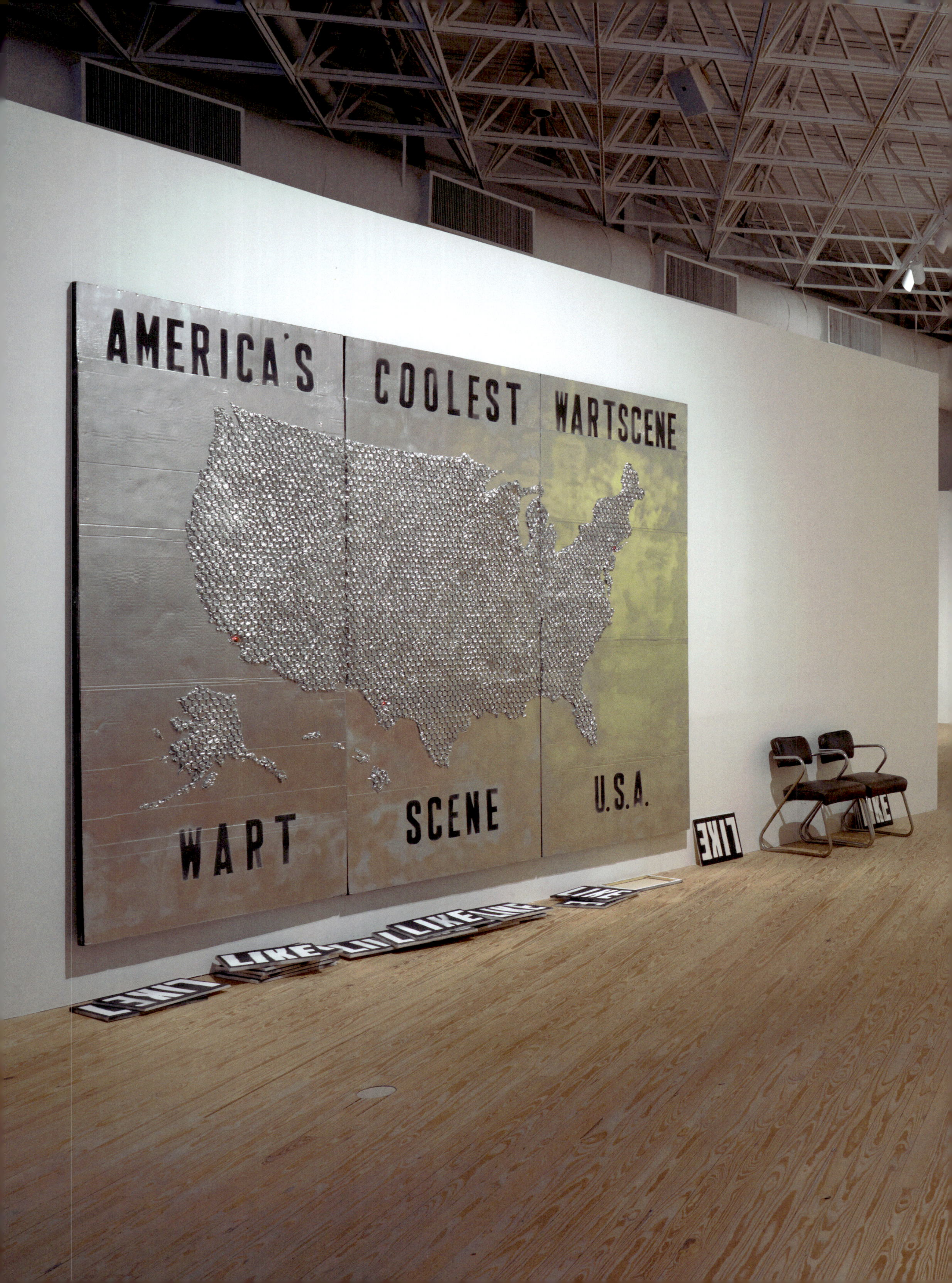

AMERICA'S
COOLEST
WARTSCENE
WART
SCENE
U.S.A.
LIKE

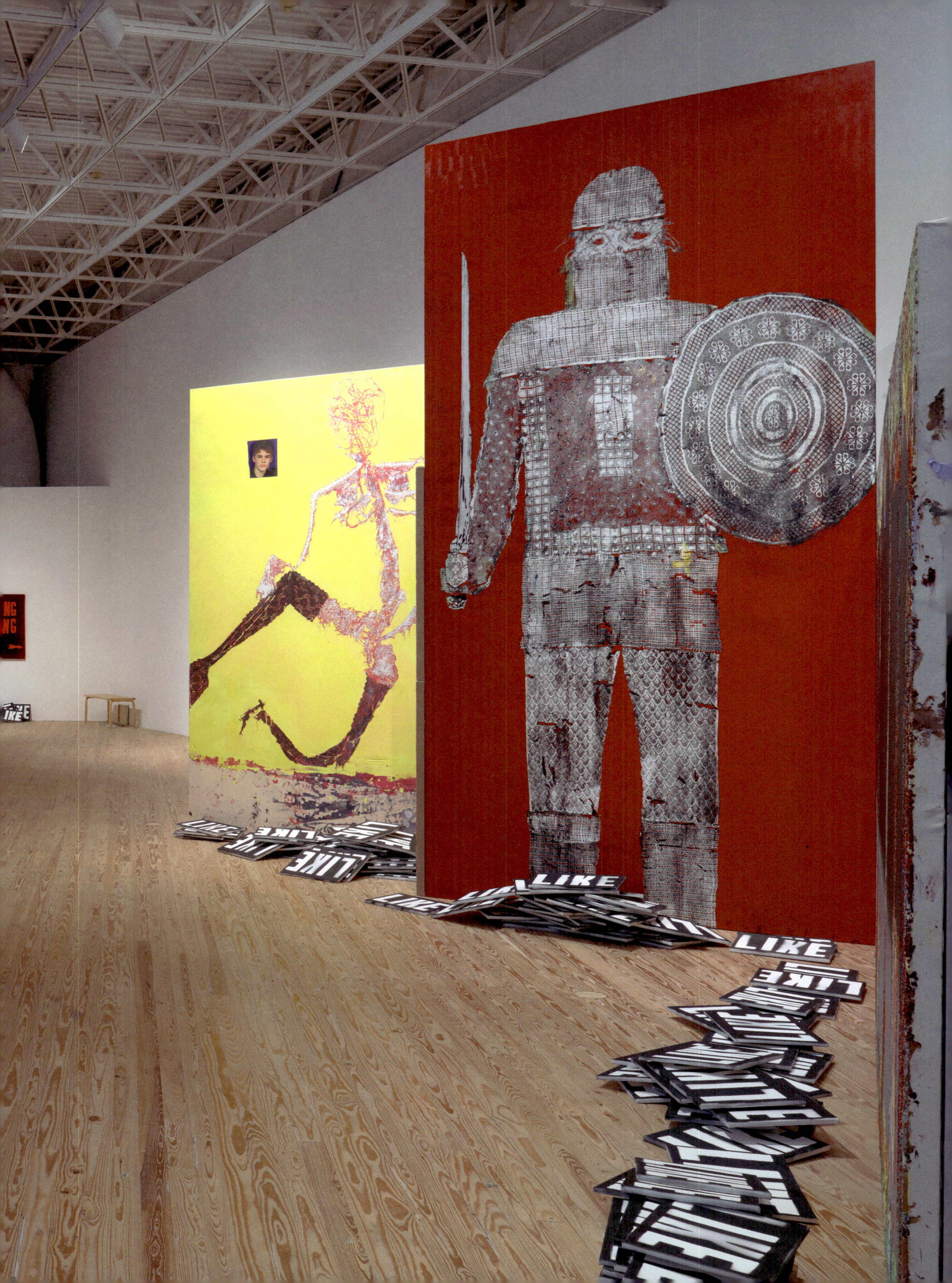
LIKE

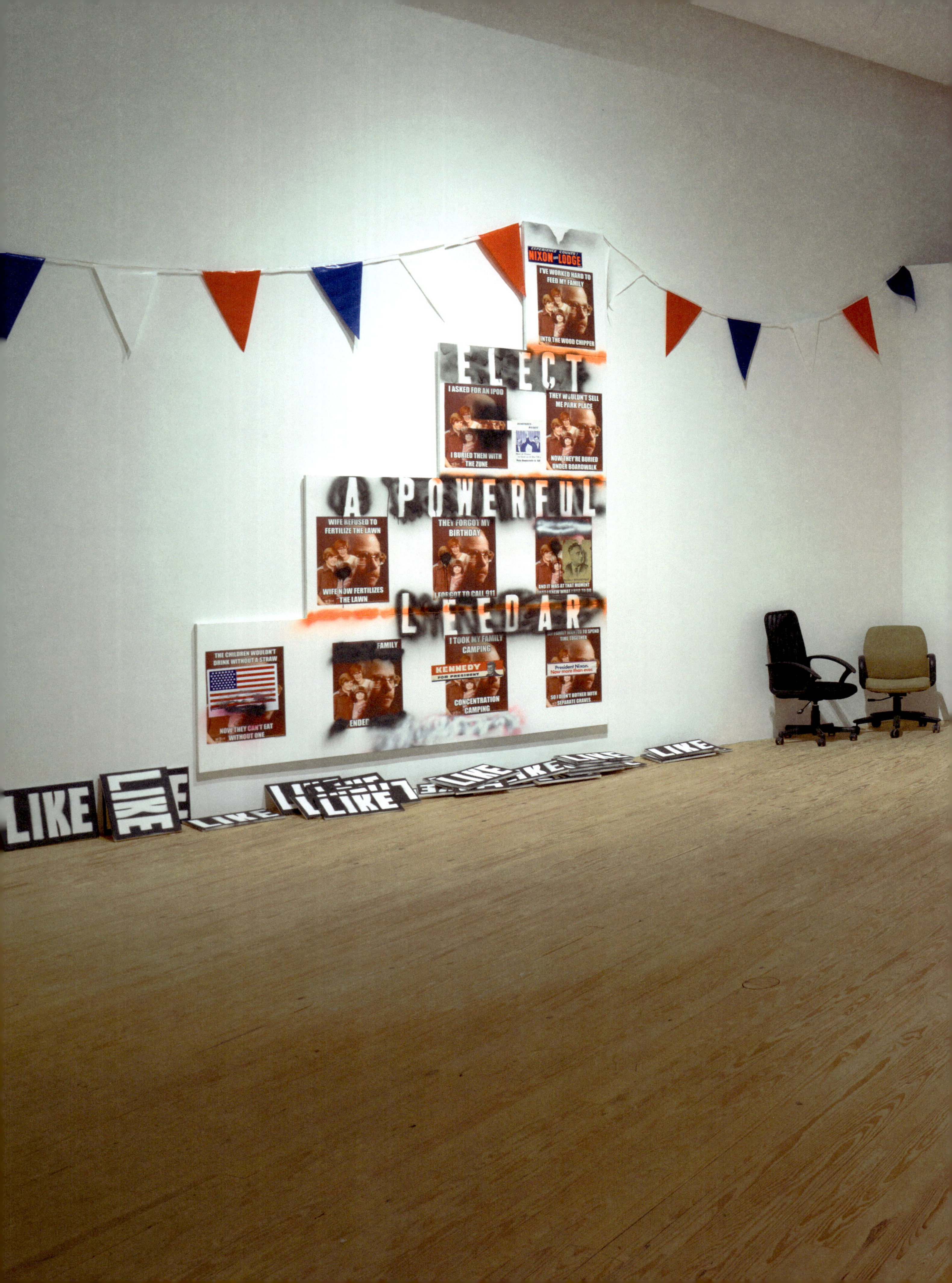
NIXON LODGE
I'VE WORKED HARD TO FEED MY FAMILY
INTO THE WOOD CHIPPER
ELECT
I ASKED FOR AN IPOD
I BURIED THEM WITH THE ZUNE
THEY WOULDN'T SELL ME PARK PLACE
NOW THEY'RE BURIED UNDER BOARDWALK
A POWERFUL
WIFE REFUSED TO FERTILIZE THE LAWN
WIFE NOW FERTILIZES THE LAWN
THEY FORGOT MY BIRTHDAY
I FORGOT TO CALL 911
LEEDAR
THE CHILDREN WOULDN'T DRINK WITHOUT A STRAW
NOW THEY CAN'T EAT WITHOUT ONE
I TOOK MY FAMILY CAMPING
KENNEDY FOR PRESIDENT
CONCENTRATION CAMPING
President Nixon. Now more than ever.
SO I DIDN'T BOTHER WITH SEPARATE GRAVES
LIKE

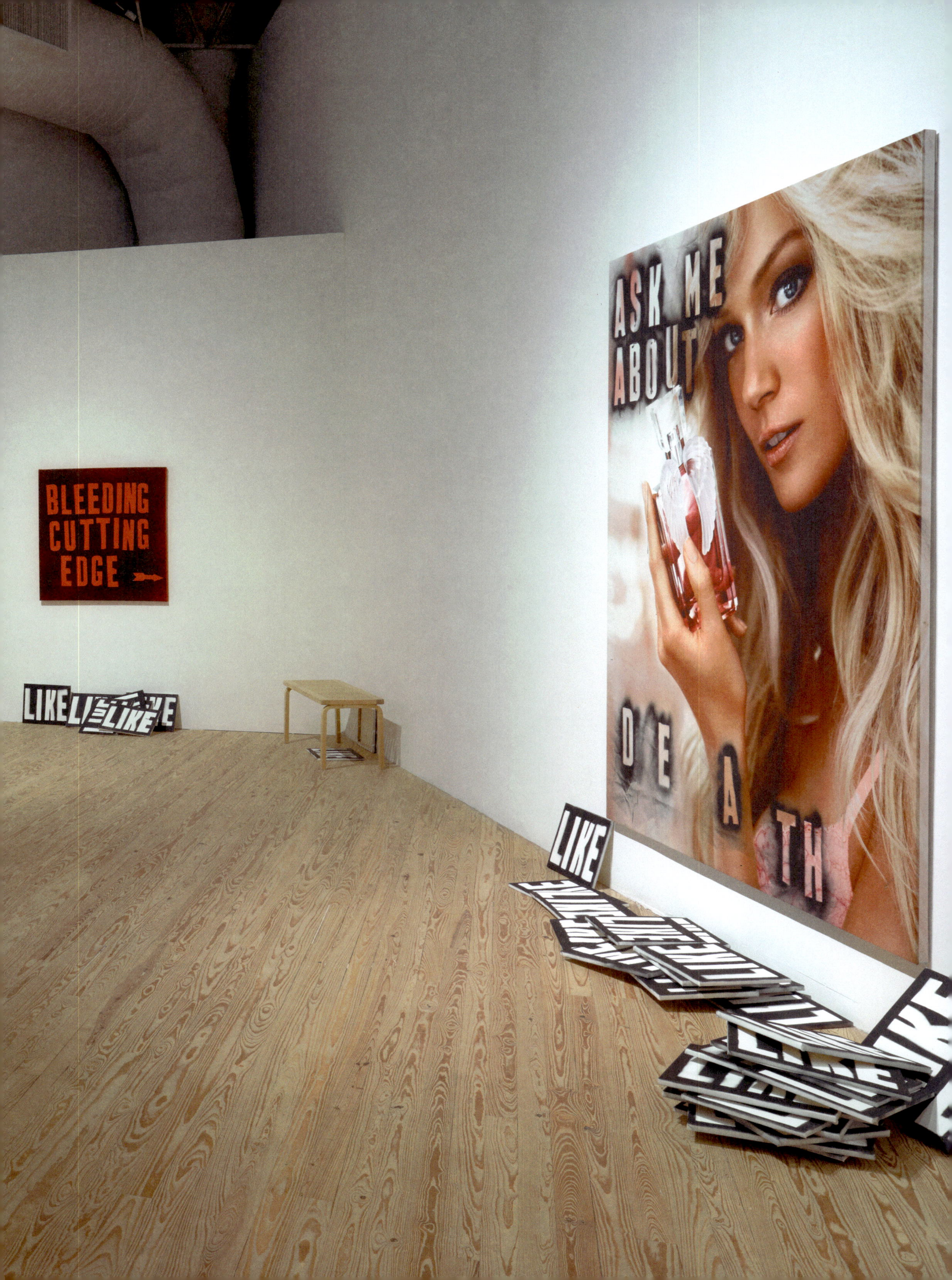
ASK ME ABOUT
DEATH
BLEEDING
CUTTING
EDGE
LIKE

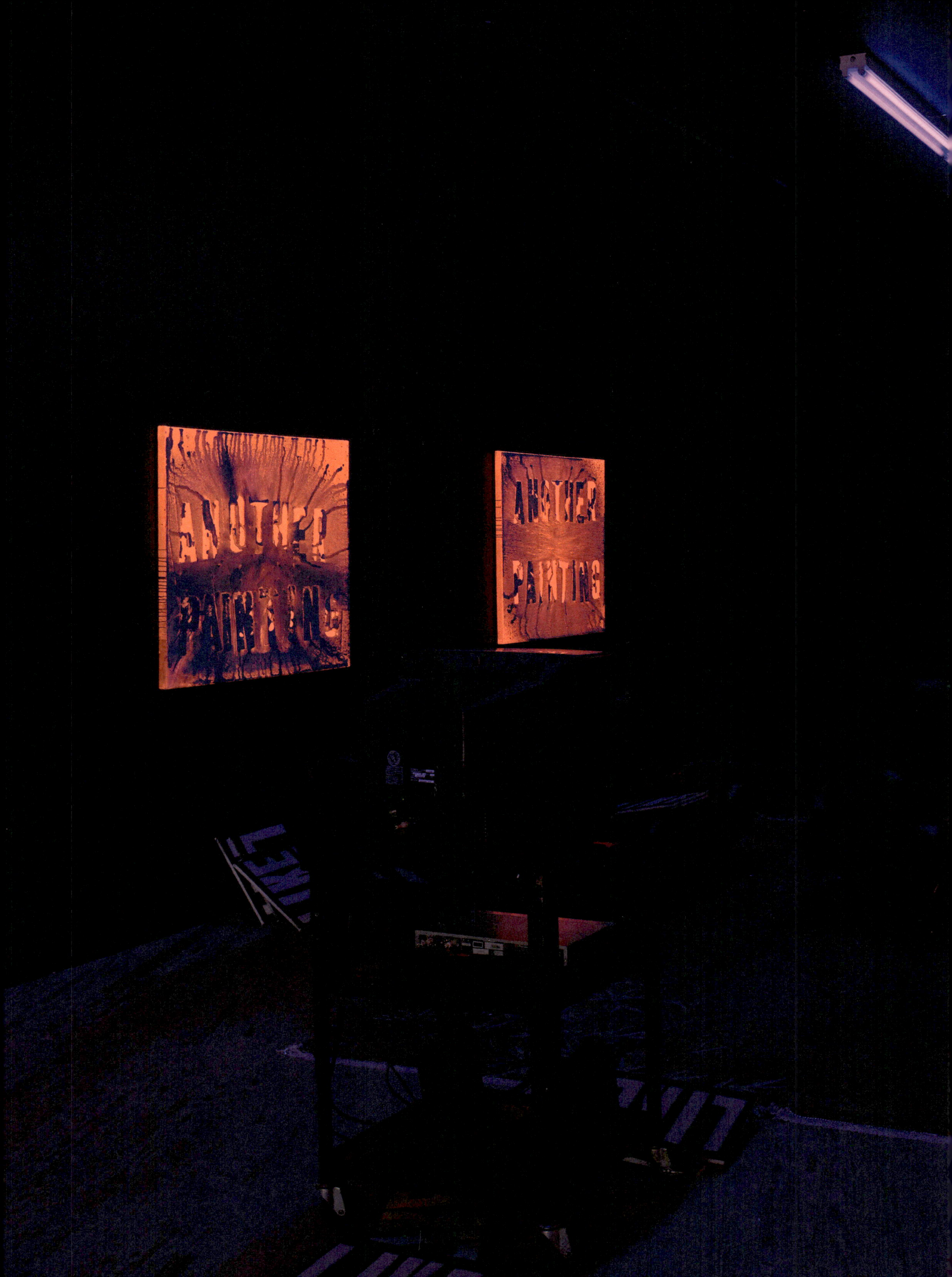
ANOTHER
PAINTING
ANOTHER
PAINTING

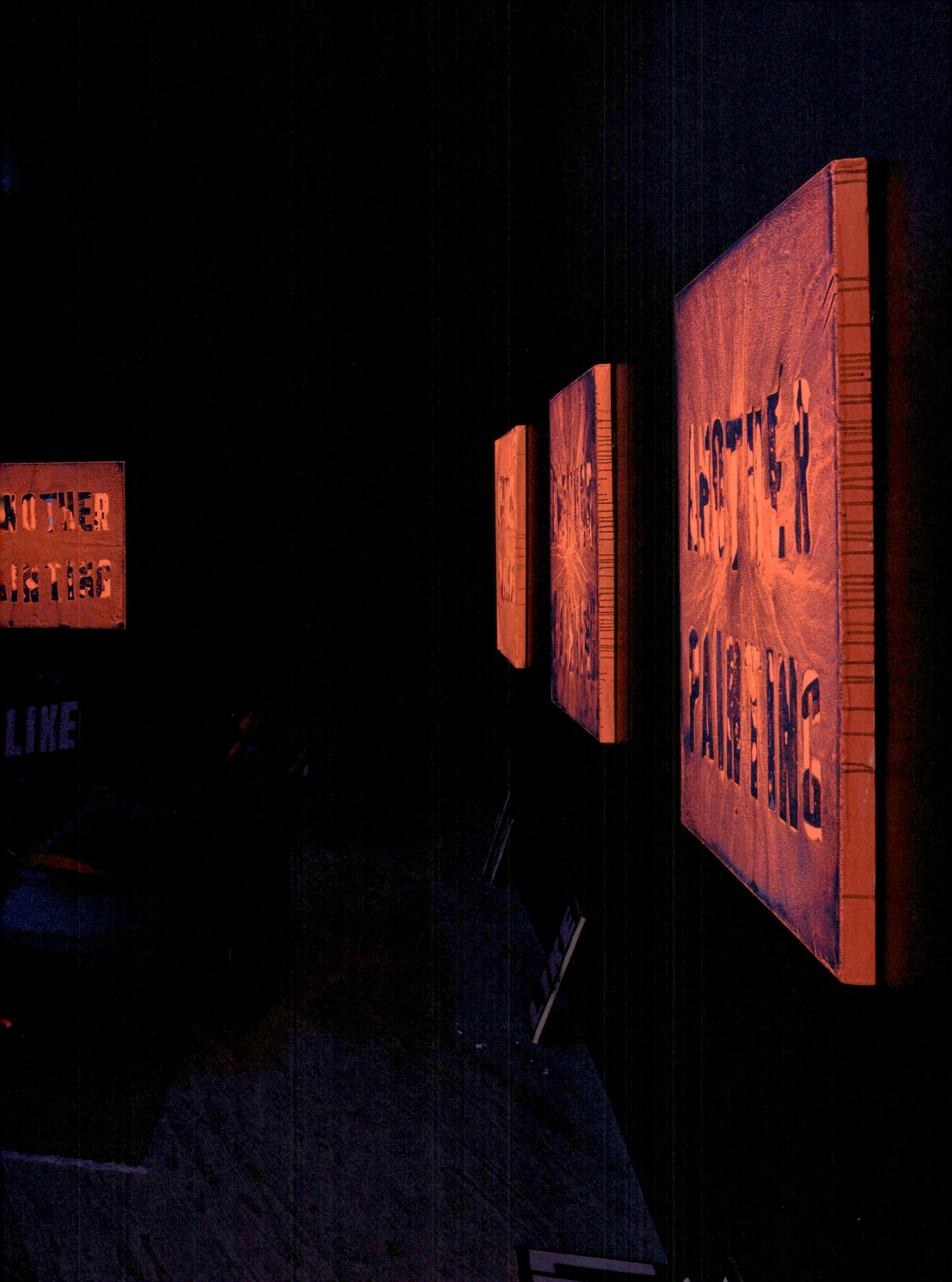
ANOTHER
LIKE

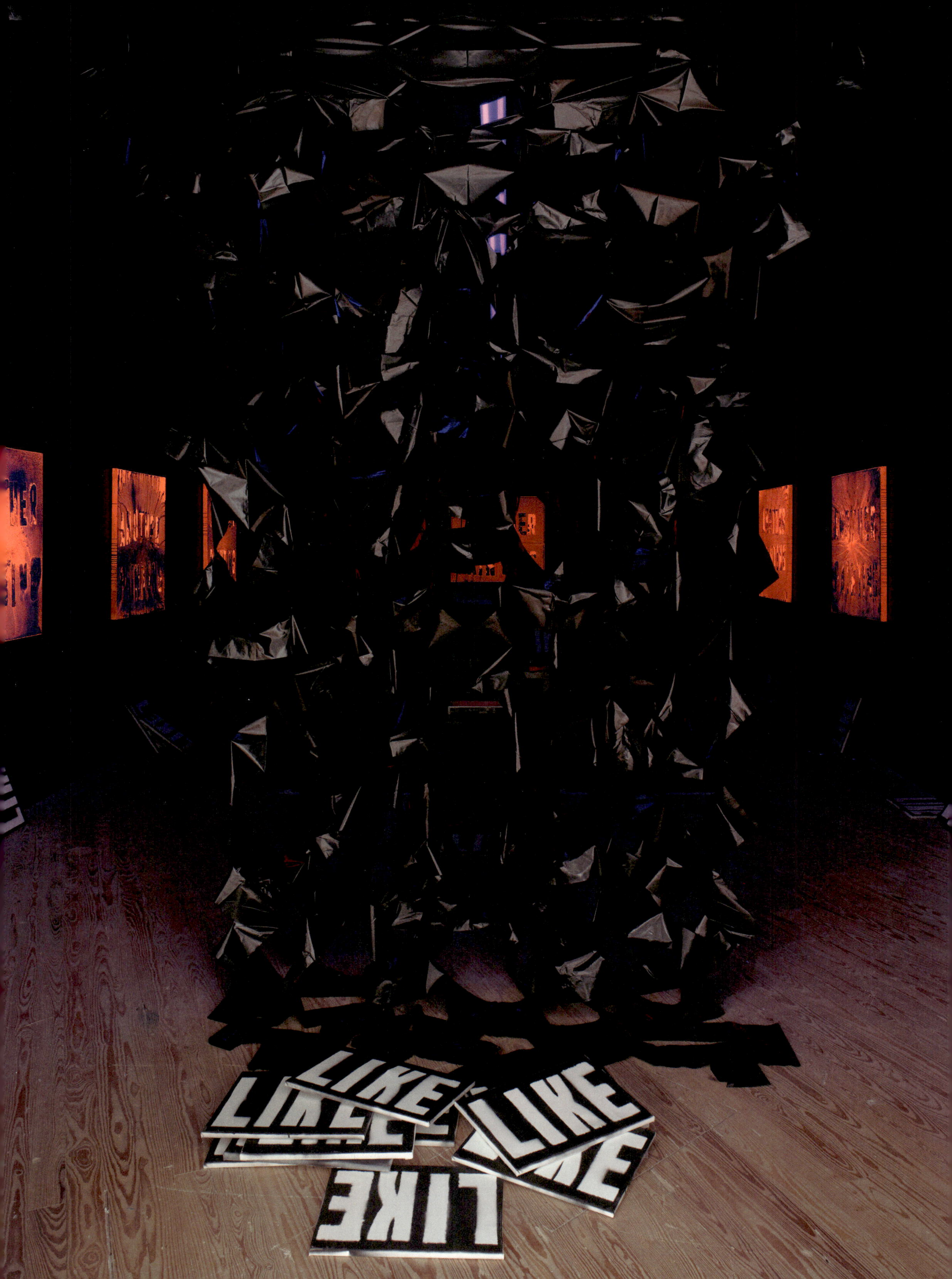
LIKE
LIKE
LIKE
LIKE

MF Hit It First

El Topito

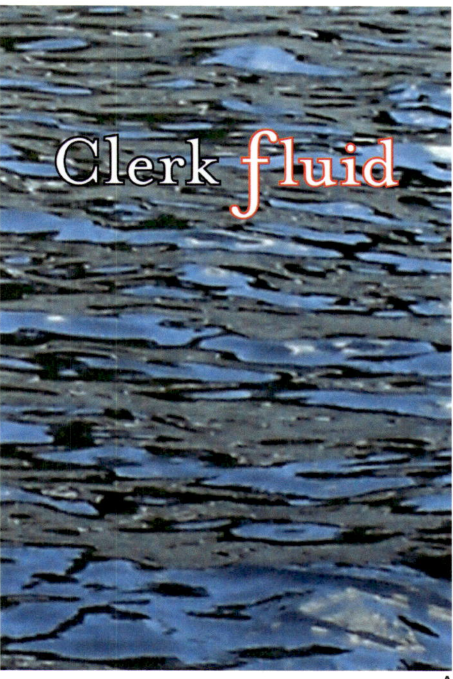

THERE WERE REJECTED TITLES TO this essay: "Save Me the Gristle: A Reluctant Foodie's Journey into the Heart of Flood's Praxis, from his Musical Peerage with Genesis Breyer P-Orridge to the Literary Genius Trapped in a Careerist's Career" was the longest. Titling a piece about Mark Flood ("MF") is difficult because his own title choices are so perfectly extracted, they render useless additional context. Whichever optical neurons his artworks stimulate, there is usually linguistic icing on the cake. How can one write about the choices of someone who recently said to an interviewer, "My own career bores me"?

Which is to say that Flood is clever with words that construct his mythos, and he has written extensively about his own career, institutional experiences, art history, and musings in general. I would put on record that anyone interested enough in Flood to be skimming this essay should go out and purchase *Clerk Fluid* (2009), his homage to the artist's book genre, available in several media. In it—much like in other great confessionals—the artist/author covers his emotional and intellectual development from mortal creature to the white rhino we now address as Mark Flood.

When I met Flood—about the time he published *Clerk Fluid*—I didn't know he was much of a writer or social satirist or engaging persona. He was another artist with a quasi-fictitious name, although already a somewhat notable one. He was disarmingly direct, as his published interviews evidence. A student of the emergence of consciousness, he was interested in and knowledgeable about the convergence of cultural histories, media, and technology. He was humble and self-effacing but not naive by a mile, generous with his time and opinions and even his working capital, already funding exhibitions, projects, and publications of his friends and/or assistants.

But I haven't come here to praise the man, I've come to vivisect his artistic integrity. But who am I to judge, you dare ask? A succubus. "One of his dealers," on the lower tier.

Oh it sounds so very romantic in retrospect. Talking to people about this man—this artist—more artist than man, but being Texan perhaps more of a man than most American males born after 1988. When I first met him we began the most American of conversations about Johnny Carson and the vernacular of those who would watch Lawrence Welk on television, moving on to obsolete technologies, and perhaps we bonded most over our lack of mutual enmity. That Johnny Carson painting, *NEXT* (2008)—how I loved its humble amalgamation of paper, Coroplast, and wood—an Intimist masterpiece. Who bought it? Maybe someone with a big wall. It spoke to that time and place that is fading from

A
Clark Flood,
Cover of *Clerk Fluid*, 2009

memory for most, but we can't let old television die. In short order I became a ground soldier in the information war of Mark Flood, spending work hours waxing ecstatic about his sexy, swelling career.

And sexy it was and has been perhaps since the dawn of the lace paintings and his *market-friendly* style of work. "Sexy" is the price of admission that isn't discussed, and sexiness is subjective of course. I find Hans Haacke's work very sexy, but you may not. I find process-based photography incredibly unsexy, but you may. In any case, Mark's paintings, sculptures, media works, and installations were incredibly complete, mature, and by mysterious birthright very photogenic; therefore they possessed sex appeal. I proselytized.

What would I say about them, and to whom? I wouldn't tell you whom, but I would say things like *"MF is making art that circumvents the allowable and goes straight for the jugular. Art that is explicitly about collecting, about other artists, but not in an oblique manner. In a time when so many careers are based on taking one thread from a more established, complex artist of the past ('standing on their shoulders')—and turning that riff into a stand-alone enterprise, MF is still bothering to create multifaceted, layered material."*

We were lucky, and there was interest in his product. The well-heeled were willing to purchase the factory samples, sometimes with little evasive maneuvering. Early on, if my memory serves correctly, Manhattanites were buying his paintings from Los Angeles, a reversal of the generally accepted universal order at the time. One of my favorite paintings was among the first that sold, with the assistance of a facilitator who admitted to me that they didn't quite "get it"—but knew enough to tell someone to buy it—a line of reasoning I fully endorsed.

The entrepreneur-as-artist, mythological self-made man. "My Dinner with Flood" was another potential title for this essay, but all he did was take me to the movies once and dinner a couple of times. The place

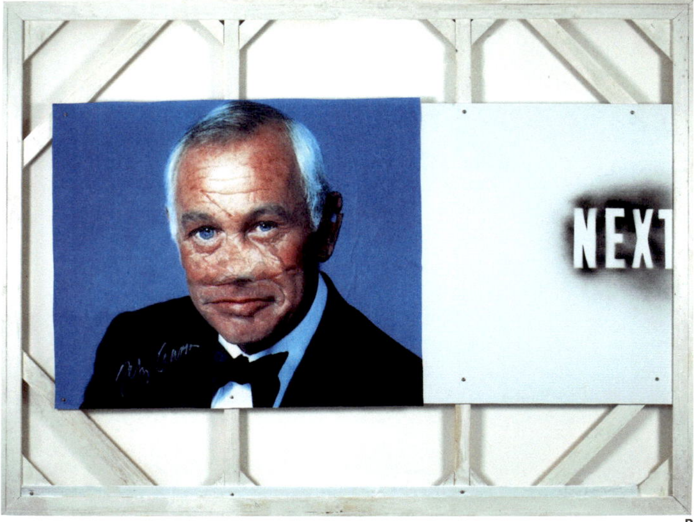

B

was expensive, but my view of a table of Russian "models" made it almost worth the price of the bill I didn't pay. MF, the lavishly tipping American who bootstrapped himself to success the un-easy way. There was some thuggish negotiation on the way up, but he was mostly fair to the vanquished. He played the harlequin, read some Carlos Castaneda, and bit the bullet until he could finally embrace financial success and the beneficence of twenty-five-year-olds from Palo Alto who refuse to purchase anything made in traditional media. But oh do they covet those digital prints on canvas.

The titles of Flood's *FANTASIZE ABOUT VIOLENCE* (2013) and *& YOUR SOUL* (2008) leave much to the imagination. Are these the commands of a deity, or the inner monologue of the artist/viewer? I would call this phenomenon the "unsubtle cock tease" of MF's work. Like a reasonable Burrovian, MF liberally draws from the ether that surrounds him and spews it back to subvert its original purpose. What differentiates him is that at every phase of production his decisions are outrageously nuanced, accurate, and brutally honest. Yet he claims to try his damnedest *not* to be a micromanager of others or his work, and I believe that statement.

Really though, MF works under the disappearing tradition of studio practitioner/flâneur who has arrived at his place in the

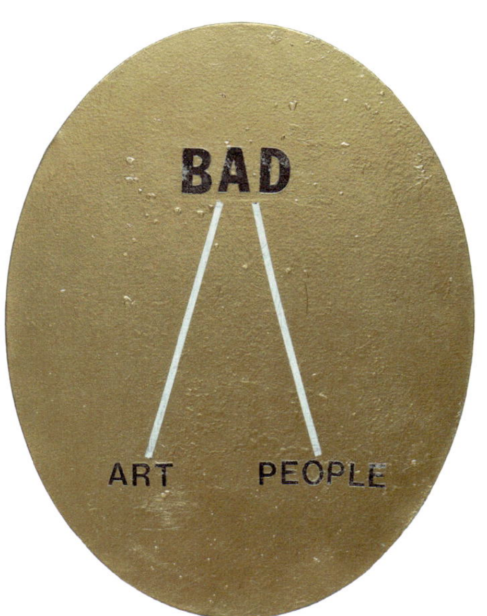

C

B
NEXT, 2008
Collage and spray paint on Coroplast on wood
80 x 108 inches

C
BAD ART / PEOPLE, 2008
Spray paint and acrylic latex on canvas
20 x 16 inches

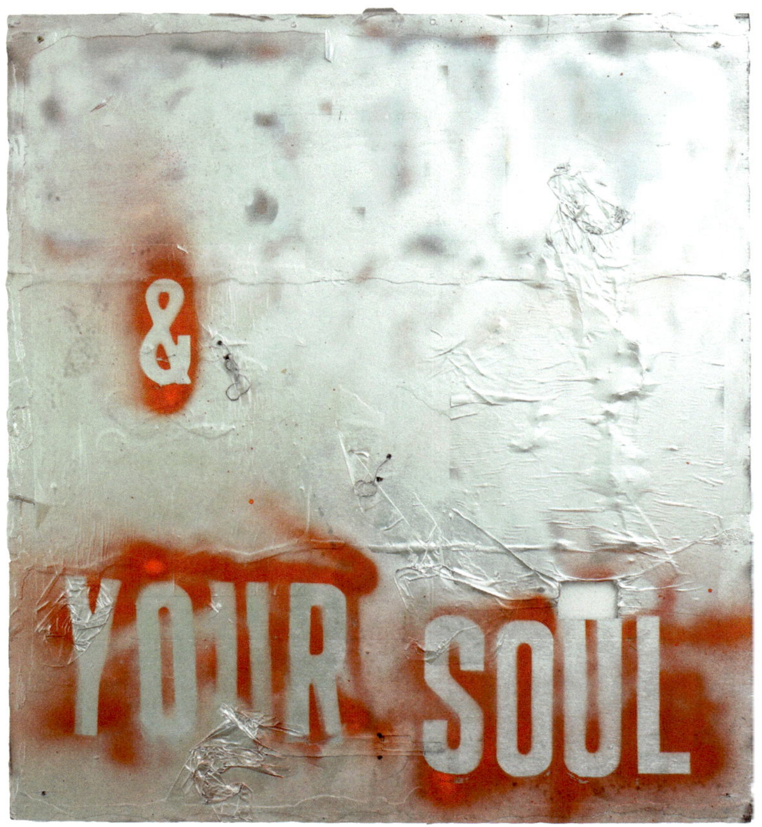

E

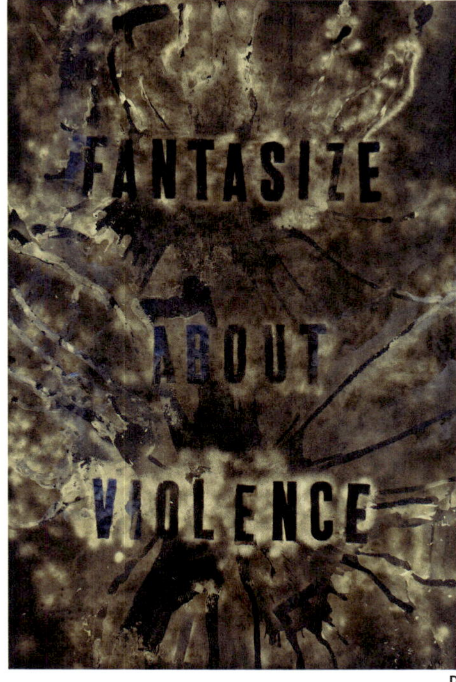

D

pantheon by swallowing nebuchadnezzars of blood, sweat, tears, pride, and self-loathing. He is Antonin Artaud and Vaslav Nijinsky in the current blind spot of history, though he rolls fluidly with the technological punches of the times, relentlessly seeking the extremes of experience while interpreting them with a laid-back flow. When Houston's beloved DJ Screw was still around, MF listened and integrated the eminent musician's postproduction techniques into his own. On the surface it is simply a knowing gesture, but when you consider the breadth and innovation of his homage to "cut and paste"—or "chopped and screwed," as it were—you glimpse the intensity of MF's distillation process.

Much has been made of the Internet and its effect on art and artist alike, but the emergence of the meme as an idiom of MF's output is particularly worth noting. Examples of this work could include his original sign paintings or the more recent meme paintings, though the motif is differentiated by stylized text that usually serves an adjacent visual metaphor rather than being "read" as a statement. "What's in a meme," you ask? It turns out that people today understand memes as a stand-alone entity with perhaps twelve million times the fan base of contemporary poetry, but memes began their existence essentially as rapidly shared visual-lingual jokes. In retrospect it is easy to trace the use of meme-like tropes through the artist's work all the way back to the beginning of his career. It is as if his adoption of this style of language was a piece of native intelligence he possessed and embraced a very long time ago, while it took society at large many years to catch on.

BAD ART/PEOPLE (2008) is a logic tree within a painting. There are earlier artistic precedents that resemble logic trees—perhaps those by Kurt Schwitters, Alighiero Boetti, et al.—but none with the straightforwardness of this one. It is a comment about an existential condition of art, or rather it is a painting that

D
FANTASIZE ABOUT VIOLENCE, 2013
Acrylic on canvas
103¾ x 69⅝ inches

E
& YOUR SOUL, 2008
Spray paint, acrylic latex, collage, and wire on wood panel
46½ x 43 inches

takes us to the edge of a decision but tactfully refuses to make the choice for us. Is bad art created by bad people for bad people? Both, neither, or only sometimes? There is pleasure in the contemplation of the unresolved. But MF resolutely and sincerely likes people—even bad ones (perhaps especially bad ones)—though his refusal to judge the actions of others does not absolve him of stirring the debate. Would we the viewer feel better if we could reach the conclusion that bad art is made by or for bad people? And, in turn, if good art is made by or for good people?

MF himself is as enigmatic a "good person" as you can meet: direct, genuine, and polite. But does his photogenic name indicate that he is operating under an artistic persona? MF is not shy about the fact that he invented this name, and it works for me so I use it when I address or speak about him. If it is a veil, he wears it without guile. But maybe it's just because he wanted a good enough *nom d'art* to make good art with a reasonable chance of finding an audience. I've heard rumblings from his entourage that it is part of a master plan, one that he hasn't shared with everyone.

MF has written and made text works about artistic communities, mocking them more often than not. Yet he fans the flames that sustain several groups or scenes, simultaneously, around him. He is perhaps bemused by the "art world" at large and has expressed his ambiguity about its implications. In December 2014, MF flew me to Florida to attend his exhibition *Mark Flood Resents* and rub elbows with his coterie. I used the experience as a "postcards from Miami" moment, although I was no Michael Herr: I crossed at the crosswalks, sat in my room until summoned, and attended the ritualistic encounters between the subspecies on hand. Assistants, managers, friends, lovers, sycophants, collectors, randoms, all were welcome though none contributed as much energy as the artist in the middle of it all. I wandered and thought of unfunny double entendres for this essay, such as "the artist and his ROLL in society," and I learned, again, that MF really does like people.

He sends frequent Instagram and e-mail blasts to his legionnaires advising them of new projects, but they mostly frustrate me because he is so talented and prolific. They make me insanely jealous and full of contempt. Who does he think I am, an unpaid quality-control inspector for his art?

A final title consideration: "Mark Flood and Mainstream American Television, 2010–15." I have witnessed a nonplussed MF work furiously and accurately on lace paintings in nondescript commercial rental spaces. I have seen a warehouse in Texas packed with his art, the living totem of all the years of struggle, the painter's secret burden. I have watched more hours of *Big Brother: After Dark* with him than I care to admit. We are riveted by the fear of a double eviction, we flies on the wall. Even in moments of extreme passivity he works, and if you scan his output he pays *Big Brother* and *Big Brother: After Dark* repeated homage. These game shows are simply structures to embrace, though the good people at Endemol are no fools and they've built the game's rules upon societal constructs that are easy to understand, fear, and crave.

In MF's hands, the rules of the game are interchangeable with the cold hard facts of modern life, evidence that the unsubtle class consciousness in his work manages to be neither bitter nor dogmatic, just biting and humorous. A further discussion of his *Big Brother*–related work would fit suitably into a TEDx Talk, or a TEDx Crossfit MF/ABMB event in his Miami Beach atelier. In a time when so many careers are based on taking one thread from a more established, complex artist of the past ("standing on their shoulders") and turning that riff into a stand-alone enterprise, MF is still bothering to create multifaceted, layered material.

Flood accepts the radical change around him, as if he knows what happens next, as if this world's self-cannibalizing chaos is of the same level of concern to him as what to watch on television later, as if he once caught a tiger by the tail and was let down by the experience. I had—and have—limitless admiration for this level of professionalism.

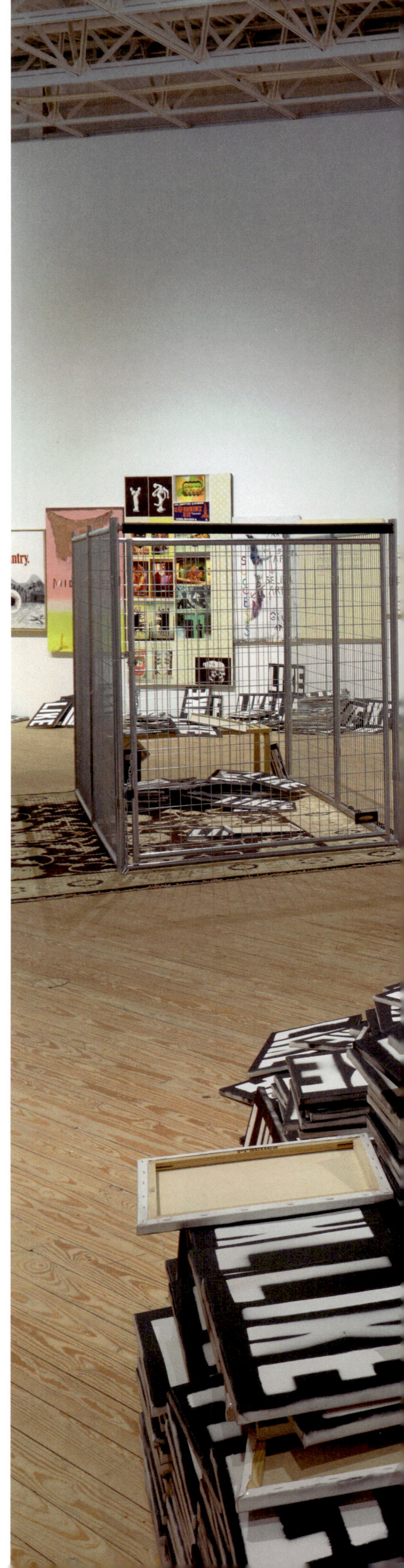

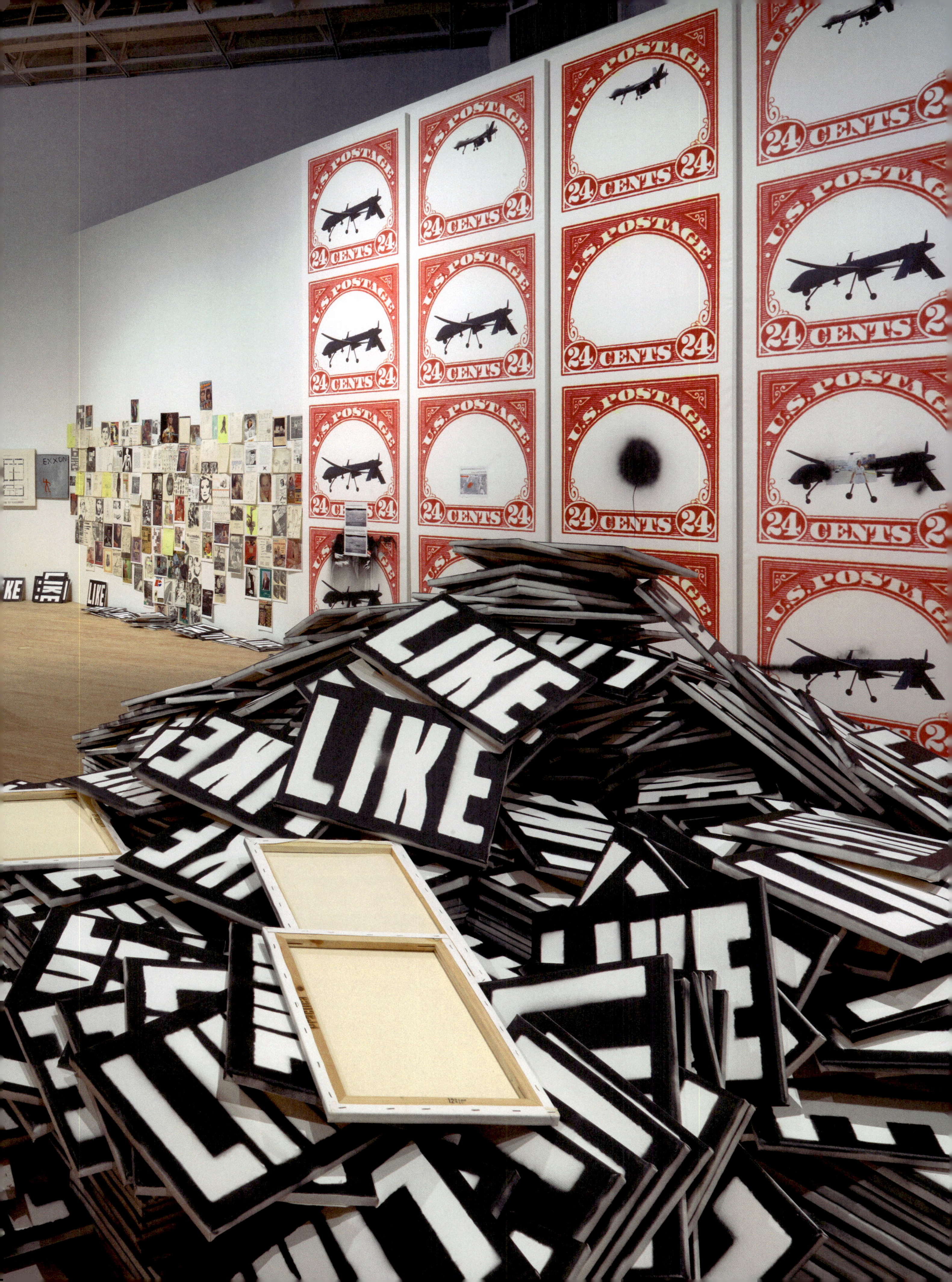
U.S. POSTAGE
24 CENTS 24
EXXON
LIKE

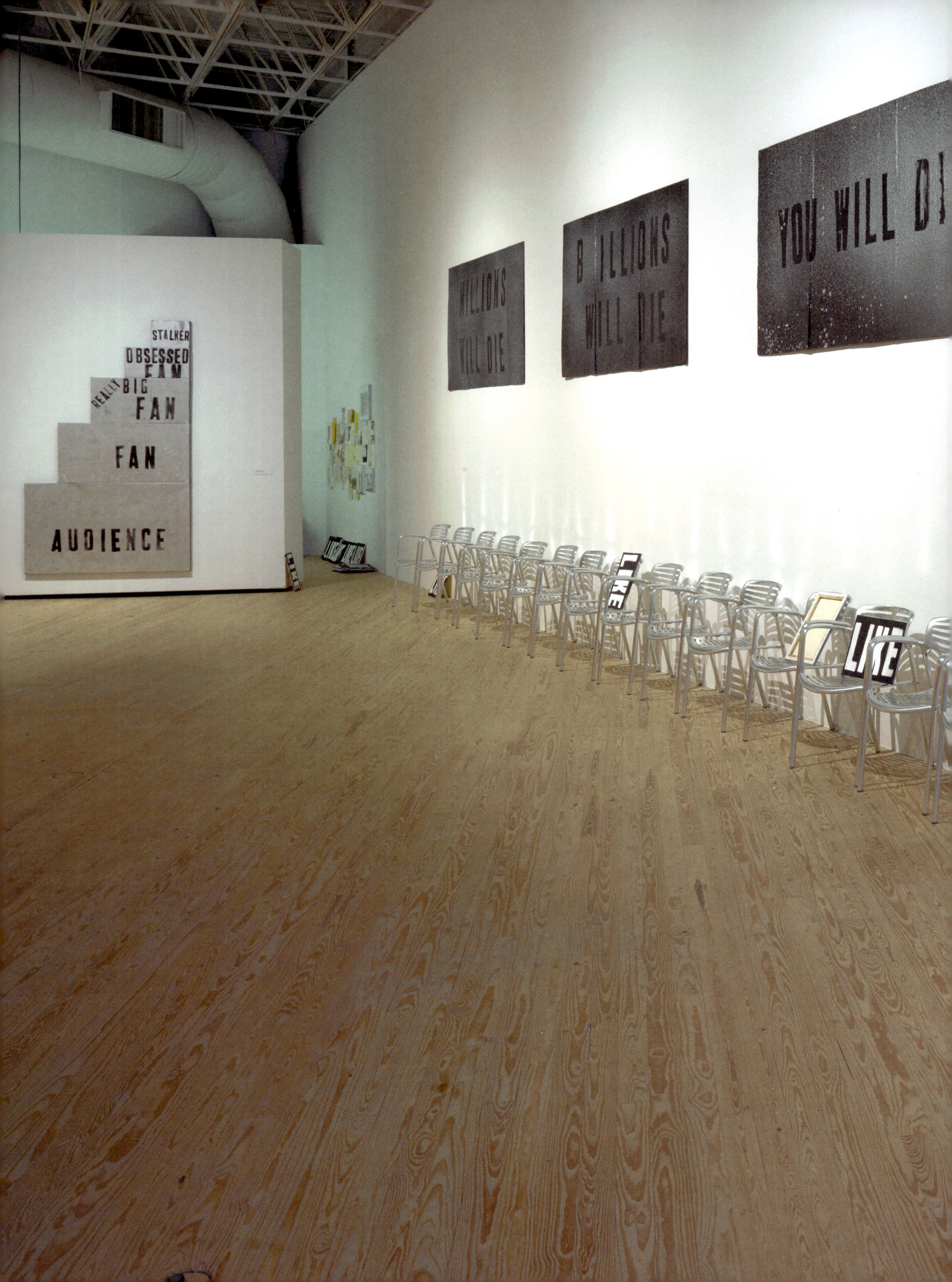
STALKER
OBSESSED FAN
REALLY BIG FAN
FAN
AUDIENCE
MILLIONS WILL DIE
BILLIONS WILL DIE
YOU WILL
LIKE
LIKE

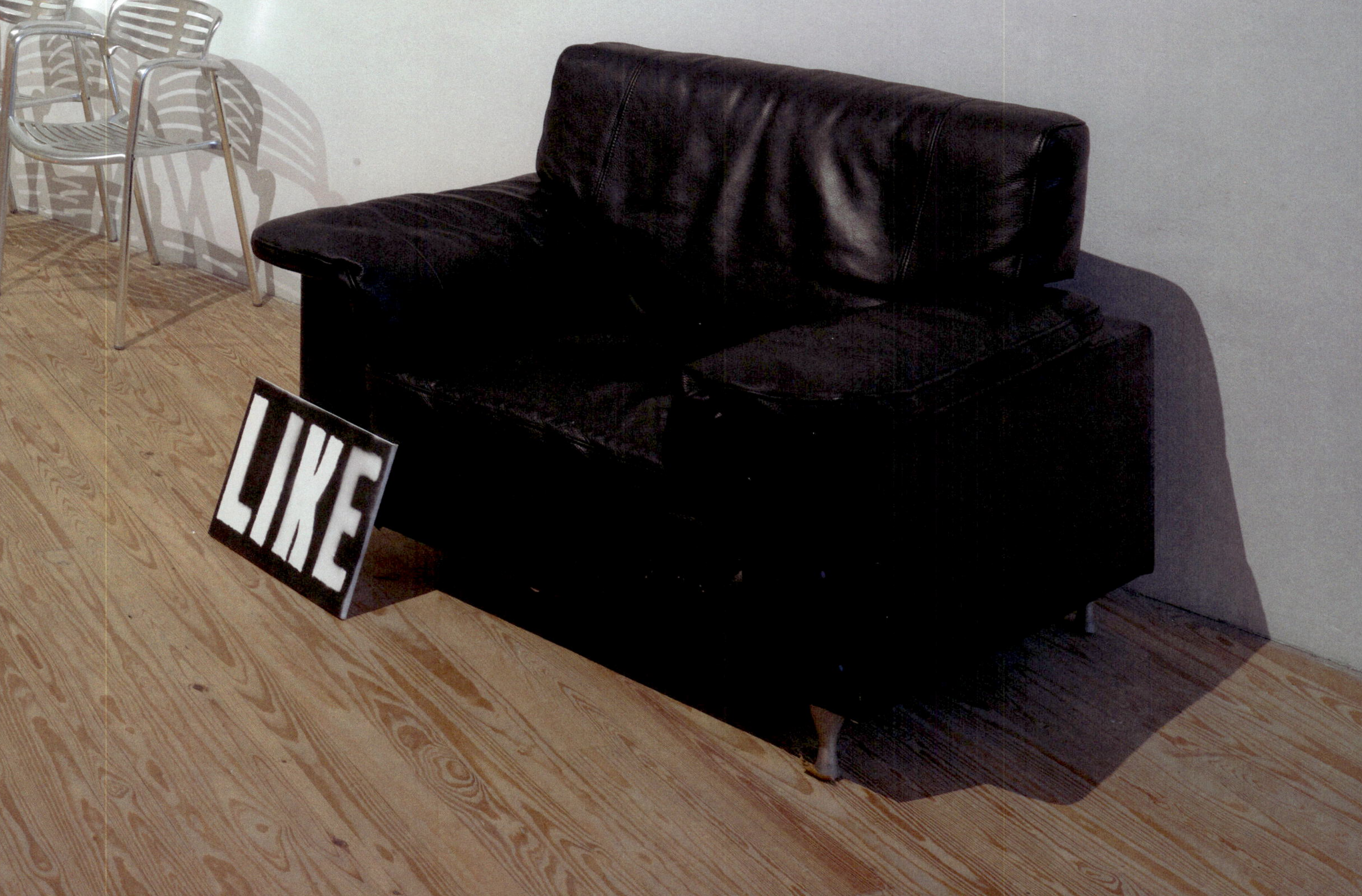
MARK
FLOOD
LIKE

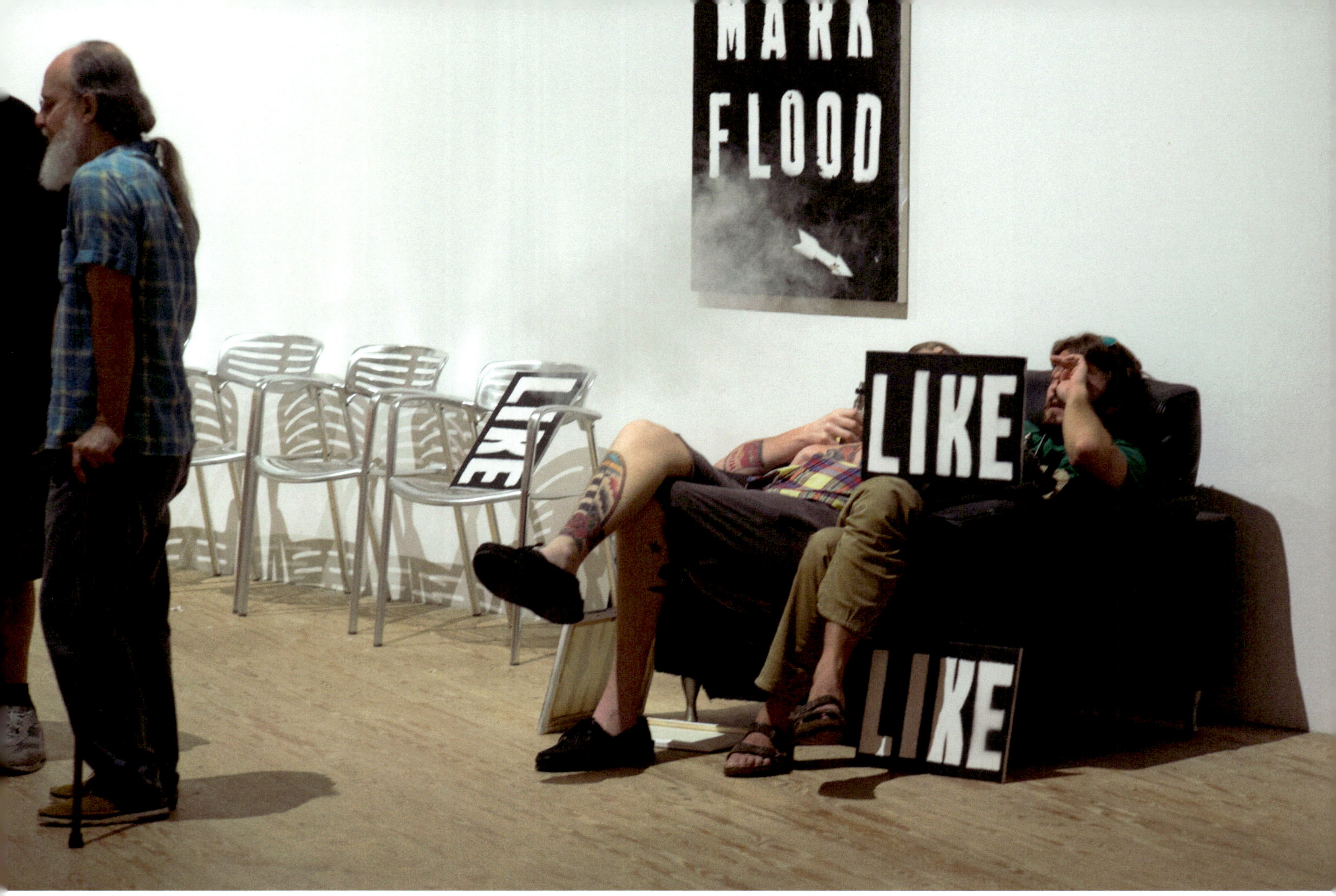

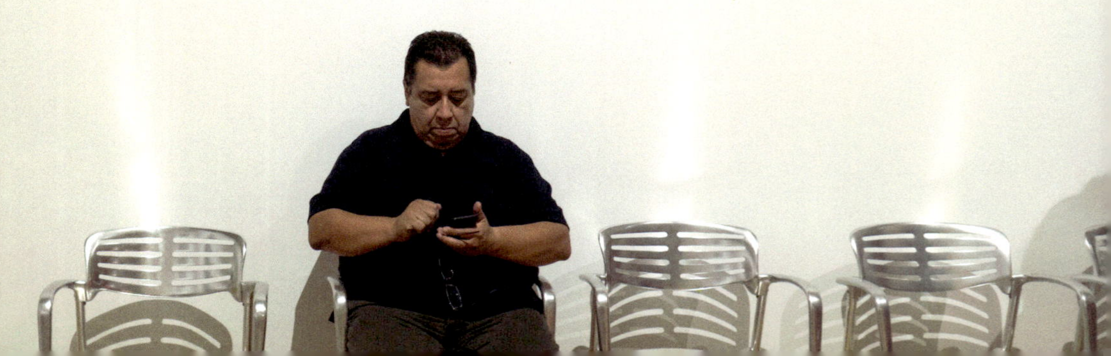
MARK
FLOOD
LIKE
LIKE
LIKE
MILLIONS 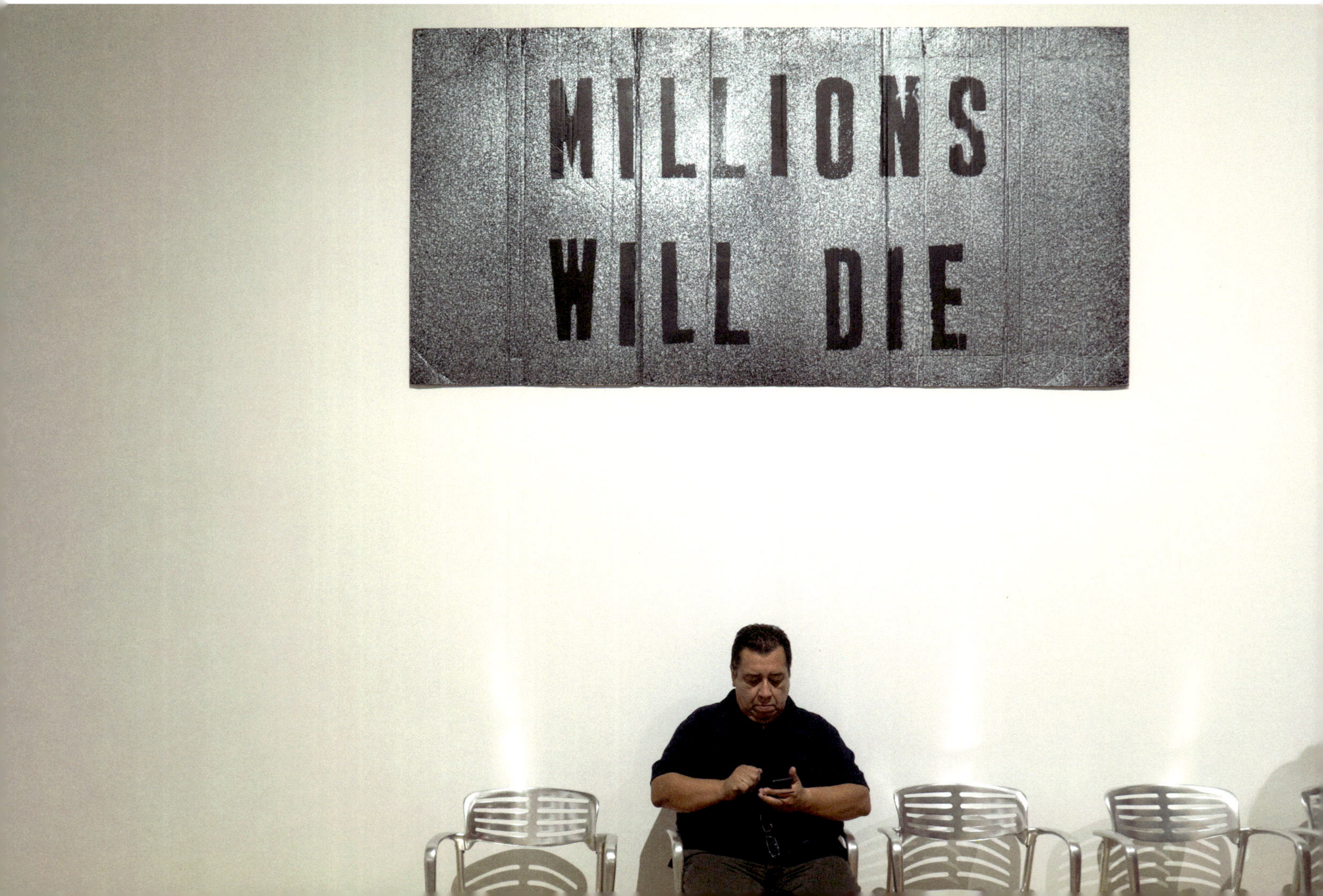
WILL DIE

AN' I HATE YOU, ONE AND ALL: SPAM YOUR EYES

Scott Indrisek

THE FIRST TIME I E-MAIL MARK FLOOD my message is automatically bounced back by a program called SpamArrest; the artist, it appears, is protecting himself from unwanted mail. There's something impossibly delicious about this. Because, of course, Flood's work—aggressive, impolite, absurd, ragged, explicit, yanking its pants off, yelling fire in a movie theater—is often engaged in the flagrant dissemination of something akin to radio signals intercepted from a foul and blistering underground. You get the message whether you want it or not. Flood shouts, exhorts, and issues vile commands ("EAT HUMAN FLESH," "ENCOURAGE SELF MUTILATION EATING DISORDERS AND HARD DRUG ABUSE," "DRINK BLOOD"). He pretends to want to make nice—look at the almost frilly, psychedelically lurid lace of *those* paintings!—and then punches you dead in the kidneys. He spams your eyes.

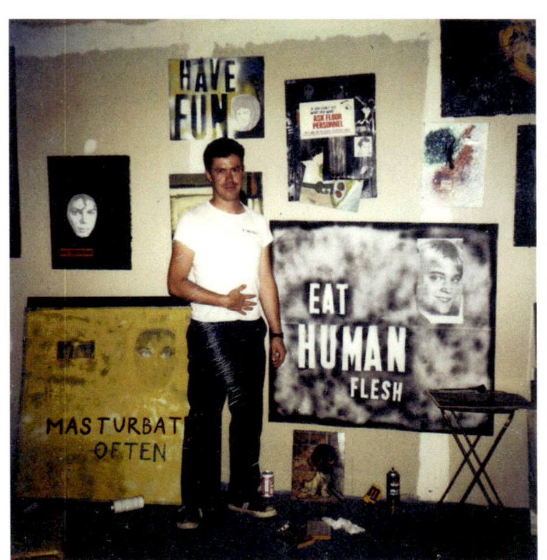

A

love and acceptance!

Flood is one of those artists whose work I admire, and, as a result—*because* of that admiration—I'm forced to doubt really big, looming things. Like my whole existence. Or at least my career. But what Flood is up to is more than simple refusal or parody. It may be surprising to learn that, despite his peculiar form of aggro-comedy, Flood doesn't think of himself as outwardly critiquing the "art world," whatever that term actually means. Not that this so-called "art world" doesn't have a heroic metabolism. Not that it isn't capable of digesting and celebrating every manner of subversion, all that snarling, screw-you-very-much disdain. The art world is perhaps the only place where you might be able to divest a high-net-worth individual of some serious cash in return for an artwork that's murderously contemptuous of the system that made such a HNWI possible in the first place. (Let's imagine the hypothetical Barbara Kruger/John Giorno collaboration, hocked at Art Basel, blazoning "RICH DICKS SUCK COCK" on the side of a glass-walled condo on the Williamsburg waterfront). This is how the wealth *cool up*—they don't just *take it*, they winkingly participate in their own degradation.

And so if you can't beat 'em... think differently about the beating, maybe. While he admits it's the category he most often finds himself constrained within, Flood wants you to forget institutional critique as a model for understanding his work. "It's more powerful to approach a social site with love and acceptance, and a sense of humor, instead of judgment," the artist tells me. "People misinterpret my art as institutional critique all the time. It's all they know, it's what they learned in art school. *He had an Insider Art Fair... he must be critiquing art fairs! Derp derp derp.*" So let's think of Mark Flood, to paraphrase Jesus Christ by way of Barry Schwabsky, as being "in the art world, but not of the art world." As the benevolent dictator of something more akin to an alternate reality that can exist as a happy parasite on the master-narrative of the contemporary. As a savvy Texan mosquito (minus the Zika). As a kind of impatient anthropologist. As someone who may be fed up, sometimes, but never really wants to quit.

Still, it's hard to imagine many viewers throwing "love and acceptance" in the same paragraph, let alone sentence, as Mark Flood. When in 2012 he exhibited a series of work

A
Mark Flood standing in front of his artwork in Houston, 1989
Photographer unknown

Cats driving cars, talking nonsense. Siouxsie and the Banshees turn radioactive. Roger Daltrey becomes a psychotic baboon with an anteater snout.

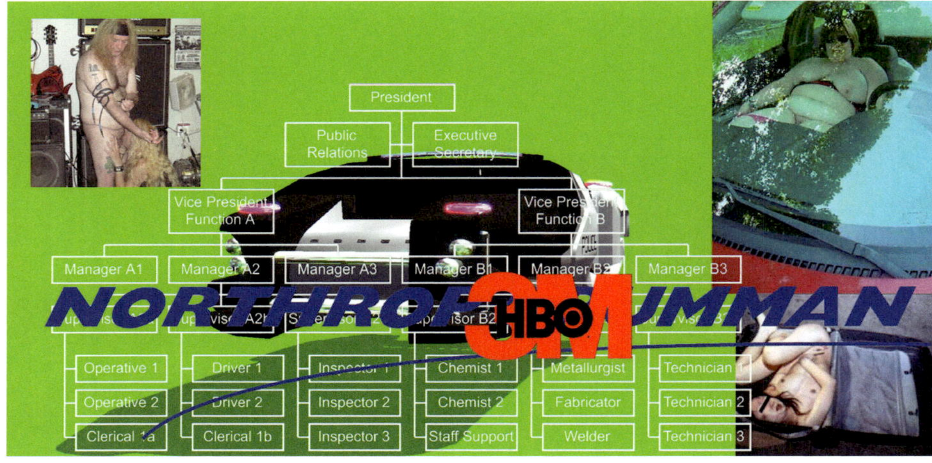

B

from the eighties at a swank townhouse gallery on New York's Upper East Side, he dubbed the show *The Hateful Years*. A print-on-canvas painting, on view recently at Marlborough Chelsea in New York, combines a corporate organization chart with found images of a girl stuffed into a suitcase and a photograph of Anal Cunt front man Seth Putnam receiving a blow job while shooting up. Perhaps that "love and acceptance" might also apply to Flood's democratic embrace of the Internet's generative swill. (Take a second to appreciate the aptness of his surname, considering how the Web is so often likened to a "sea of images": something that could overtake us, something we could drown in.)

There is a certain leveling of images in his work, no matter the source: everything is possible content. Flood is a promiscuous post-punk vacuum hoovering all kinds of culture—movies, music, social media, advertising, vulgar highbrow art speak—and coughing it back up into a smoggy, grungy cloud. His relationship with popular culture is akin to his relationship with the art world: somewhere slippery between antagonism and admiration; he's an outsider who's not sure if he even *wants* in. Consider the collaged violence done to well-known mugs (Anderson Cooper, Billy Idol). The sly parody of celeb-stalker culture in *The Edge of Fame* (made from 6,000 Lindsay Lohan clippings). At the Contemporary Arts Museum Houston: 5,000 paintings based on Facebook's LIKE button, which are meant to be positioned around the gallery by viewers. Social-network tokens flush against images of pure trauma. Cats driving cars, talking nonsense. Siouxsie and the Banshees turn radioactive. Roger Daltrey becomes a psychotic baboon with an anteater snout. The slick facade of popular, celebrity, digital, and news culture has its face ripped off, and what's underneath isn't often pretty. At full tilt, this barrage of images achieves a queasy frisson that is actually shocking (in that it's shocking to find oneself shocked by contemporary art, anymore). As with Thomas Hirschhorn's parades of war imagery, we're reminded that our supposed desensitization to all things visual is mostly false. We can still be made to want to turn away.

can't go on, must go on

I've been thinking a lot about exhaustion lately: what it means, what comes after, and if it can be productive. Mark Flood makes art from a position of a certain kind of exhaustion, or exasperation, which I feel is different from desperation, and different from pure, bile-flecked cynicism. A series of spray-paint pieces in *Gratest Hits* replay the phrase "ANOTHER PAINTING," as if flaying that medium's supposed corpse again and again. A four-paneled sculptural work of stacked canvases, titled *Endless Column* after Constantin Brancusi, sings of a putrid quartet: "WHORE MUSEUMS / GUTLESS COLLECTORS / BLIND COLLECTORS / ALLEGED ARTISTS."

But exhausted is not the same thing as dead, or nihilistic. Flood has kept the faith, both in certain media forms (even if his newest works rely more on computers, digital printing, and 4chan scavenger hunts) and in the public, collecting or otherwise. As such he is part of a small and unconnected cluster of artists—

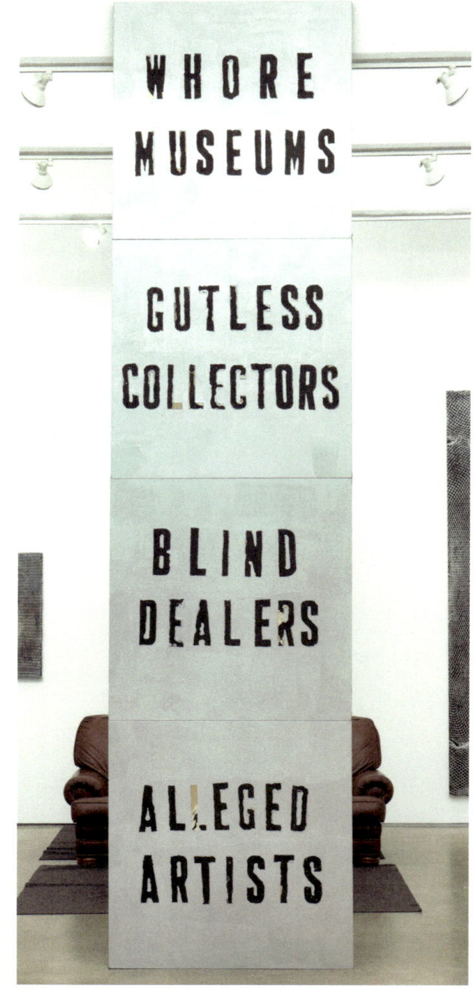

C

B
Executive Secretary, 2015
Archival ink on canvas
60 x 144 inches

C
Endless Column, 2012
Acrylic on canvas
192 x 48 inches

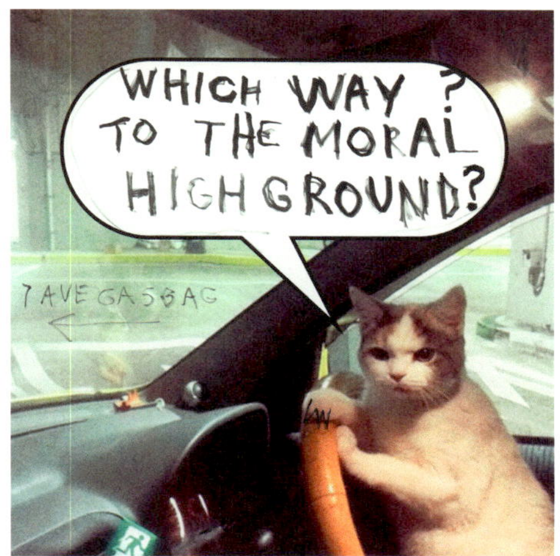

D

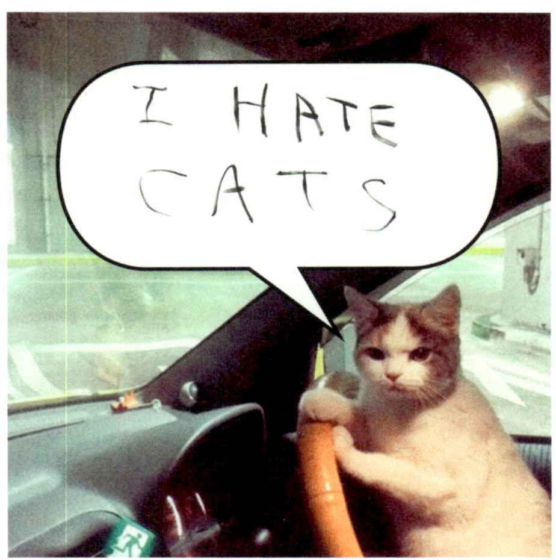

E

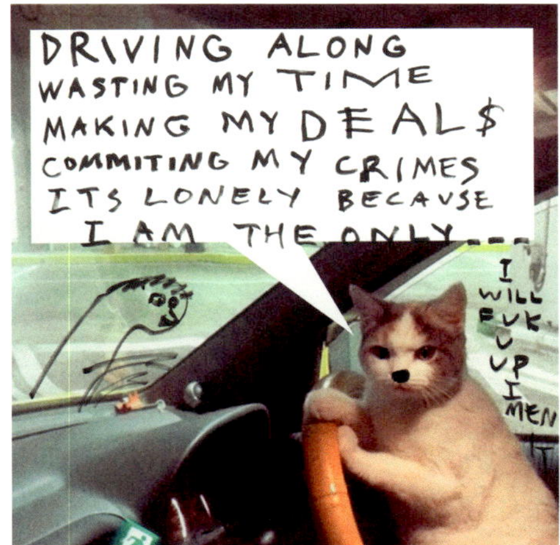

F

"I'm continuing to develop the idea of... paintings sitting on the floor like walls, joined together to make rooms, where there's a sense of privacy with the work. Having people walk through curtains so there's a sense of progression."

from Alex Bag to William Powhida, to name two semi-random examples—who question whether there even is an "outside" to begin with, but proceed as if there *might* be. They are simultaneously willing participants and gadflies; like them, Flood is tough to put your finger on. He can front with what seems to be the cruelest mockery, and then claim he comes in peace. In a digital trailer for the last show he curated in New York, he boldly stated that "brushstrokes are for bitches"; this, however, seemed less of a judgment on the viability of old-fashioned paint than a way to increase his own feverish production, a way to keep up with the vicious tempo of the image-cycle that feeds him, as if any exhaustion was countered by gorging on that creative commons.

And rather than complain and critique, Flood offers alternatives; namely, to the tired standards we've grown to accept as the boundaries of the art-viewing experience. His description of the installation plan for *Gratest Hits* could read equally well, out of context, as a proposal for a high-end brothel: "I'm continuing to develop the idea of dimly lit spaces, with lots of furniture so viewers can sit, or lie, down," he muses. "Paintings sitting on the floor like walls, joined together to make rooms, where there's a sense of privacy with the work. Having people walk through curtains so there's a sense of progression."

splatter the viewer

But how far should we even trust what Flood says—or rather what his paintings say, in bold blaring white ALL CAPS? "Reading simulates an auditory hallucination, which is a primal religious experience," the artist tells me. "Even the humblest text is imbued with the qualities of the sacred—it contains enormous power in every detail of its physical presence." What to do with The Word: "Write it, distort it, misspell it. Cut it up like Burroughs and Gysin. Watch it explode. Tap into the power of text, but just to revel in it, to splatter the viewer with it."

MILLIONS WILL DIE
B ILLIONS WILL DIE
SAY CHEESE
USE YOUR FAMILY AS AN EXCUSE
TOTINO'S PIZZA ROLES

Rendered in rigid, stenciled letterforms, Flood's text is caveman concrete poetry; it's language ingested and eructated as brutal slogan, looming threat, or perverse typo. Some of it is linguistic détournement, pace the Situationist International: "I do have my unpopular, unstylish, and obsolete non-Marxist intellectual sources," the artist muses, "plus Guy Debord." Flood's cannibalization of common phrases plays with how they can feel, strangely, in the mouth—divorce "say cheese" from its smile-for-the-camera context, for instance—or what they remind us of, sickly (the "Billions and Billions Served" of McDonald's highway signs). The title of John Travolta's 1983 disco sequel becomes a veiled plea. Flood may love a good pun ("pressed release" for "press release"), but the way he marshals text can force a wry turn of phrase into uncomfortable positions: the territory of protest signs, ransom notes, a stalker's rants, or the violent verbal bludgeons of the Internet commentariat.

lone star guts

When Flood isn't utilizing the "auditory hallucination" of the written word, he's pushing the retinal force of pure images (often removed from their original context, making them even harder to digest or conveniently classify). "It's about finding the power of images and using

D
Seeker Cat, 2014
Inkjet print and marker on canvas
48 x 48 inches

E
Hateful Cat, 2014
Inkjet print and marker on canvas
48 x 48 inches

F
Available Nasdaq Cat, 2014
Inkjet print and marker on canvas
48 x 48 inches

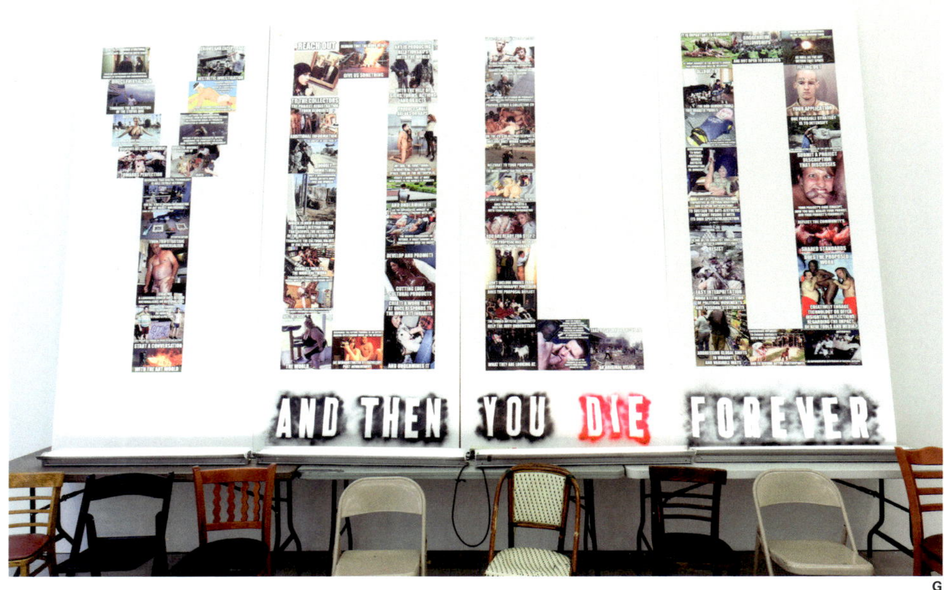

G

them in a brutal, irrational way," Flood told me during an interview earlier this year in New York. "I go for the gut, not the intellect." In that sense, Flood's work actually earns the adjective "visceral," one of contemporary art criticism's most tired and misused clichés; what's born of his gut causes *ours* to churn. (Fellow-Texan-cum-war-criminal George W. Bush may find something perverse to celebrate in the artist's sentiment: now *there's* a man who knew how to privilege gut over intellect; who thrilled at the brutal, irrational use of powerful images—but at the risk of destroying several nations, not just art-world complacency.)

One of the thorniest problems within Flood's body of work, to me, is the apparent discrepancy between the bulk of his output and the comparatively baroque, seductive depictions of torn textiles surrounding gaping voids—the so-called "lace paintings," several of which are on view at CAMH. I can't imagine anyone not previously clued in to the artist's full oeuvre would ever assume that these pretty, quasi-delicate things came from the same hand that gave us the pop-album-as-horror-film of *Julio Is Moving In* (1984); or the snide pharmaceutical-commercial riff *ASK YOUR DRUG DEALER* (2011); or *YOLO (AND THEN YOU DIE FOREVER)* (2015), with its collision of text culled from artist grant applications and the most casually appalling images the Internet has to offer; or *SUCK 2 DICKS* (2014), in which the phrase is sprayed over a pair of Abercrombie-ready hunks. But bring up this discrepancy and Flood can seem surprised; to him, the effect is somewhat the same: "Super beautiful stuff gets this gut response," he says, simply, "and these viral images are so intense, they also go for the gut." It's the one leap of faith I have trouble making, and this is perhaps why the lace paintings remain such a fascinating wrinkle in his practice, especially when exhibited in conjunction with what is comparatively more unforgiving, vulgar, and willfully raw. Some of Flood's work wants you to love it, to linger on it; other pieces want you to go fuck yourself. It's like meeting a furniture maker well-known for both sleek, Nakashima-inspired coffee tables and couches built of foam, duct tape, and used syringes.

Maybe, in the end, we just let the final words be the artist's own, as seen on the most recent work in this exhibition: a... well... suitably deadpan obituary titled *Tombstone* (2016). "Mark Flood is somebody who did something somewhere formerly nowhere," it reads, standing nearly seventeen feet tall. "Mark Flood doesn't like explaining he lets the audience figure it out" Amen, indeed.

G
YOLO (AND THEN YOU DIE FOREVER), 2015
Archival ink on canvas (4 parts)
110 x 200 inches overall

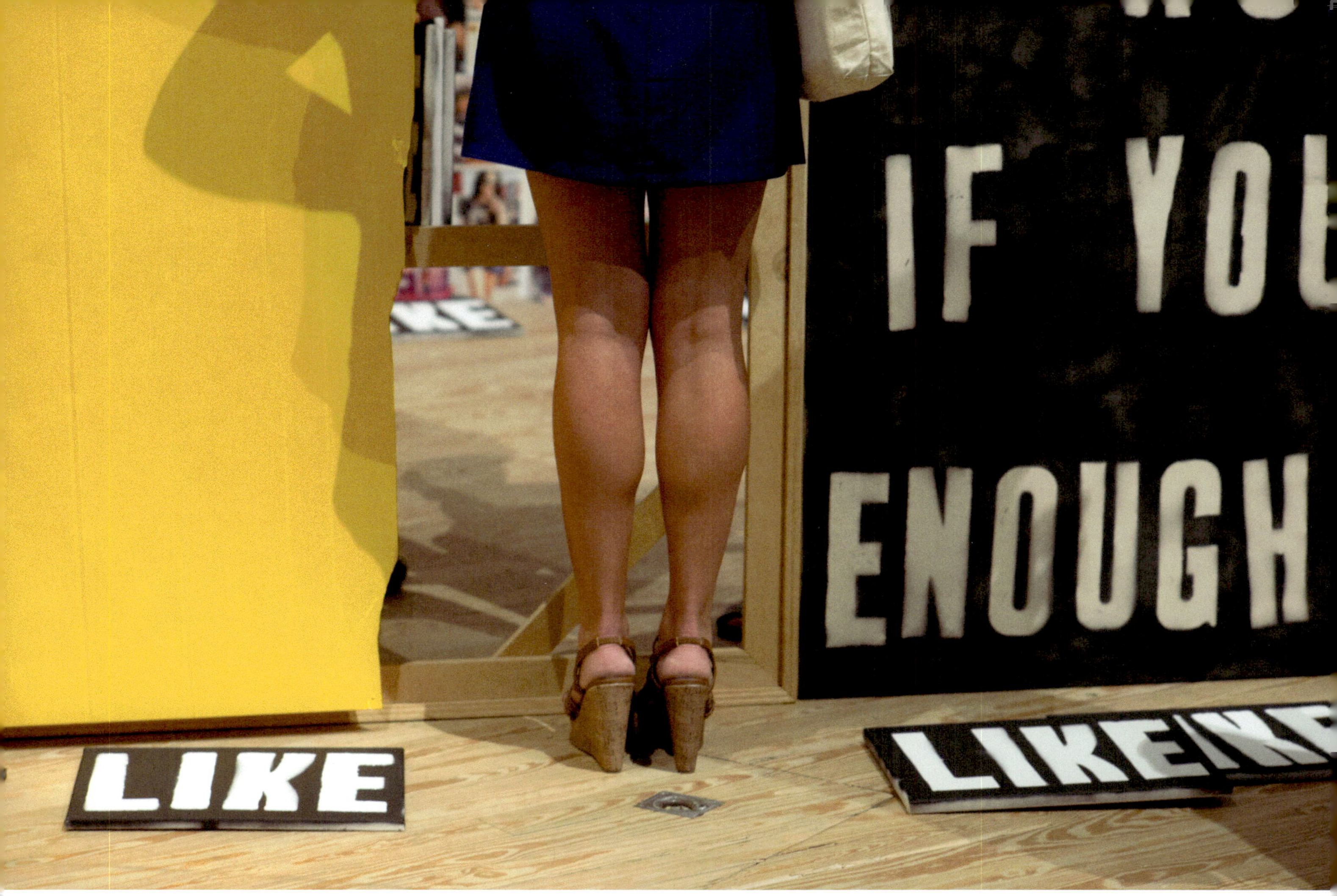

IF YOU
ENOUGH
LIKE
LIKE
DISGUSTING 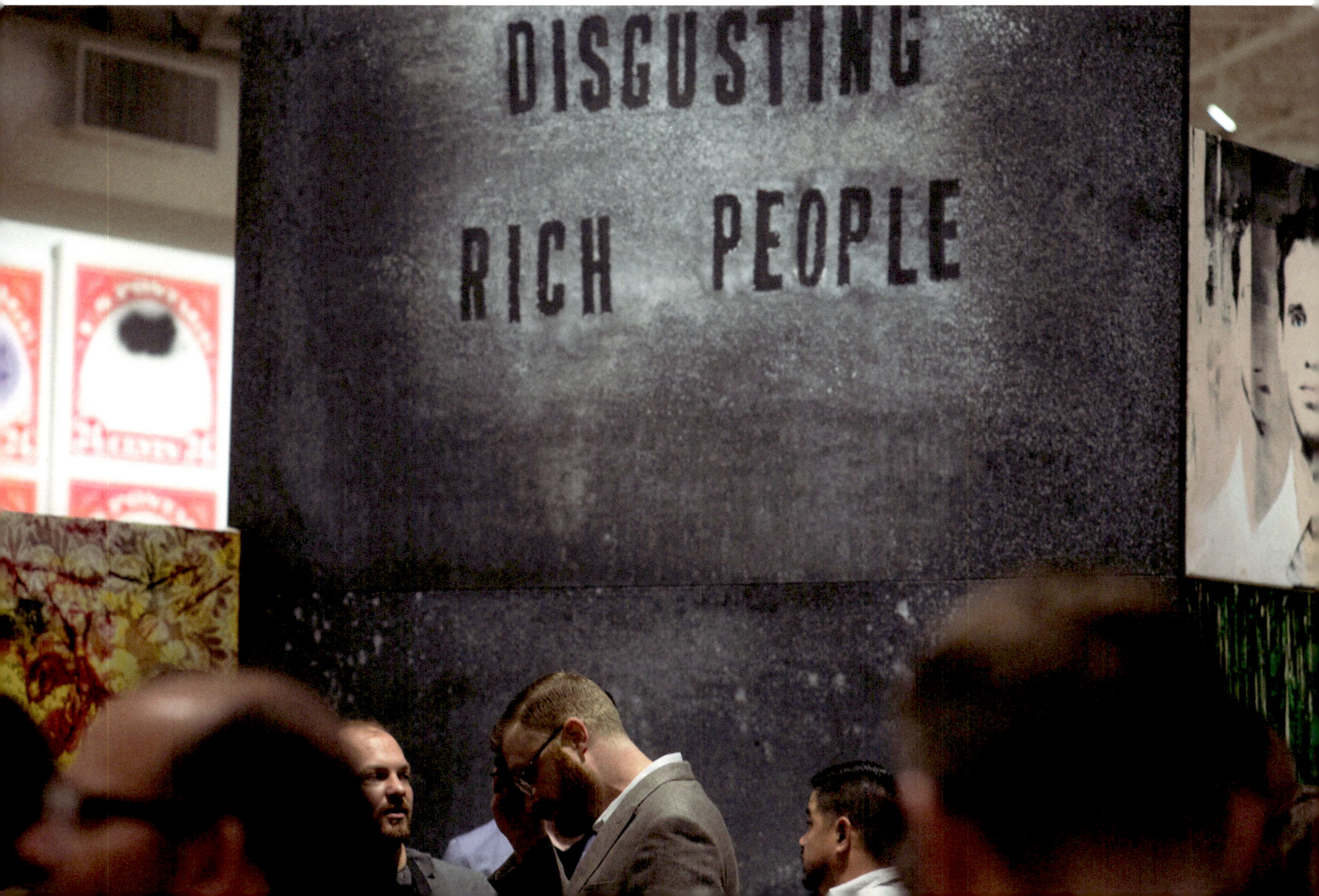
RICH PEOPLE

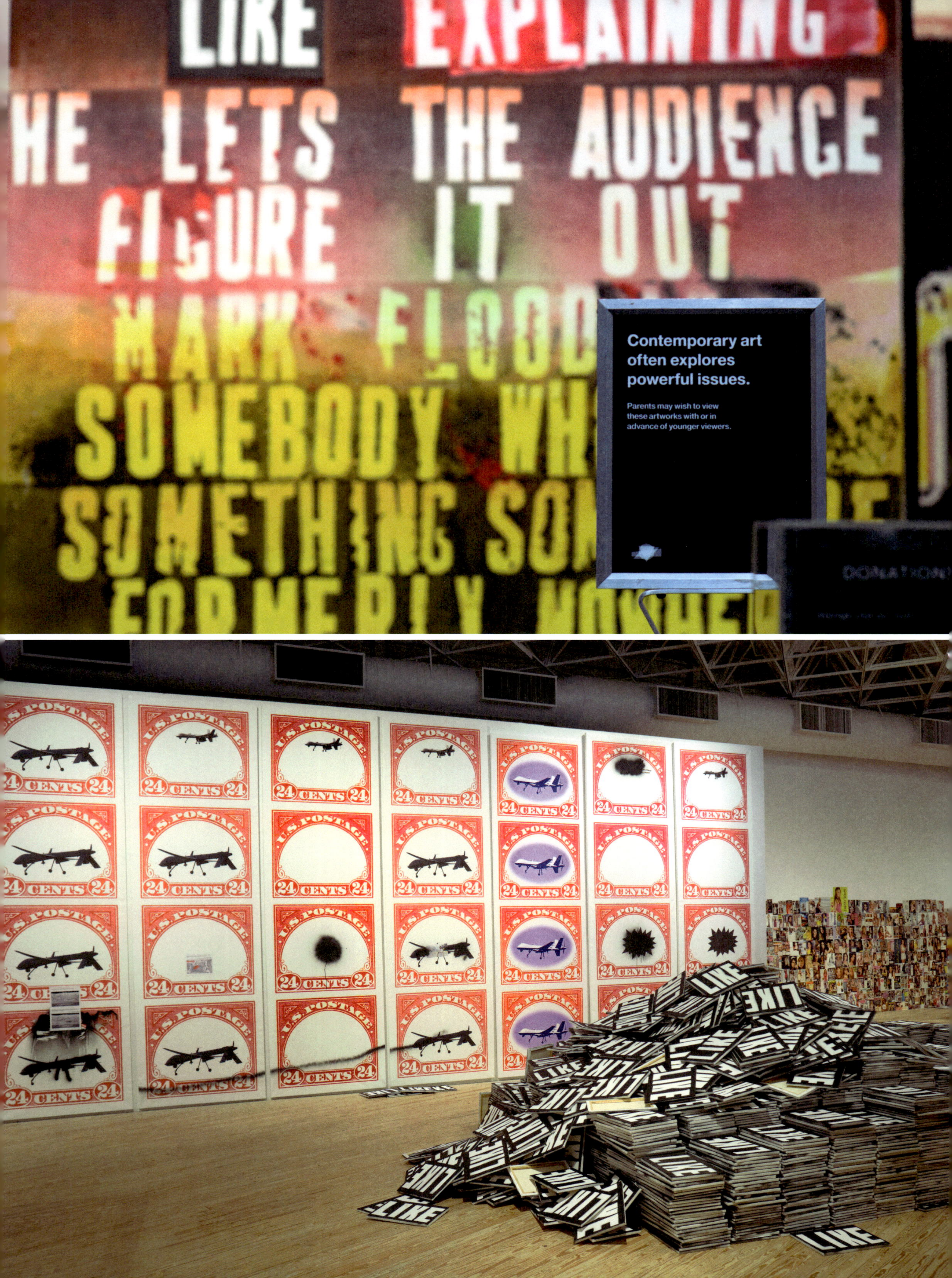

LIKE EXPLAINING
HE LETS THE AUDIENCE
FIGURE IT OUT
MARK FLOOD
SOMEBODY
SOMETHING
Contemporary art often explores powerful issues.
Parents may wish to view these artworks with or in advance of younger viewers.
U.S. POSTAGE
24 CENTS 24
LIKE

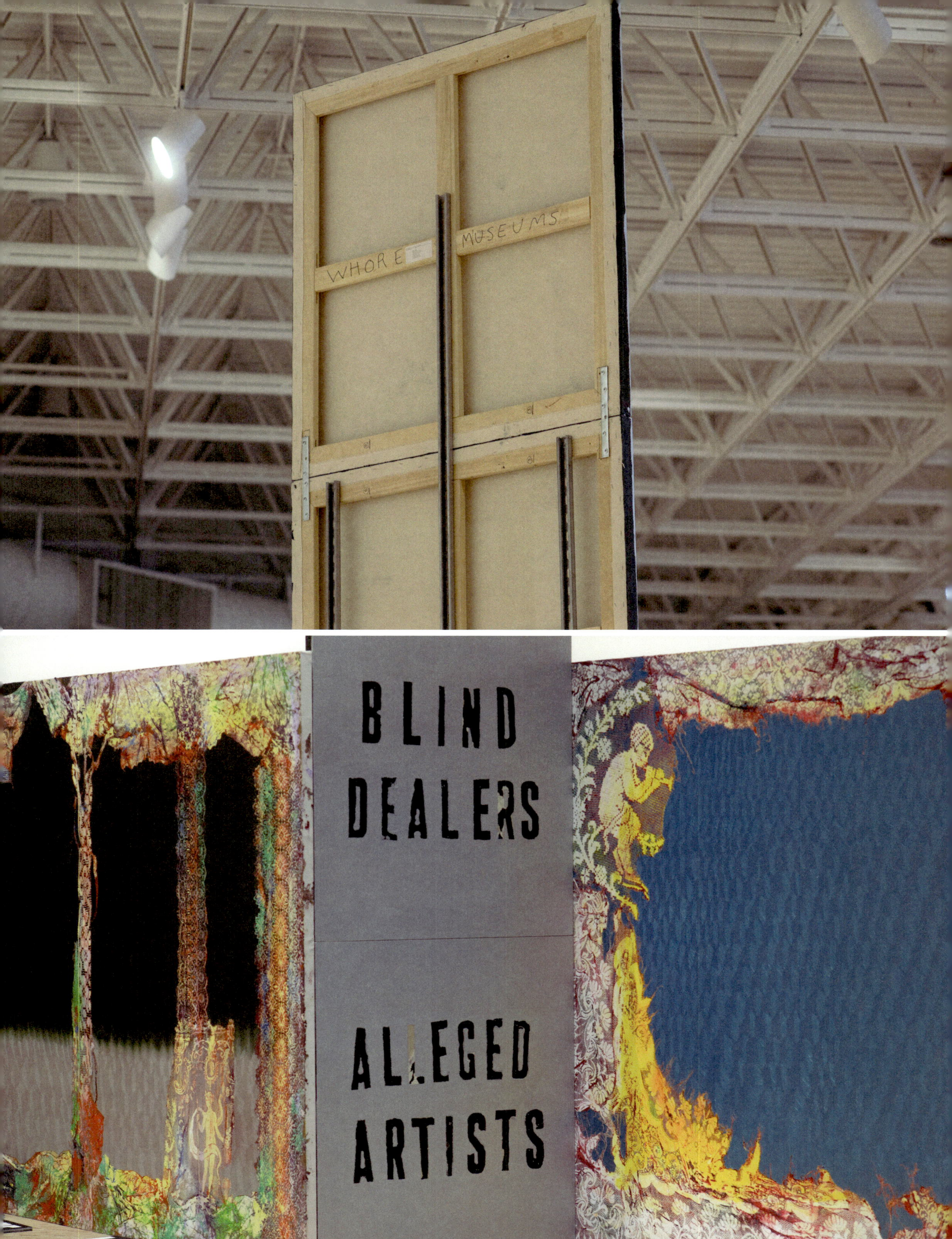
WHORE
MUSEUMS
BLIND
DEALERS
ALLEGED
ARTISTS

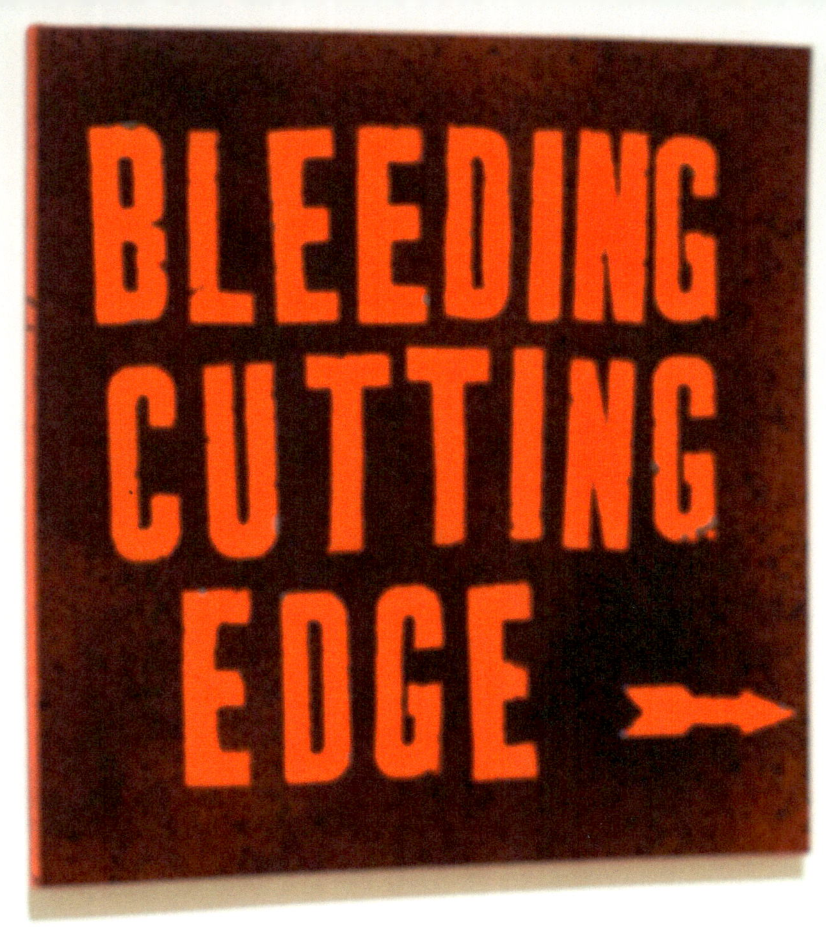
BLEEDING
CUTTING
EDGE

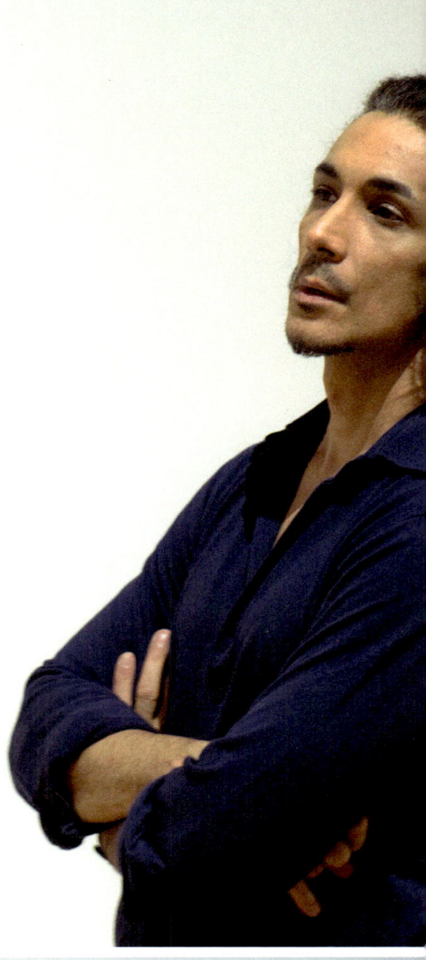

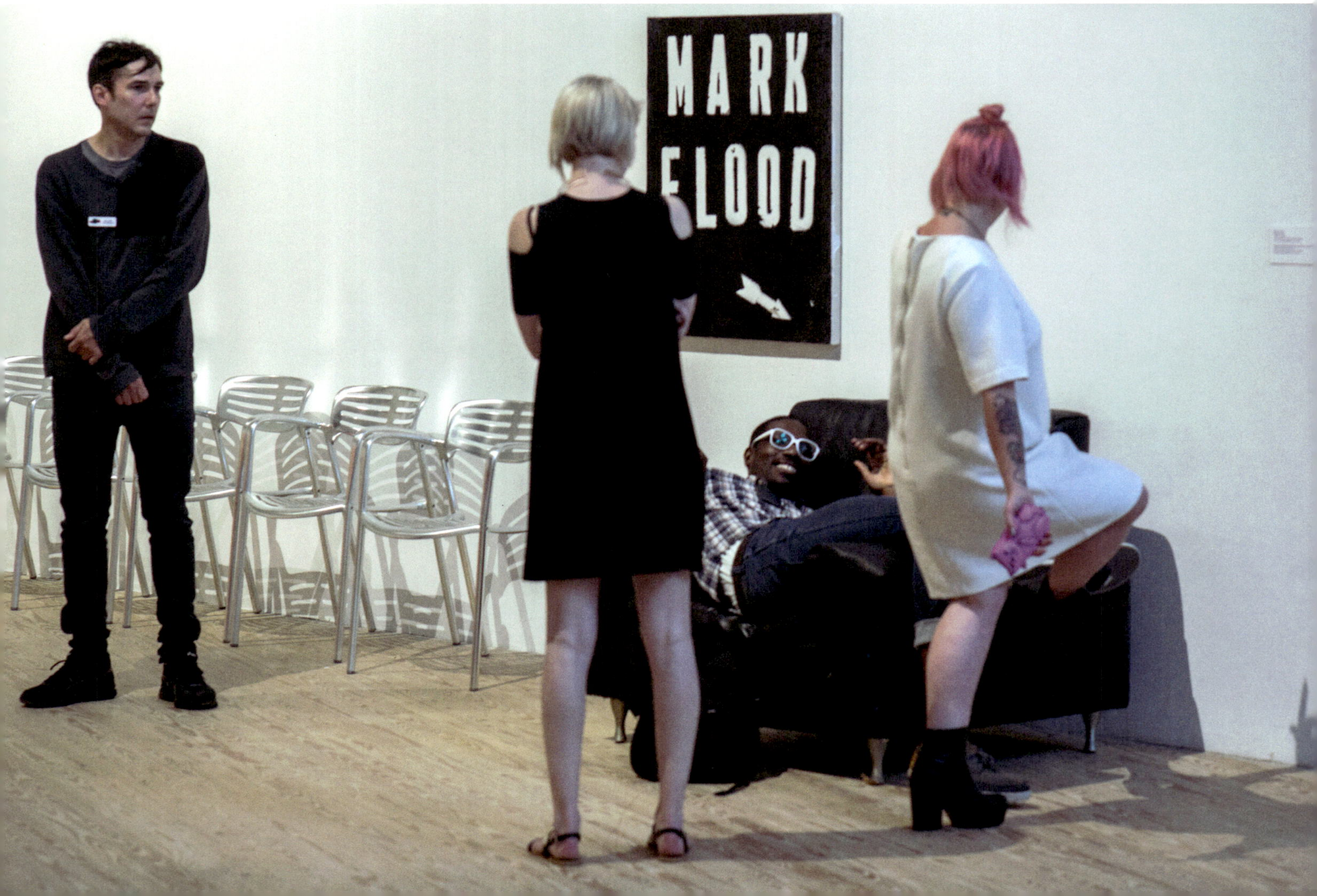

MARK
FLOOD

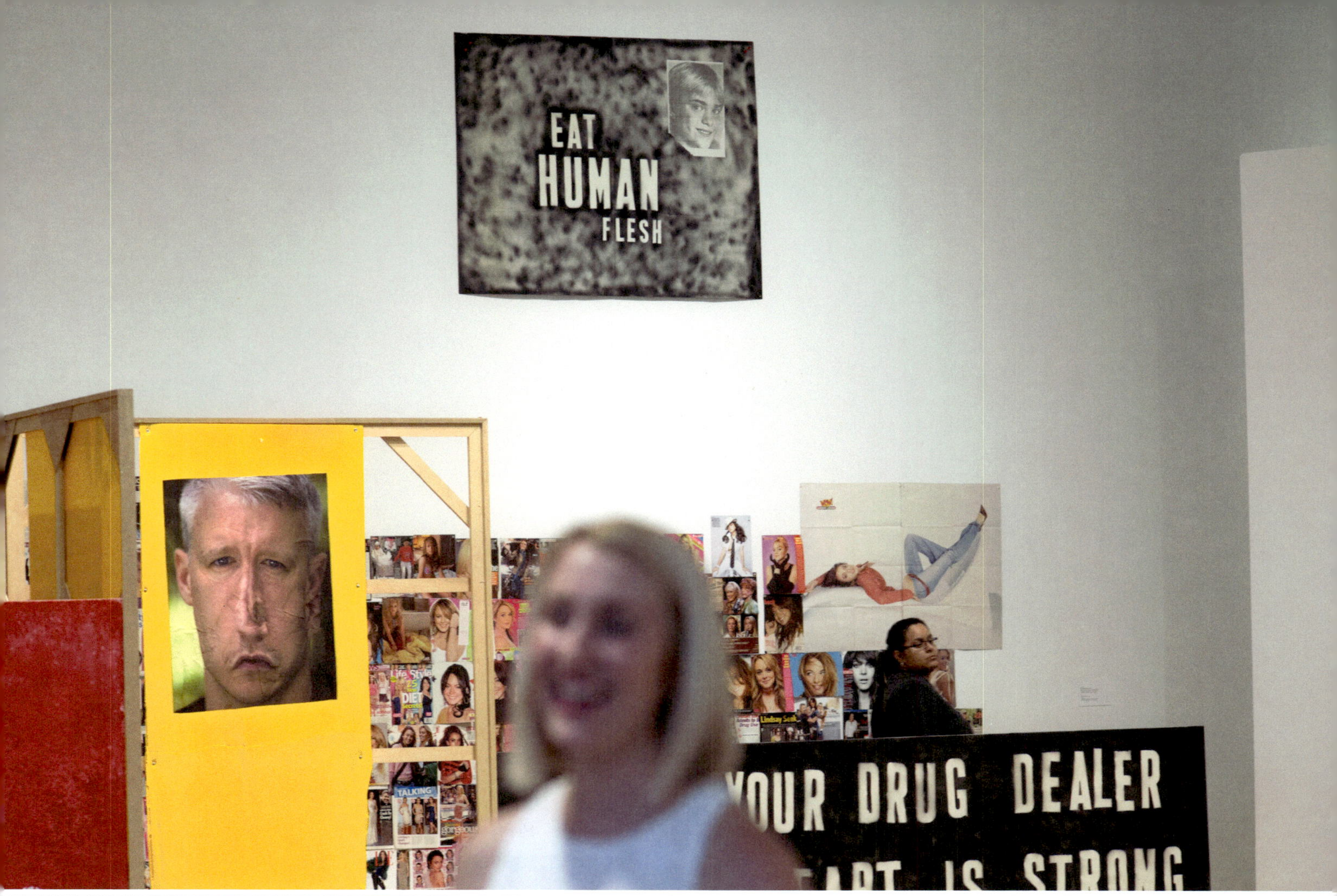

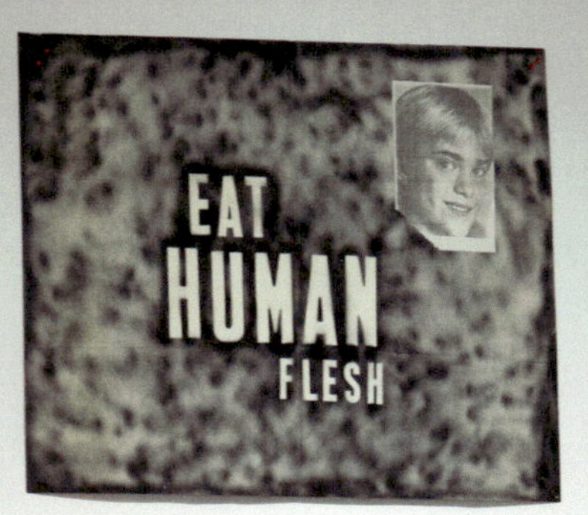
EAT
HUMAN
FLESH

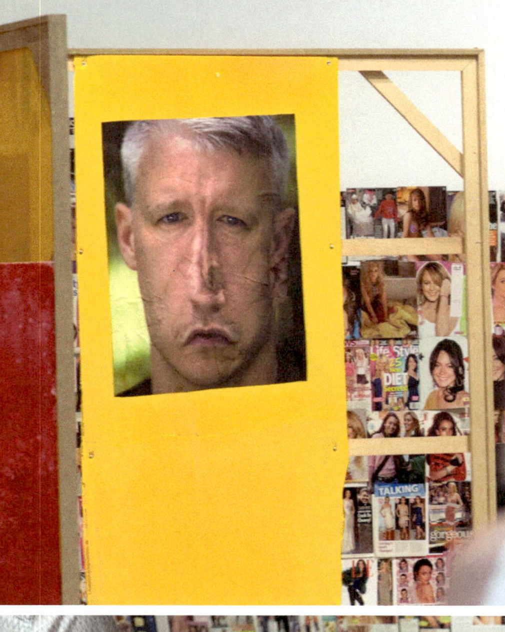

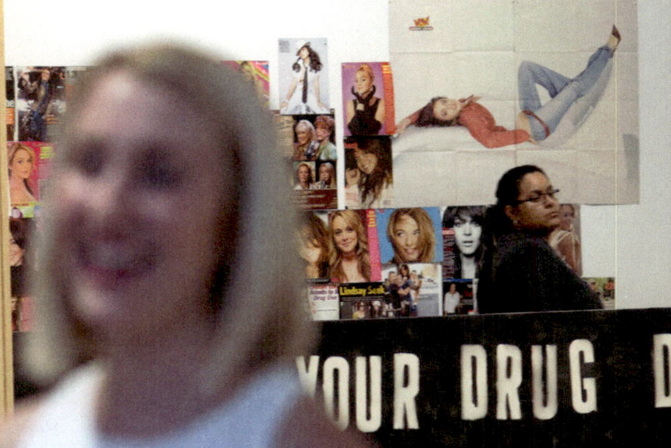
YOUR DRUG DEALER

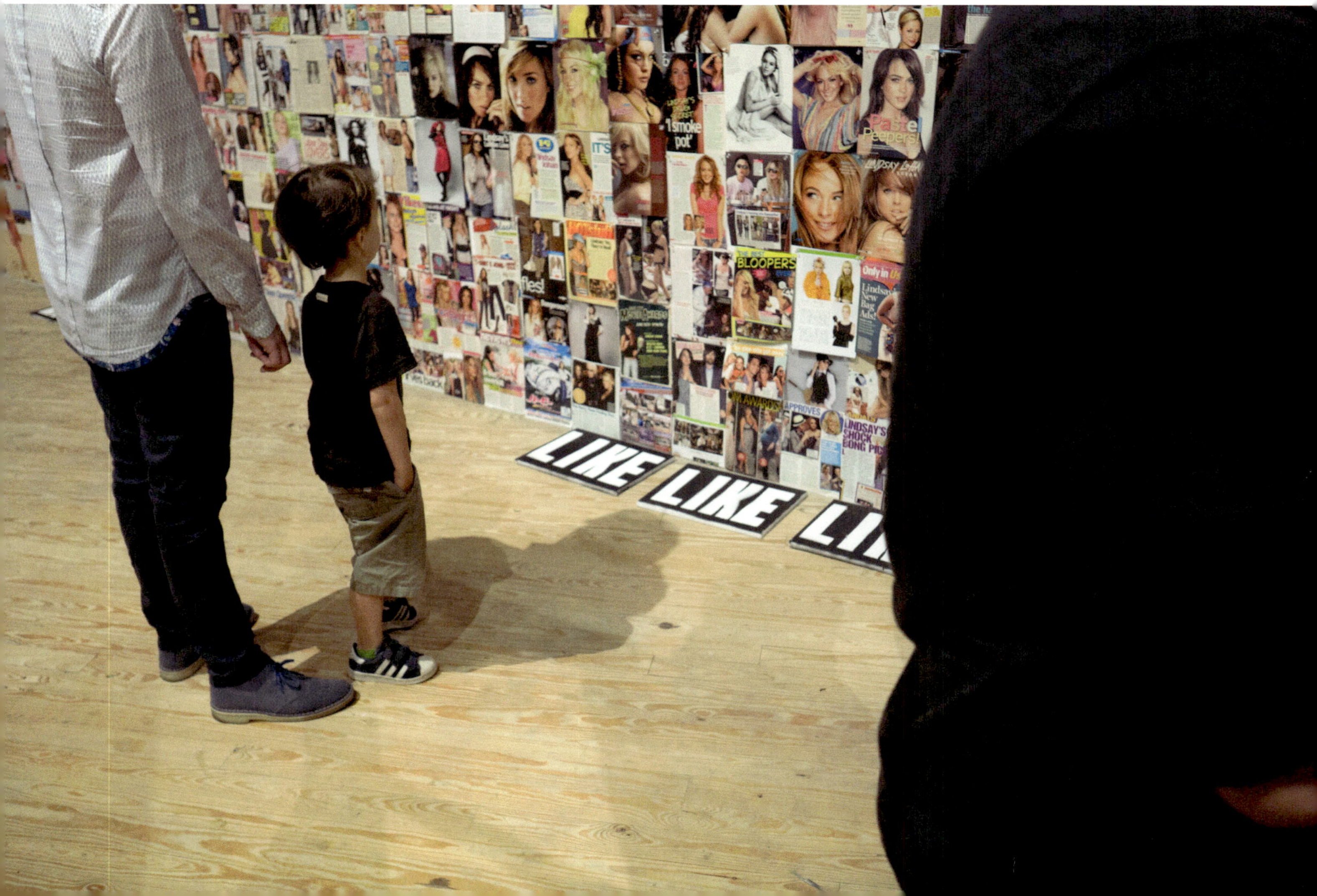

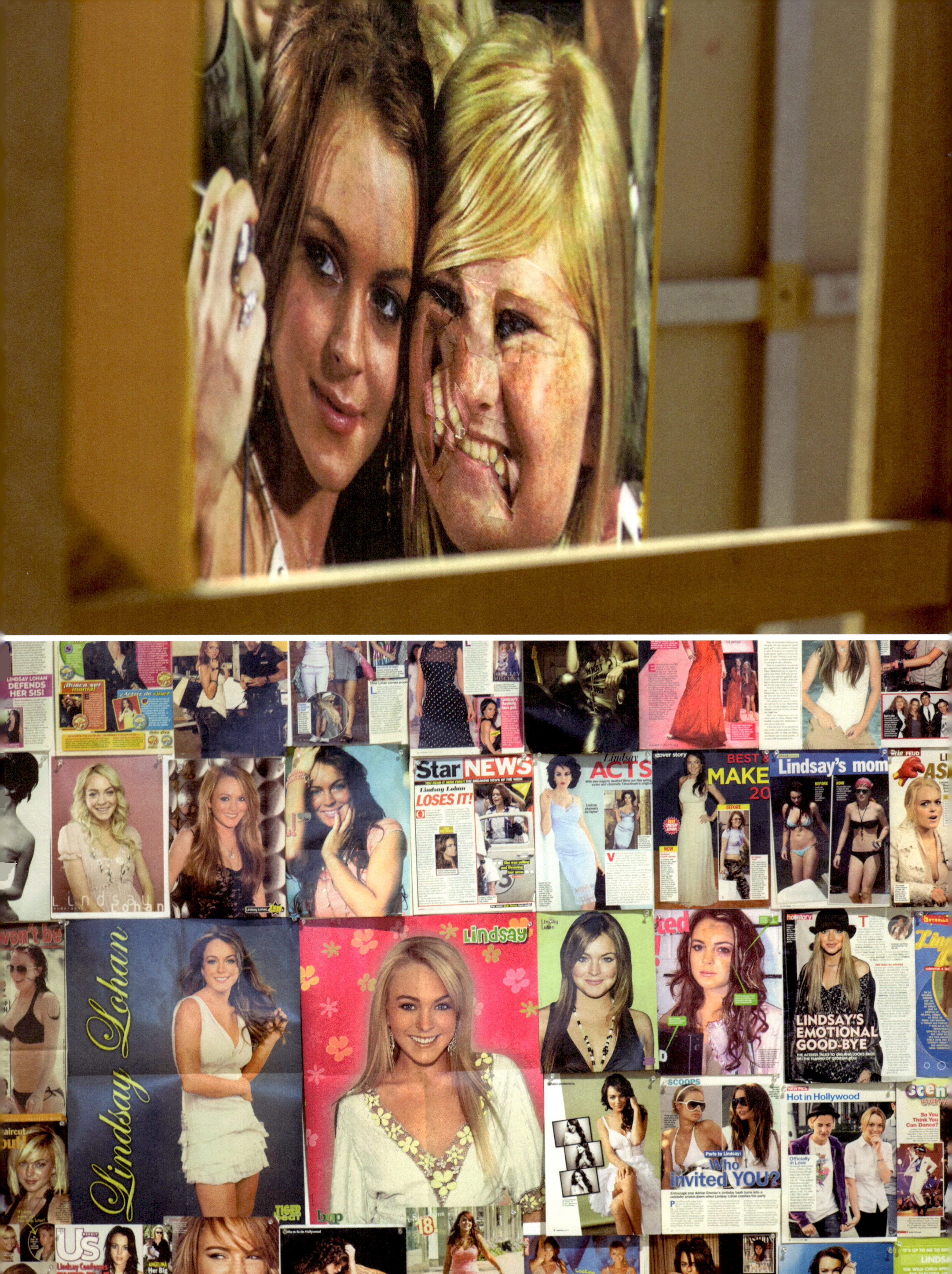

LINDSAY LOHAN DEFENDS HER SISI
Star NEWS
Lindsay Lohan LOSES IT!
ACTS
cover story
MAKE
Lindsay's mom
Lindsay Lohan
Lindsay
LINDSAY'S EMOTIONAL GOOD-BYE
SCOOPS
Who Invited YOU?
Hot in Hollywood
Us

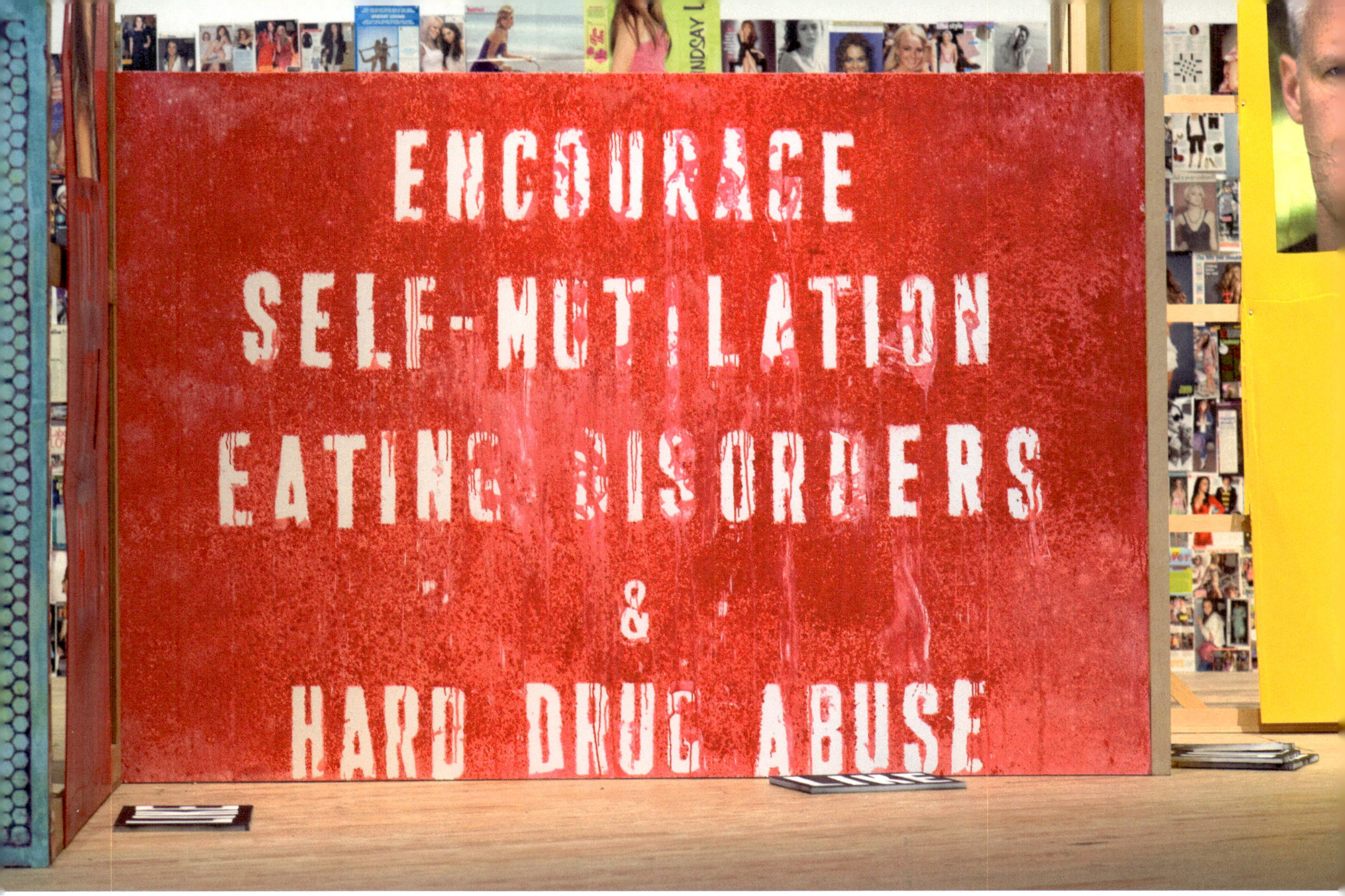

ENCOURAGE
SELF-MUTILATION
EATING DISORDERS
&
HARD DRUG ABUSE

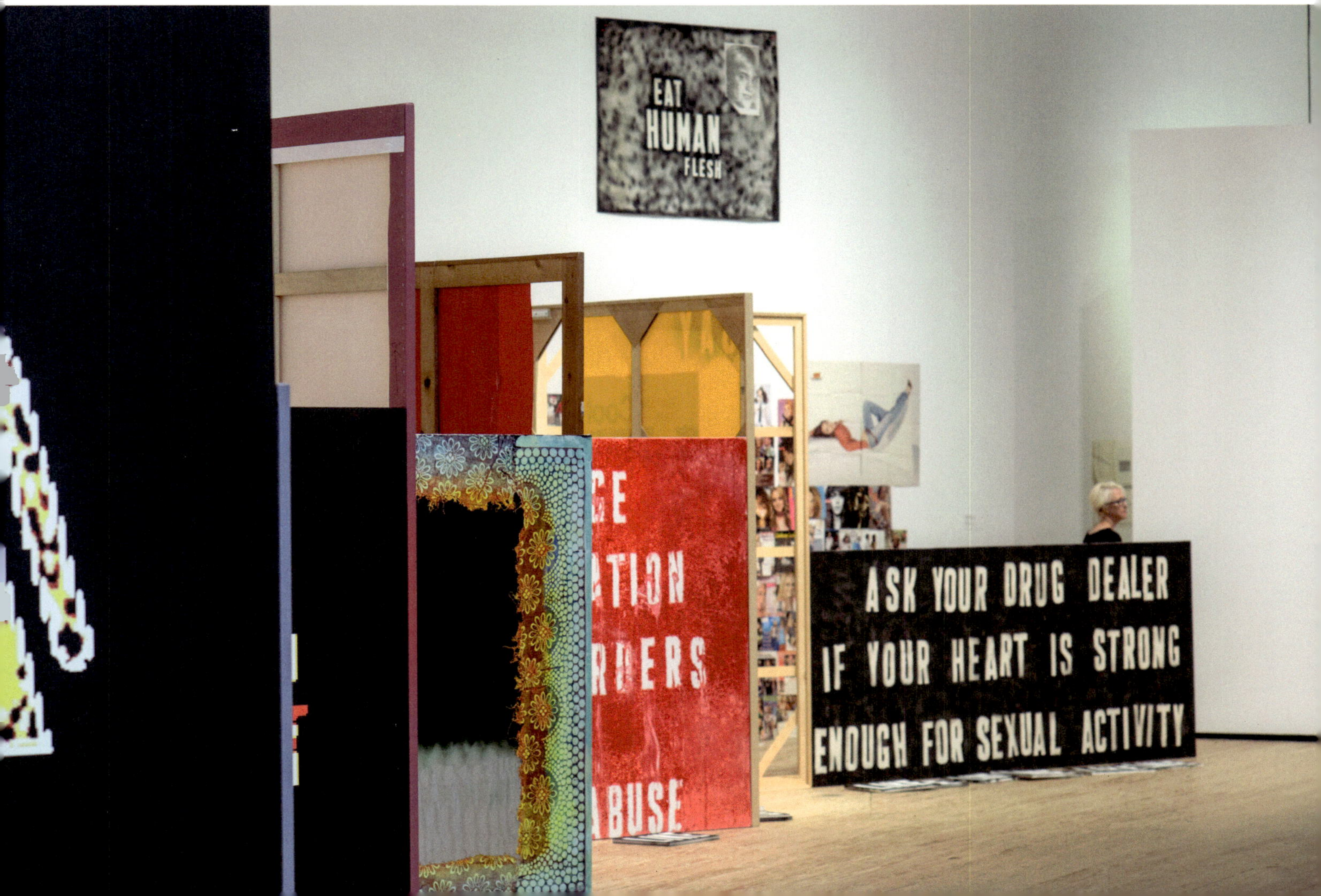

EAT
HUMAN
FLESH

ASK YOUR DRUG DEALER
IF YOUR HEART IS STRONG
ENOUGH FOR SEXUAL ACTIVITY

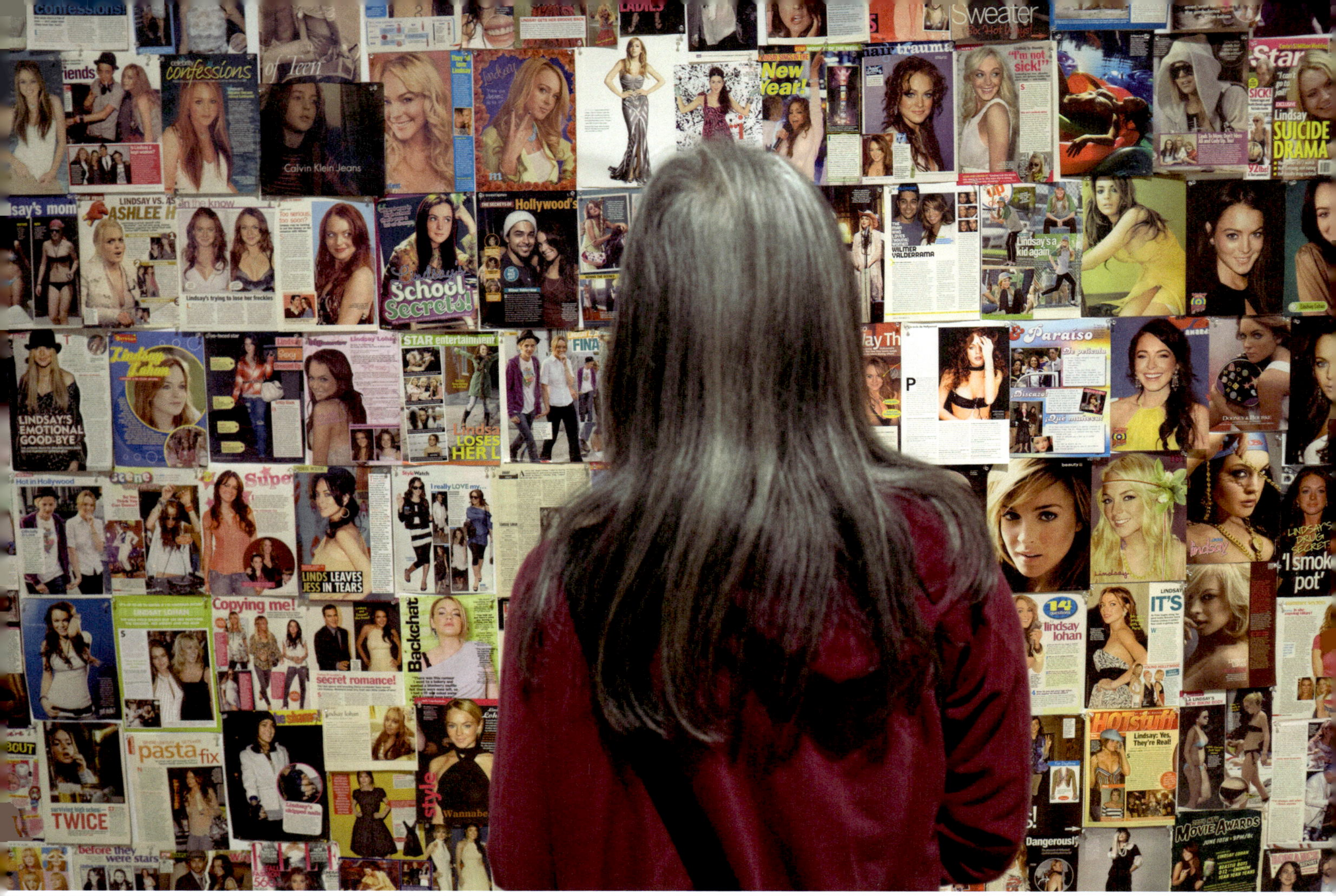

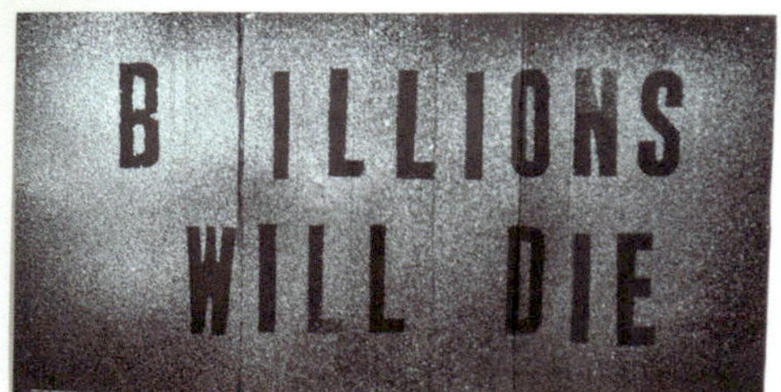
B ILLIONS
WILL DIE

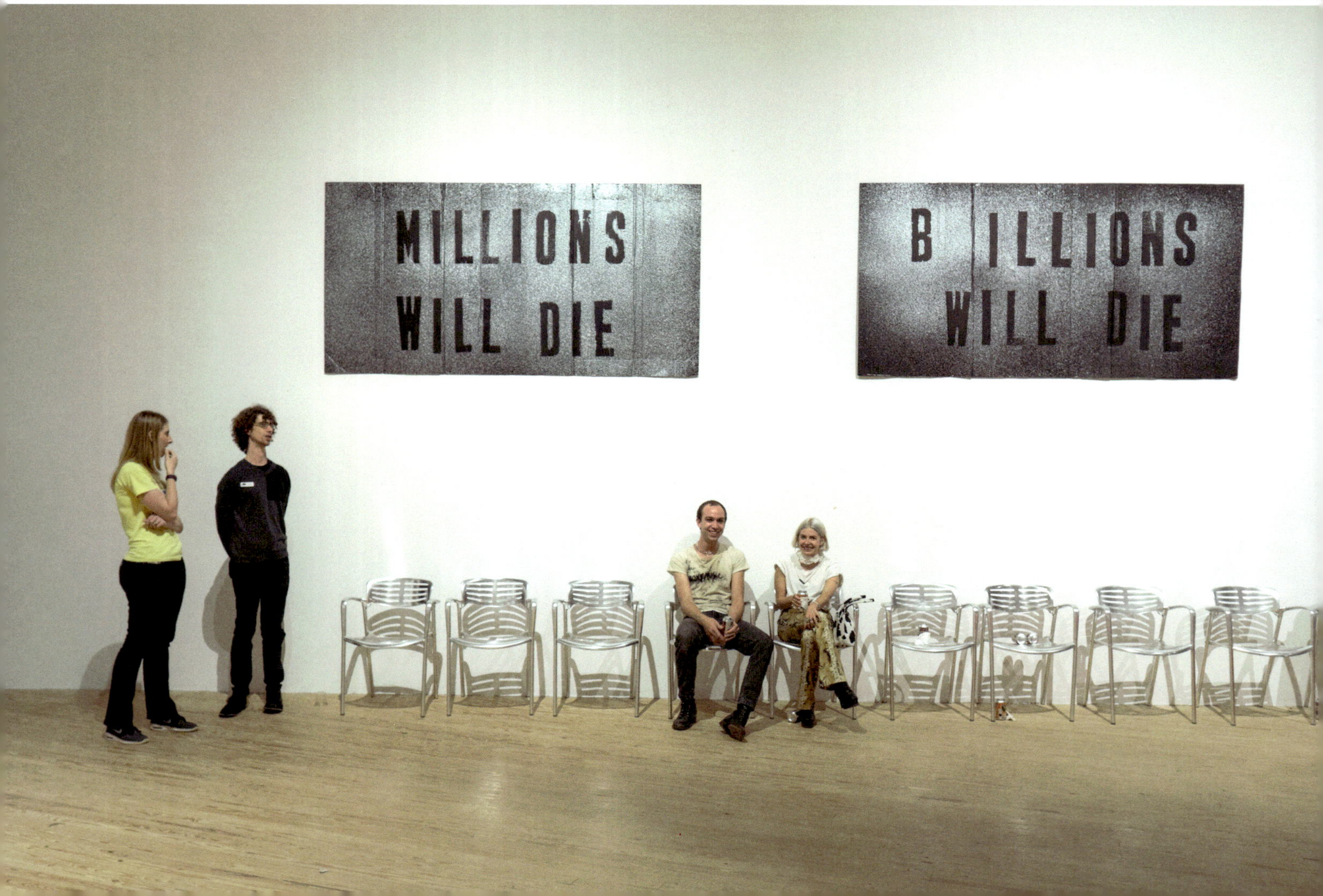

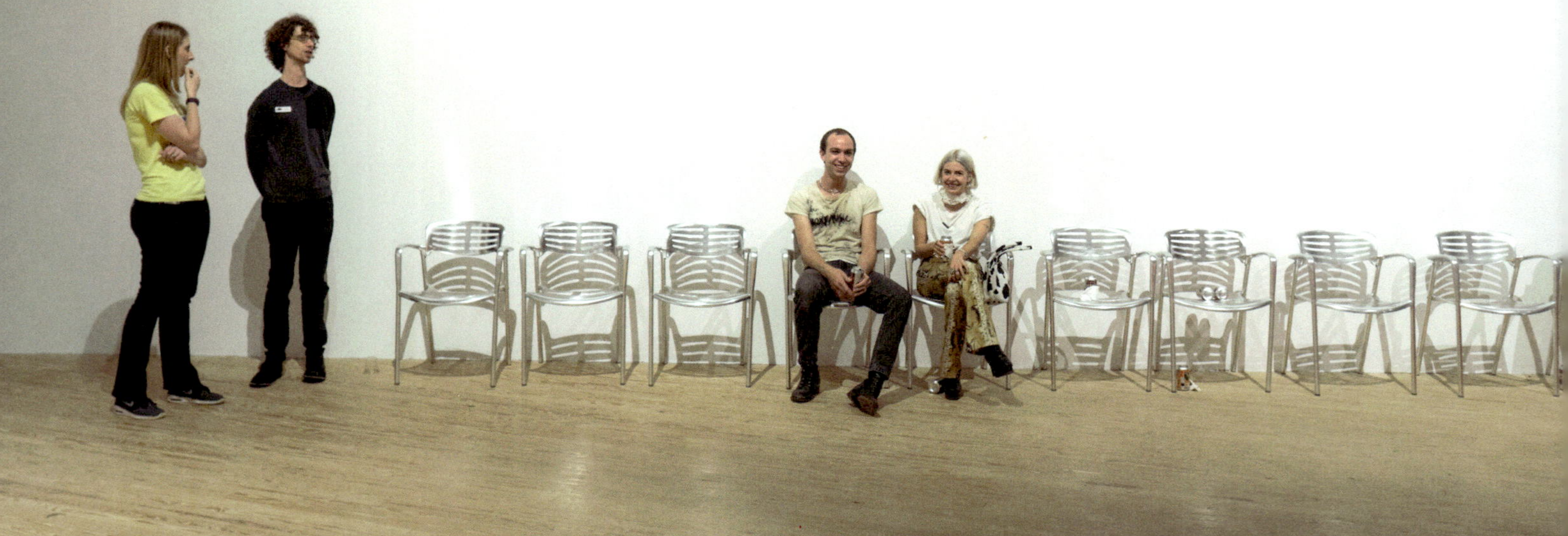

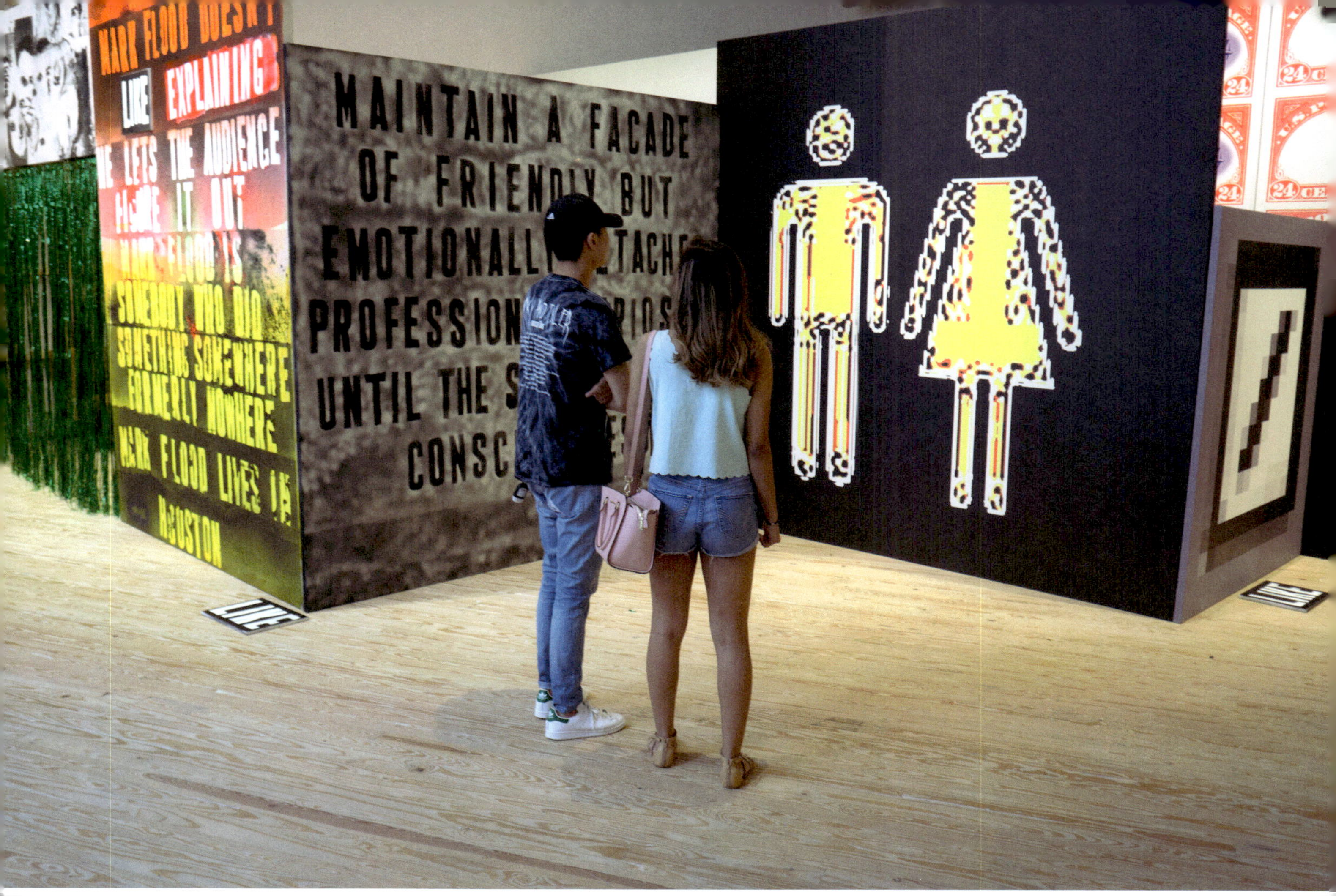

LIKE
EXPLAINING
THE AUDIENCE
IT OUT
SOMETHING SOMEWHERE
FORMERLY NOWHERE
MARK FLOOD LIVES IN
MAINTAIN A FACADE
OF FRIEND BUT
EMOTIONALL TACHE
PROFESSION
UNTIL THE S
CONSC
LIKE
PEOPLE

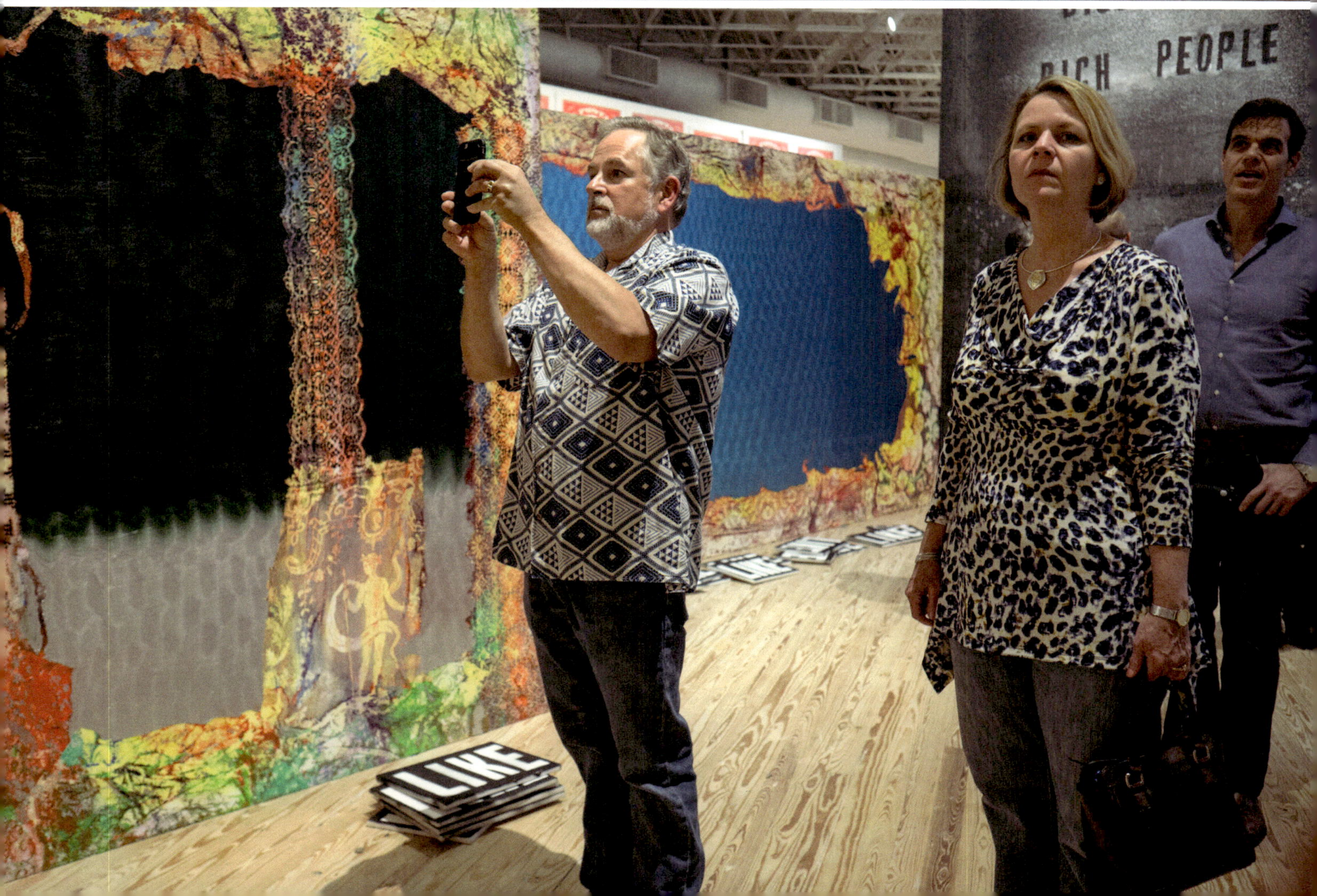

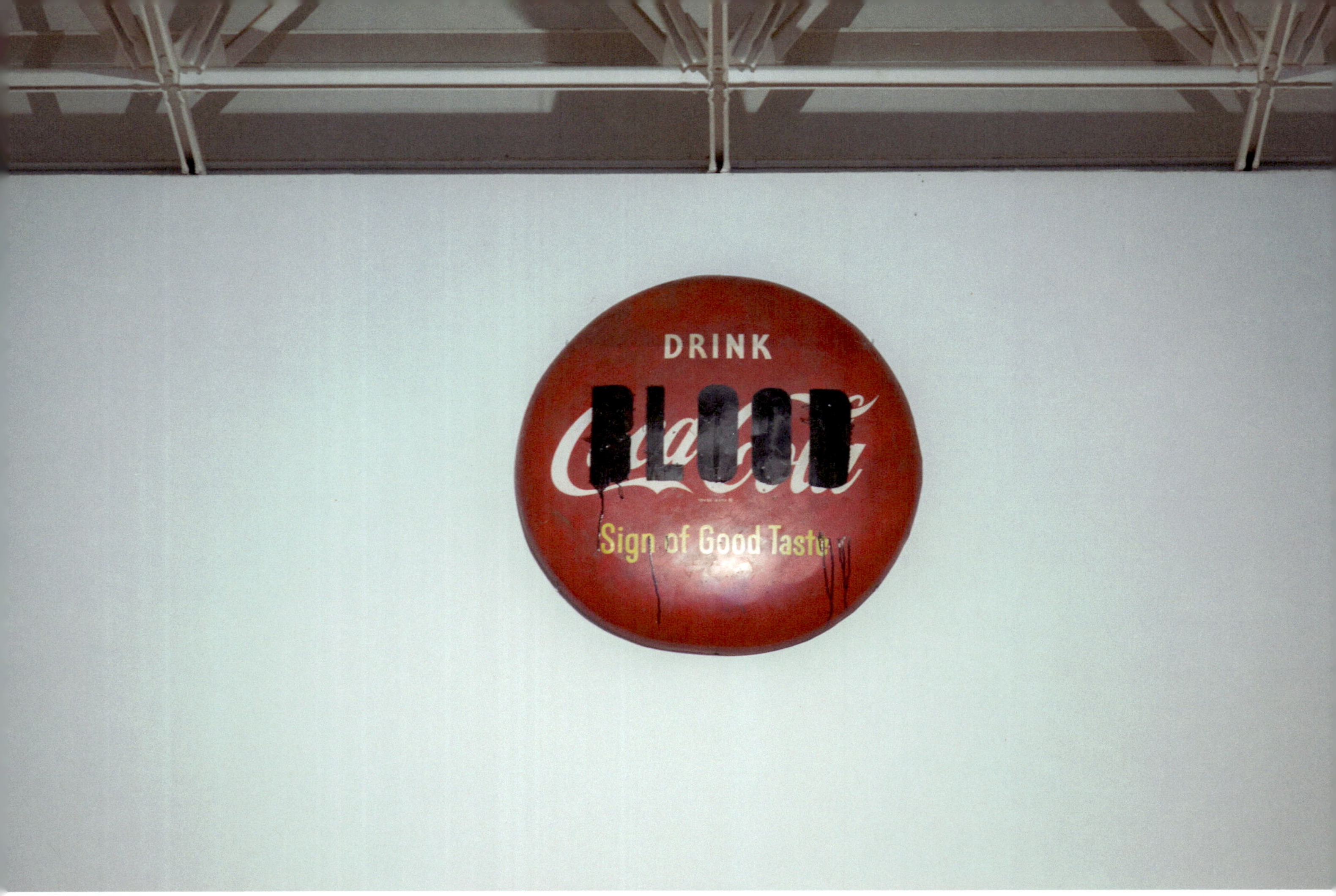

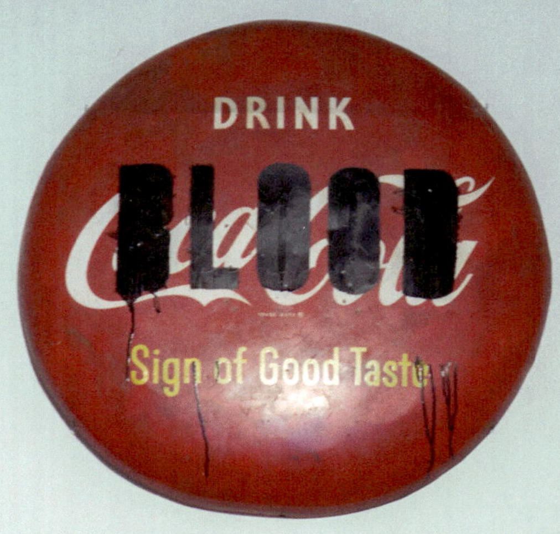
DRINK
BLOOD
Sign of Good Taste

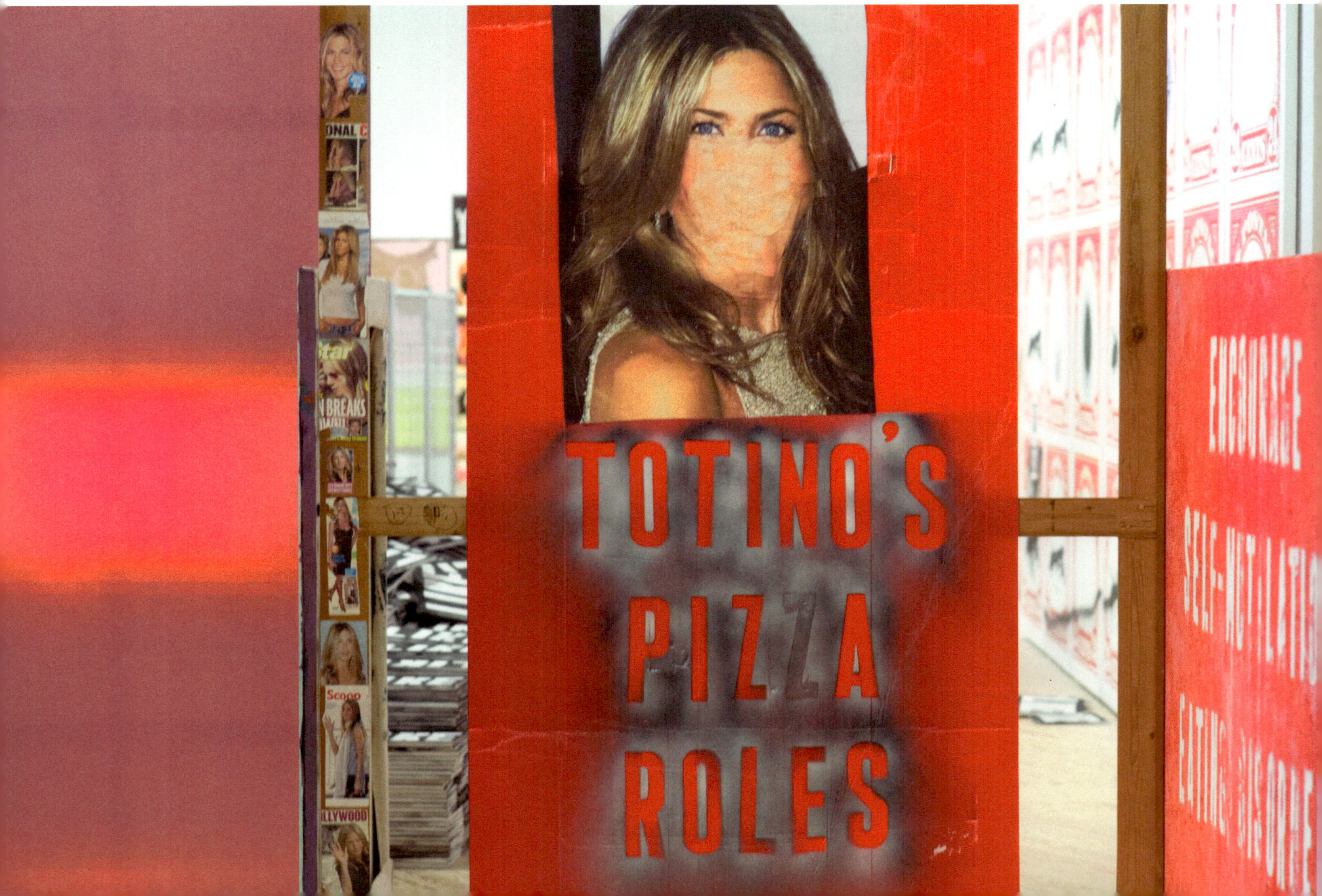

TOTINO'S
PIZZA
ROLES
ENCOURAGE

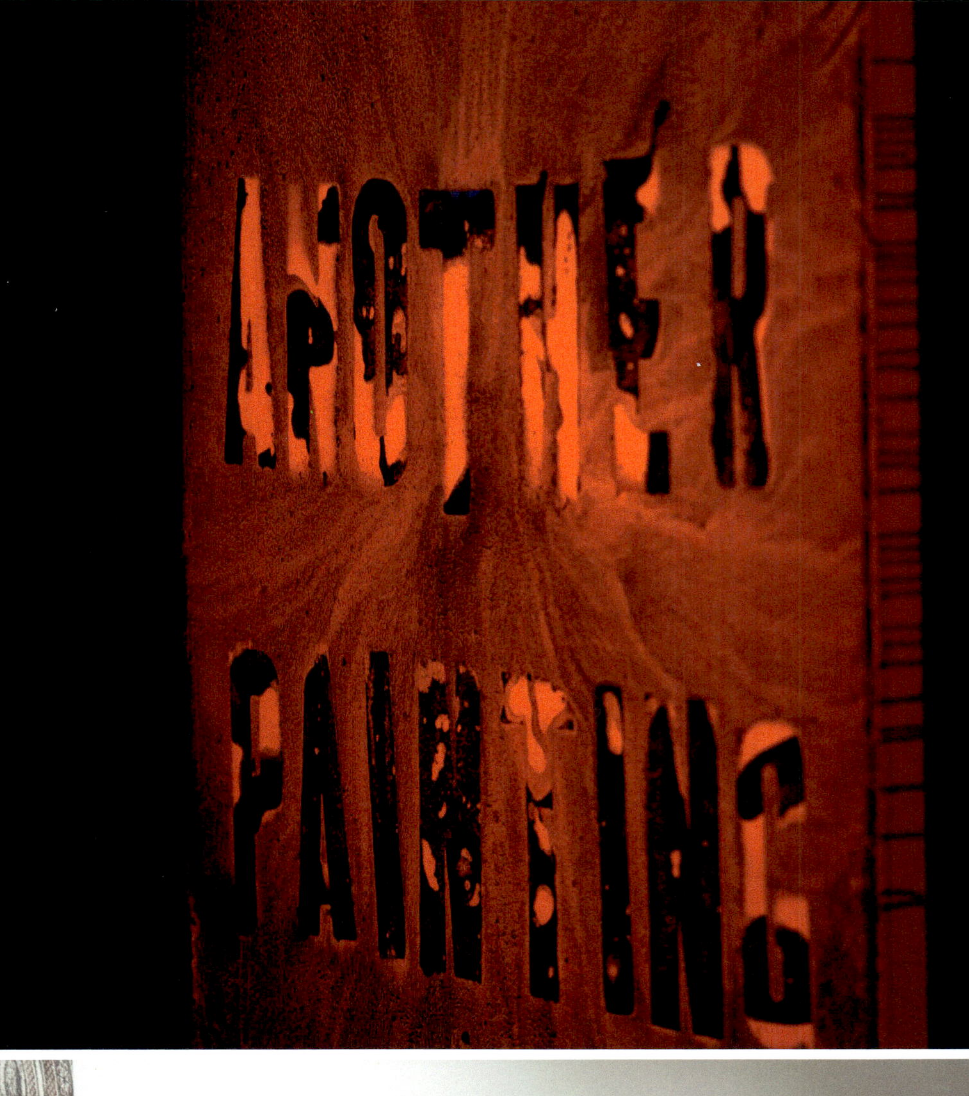
ANOTHER
PAINTING

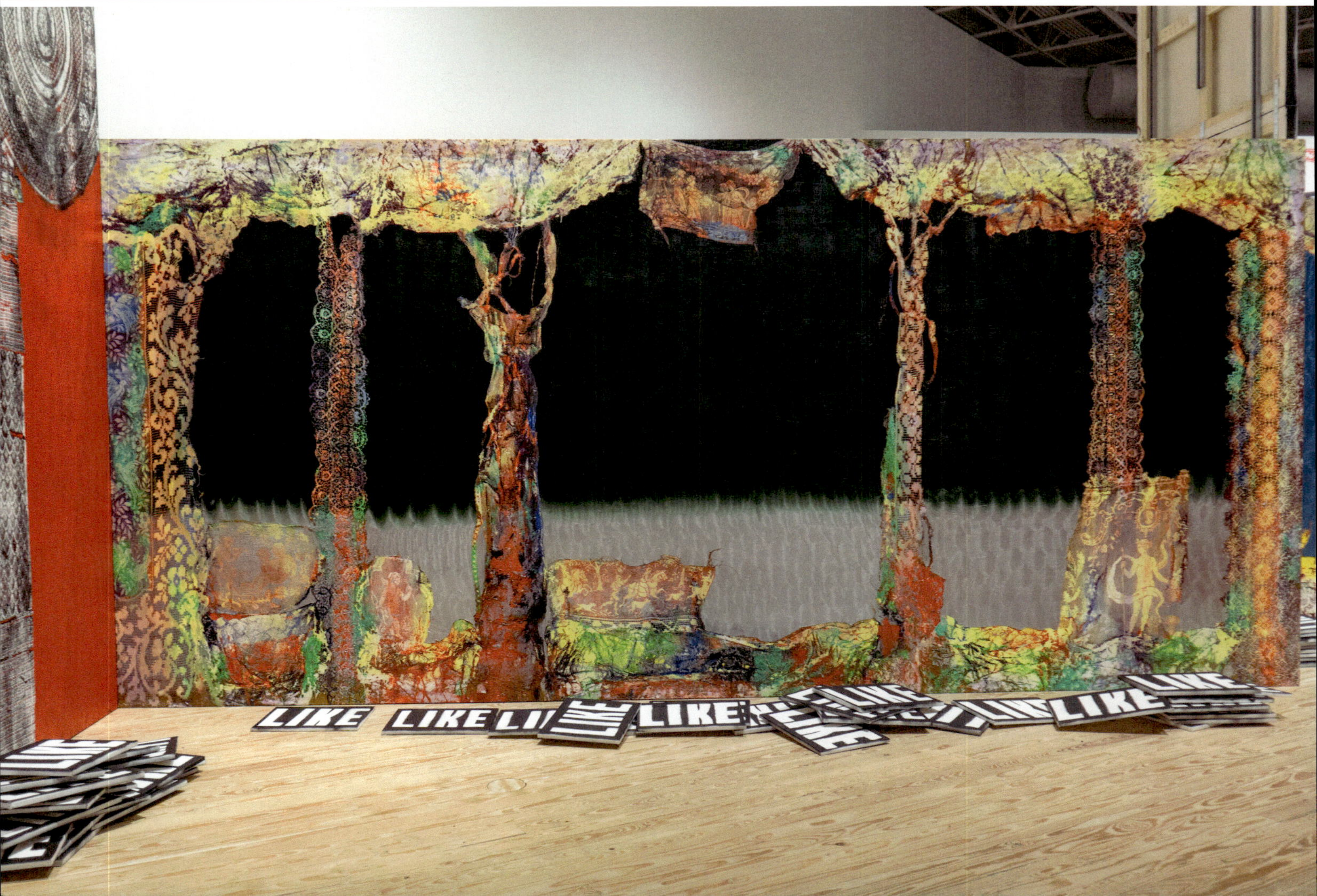

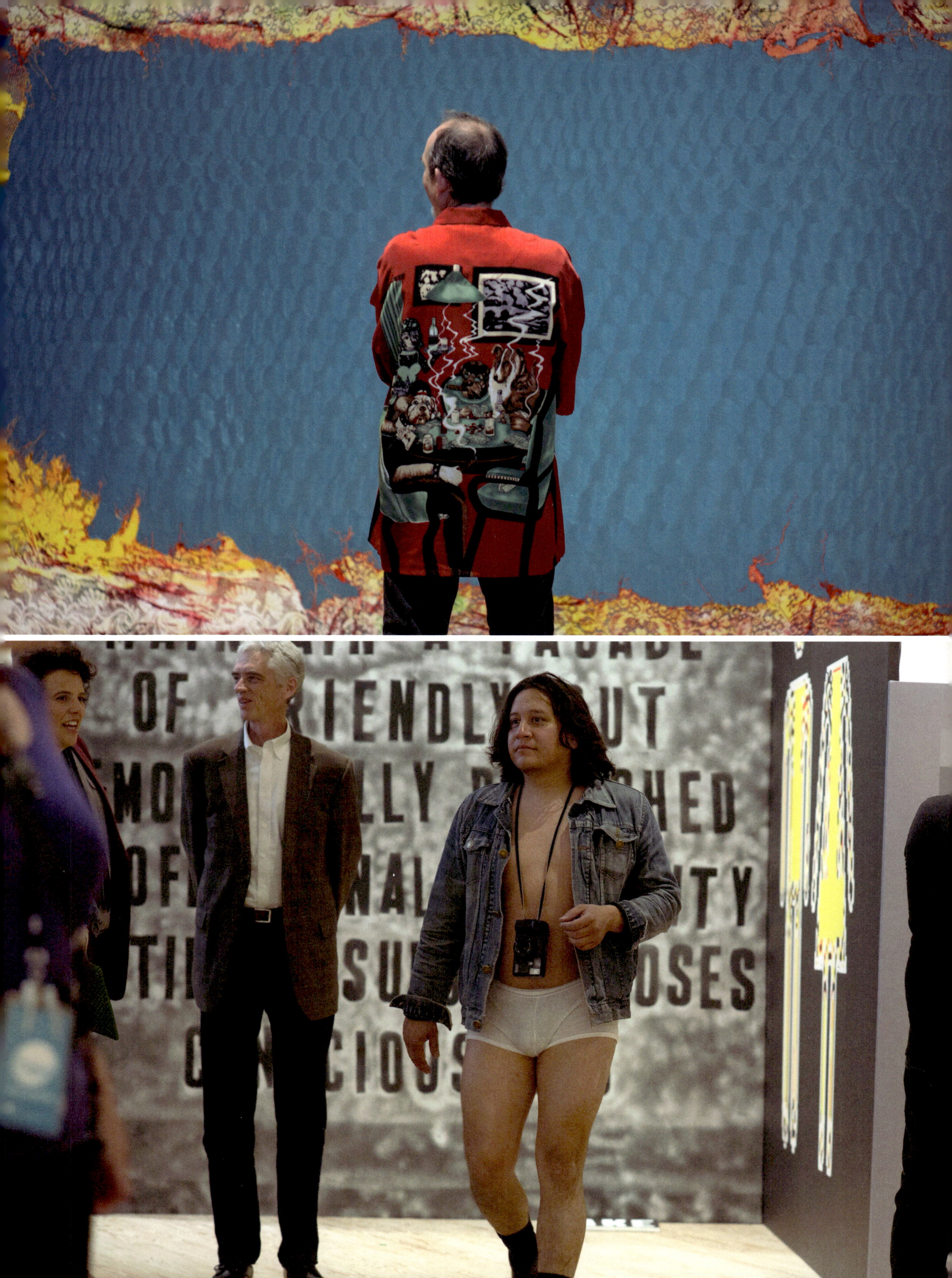

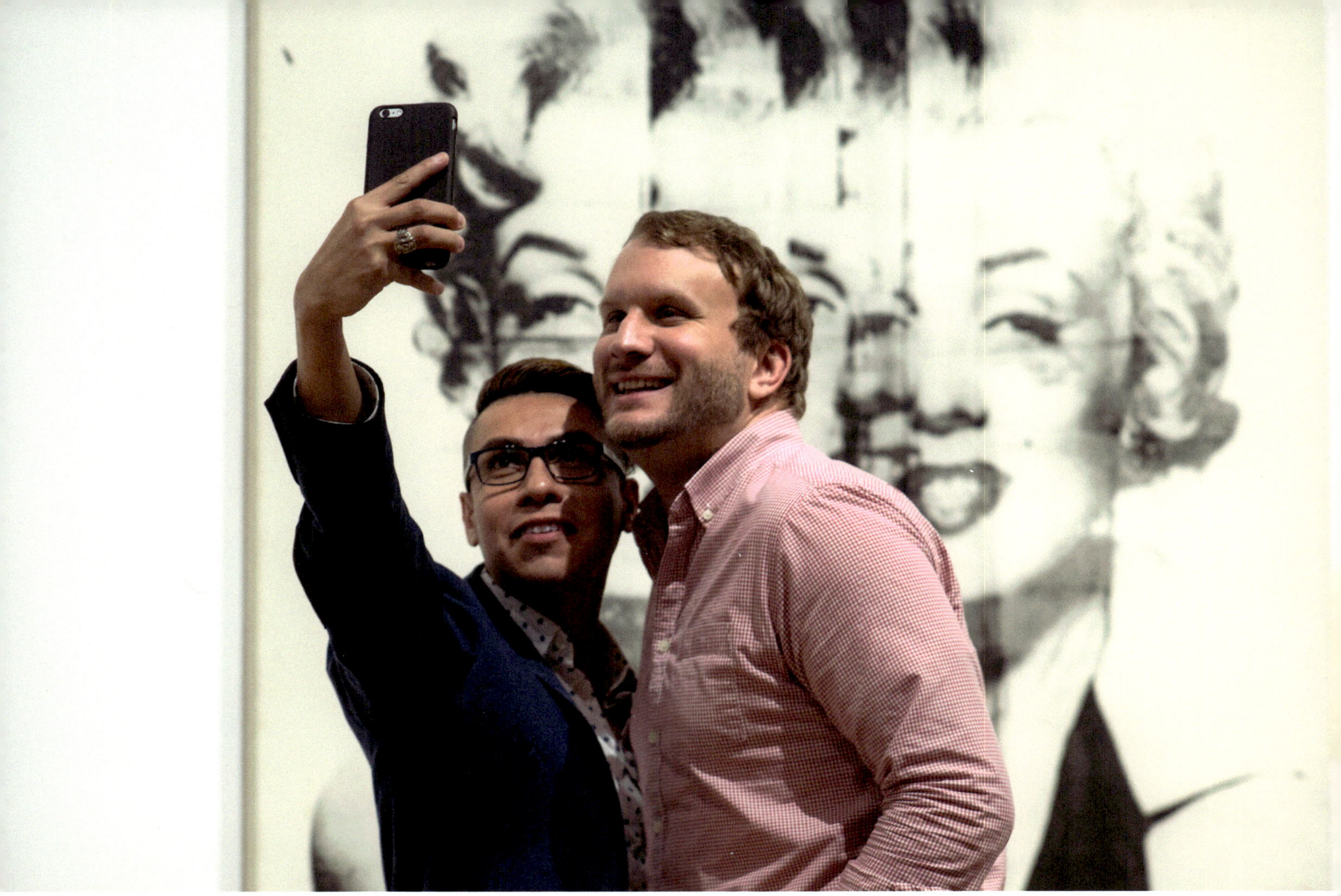

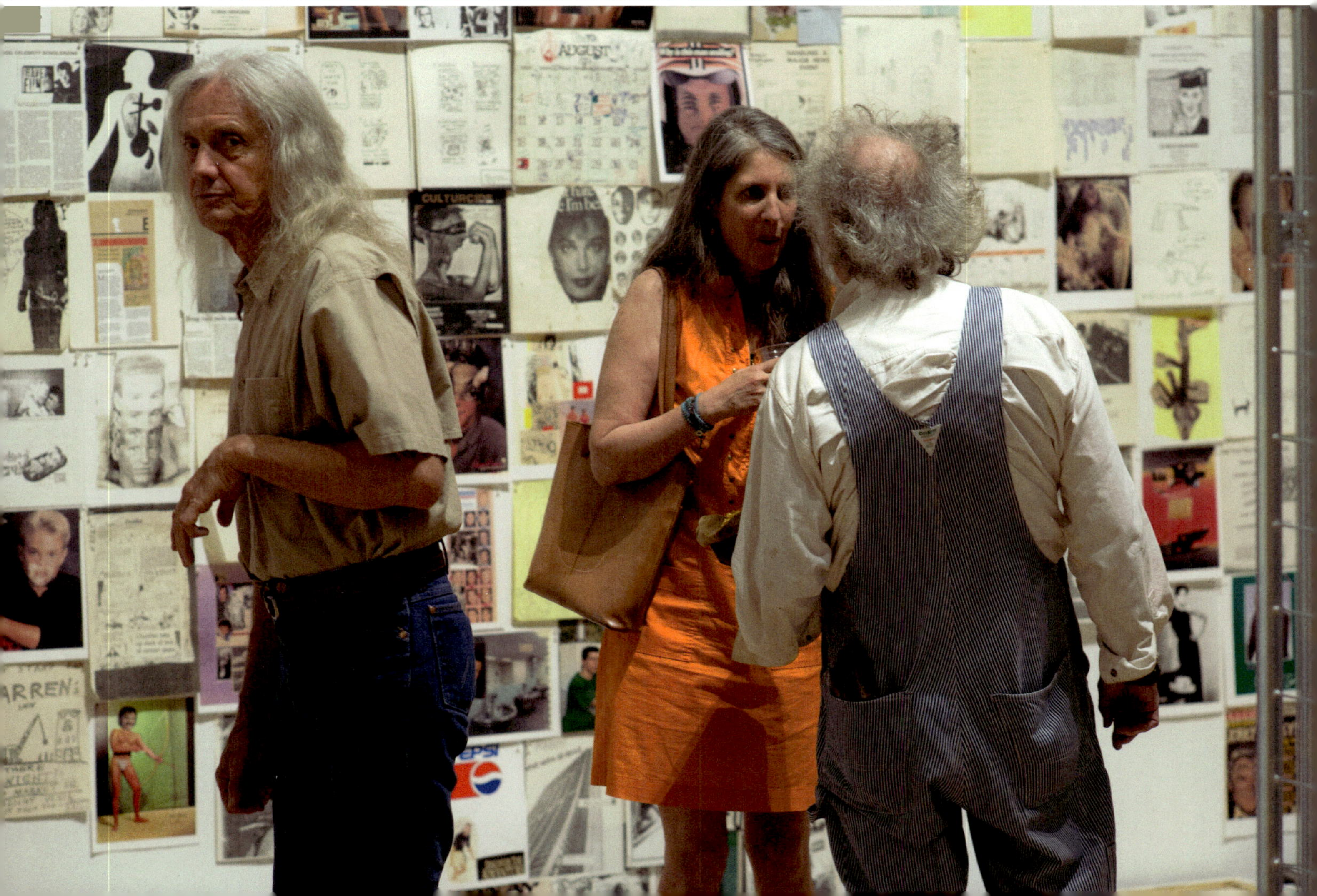

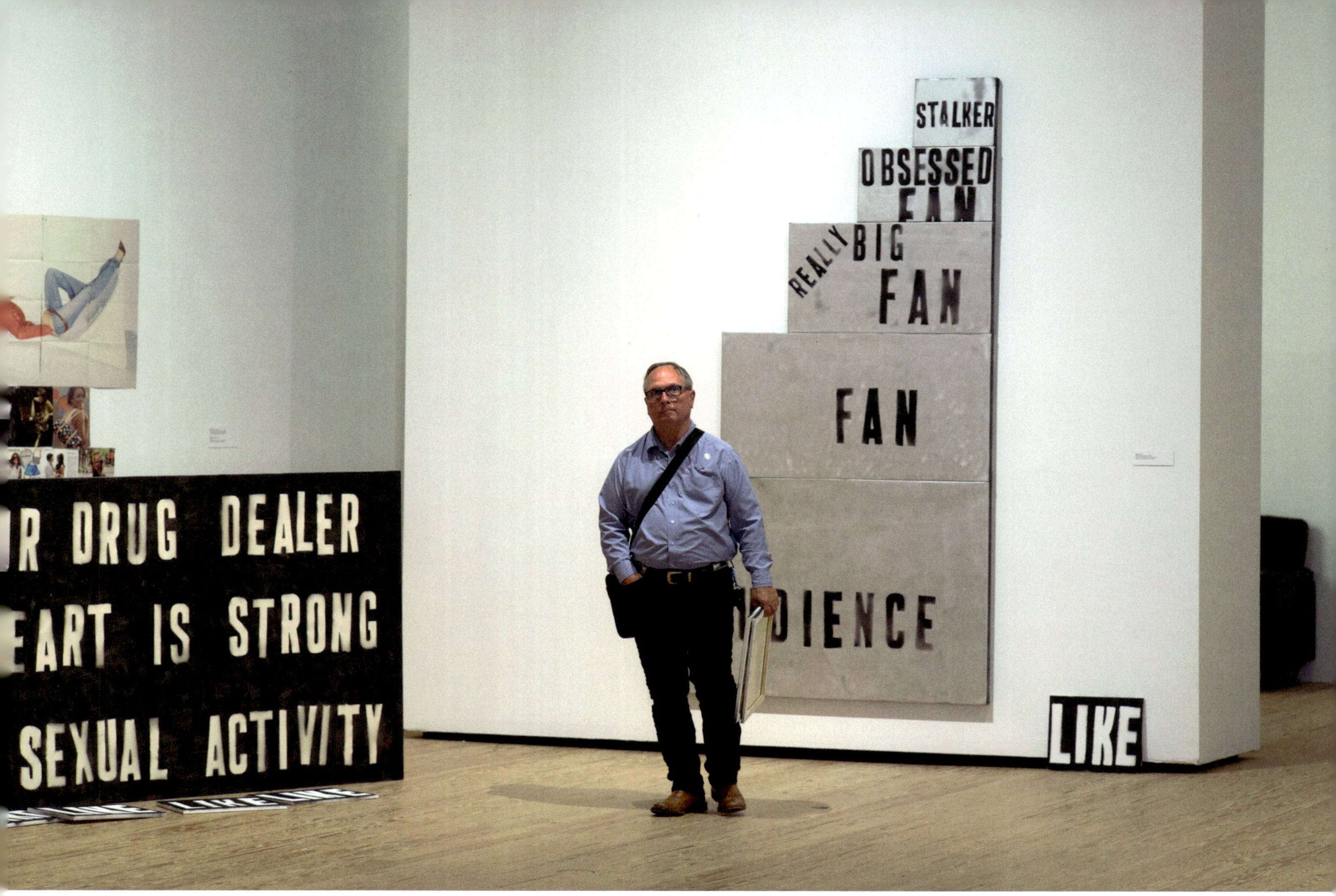

STALKER
OBSESSED FAN
REALLY BIG FAN
FAN
DIENCE
LIKE
R DRUG DEALER
EART IS STRONG
SEXUAL ACTIVITY
LIKE LIKE

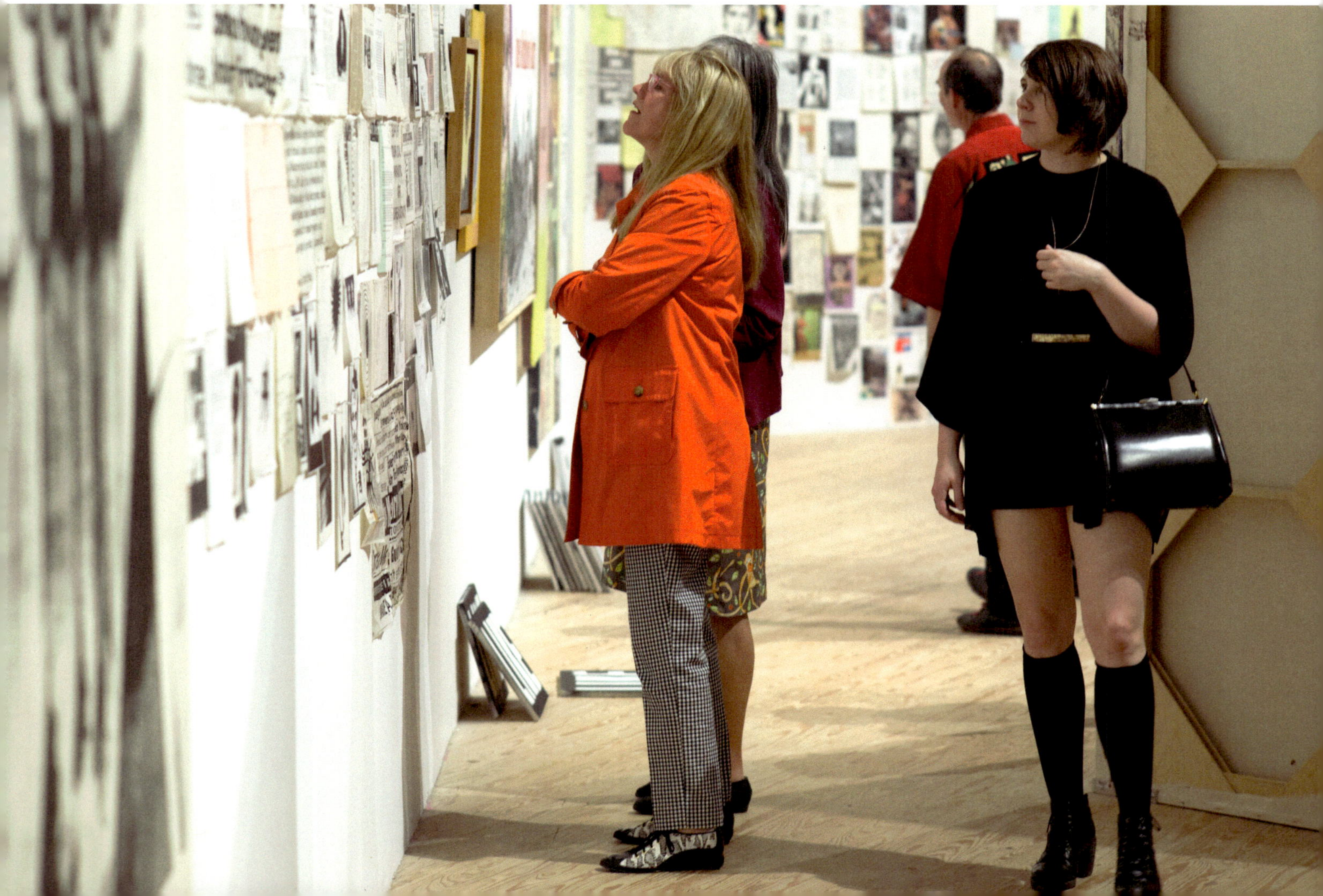

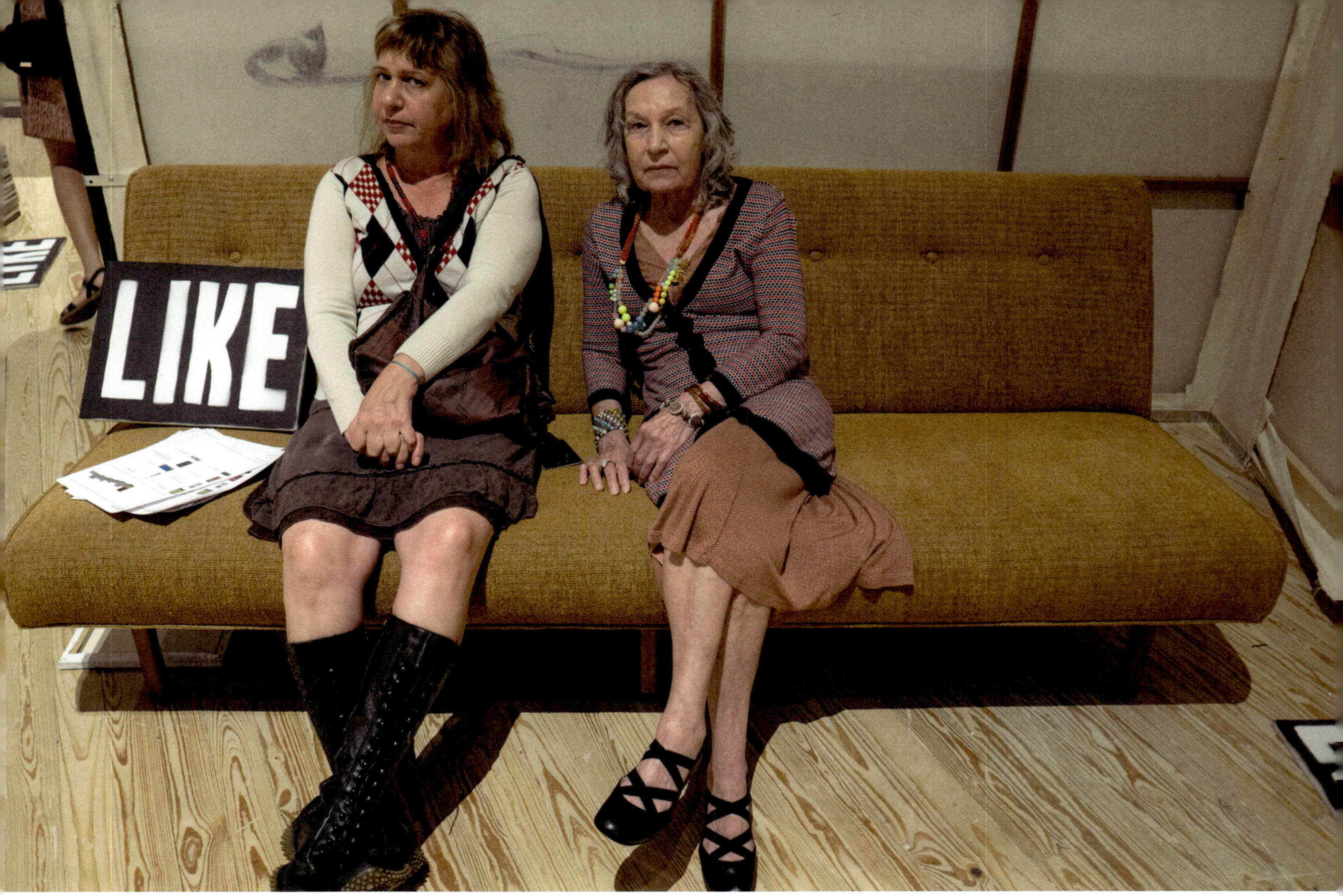

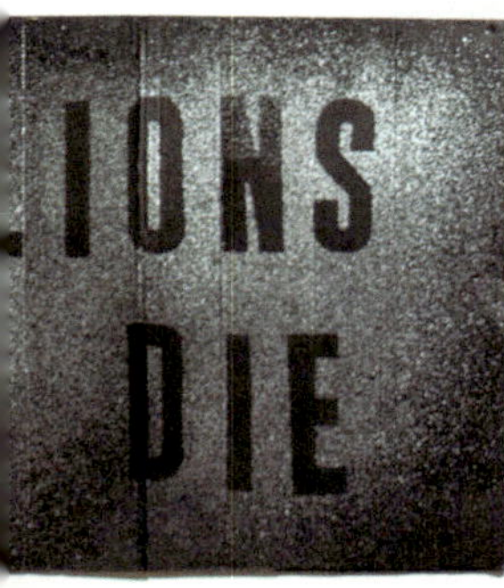
IONS
DIE

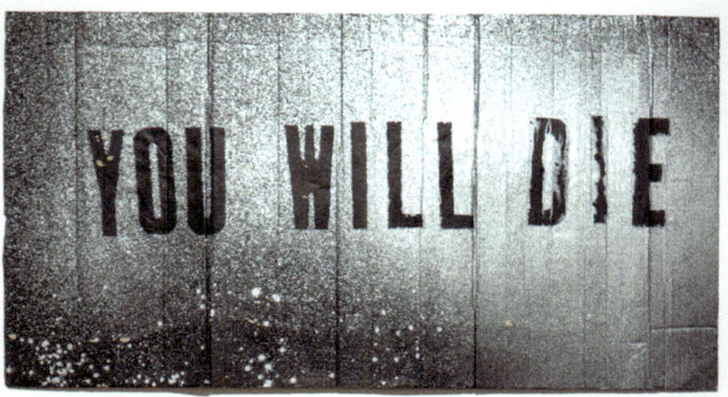
YOU WILL DIE

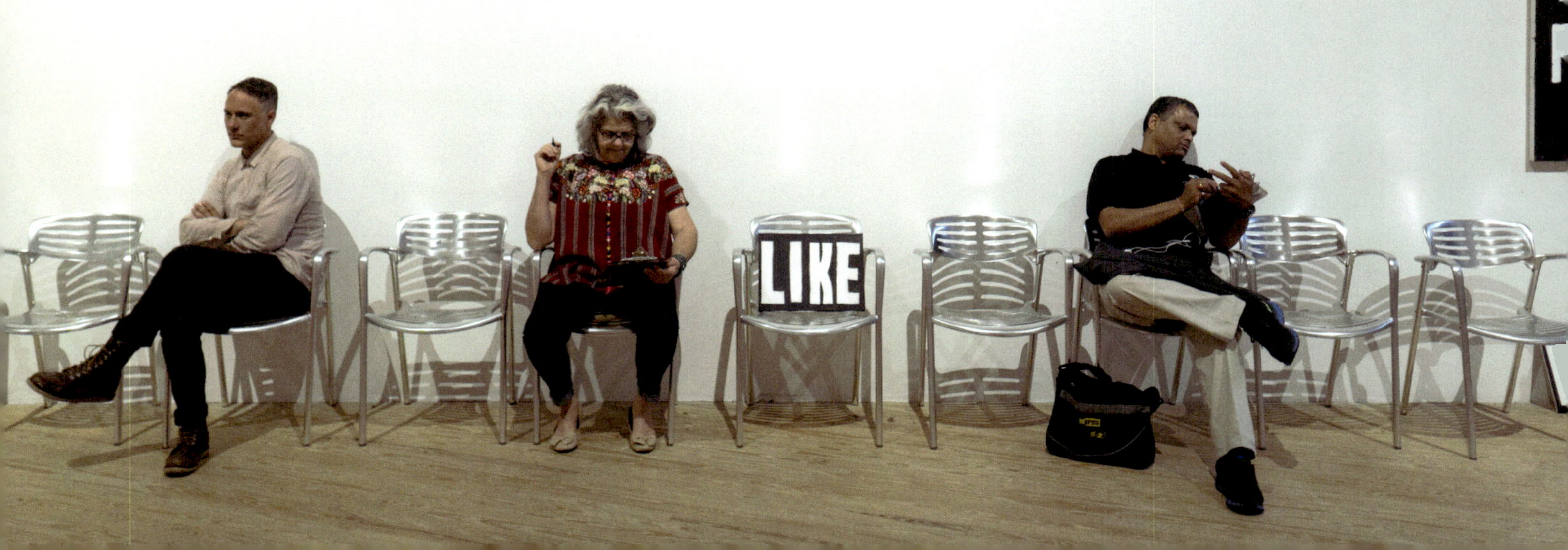
LIKE

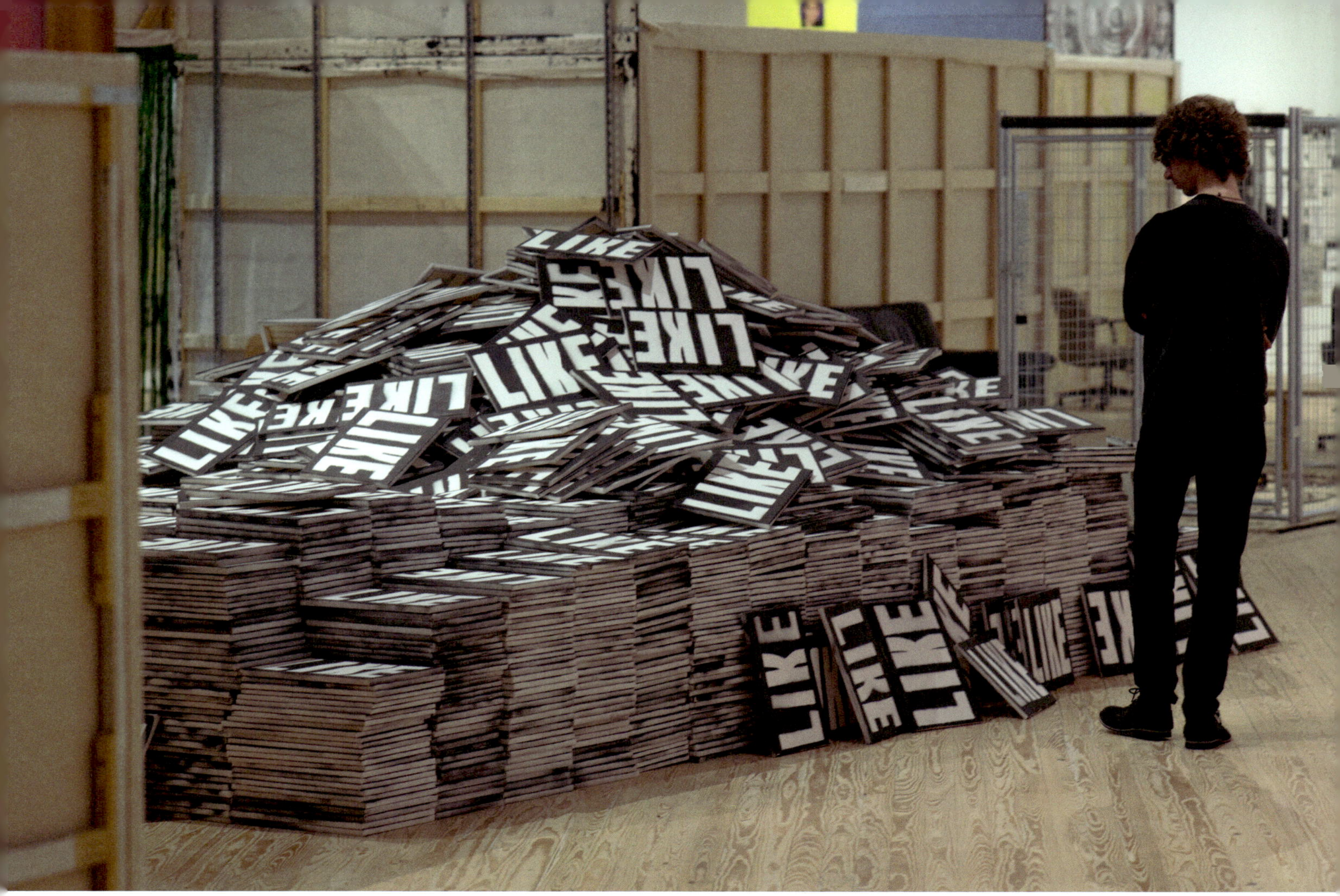

LIKE

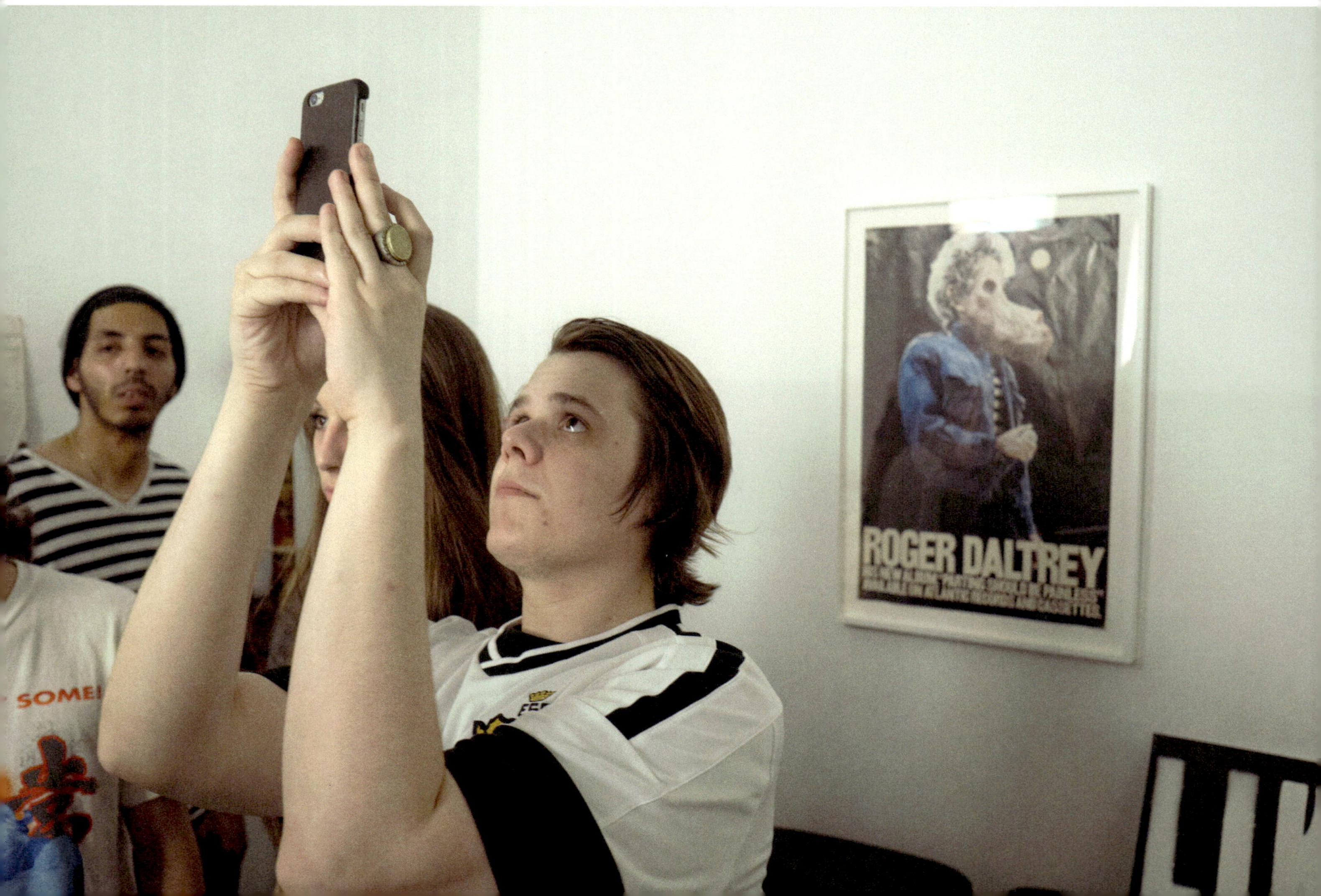

ROGER DALTREY

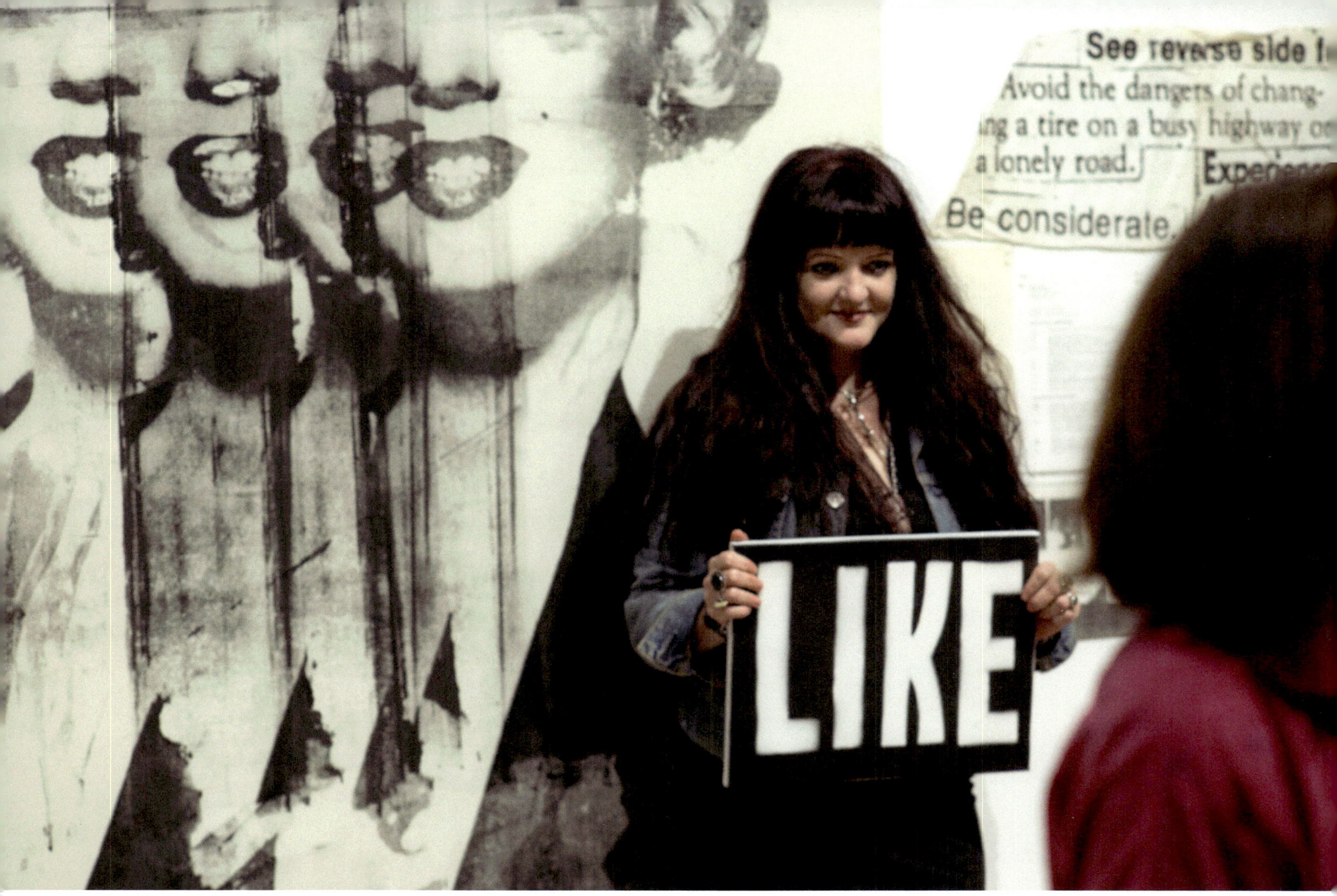

See reverse side f
Avoid the dangers of chang-
ing a tire on a busy highway on
a lonely road.
Be considerate.
LIKE
Lindsay 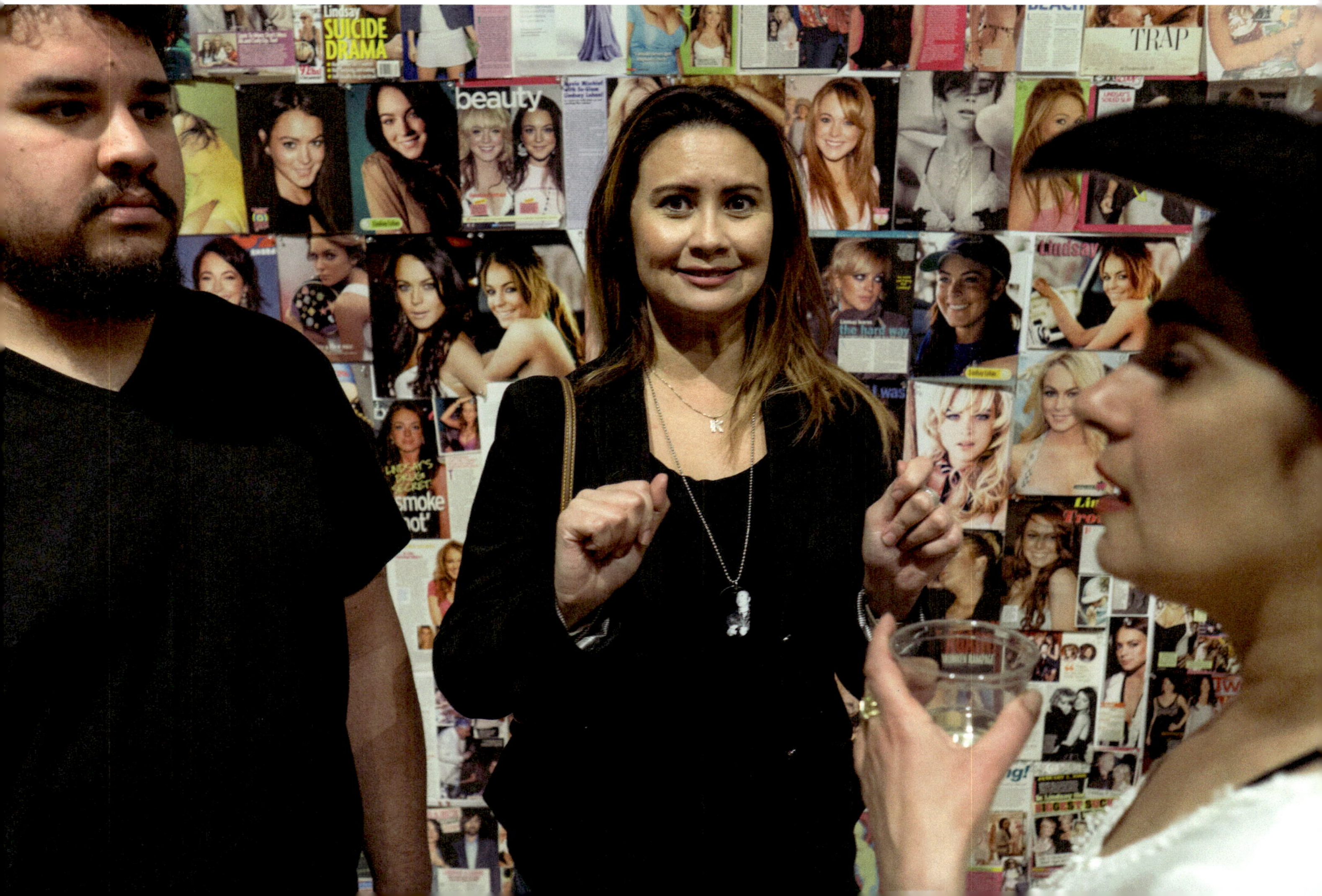
SUICIDE
DRAMA
beauty
TRAP
the hard way
smoke

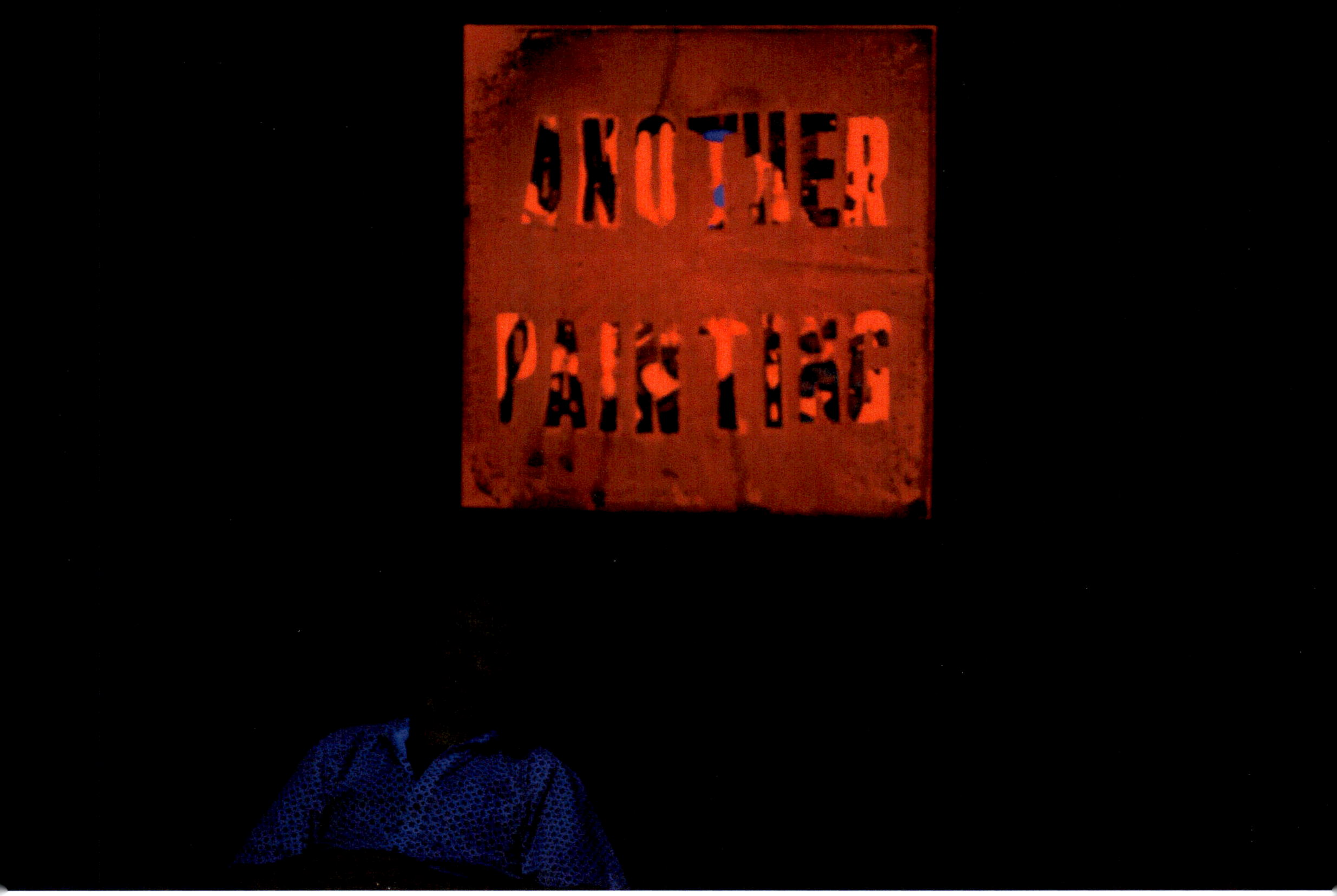

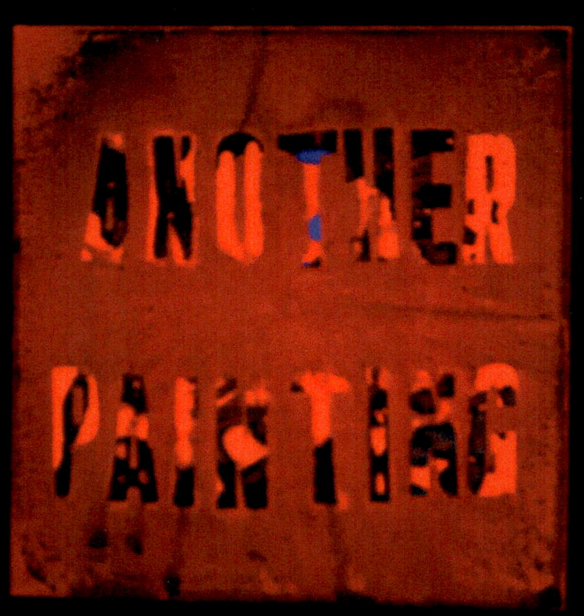
ANOTHER
PAINTING

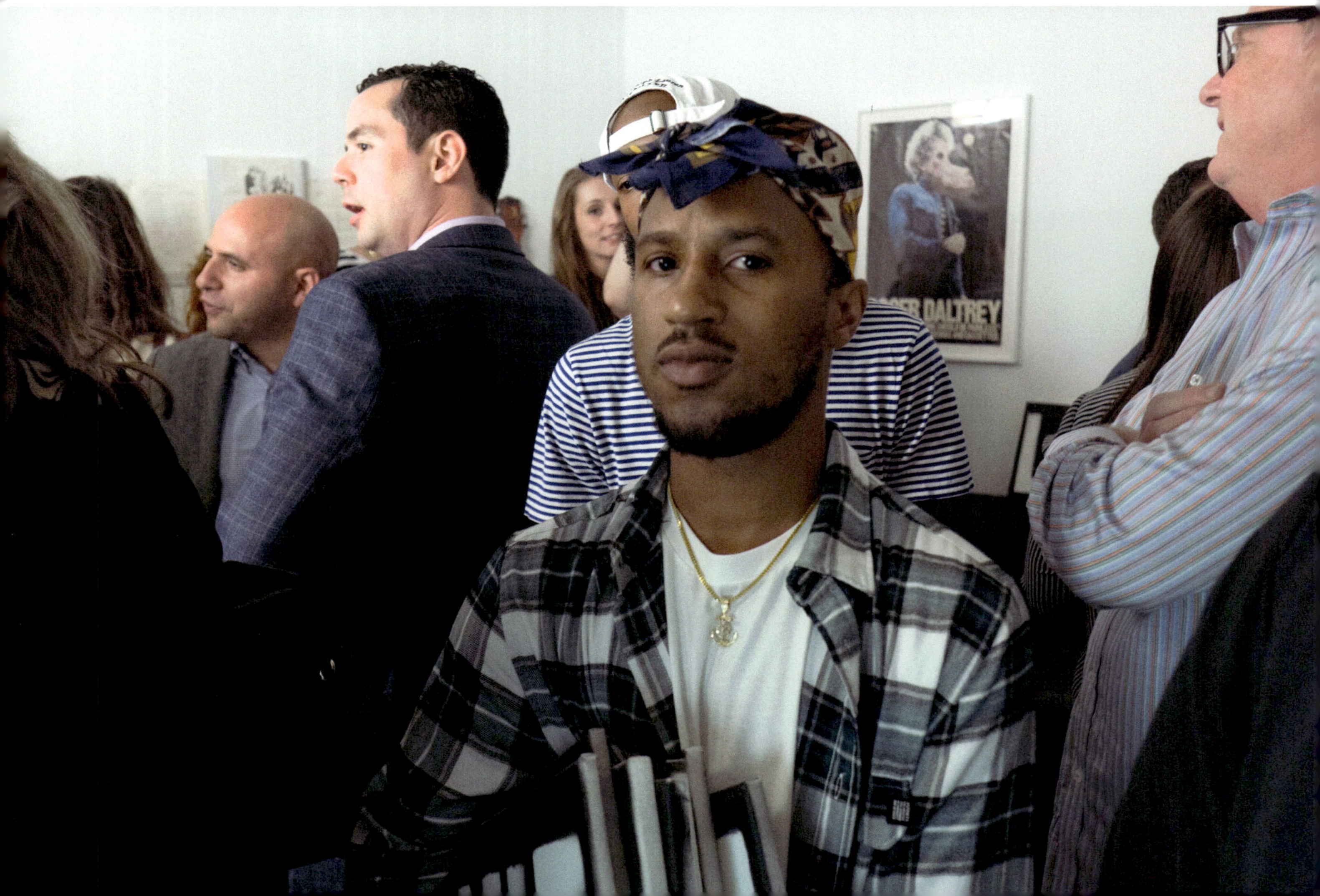

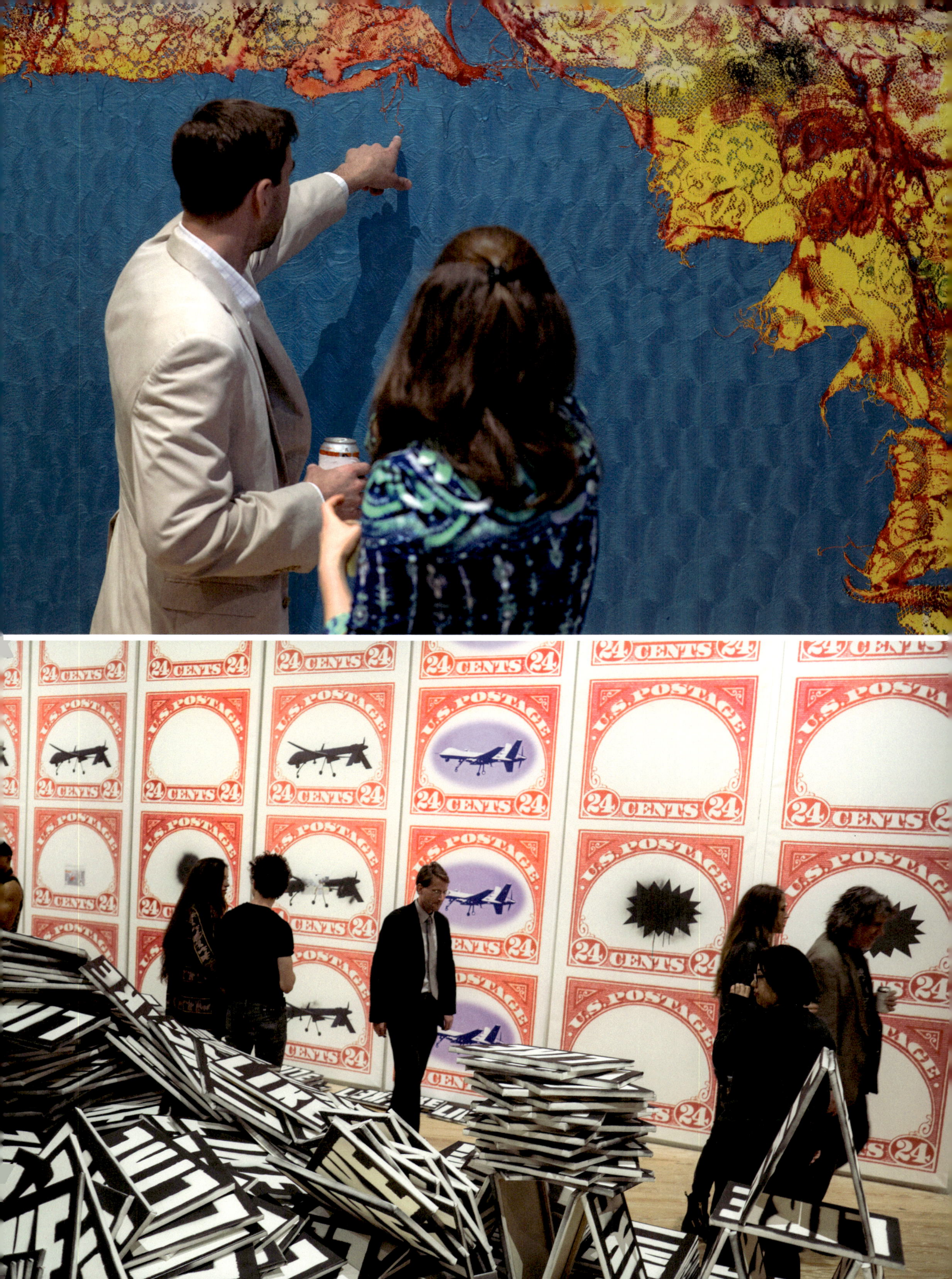
24 CENTS 24
U.S. POSTAGE
24 CENTS 24

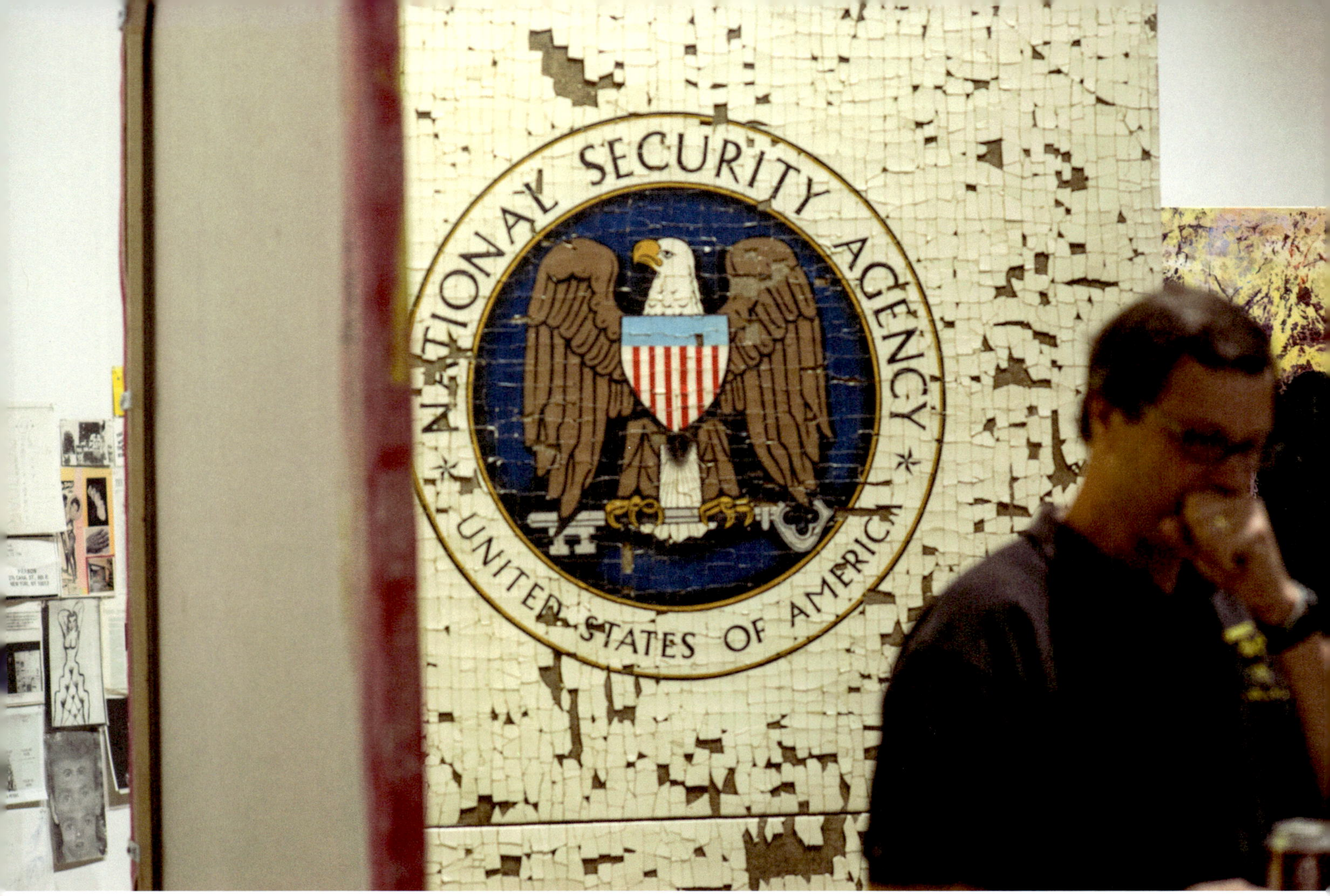

NATIONAL SECURITY AGENCY
UNITED STATES OF AMERICA
EOS 50D

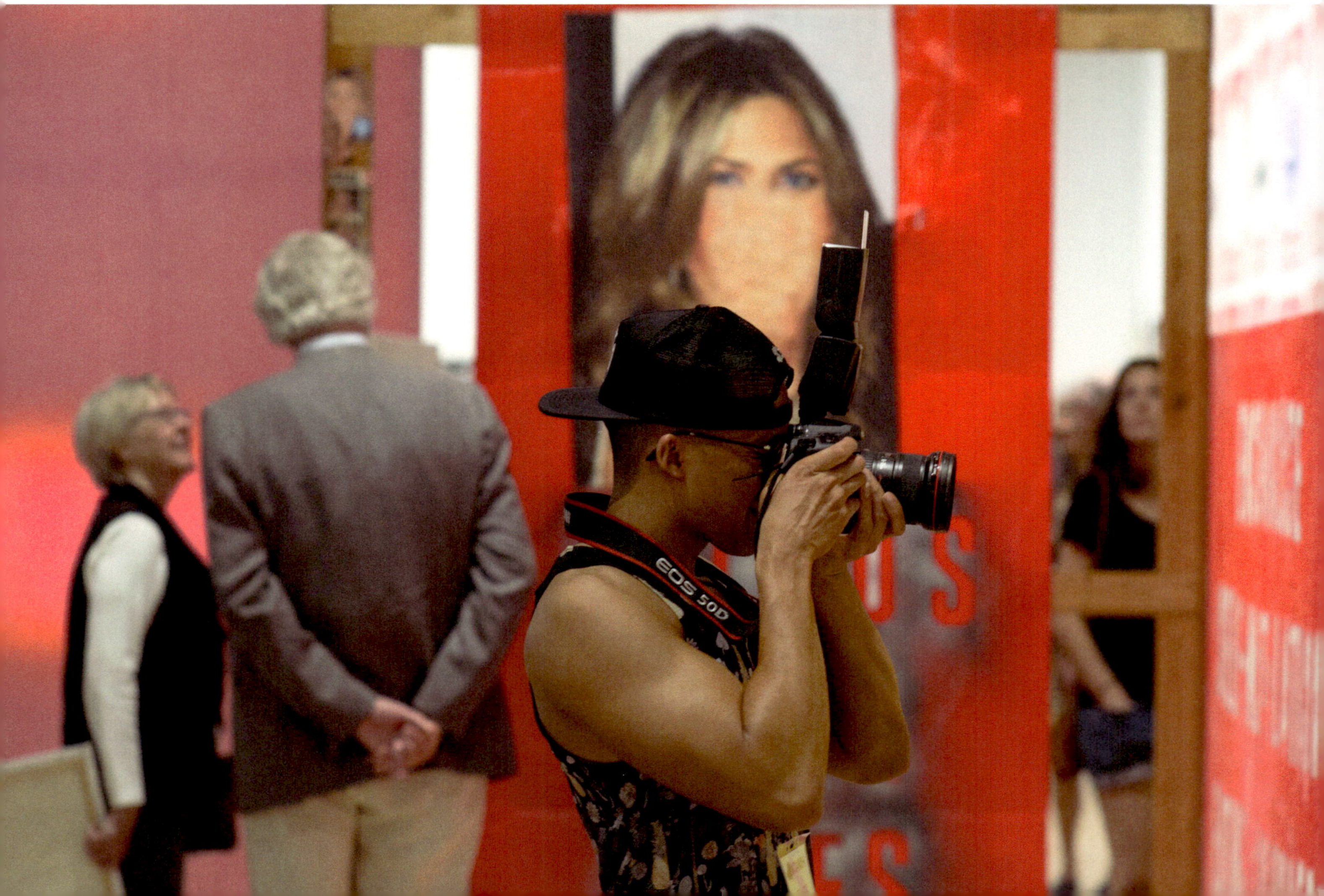

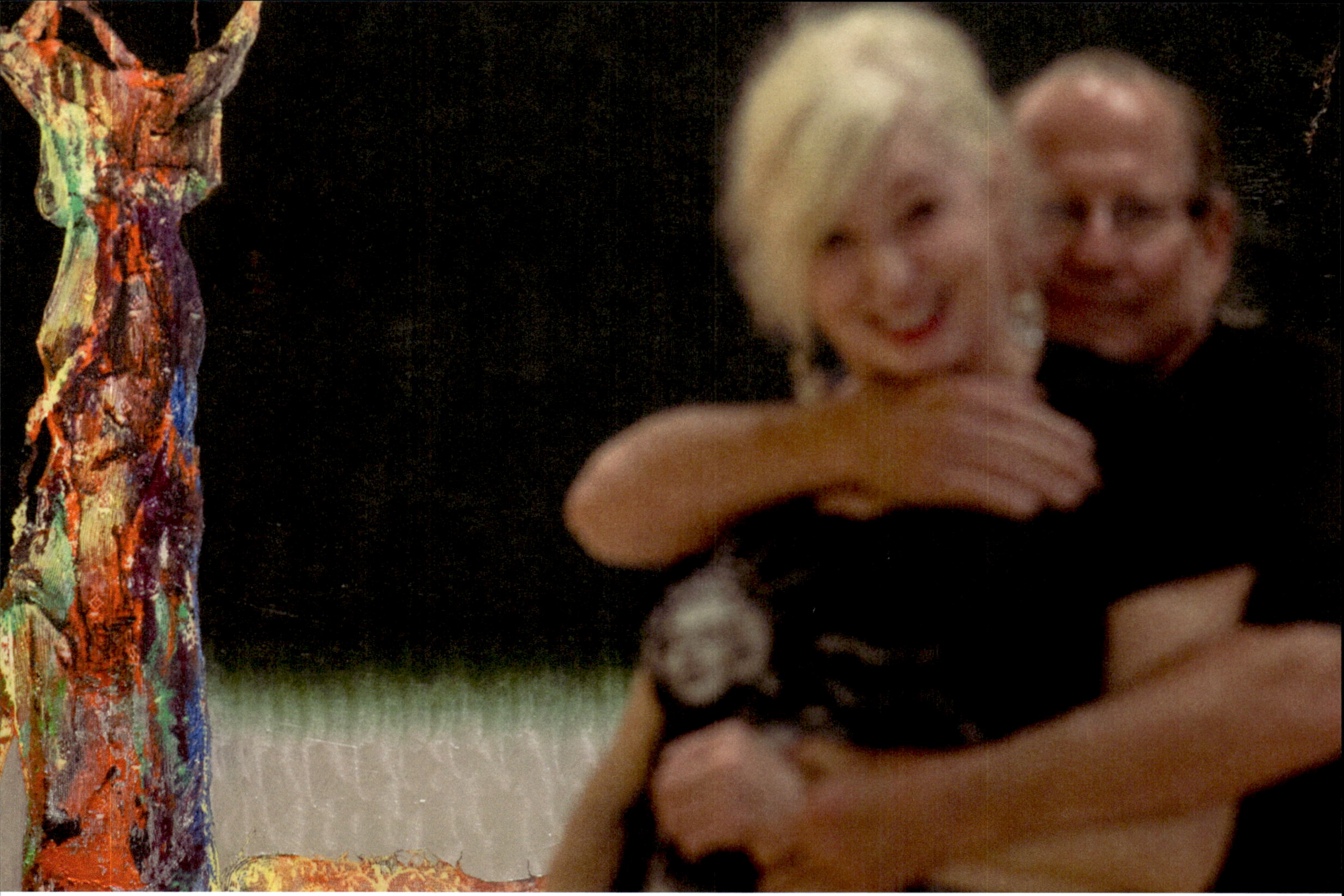

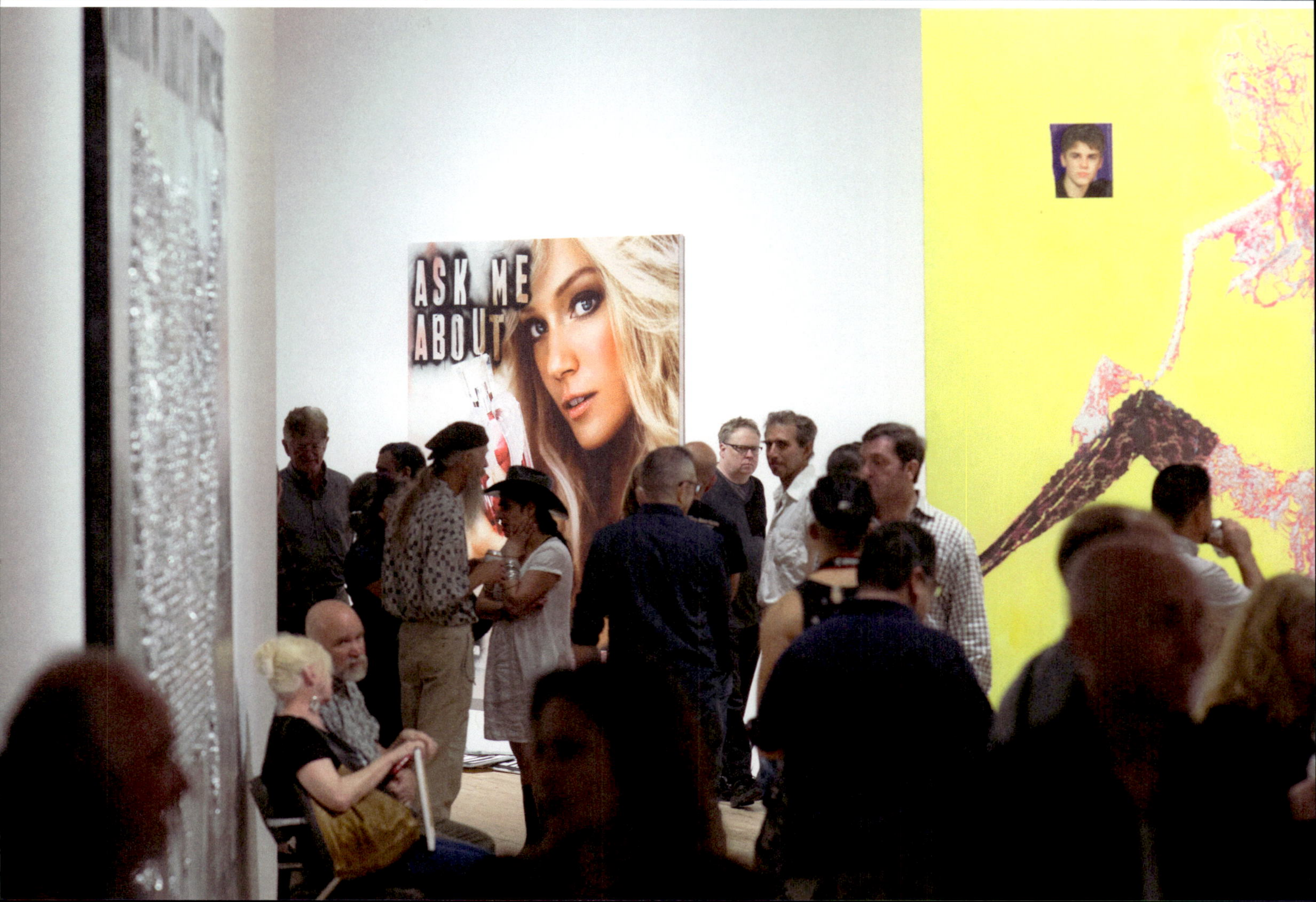

ASK ME
ABOUT

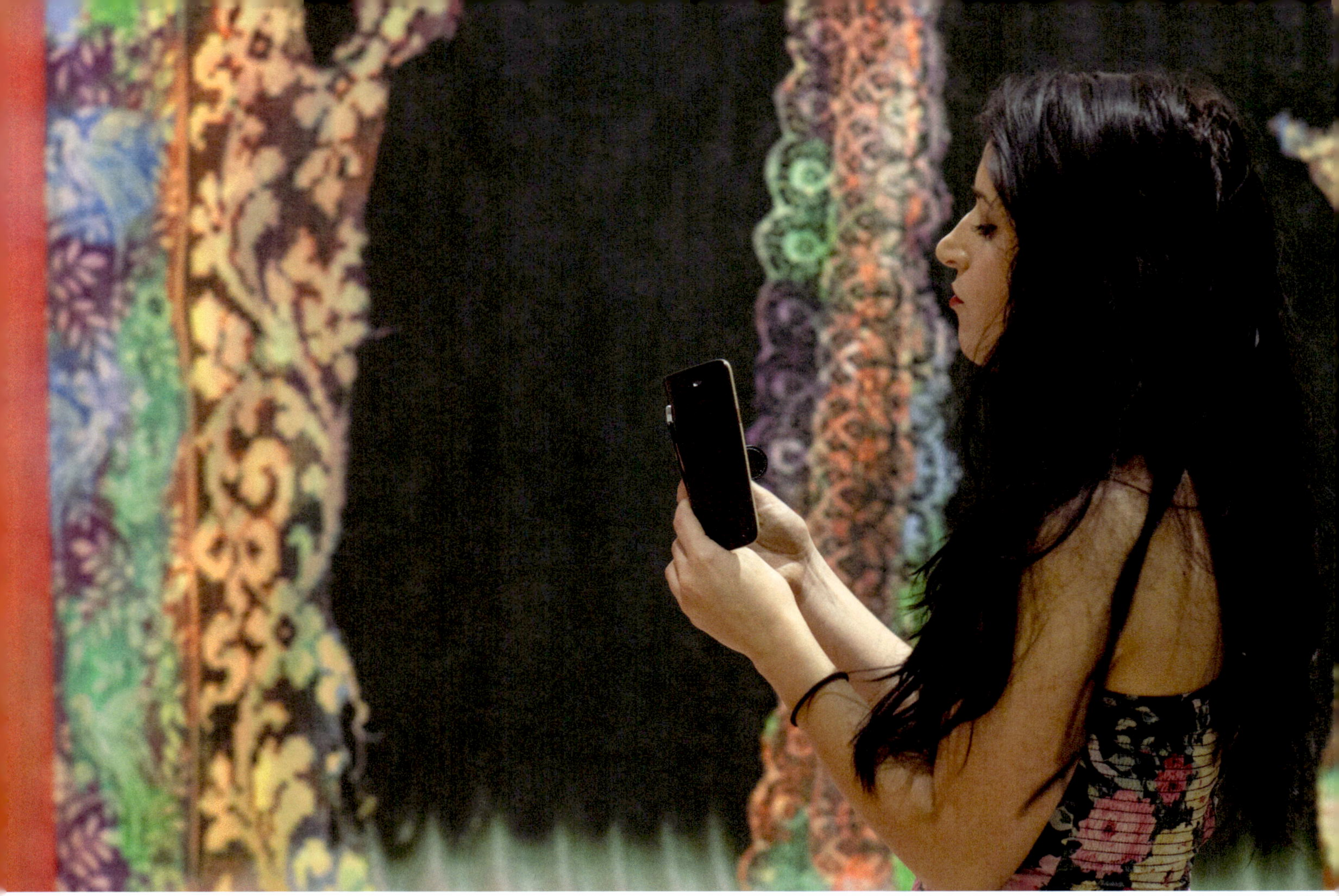

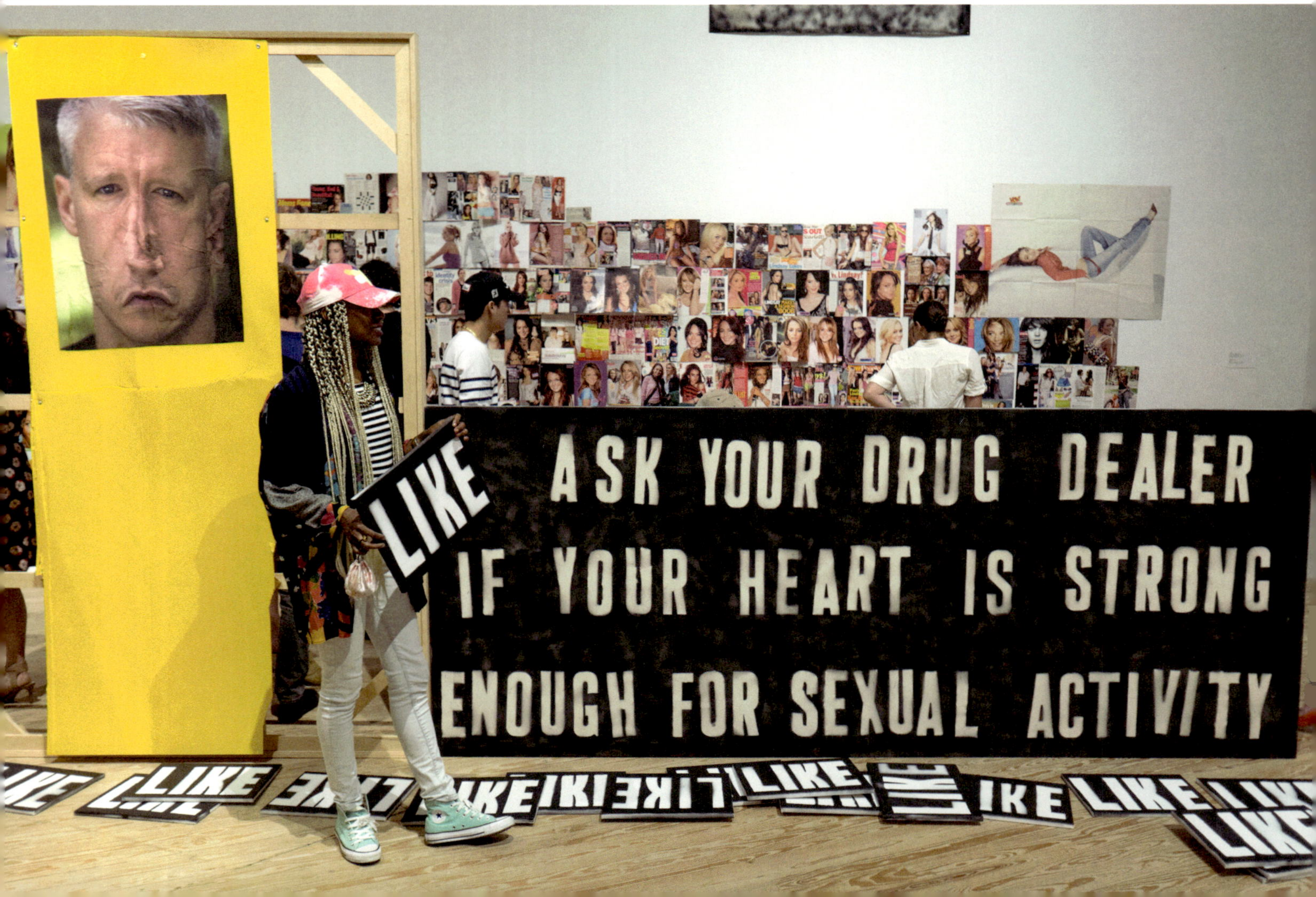

ASK YOUR DRUG DEALER
IF YOUR HEART IS STRONG
ENOUGH FOR SEXUAL ACTIVITY
LIKE

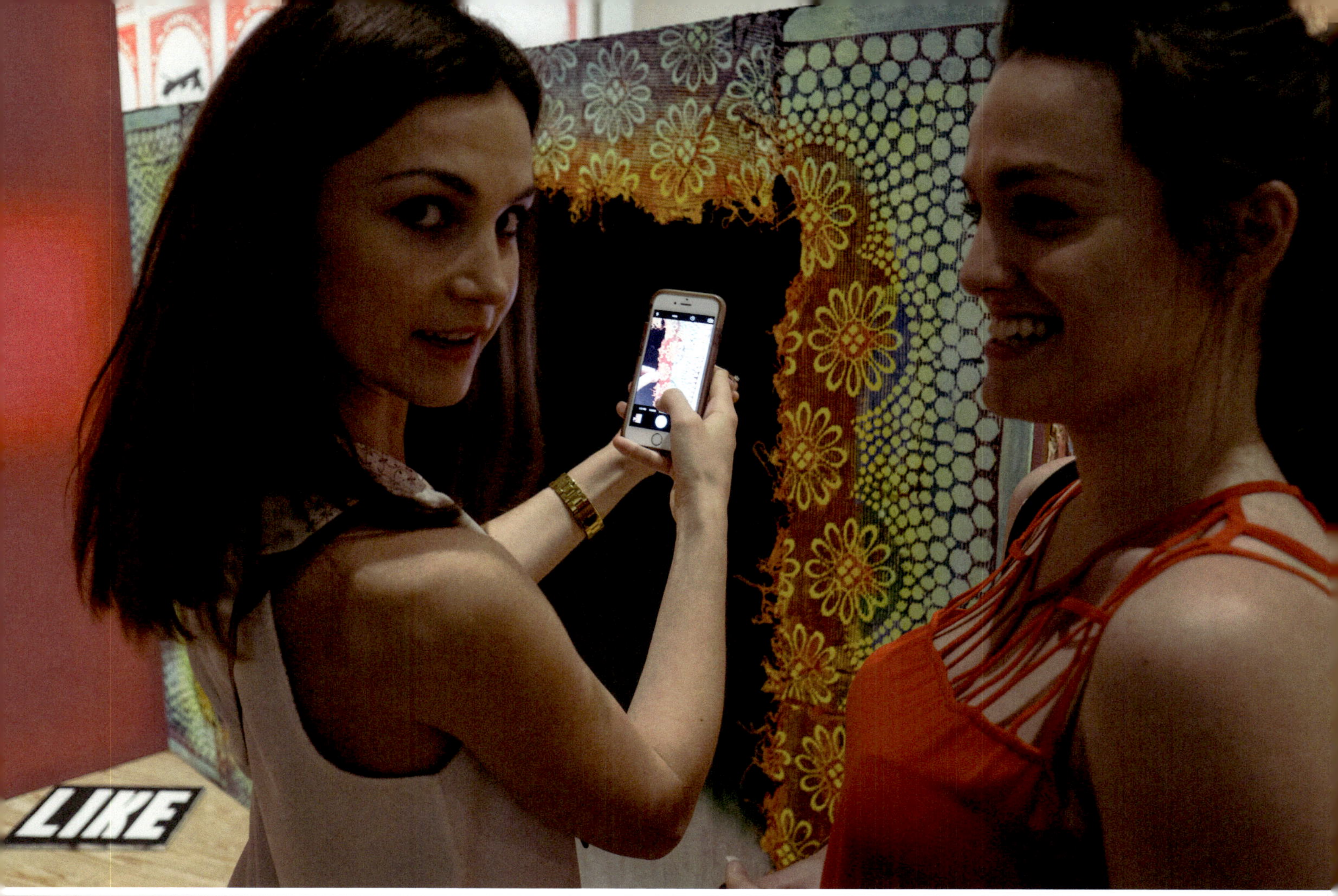

LIKE
STALKER 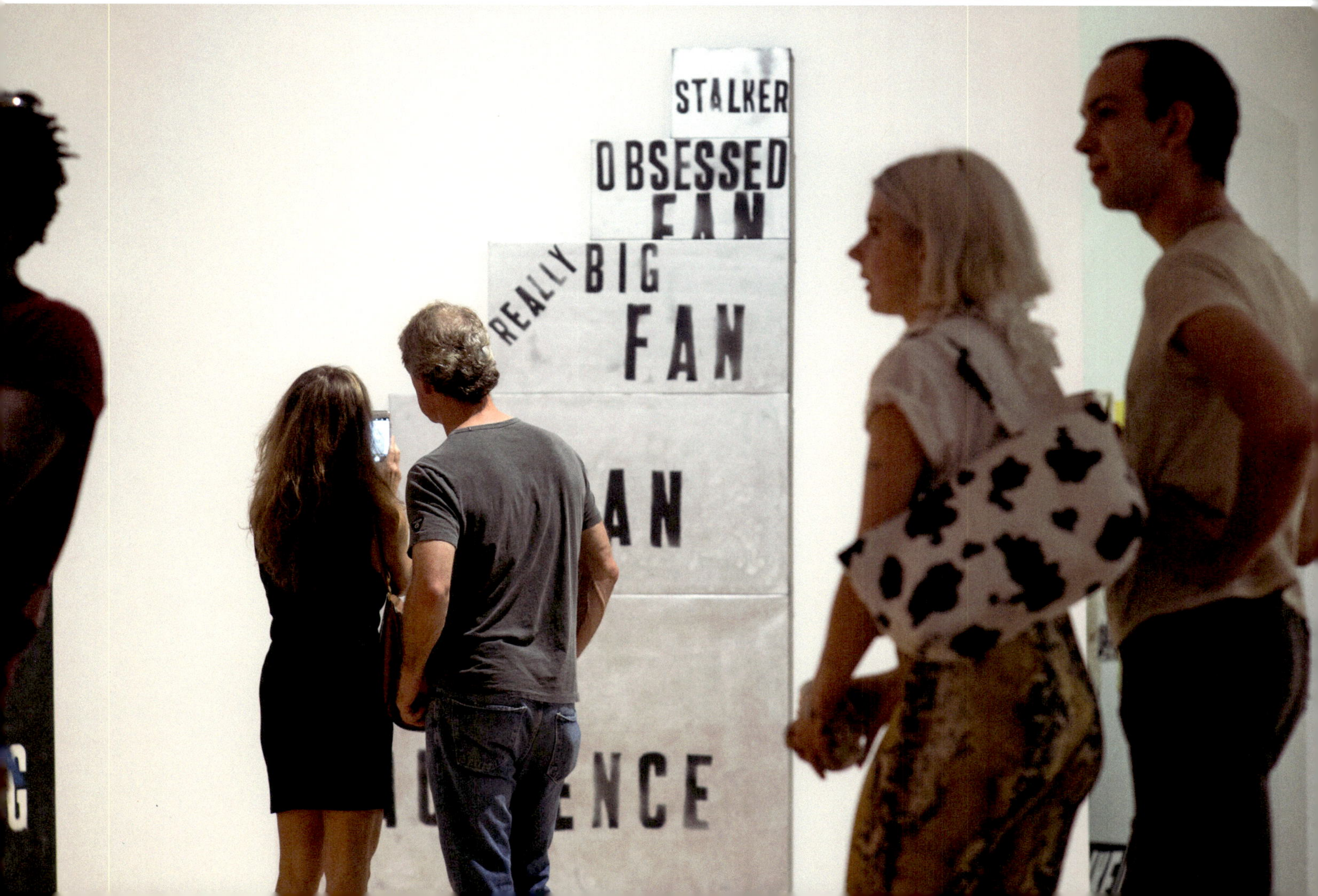
OBSESSED FAN
REALLY BIG FAN

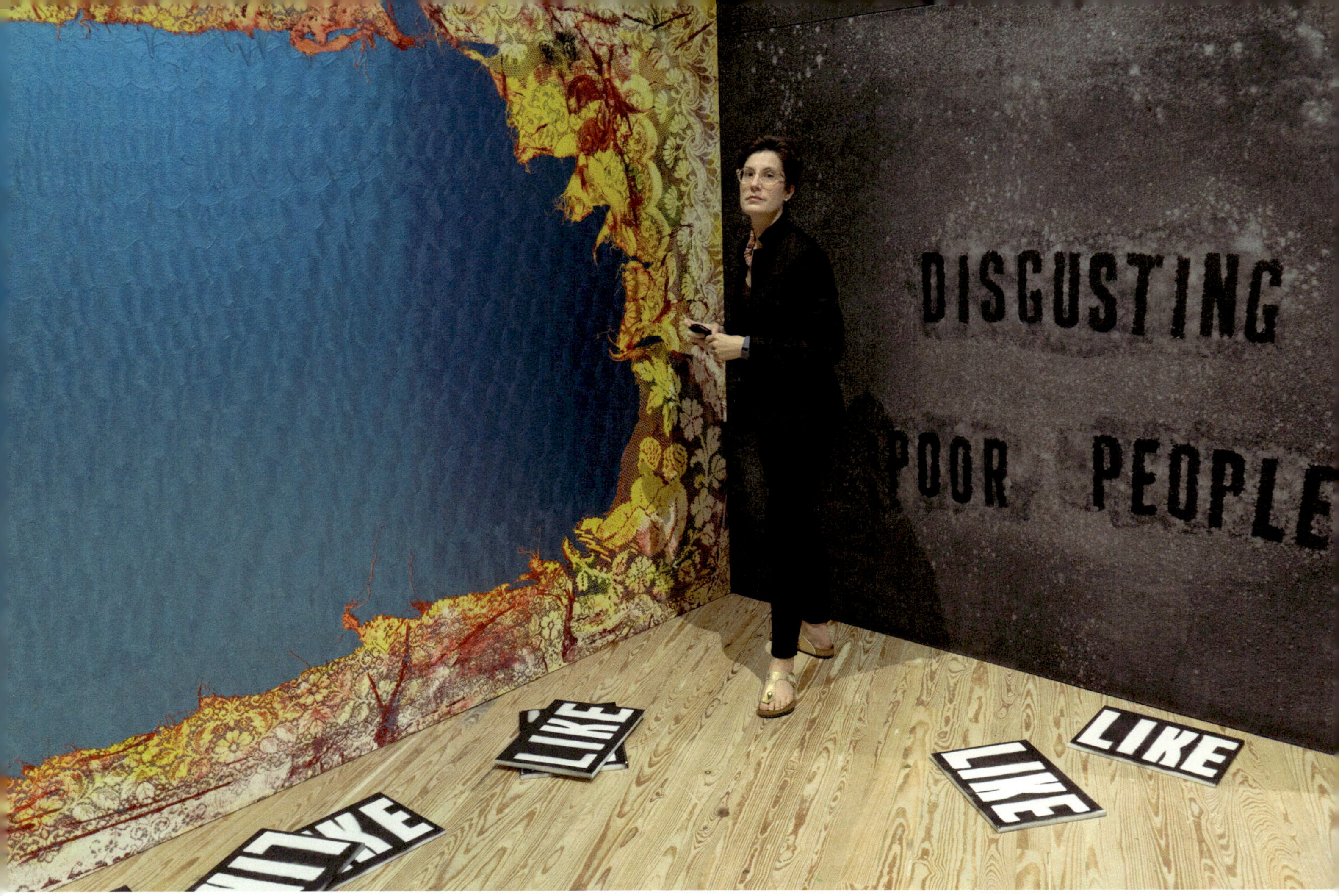

DISGUSTING
POOR PEOPLE
LIKE
LIKE
LIKE

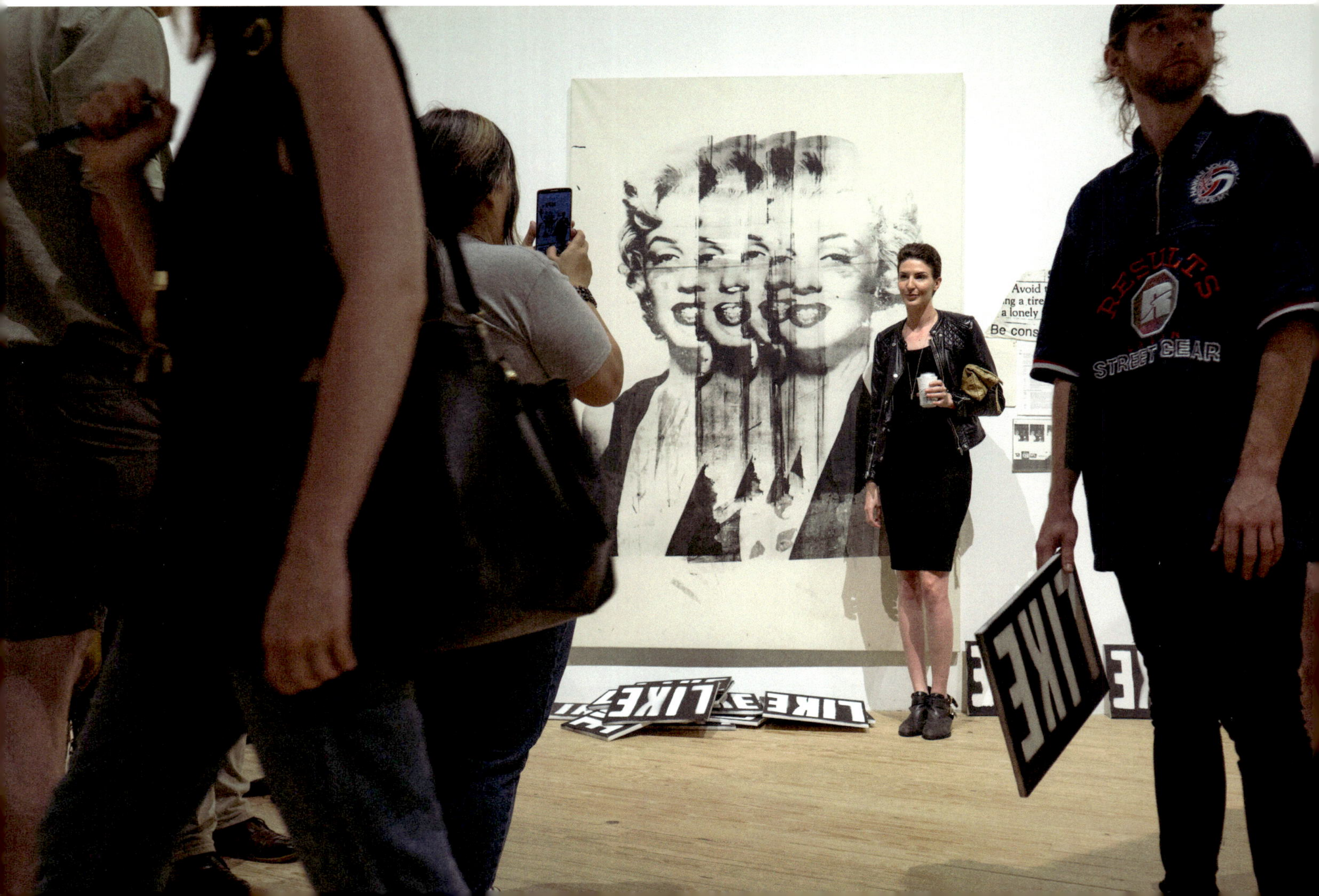

RESULTS
STREET GEAR
LIKE

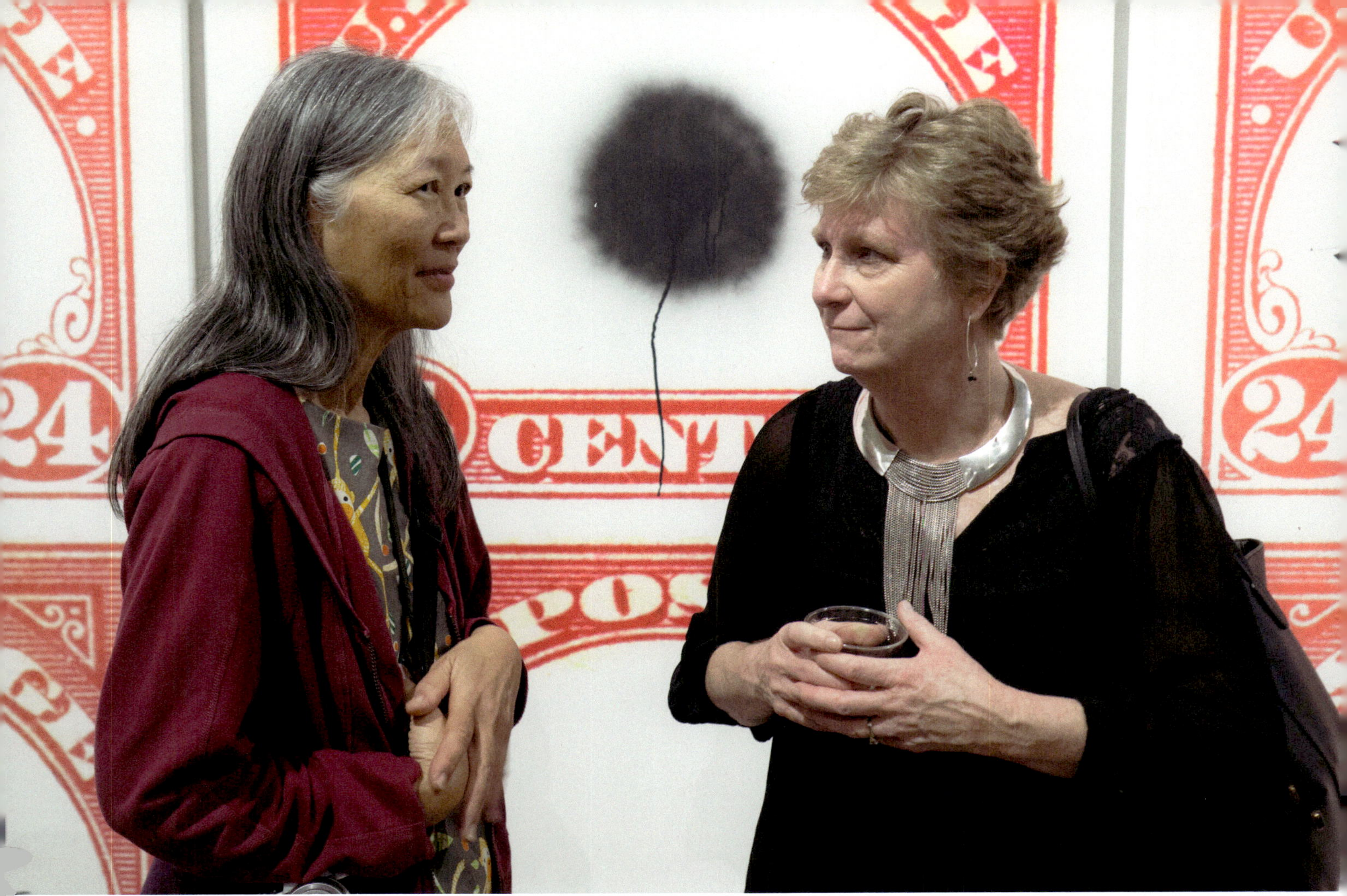

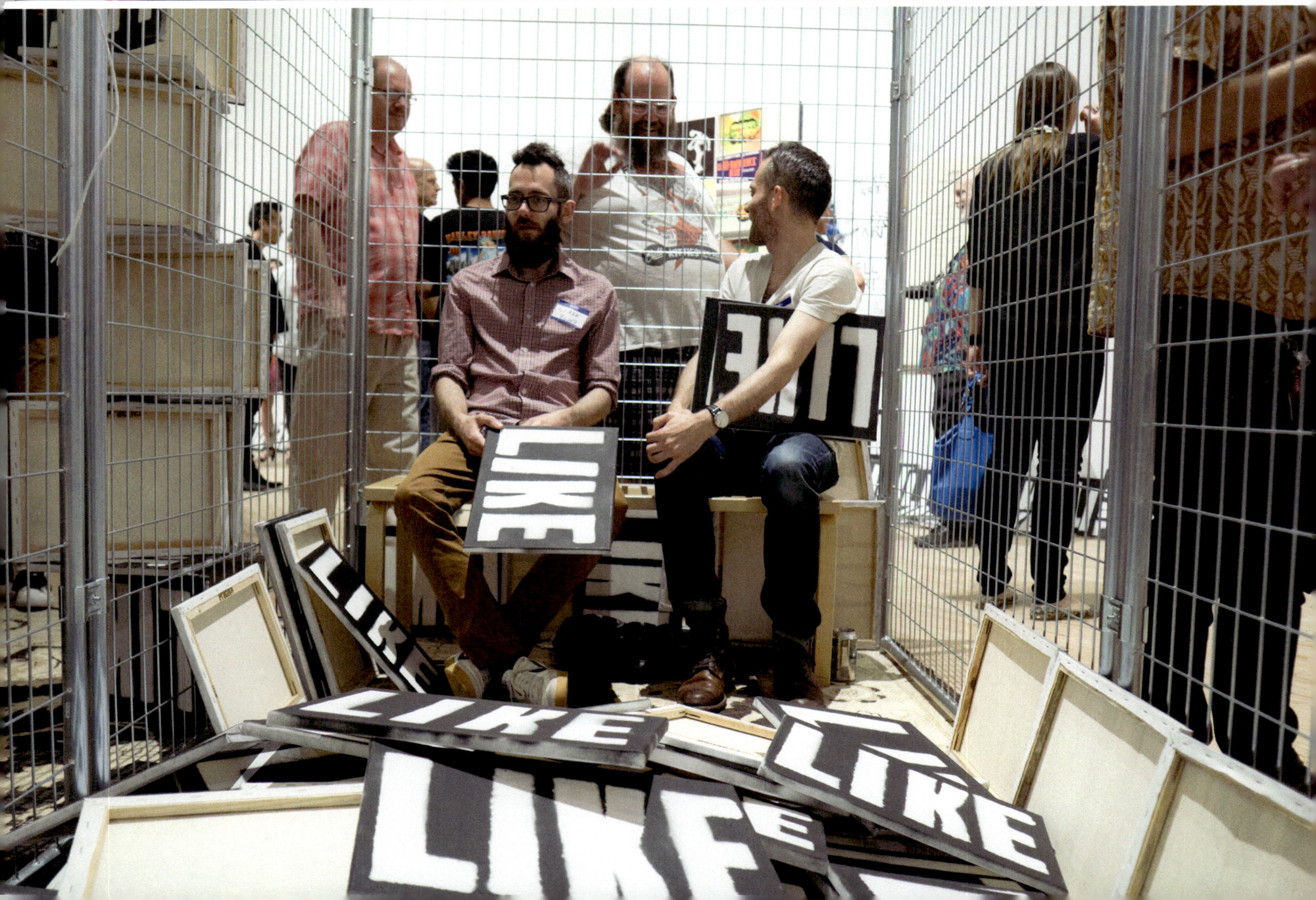

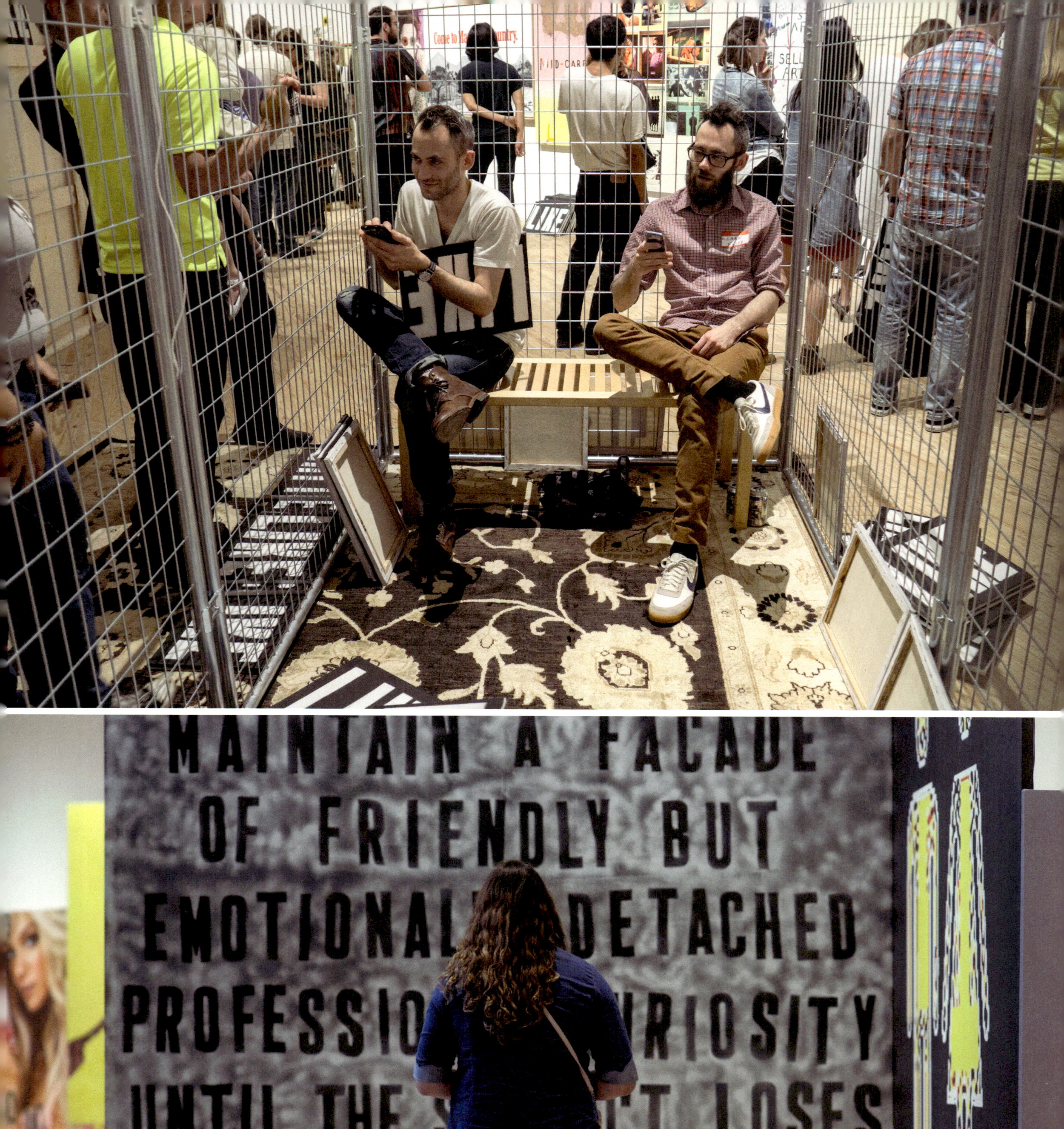
MAINTAIN A FACADE
OF FRIENDLY BUT
EMOTIONAL DETACHED
PROFESSIO URIOSITY
UNTIL THE S CT LOSES
CONSCI NESS

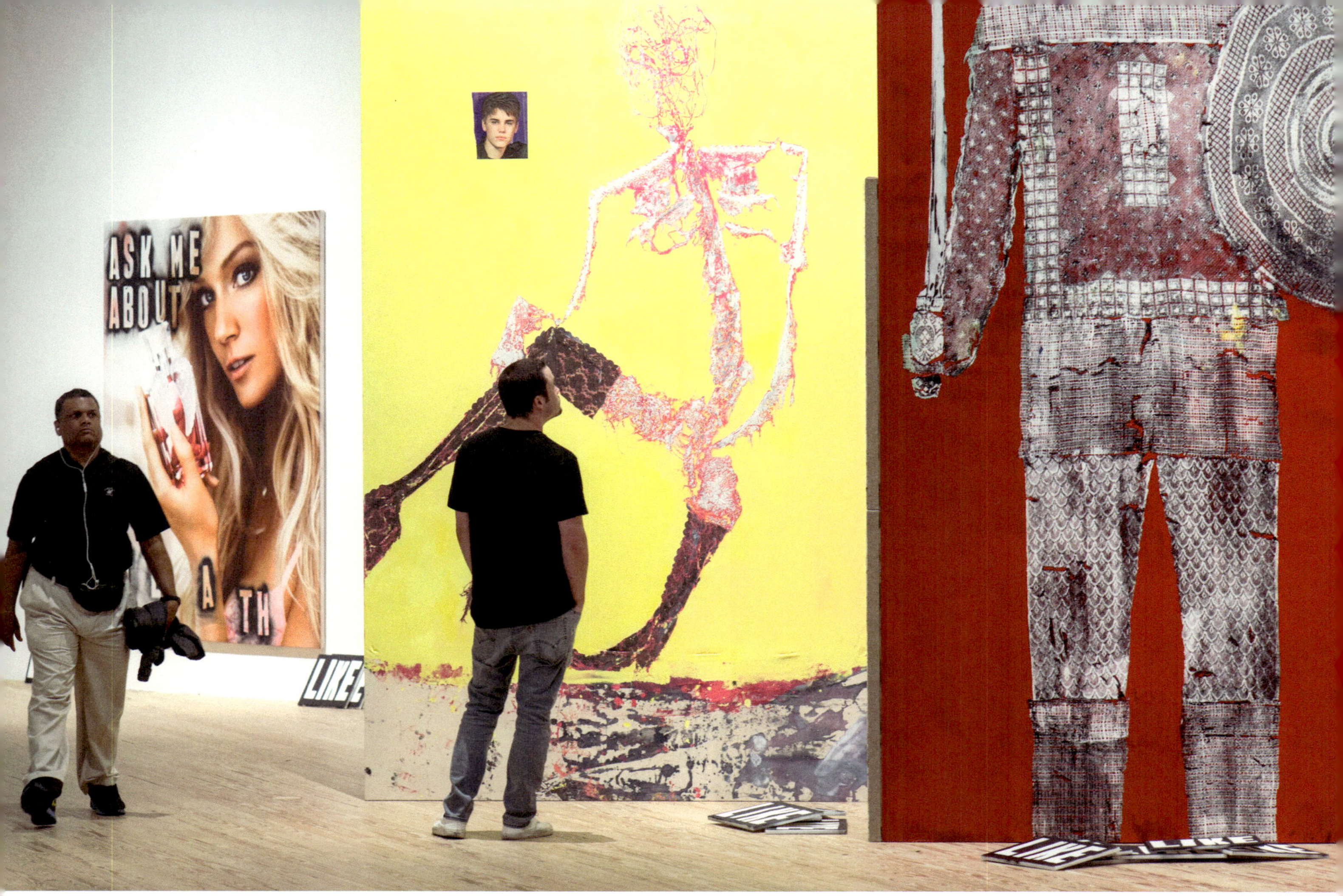

ASK ME
ABOUT
LIKE
SEUMS 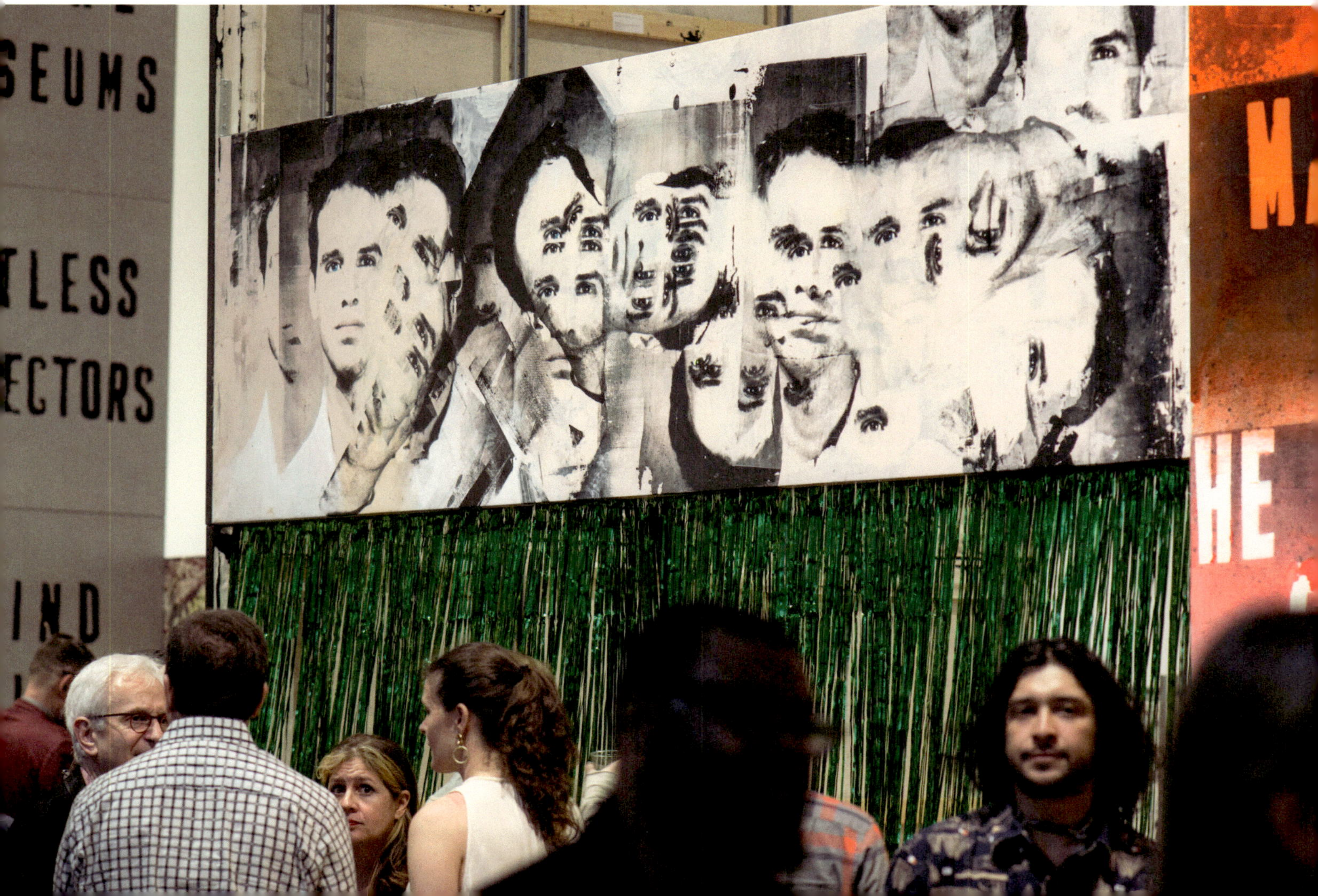
TLESS
ECTORS
IND
HE

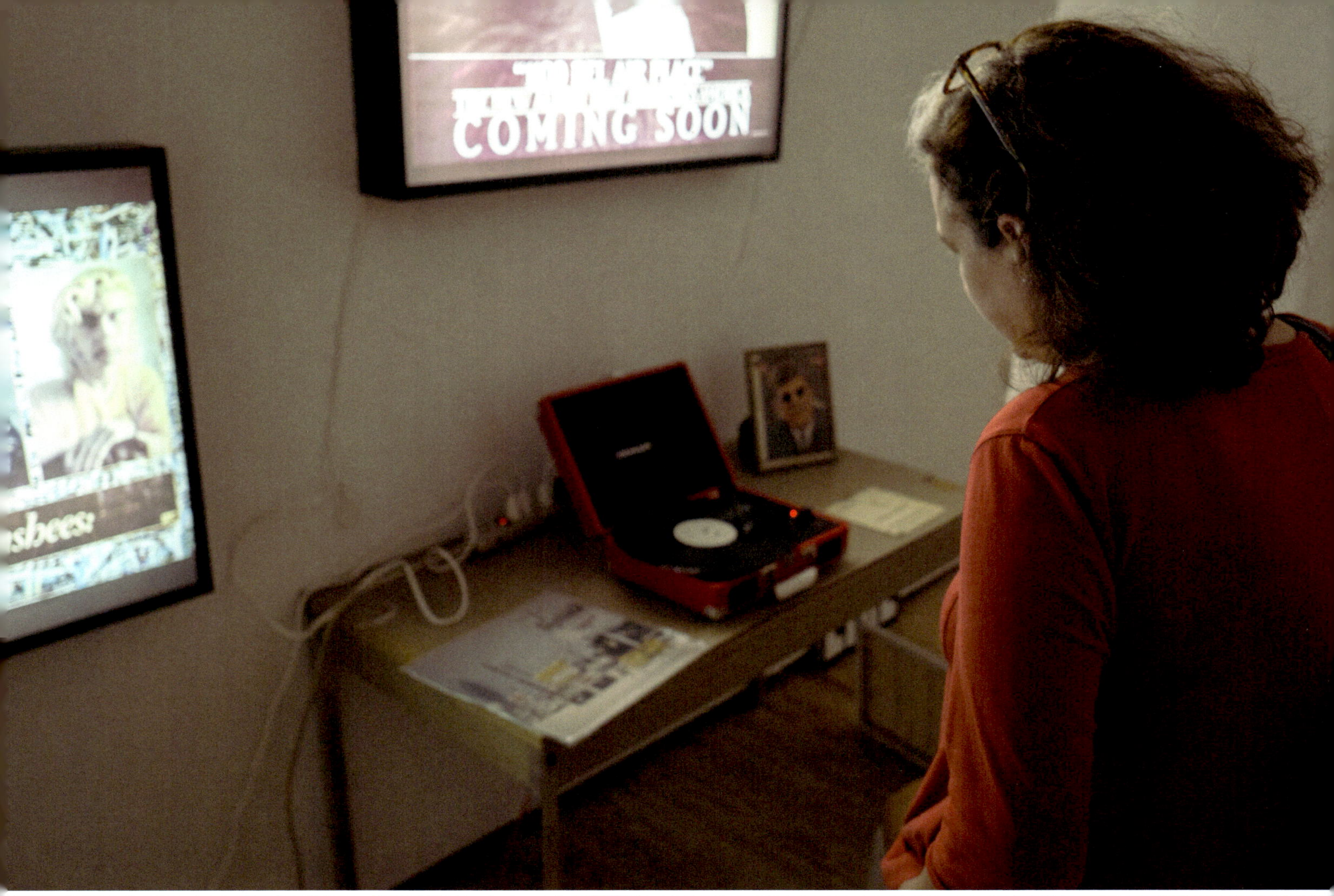

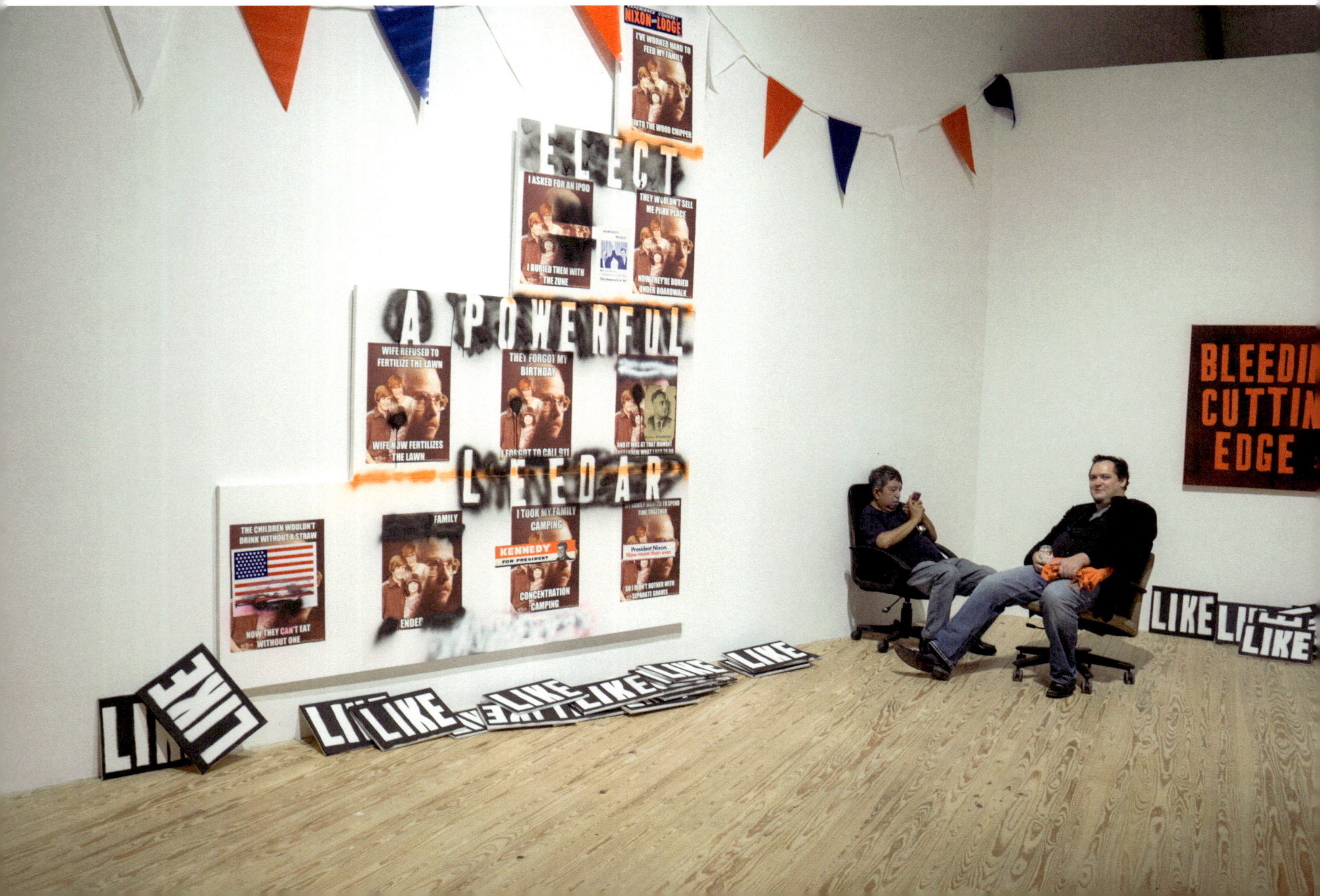

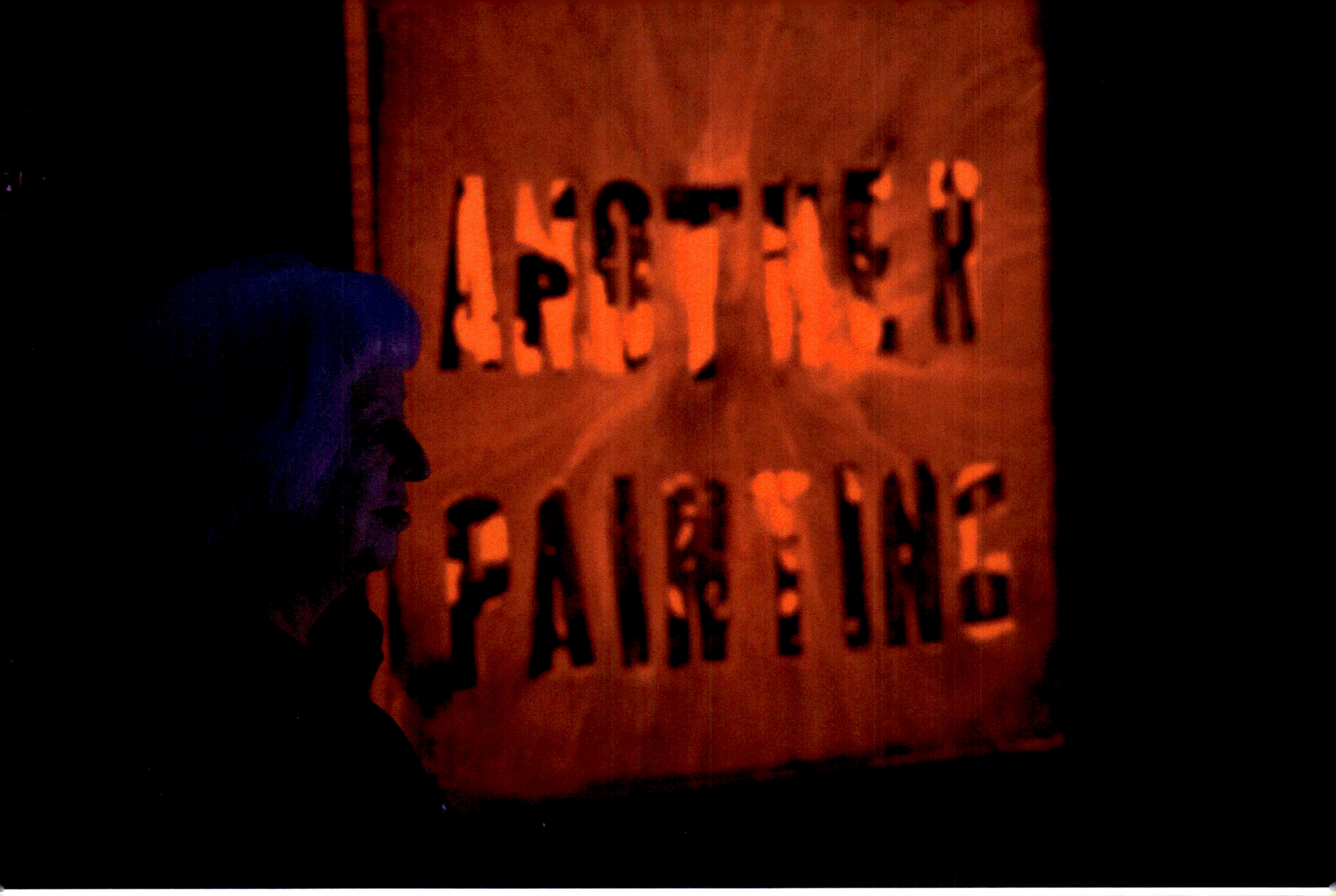

ANOTHER 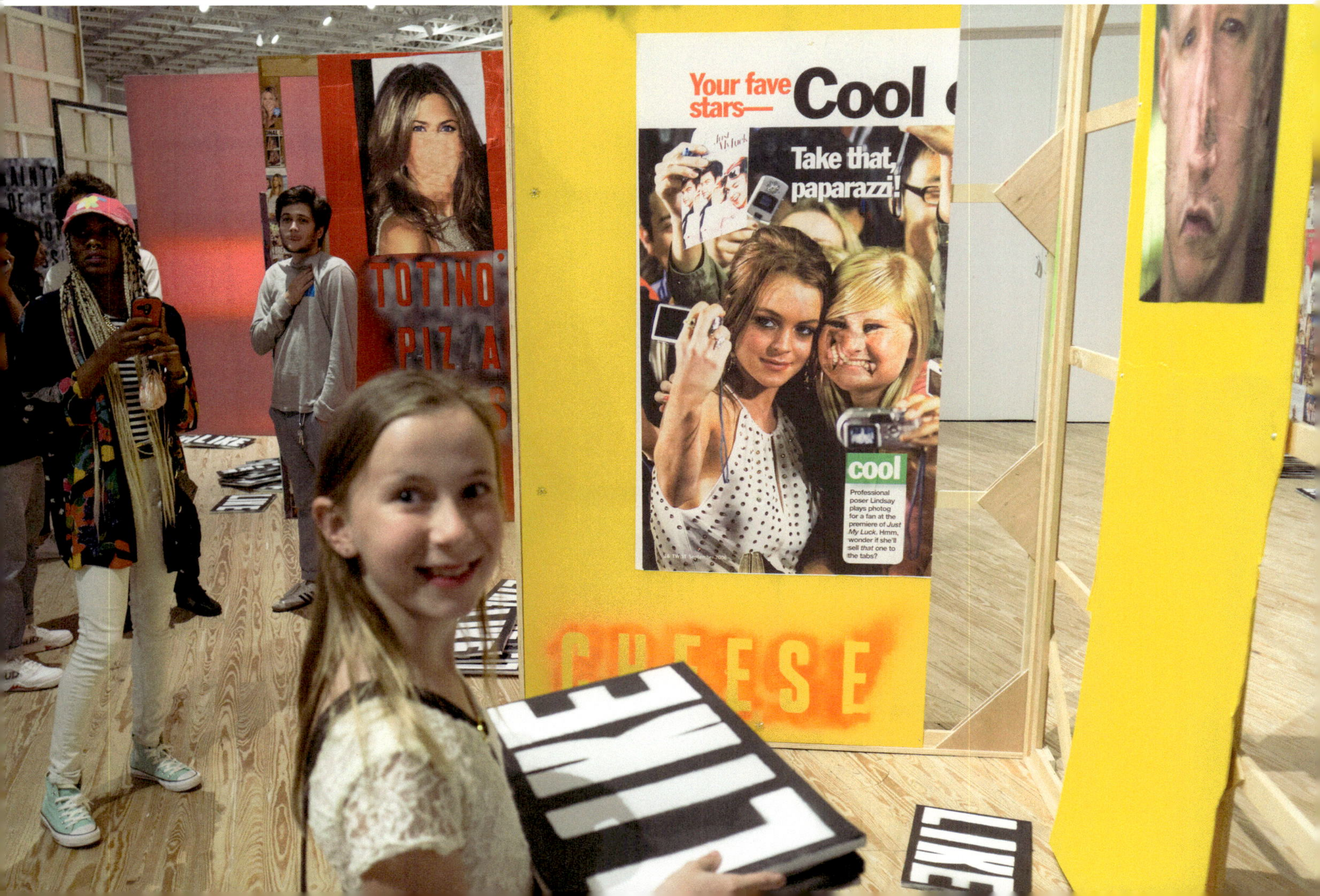
PAINTING

TOTINO
PIZ A
Your fave stars—
Cool
Take that, paparazzi!
cool
Professional poser Lindsay plays photog for a fan at the premiere of *Just My Luck*. Hmm, wonder if she'll sell *that* one to the tabs?
CHEESE
LIKE

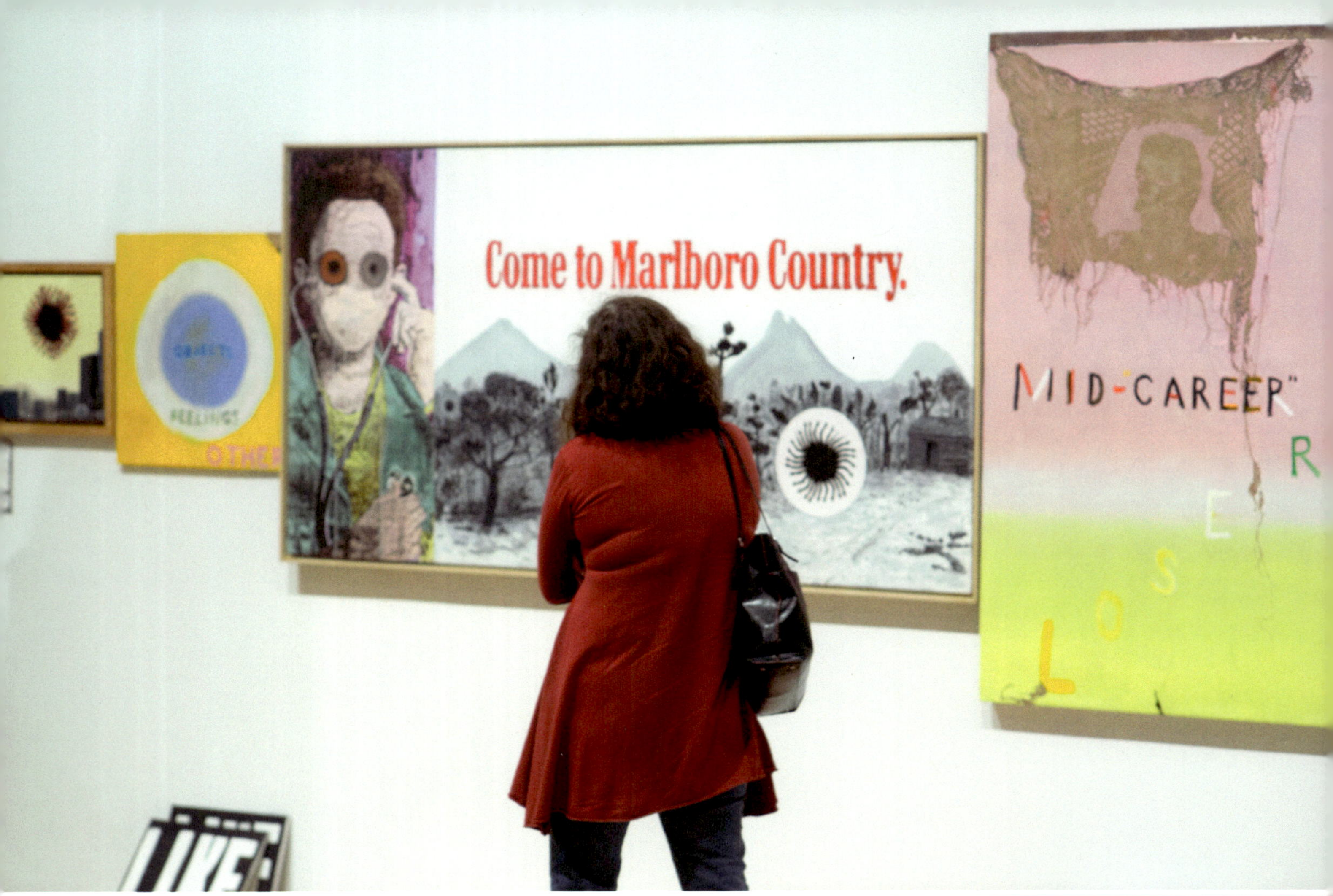

Come to Marlboro Country.
MID-CAREER"
LOSER

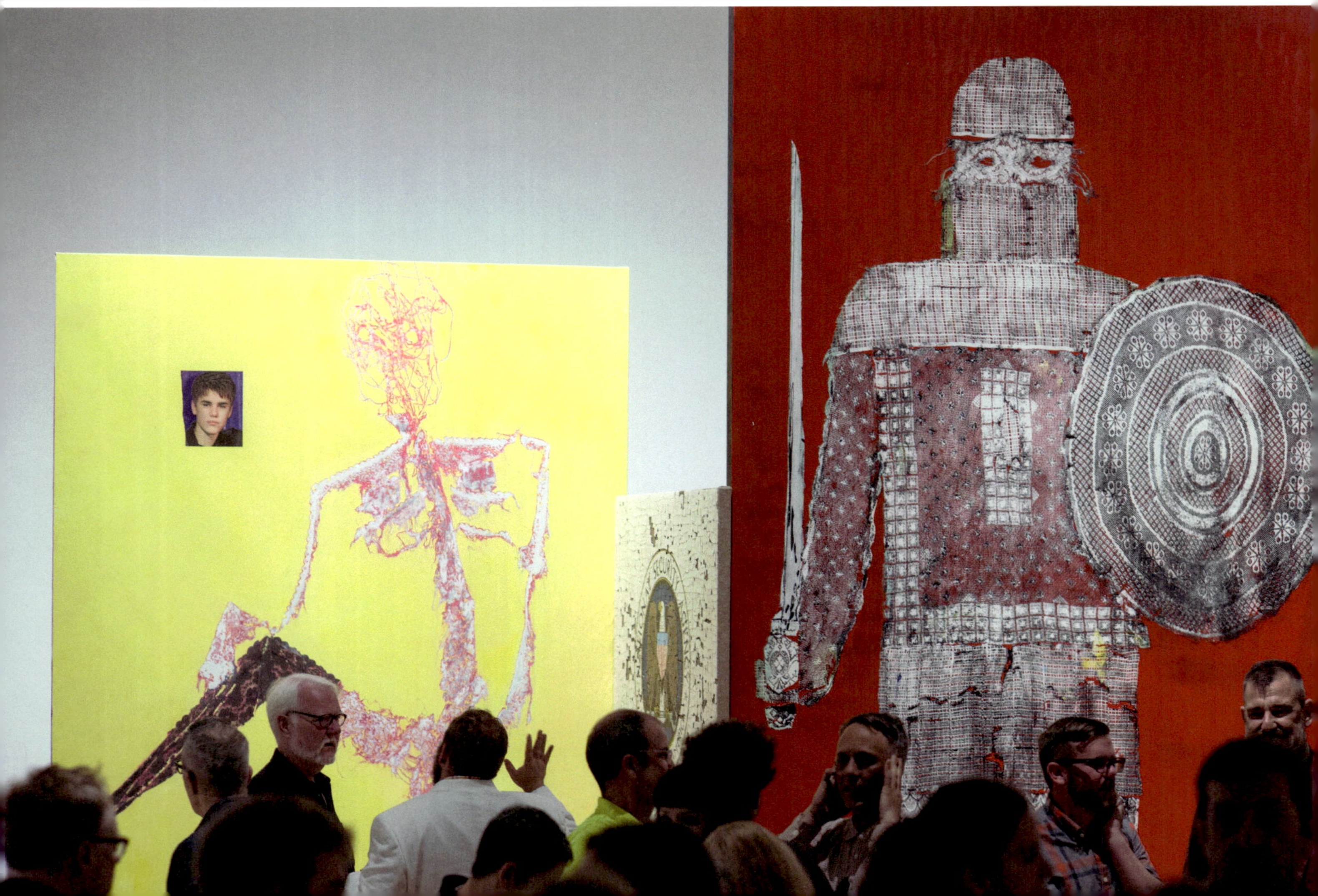

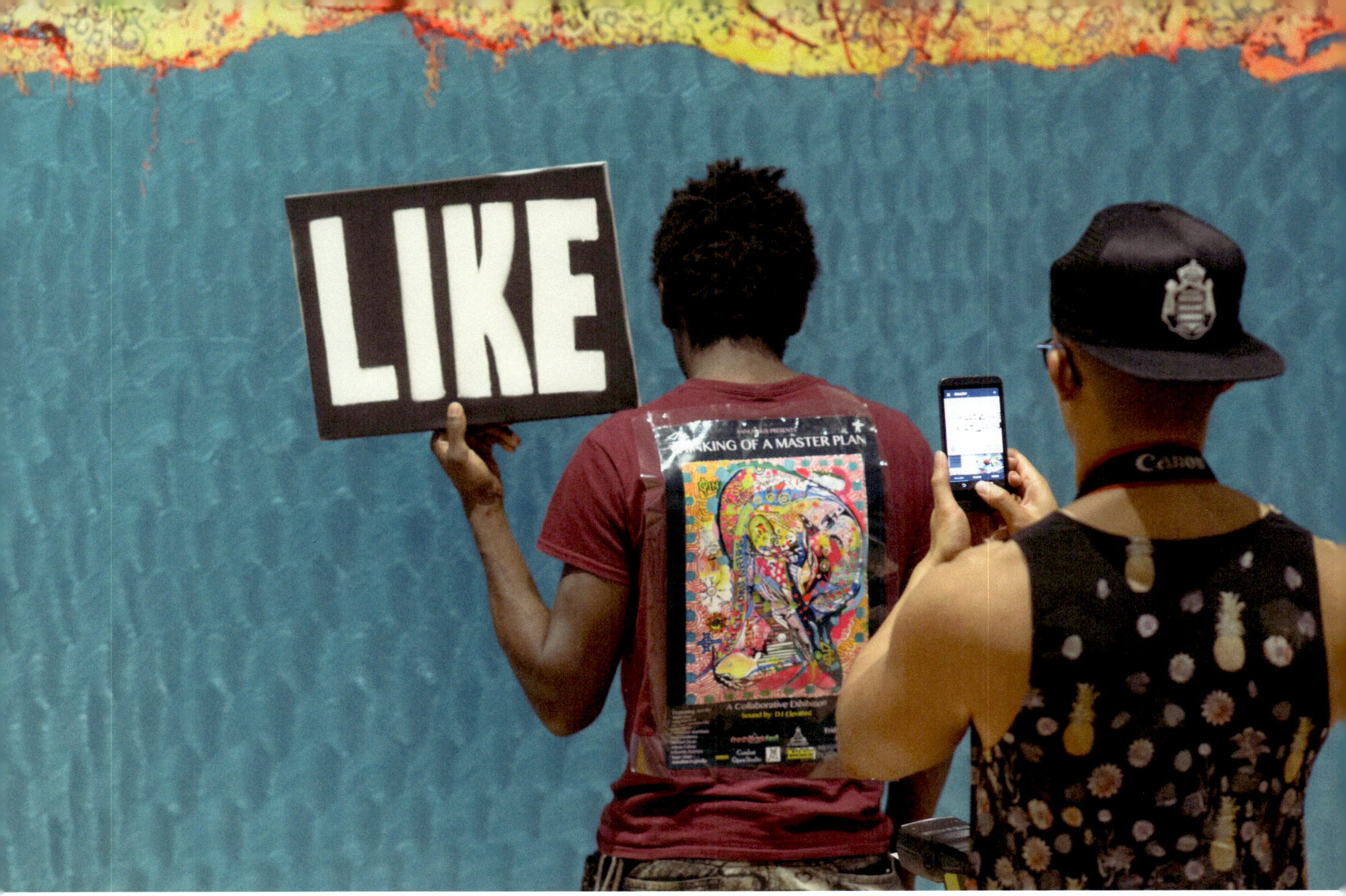

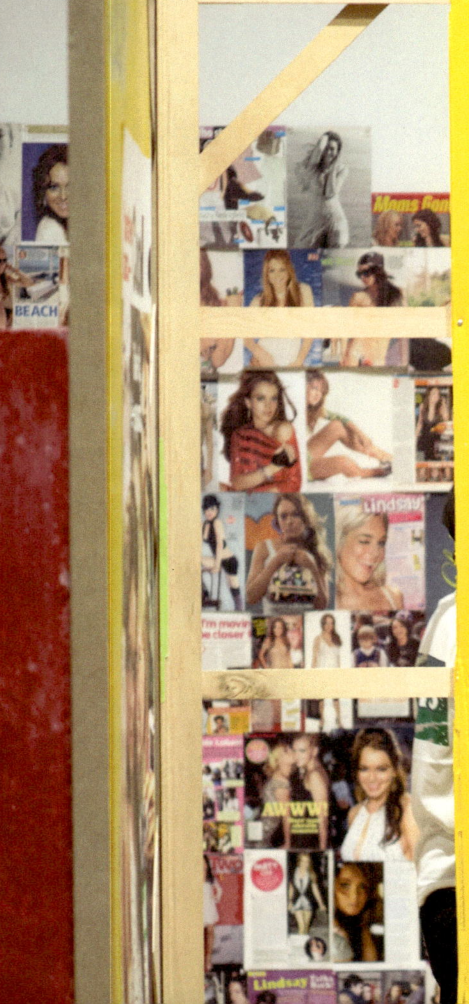

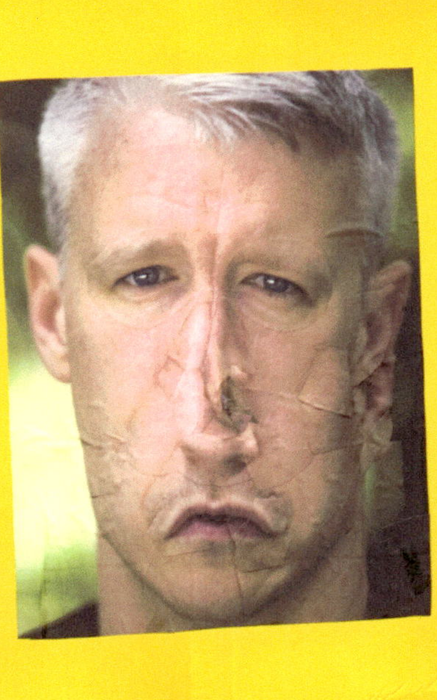

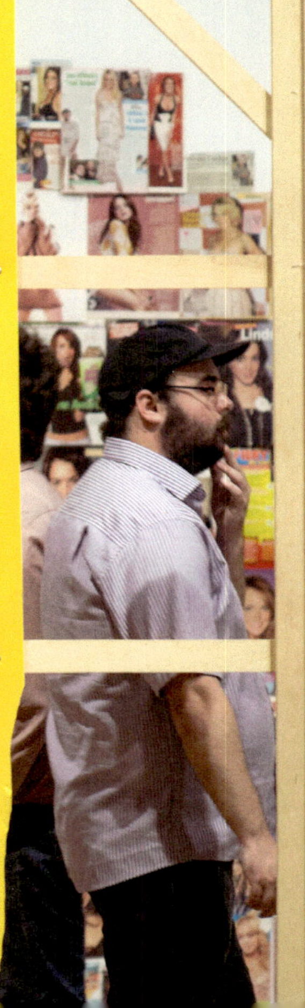

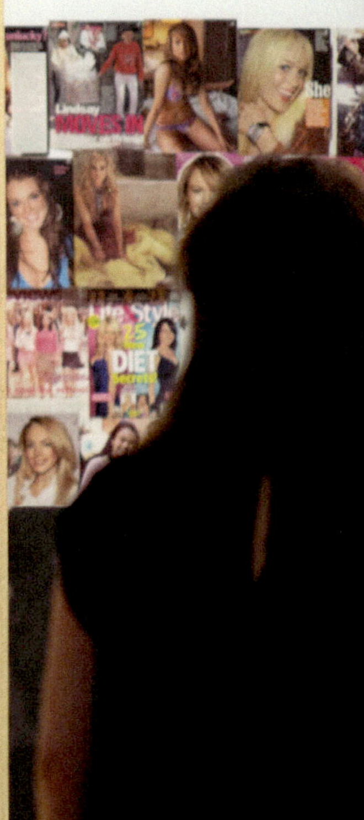

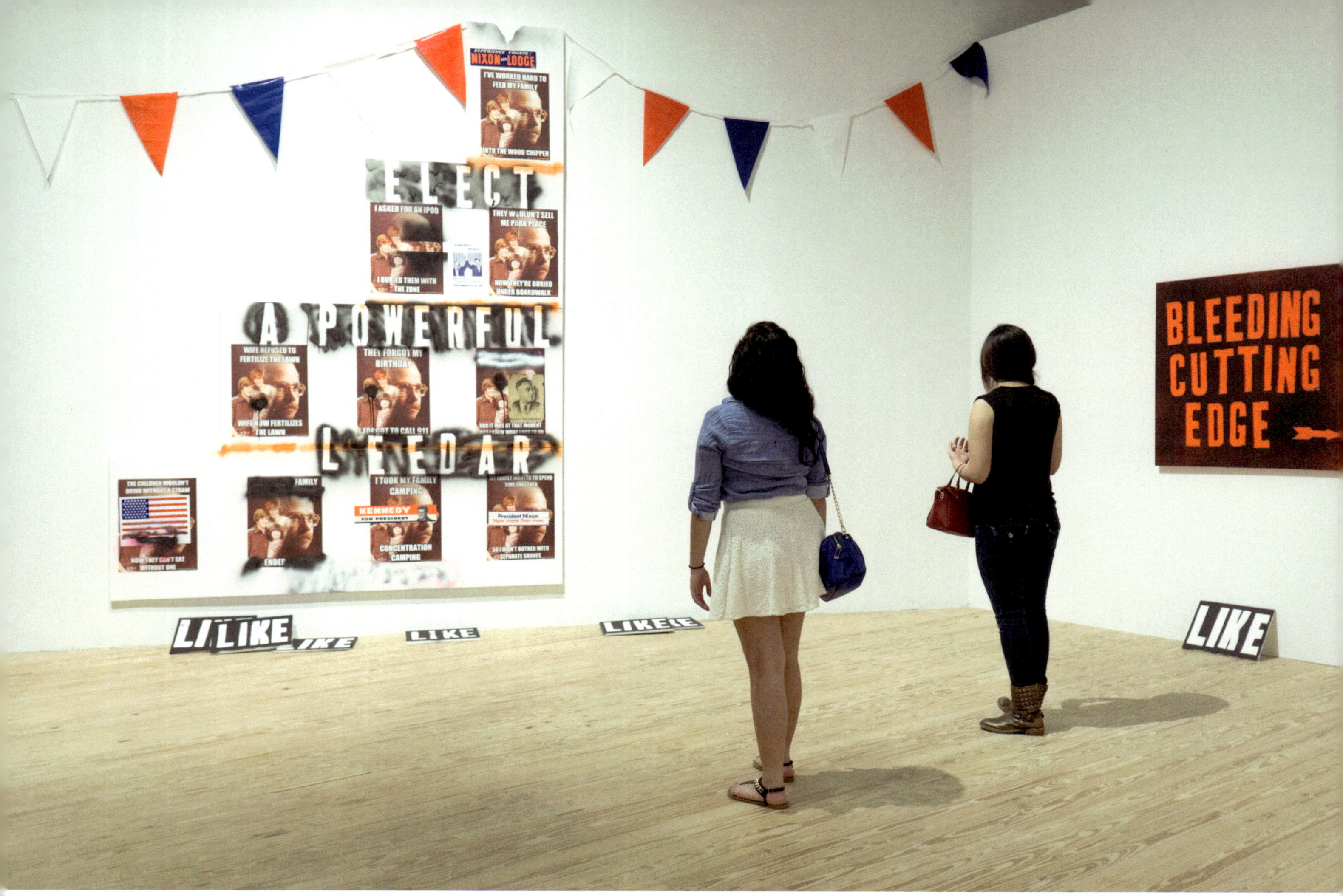
NIXON LODGE
I'VE WORKED HARD TO FEED MY FAMILY
INTO THE WOOD CHIPPER
ELECT
I ASKED FOR AN IPOD
A POWERFUL
THEY FORGOT MY BIRTHDAY
LEEDAR
I TOOK MY FAMILY CAMPING
KENNEDY FOR PRESIDENT
CONCENTRATION CAMPING
President Nixon
LIKE
BLEEDING
CUTTING
EDGE

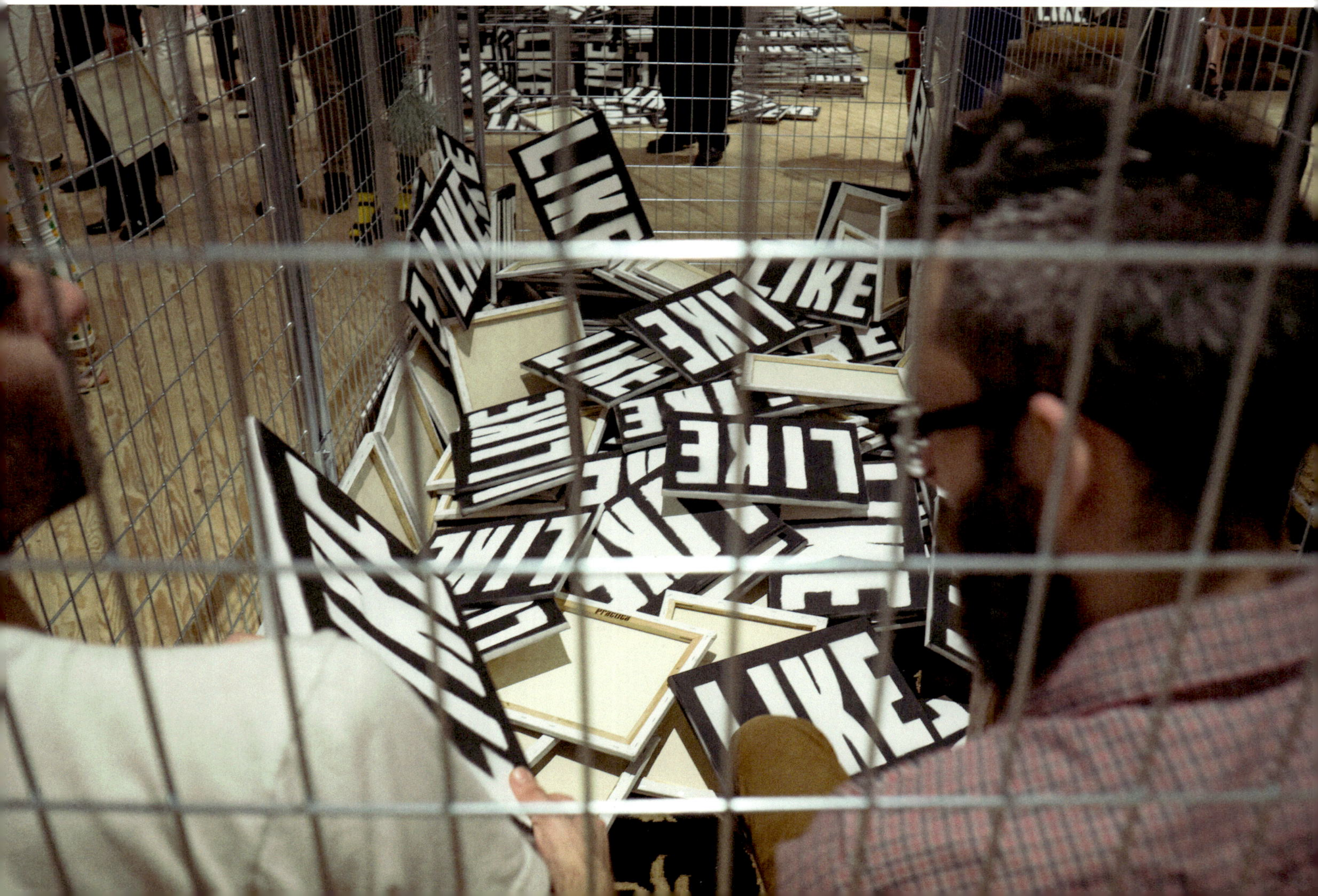
LIKE

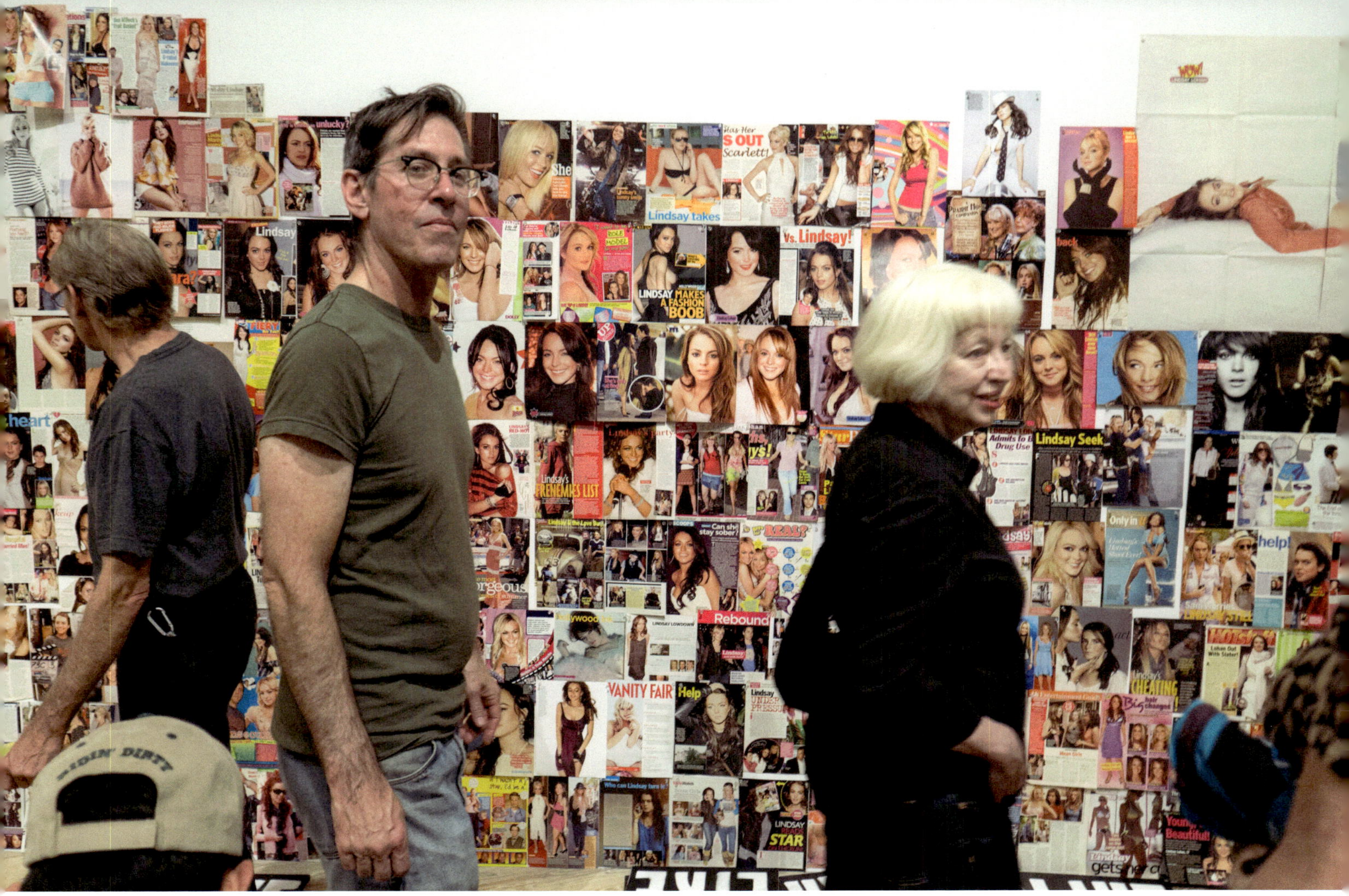

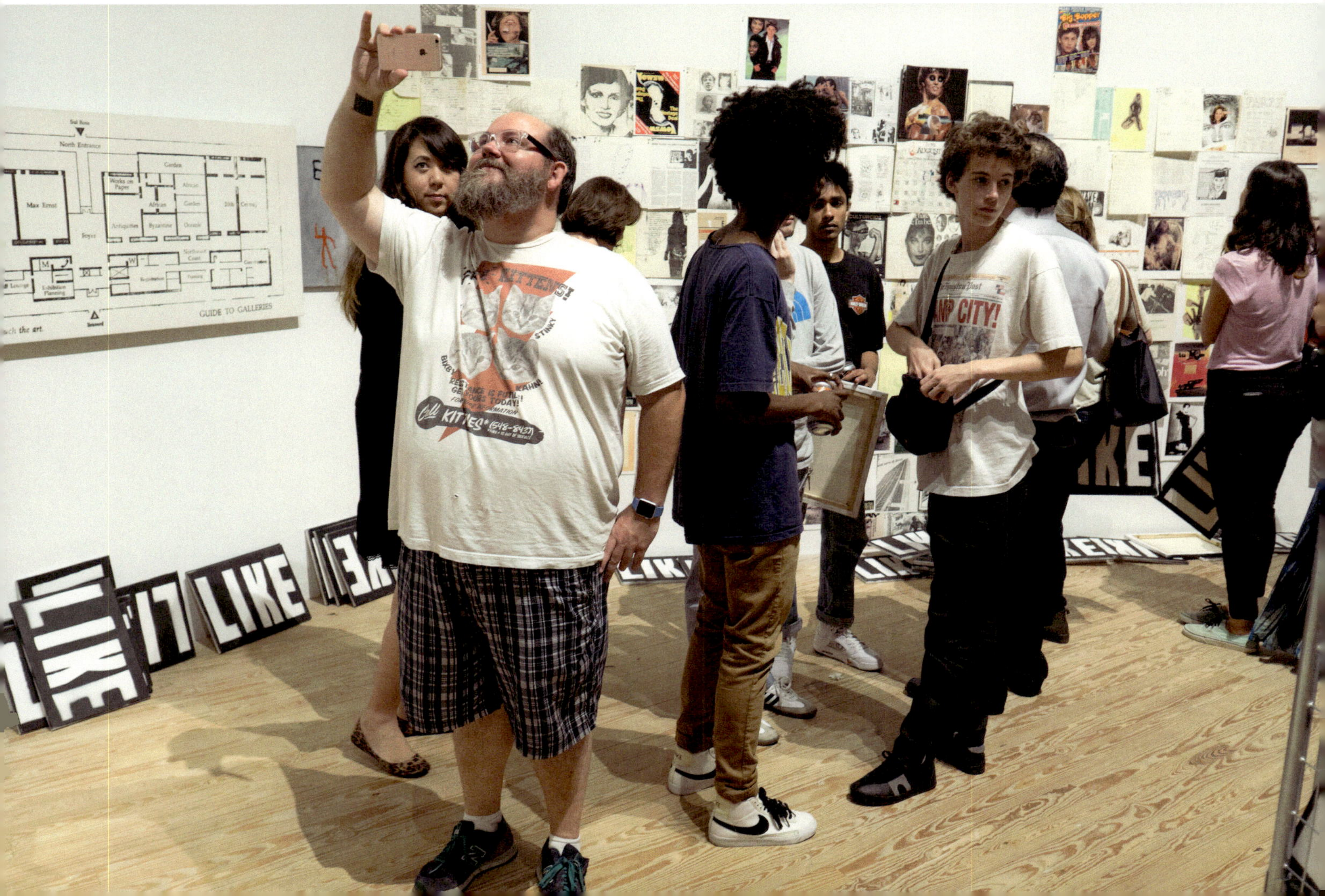

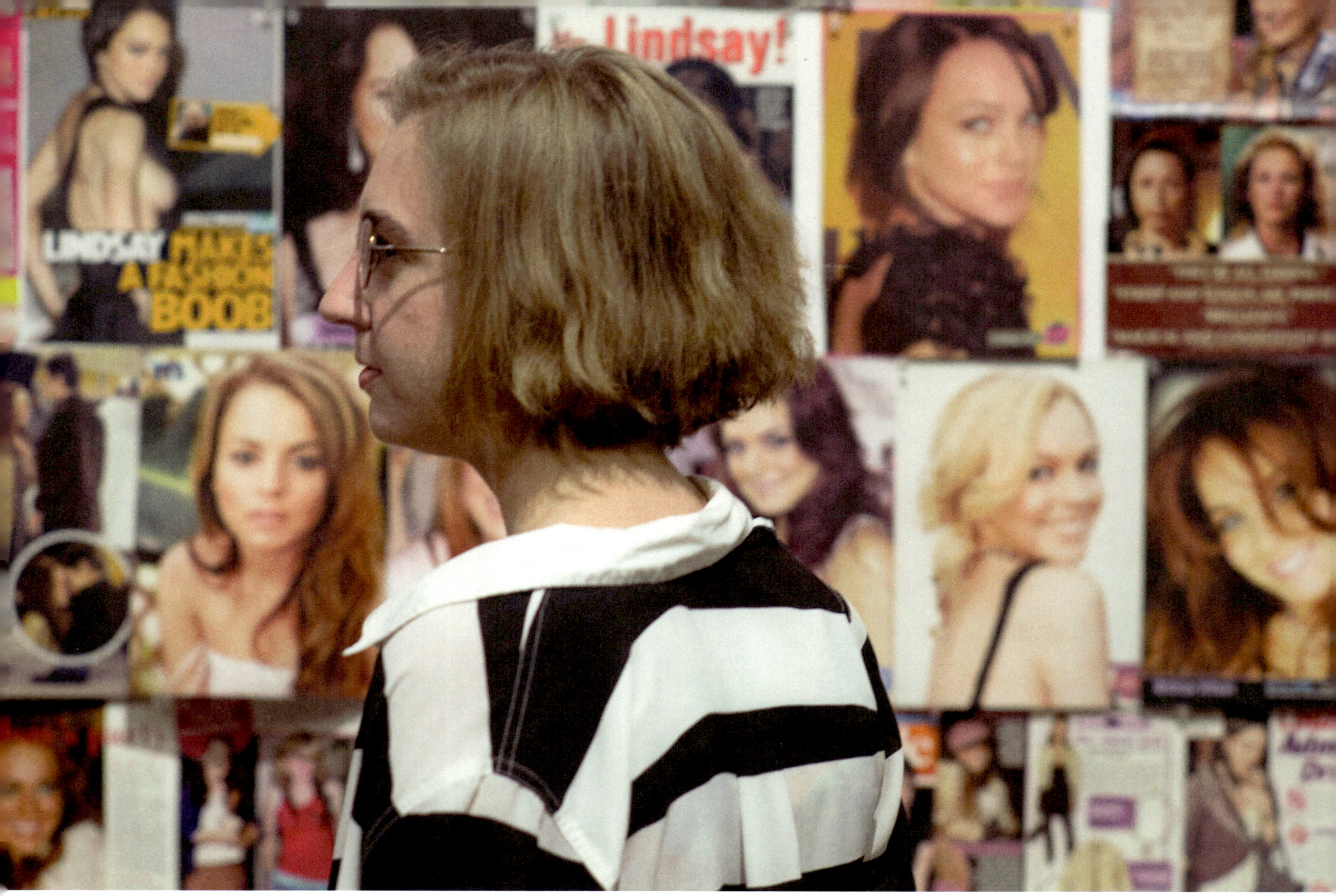

Lindsay!
LINDSAY MAKES A FASHION BOOB
24 CENTS 24 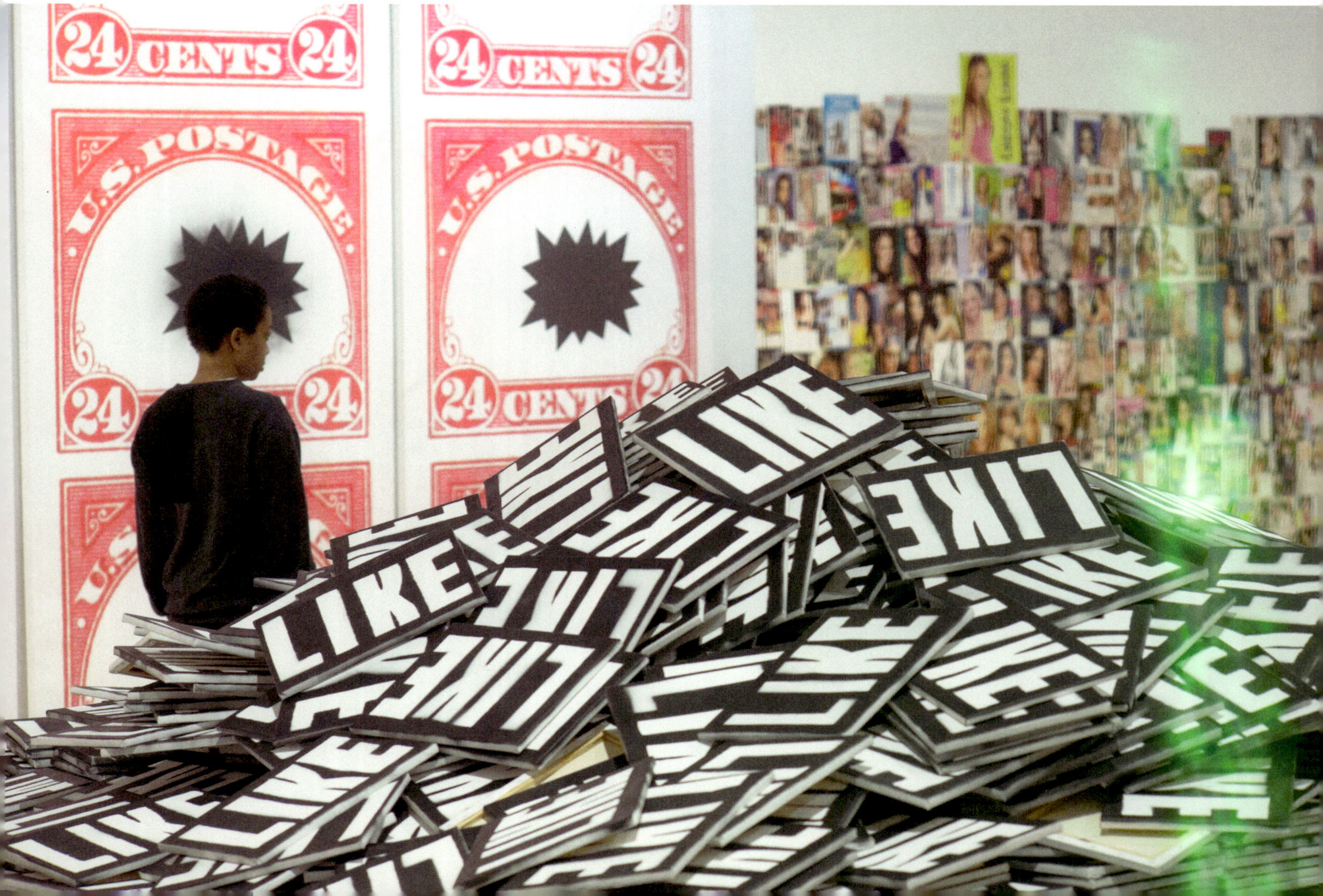
U.S. POSTAGE
24 CENTS 24
LIKE

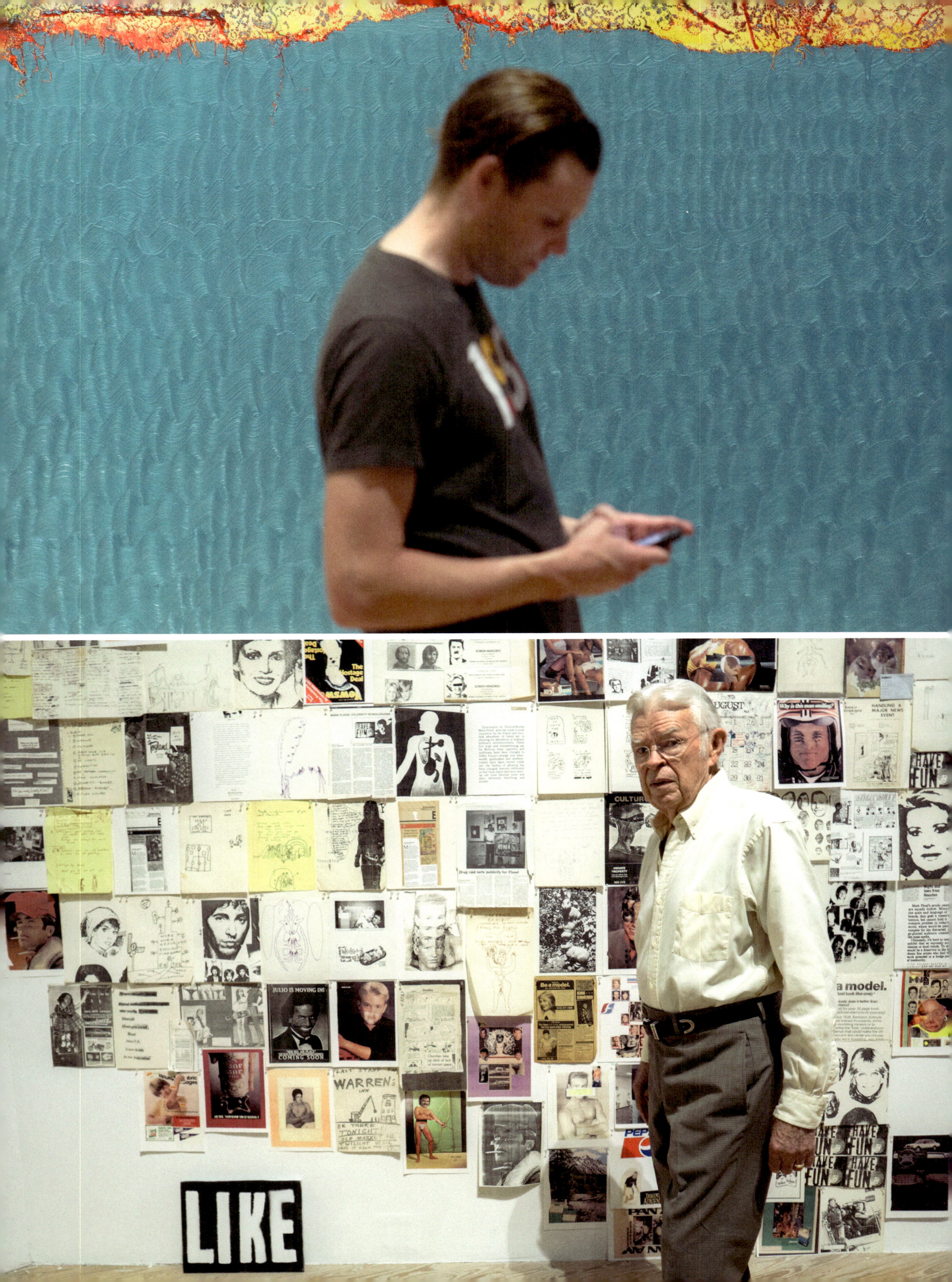

The Hostage Deal
JULIO IS MOVING IN!
COMING SOON
WARREN
Be a model.
a model.
CULTURE
HAVE FUN
LIKE

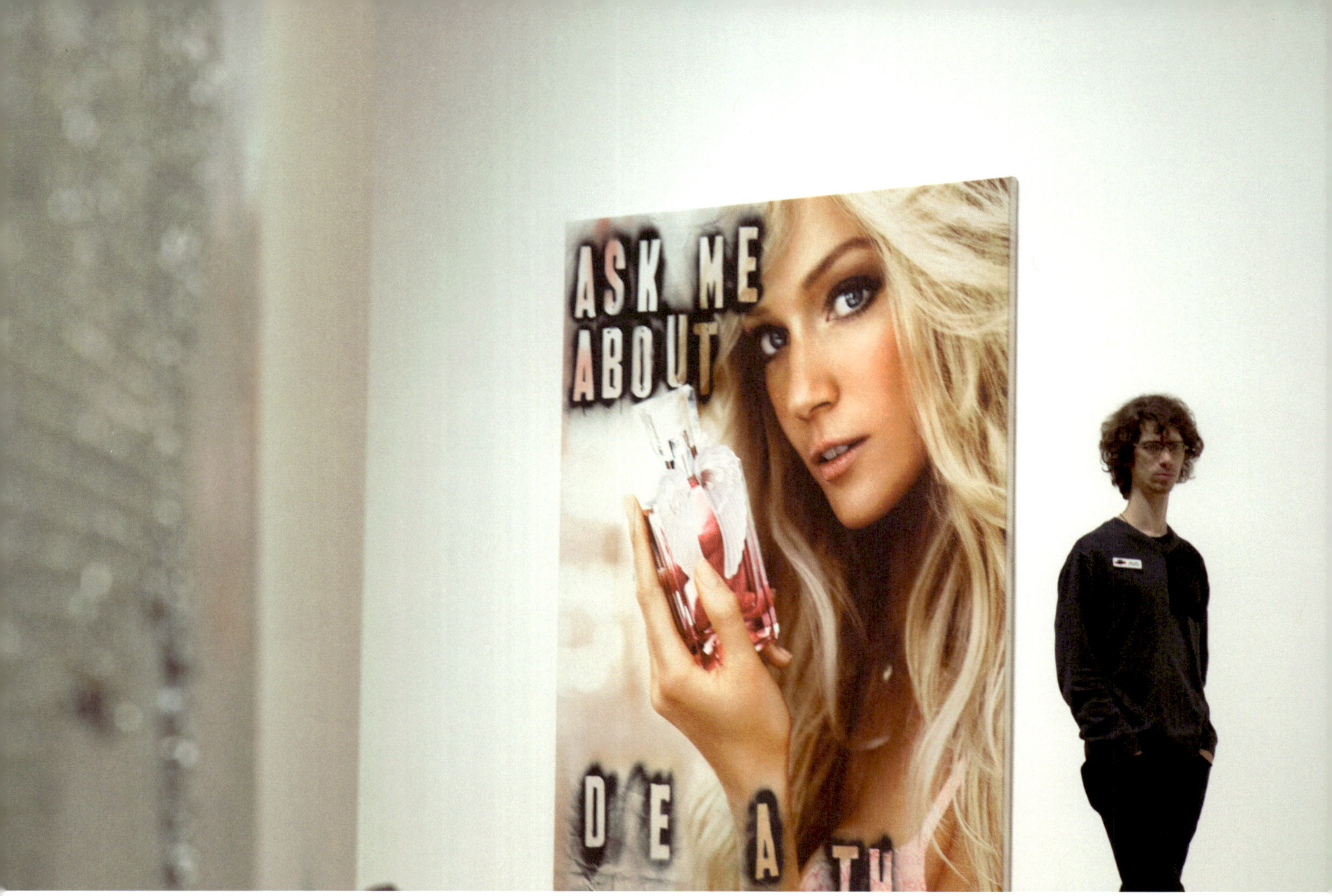
ASK ME
ABOUT
D E A TH

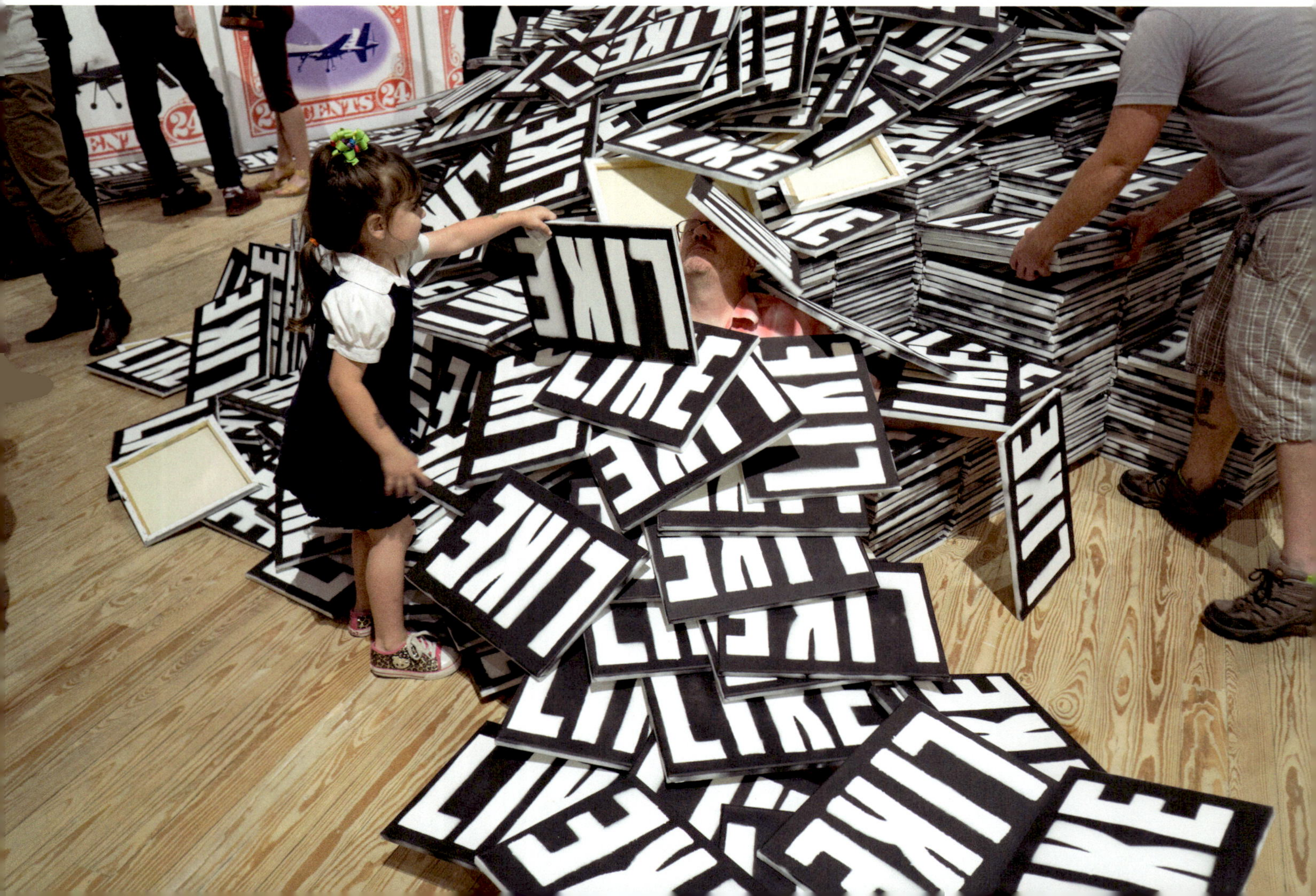
LIKE
CENTS 24

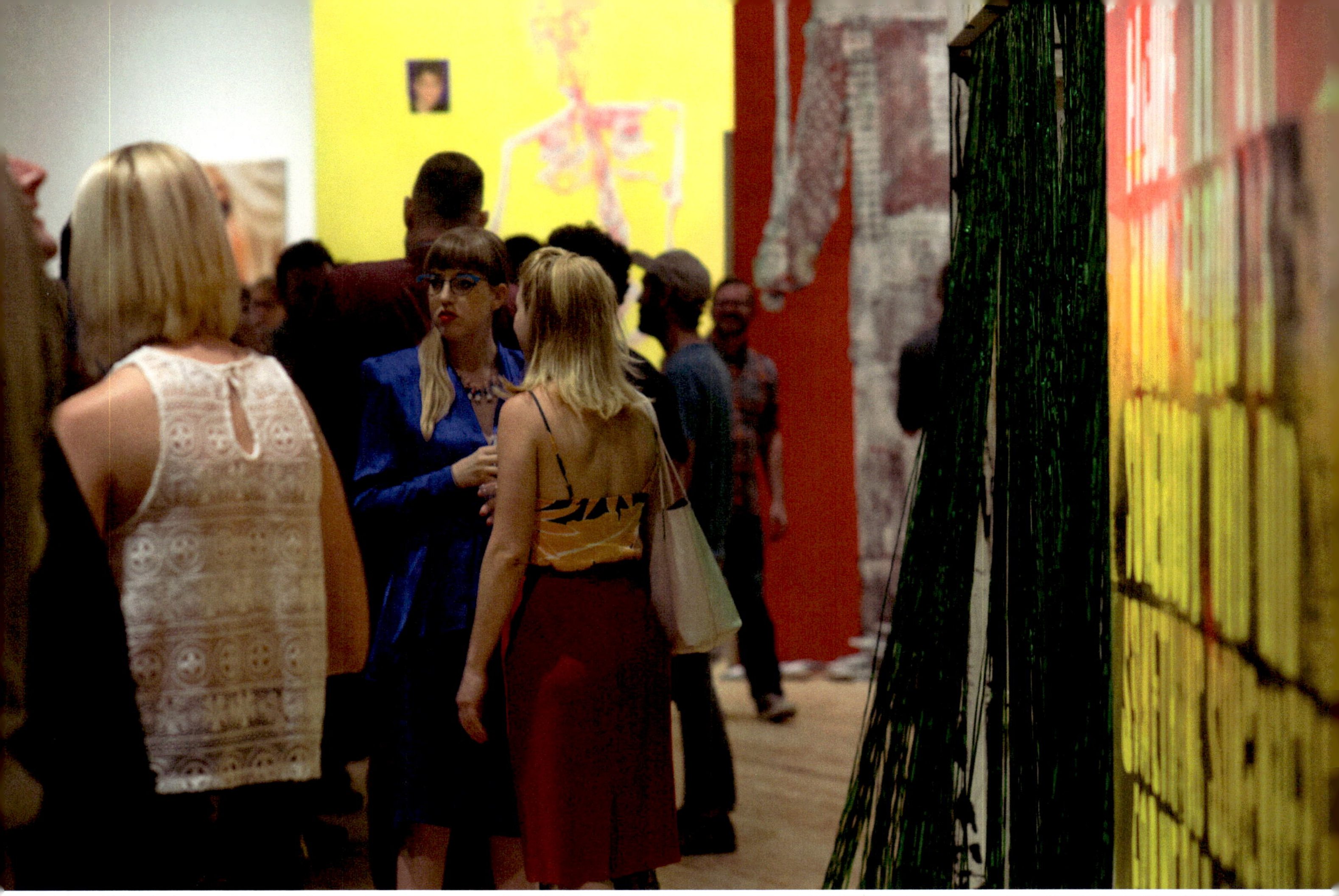

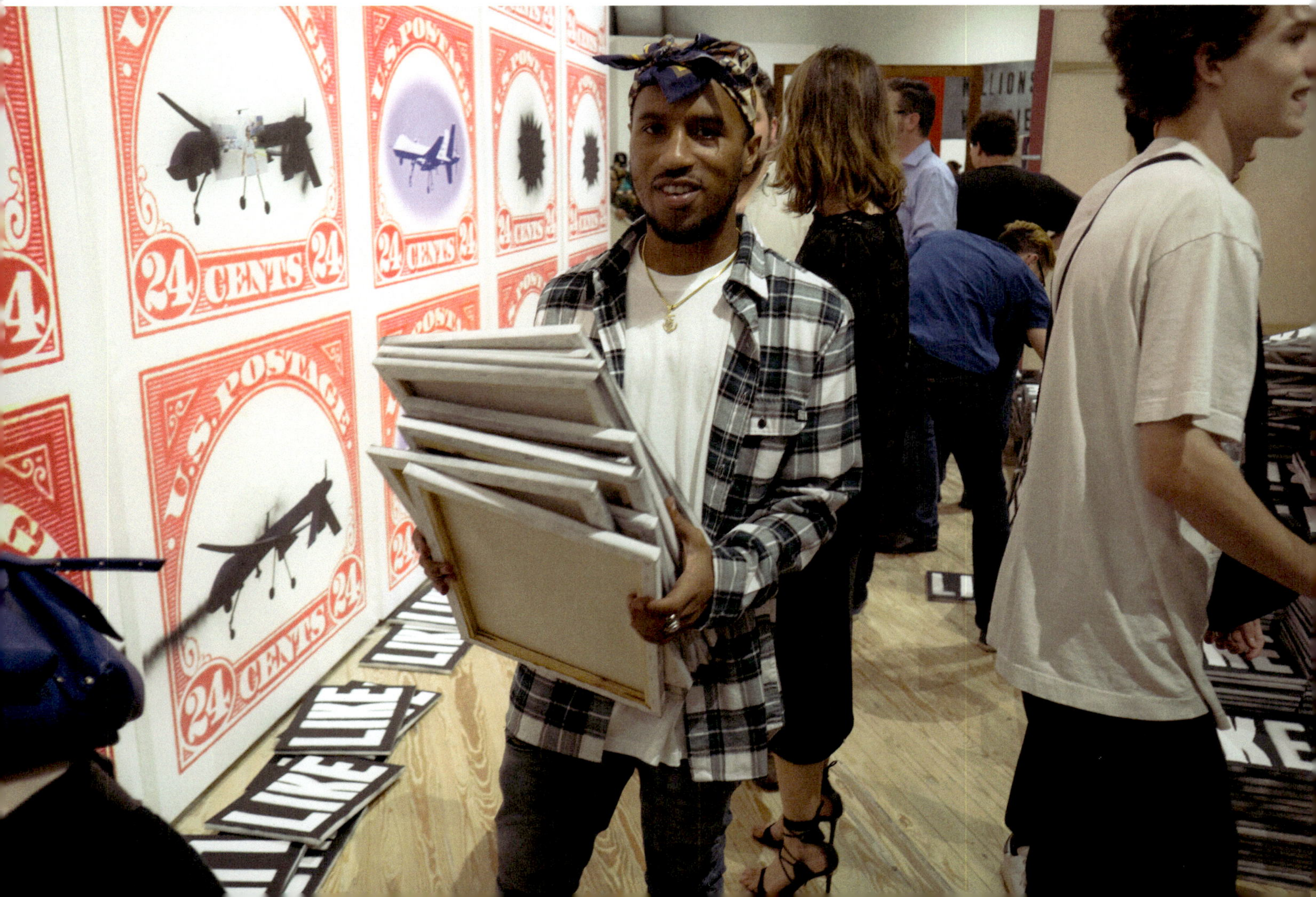

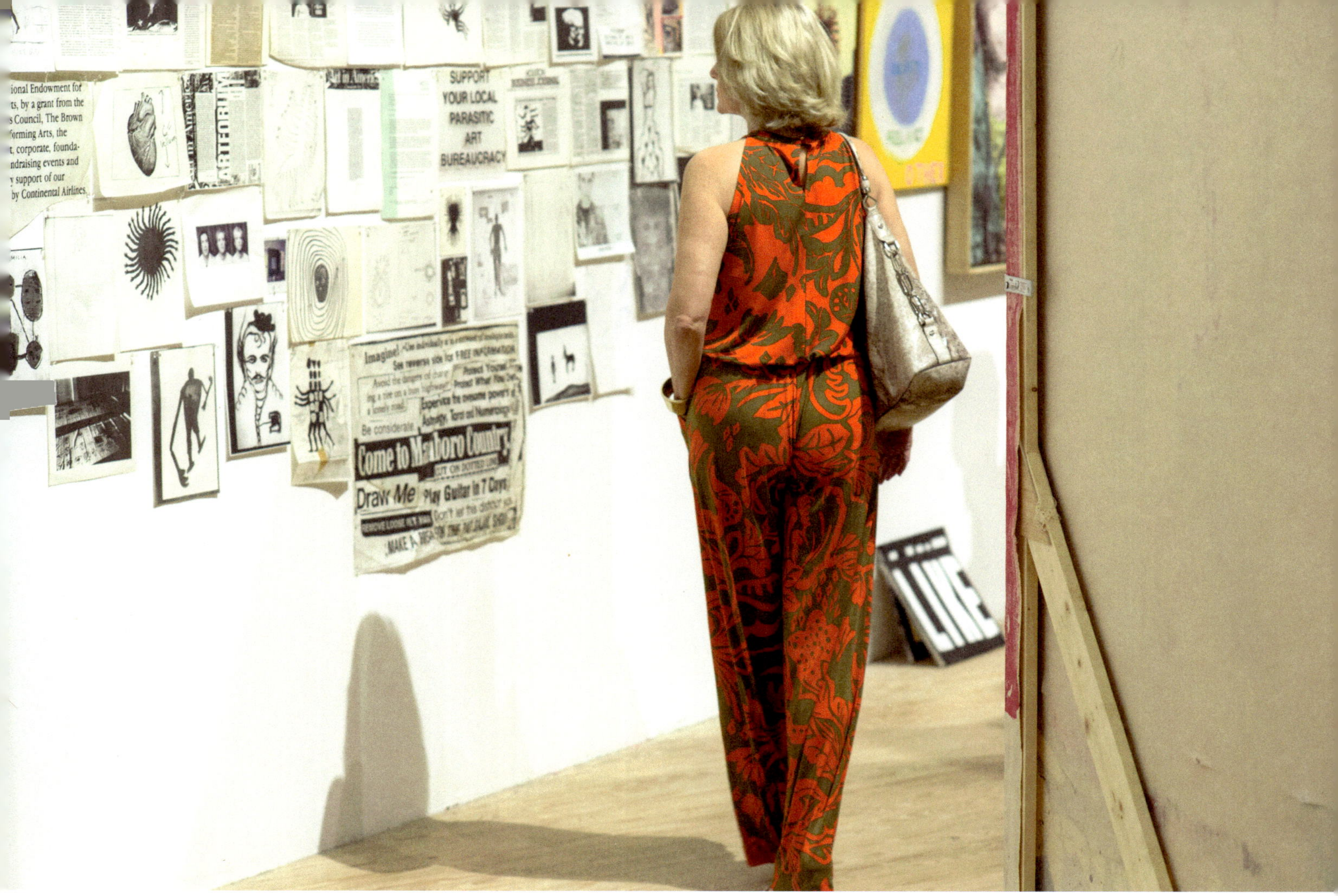

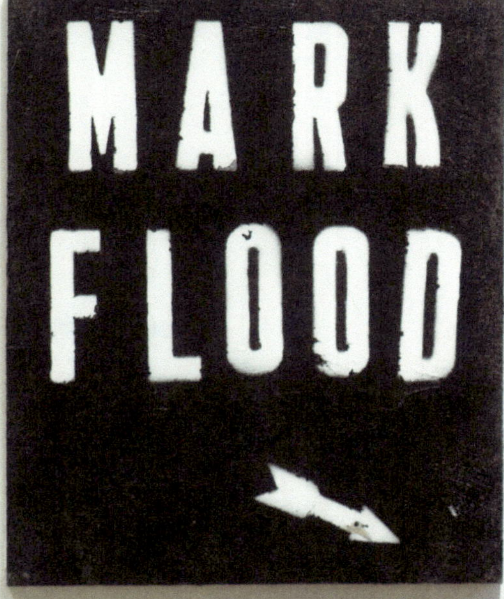
MARK
FLOOD

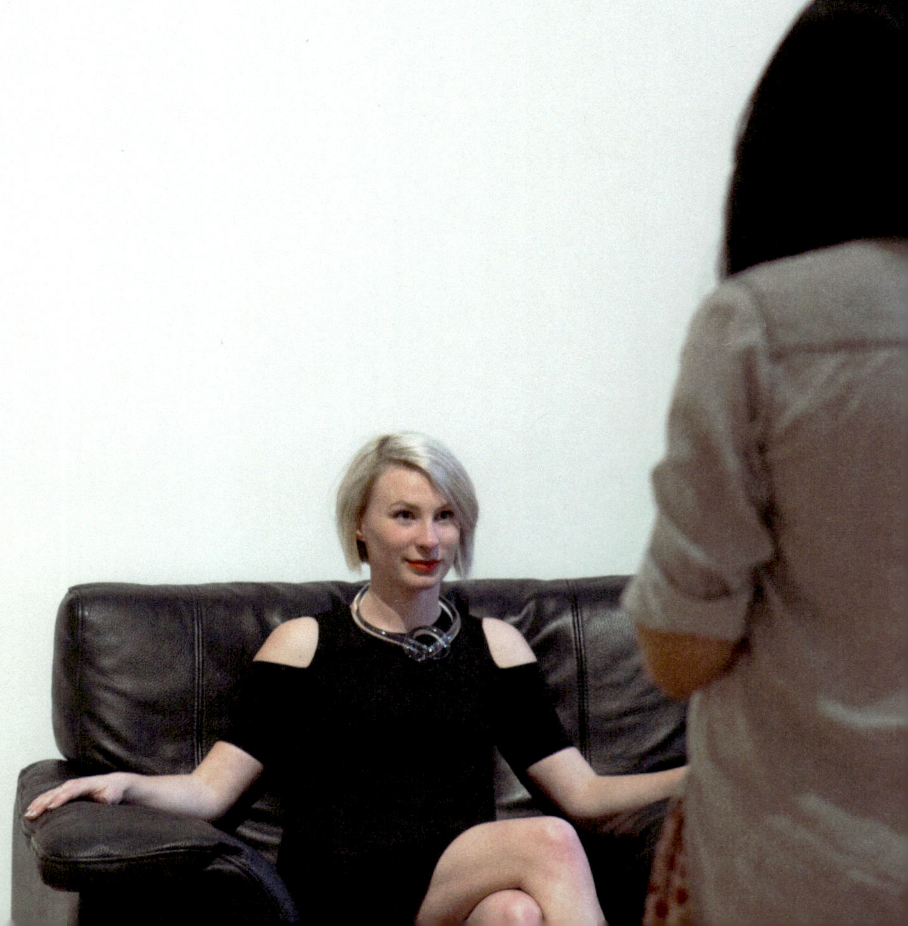

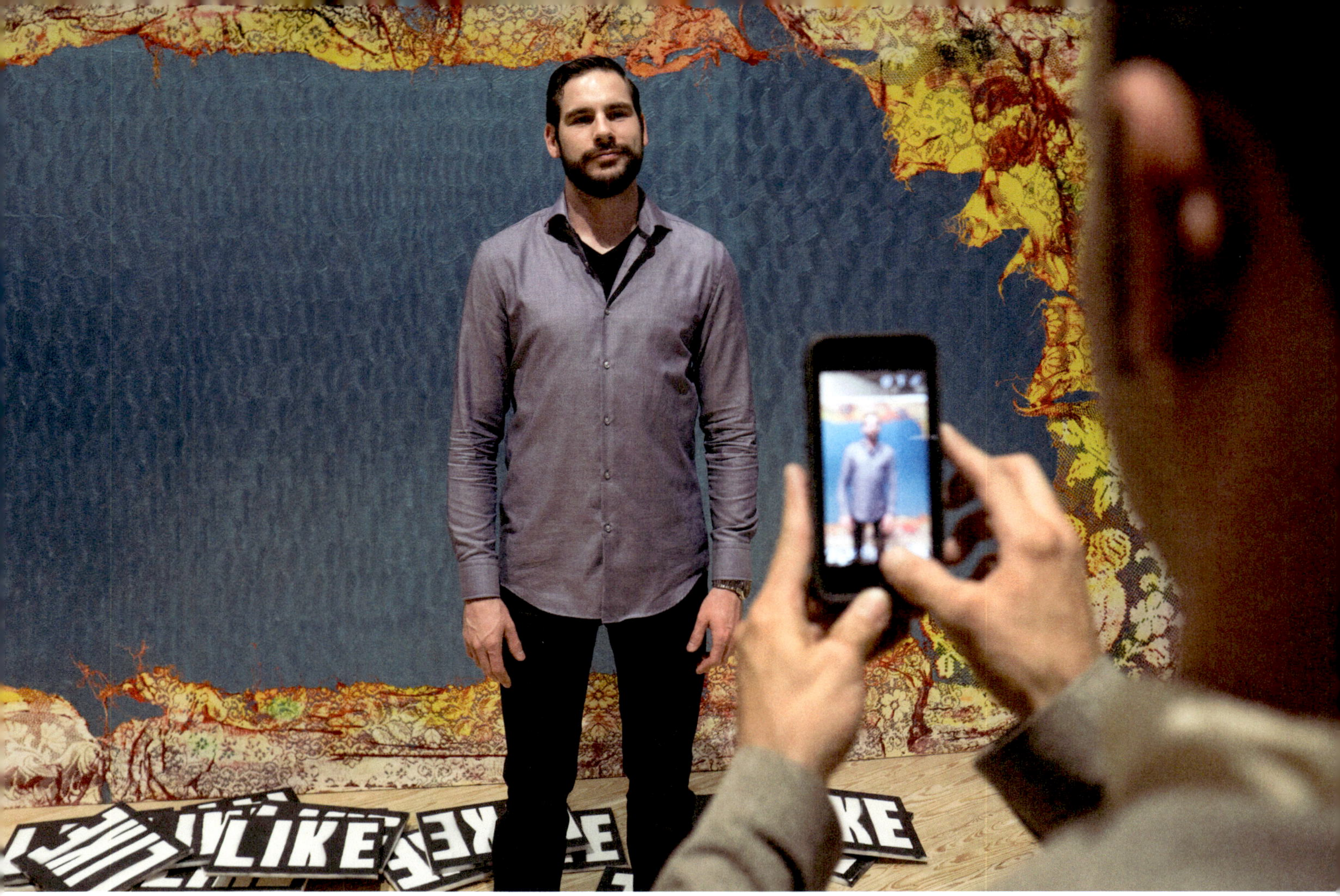

LIKE
WORLD PREMIERE 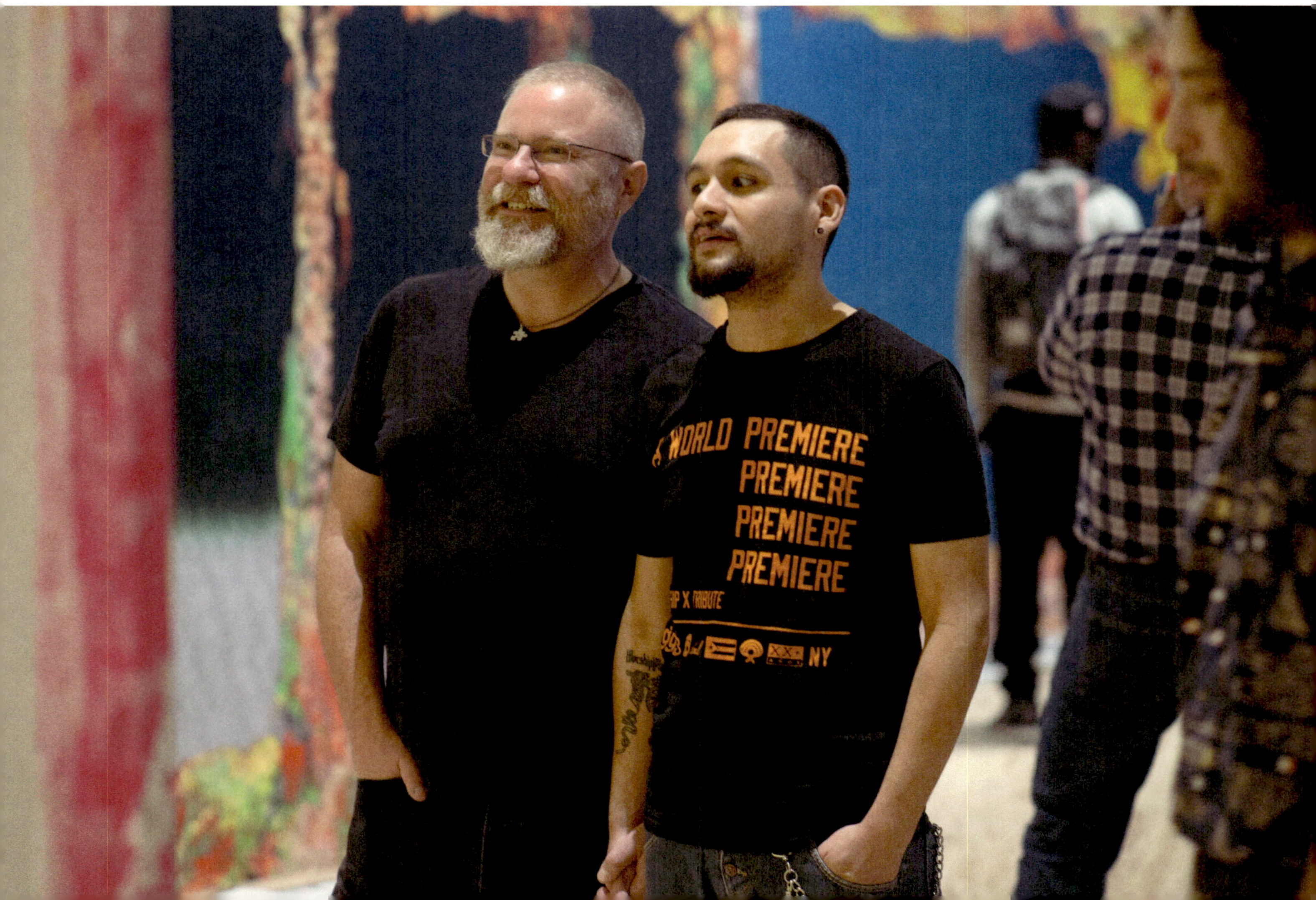
PREMIERE
PREMIERE
PREMIERE
NY

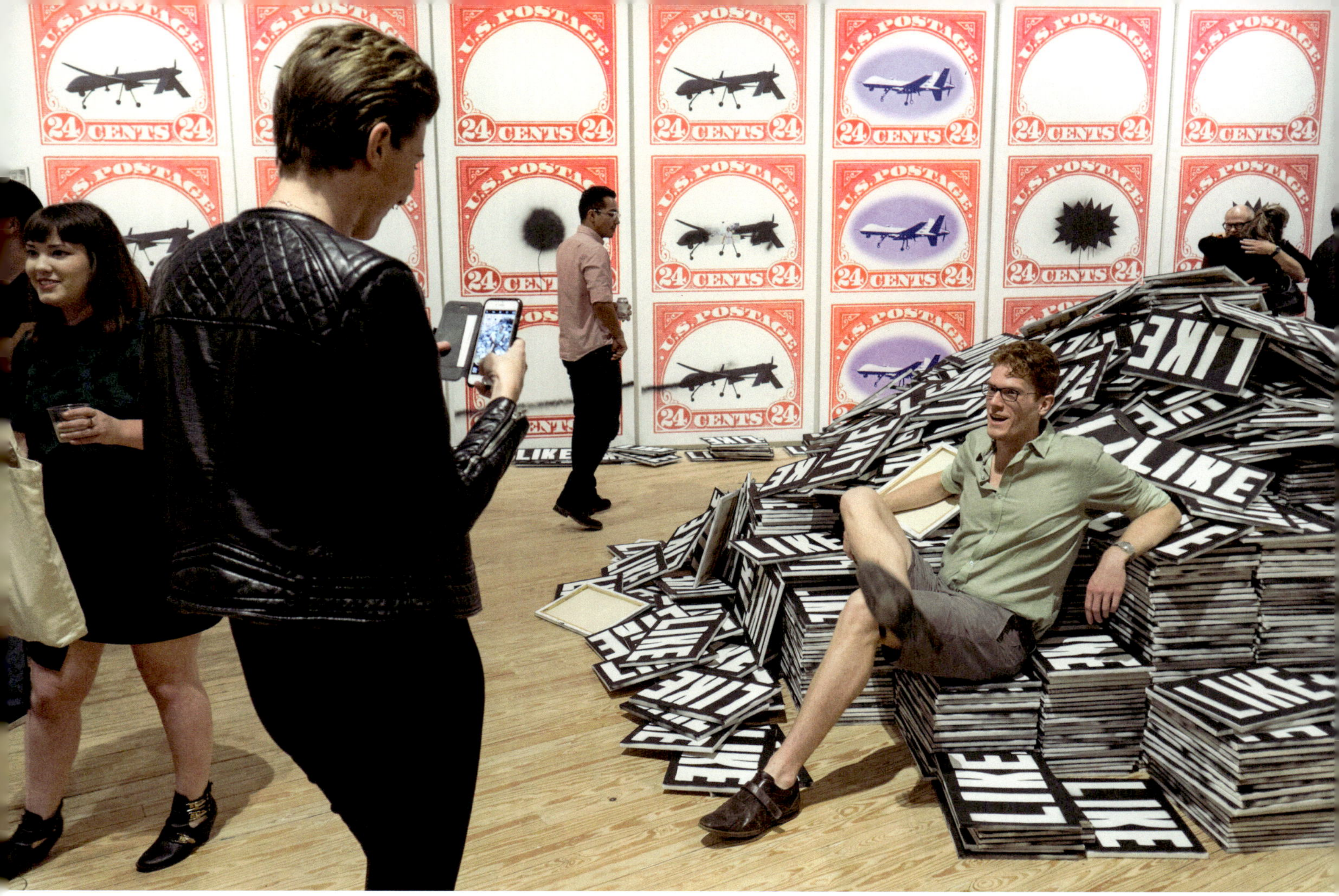

U.S. POSTAGE
24 CENTS 24
LIKE
Come to Marl Countr

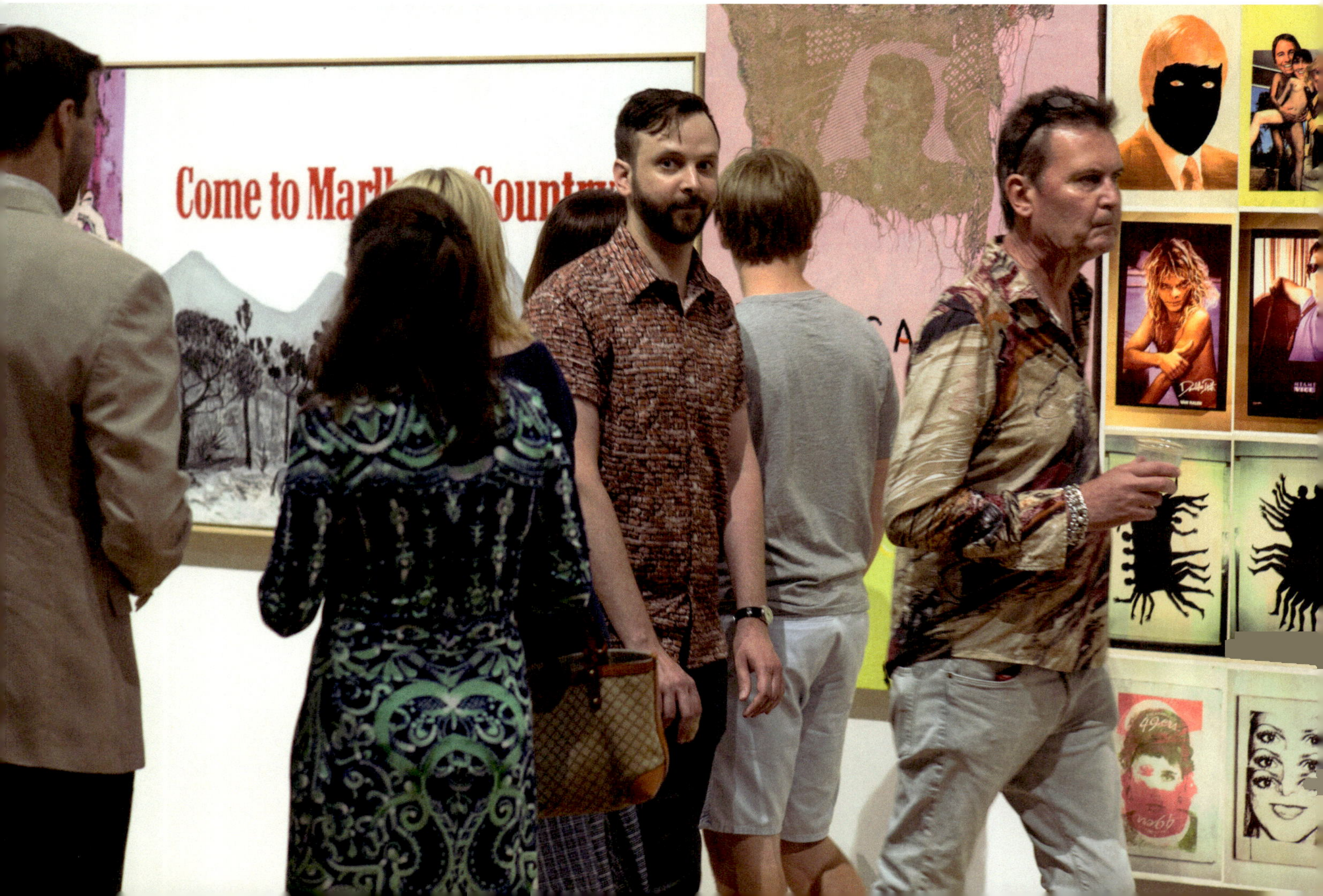

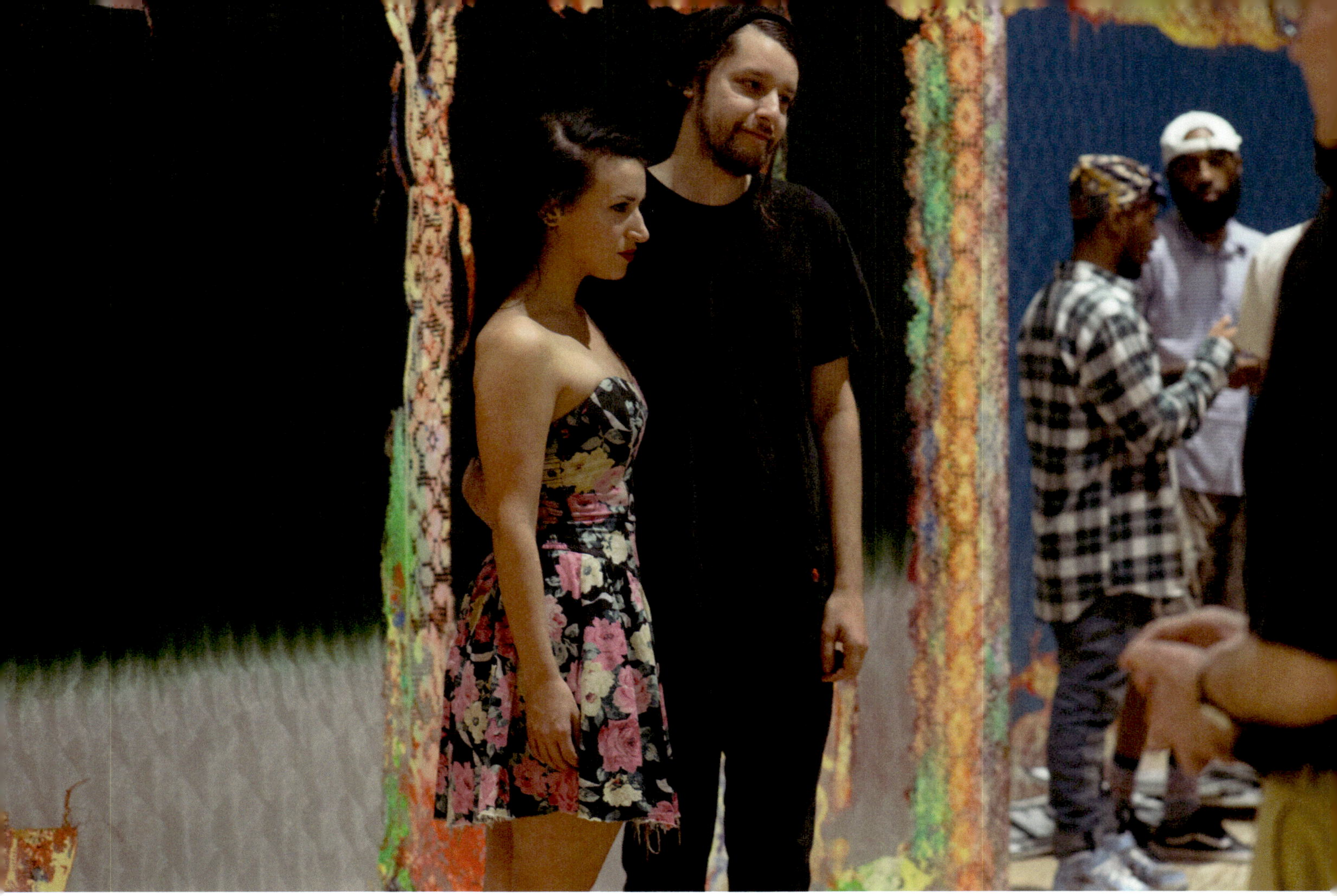

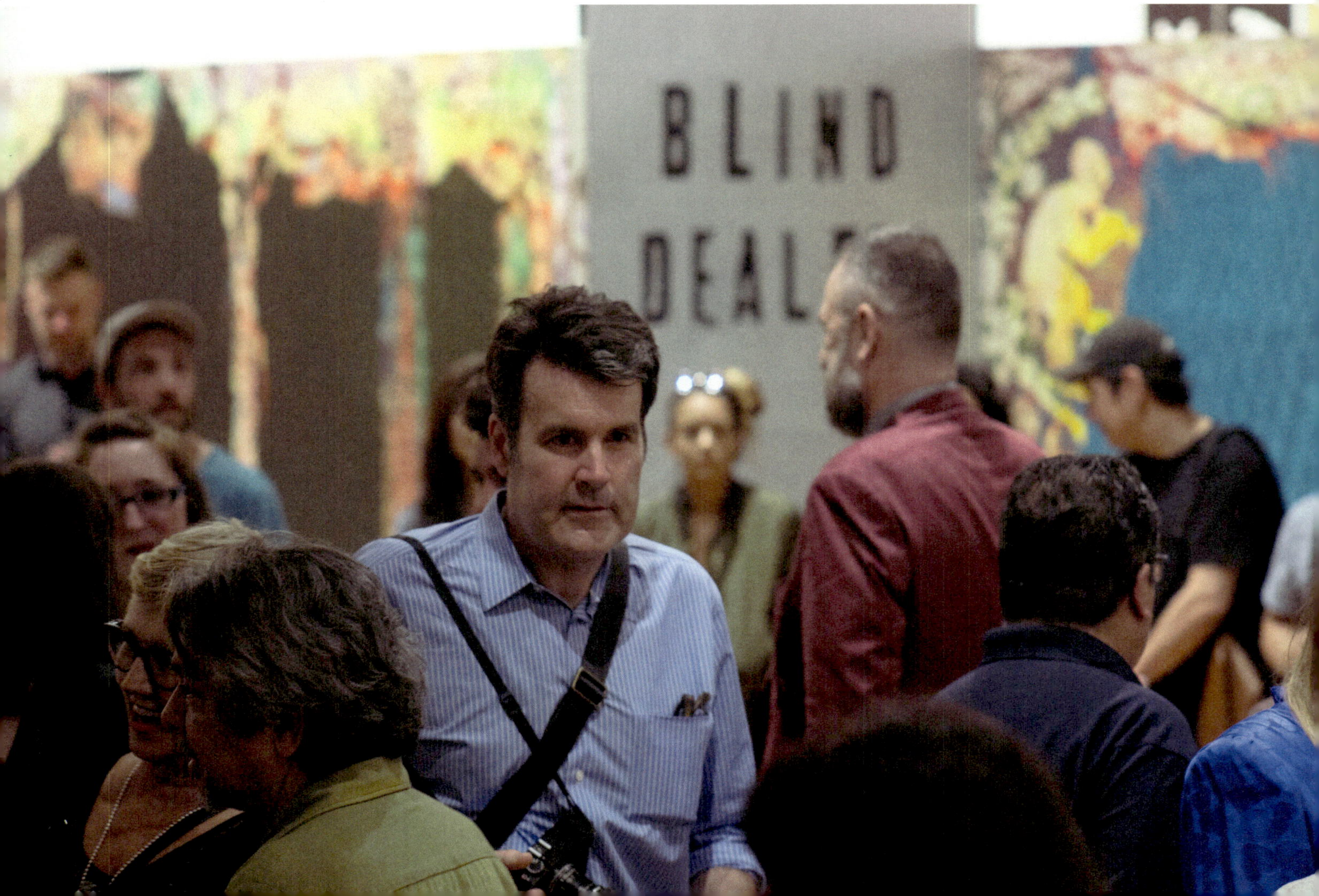

BLIND
DEAL

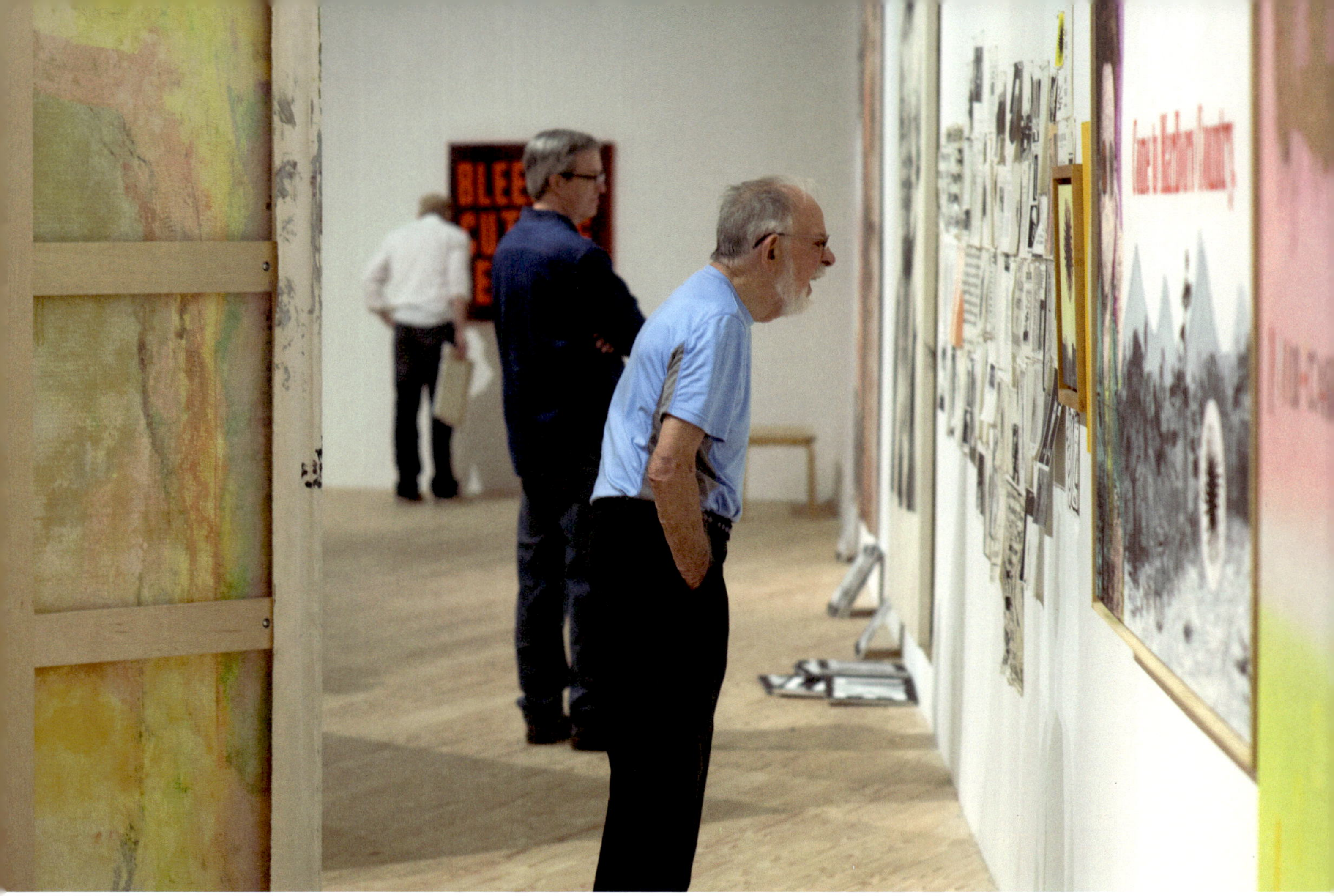

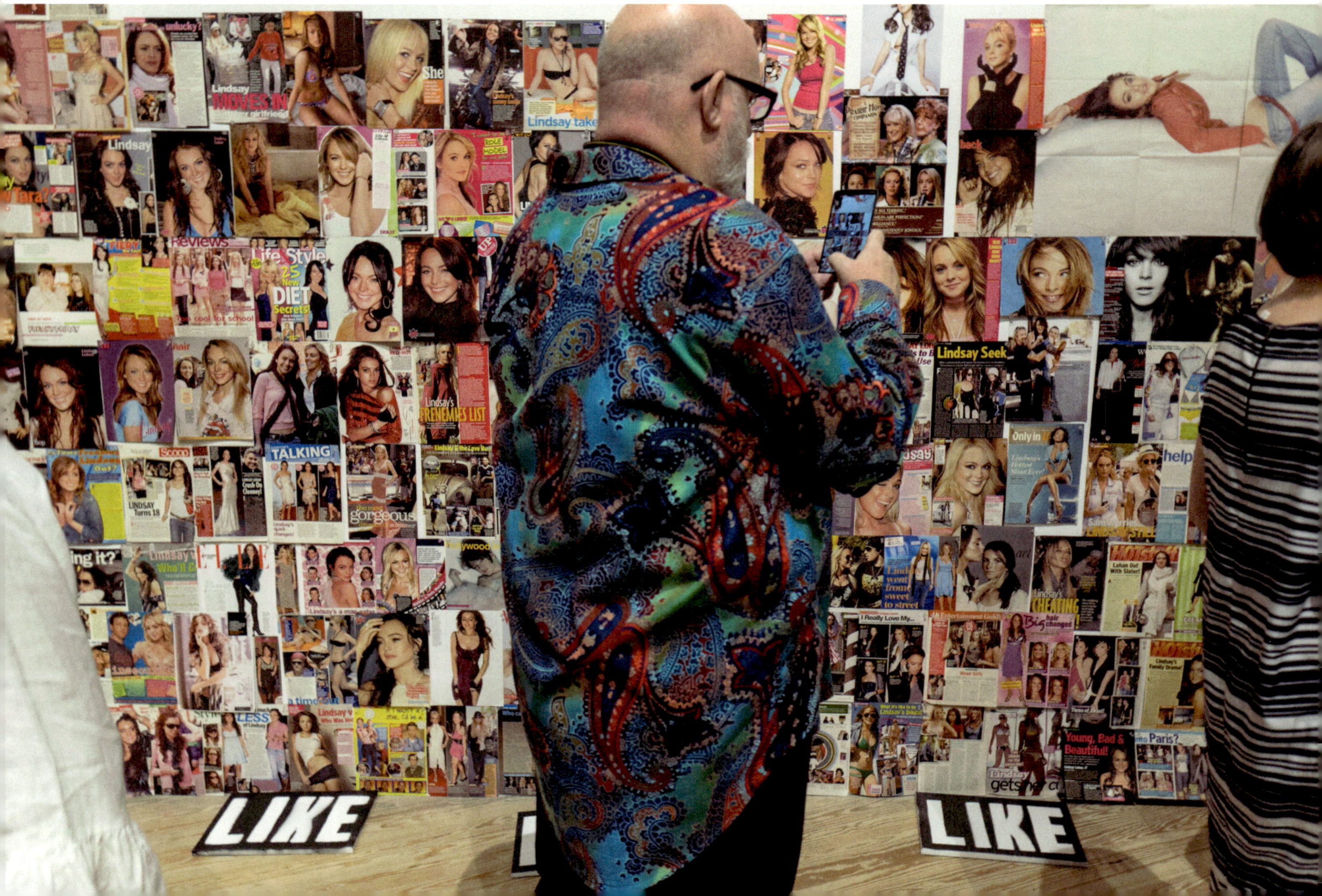

LIKE
LIKE

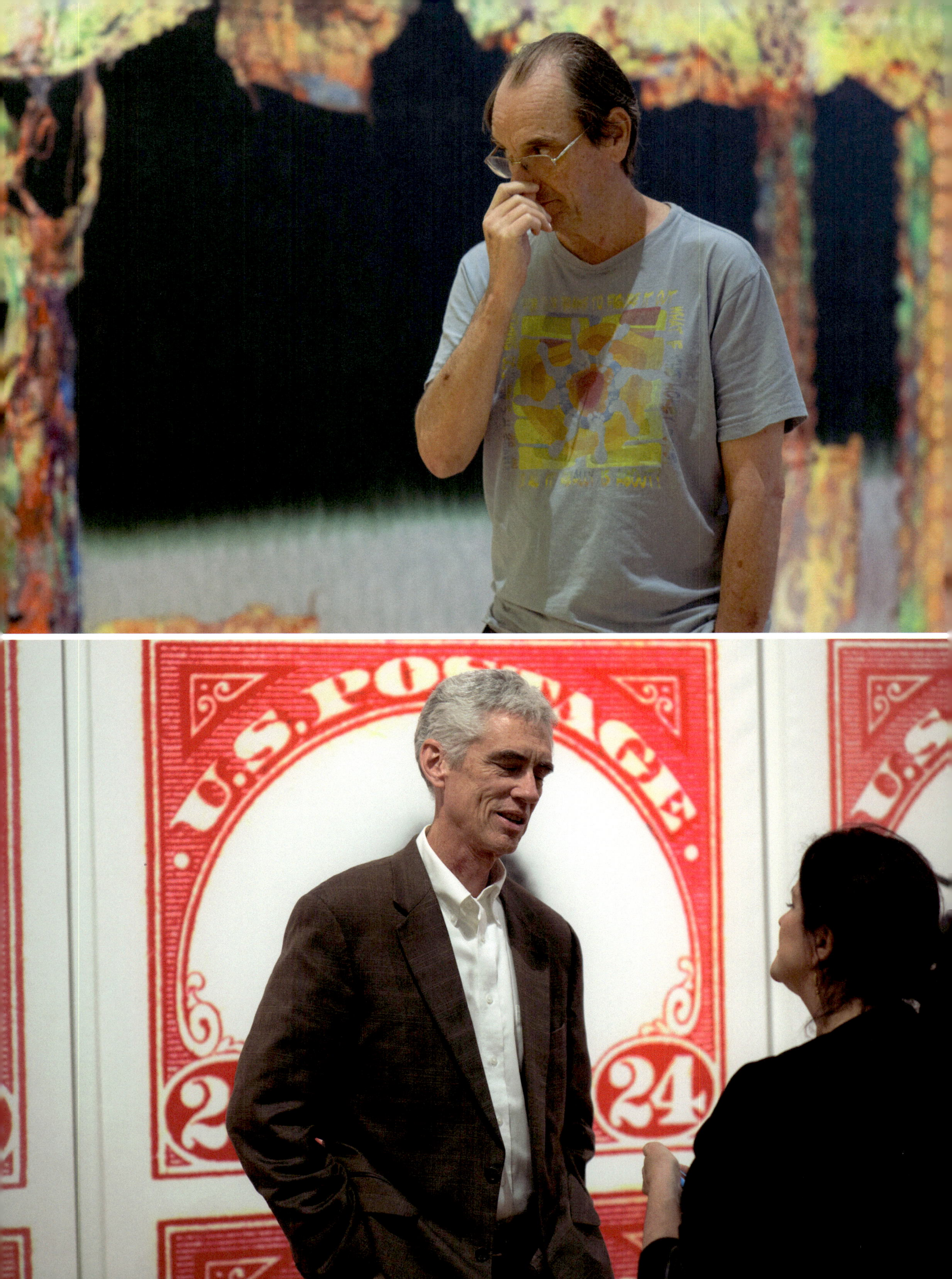
U.S. PO
AGE
24

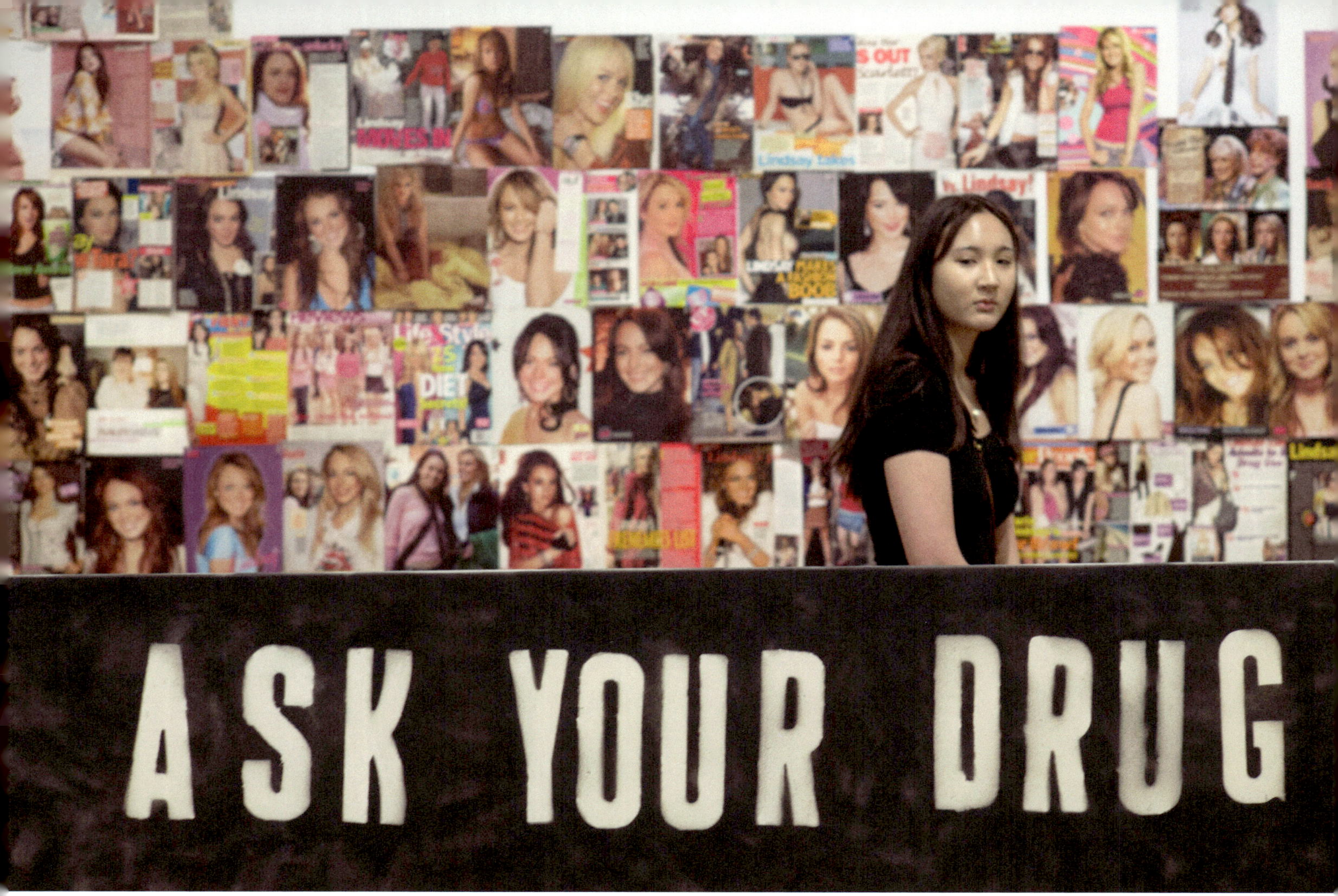

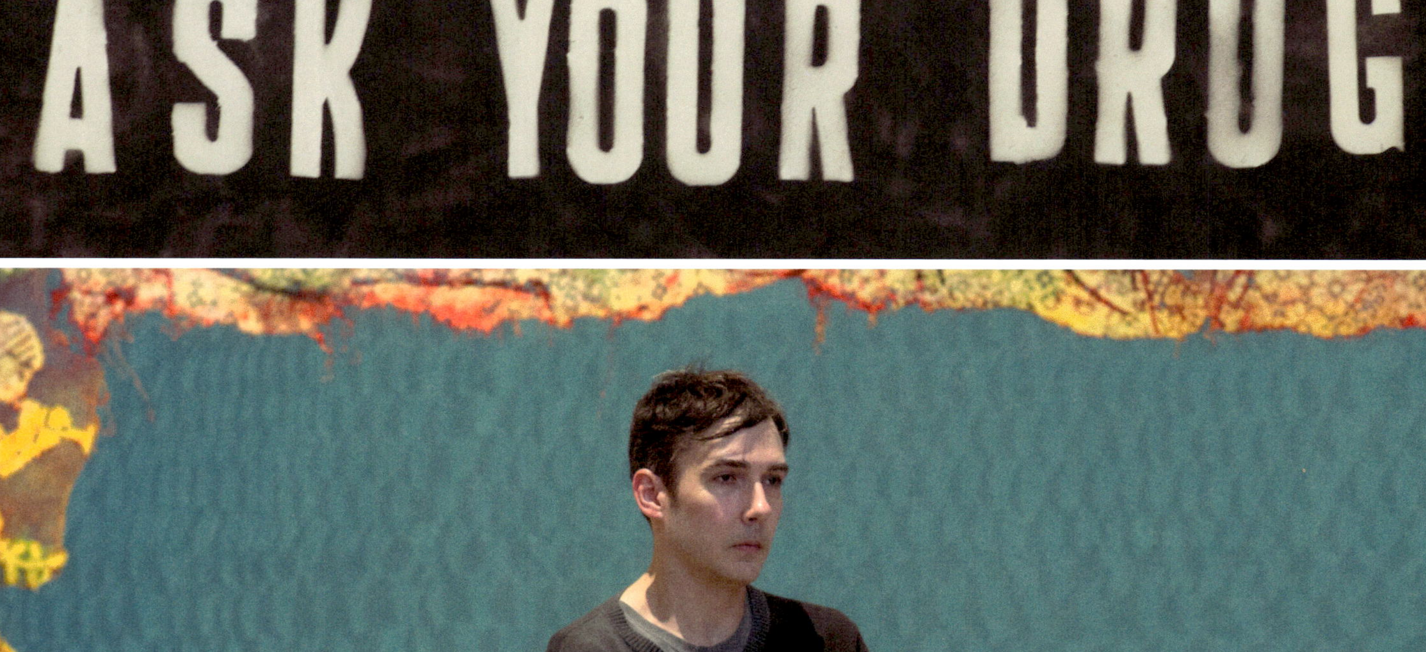
ASK YOUR DRUG

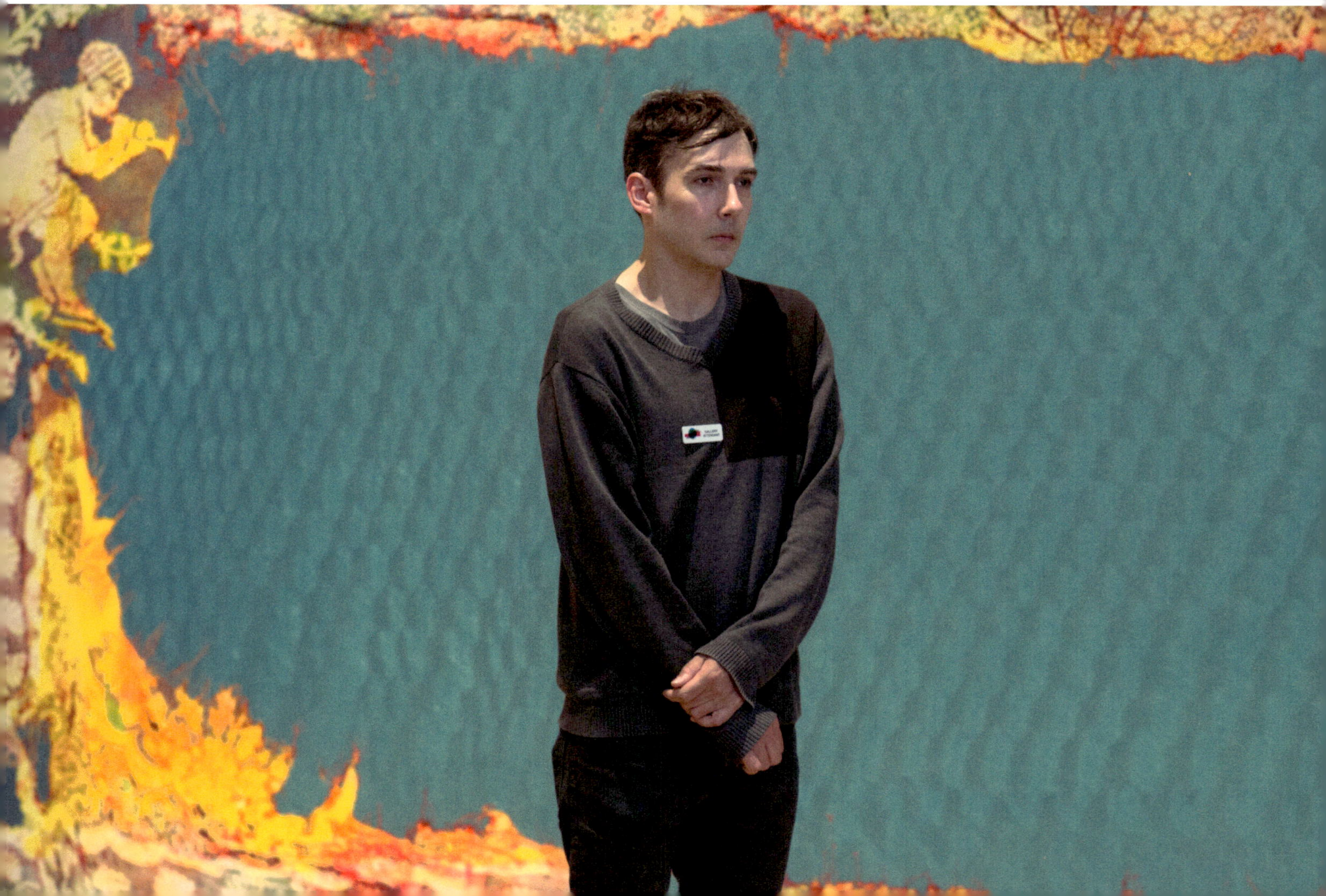

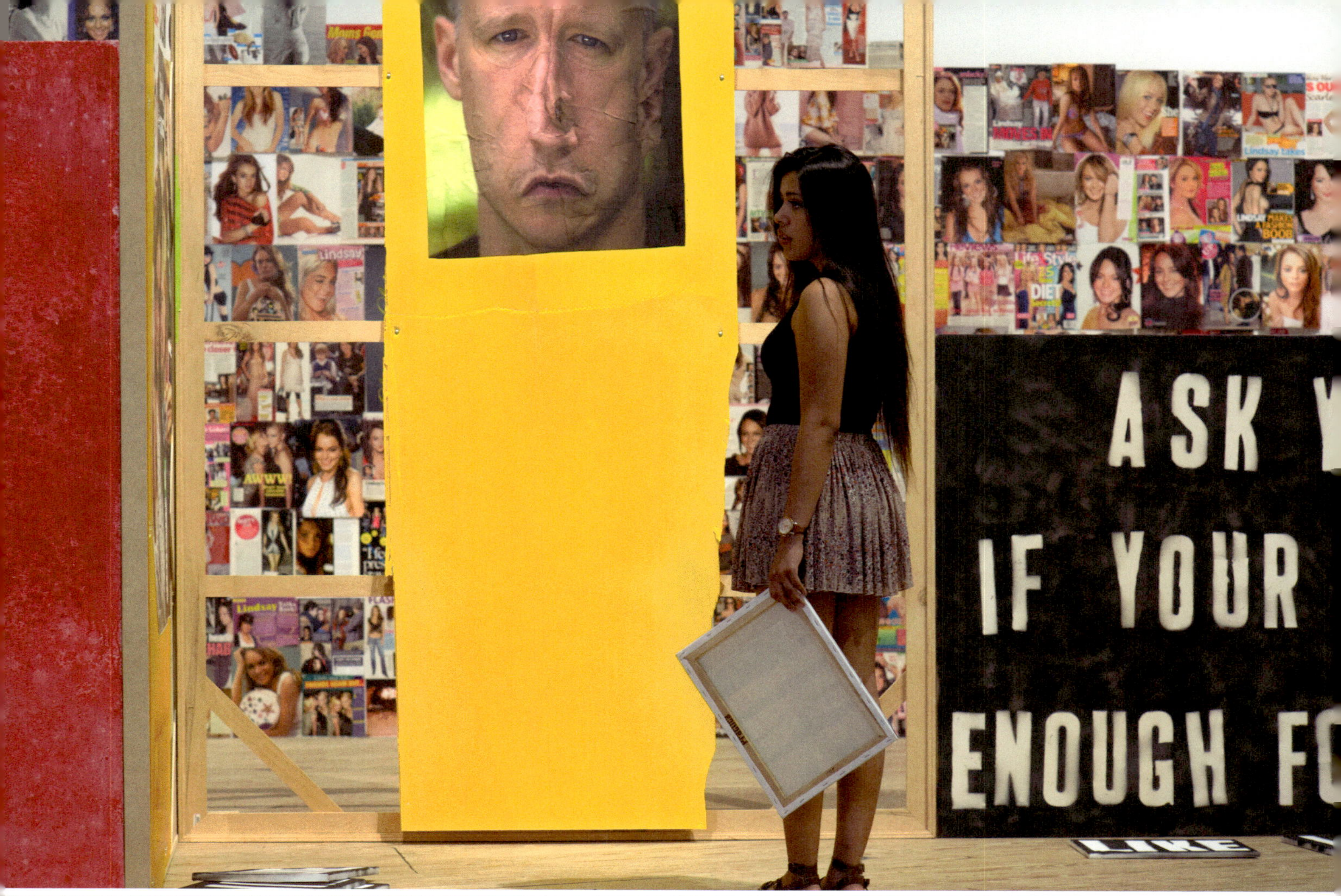

ASK Y
IF YOUR
ENOUGH FO
LIKE

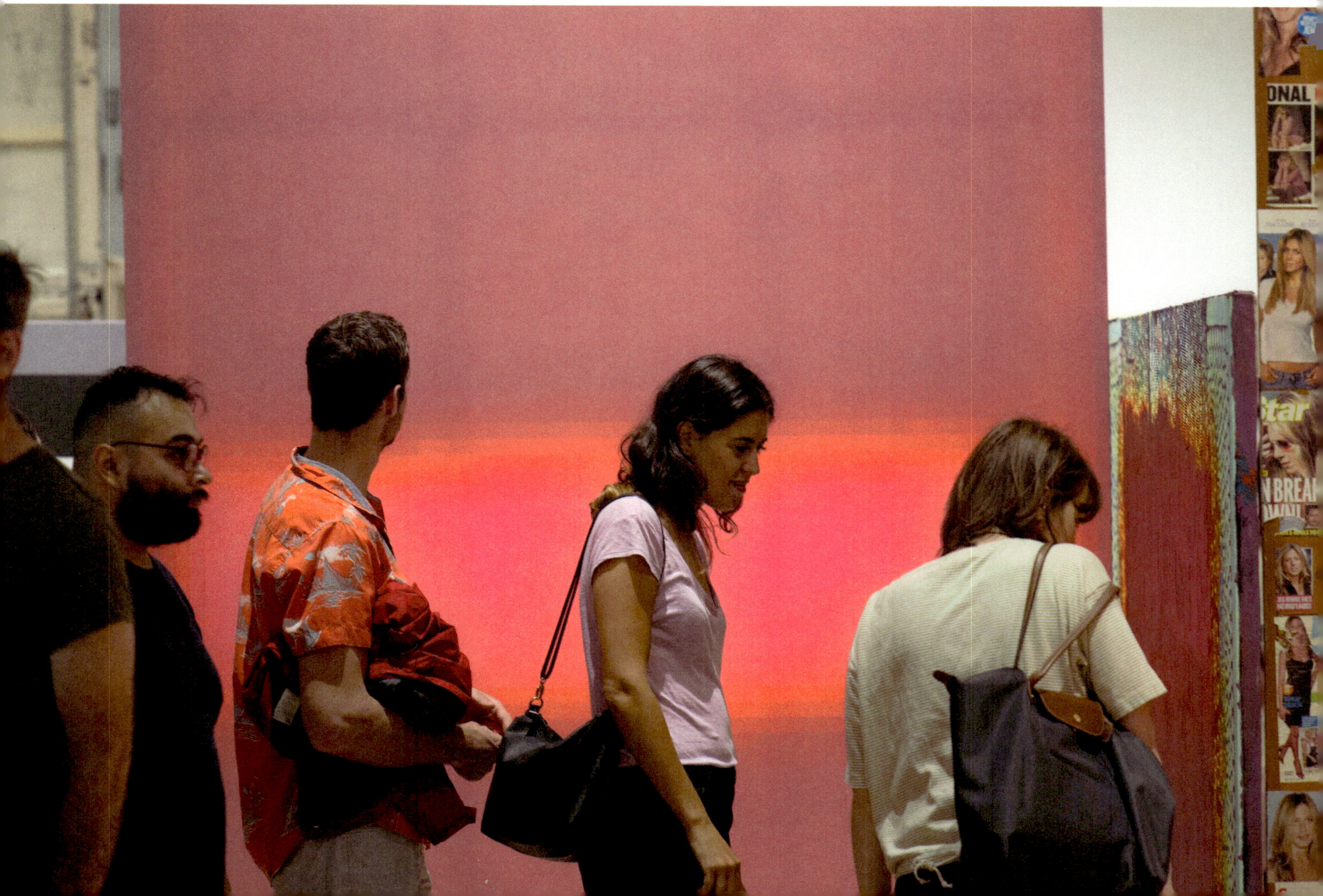

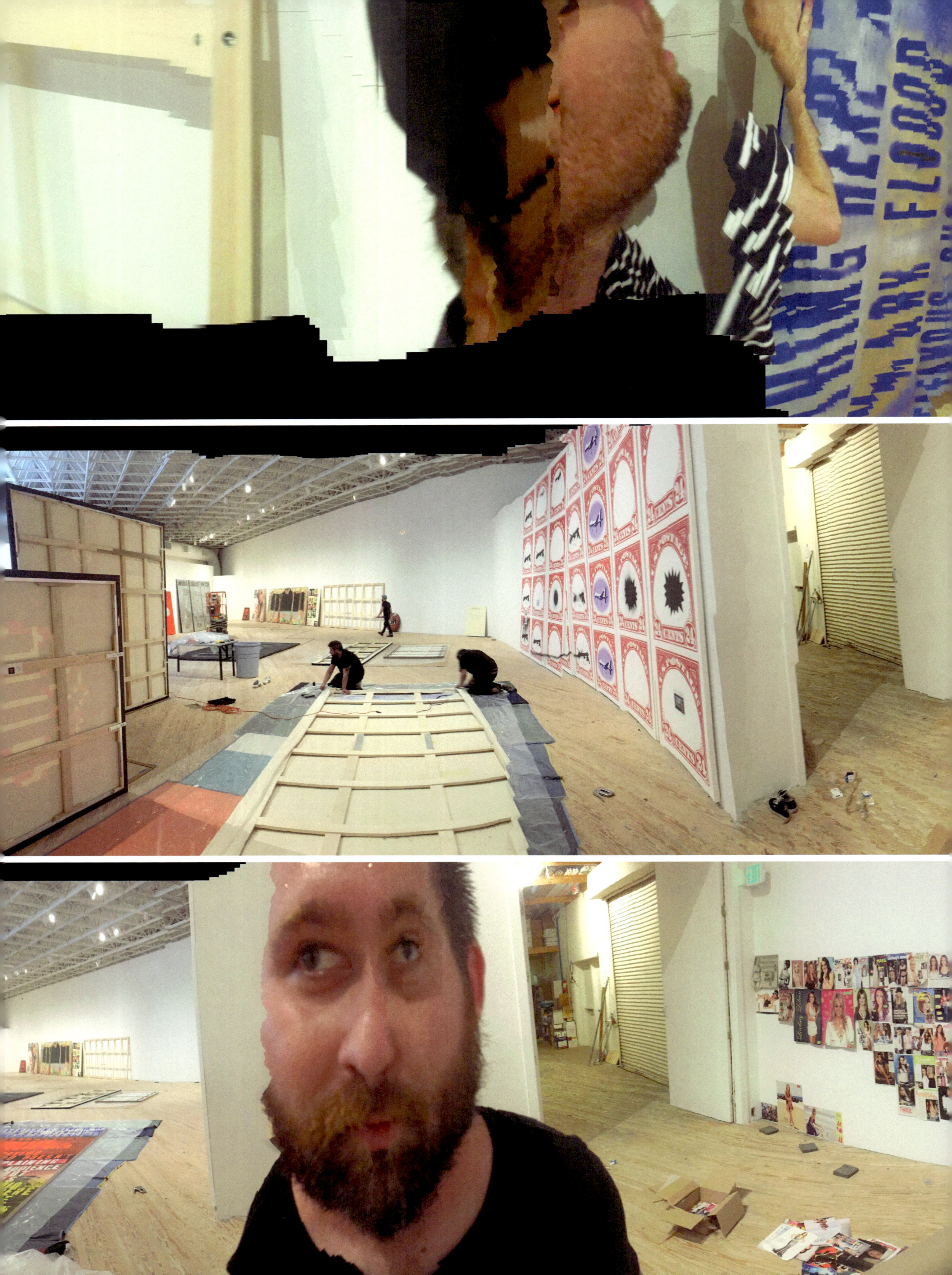

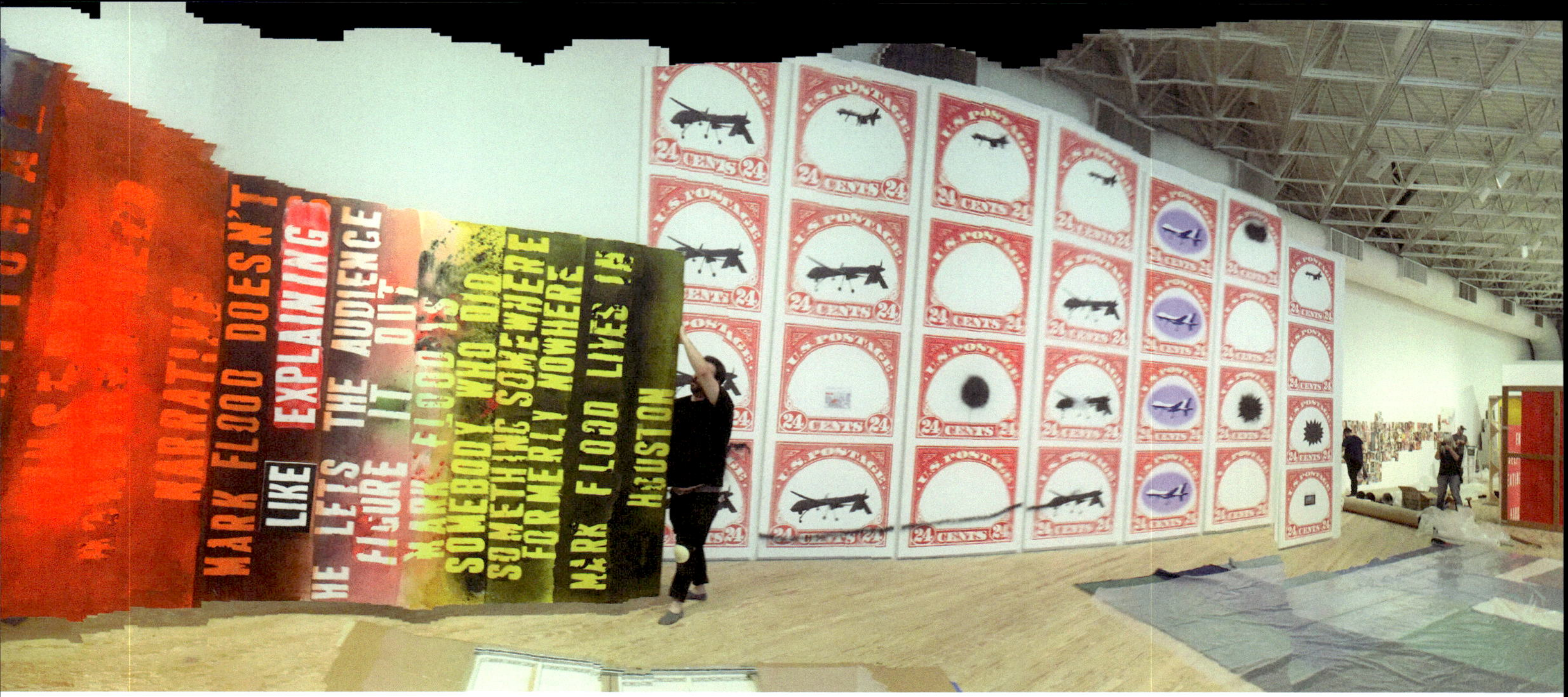

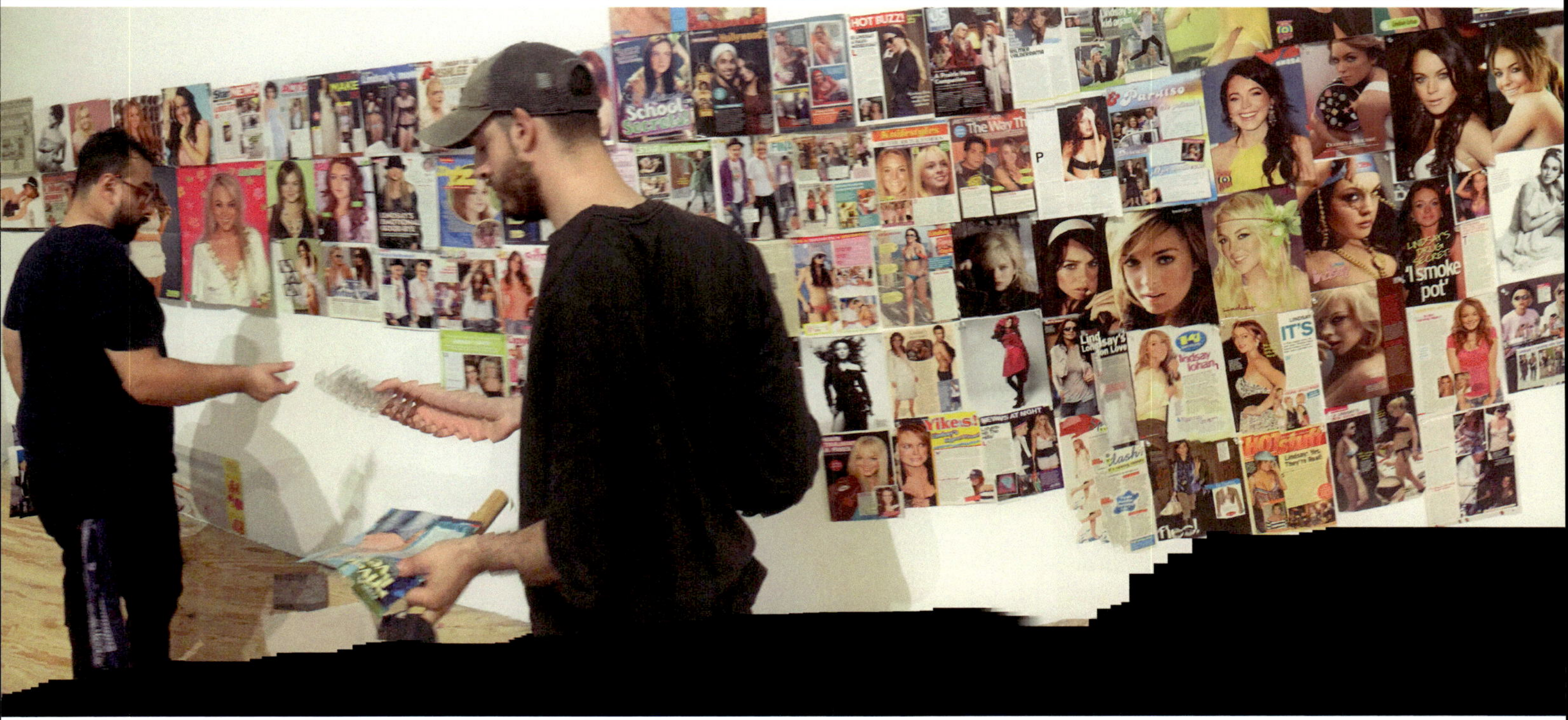

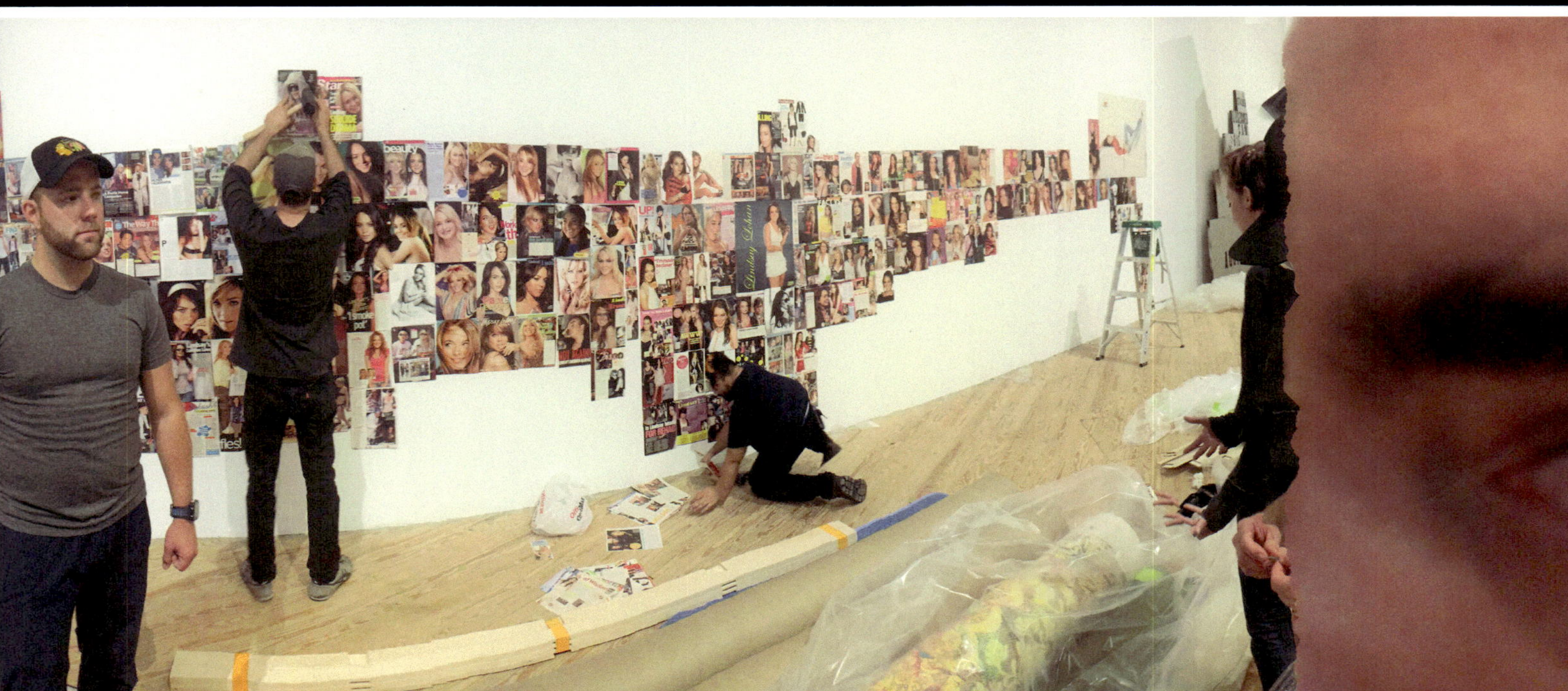

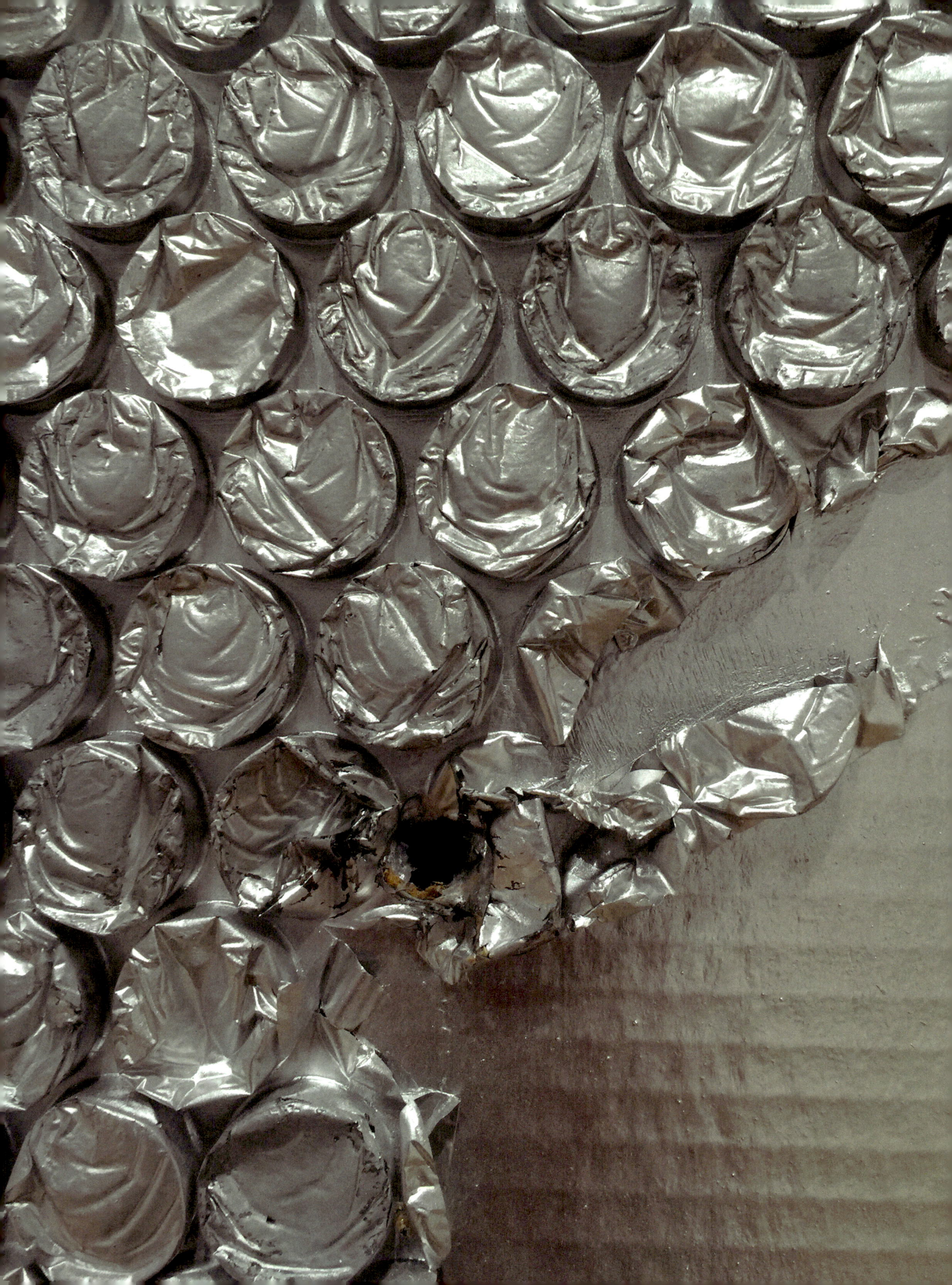

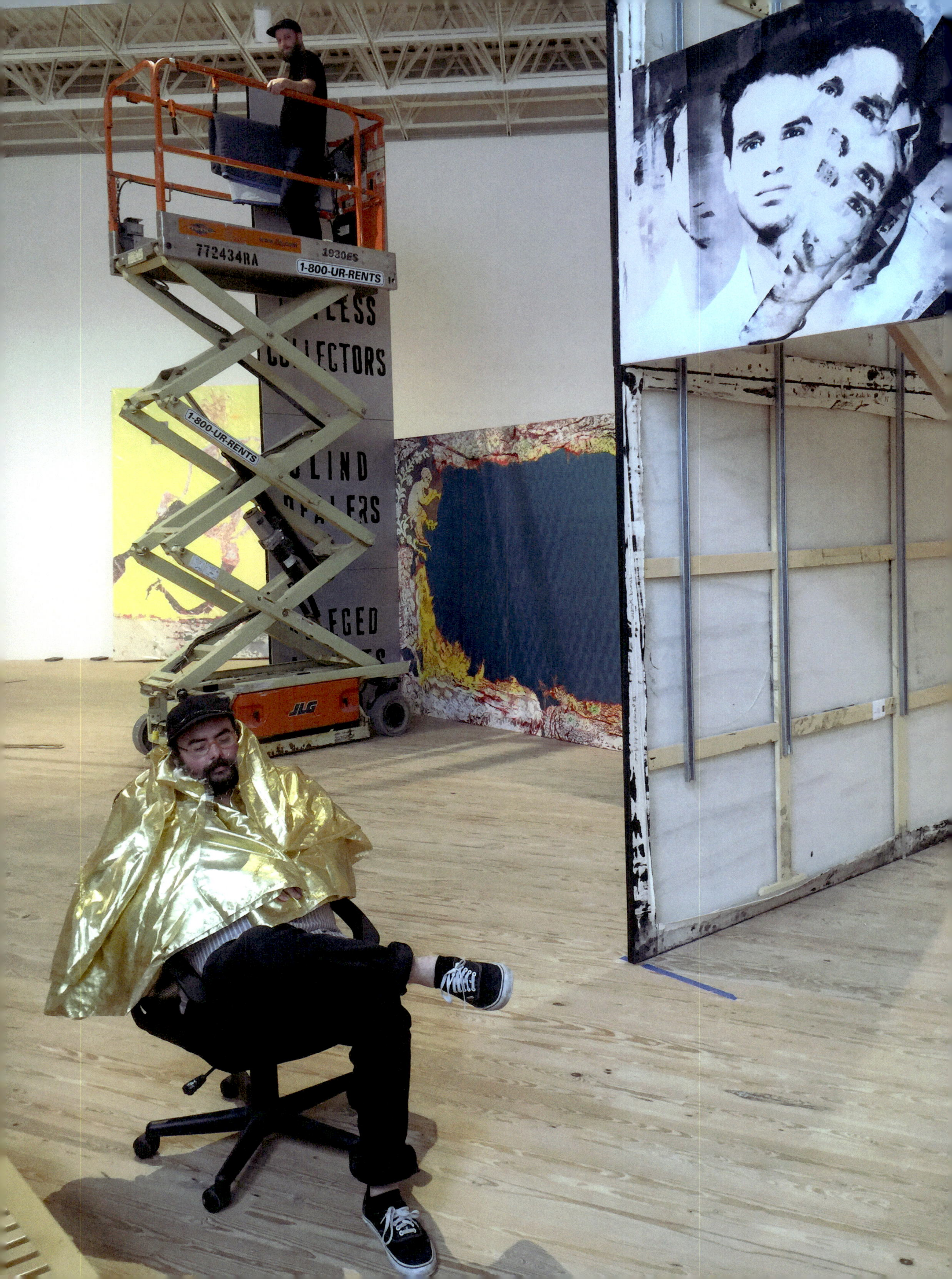
772434RA
1930ES
1-800-UR-RENTS
COLLECTORS
1-800-UR-RENTS
JLG

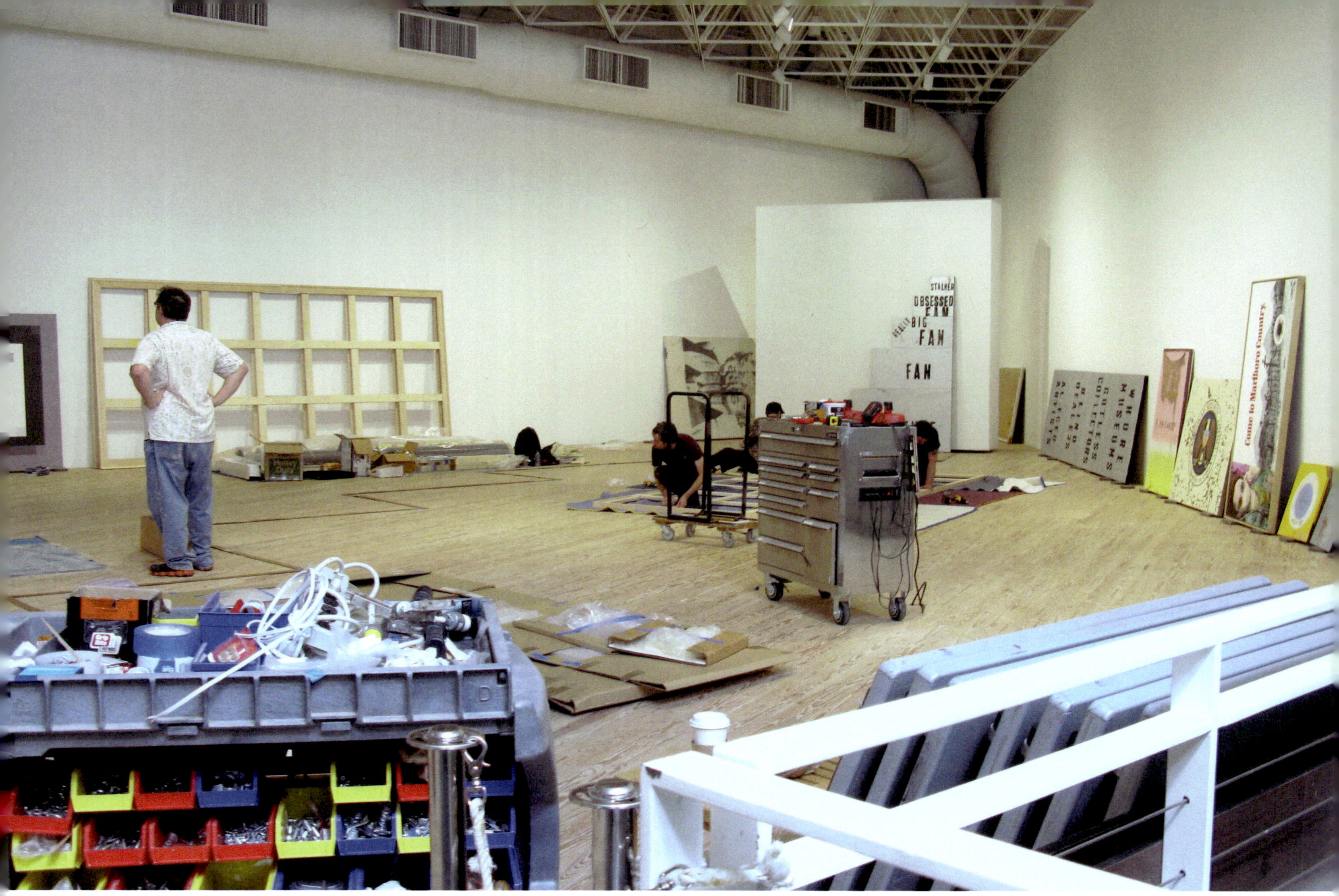

STALKER
OBSESSED
FAN
BIG
FAN
FAN
Come to Marlboro Country.
U.S. POSTAGE 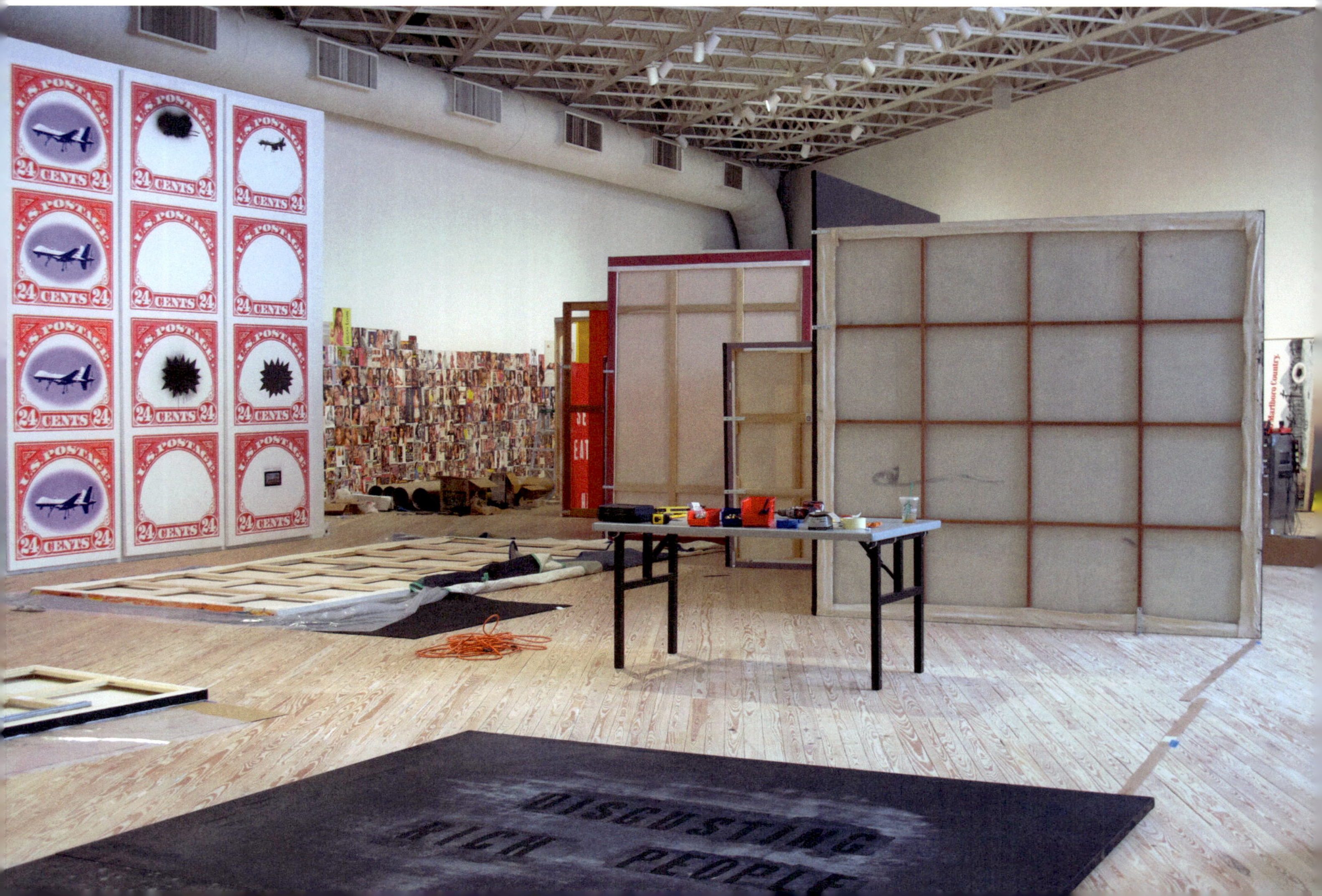
24 CENTS 24
DISGUSTING
RICH PEOPLE

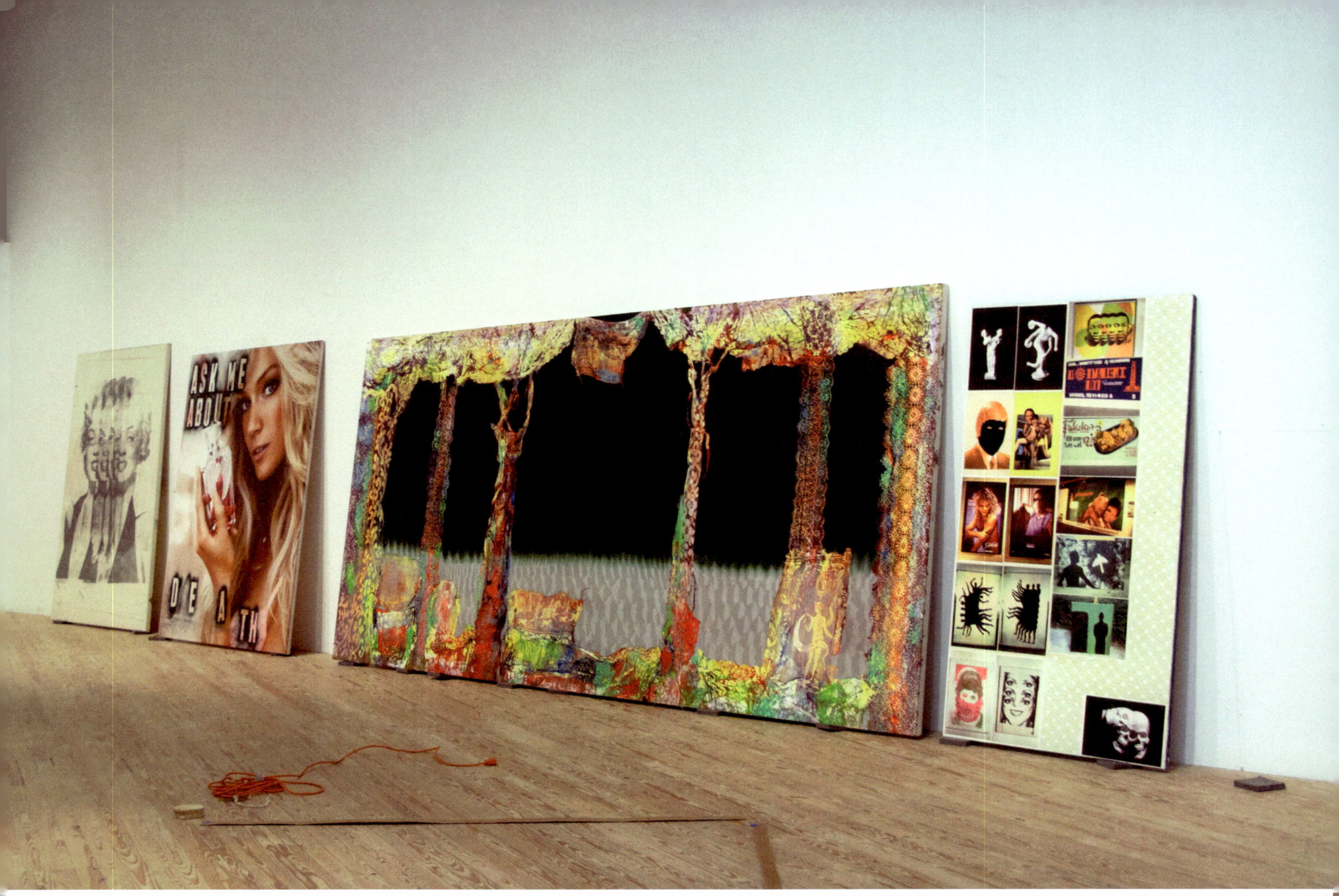
ASK ME
D E A TH

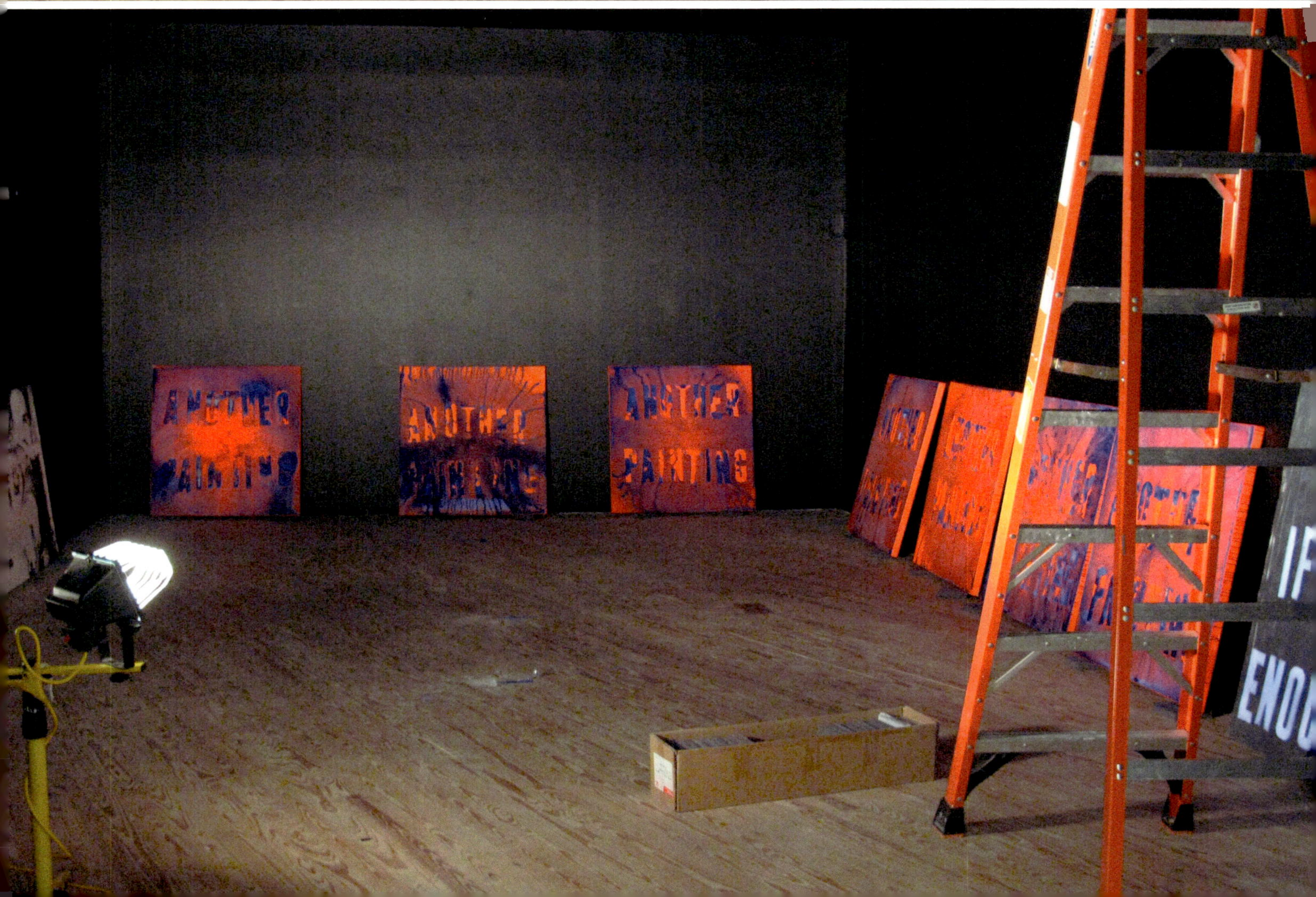
ANOTHER
PAINTING
IF

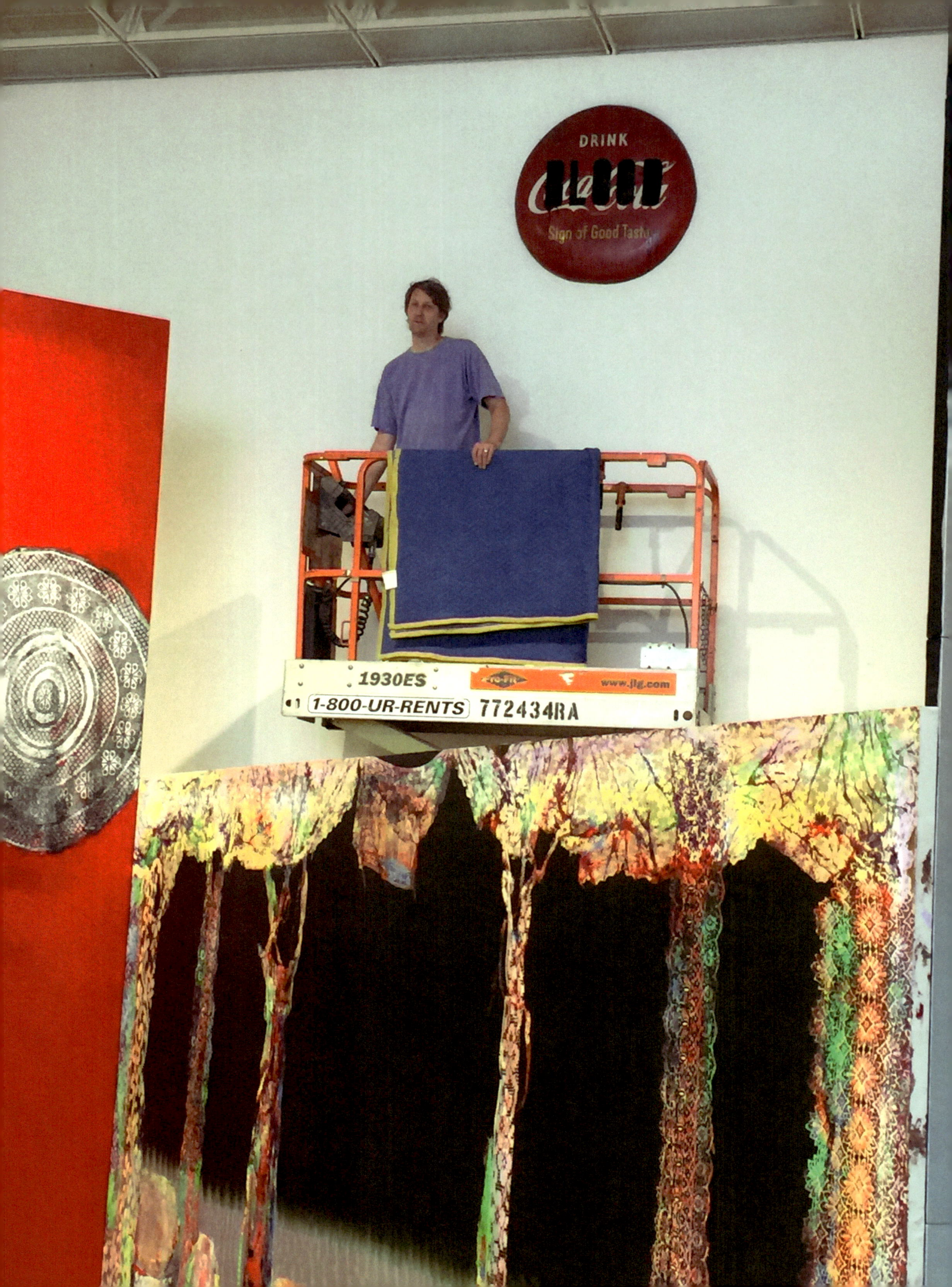
DRINK
BLOOD
Sign of Good Taste
1930ES
www.jlg.com
1-800-UR-RENTS
772434RA

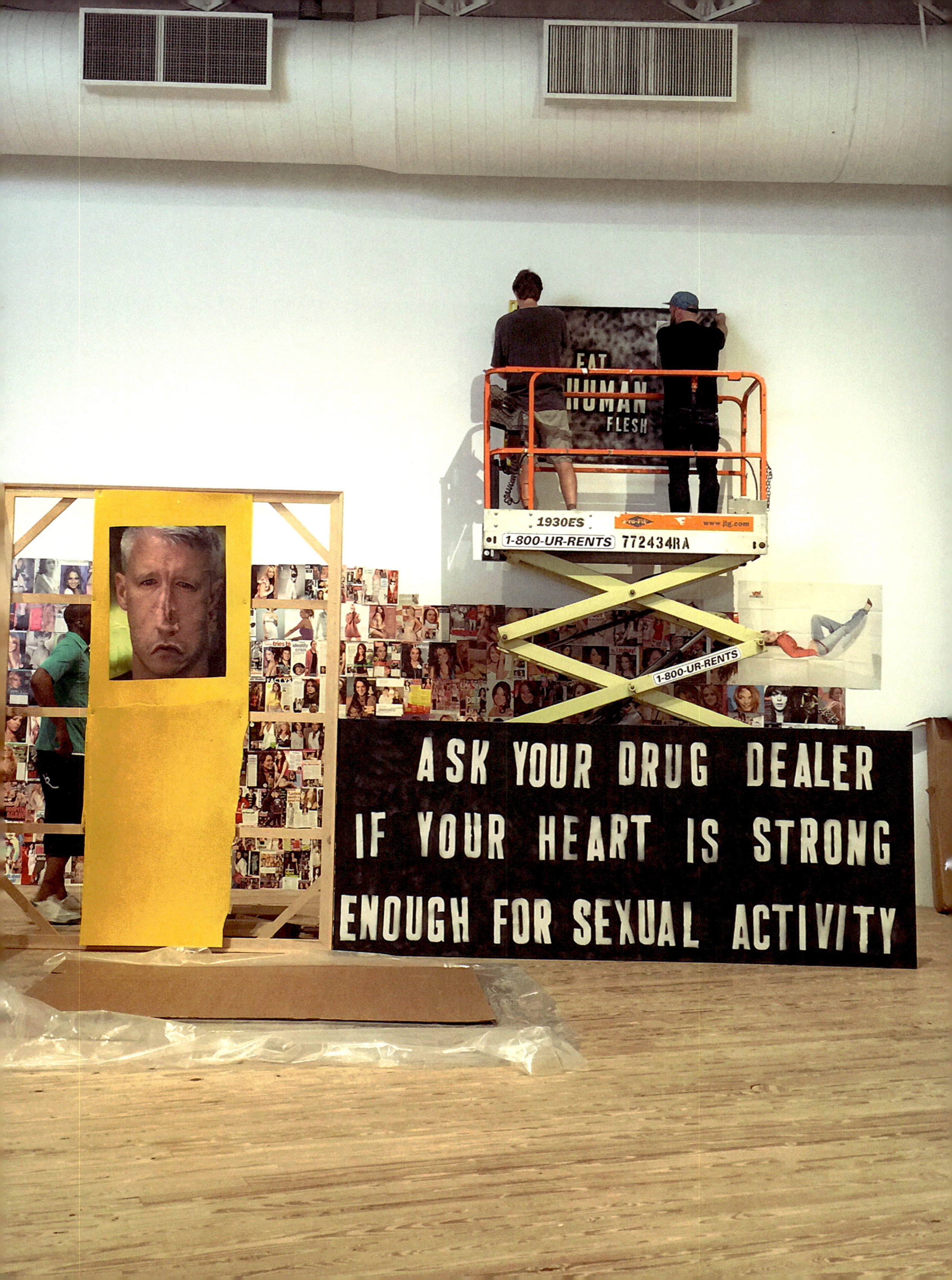
EAT
HUMAN
FLESH
1930ES
1-800-UR-RENTS
772434RA
1-800-UR-RENTS
ASK YOUR DRUG DEALER
IF YOUR HEART IS STRONG
ENOUGH FOR SEXUAL ACTIVITY

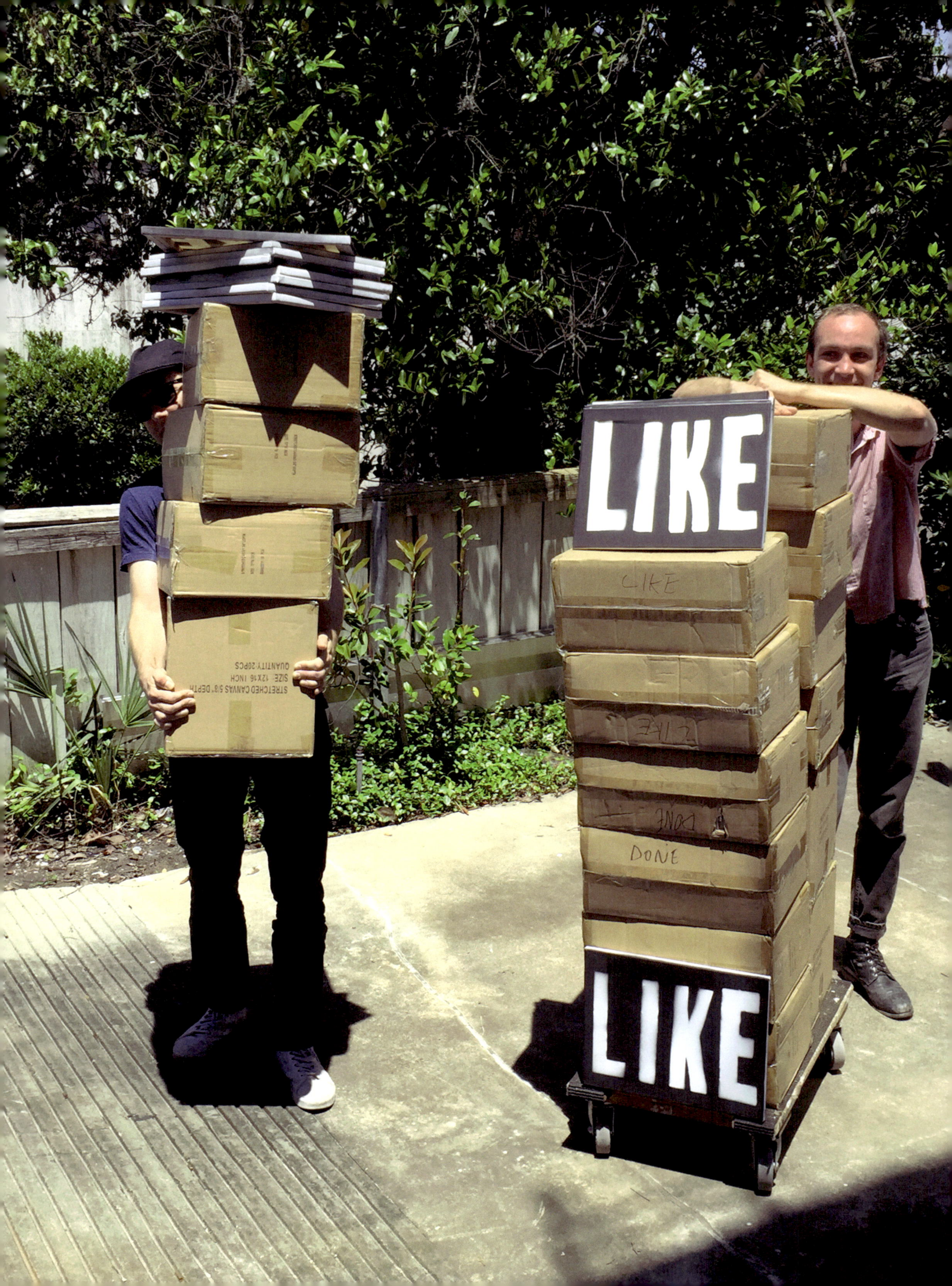
LIKE
LIKE
DONE
STRETCHED CANVAS 5/8"DEPTH
SIZE: 12X16 INCH
QUANTITY: 20PCS
LIKE

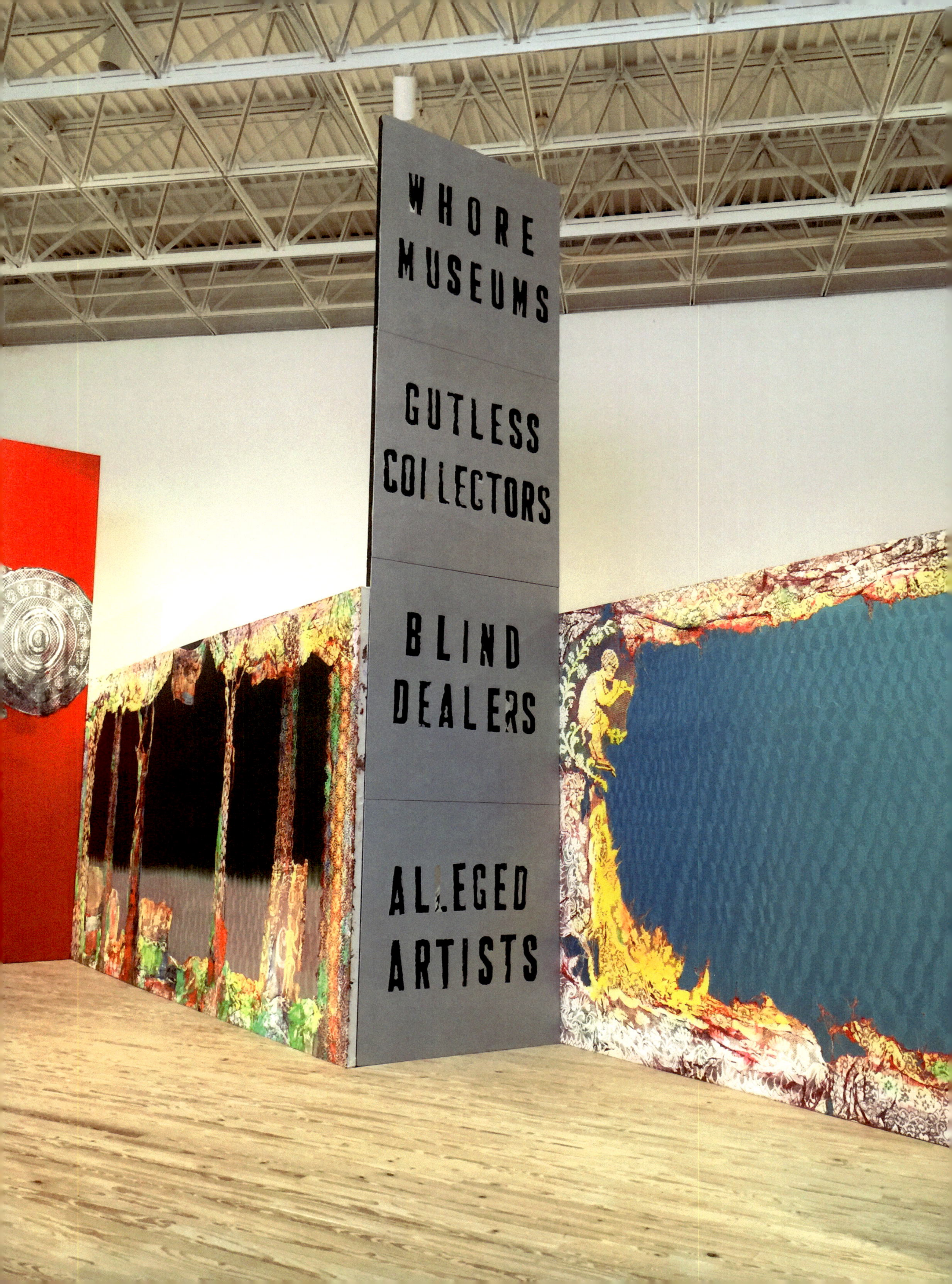
WHORE
MUSEUMS
GUTLESS
COLLECTORS
BLIND
DEALERS
ALLEGED
ARTISTS

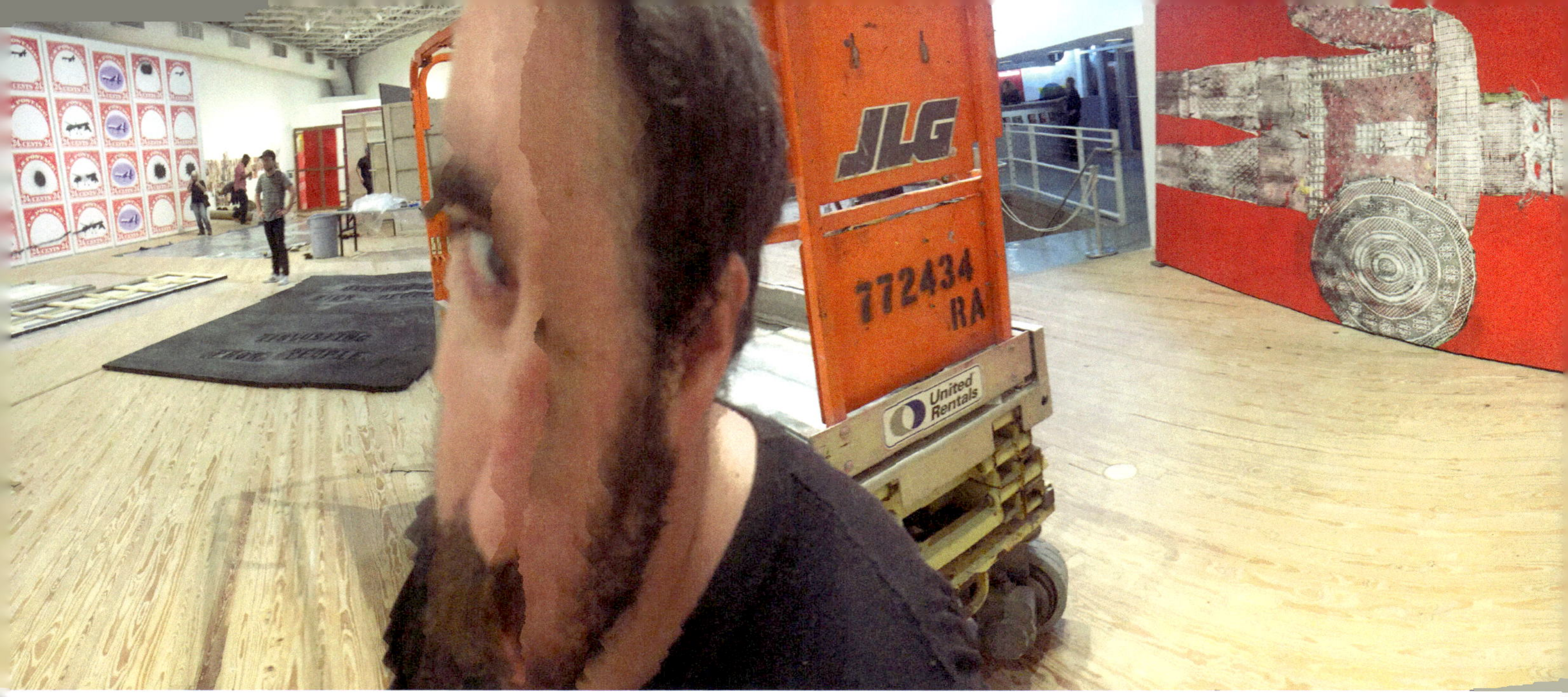

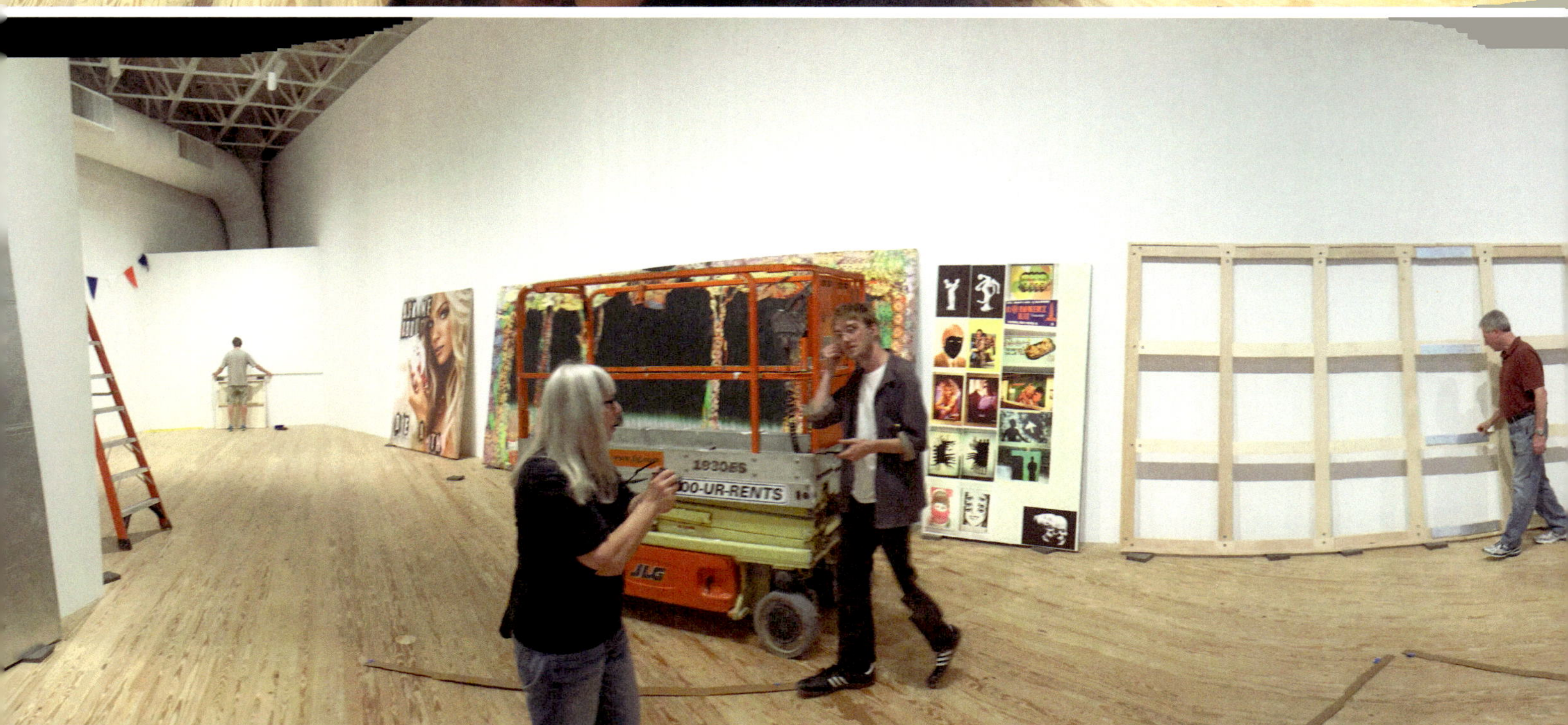
1830ES
JLG

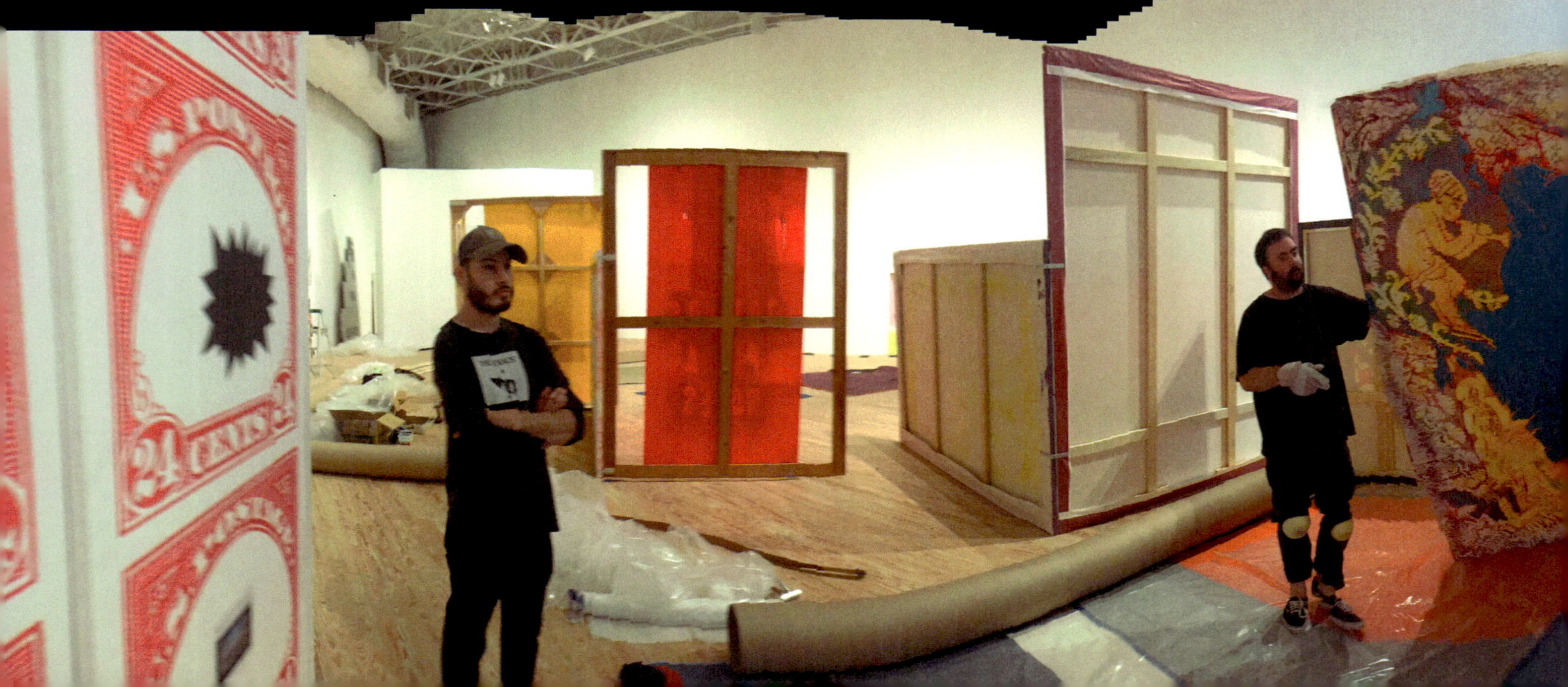

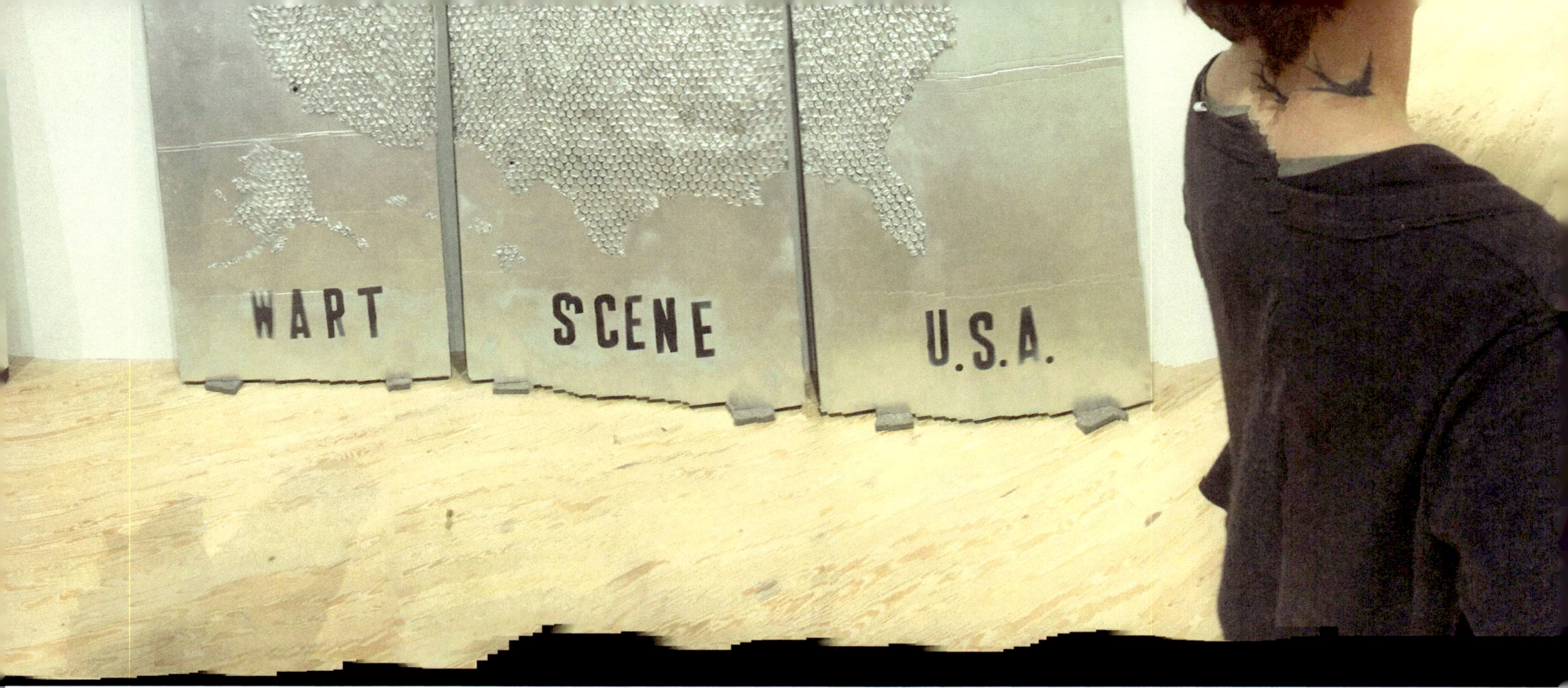

WART SCENE U.S.A.

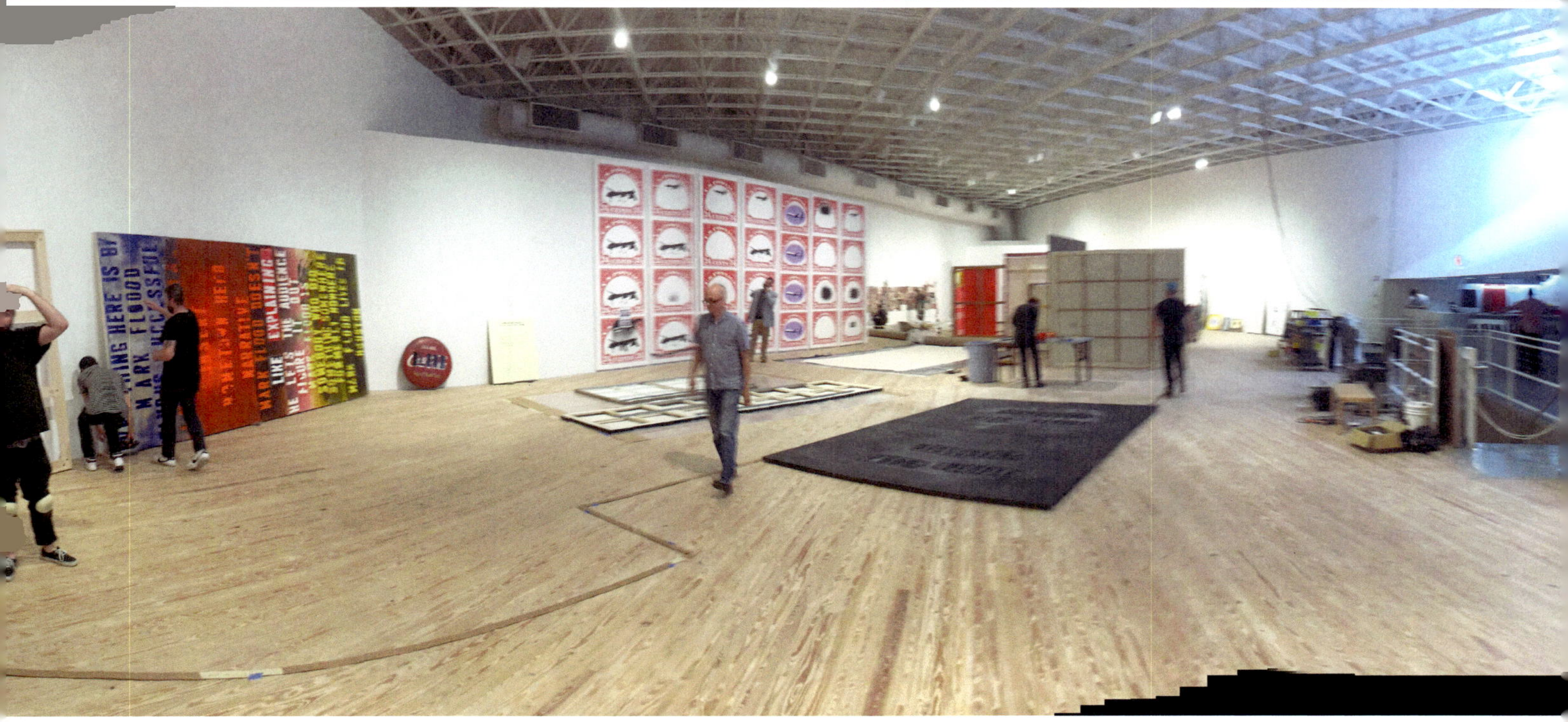

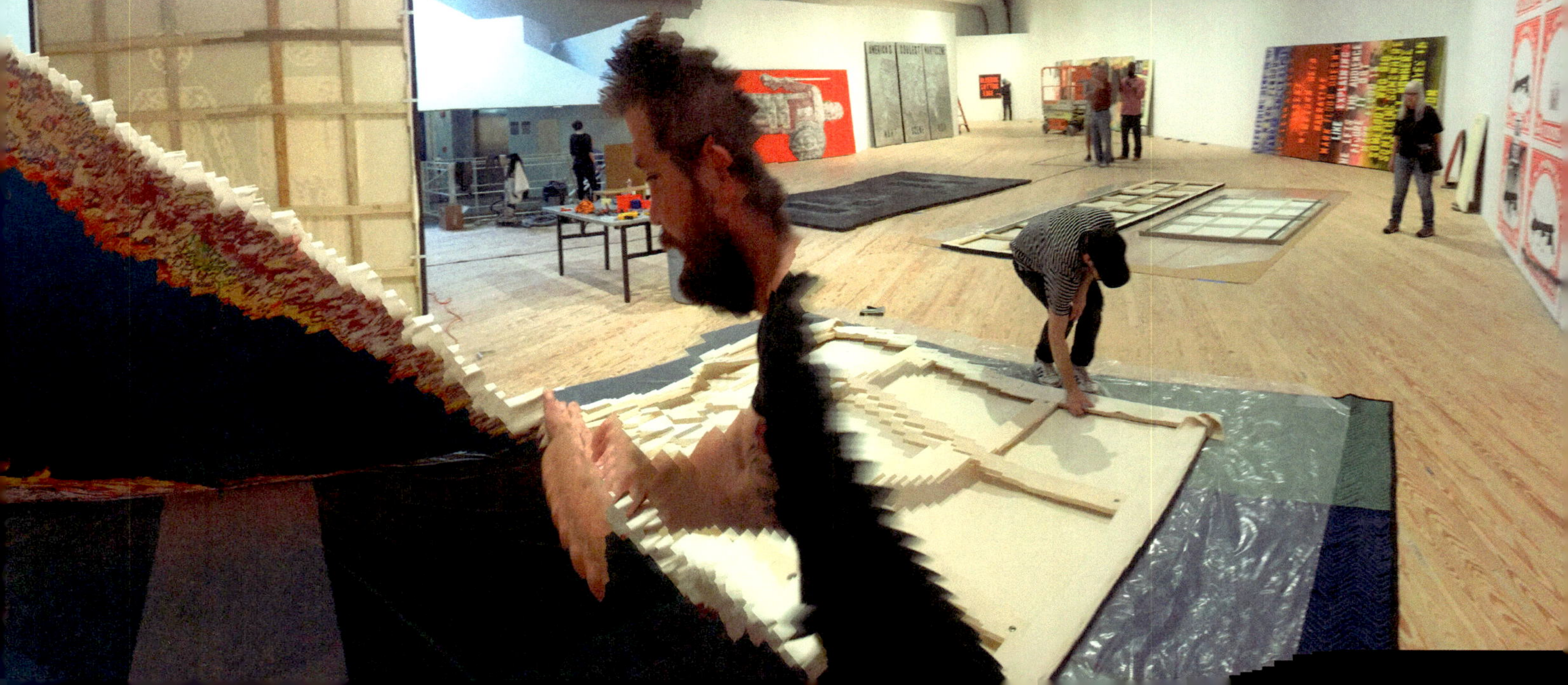

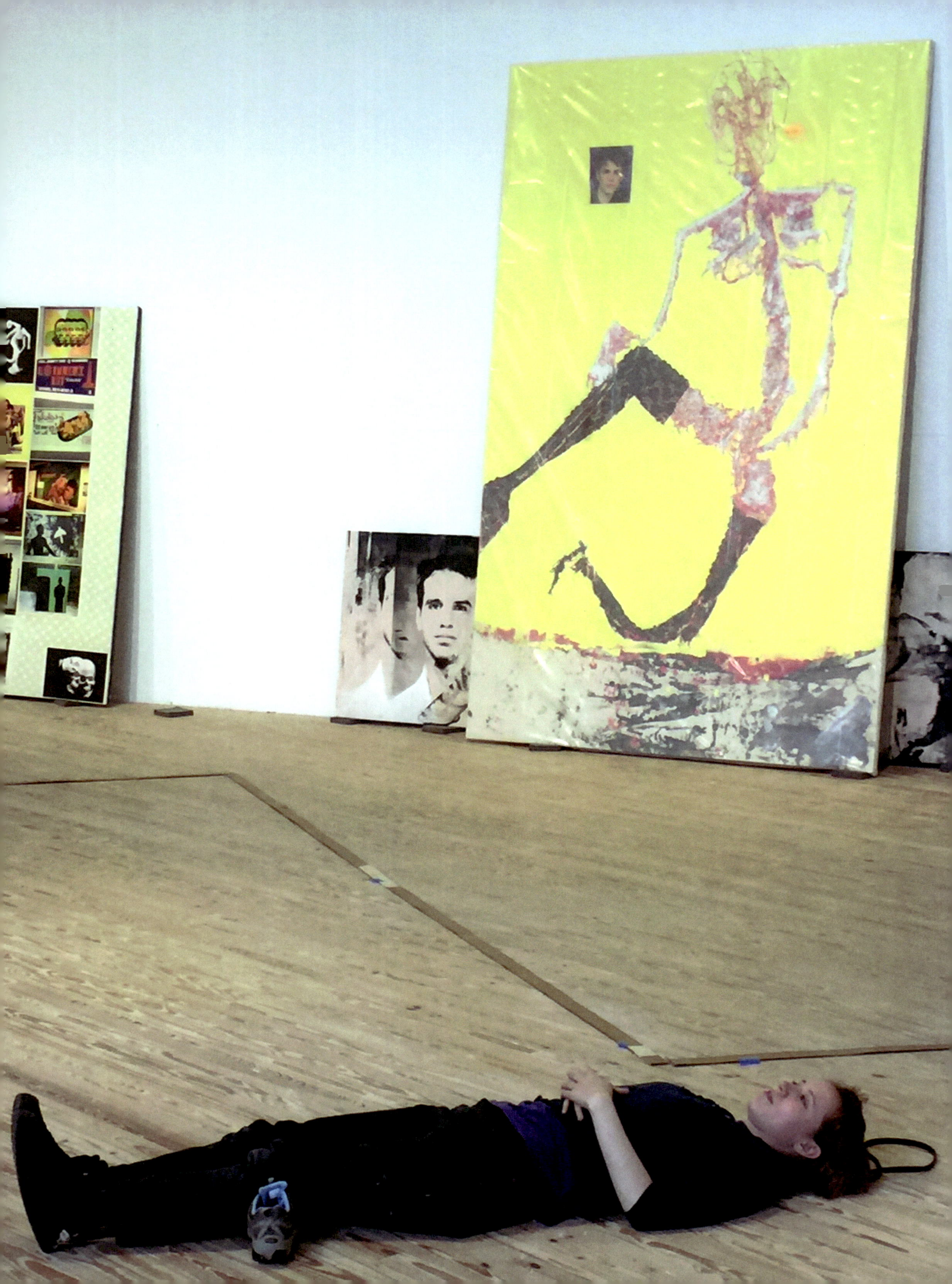

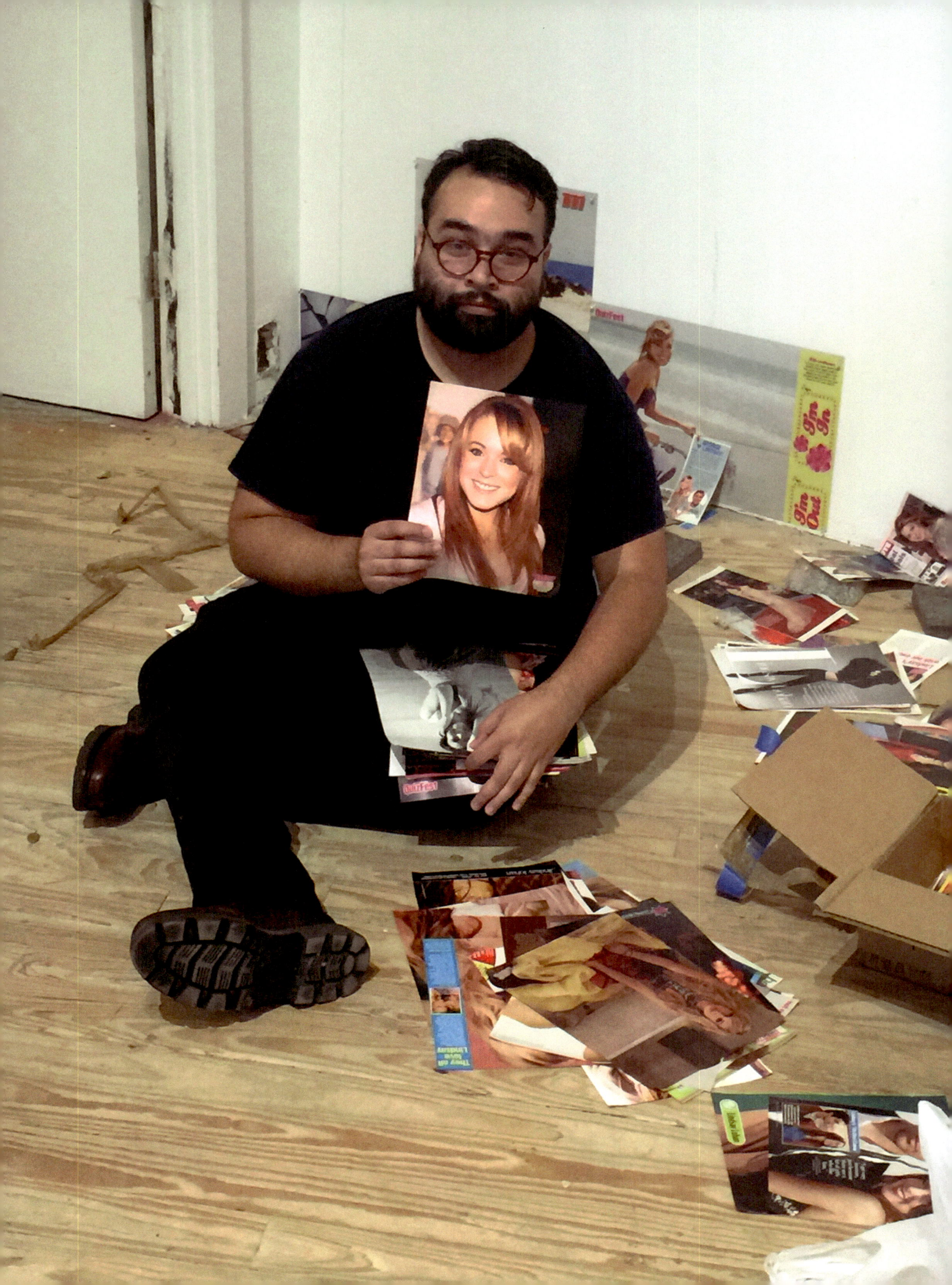
QuizFest
I'm In
I'm Out
QuizFest

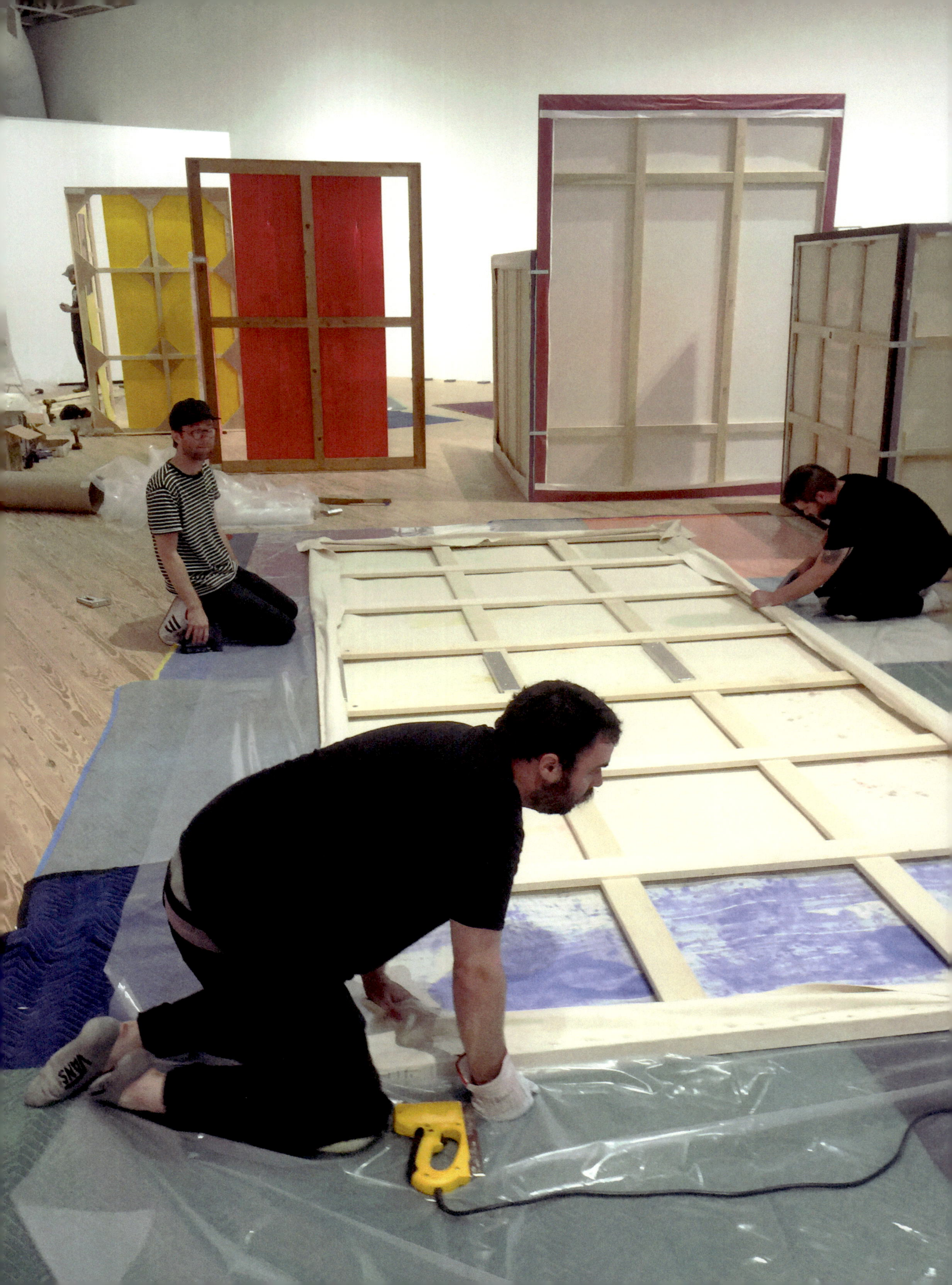
VANS

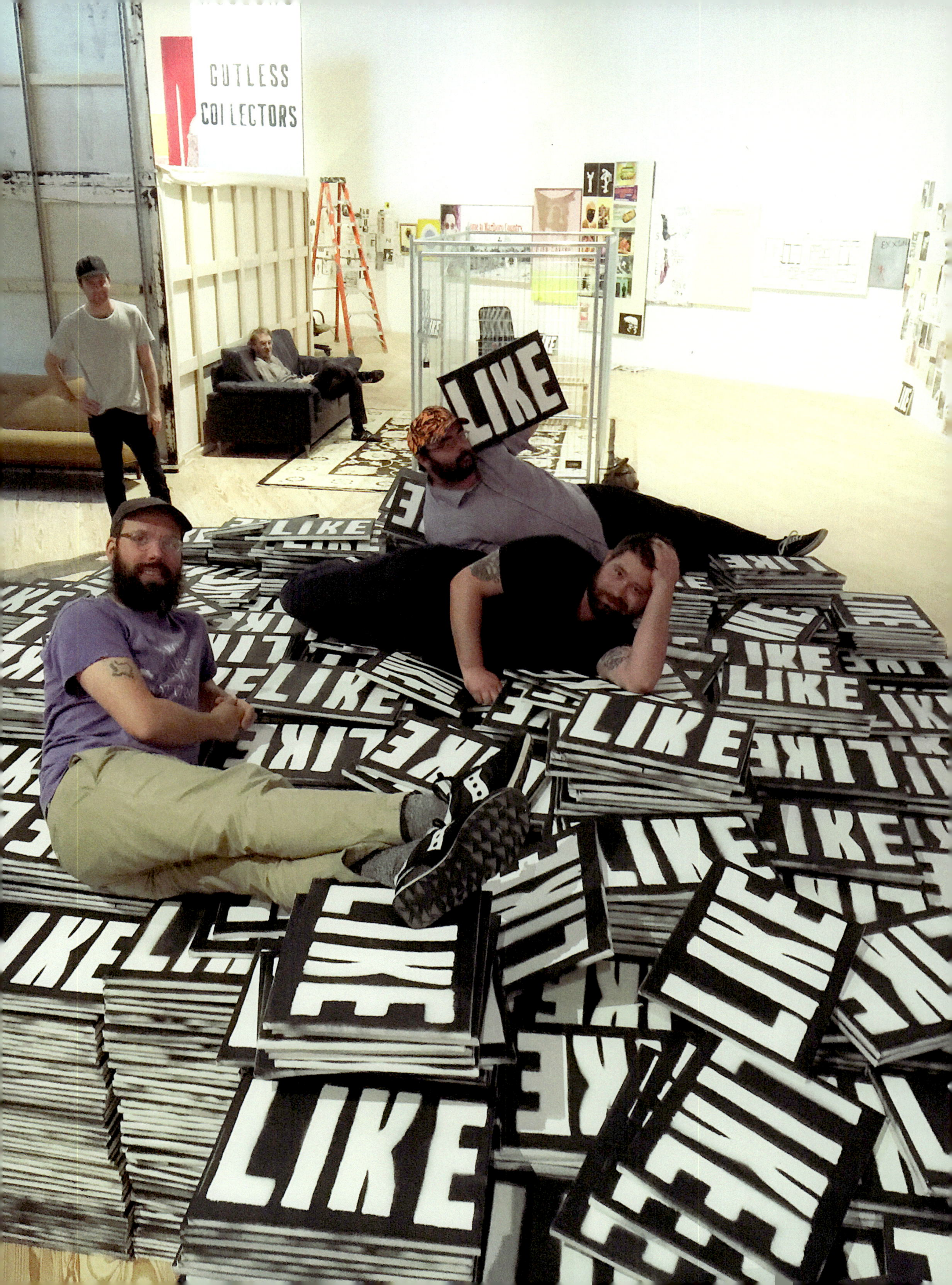
GUTLESS
COLLECTORS
LIKE

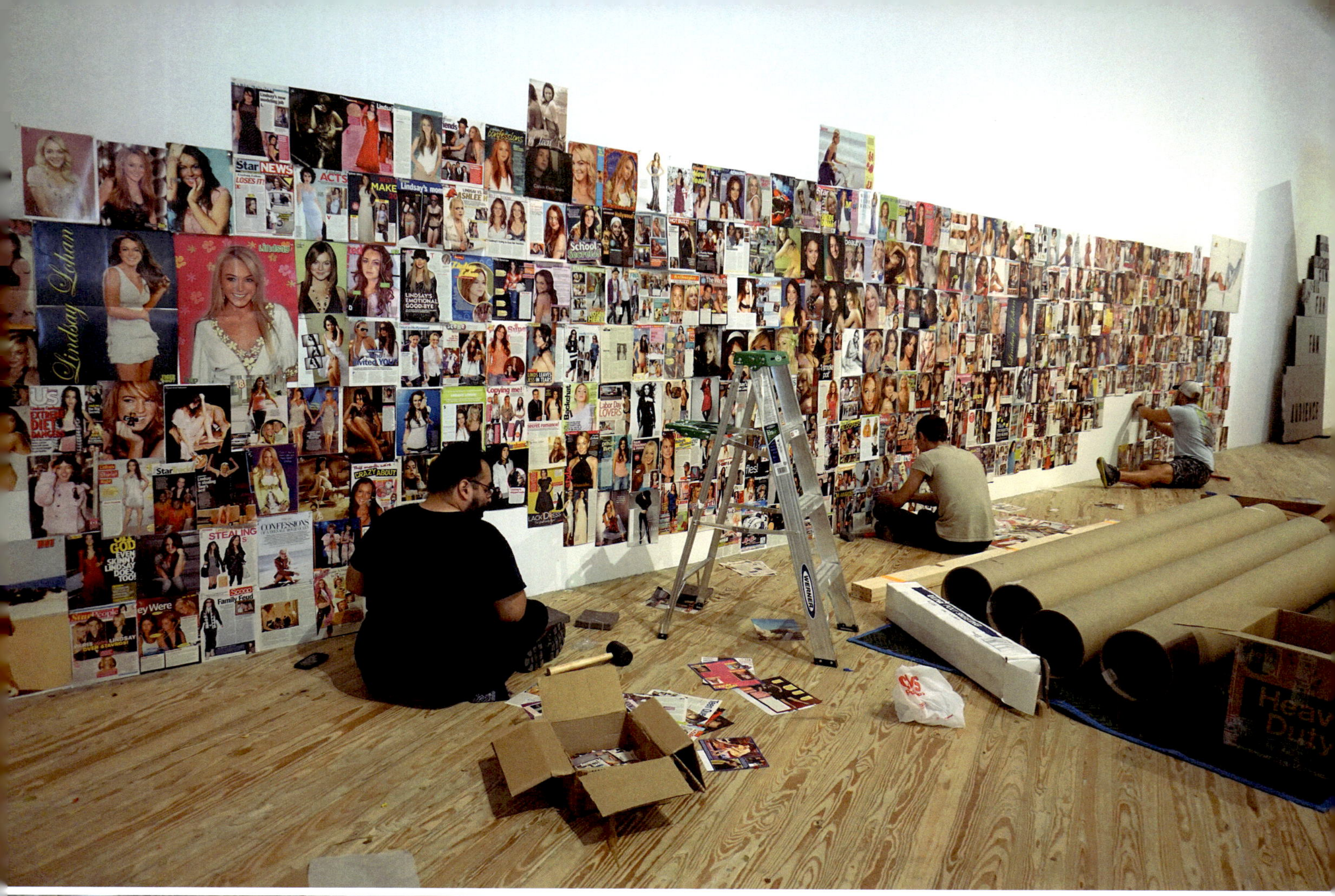

ASK YOUR DRUG DEALER
IF YOUR HEART IS STRONG
ENOUGH FOR SEXUAL ACTIVITY

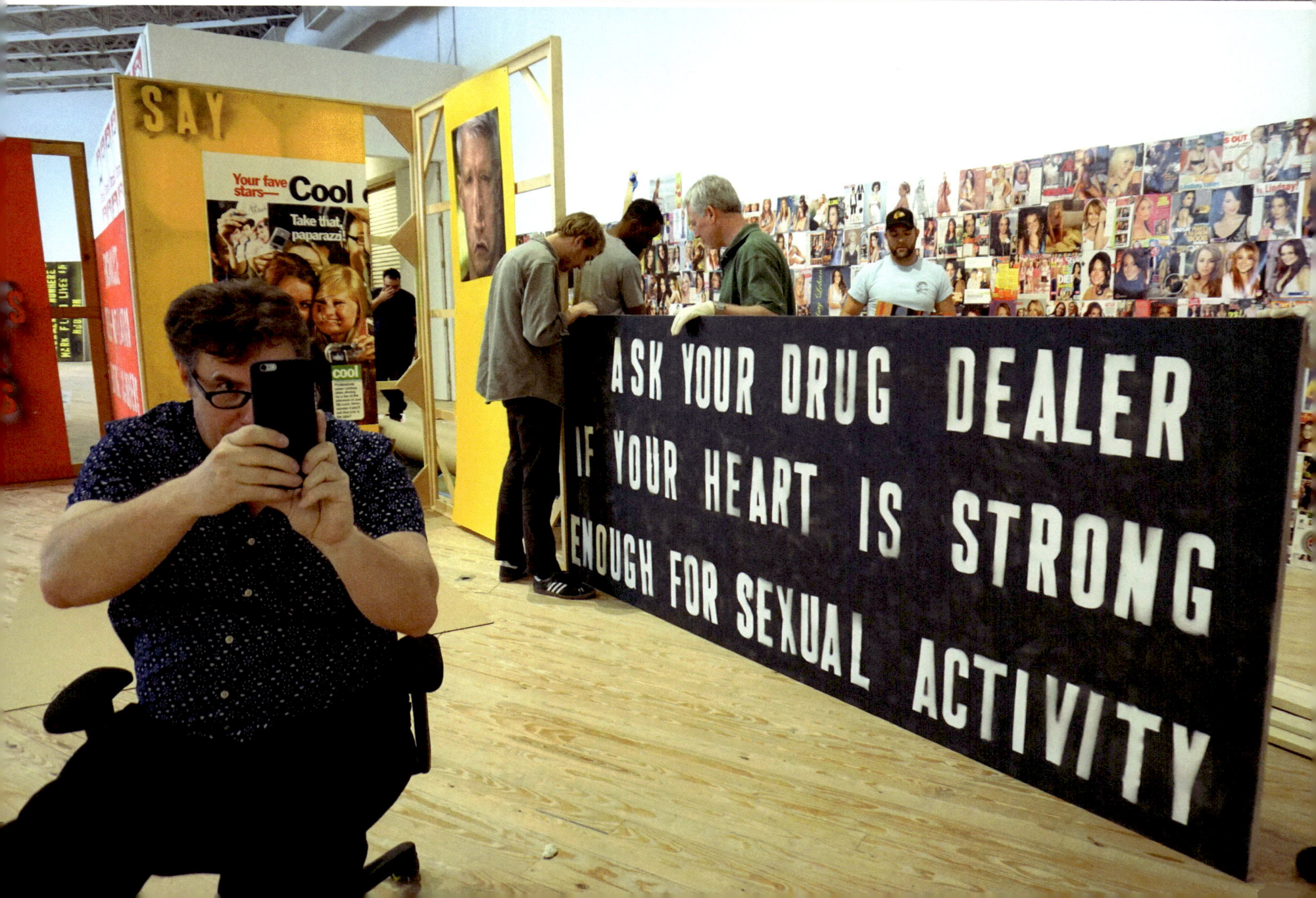

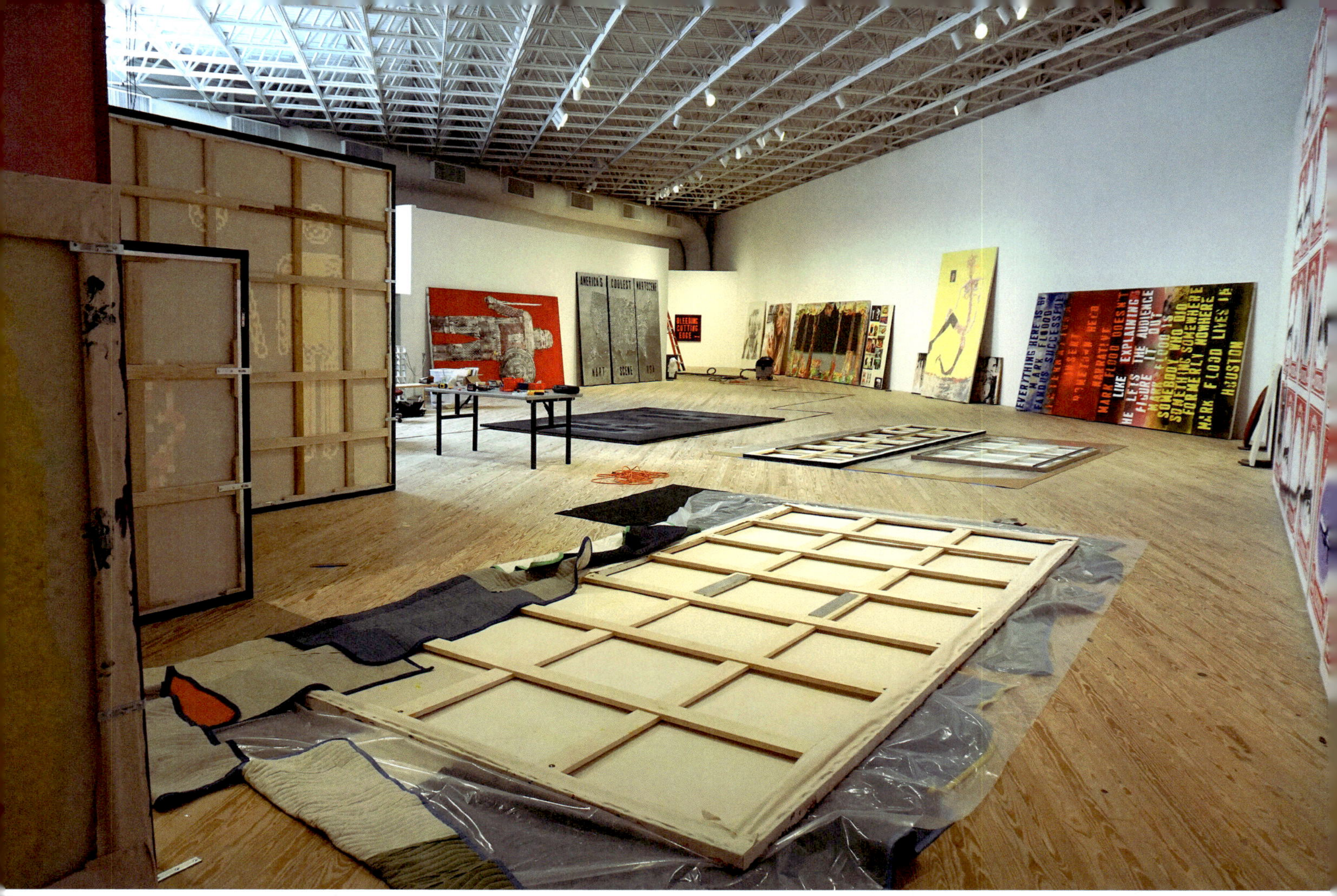

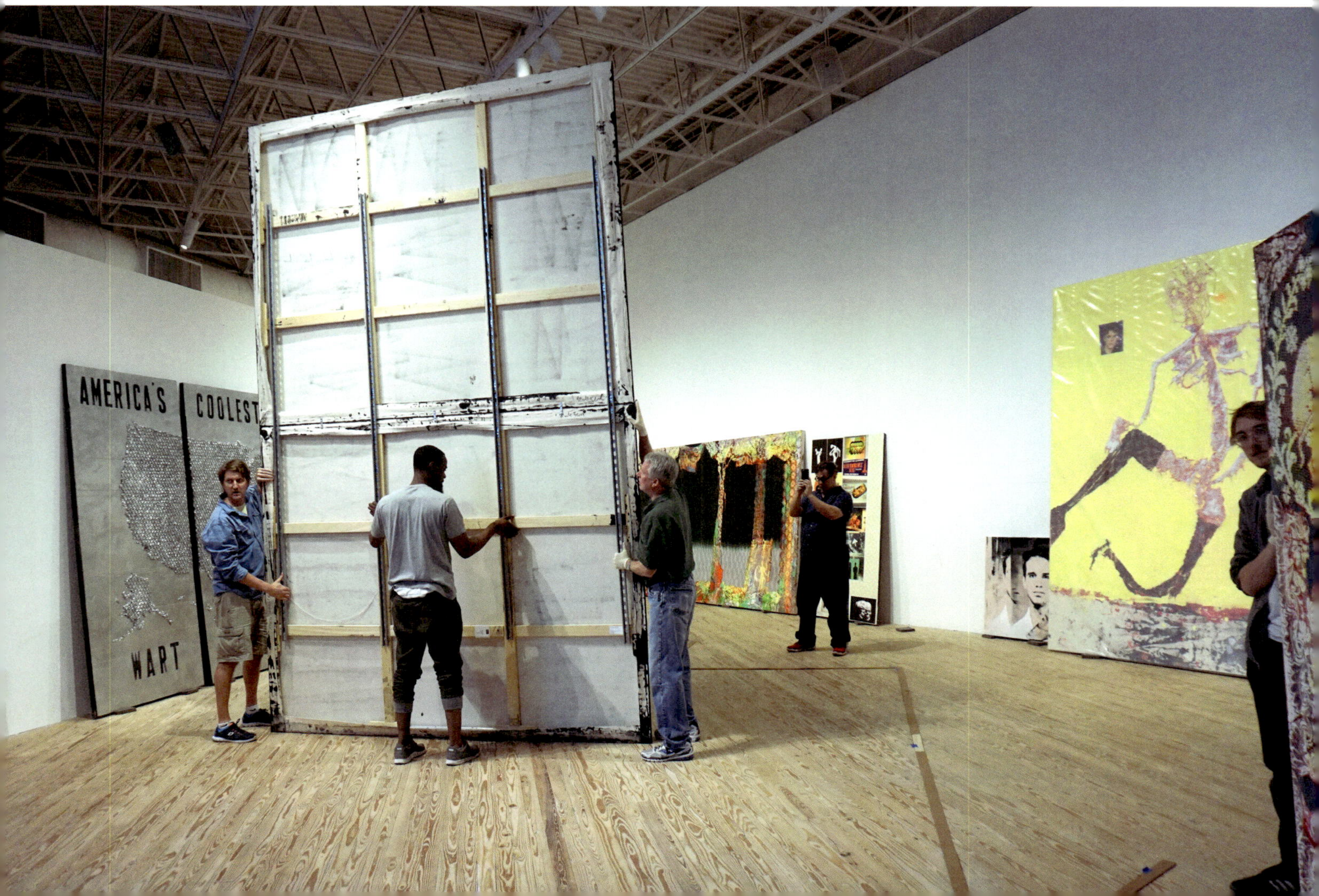

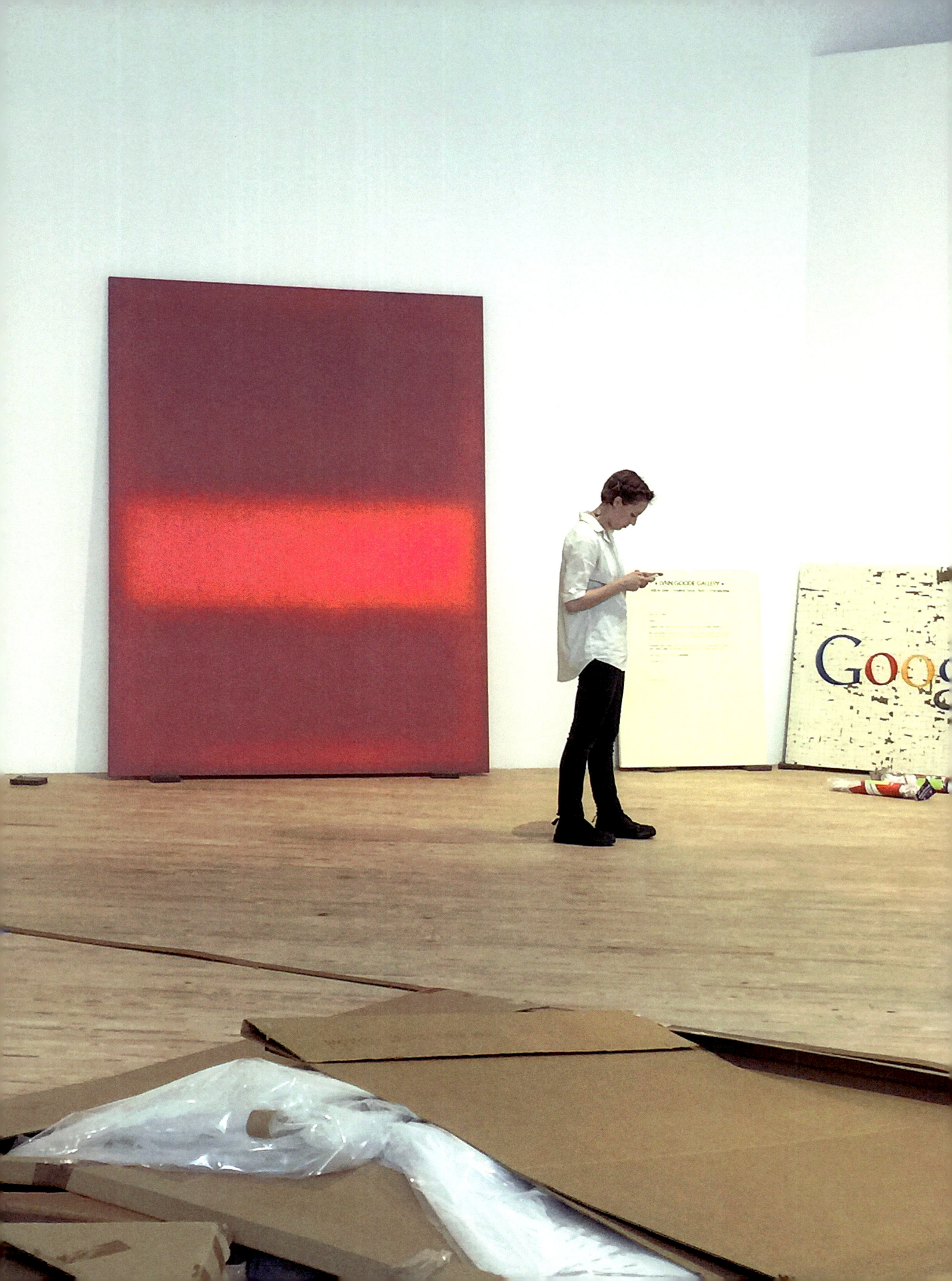

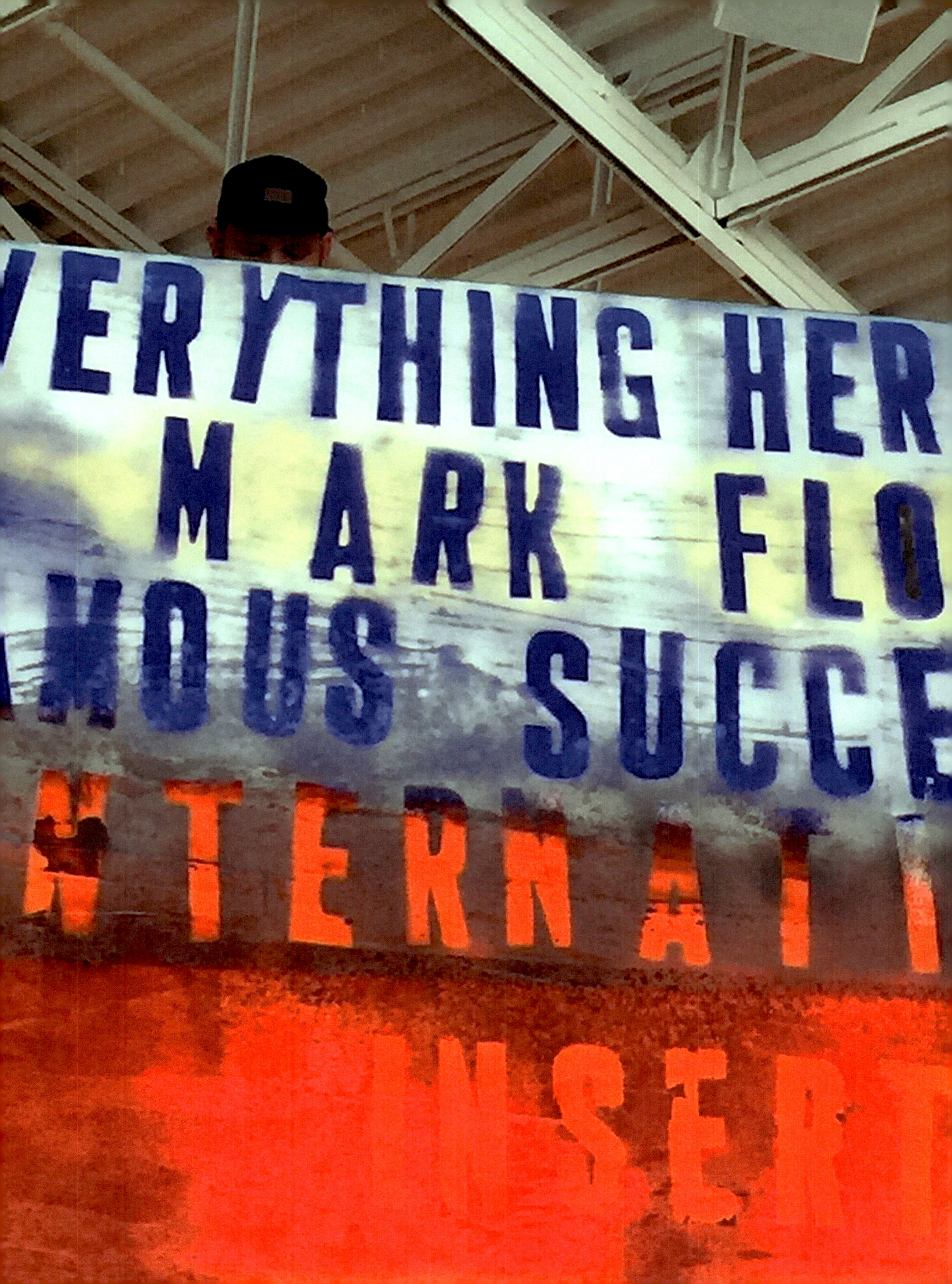
VERYTHING HER
M ARK FLO
MOUS SUCCE
NTERNATI
NSER

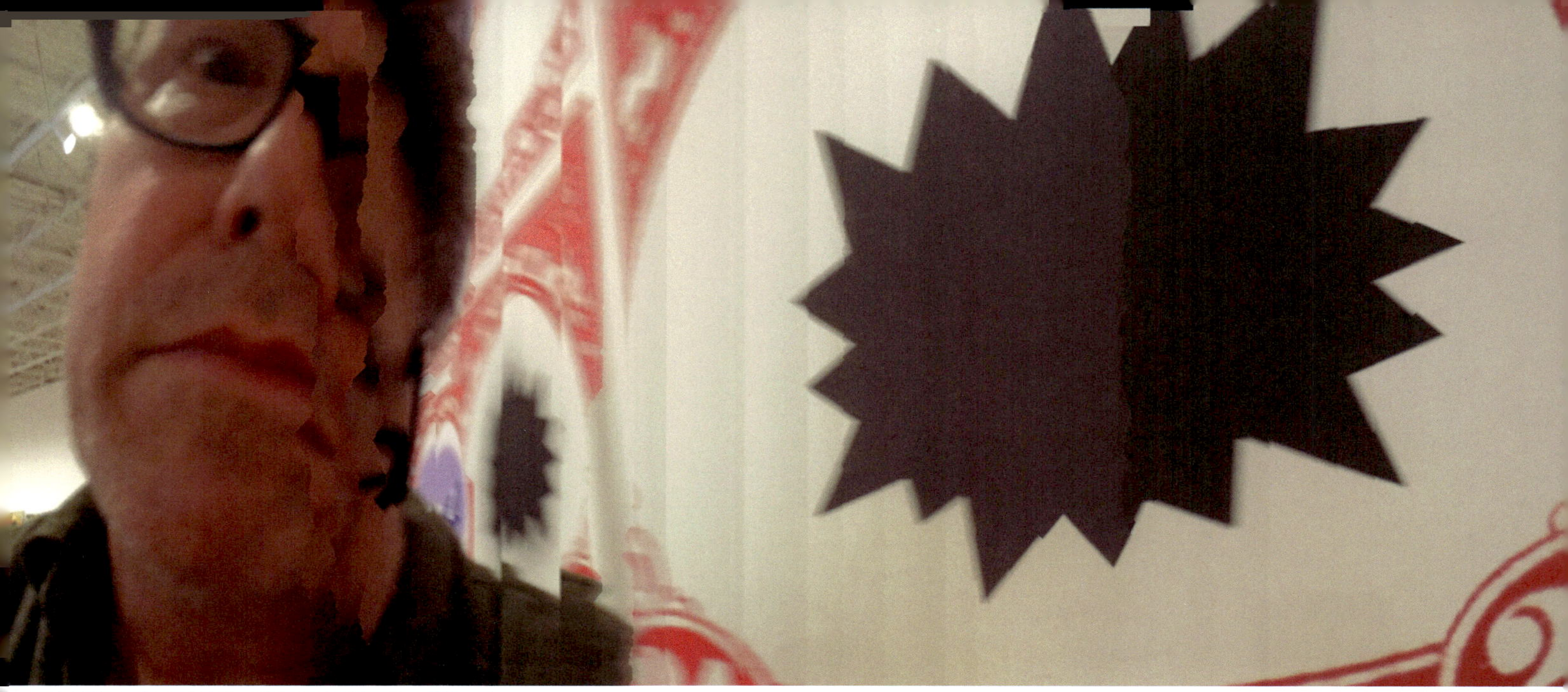

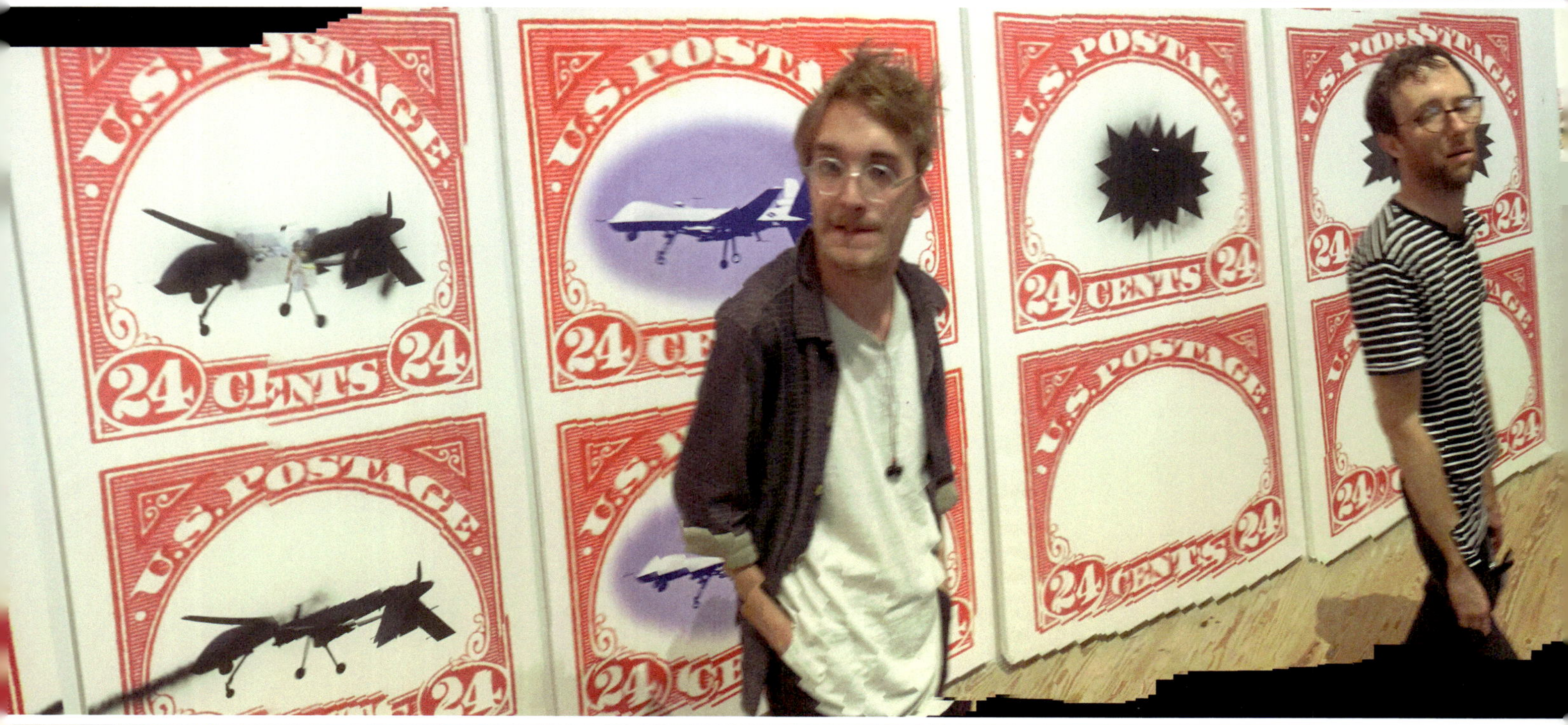

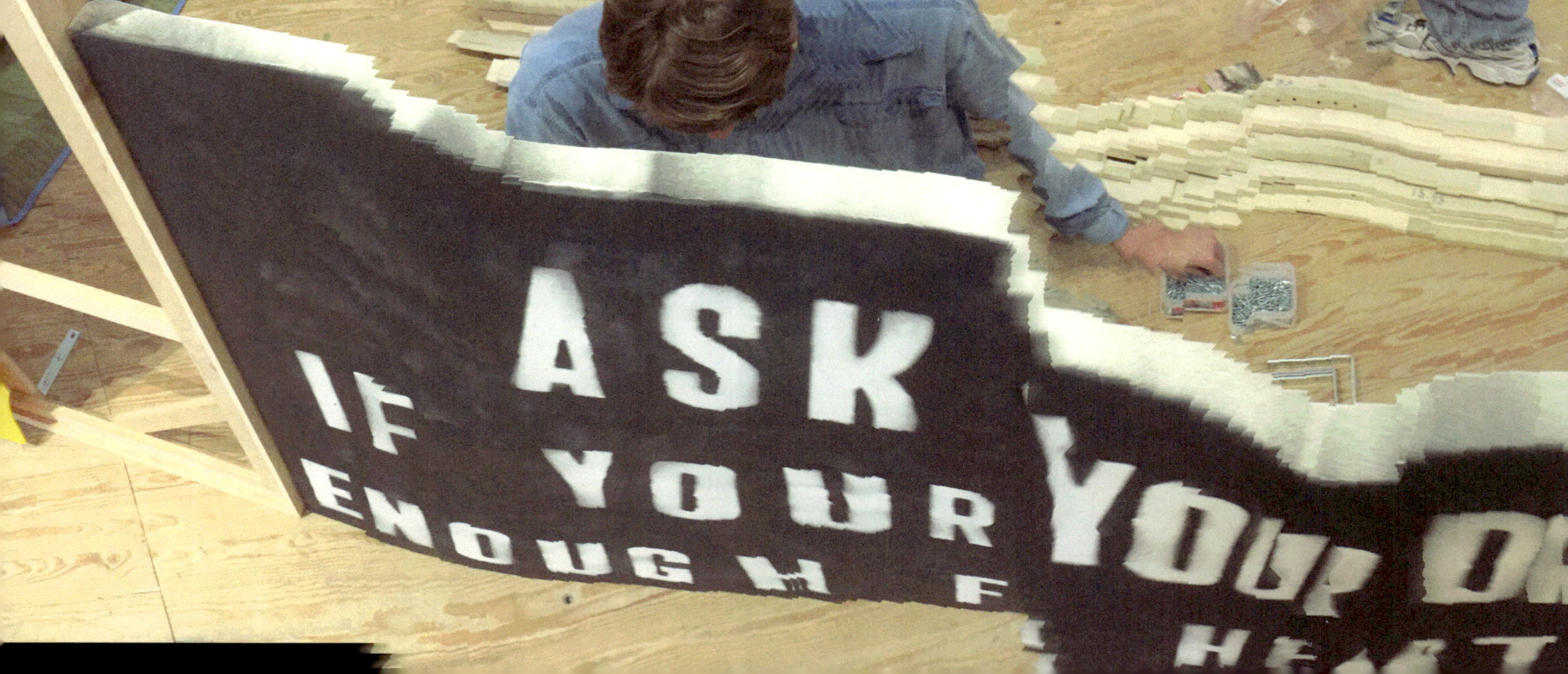
ASK
IF YOUR

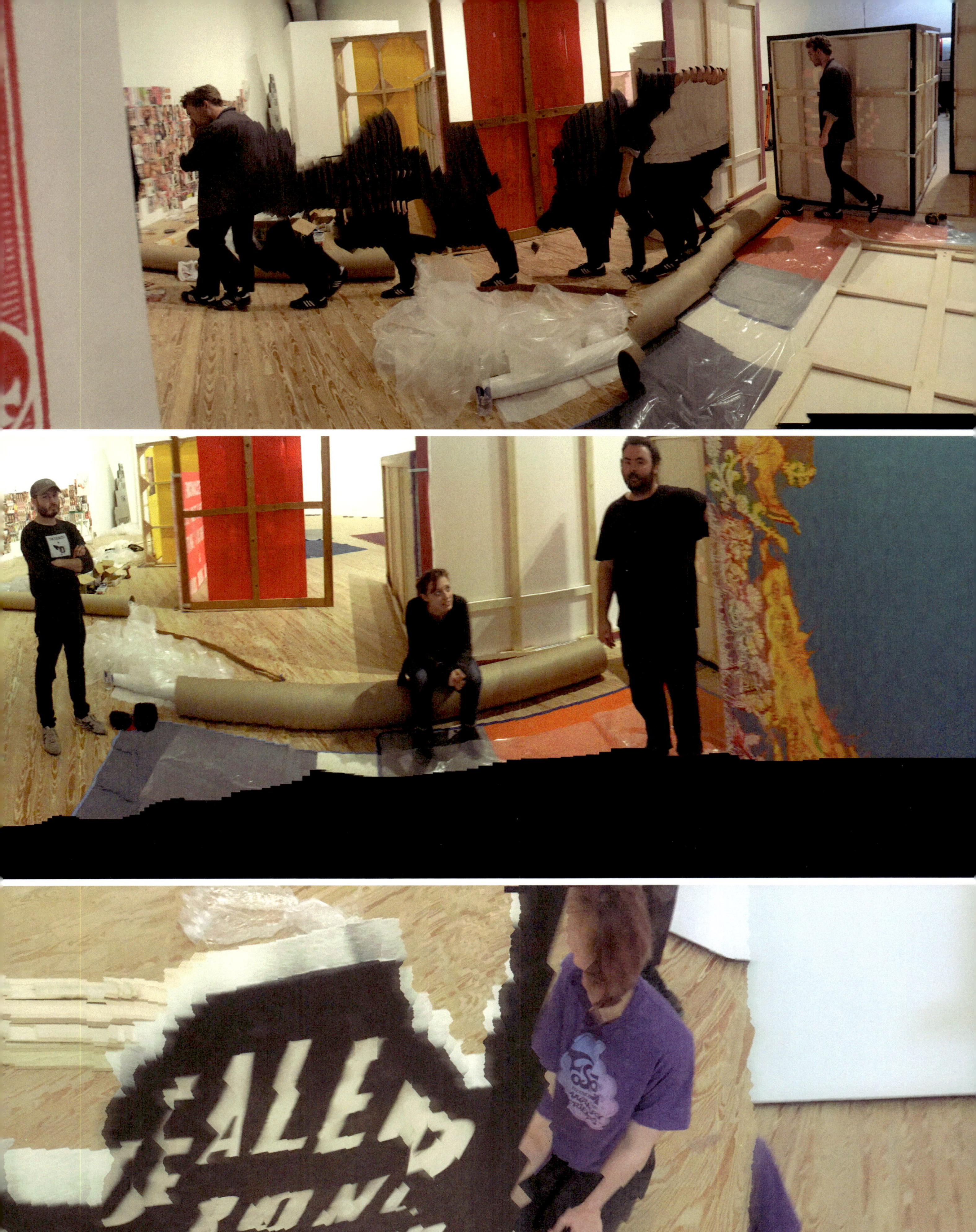

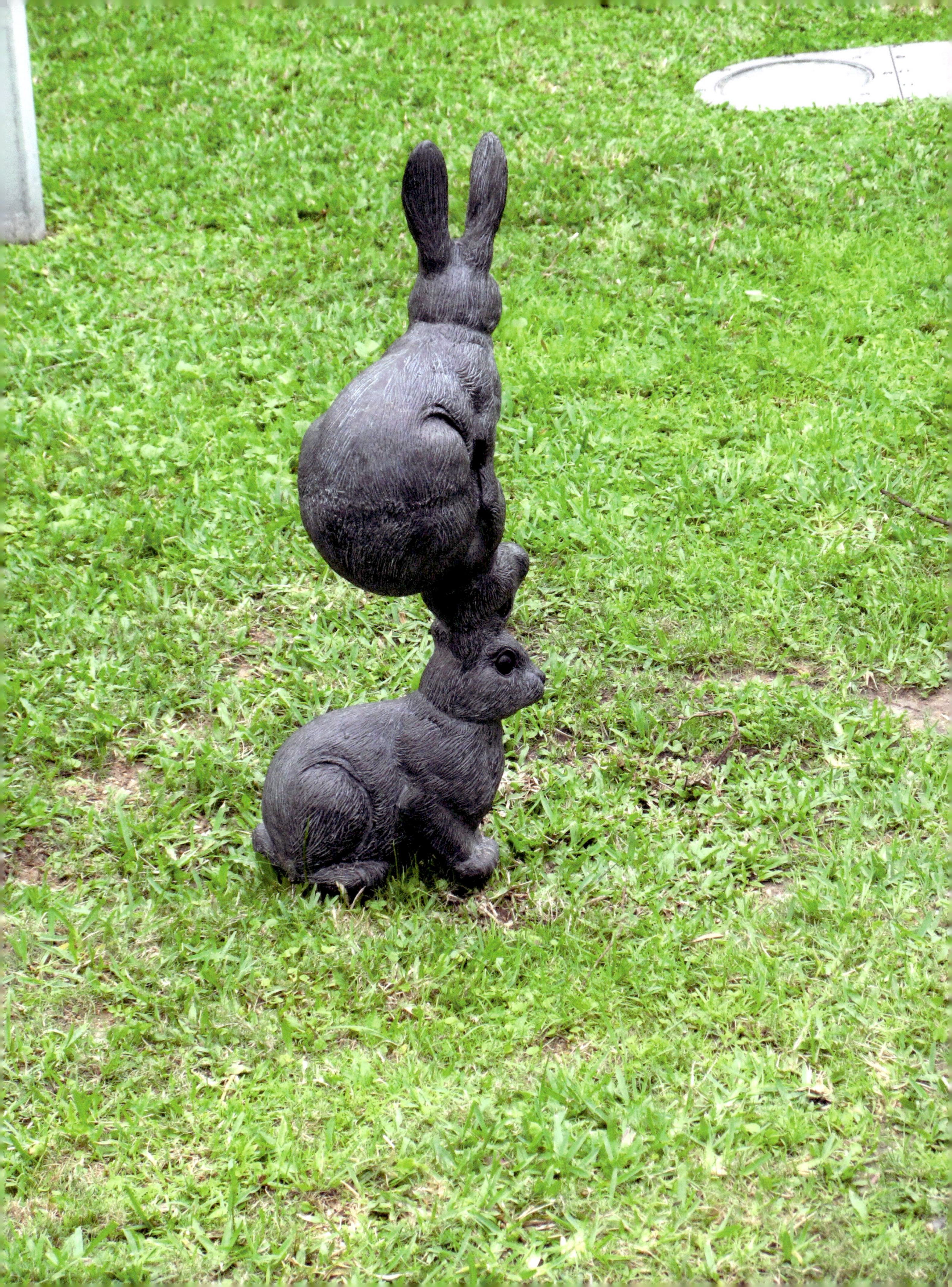

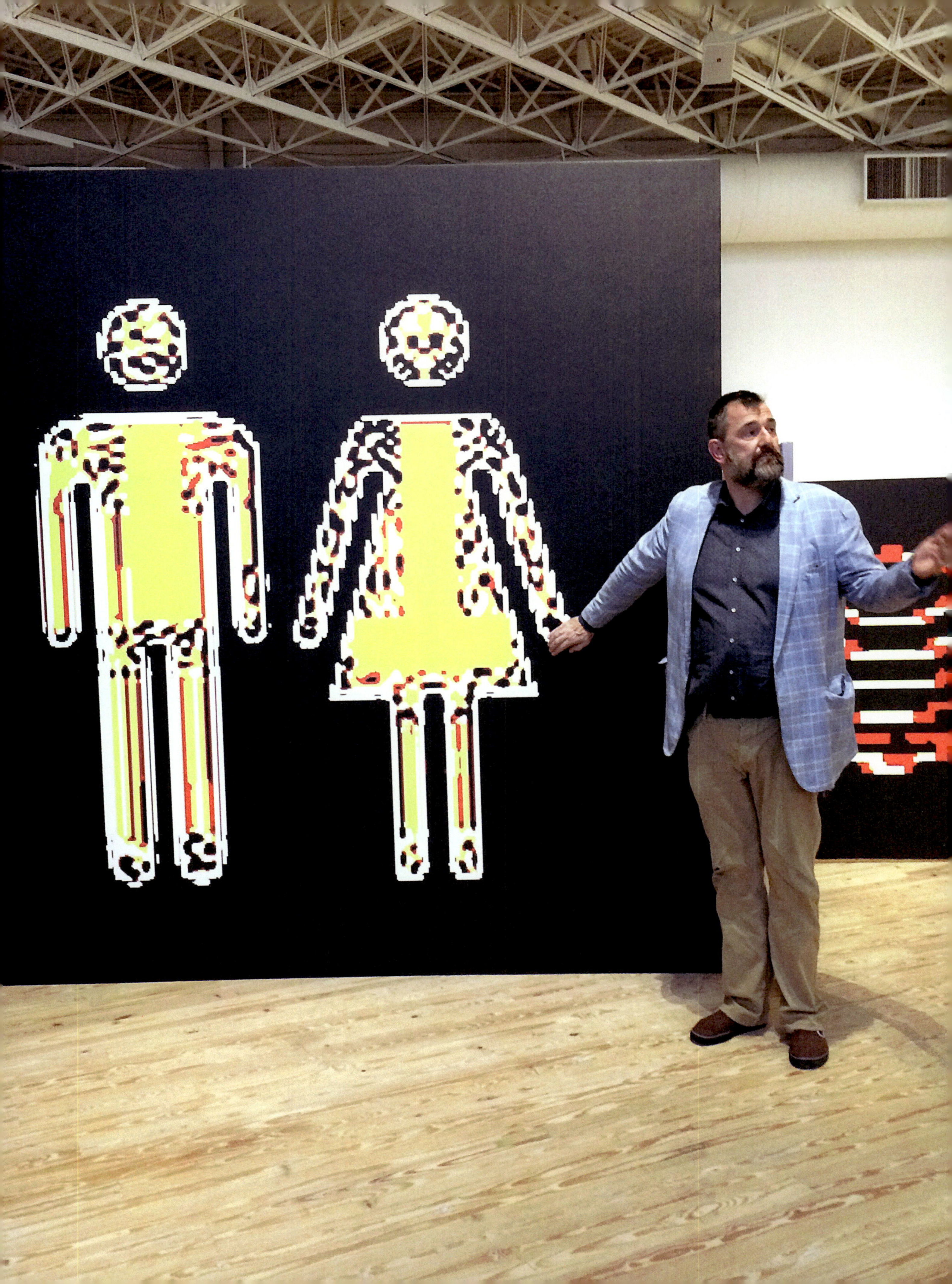

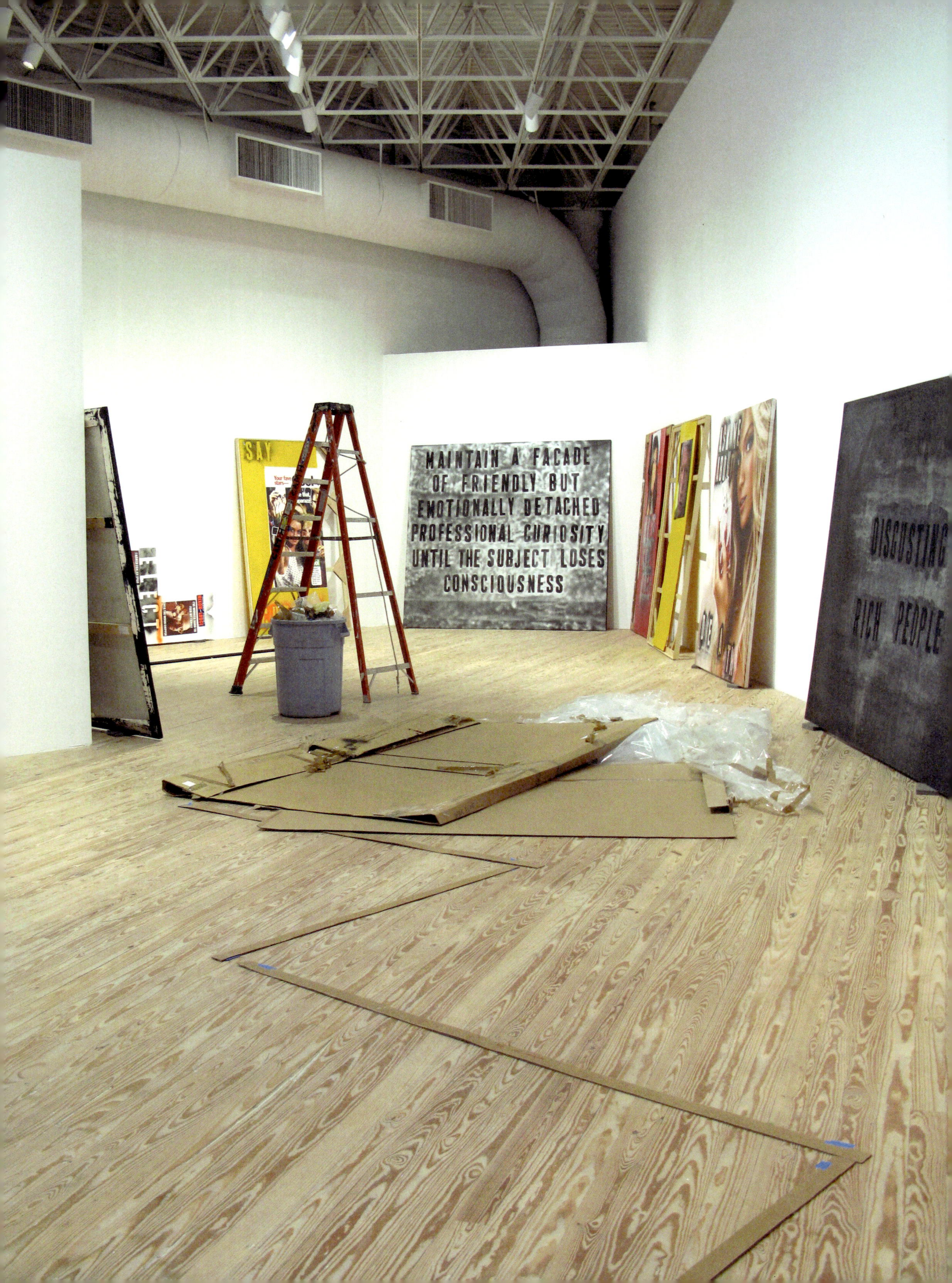
SAY
MAINTAIN A FACADE OF FRIENDLY BUT EMOTIONALLY DETACHED PROFESSIONAL CURIOSITY UNTIL THE SUBJECT LOSES CONSCIOUSNESS
DISGUSTING RICH PEOPLE

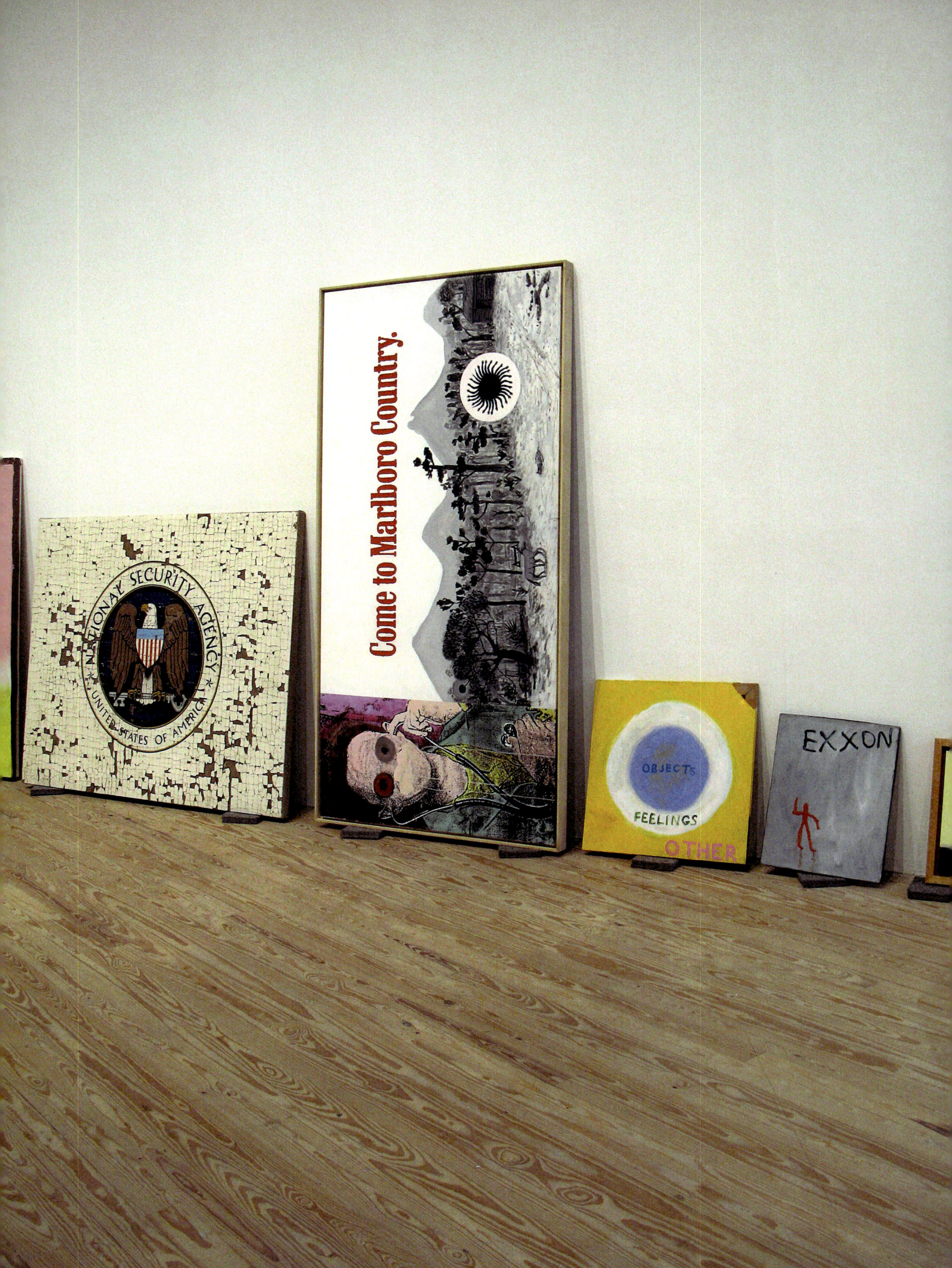

NATIONAL SECURITY AGENCY
UNITED STATES OF AMERICA
Come to Marlboro Country.
OBJECTS
FEELINGS
OTHER
EXXON

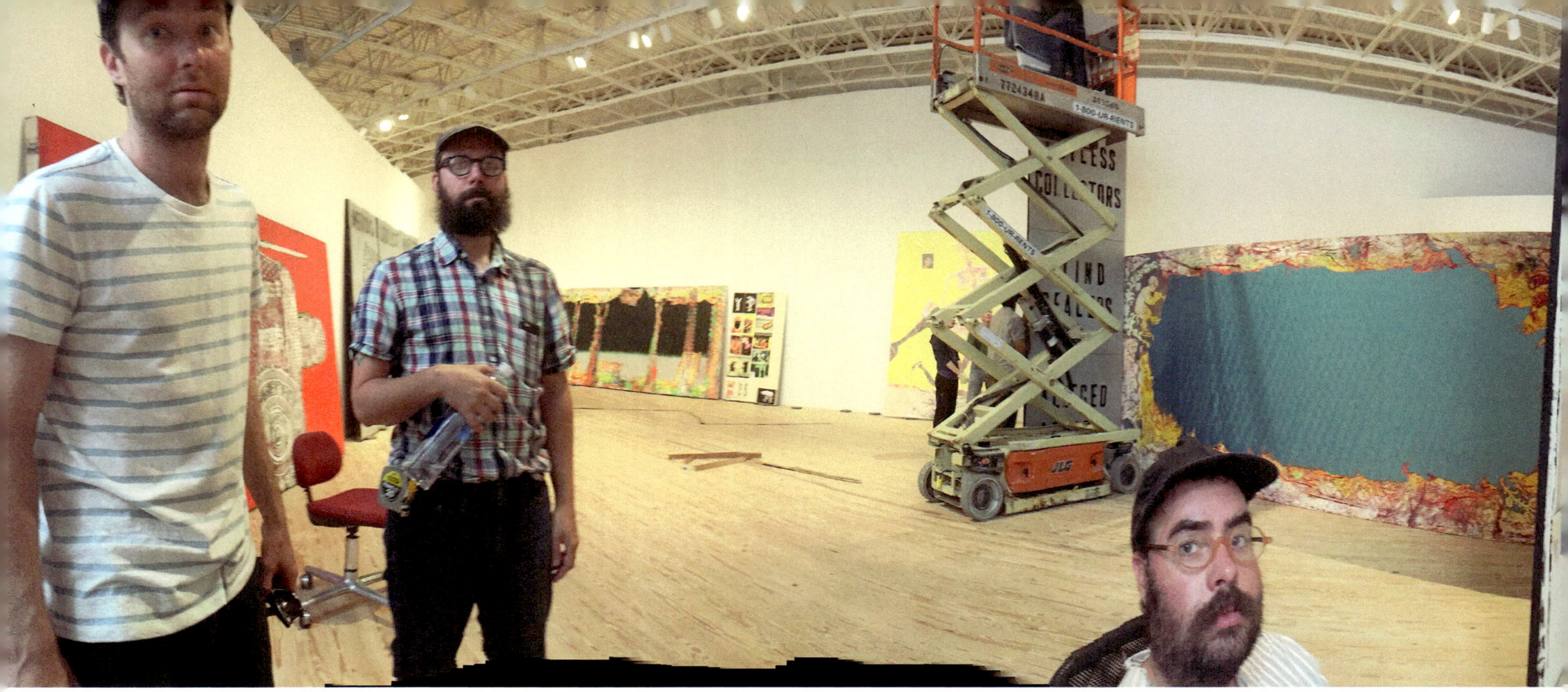

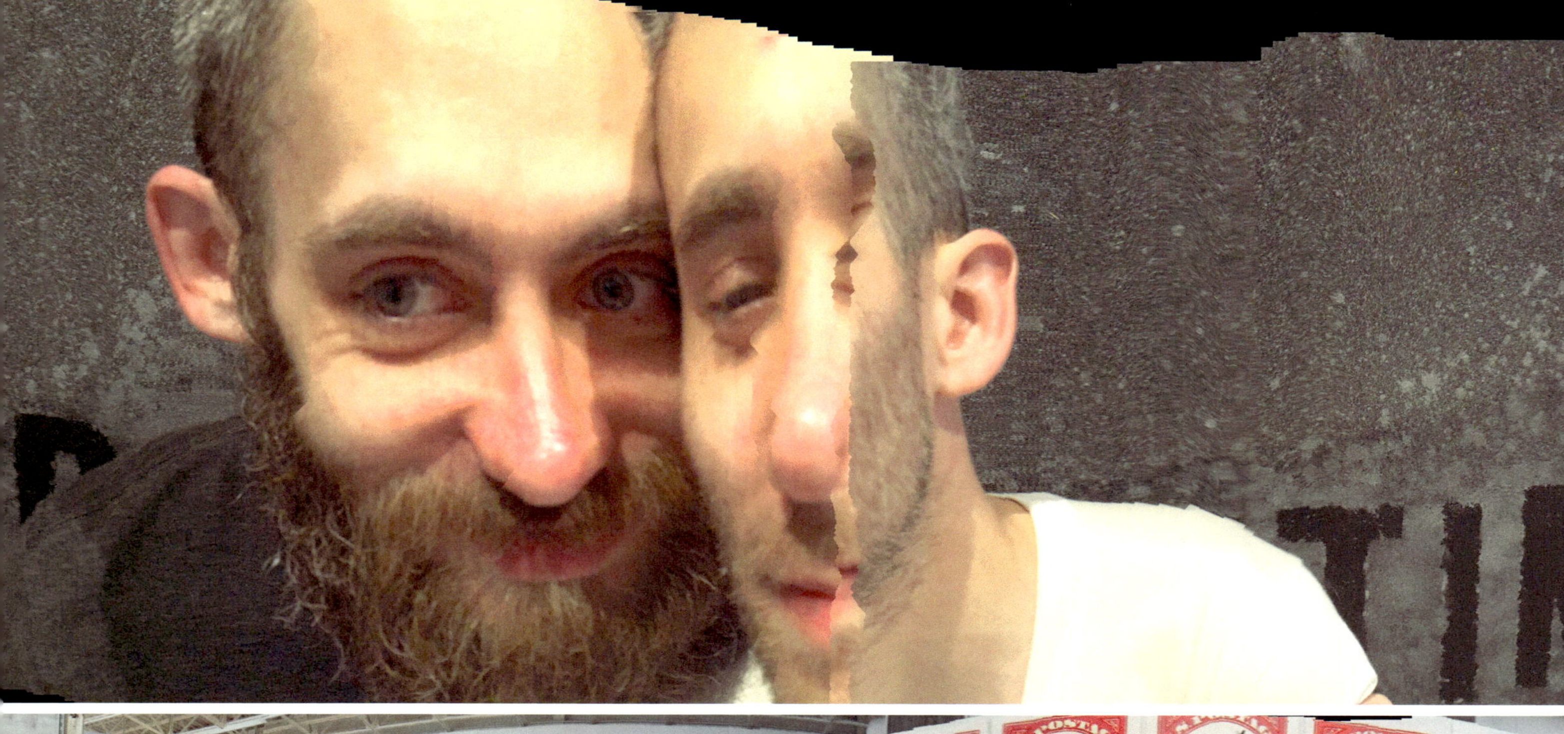

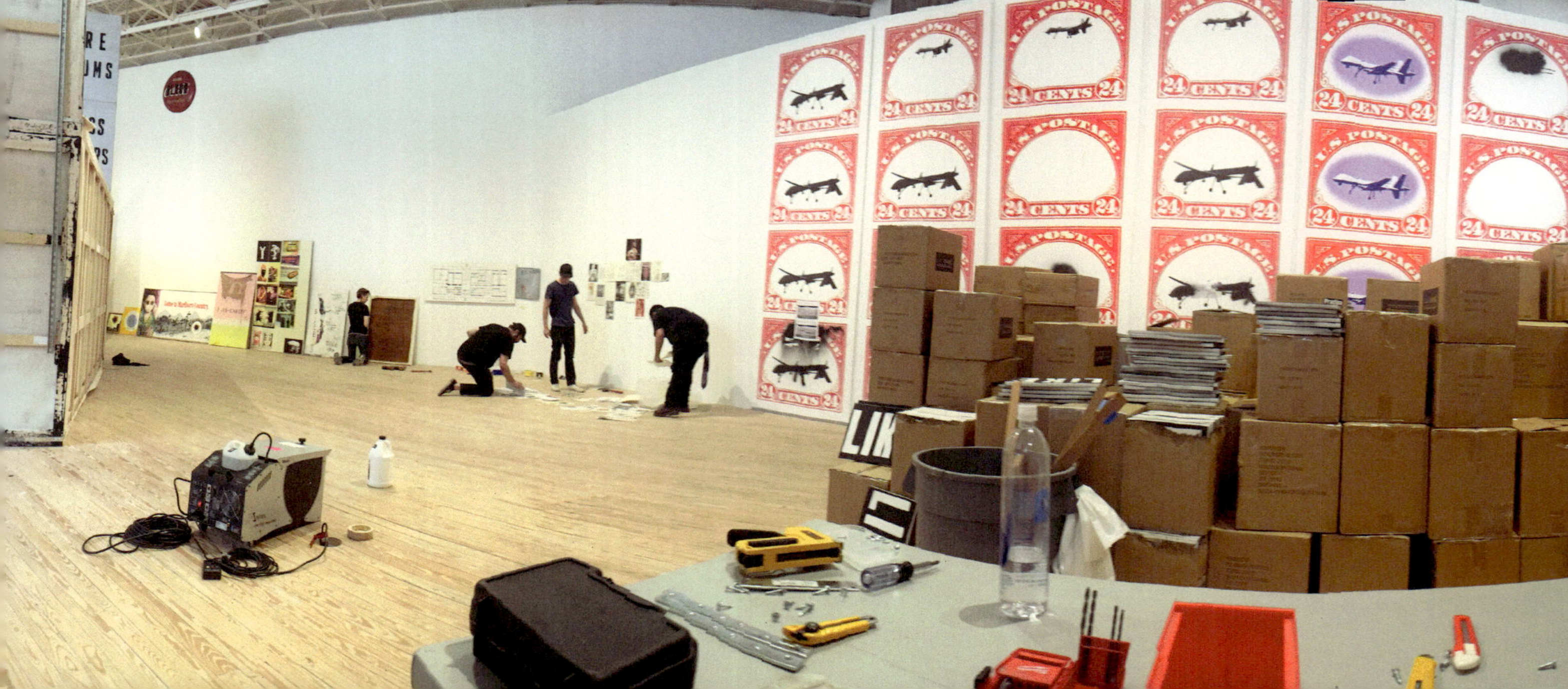
U.S. POSTAGE
24 CENTS 24

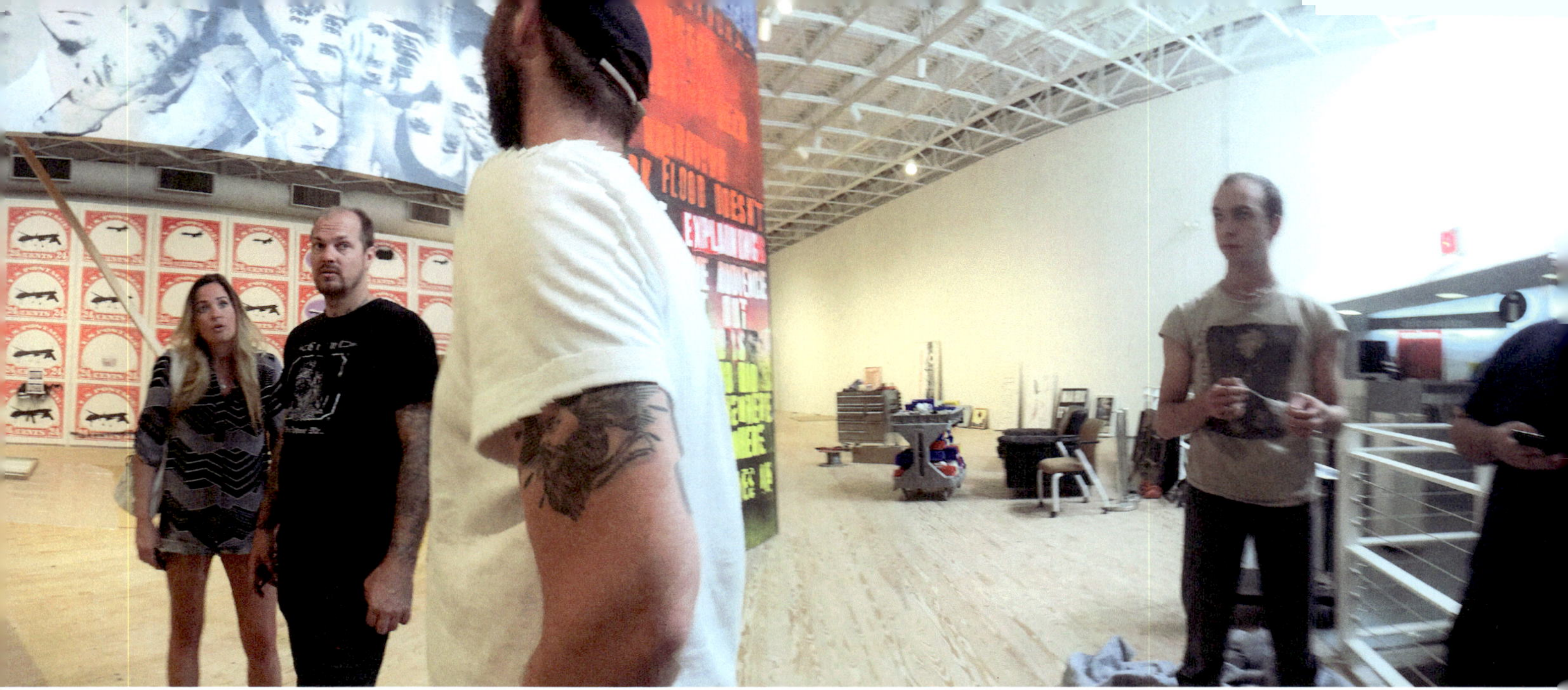

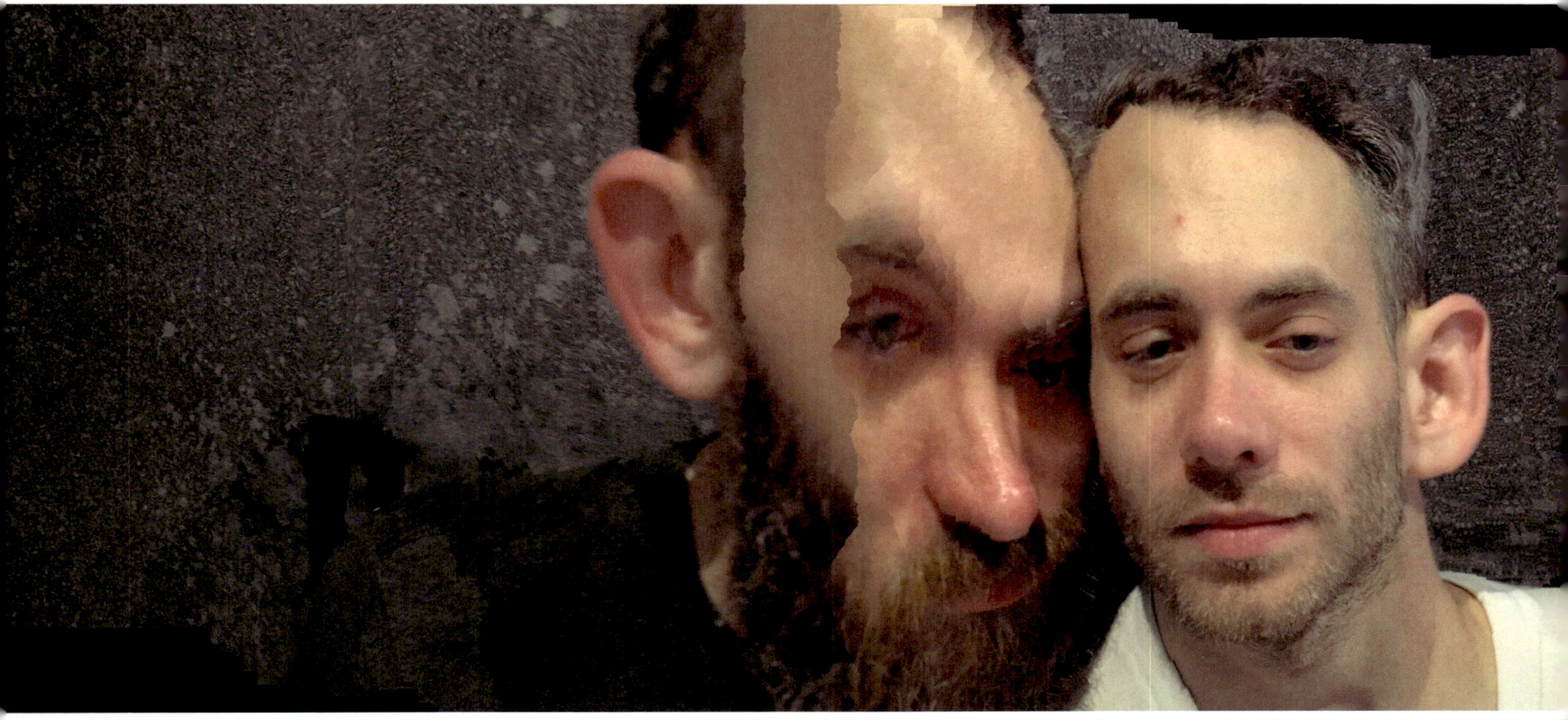

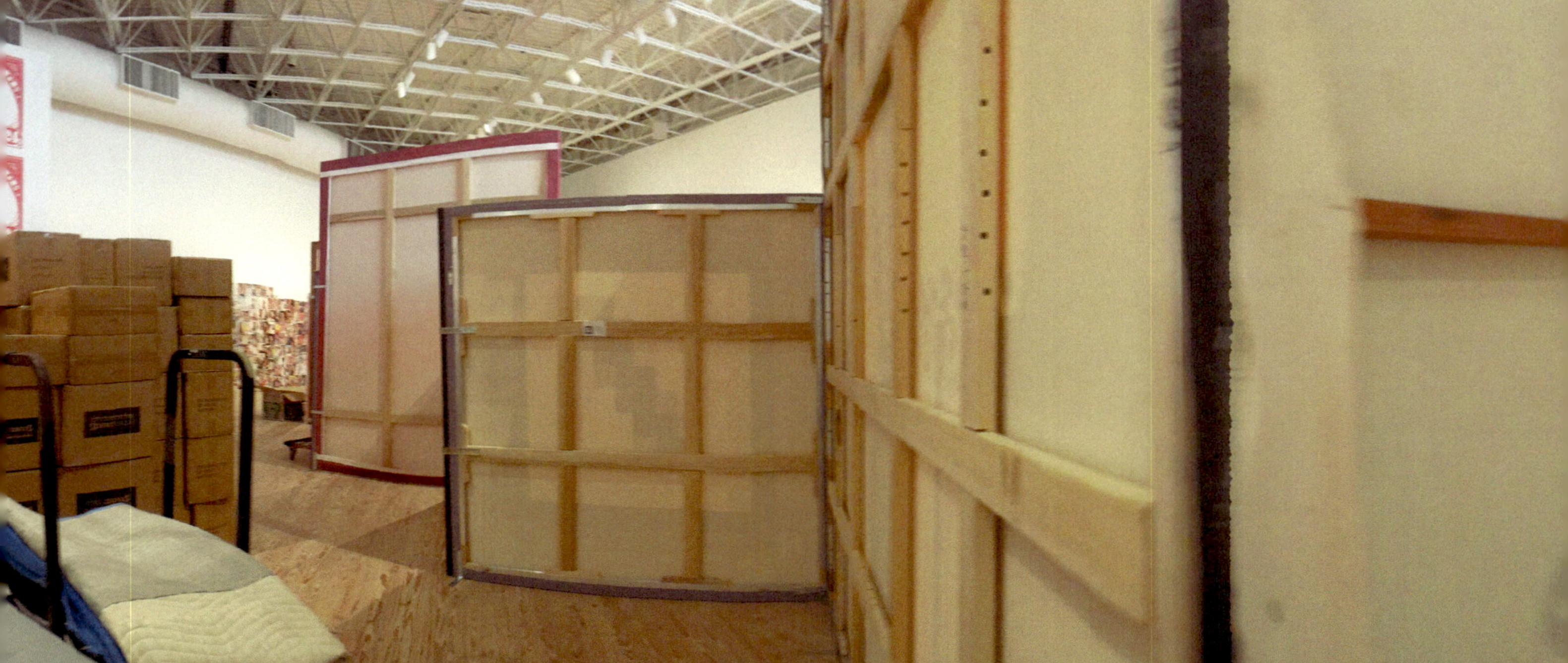

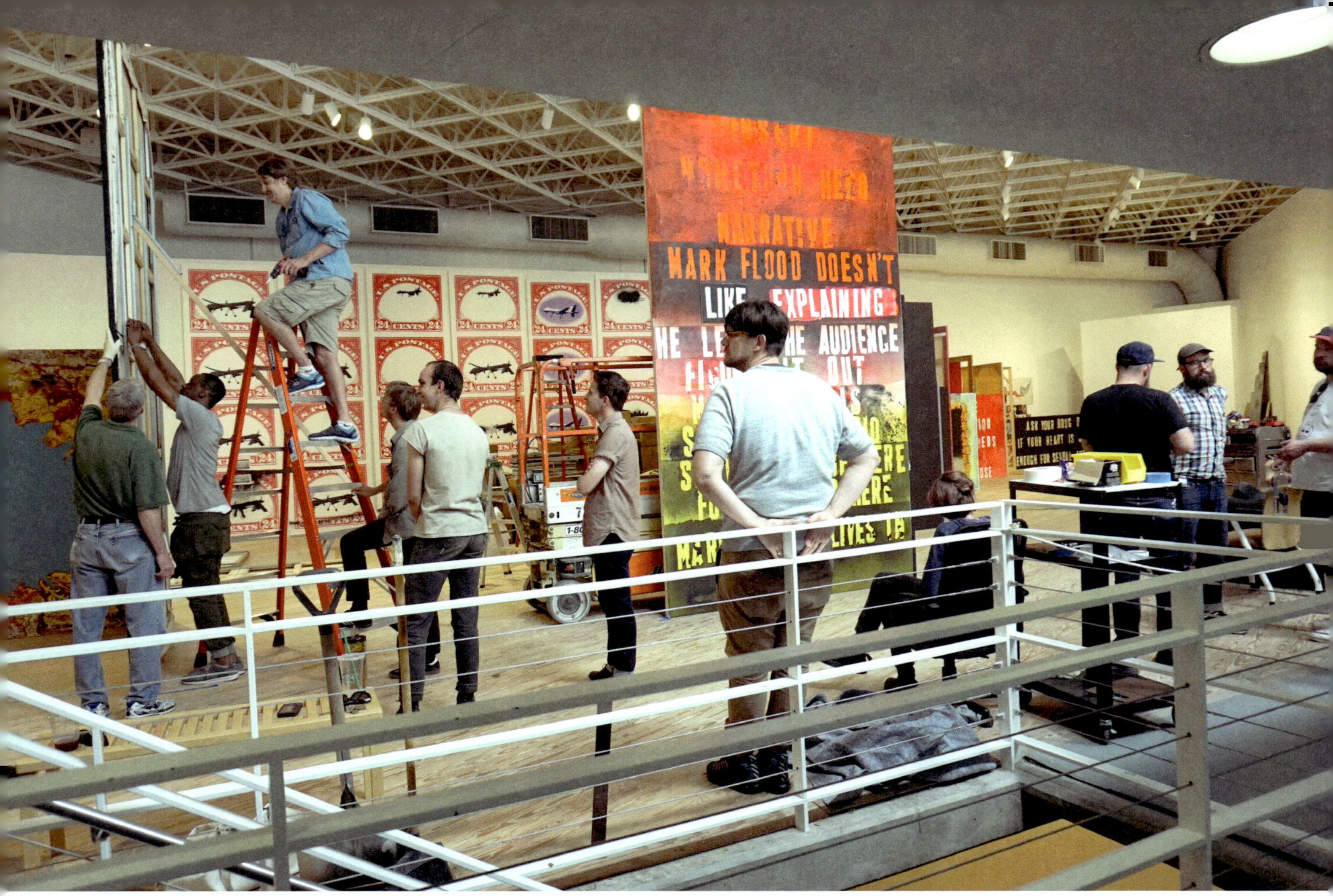

NARRATIVE
MARK FLOOD DOESN'T
LIKE EXPLAINING
HE LE THE AUDIENCE
Come to Marlboro Country. 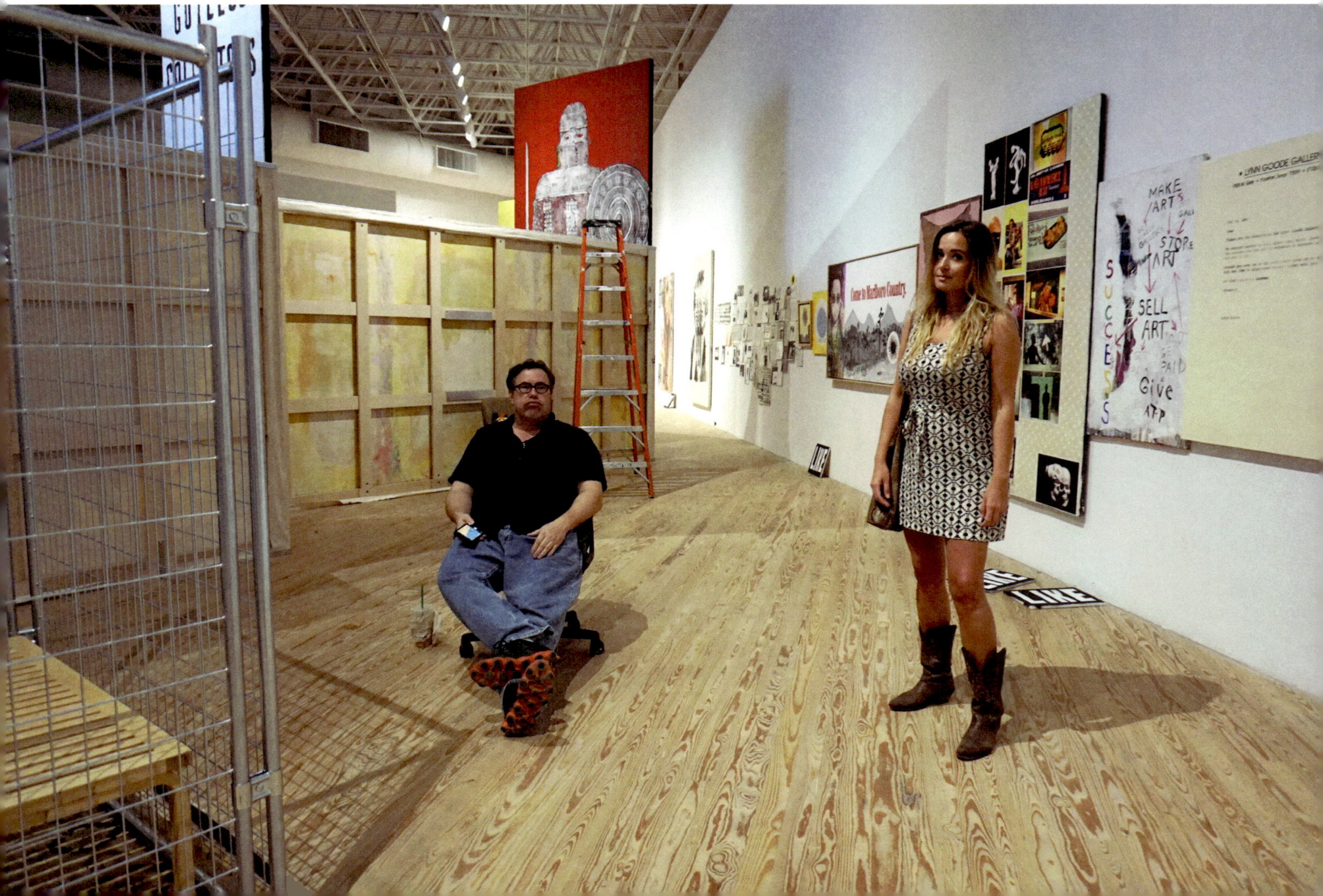
MAKE ART
SELL ART
Give
SUCCESS
LYNN GOODE GALLERY
LIKE

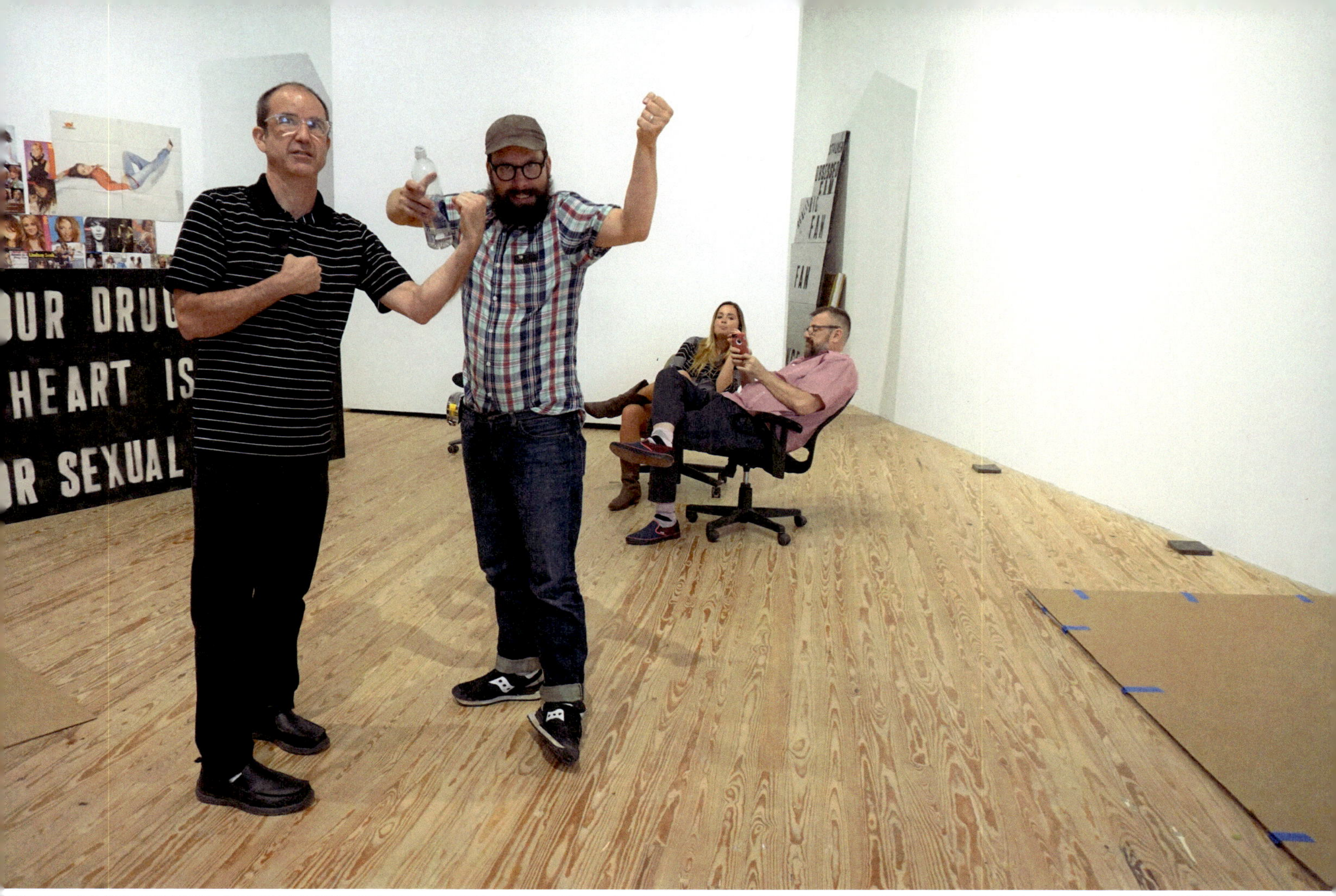

OUR DRUG
HEART IS
R SEXUAL

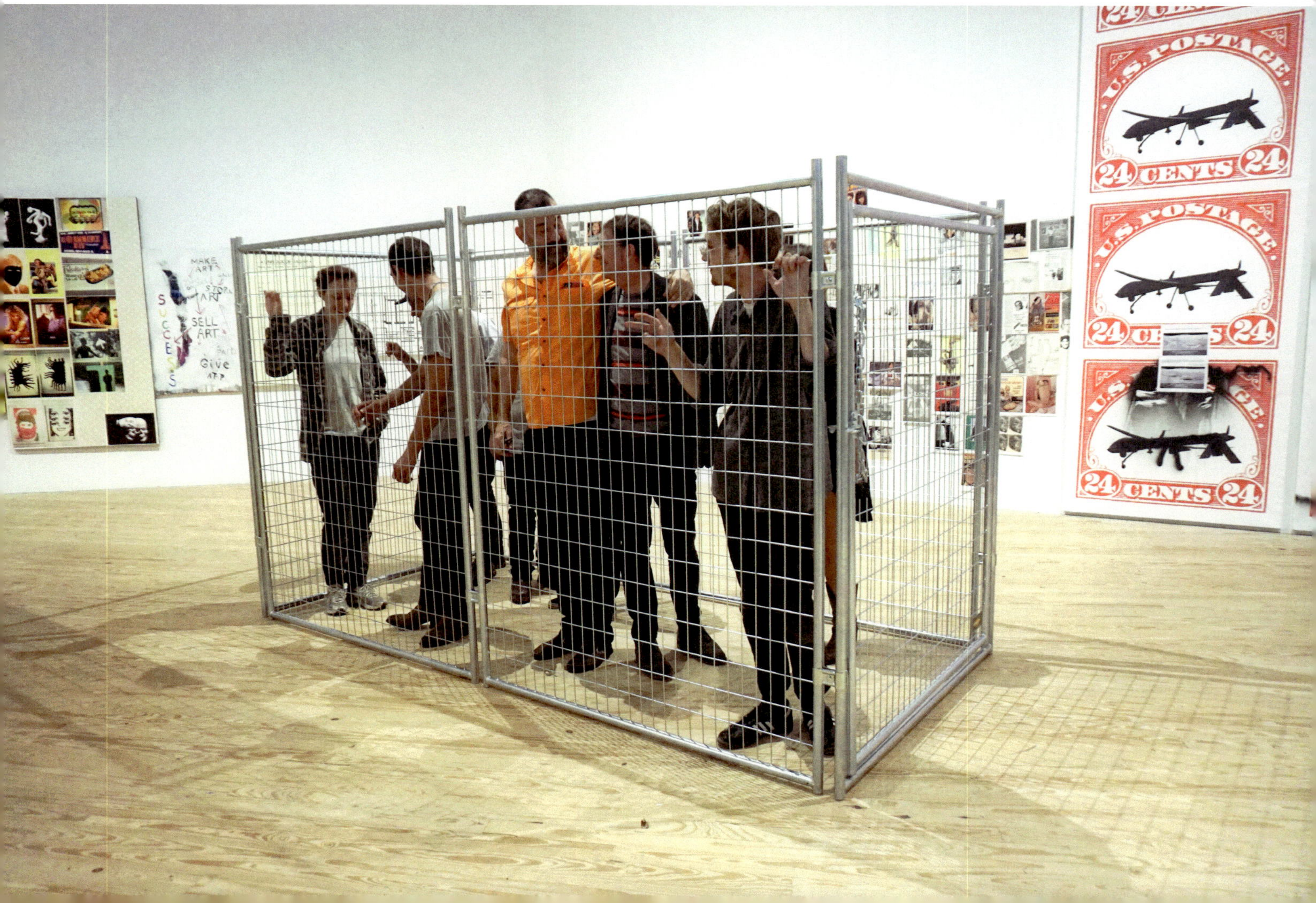

U.S. POSTAGE
24 CENTS 24
U.S. POSTAGE
24 CENTS 24
24 CENTS 24

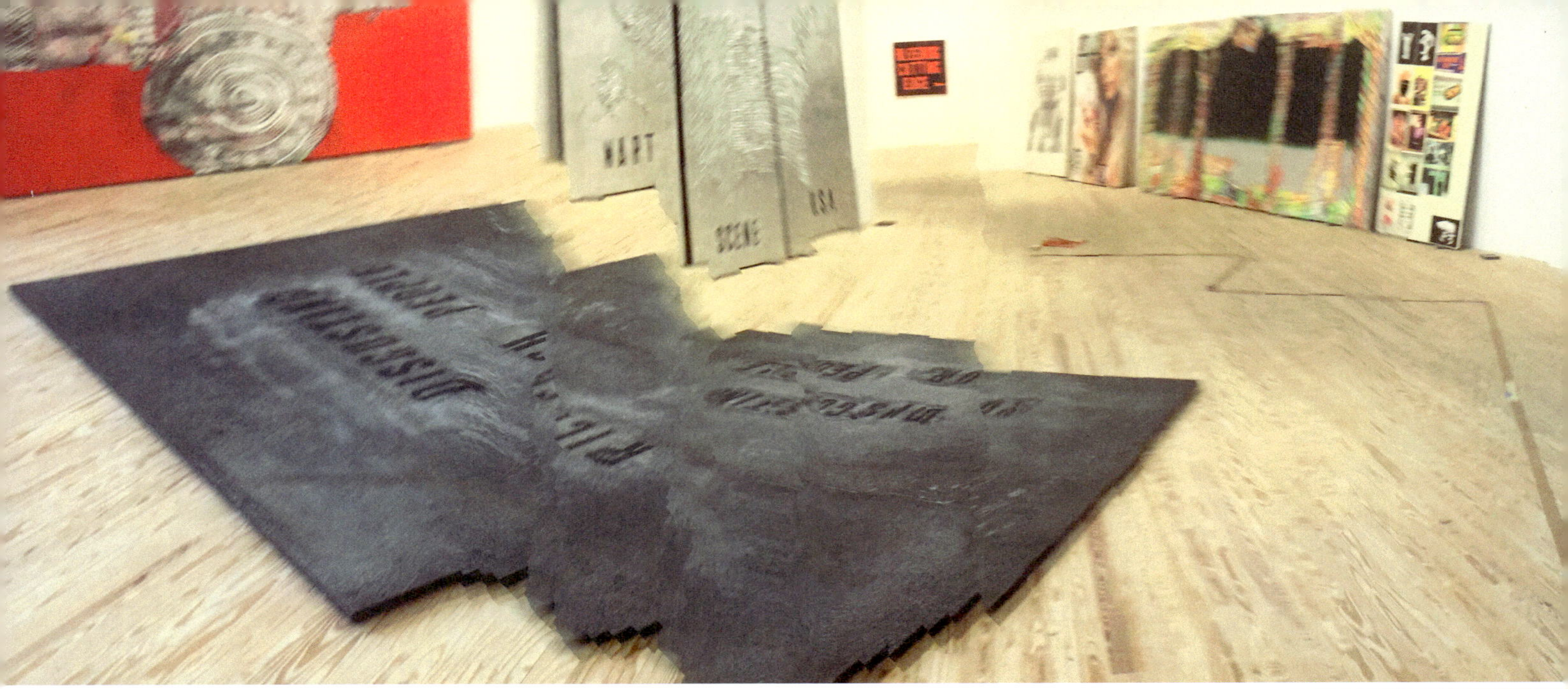

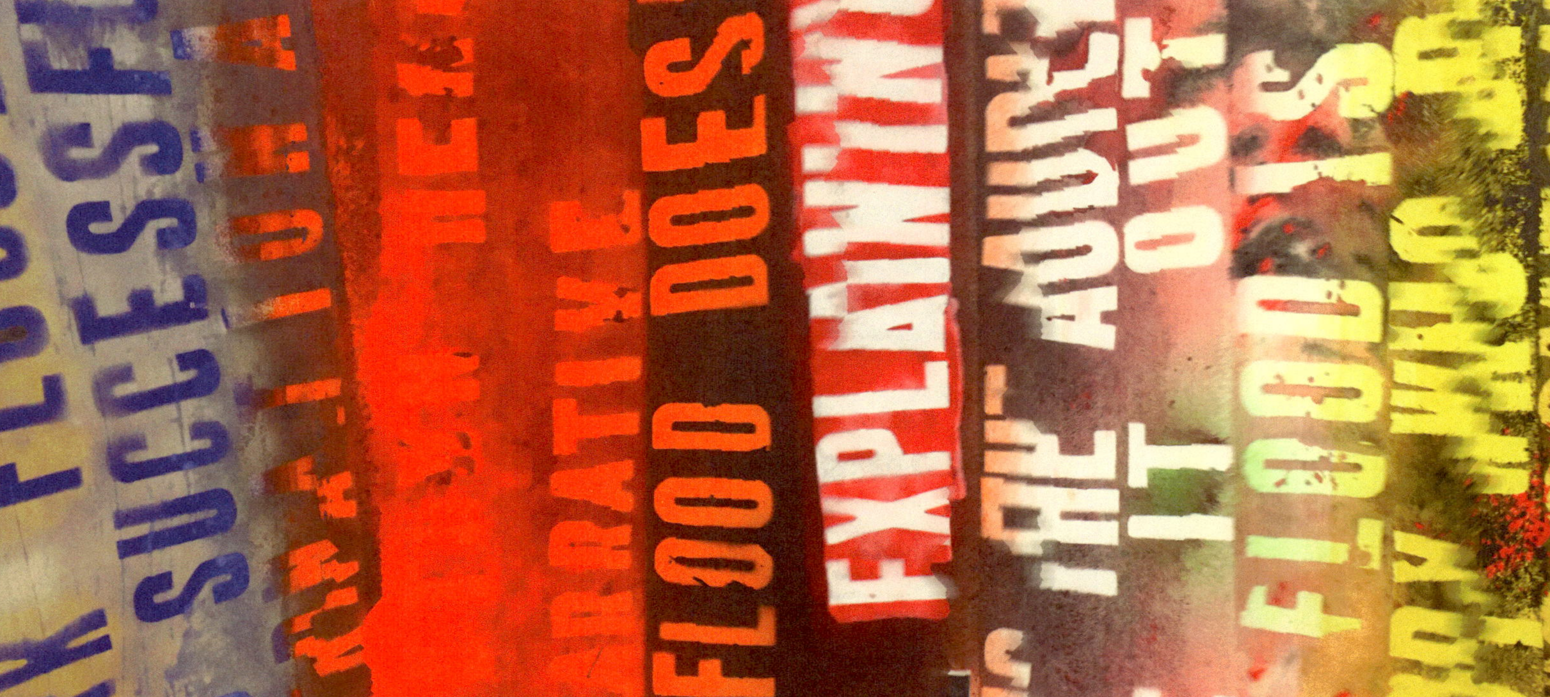
FLOOD DOES

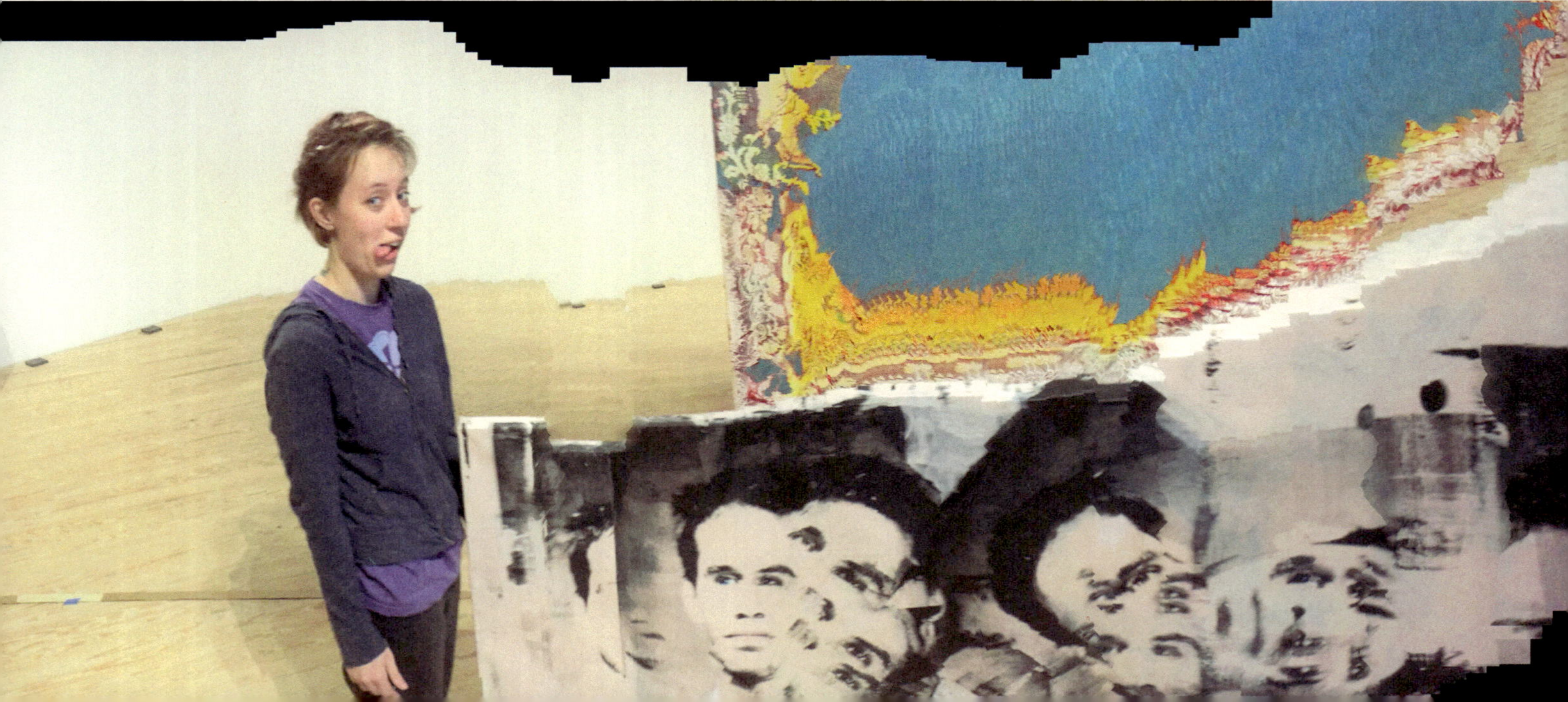

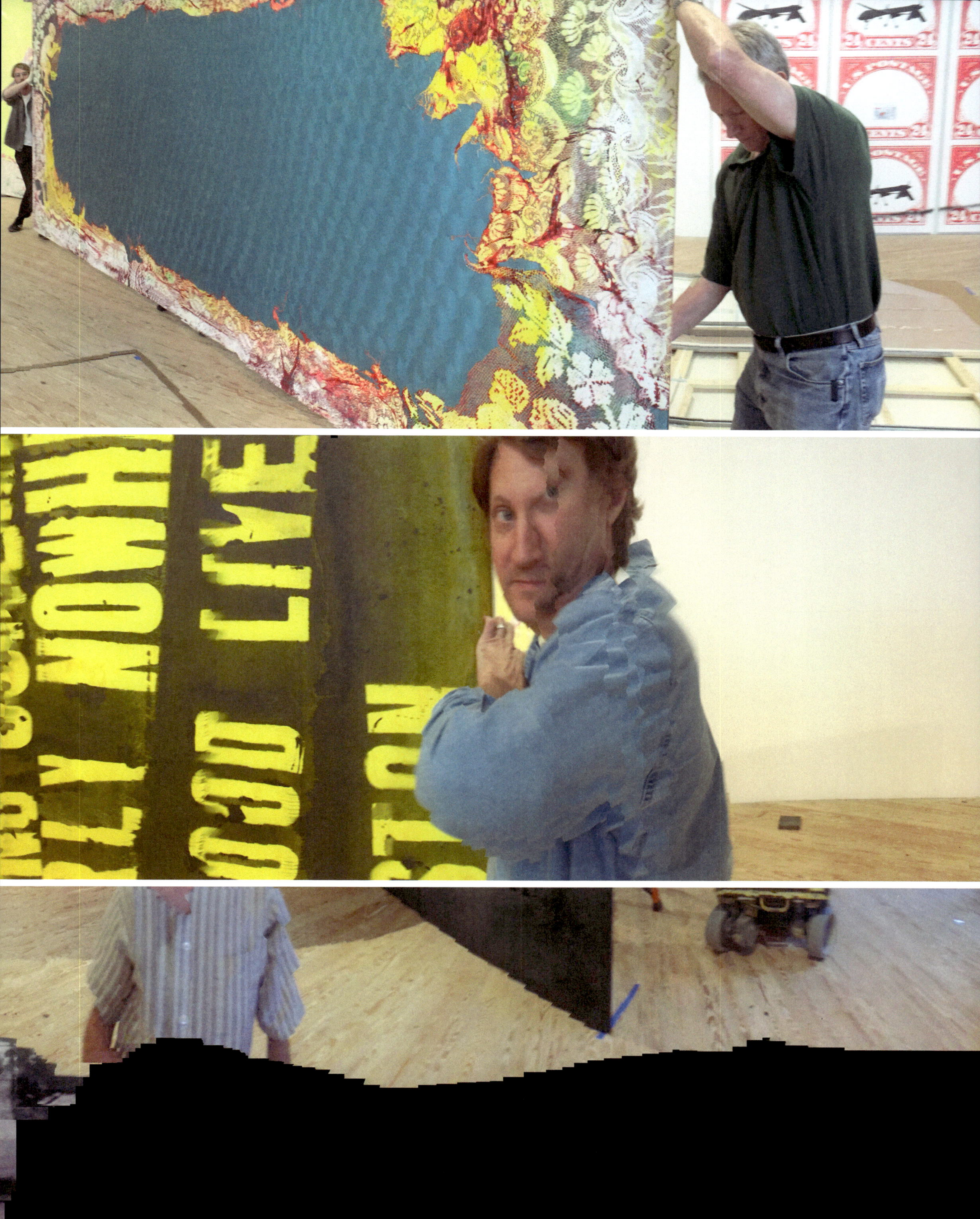

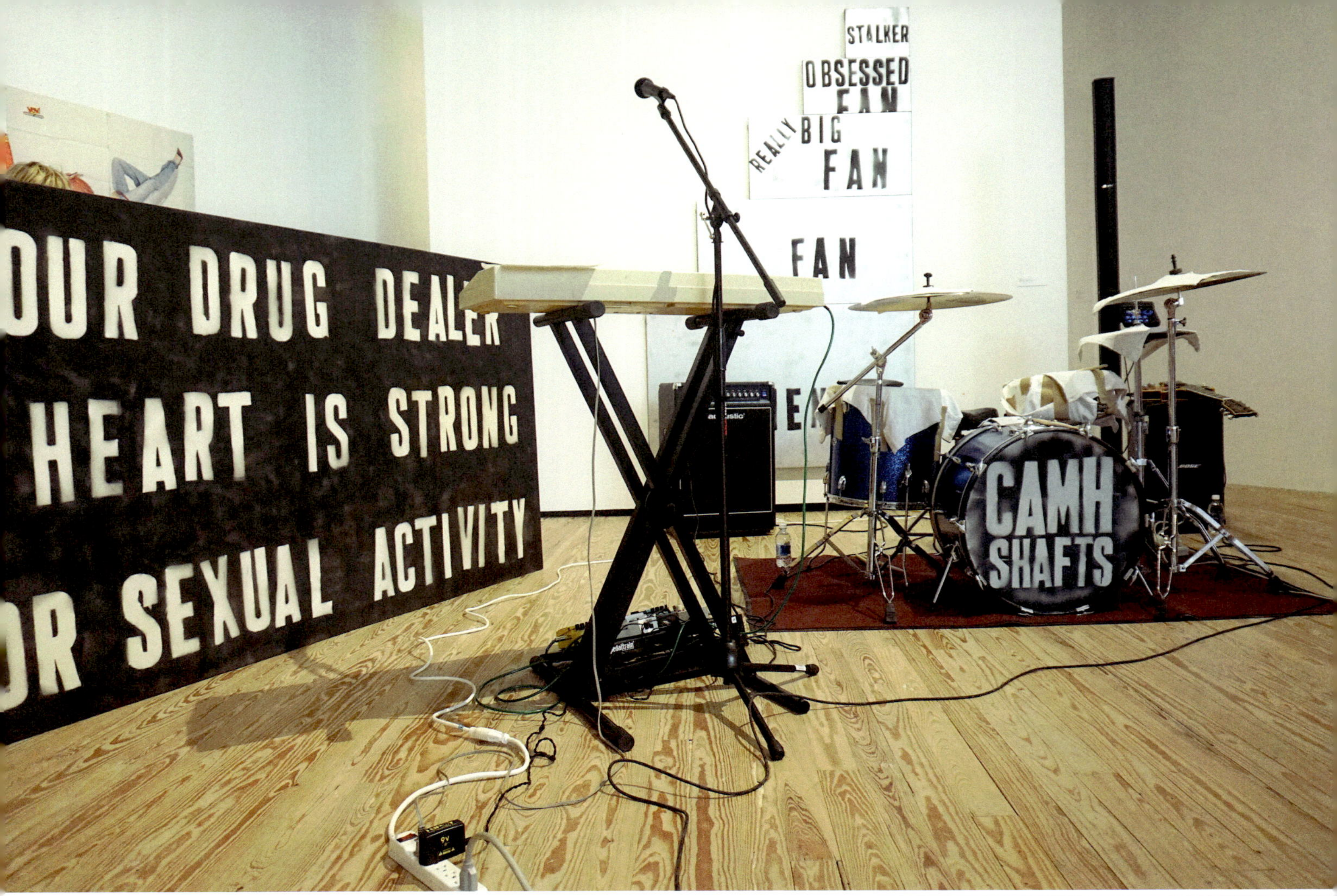

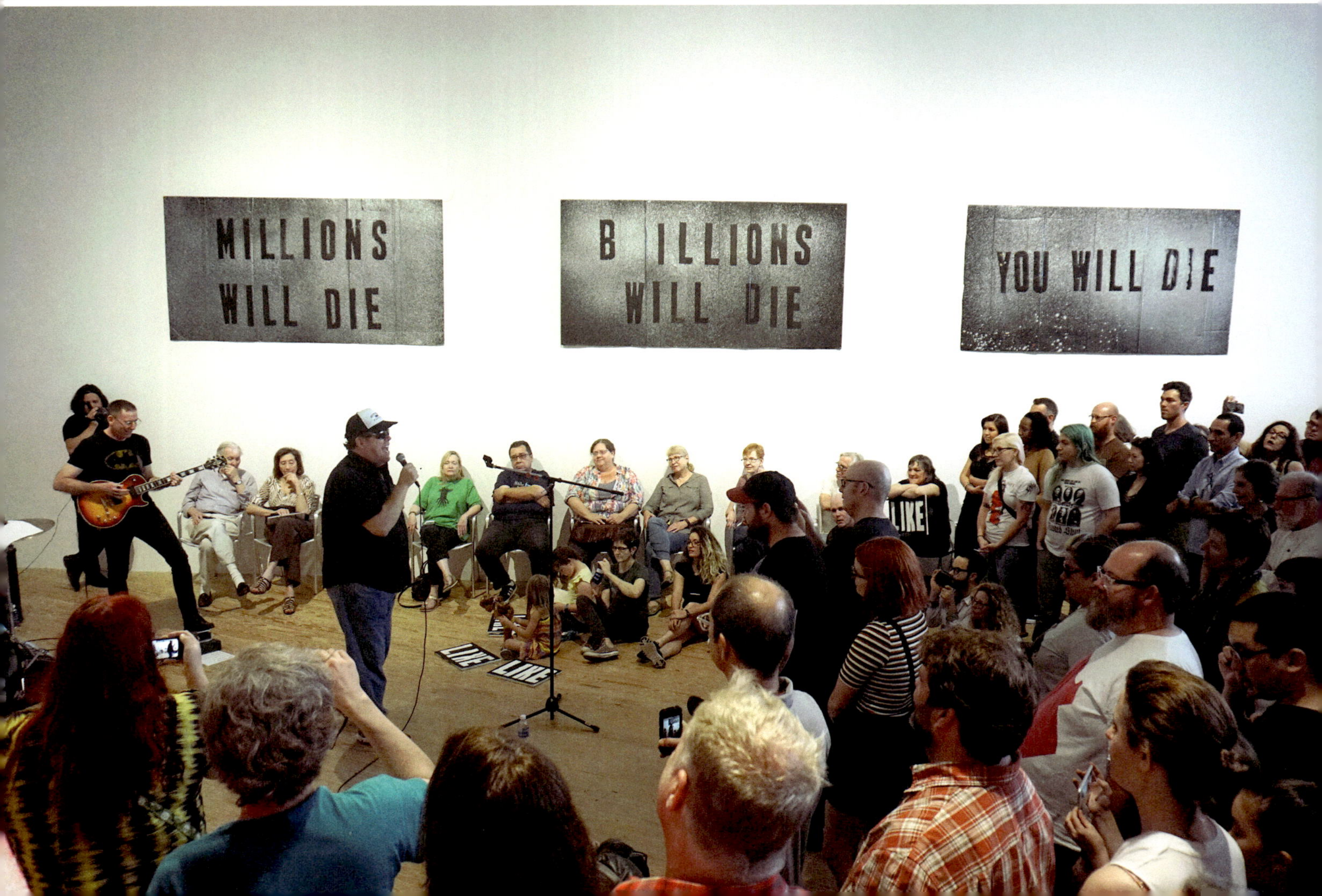

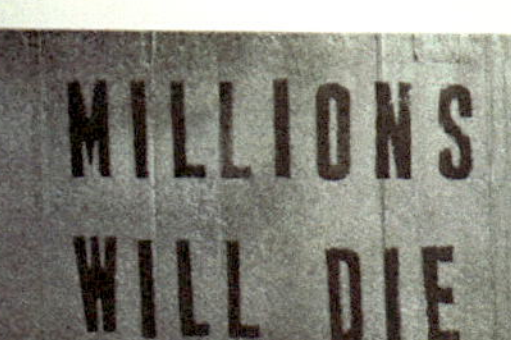
MILLIONS
WILL DIE

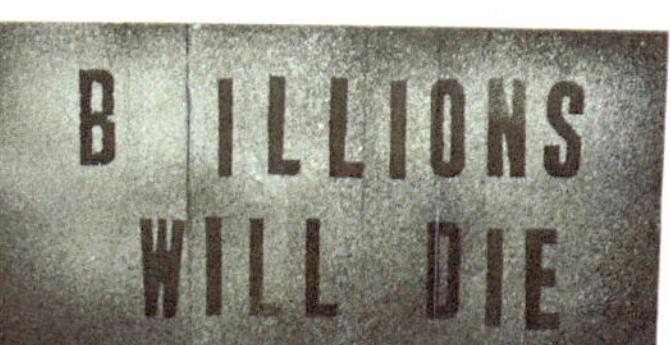
B ILLIONS
WILL DIE

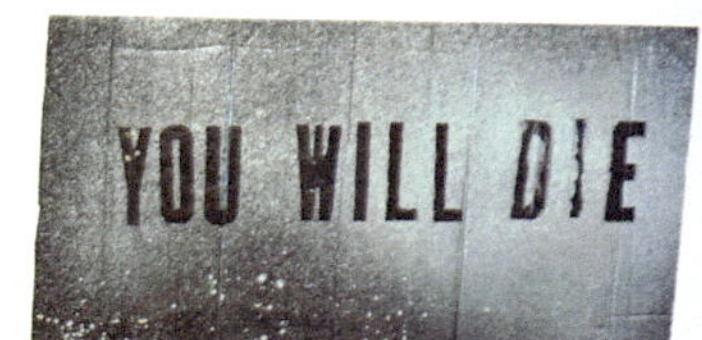
YOU WILL DIE

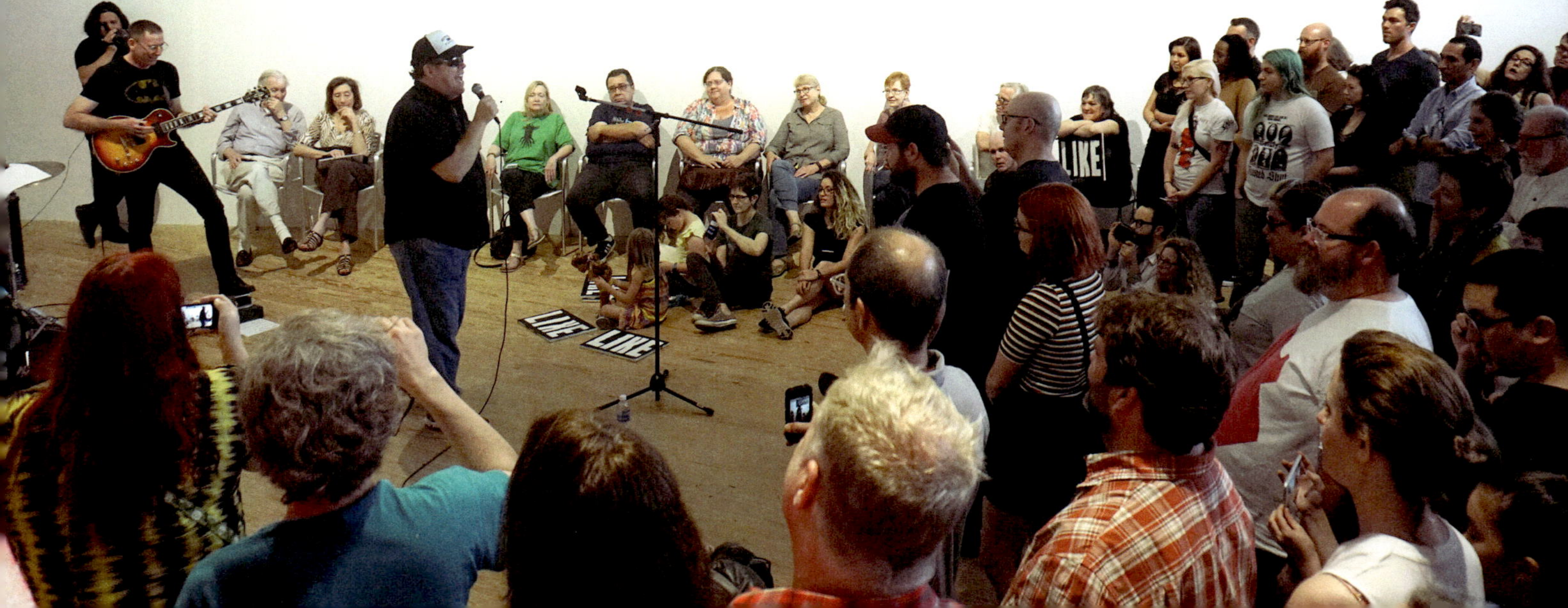
LIKE

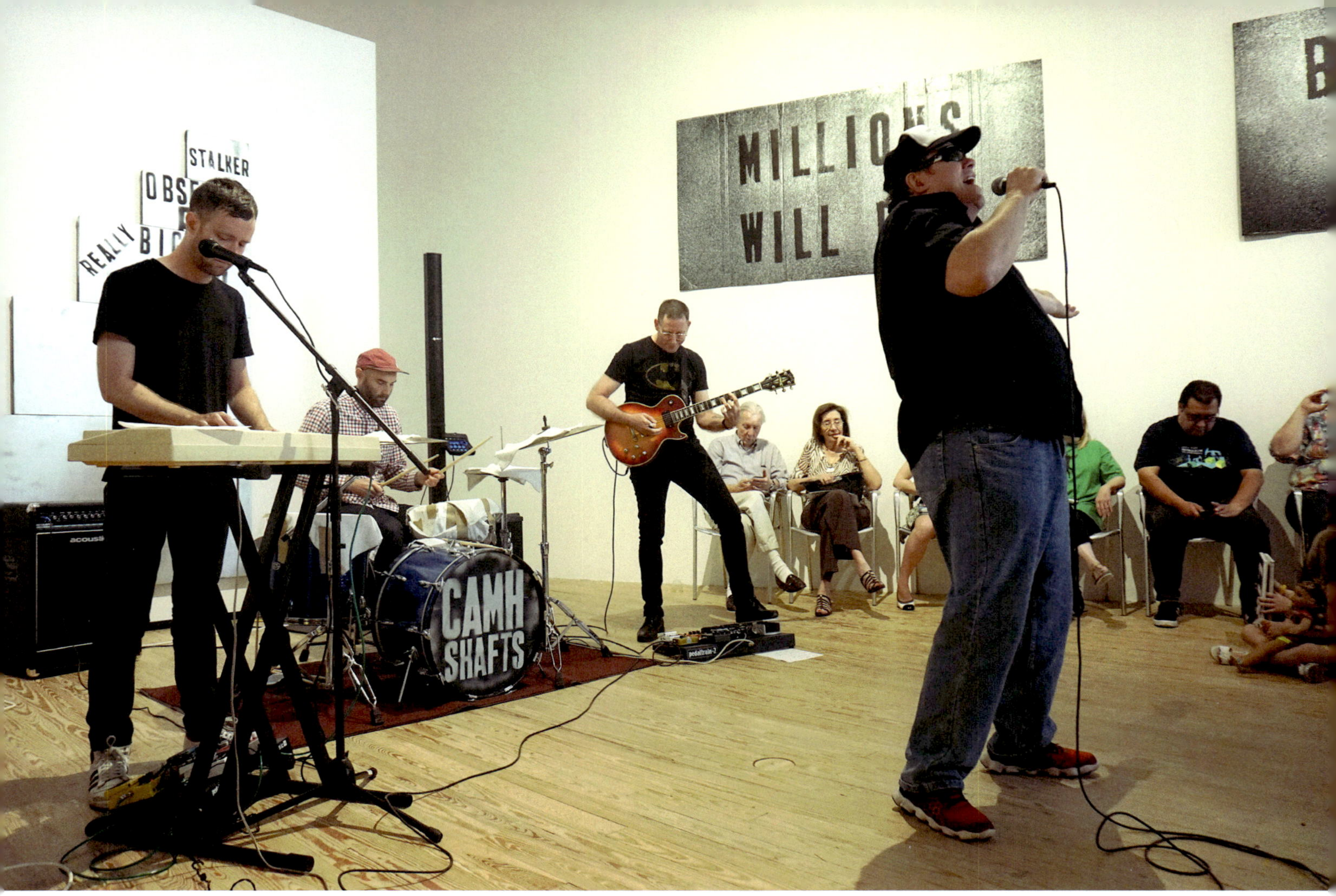

STALKER
OBSE
REALLY
BIG
MILLIONS
WILL
CAMH
SHAFTS
SAY 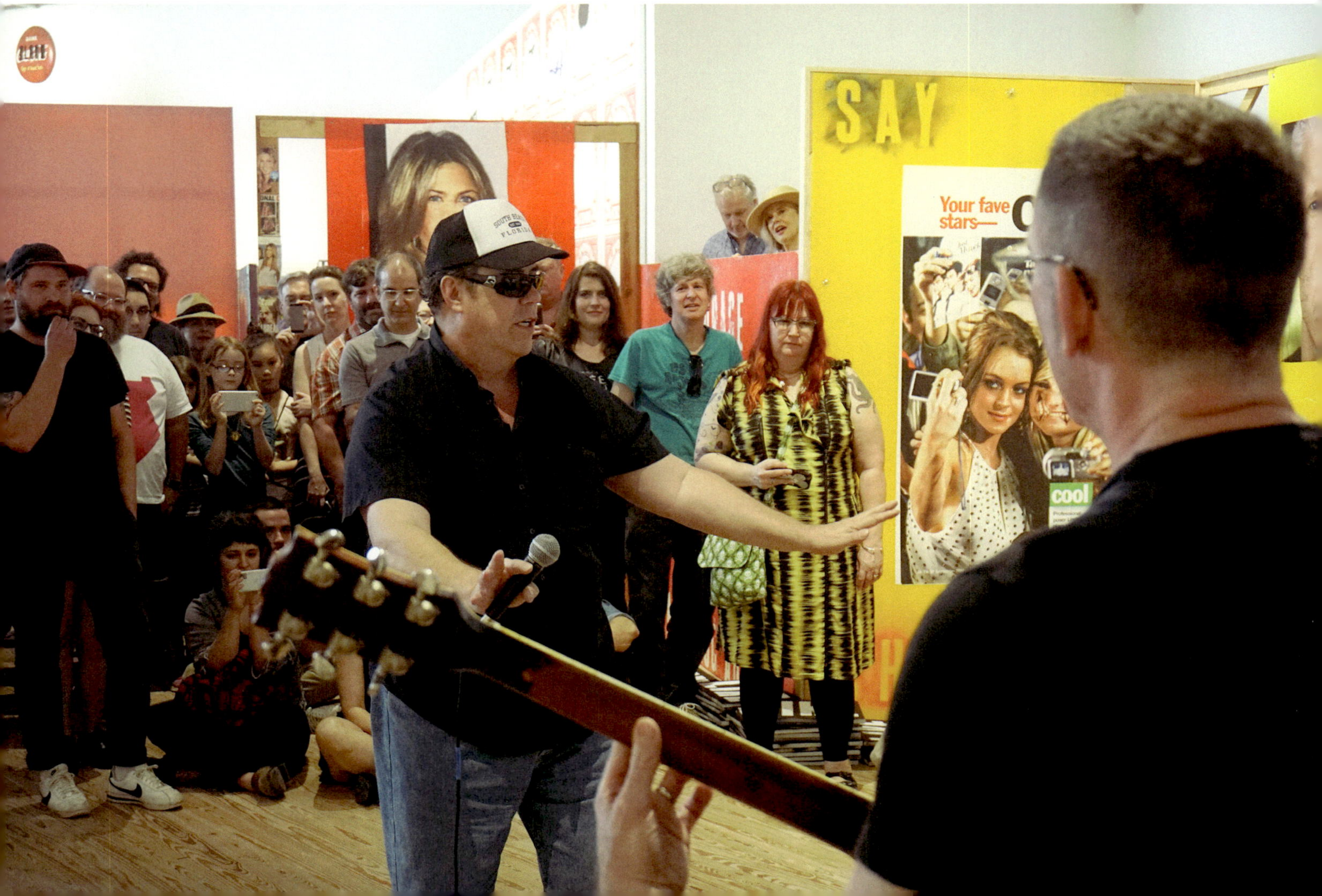
Your fave
stars—
cool

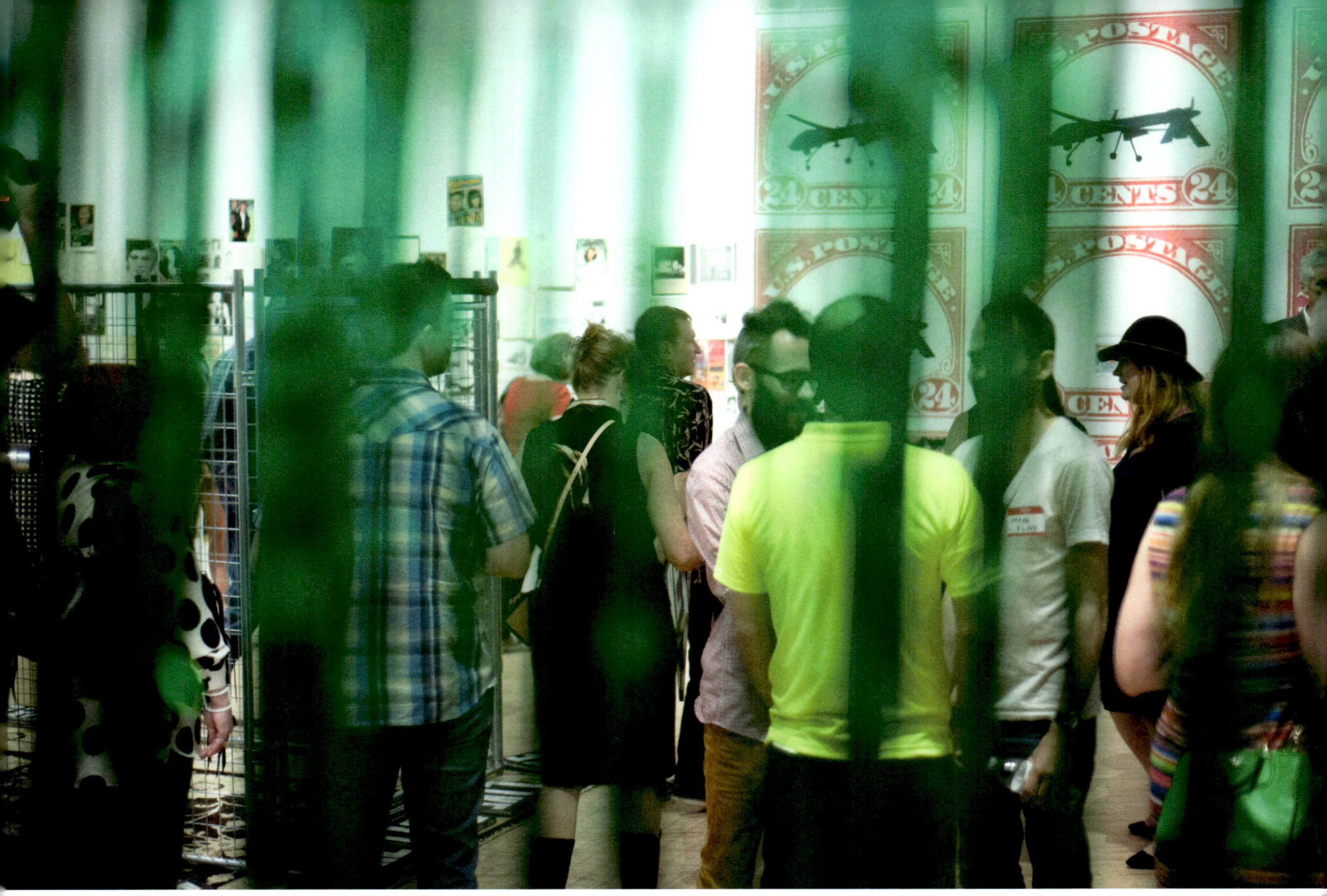

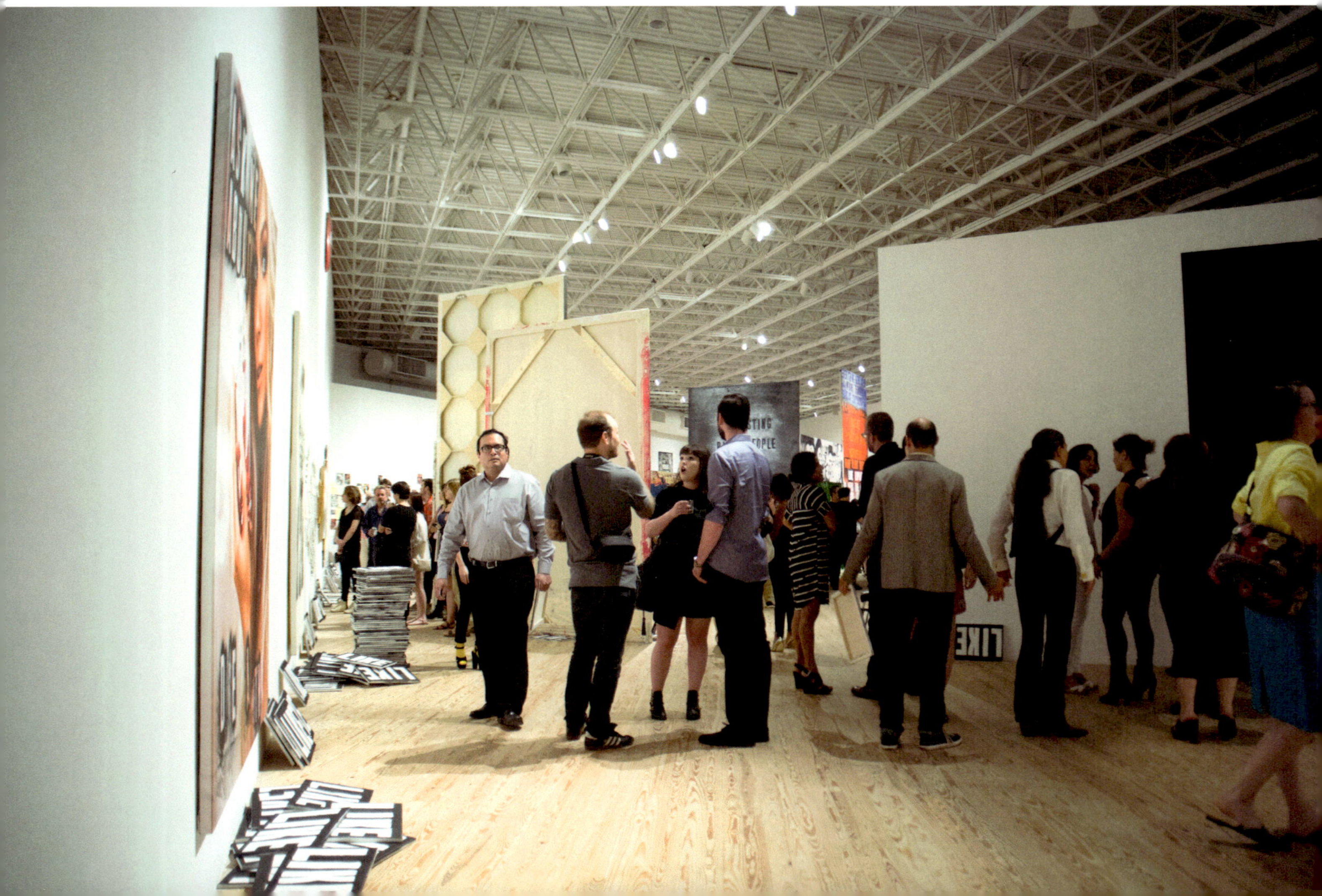

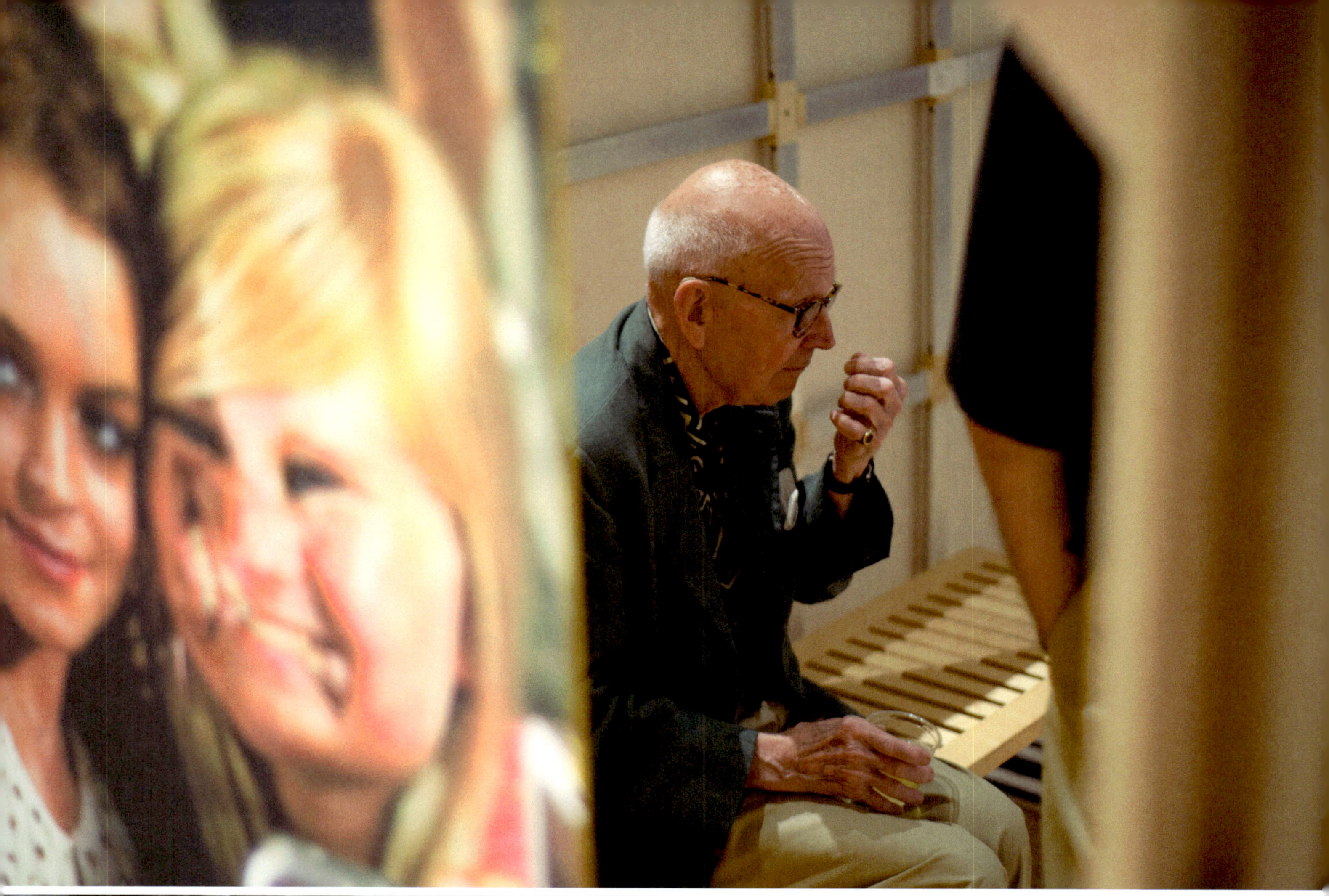

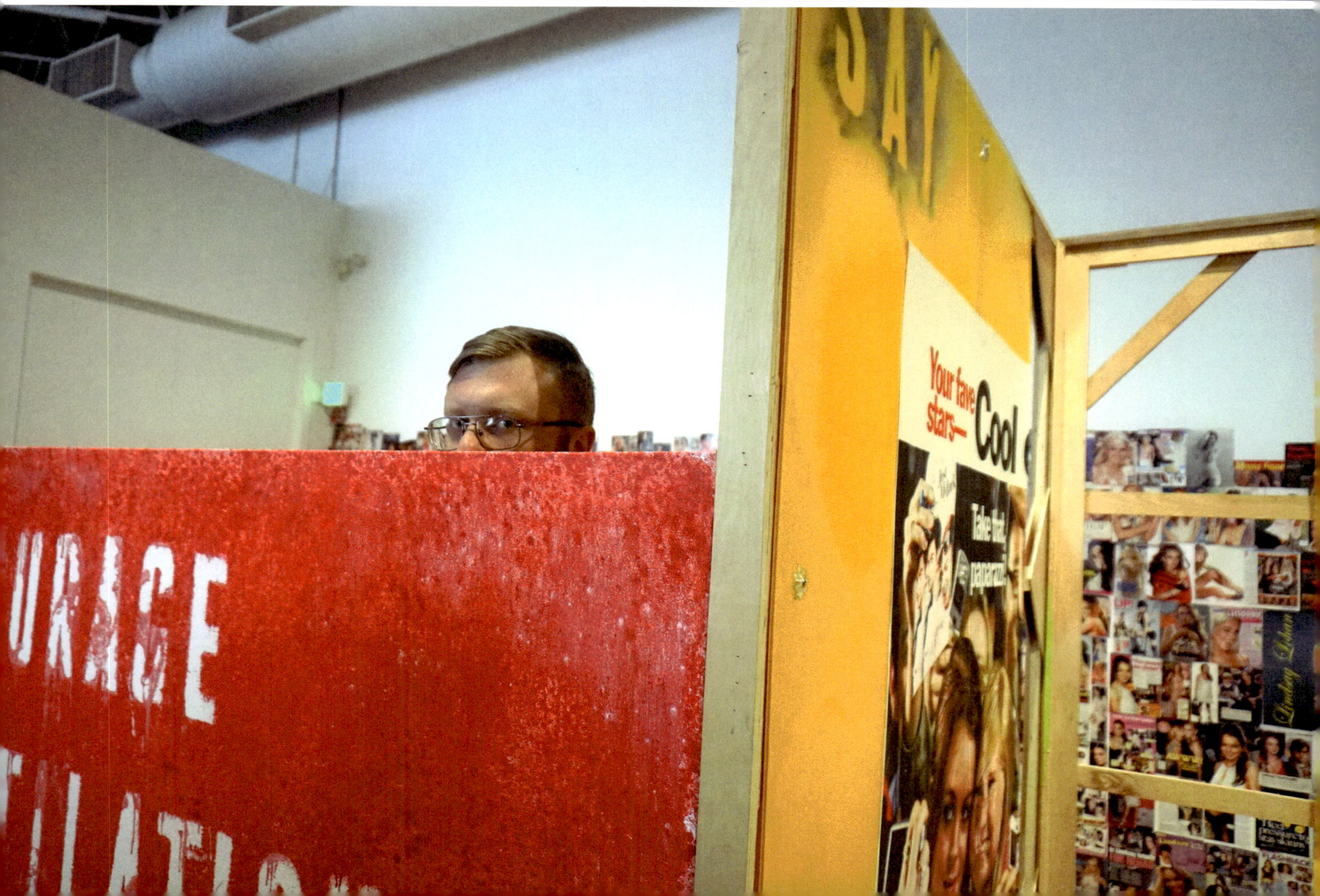

SAY
URAGE
Your fave stars—
Cool

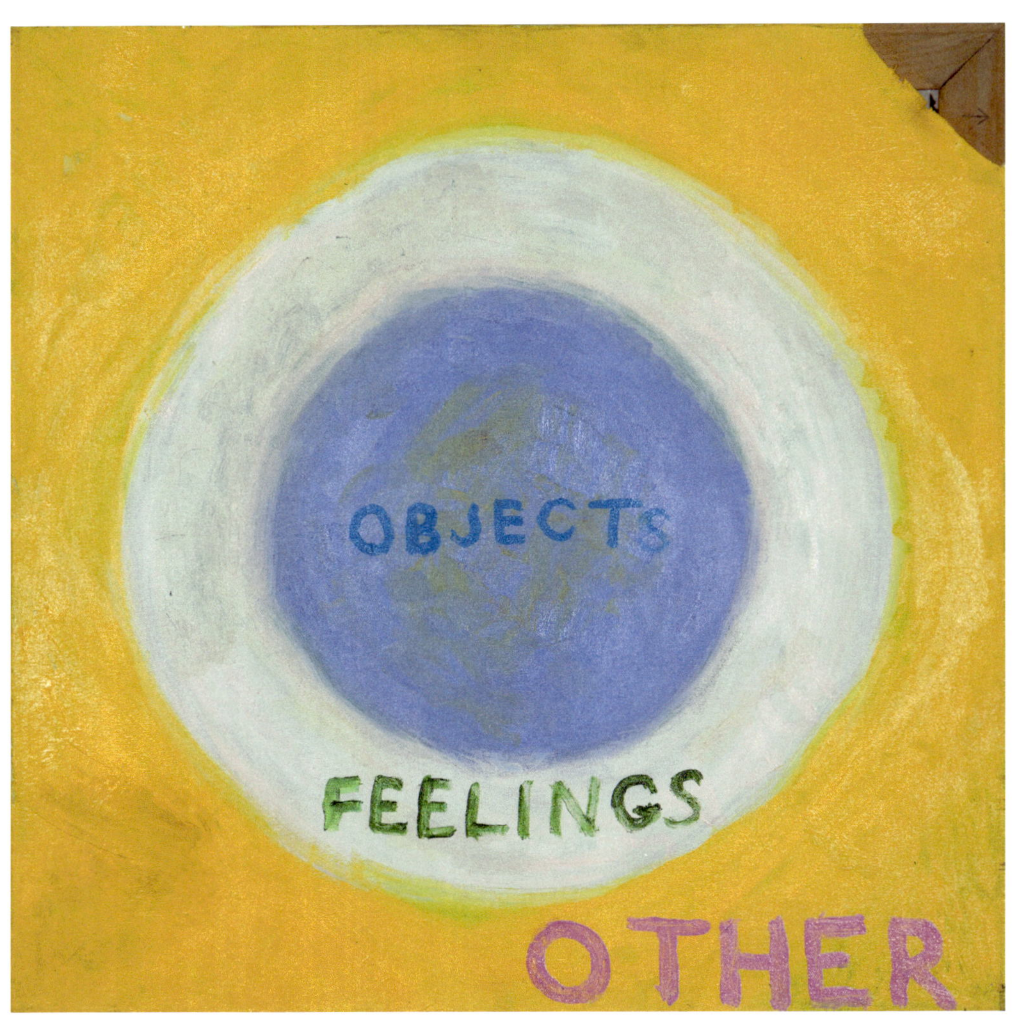

OBJECTS/FEELINGS/OTHER 1997 acrylic on canvas 24 x 24 inches

Excerpts from *Clerk Fluid*

Clark Flood

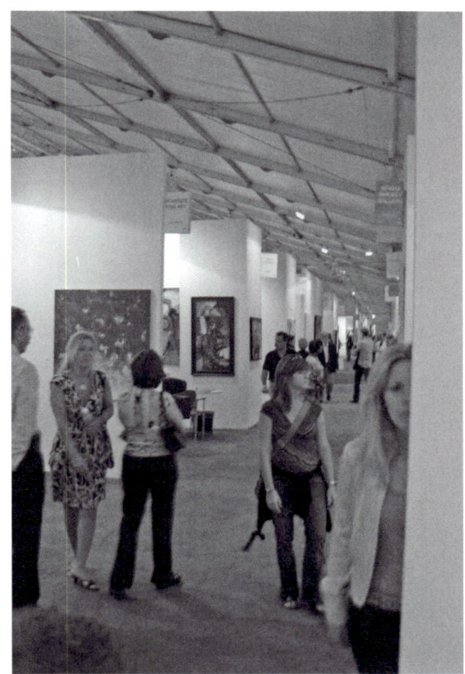

#2: Art Fair Incident

SOME TIME AGO I WENT TO THE Clear Lake City Art Fair. For those who don't know, art fairs are the way of the art world these days. They are as inevitable as kissing the anuses of those more powerful than you, and just as enjoyable.

Like the whole world, they make a lot of sense when looked at from the point of view of the very wealthy, because art fairs, like the whole world, are entirely set up to service the very wealthy. The rich art-buying class is like a swarm of fickle locusts, always searching for a new spot to chew to death with their money. If you put on an art fair in the right destination city, the plague-cloud swoops in to party (and to buy art) and everybody's happy.

It's a wretched experience for artists, who are advised to stay away. Otherwise, you get to see just how pathetic and unimportant you really are, unless you've been dead for about 50 years. Your art is exhibited with all the curatorial finesse of the detergent displays at Fiesta, and with as much honor, but you're lucky just to get product onto these supermarket shelves. Not to be present is the worst. You don't exist if you're not at the fairs. You need to be on a good shelf in a cool booth at a happening art fair just to be in the game! Then you can enjoy watching a bunch of clueless tourists, blind art professionals, manipulative collectors and gutless dealers walk around feeling important, dissing each other, and equating the state of their personal financial health with the state of Art Today. In the best case scenario, they haggle over your work the way old peasant women at a street market in Caracas might haggle over a particularly attractive gourd. That's called being a big hit at the art fair.

Again, it's best for artists to stay away. Otherwise, your childish emotions get engaged and you can become depressed. The Armory Show fair in NYC is held on piers and at the end of each pier, a lot of artists just jump right off into the sea.

Anyway, a happening international burg like Clear Lake is just the sort of hip crossroads that attracts the collector plague-cloud, and the fair has been held there for years now. It's actually a cluster of fairs, anchored by the big international Clear Lake-Moscow fair, where all the blue chip and wannabe blue chip dealers hunker down in their $50,000 booths. It's held at the Clear Lake City Civic Auditorium. There's also a bunch of smaller fairs, living on the big fair's spillover the way the grackles at Mission Burrito live on the spillage from everyone's fish tacos. You've got your Nova Fair, your Scope Fair and your Pulse Fair, held respectively at the Clear Lake High School Cafetorium, the Clear Lake Holiday Inn Grand Ballroom and the Clear Lake Knights of Columbus Bingo Hall. A lot of collectors prefer these smaller fairs, where lesser dealers and lesser artists

Clark Flood, "#2: Art Fair Incident," in *Clerk Fluid*, ed. Mark Flood, 4th ed. (Houston: Self-published, 2009), pp. 14–22.

can be bought for lesser investments. It can get quite competitive on the opening nights, when the collectors stampede inside all at once. They sometimes end up tussling rabidly over bargains. Subsequently, their big thrill is walking around sizing up their portfolios, as in "that Clayton Brothers painting is $15K; I only paid 8 for mine last year. YES!!!"

I had good reason to be in CL for the fairs. I was meeting a cool big-time collector there and he was to hook me up with a local art dealer. I was going to crack the crucial Clear Lake market through those backstage art-world machinations that seem glamorous, but are actually entirely tedious, until the magical moment when somebody's check clears. Anyway, it was wonderful for me that this man was going to make a connection for me. I know from experience that dealers hate it when artists try to promote themselves! It's a deadly faux pas to reveal that one has one's own ideas about one's career, let alone to challenge the dealer practice of silently studying art scenes the way foxes survey moonlit henhouses, looking for the plumpest, stupidest birds. No, it's much better to have these fateful marriages pre-arranged by parties as wise and disinterested as collectors. What could go wrong?

Well, first of all we couldn't find the bastard. He wasn't at his famous, trendy, edgy gallery which turned out to be a repellent, low-ceilinged storefront in a neighborhood as suitable for tossing murdered hookers as for investing in objets d'art. I looked around, grinning like a plucky orphan at what I thought was to be my new home. The art on display was generic, some adolescent's perfunctorily executed art-school homework: a homemade chandelier, a video, a wall of photos, a need to nap 30 seconds later. That's OK; everybody else's art always sucks. I checked out the storage rack, a crudely divided cubbyhole full of the remnants of previous exhibits now left to die, unwrapped and unprotected, on a bare cement floor. OK, so they're not big on sales after the show. I'll fly back and wrap everything up myself after my CL triumph. I told the Collector "I love this place." He was irritated, incredulous that the dealer had stood him up. I tried to calm him. I'm an artist: I'm used to abuse.

We found the Dealer at his booth at one of the fairs. He embodied evil. When I finally saw *Star Wars*, which was not till the 25th anniversary re-release, I didn't find the Dark Lord evil. He reminded me of myself: a pale, creepy old man with a smoker's rasp, lurking in the shadows, manipulating other people's lives. I related. I thought he was the hero. But this dealer! He was clearly bad. I can't explain it, but one look into his black, dead-fish eyes and I knew that I was far more likely to be found rotting in the trunk of my car than to ever get paid for any art of mine he sold.

He seemed puzzled by our presence, and reacted to my introduction as one might react to the discovery of a small, unidentifiable stain on the cement floor of one's carport while unloading some enticing groceries. Apparently, he'd never heard of me, never seen my work, and all the support materials I'd previously sent were moldering, unexamined, in some dusty pile in the gallery. The Collector drifted off and I was left alone with this devil. I thought of my herpetologist friend, of calling him to share my discovery of this new species, a poisonous snake that walked upright on two legs. But I wanted to make the best of it so I attempted small talk. The Dealer smiled coldly, and asked me if the Collector bought my work. I said Not yet. The dealer asked Why not? I said He's waiting to buy it from you. I thought I saw a flicker of interest. I always feel like shaking these sphinxes and screaming into their faces, "Don'tcha wanna make some fuckin' money?" But they don't like plain talk. They like creative types. The plumpest, stupidest birds.

I partied my frustrations away that night. For dinner I had sushi at a joint on Clear Lake's famous Crawdad Row. There was one bite I would have spit into my napkin if I'd been alone. It tasted just a little bit funky. But I wasn't alone. I was at a tiny little table with a bunch of cool collectors and art scenesters in the middle of a crowded, trendy joint. So I swallowed it.

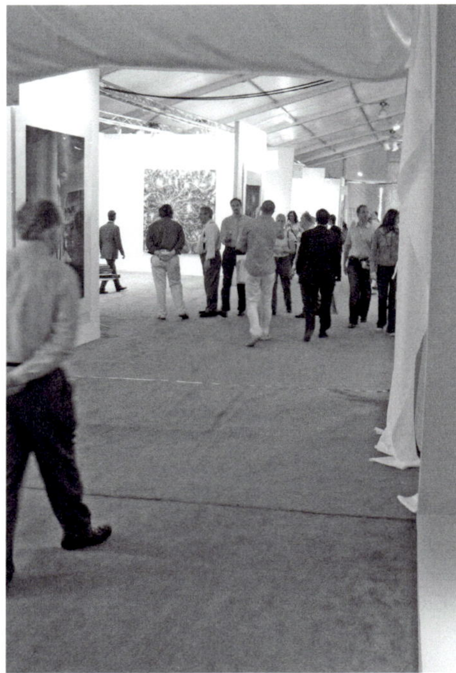

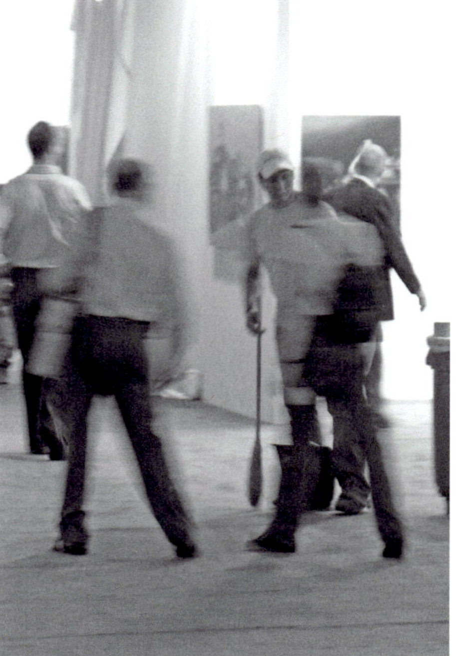

When I finally saw *Star Wars*, which was not till the 25th anniversary re-release, I didn't find the Dark Lord evil.

He reminded me of myself: a pale, creepy old man with a smoker's rasp, lurking in the shadows, manipulating other people's lives. I related.

I thought he was the hero.

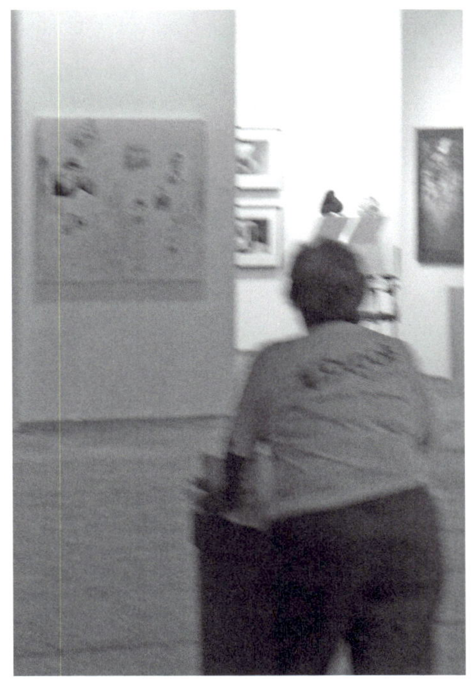

I woke up about 3AM with wretched heartburn. It felt like I'd swallowed large nails without properly chewing them. I have a history of GERD and I'm on substantial meds and this wasn't supposed to happen but it was happening to me, and it's happened before. I ate antacids and took hot showers and did all the other things I do to distract myself from the horrible pain. Nothing works very well except waiting, and sometimes exercising in place. So there I was in my fabulous Clear Lake suite in the middle of that fabulous night, suffering like something out of a Francis Bacon triptych, exercising and waiting for my pain to recede. That goddamn sushi bite, I thought.

I flew back to Houston eventually. I talked over the whole trip with the healer witch. The heartburn incident. The evil Dealer. I was still hopeful something would happen with him. She said it was a bad idea to do business with someone I instinctively thought was the devil. She compared him to the bite of bad sushi. She said Don't swallow it this time.

Good advice. Naturally, I didn't follow it. I kept bugging the Collector to pull the string. I didn't want to cold-call other galleries. I wanted to work my connection! I wanted to crack the Clear Lake market with a killer show at the devil's storefront!

It took forever, but the Collector finally had the conversation with the Dealer. The Dealer had looked at my stuff. He wasn't interested. He wasn't interested, but he had kindly offered to suggest some other places. He wasn't interested! The bad sushi wouldn't swallow me! Ouch! Something was said about "the cutting edge" of art. The inference, clearly, was that I wasn't on it.

So that's how I came to be in Folsom prison. Not really. I'm an artist, I'm used to abuse.

The healer witch says she doesn't eat sushi. She says no matter how good the restaurant is, you end up with internal parasites. She treats herself periodically for internal parasites, with herbs and whatever. She says most people have internal parasites and don't even know it. The parasites live on and on. CF

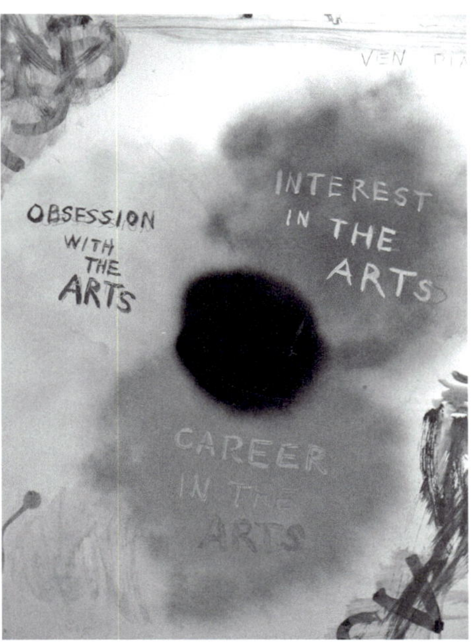

#9 Legend Buster

I like those sites where you can check out stories your friends tell you and find out if they're just urban legends. I think I'm gonna retool my column to be the art-world version. My tentative attempts at humor aren't working out, so now I'll devote this space to a critical examination of the many myths, fables and half truths that swirl around our happening Houston art scene. Please email me your most cherished beliefs so I can "CRED 'EM OR SHRED 'EM!"™

My parents want me to be an engineer but I'm "drawn" to the creative life, ha ha. I've tried to explain to them that being an artist is cool and that society values artists, and builds museums for them, and ladles out lots of cash to keep their precious creativity flowing. They act like I'm jumping off a bridge. Please explain to them that artists being poor until after they're dead is just a myth.

To be merely poor would be a step up for an artist. Not to be persecuted, hounded, driven from town to town by angry mobs, with the smell of tar, feathers and one's own shat pants in one's nostrils—that's the dream.

Clark Flood, "#9: Legend Buster," in *Clerk Fluid*, ed. Mark Flood, 4th ed. (Houston: Self-published, 2009), pp. 78–86.

It's a myth that something wonderful happens to artists' net worth when they die. Actually, as their bodies decompose in whatever Potter's field or vacant lot the authorities use for dumping miscellaneous corpses, their income level stays about the same. They may be working some minimum wage job down in Hell, but no accurate figures are available on that.

I pity your parents. They have every right to be horrified by your career choice. "Artist" is a despised professional category, located somewhere between "contagious leper" and "lap-dancing crack whore" on the social scale. Most moms and dads want something better for their children.

A tiny fraction of the art that gets made is good and becomes valuable. A weak mind like yours might distort this fact into a belief that artists are valuable too, but that's wishful thinking. People value gold but they don't give a damn about gold miners. They value wool sweaters but they don't mind if the sheep have to sleep outdoors.

Your parents will probably eventually find a way to accept you, just like they would if you were a serial killer, or a child molester, or a Democrat. They'll learn to smile and choke out the words, "We're proud of you." But rest assured, you're breaking their hearts and crushing their spirit.

How selfish are you? Maybe you should give them a break and go into porn instead.

I start feeling like a real artist, like ones I'm studying, after I get my post-graduate degree, right?

I don't know why you would want to feel like an artist, but if that's all you want, just throw away your money, stop bathing or doing any personal grooming, steal some art supplies, make your crap and humiliate yourself trying to get professionals to like it. Then, gently buffer the pain of their rejection with a soothing medley of drug and alcohol problems. For God's sake, don't go near any art classes.

Art education is best understood as a slow motion Ponzi, or pyramid, scheme, one that takes years instead of weeks or months to become an obvious rip-off. Wikipedia notes that *A Ponzi scheme is a fraudulent investment operation that involves paying abnormally high returns ("profits") to investors out of the money paid in by subsequent investors, rather than from net revenues generated by any real business.* We might add that Art Education is a fraudulent investment operation that involves turning abnormally "high" artists into academics, who support themselves with the tuition paid by the parents of art students, rather than with real art careers.

Hey, goof-ball. Your art school has apparently let you vaguely imagine that your education was turning you into a more-or-less successful artist. The only bad thing that might possibly be happening outside of your conscious awareness is that you're wasting years of your life, going into super-debt and totally fucking up your creativity.

The good news is that someday you might get some pieces of paper, which will signify that you are officially "in" on the academic con job, and that you got there the hard way. If it's an advanced degree, you'll have learned all about working the con, too. You will believe in the con and you will make others believe in it. Your career will not be living off your own art as you once dreamed, but rather a series of teaching gigs that allows you to drift all around the country like an infectious professional tumbleweed.

You will be grateful, bitch, and the cycle of abuse will continue. These art education pyramids make the ones in Egypt look like tater tots.

Which Houston gallery does the best job of hooking up local artists with the New York City scene?

That would be the snazzy Aint Gonna Happen Gallery, located near the intersection of Wannabe Street and Gullible Road, aka "the road to nowhere." My understanding is that they usually schedule the career-making New

A weak mind like yours might distort this fact into a belief that artists are valuable too, but that's wishful thinking.

People value gold but they don't give a damn about gold miners. They value wool sweaters but they don't mind if the sheep have to sleep outdoors.

York City Express exhibits on the twelfth of Never, with a self-congratulatory champagne reception at 13 o'clock sharp. Don't be late for your appointment with destiny.

What a scene it will be! All the trend-making New York dealers, and loads of canny, big-spending New York collectors will be there, staring like cheetahs eyeing a shaky newborn gazelle. They're so desperate for new art thrills that they spend all their time out here in the sticks, searching, always searching. They're desperate for raw uncut peasant creativity, soul-sick with the need for it.

They're not here for the climate. They're here because hardly any good artists go to New York City anymore and the few that do just don't have what it takes, can't really go the distance, aren't prepared to make all the right moves. They're too local, too close at hand, maybe just not quite new enough, not fresh, not fresh with the glistening dew that seeps out of a genuine provincial atmosphere like ours, all humid with evaporated talent. They'll be looking at you with calculating eyes, those savvy New York svengalis, while stroking their chins, upper torsos and groin areas. If you playfully struggle just a little bit, once you're down, they'll really pile on the cash, to try and immobilize you. New York City art-vampires are crazy with their need for new blood, so go ahead, tie that tourniquet around your neck and display some youthful vascularity.

You have been chosen by an art professional eye! That makes your success in New York as certain as finding weapons of mass destruction in Iraq, and as dependable as a carny's sense of basic human decency. Every bored divorcee or dreamy retiree who opens an art gallery to satisfy a vague spiritual longing is automatically, magically in league with the ruthless power brokers of Manhattan's art world. Similarly, diligently digging a hole in your backyard will connect you to China.

You're on your way, straight to the top! Try to get it in writing.

Watching local galleries compete over local artists is like watching drunk revelers at Mardi Gras get into fistfights over plastic beads. Duh, some galleries will say anything to get what they want. Meanwhile, artists seeking a surrogate mommy or daddy, to tend their needs while they concentrate on making art-caca in their diapers, will hear whatever they want to hear. Everybody has a soft spot for the beautiful fairy tale of Cowtown tonight, Chelsea tomorrow.

Maybe you should try going to New York yourself, living there for 200 years, and seriously studying how to crack that old nut, so you can sample the delicious nut meat supposedly within.

Yum. Open wide for the spicy rush of success, the sour tang of fame, and the chewy sweetness of a big income. Bon apetit! Perhaps you'll also have some opportunities, along the way, to familiarize yourself with other popular New York City art-career flavors like ass, despair, crow and humble pie. CF

#15 Useless Mediocrity

The Center for Useless Mediocrity Houston occupies the space where a museum of contemporary art might have gone. Loads of people wander around inside its galleries, under the impression that it's a museum of

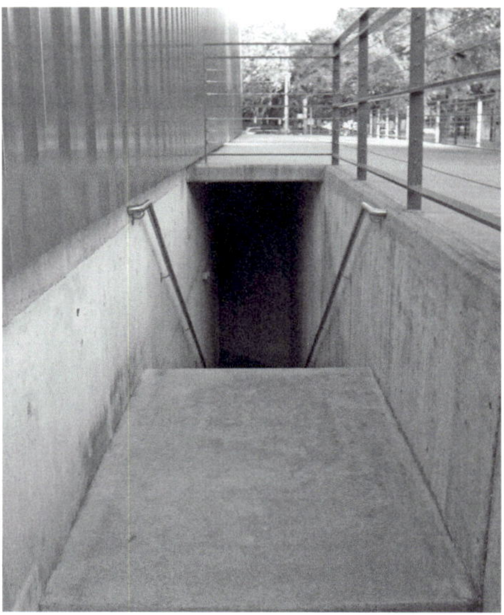

Clark Flood, "#15: Useless Mediocrity," in *Clerk Fluid*, ed. Mark Flood, 4th ed. (Houston: Self-published, 2009), pp. 125–34.

contemporary art, and it greedily sucks up all the money and all the energy the community has for that purpose. But it's not really a museum, because no Muses live there. It's not a sacred place where local artists can go to invoke the Muses for inspiration and protection. The Muses were all evicted a long time ago, because they created image problems and negatively impacted the bottom line.

Oh, the trouble the Center had! Way back, in the misty never-was, someone accidentally hired a radical director for the place. Instead of hoarding all the power and tossing stingy little crumbs of it to artists, the way a tweaked-out coke dealer parcels out dirty eight-balls, this director let artists run wild. You can imagine the result. There were parties at which liquor was served to poor people. There was crazy art. Things we're written on a wall in the men's room, and a big spit-wad got stuck on a light fixture in the gallery.

Anarchy engulfed the city. The board of directors had to interrupt their vacations and jet back to town, in the off-season, to fire the willful servant. They listened to the shocking story of an unlucky board member who had actually attended one of the Center's wild openings. She compared it to a Witch's Sabbath. She had been hit on her left shoulder by a spit-wad. Oh my! the others murmured, sympathetic and concerned. If that had been a steel-tipped cop-killer bullet fired directly into your face by a dangerous radical terrorist-drug-dealer-child-molester-labor-organizer, you could've lost an eye!

The board vowed, Never again! Never again would anyone creative have a chance to embarrass them in front of their friends at the club. No more Muses. No more experiments. No more fun. Absolutely no more artists doing whatever they wanted. They demanded safe, sane, responsible directors, preferably ones with experience in law enforcement, directors with the kind of servile vision that focuses more-or-less exclusively on the social pecking order, and takes orders accordingly. They vowed to keep art and artists in their proper place. For God's sake, they muttered over brandy and Xanax, just because the grease monkeys change the oil doesn't mean they should get to drive the Mercedes!

Some board members still dabbled in the business world, and they nobly volunteered to show how the Center could be reorganized to run just like a business, just like a big corporation. Everyone said, Three cheers for corporations! Hooray for their layers of incompetent, unresponsive management! Hooray for their institutionalized censorship and their suffocation of public dialogue!

Hooray for prioritizing profitability over yucky balls of red tape like the law, common decency and the survival of the human race! Let's run our museum like a corporation! These courageous, Wall-Street-Journal-thumping idealists accomplished their revolution, and made the Center for Useless Mediocrity more fiscally responsible, like Enron, and more ethical, like Exxon Mobil.

The original building had been designed by Frank Lloyd Wrong to resemble a giant cinder, like the cinders that sometimes get painfully stuck in one's eye. It was a clever play on the negative reaction many people had to contemporary art in those days. The rededicated board decided it was all a bit too clever, and they ordered an architectural makeover, to symbolize a bold new commitment to mediocrity. A big trigger was installed on the exterior, turning the Center into an image of a futuristic gun. It was a clever play on the idea that from then on, local artists would be encouraged to commit suicide.

The board's safe, sane, business-oriented vision triumphed, and indeed, spread far and wide throughout the art world, like a burger franchise. Today, it's the only vision of a contemporary art center most of us have ever known. We accept it as part of the natural order of things, like the torturing of helpless prisoners and the breathing of carcinogenic air. Nowadays, everyone intuitively understands that it's unfair to show artwork that's not mediocre, because it might bother somebody or cause a ruckus. It seems completely natural that only certified

A big trigger was installed on the exterior, turning the Center into an image of a futuristic gun. It was a clever play on the idea that from then on, local artists would be encouraged to commit suicide.

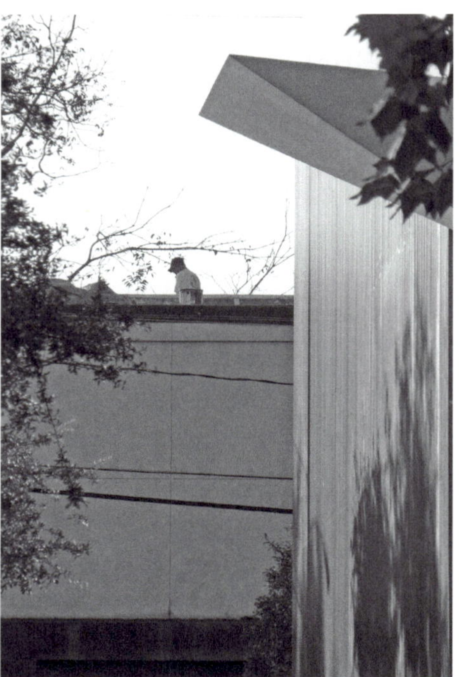

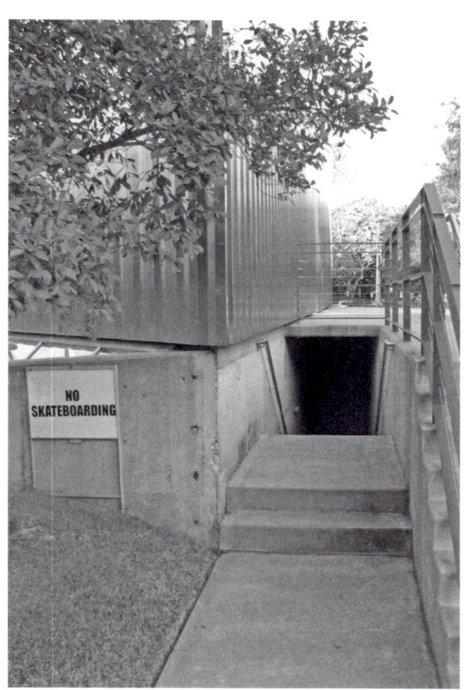

So many artists are working hard to achieve mediocrity. They're developing the kind of safe, familiar art that might someday land them an exhibit in the prestigious basement holding cell of the Center, between the gift shop and the toilets.

art-professional gatekeepers, festooned with degrees and skilled at reassuring the powerful, get to make decisions on what the Center shows. Otherwise, the world would stop and the universe would burst into flames. Otherwise, a giant corporation, busily exterminating an indigenous tribe to steal their mineral rights, might get its feelings hurt and stop funding the Free Day that bears its name, the one carved in 12 foot tall letters across the Center's marble facade. Otherwise, a Christian, maybe even a Christian child, might see a tit.

Mediocrity is a slippery tightrope. On one side lies embarrassing failure, with its mortifying absurdity and its bad press. On the other side lies frightening success, with its dangerous empowerment of new ideas and independent people. The trick is to never fall either way, to slowly and carefully creep forward, without ever making a big fuss or attracting too much intelligent attention. That kind of sustained, high profile mediocrity doesn't just happen by itself. It demands careful planning and constant vigilance. Human creativity is always squirming around, trying to break free and do God-knows-what. The job of the Center is to keep everyone from finding out just what that what might be.

Most artists quickly internalize the Center's program. Like children, they respect and trust the authority figures who carelessly exploit them. They're glad that the grown-ups manage the big scary art world, and they're grateful in advance for the little crumbs they expect may one day fall off the Center's art professional table, right into their hungry mouths. They never question why all the money for supporting the arts goes into paying the salaries of an ever-changing gang of bureaucratic gatekeepers, instead of to supporting artists. What would an artist want with money?

This cursory review of the Center's history may startle them. They'll be surprised to read that there was once an artist destiny that didn't involve total submission to the Big Book of Art Rules, the one they paid so much tuition to open.

Creativity? That's something you can go to college for nine years to learn. Be careful! It's potentially a bad habit, like masturbation. It can ruin your life and the lives of those around you unless you learn how to channel it into acceptable forms. Try 1) aestheticized cries of ineffectual protest on the politically correct side of dated and over-simplified social issues 2) Ironic or confessional rehashings of your personal habitrail of popular culture 3) Ugly, boring conceptual crap with long, explanatory labels or 4) tediously detailed, impressively skillful realistic drawings!

So many artists are working hard to achieve mediocrity. They're developing the kind of safe, familiar art that might someday land them an exhibit in the prestigious basement holding cell of the Center, between the gift shop and the toilets. For those whose ambition is to do as they're told, a show down there is an important milestone on the road to nowhere. CF

#19 Context

Context determines meaning. *I smell bacon* means one thing when I exclaim it in the kitchen of granny's cottage as she cooks breakfast. It means something different when I mutter it while strolling past a chubby security guard at the Galleria.

That's why it's important where one exhibits one's art. Whatever awesome or dank projection of the artist's very soul constitutes the work, and whichever inspirational message or blood-curdling battle-cry is cleverly secreted therein, will be shaded, perhaps even contradicted, by its exhibition context.

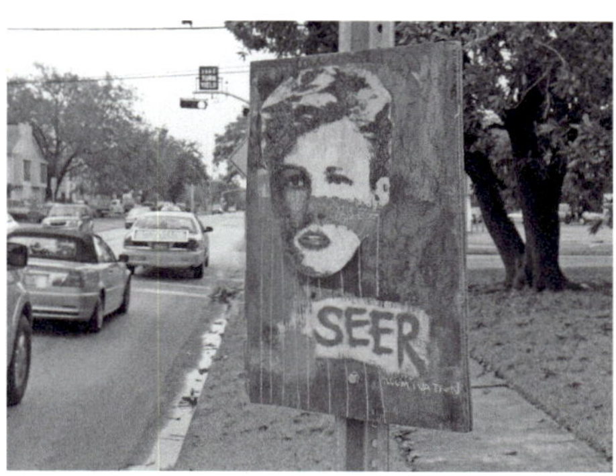

Clark Flood, "#19: Context," in *Clerk Fluid*, ed. Mark Flood, 4th ed. (Houston: Self-published, 2009), pp. 162–77.

I used to think my work had some internal integrity that would persist whether it was hung in the lobby of the Museum of Modern Art or used as a urinal cake at Poison Girl. Now I understand that it would lose something very important if it were ever exhibited at MoMA.

If I were tied to a board and repeatedly dunked under water, held under each time till I began inhaling the H2O and drowning, which Bill O'Reilly told Oprah Winfrey he had, after much soul-searching, accepted as a method of interrogating persons who might have information about terrorist plots against the U.S. of A., I would eventually confess that there are approximately three categories of places where so-called artists might exhibit. If my interrogators then followed the CIA torture manual approved in the nineteen-eighties for use against Central American "rebels," and peeled the flesh off one of my fingers as they held it in front of my face, I would probably name those categories. Between sobs and moans I would offer, 1. Art dealers. 2. Nonprofit spaces, and 3. Other… aaaa!… the street.

1. Art dealers theoretically are in business to sell art. Some people find that prospect disturbing, the way virgins find rumors of orgies disturbing. Exhibiting one's art in the context of a commercial gallery inextricably links one's creativity to the exotic activity of buying and selling things, and there are artists who deem such linkage inappropriate. They're sensitive souls, and they get disgusted by sell-out art whores resignedly spreading their aesthetic legs to make a living.

For some work, specifically hardcore attempts to bring integrated global capitalism to a screeching halt, I agree that the gallery context would be a compromise, even a betrayal, but I don't think that work exists. Last time I checked, it was ludicrous for any painting, sculpture, performance, film or installation to claim to be the revolution in human consciousness and social relationships that some are vaguely anticipating. We who live in the belly of the beast know all too well that capitalism can digest anything, certainly anything arty.

The legendary big R is not to be confused with the likes of Tide's revolutions in fabric softening, or Charmin's revolutions in anal buffing. My guess is that, when it comes, it will run into all the military hardware in the world, after beginning in a remote Third World locale where the brainwashing is lax. I'm certain it won't involve arty art, except perhaps as kindling.

If you're not isolated in a tiny prison cell where your meals are delivered by a robot, or being targeted for assassination by rogue federal law enforcement agencies (I'm sorry, was "rogue" redundant?), you're probably not a revolutionary artist. Thinking you're too noble, too anti-social, or too underground for galleries may be wishful thinking, which closely resembles you positioning yourself to sell out your alleged integrity five or ten minutes from now. Maybe you should reword your business card. Add some fine print that says you're a phony, marketing pseudo-rebellion to youngsters still not able to see through your crap, or rich old ex-rebels, sentimental enough not to laugh in your face. A pretentious commercial gallery will be perfect for you, whenever you're ready.

But which gallery; which dealer? Most galleries are vanity galleries and they exist not to sell art or to build art careers, but as therapy for their owners. They exist to entertain aimless, wealthy retirees who choose art dealing as a project the way a child chooses mango sherbet at Baskin-Robbins; to fulfill empty-nest housewives, determined to reinvent themselves at the expense of their philandering husbands; to enable obsessed collectors who must deal the art-drug in order to support their own art-addiction; and to validate haunted, moonlighting corporate executives who mistakenly believe such props are necessary to gain entrée to some secret world of art they've imagined.

These wannabes often spend a fortune making their dream into reality, creating elaborate exhibition spaces and impressive offices. Then they sit around, waiting impatiently for the miracle of art sales to happen. Soon they're glaring at the staff as if it were the staff's fault that water flows downhill and the sun sets in the west. Many come to resent the

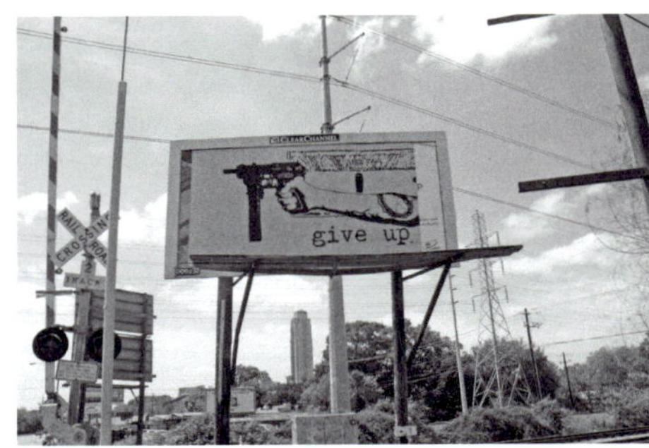

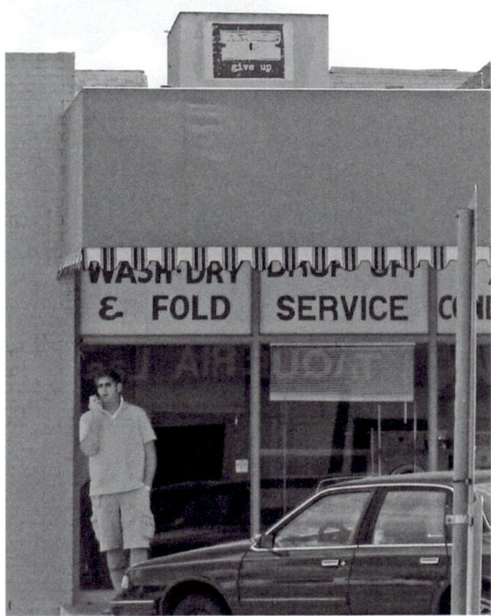

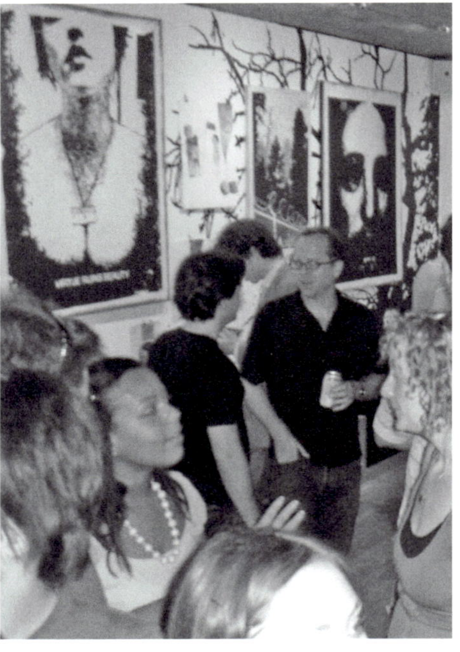

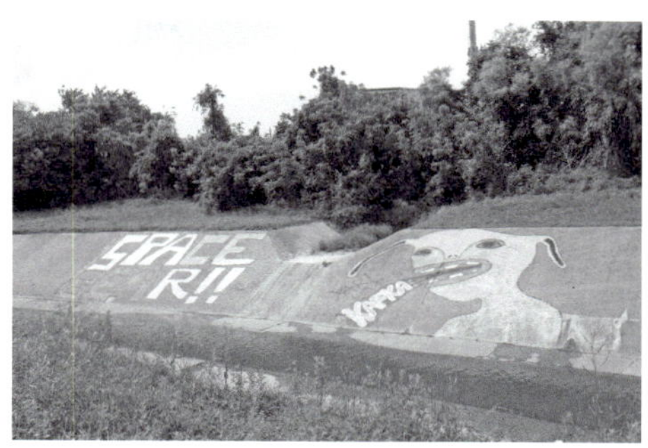

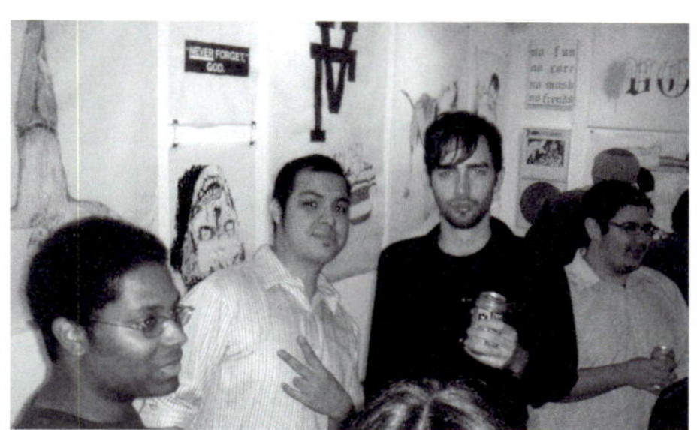

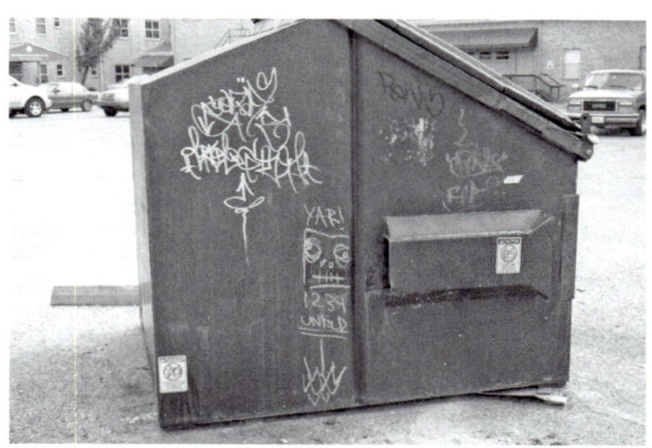

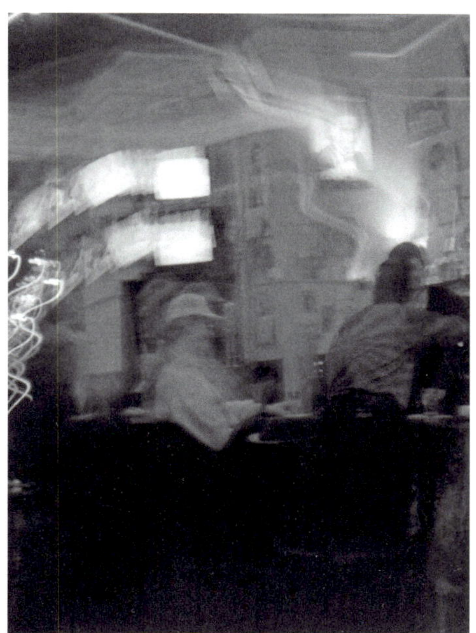

artists who, like baby mastodons in a tar-pit, have foolishly become involved with their disaster. Eventually, incompetent dealers embarrass everyone with fruitless, ignorant attempts to create desire for their motionless inventory. They offer disorienting discounts, they mount thematic sales events more appropriate to car dealerships or furniture outlets, they play pathetic games with red dots on the wall.

Turning useless, worthless, dirt-common art into lovely, spendable, cash money is a magic trick of the most extraordinary sort, and whatever they boast, very few dealers can perform it. That they posses such a talent is the one and only reason for any artist to associate his or her art with a representative of that scummy caste. It's also the only reason to overlook the character defects and associated financial irregularities that the species invariably displays. Don't wait for a charming, trustworthy, nicely-scented dealer who has enthusiasm and ideas. Grab the smelly hunchback who actually has some collector clients and don't let go.

2. The gulag of non-profit art-org corporations is always looking for new talent to exploit. "Alternative" spaces, prestigious museums, respected artist's workshops, self-congratulatory grant-mongers: they all pretend to administer human creativity the way religions pretend to administer human spirituality, with comparable results. If you've read this column before, you've already heard me hint at my problems with this context, so I'll summarize:

Artists, if your work is not academic, rated PG-13, politically correct, bureaucrat-friendly and weak, don't waste a moment of your time with these self-serving mediocrities. They promise everything and they deliver only themselves, season after dreary season. Their only purpose is the perpetuation of their institutional existence, and in their hands, you will never be more than a means to that end. However unique your vision, it will be reduced to one perky paragraph in an infinite series of perky paragraphs on an endless schedule that stretches to a necessarily meaningless, fund-raising future. However breathtakingly experiential your art may be, it will be ruthlessly chipped into a pile of incompetently written words by the heartless and soul-less necessities of the blurb, the resume, the press release and the artist's statement. It's not unusual, just like slaughtering cattle isn't unusual in a slaughterhouse. It's merely wrong.

Non-profit corporations are immortal, but you are not. Don't waste a moment of your precious time.

3. Artists find other contexts. Many today apparently prefer tagging dumpsters and wheat-pasting images on industrial barriers, to figuring out which kooky art doo-dad might titillate the wooden eyes of a neurotic dealer, or embody the quota-determined vision of a hamstrung CAM curator. They could correct their misguided habits with a few semesters in the pain amplifier of art education, but are they willing? Is it possible they could be satisfied with a following among those similarly disaffected, and with earning a living in economies less fantasy-based then those of the art desert, with its shimmering mirages of stardom, careers, gallery sales and grants?

Given the art world, the non-art world looks rather inviting. Marginal places where total control isn't yet total radiate an unauthorized, dignified reality that makes the white cube context look like a job application. Streets and alleys, walls and fences, concrete and sheet metal, asphalt and glass: the city's brutal exoskeleton beckons those who would make their mark without getting permission first. Likewise, the skin of one's own body is currently available, as is every computer screen in the world.

People who don't know a thing about art sometimes turn out to be a surprisingly perceptive, discriminating art audience. Other times, they want you arrested. Welcome to Pottersville, where everybody loves creativity in just the same creepy, hypocritical way they love freedom and democracy. Everybody loves art and artists; so much so that they've gone ahead and figured out your whole life and career for you, for your own good and for everybody's safety and security.

I smell bacon. CF

#21 AT THE CINEMA

Hi, I'm Clark Flood, Scorpio, and I'm probably best known to you as a pattern of pixels quietly glowing in your home. Most of you have probably never thought about me having a corporeal body, and a corresponding time-boundaried physical existence, and that's understandable, given the godlike quality of my prose and my supernatural talent and all. Nonetheless I am a person too, technically.

If you were ever to penetrate my security far enough to come within viewing distance of my high-tech cocoon I might even wave a pale human limb at you, tricep wobbling. But I usually forego such intimate social interactions. I prefer to making my life meaningful by having low-wattage aesthetic epiphanies; typically with my vast accumulation of found, purchased and stolen signage.

The other night I was stealing the VIP PARKING AVAILABLE sign from the Edward's Cinema and I felt a pang of concern. Was my collecting out of control?

My companions were disgusted when I dragged this large sticky piece of trash out of a stairwell in the parking garage. They made fun of me because I said, Can I stick it in your trunk?

The joy and excitement I felt at acquiring the sign outweighed the social backlash. Now, staring into its coolly resolved blue and white lettering I get the feeling I get when I look at great art. That feeling always helps me forget about pesky human relationships.

Maybe I'm too compulsive about acquiring these poignant souvenirs of our civilization. I have approximately 25,000 signs now, crammed into a warehouse. Part of my rationale is that no one else seems to understand how beautiful and important they are. If I don't drag them down off their poles and fences and enshrine them as objects worthy of contemplation, maybe nobody ever will.

Yes, I'll admit, it's a compulsion.

How did it begin? When I was young my family and I spent a lot of time in Mexico and Central America. Mom was a witch, more specifically a priestess in the 1960s version of what later became known as Santeria. We spent a lot of time performing rituals and power-gathering ceremonies in moonlit fields and abandoned buildings, killing the occasional stray tourist so we could drink his or her warm pulsing blood; cooking the bodies down into invigorating stews. Good times.

We visited pre-Columbian ruin sites seeing what demonic entities might still be lurking around, ready to barter with mortals. It was from these ruins, rather than from the antibiotic swabs of museums or the drone-zone of books, that I received all my ideas about art.

I loved the design ethos of those ancient cultures and as I played around their massive stone remains I observed how that ethos inflected every single inch of their material culture. The "art" permeated everything; it wasn't segregated in some chamber of aesthetics perched on top of the pyramid, although it might've climaxed there, red, wet and hot, all over a now long-gone set of costumes, implements, paintings and social types. I wandered attentively through vast fields and courtyards almost paved with broken ancient pottery. I would pick up tiny shards with the familiar whorls or zigzags painted on them. Those broken vessels must have been everyday objects, yet they contained the magic.

Back in H-town, I concluded that the same rules applied. I perceived that the green fluted Coke bottle, from which I daily chugged, embodied the multiplicitous soul of the U.S.A; hard, grotesquely beautiful and menacing; sometimes full of a pseudo-nutritional, purely symbolic, foaming black bile of a capitalist product; sometimes empty, like our religion, our political platforms and our civic life. The Coke bottle was us; and when all that was left of us was an endless field of broken Coke bottles, some future consciousness would catch our reflection there, gleaming off the jagged fragments of green fluted glass.

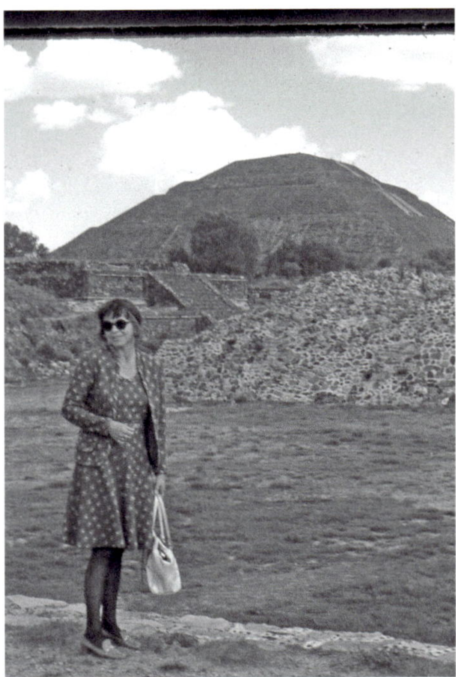

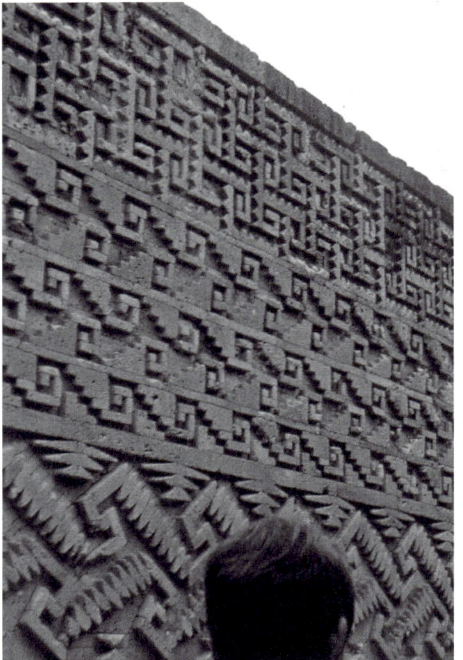

Clark Flood, "#21: AT THE CINEMA," in *Clerk Fluid*, ed. Mark Flood, 4th ed. (Houston: Self-published, 2009), pp. 282–297.

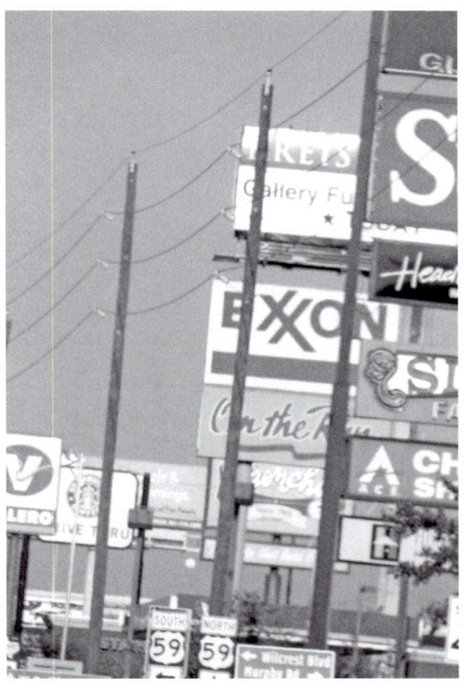

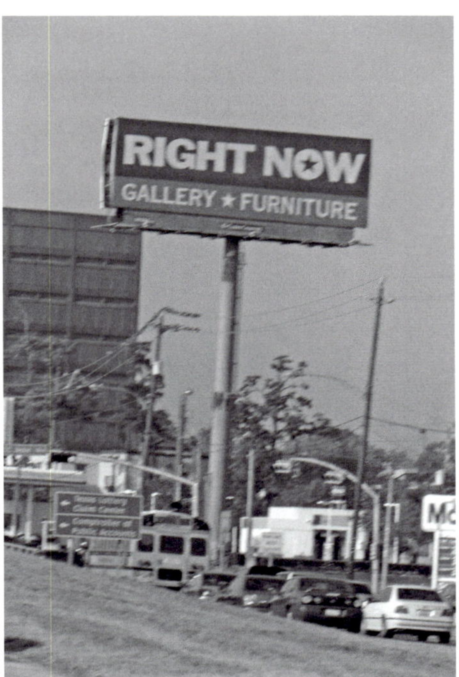

Billboards seemed to be the dominant pictorial manifestations of our spiritual life. Invisible behind masks of familiarity and triviality were the looming impassive faces of our implacable gods, their superhuman cruelty demonstrated in the shaming taunts and manipulative teases of advertising, their divine arrogance embodied in monstrous size and overwhelming scale. Every piece of commercial signage was our version of a stele, covered with our hieroglyphs, delineating the agitated passage of our fifth-wheel souls. The Mayans had marked their species of time with date-obsessed singularities carved in stone; we indicated our sinister achronicity by carelessly exhibiting and indifferently discarding millions of craven pitches, plugs and notices; our time dissolved into a murky puddle of perpetual present, perfect for compulsive shopping, and resigned wage-slavery.

I began worshiping billboards then; back when they were still printed paper pasted onto huge wood and metal frames sat atop giant poles. Nowadays billboards are digitally printed on enormous length of lightweight, translucent vinyl and then stretched over those frames. After a month or two they're taken down and sold to junk dealers who resell them to be used for tarps by grubby businesses.

It reminds me of how they used the blocks of the pyramids to build a Catholic cathedral.

Sure, I have a few hundred paper billboards of yore, neatly folded, pulled out of the dumpsters of various printing companies or otherwise acquired. Sure I burst two discs in my spine trying to salvage massive pieces of billboard wreckage left behind by hurricanes. Does that mean I have a problem?

I used to have rules, but over the years they have fallen away. Now I'm approaching some kind of total indiscrimination. I'm entranced by the little phone cards in Spanish lying near the few remaining pay phones. The scratched off gambling cards. Club bracelets. ATM signs.

I'm compulsively gathering up those cheap little numbers that spring up like toadstools along the road, vinyl on vinyl. Need a lawyer? Sell us your ugly house. Marriage problems? Earn money at home.

Don't judge me.

Even the humble garage sale signs look to me like exquisite mementos of vanishing moments. Big Garage Sale. The sacred event. Multi-family. A community event. The beautiful pointing arrow, like a direct instruction from a god. The addresses and the date, sacred time and sacred space co-joined in one event, a household flung open and all its secret inner stuff displayed for judgment in the burning light of a lawn; laid out for all to see like an open beating heart! It's who we are, and it's beautiful to me. One day only.

I'm dumbfounded by the current trend to display arrays of corporate logos, row atop row of trademarks indicating just which of the many dark gods of capital are involved in any particular product or performance. It looks like a grid of glyphs to me.

Lately I've been casting some cold eyes at lost cat and dog flyers. Needless to say, it isn't concern for the missing pet that turns my head. It's the mania, the sickness. I wonder, Did Schwitters have this? Cornell?

I even get the feeling from stop-signs. Are they beautiful because they're ubiquitous? Of course not. Thats what makes them ugly and invisible. But isn't it wonderful how the entire spectrum of society's need for control, to deter individuals from doing what they want, is summed up in that screaming red octagon?

It's easy enough to see the artiness of the whole road construct, the formalist compositions of yellow and white stripes, the forest of instructional and coercive messages all around. An incalculable weight of steel and concrete, enough to make the spinning earth stumble on its axis, has been deposited so that we can approach, in driving, a spiritual ideal of weightless freedom. We hurry from nowhere to nowhere driven by the supernatural necessities of consumption and production, whipped along by the gentle stings of slogans and spokespersons, eager to establish and immortalize our personal existences.

Our individual statuses, elaborately embodied in our whizzing metallic tombs on wheels, are poised to explode at any moment into fiery hells of sacrificial destruction. If you've never observed one of the human insects fatally roasting inside a flaming disaster beneath the ominous full moon of an indifferent billboard, I can tell you what it says with its eyes as it looks beseechingly out at the receding world through smoke, heat and a shattered windshield.

Remember me!

I love this VIP parking sign. A little bit of the stardust of existence has drifted down from the Milky Way, from whence we all drift, and gotten carved into this VIP sign and it feels like all the good times at the movies and the special feeling of being a VIP and driving. It's all so obvious it's invisible, but not to me. I can see it. The faint afterglow of warmth that spots the places where nearby passing human hearts have pumped human blood over and over through those beautiful interlacing networks of veins. Somebody was here. They left a mark.

I guess one can never leave enough behind to express oneself to a future where one no longer exists, if one is the sort that imagines such futures.

Remember me! I was one of the billion gnats on that sunny day of our civilization, frenetically circulating in a confused cloud of desire and imminent death. CF

1. QUOTES

alleged Duchamp quotes

from the Calvin Tompkins' TimeLife DUCHAMP *and his followers*

"We must remember that critics, dealers and collectors are only so many lice on the back of artists..."

That's the quote that's fun to play with for hours, like one's sex organs or even somebody else's, if you're still young.

I like to try updating it. My current version goes something like...

We must remember that administrators, advertisers, advisors, alternative spaces, amateurs, applicants, art-bloggers, art-handlers, art-lovers, art-therapists, assistants, associates, audience members, bean-counters, benefits, board members, bores, collectors, commissioners, committees, concerned citizens, competitions, conservators, consultants, contests, contributors, corporate sponsors, councils, critics, curators and curatorial teams, dealers, degree-holders, designers, developers, directors, diversity-champions, deadbeats, docents, donors, editors, emerging talents, excellence-rewarders, executives, exhibitors, experts, exposure-mongers, faculty members, fellowships, foundations and their founders, fund-raisers, galleries, guards, gasbags, glory-hogs, graduates, grant programs, greeters, groups, guests, hard workers, has-beens, historians, human resource coordinators, honorary position holders, interns, instructors, interdisciplinarians, jurors, kunsthalles, leaders, major donors, managers, masters, mavens, moderators, motivators, multi-taskers, museums, museographers, non-profits, organizers, organizations, panelists, paper-shufflers, patrons, passers-by, people-persons, photographers, PHDs, planners, post-grads, programmers, professionals, professors, project managers, producers, quota-stuffers, registrars, reporters, resource coordinators, responsible adults, riggers, role models, salespersons, specialists, seasoned veterans, sell-outs, self-styled "good eyes," showcasers, staff, students, supervisors, supporters, tail-riders, talent nourishers, task-forces, teachers, technicians, would-be art directors, VIPs, volunteers, wannabes, web-masters, wind-sniffers, and writers...

ARE SO MANY LICE ON THE BACKS OF ARTISTS! So many filthy, tiny, disease-carrying, itchy, scaly, scabby, crawling, biting, burrowing, disgusting, infectious, six-legged vermin...

Remember me! I was one of the billion gnats on that sunny day of our civilization, frenetically circulating in a confused cloud of desire and imminent death.

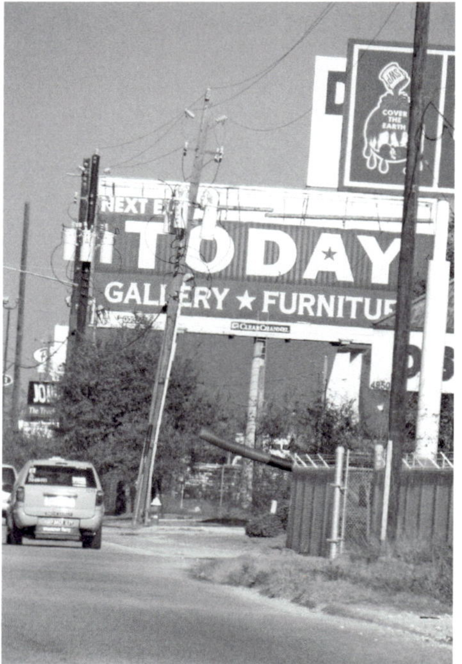

Clark Flood, "1. QUOTES," in *Clerk Fluid*, ed. Mark Flood, 4th ed. (Houston: Self-published, 2009), pp. 484–89.

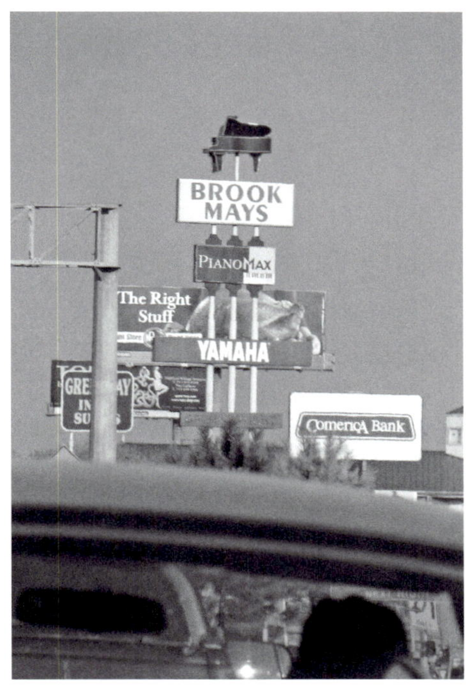

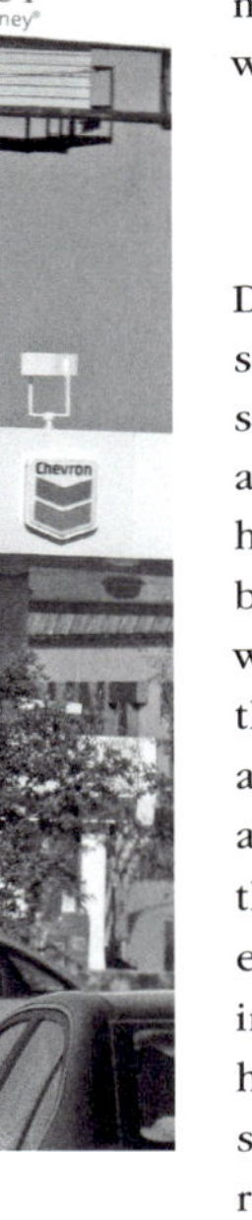

It fits right in with the next quote –
The artist must go underground.

I like to think Duchamp is suggesting that artists operate secretly and stealthily and anonymously instead of trying to promote one's self and one's art by performing like a monkey for the parasitic art bureaucracies and the dealers and everyone else mentioned. The implication is that those activities are harmful for the art and the artists and I certainly agree with that. It goes against everyone's instincts these days, which is another plus.

Immature artists imitate; mature artists steal
attributed to Matisse and so many others

You can't drive down the streets of Houston without seeing the work of anonymous taggers who, if still seeking some sort of audience, at least have no interest in the parasitic art bureaucratic artworld.

I like to be reminded that I can still get enormous self-satisfaction out of my creative acts even if no one is around to see them, praise me or hand me cash, or sex, all gratifying as well. But... The greatest sat is in the doing.

Duchamp left us the example of his own stealthily cerated and deployed *etan donne*, secretly assembled over a twenty year period and only released, already museumified, after his death. It came with assembly instructions but no explanatory label. I like to line it up with Hickey's theories about beauty being the artistic end run around the academic art concentration camps. I doubt Duchamp anticipated CACH, even though he did live through ww2. I think his concern with extending the shelf life of his art, and his interest in overarching designs unifying his own work, and the example of cornell's surrealism- in-a-box, led to a work that recapitulates his themes with a contradiction of his own anti-retinal stance. It doesn't matter why, but it's helpful as a pointer out of the current mess.

Still helpful.

Plus, its good to be reminded that art, from the caves to the twenty-Fist century, is all about fucking. If the ancients weren't masturbating to their neolithic Venuses, they had more self control than I have.

Quote about art education.

He started it but his work floats way above it, maybe because he wrote his own labels.

The dealers used to think they controlled it. Then the curators tried controlling it. Now the collectors think they control it. The mechanism of the art world. But only are-tists control it. And only the good ones.

How long is the coastline of bad art?

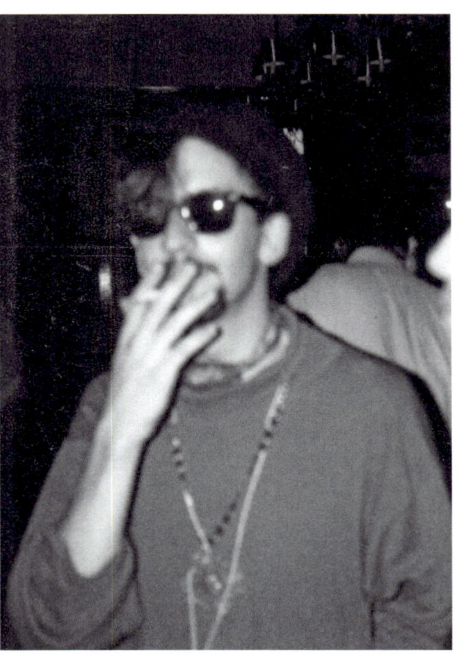

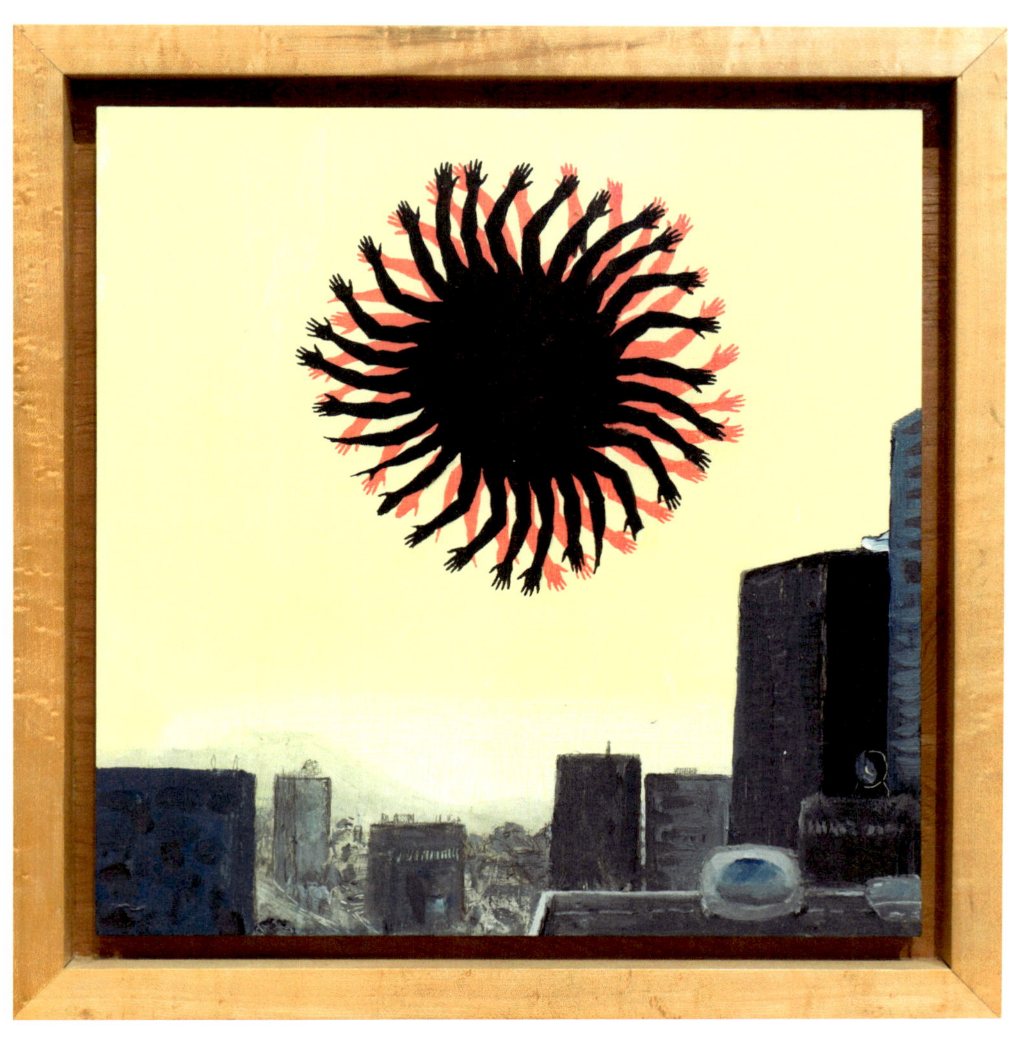

Mexico City 1996 acrylic on wood 15 x 15 inches

Contributors

Bill Arning is the director of the Contemporary Arts Museum Houston. Since arriving at CAMH in 2009, he has organized solo exhibitions on Marc Swanson, Melanie Smith, Matthew Day Jackson, and the late Stan VanDerBeek. In 2015, along with curator Elissa Auther and the Museum of Contemporary Art Denver, he co-organized the survey show *Marilyn Minter: Pretty/Dirty*. Previously, Arning was curator at MIT's List Visual Arts Center (2000–2009), curating shows on AA Bronson, Cerith Wyn Evans, and Kate Ericson and Mel Ziegler. From 1985 to 1996, Arning was director of White Columns in New York, where he organized groundbreaking first solo shows for artists such as John Currin, Marilyn Minter, Andres Serrano, Richard Phillips, Cady Noland, and Jim Hodges. His writing has appeared in *Artforum*, *Art in America*, *Out*, and *Parkett*, and he has contributed to many international publications, including exhibition catalogues on Keith Haring, Christian Jankowski, and Donald Moffett. Most recently, he wrote an essay on the art market and AIDS for *Art AIDS America*, organized by the Tacoma Art Museum.

Alison M. Gingeras is a curator and writer based in New York and Warsaw. She has held curatorial positions at the Solomon R. Guggenheim Museum, New York; Musée National d'Art Moderne, Centre Georges Pompidou, Paris; and Palazzo Grassi, Venice. She is currently an adjunct curator at Dallas Contemporary in addition to working independently. Her writing regularly appears in *Artforum*, *Tate Etc.*, and *Mousse*, as well as in many books and exhibition catalogues. Notable recent publications have addressed the work of William N. Copley, Ella Kruglyanskaya, Bjarne Melgaard, Martial Raysse, and Francesca Woodman.

Carlo McCormick is a critic and curator based in New York. A senior editor of *PAPER*, he has contributed to numerous monographs and exhibition catalogues and to such journals as *Aperture*, *Art in America*, *Artnews*, *Spin*, and *Vice*. In 2006 he organized the exhibition *The Downtown Show: The New York Art Scene, 1974–1984* at the Grey Art Gallery and Fales Library at New York University. His monograph on the work of Jean-Michel Basquiat is forthcoming from Taschen.

El Topito is the pen name of someone formerly employed by one of Mark Flood's dealers. He came out of college swinging and, after early promise and no realization, finds solace in beautiful bottles of alcohol (when his budget permits) because they allow him to "travel" outside of his region. A favorite childhood memory: "… visiting friends of my parents in Cape May, New Jersey. A small cream house near the train tracks. Dusk finds me throwing things at passing freight cars. That night I am permitted to watch *A Nightmare on Elm Street* on cable television. I don't find the film particularly scary, but later in the strange guest bed I dream of large houseflies imploring me to 'please urinate now.' I comply."

Scott Indrisek is the Editor in Chief of *Modern Painters* and a senior staff writer at Artinfo.com. His work has also appeared in a wide variety of publications, including *The Believer*, *Village Voice*, *Bookforum*, *BlackBook*, *Artnews*, and *Whitewall*. Indrisek also runs a small network of extracurricular blogs on topics from art-world socialites to Marina Abramović and the worst of the *New York Times*; more information can be found at Heavypurring.com. He resides in Bedford-Stuyvesant, Brooklyn, with two erudite cats.

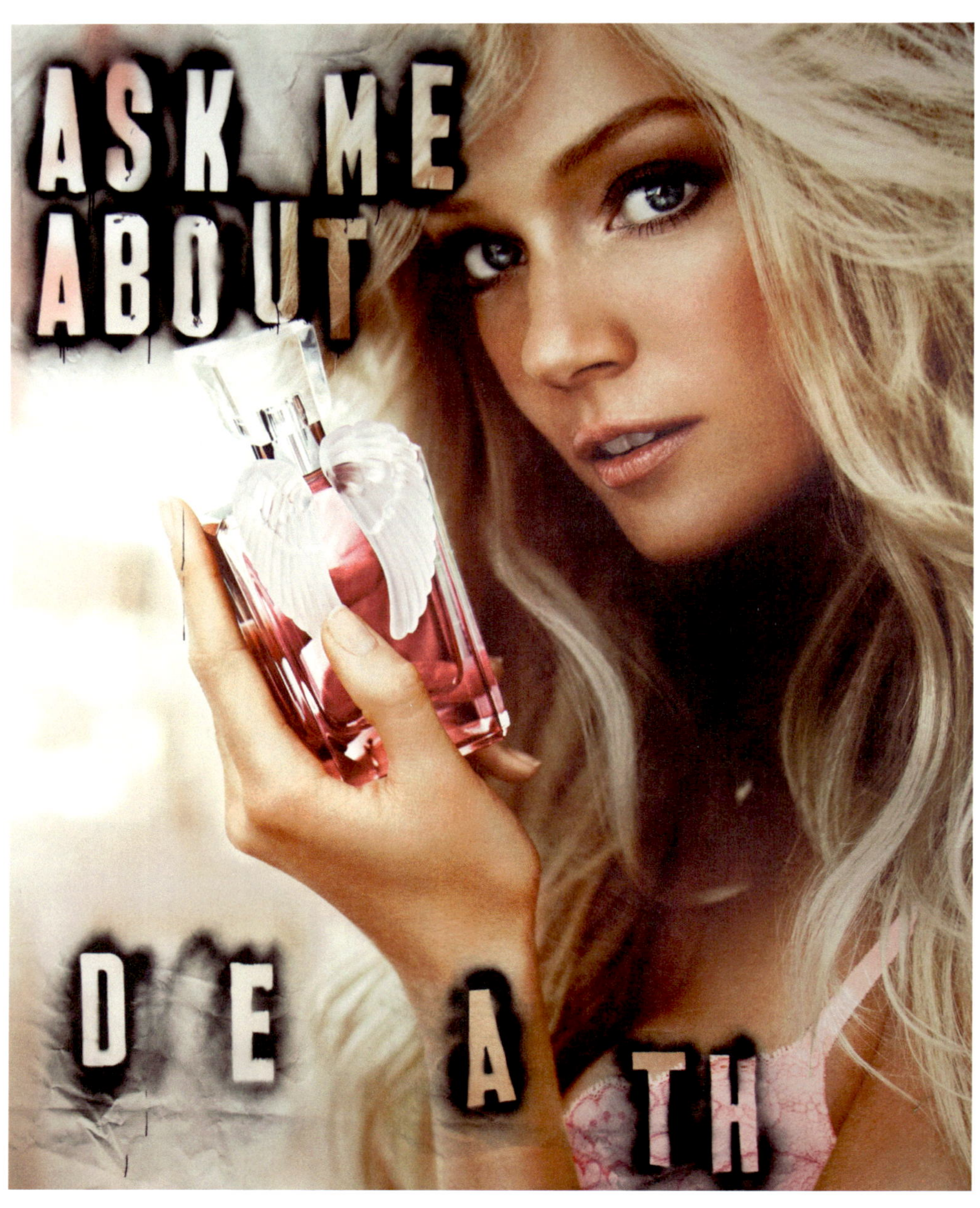

ASK ME 2015 spray paint on printed advertisement on canvas 92 x 76 inches

Exhibition History

Mark Flood

Born 1957, Houston
Lives and works in Houston

Selected Solo Exhibitions

2016

Mark Flood: Gratest Hits
Contemporary Arts Museum Houston

2015

American Buffet Upgrade
Stuart Shave/Modern Art, London

Astroturf Yelp Review Says Yes
Peres Projects, Berlin

Untitled Solo Exhibition
Rubell Family Collection, Miami

2014

Mark Flood
Stuart Shave/Modern Art, London

Available NASDAQ Symbol
Zach Feuer Gallery, New York

Insider Art Fair
Center 548, New York

Another Painting
Contemporary Art Museum, St. Louis

2013

Facebook Farm
Beta Pictoris, Birmingham, Alabama

Mike Lood / Ask Officer Pepperspray
Peres Projects, Berlin

2012

Bushwick Basement
Grimm Schultz, Brooklyn, New York

YES YES YAWN
Home Alone 2 Gallery, New York

ARTSTAR
Zach Feuer Gallery, New York

The Hateful Years
Luxembourg and Dayan, New York

People Are Strangle
Peres Projects, Berlin

ECU
Marfa Book Company, Marfa, Texas

2011

Murk Fluid
Zach Feuer Gallery, New York

Monument to the Responsible Management of the Earth
Maccarone, New York

The Bitterness of the Red Pill
Cardoza Fine Art, Houston

2010

Bitch Moves
Peres Projects, Berlin

Decorations on Her Body
Galerie Rüdiger Schöttle, Munich

Green Cube
Noma Gallery, San Francisco

2009

Chelsea Whores
Zach Feuer Gallery, New York

Wart Exhibit
Peres Projects, Berlin

2008

Entertainment Weakly
Peres Projects, Los Angeles

Vote Demon Replicant
Locker Plant, Chinati Foundation, Marfa, Texas

Nondifference Personified
Brasil, Houston

2007

People in the Leaves
Hiram Butler Devin Borden Gallery, Houston

2006

Assorted Rags
Arthur Roger Gallery, New Orleans

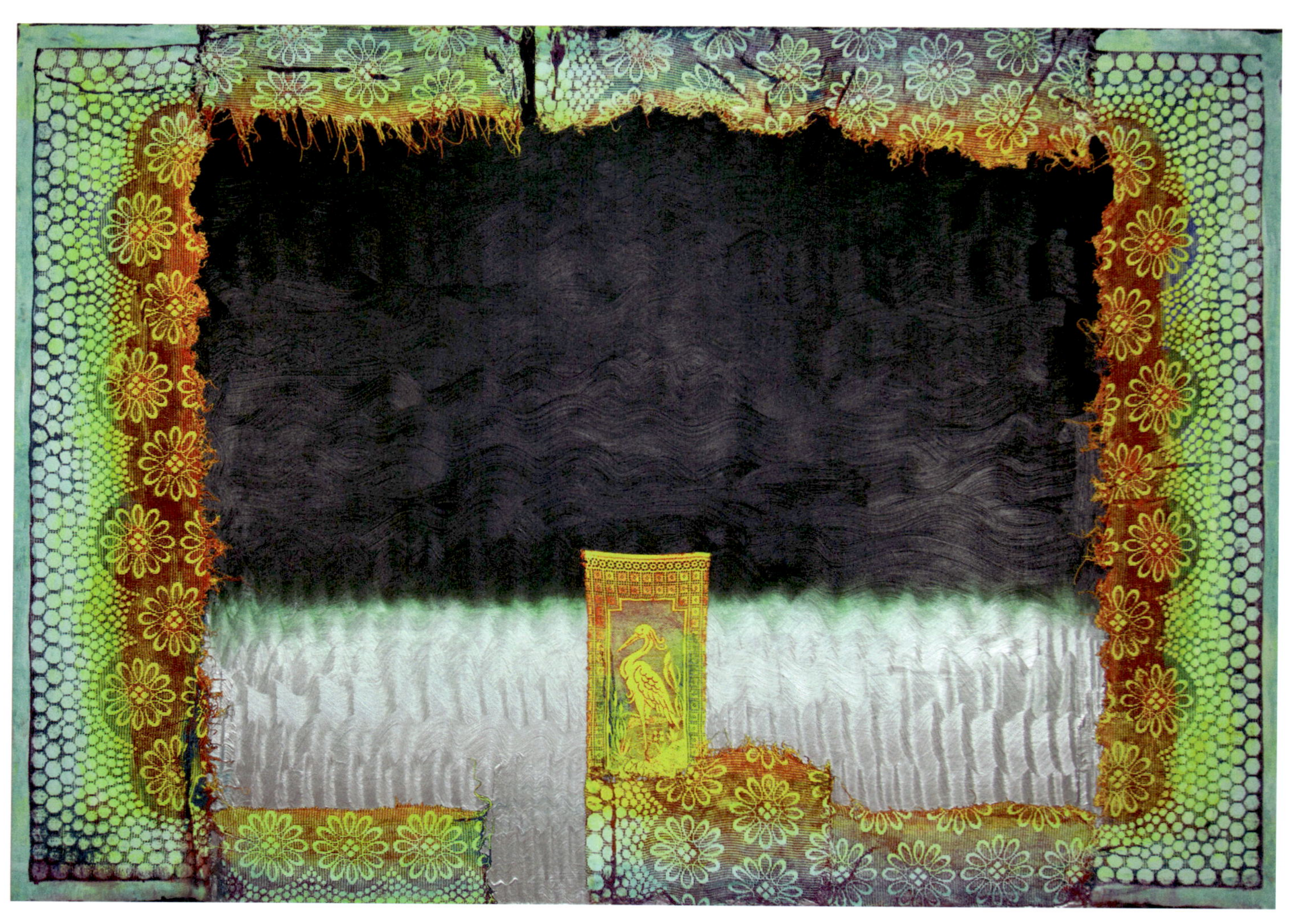

Heaven's Gate 2015 acrylic on canvas 70 x 101 inches

Exhibition History *cont'd*

2006 cont'd

Lace Paintings
Marty Walker Gallery, Dallas

Lace Paintings
Finesilver Gallery, San Antonio

2005

Surprise Your Loved Ones
Machine Project, Los Angeles

Support Your Local Parasitic Art Bureaucracy
Brasil, Houston

2004

Lace Paintings
American Fine Art, New York

Lace Paintings
Angstrom Gallery, Dallas

Lace Paintings
Mixture Gallery, Houston

2002

Lace Paintings
Solway Jones Gallery, Los Angeles

Mark Flood
Marfa Book Company, Marfa, Texas

Lace Paintings
Mixture Gallery, Houston

Mark Flood
Angstrom Gallery, Dallas

2001

Lace Paintings
Sala Diaz, San Antonio

2000

An Exhibition of Work by Mark Flood Organized by Rob Weiner
Marfa, Texas

1998

Temple Signage
Commerce Street Artists' Warehouse, Houston

1997

More Mark Flood
Brasil, Houston

1994

Mark Flood
Lynn Goode Gallery, Houston

1993

Trophy Paintings
Zero One Gallery, Los Angeles

1992

Art Management
Lynn Goode Gallery, Houston

1991

Social Bodies
GVG Gallery, Houston

1989

Imperatives
GVG Gallery, Houston

Celebrity Idolatry
Commerce Street Gallery, Houston

1988

Billboard Alterations
DiverseWorks, Houston

1987

My Relationship with My Co-Workers
Instituto Stato di Cultura, Houston

1981

And Man Chose
3221 Milam Gallery, Houston

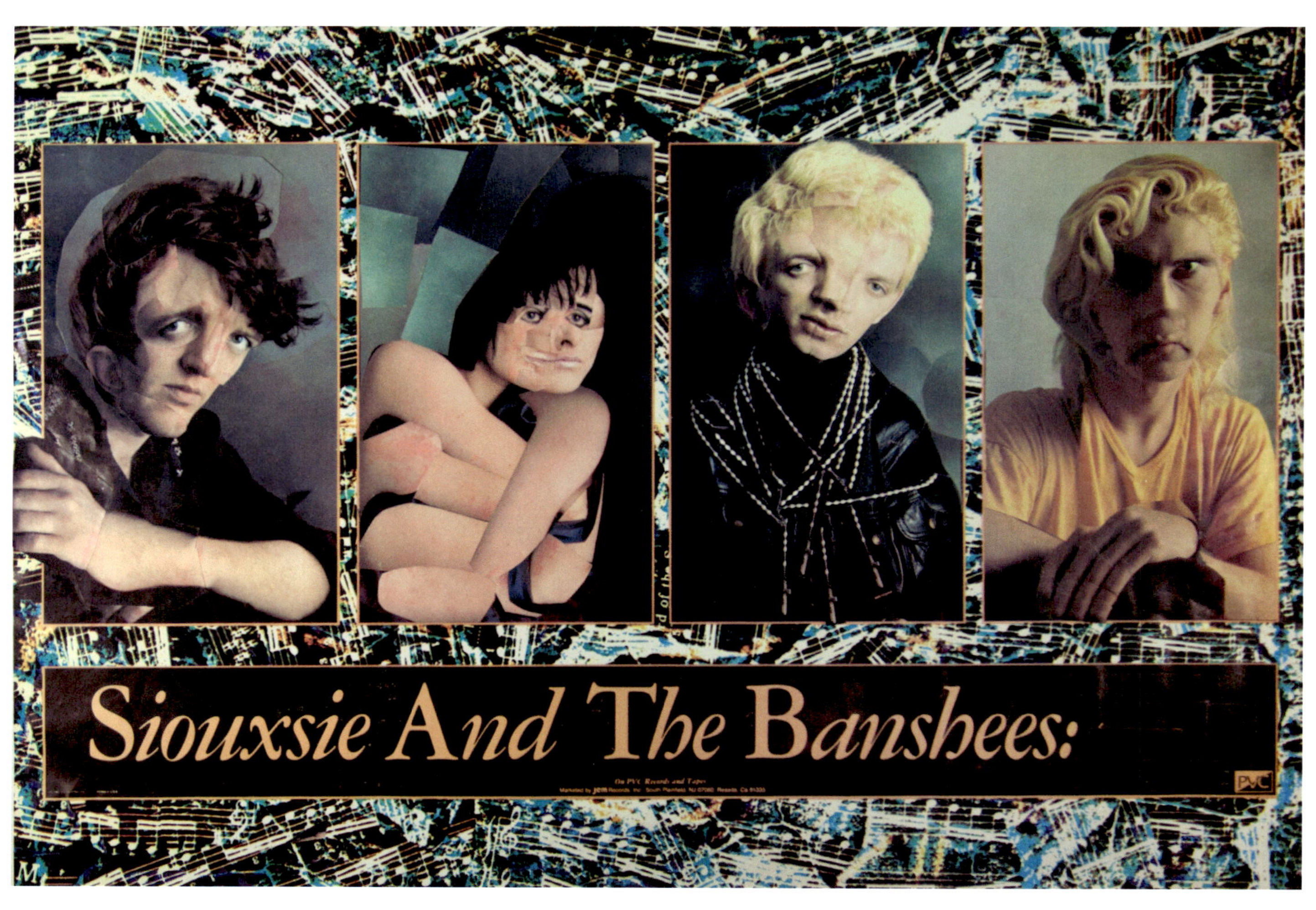

Siouxsie and the Banshees 1983 collage, ultraviolet ink, acrylic panel, aluminum, and florescent light bulbs 24 x 30 inches

Selected Group Exhibitions

2016

Walkers: Hollywood Afterlives in Art and Artifact
Museum of the Moving Image, New York

The Future Is Ow
Marlborough Gallery, New York

2015

Theories on Forgetting
Gagosian Gallery, Los Angeles

#RAWHIDE
Venus Over Manhattan, New York

Word by Word
Luxembourg and Dayan, London

Serialize
Peres Projects, Berlin

2014

Summer in Gstaad
Patricia Low Contemporary, Gstaad, Switzerland

Group Spirit
Peres Projects, Berlin

New Hells
Derek Eller Gallery, New York

2013

Happy Birthday, Galerie Perrotin/25 Years
Tripostal, Lille, France

Art for Rollins: The Alfond Collection of Contemporary Art
Cornell Fine Arts Museum, Rollins College, Winter Park, Florida

Analogital
Utah Museum of Contemporary Art, Salt Lake City

Harold Ancart, Kristin Baker, Mark Barrow, Nina Beier, Anna Betbeze, Mark Flood, Thilo Heinzmann, John Henderson, Scott Lyall, Jayson Musson, Renaud Regnery, and Pae White
Galerie Perrotin, Paris

2013 cont'd

The Writing Is on the Wall
Jonathan Viner Gallery, London

Art for Art's Sake
Frederick R. Weisman Museum of Art, Pepperdine University, Malibu, California

LAME LEWD AND DEPRESSED: Lane Hagood, Mark Flood, and Jeremy DePrez
Co-Lab Projects, Austin

Outside the Lines: UIA (Unlikely Iterations of the Abstract)
Contemporary Arts Museum Houston

Double Hamburger Deluxe
Marlborough Chelsea, New York

Anamericana
American Academy in Rome

2012

Idealizing the Imaginary: Illusion and Invention in Contemporary Painting
Oakland University Art Gallery, Rochester, Michigan

Blind Cut
Marlborough Gallery, New York

Collaborations and Interventions
CCA Andratx (Kunsthalle), Mallorca, Spain

Grisaille, Part II
Luxembourg and Dayan, New York

CineMarfa
Marfa Film Festival, Marfa, Texas

Files, Desks, Chairs
1100 E 5th Street, Austin

It's Always Summer on the Inside
Anton Kern Gallery, New York

Détournement: Signs of the Times
Jonathan LeVine Gallery, New York

In Plain Sight
McClain Gallery, Houston

Eagles: Contemporary American Artists
Marlborough Gallery, Madrid

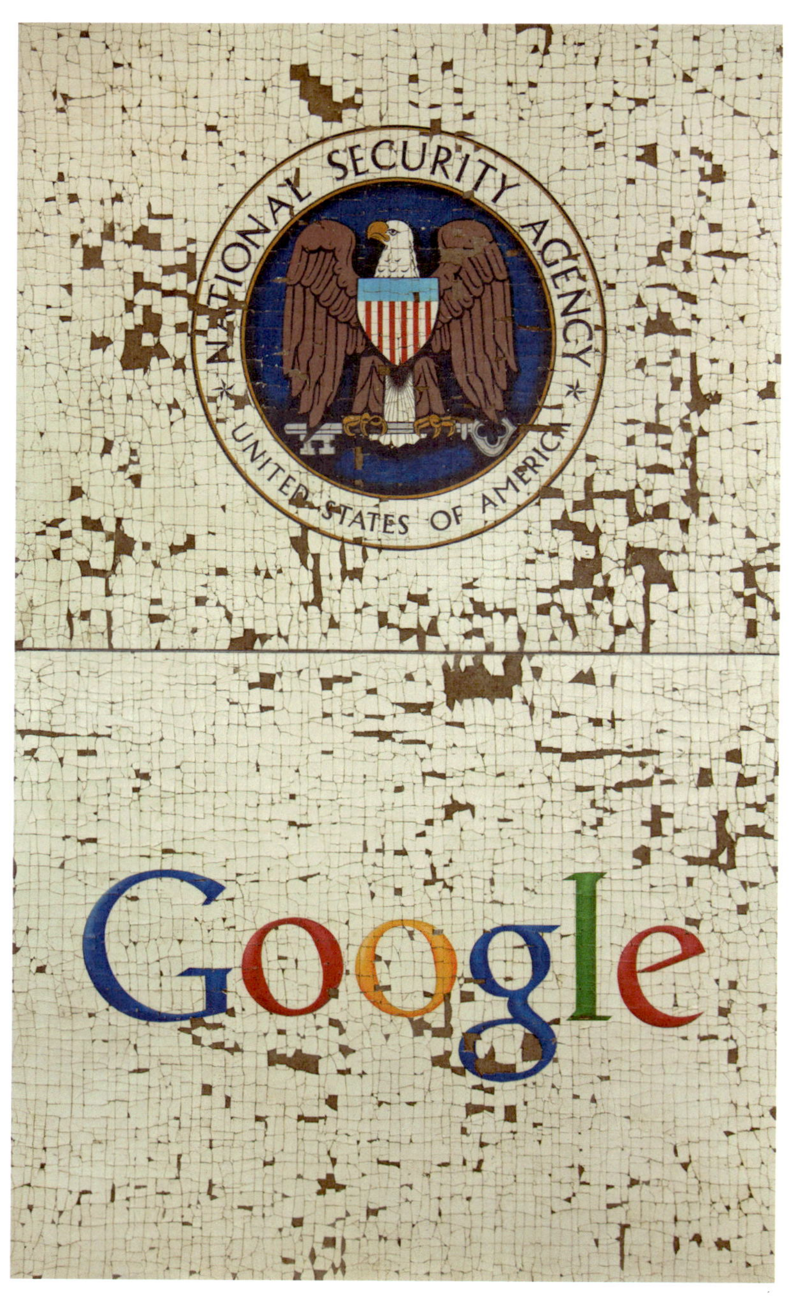

NSA/Google Diptych 2016 oil on plaster on burlap on wood panels 96 x 60 inches

Exhibition History *cont'd*

2011

The Cannibal's Muse II
Autocenter, Berlin

A Painting Show
Autocenter, Berlin

Grisaille
Luxembourg and Dayan, New York

2010

Preconceived Iconography
Museum 52, New York

SHRED
Perry Rubenstein Gallery, New York

Open
Zach Feuer Gallery, New York

2009

there's something I've been meaning to tell you...
Marty Walker Gallery, Dallas

Reality Sandwiches
Artnews Projects, Berlin

Minneapolis
Peres Projects, Los Angeles

Mark Flood and John Kleckner: Additional Paintings
ReMap2, Athens, Greece

Geography of the Imagination
Lead Apron, Los Angeles

2008

Pretty Ugly
Maccarone, New York

Sack of Bones
Asia Song Society, New York, and Peres Projects, Los Angeles

2007

BIG
Cameron Art Museum, Wilmington, North Carolina

2007 cont'd

Group Exhibition by Gallery Artists
Marty Walker Gallery, Dallas

New Paintings by Jeff Elrod, Mark Flood, and Jeff Zilm
Marty Walker Gallery, Dallas

2006

Mark Flood, Jeff Elrod, and Jack Pierson
Marfa Book Company, Marfa, Texas

Inaugural Group Show
Marty Walker Gallery, Dallas

2005

Return of the Boys in the Bubble
Anton Kern Gallery, New York

Restless
Glassell School of Art, Museum of Fine Arts, Houston

2002

Blip
University of South Florida Contemporary Art Museum, Tampa

Bitchin' Pictures
Solway Jones Gallery, Los Angeles

Untitled Group Show
Million Dollar Hotel, Houston

2001

Show People
CB's 313 Gallery, New York

Kick the Habit
Good/Bad, New York

Postmodern Americans: A Selection
Menil Collection, Houston

Trying Too Hard
Commerce Street Gallery, Houston

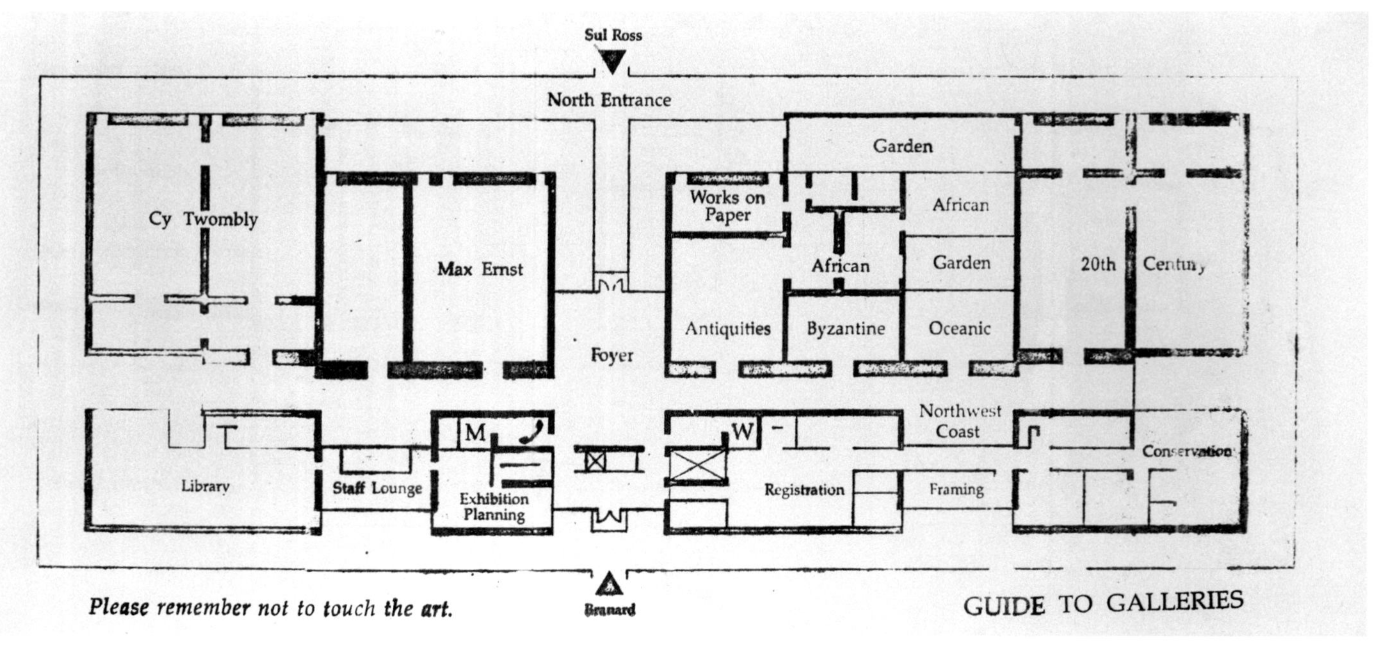

Menil Collection Floorplan 1992 acrylic on canvas 26½ x 60 inches

Exhibition History *cont'd*

2000

Broken Pictures: Mark Flood and David West

Hofstra University Museum,
Hempstead, New York

The Boys in Bubbles: Dan McCarthy, Mark Flood, and Jack Pierson

Anton Kern Gallery, New York

1999

Texas Draws

Contemporary Arts Museum Houston

1998

Elrod/Flood/Tucker

Angstrom Gallery, Dallas

1997

Monstrous Double

Lawndale Art Center, Houston

Uncommon Sense

Geffen Contemporary,
Museum of Contemporary Art, Los Angeles

1996

Unmade in the U.S.A.

La Panadería, Mexico City

1995

City Folk

Holly Solomon Gallery, New York

1994

Made in the U.S.A.: A 2000 Year Survey

Thicket Gallery, New York

1993

Texas Contemporary: Acquisitions of the '90s

Museum of Fine Arts, Houston

Darkness and Light: Twentieth-Century Works from Texas Collections

Blaffer Gallery, University of Houston

1993 cont'd

Faces

River Oaks Theater, Houston

100 Viewings of the Rodney King Beating

Catal Huyuk Gallery, Houston

1992

Paint by Numbers

Bridgewater/Lustberg Gallery, New York

Avenues of Departure

Contemporary Arts Center, New Orleans

Primarily Paint

Laguna Gloria Art Museum, Austin

Crosses

Jamison/Thomas Gallery, Portland, Oregon

1991

Texas Selections from the Menil Collection

Galveston Art Center, Texas

Animals

Max Fish, New York

Perfect World

San Antonio Museum of Art

Mutilations

Max Fish, New York

Pop Art: The Object Transformed

Museum of Fine Arts, Houston

1990

The Art of Assemblage

Lynn Goode Gallery, Houston

Texas Art Celebration '90

1600 Smith Gallery, Houston

1989

Primal Screen: A Fake Art Movement

Treebeards, Houston

1988

Untitled Group Show

Club Proteus, Houston

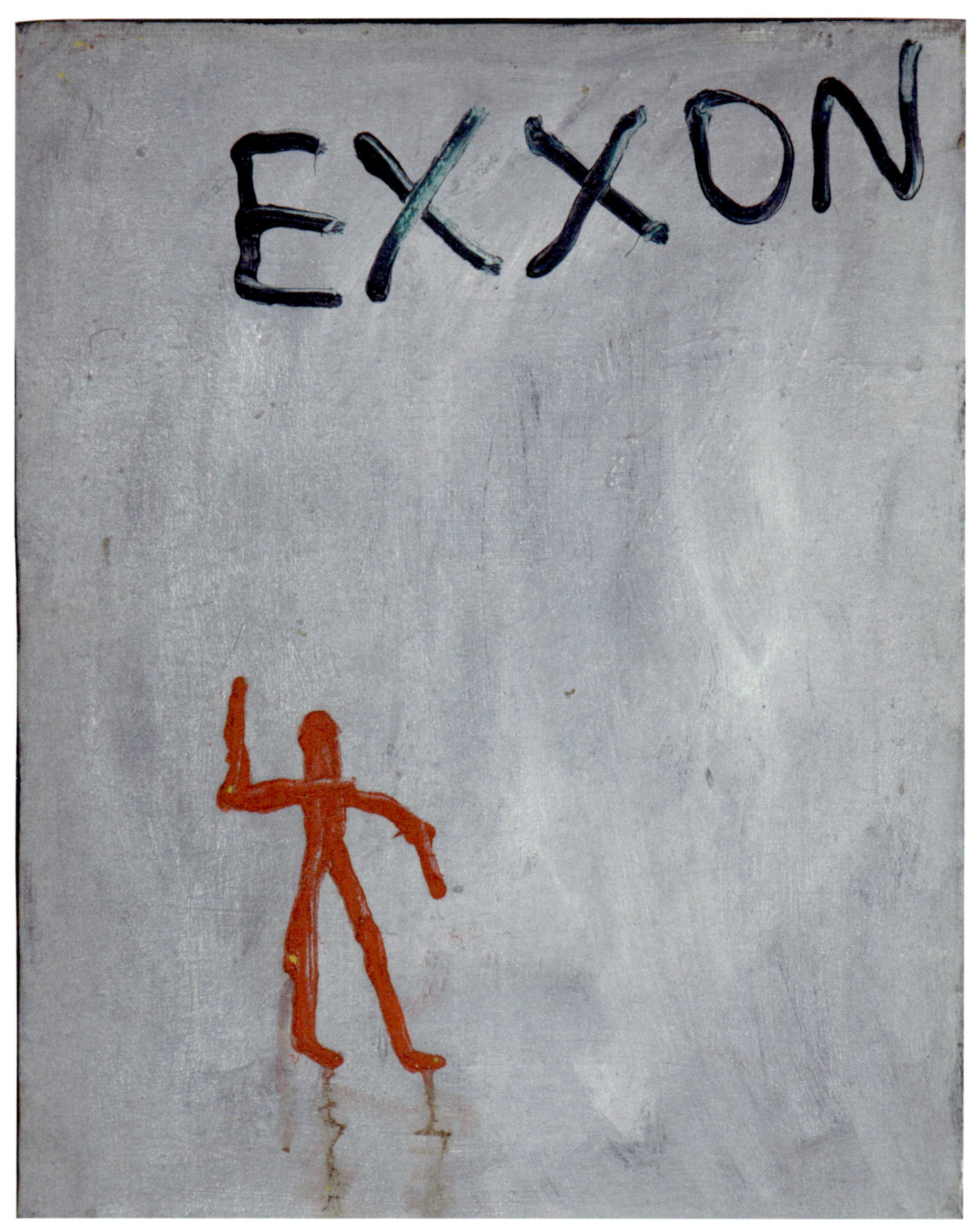

Exxon Man 1979 oil and acrylic on canvas 20 x 16 inches

1988 cont'd

Synergy
Glassell School of Art, Houston

Houston 88
1600 Smith Gallery, Houston

1987

Vandalism
Screen Memories, Houston

One Eye
Houston Center for Photography, Houston

True Wit: Humor in Texas Art
1600 Smith Gallery, Houston

Found
DiverseWorks, Houston

1986

3 to 5
DiverseWorks, Houston

1985

Propaganda
Mid-Town Arts Center, Houston

Group Show
DiverseWorks, Houston

1982

Prisoners of Conscience
Studio One Alternative Space, Houston

1981

Five Unimportant Artists
3221 Milam Gallery, Houston

Untitled Group Show
Studio One Alternative Space, Houston

Collections

Dallas Museum of Art
Menil Collection, Houston
Modern Art Museum of Fort Worth, Texas
Museum of Fine Arts, Houston

Bibliography

Catalogues and Essays

Alsoudani, Ahmed, and Max Levai. *Eagles: Artistas contemporáneos americanos.* Exh. cat. Madrid: Marlborough Gallery, 2012.

De Bellis, Vincenzo. *Anamericana.* Exh. cat. Rome: Nero, 2013.

Freeman, Jonah, and Vera Neykov. *Blind Cut.* Exh. cat. New York: Marlborough Gallery, 2012.

Gingeras, Alison M. *Pressed Release: Notes on Mark Flood's Hateful Years,* 1979–1989. Exh. cat. New York: Luxembourg and Dayan, 2012.

Goody, Dick, ed. *Idealizing the Imaginary: Illusion and Invention in Contemporary Painting.* Exh. cat. Rochester, Mich.: Oakland University Art Gallery, 2012.

McCormick, Carlo. *Broken Pictures: Mark Flood and David West.* Exh. brochure. Hempstead, N.Y.: Hofstra University Museum, 2000.

Parazette, Aaron. *In Plain Sight.* Exh. cat. Houston: McClain Gallery, 2012.

Parrish, Sarah. "Mark Flood." In *Art for Rollins: The Alfond Collection of Contemporary Art Vol. 1,* edited by Abigail Ross Goodman, pp. 40–41. Winter Park, Fla.: Cornell Fine Arts Museum, 2013.

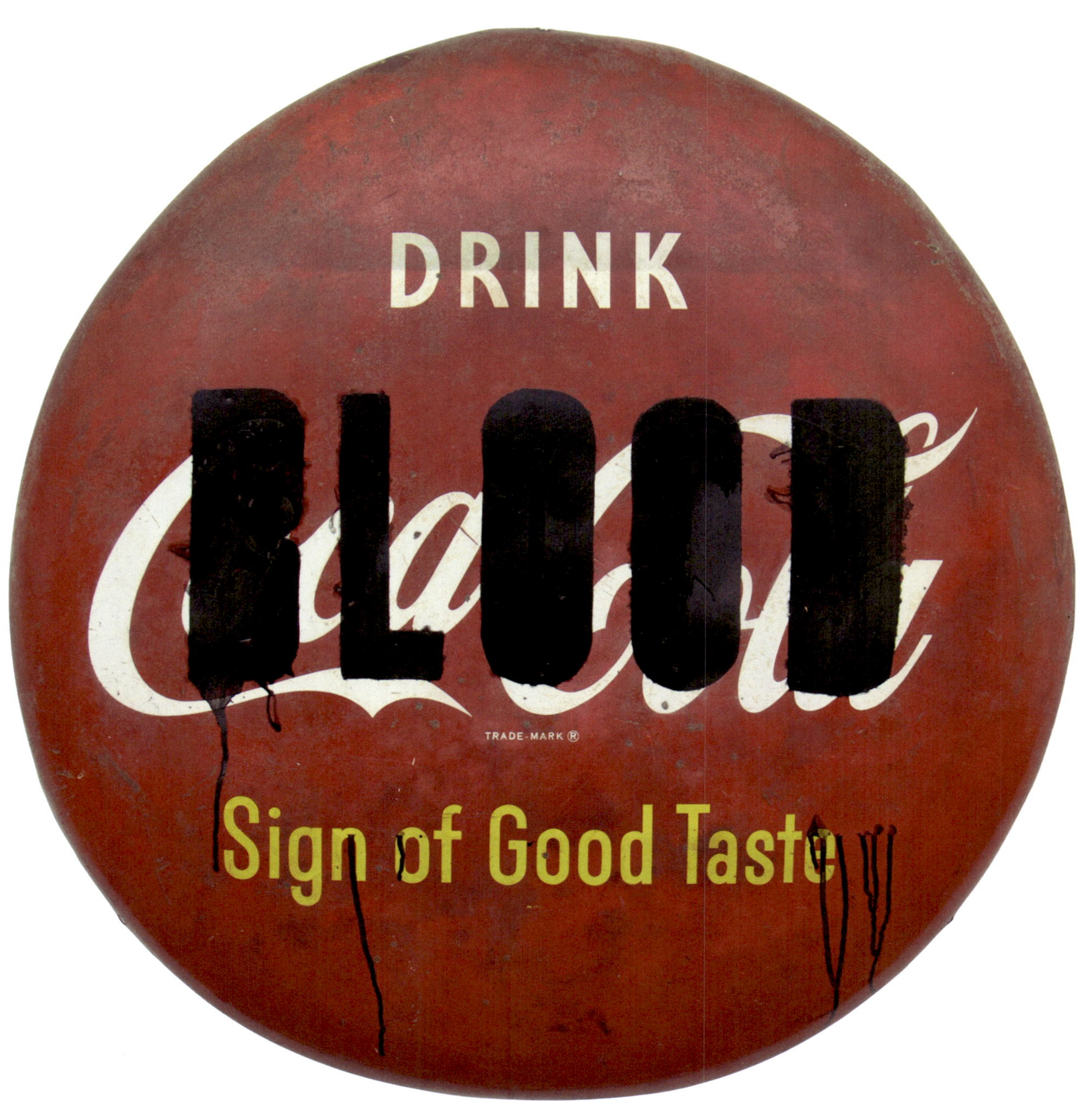

Bevilacqua's BLOOD 2016 spray paint on metal sign 36 x 36 inches

Selected Reviews

Akel, Joseph. "Mark Flood's Hateful Years Weren't Extra Bad." Interviewmagazine.com, August 6, 2012.

Anspon, Catherine. "Monstrous Doubles." *Public News*, August 6, 1997.

Babcock, Mark. "New and Interesting in Dallas." Glasstire.com, July 2, 2006.

Baker, R. C. "Houstonian Mark Flood's Capacity for Art-World Irony Is as Big as Texas." *Village Voice*, May 21, 2014.

Ballou, Chris. "You Can't Say No to the Beauty and the Beast." Glasstire.com, April 2, 2002.

"Bones' Beat: Mark Flood's Chelsea Whores." *Village Voice*, June 4, 2009.

Boucher, Brian. "Mark Flood's Insider Art Fair Is Coming to Chelsea." Artinamericamagazine.com, May 1, 2014.

Boyd, Robert. "Mark Flood at Cardoza Gallery." *The Great God Pan Is Dead*, October 16, 2011.

Chayka, Kyle. "At Luxembourg and Dayan, Mark Flood Spins Frustrated Poetry Out of America's Psychic Underground." Blouinartinfo.com, July 24, 2012.

Chen, Aric. "Lace Is More." Hintmag.com, June 28, 2004.

Corbett, Rachel. "Armory Show 2012." Artnet.com, March 8, 2012.

Creahan, D. "Mark Flood: 'Insider Art Fair' and 'Available NASDAQ Symbol' at Center 548 and Zach Feuer." Artobserved.com, May 31, 2014.

del Valle, Robert. "Stage and Canvas: Seeing the Results." *Real Detroit Weekly*, January 11–17, 2012, p. 18.

Deliso, Meredith. "Mark Flood Has Tasted the Red Pill, and It Is Bitter." Houstonpress.com, October 18, 2011.

Dempsey, Dean. "Mark Flood: The Information Sequence." *San Francisco Arts Quarterly* (October 2013): pp. 56–71.

Dewan, Shaila. "Playing Around." Houstonpress.com, October 2, 1997.

Duncan, David. "Mark Flood." *Art Lies* 63 (Fall 2009): p. 96.

Elmquist, Becky. "Mentally Yours, Mark Flood." *Muse* (Winter 2012): pp. 152–57.

Fowler, Brendan. "Mark Flood." *ANP Quarterly* 2, no. 2 (2008).

Halle, Howard. "Mark Flood, 'Chelsea Whores.'" *Time Out New York*, June 11, 2009, p. 51.

Halperin, Julia, "Mark Flood Installs Ad-Hoc Exhibition in Miami Hotel Room." Blouinartinfo.com, December 6, 2012.

Holte, Michael Ned. "Mark Flood." *Artforum* (March 2009): pp. 251–52.

Huebner, Michael. "Mark Flood's 'Facebook Farm' Opens Friday at Beta Pictoris." AL.com, May 1, 2013.

Jablon, Samuel. "'My Own Career Bores Me': Mark Flood on His Gallery Experiment." Hyperallergic.com, January 2015.

Johnson, Ken. "Mark Flood: Chelsea Whores." *New York Times*, May 29, 2009, p. C29.

Johnson, Patricia C. "'Lace Paintings' Finds a Delicate Balance." *Houston Chronicle*, May 18, 2002.

Jones, Justin. "10 Works to See at the Armory Show in New York City." Thedailybeast.com, March 6, 2014.

Jovanovic, Rozalia. "There's Something about Mark Flood: Cameron Diaz Turns Up for 'Hateful Years.'" Observer.com, July 20, 2012.

Kalil, Susie. "Art and Commerce." Houstonpress.com, February 27, 1992.

Kennedy, Randy. "No 'Sacred Monster,' Just a His-Way Artist." *New York Times*, July 8, 2012, p. AR3.

Kutner, Janet. "A Gallery of Talent." *Dallas Morning News*, February 22, 2006.

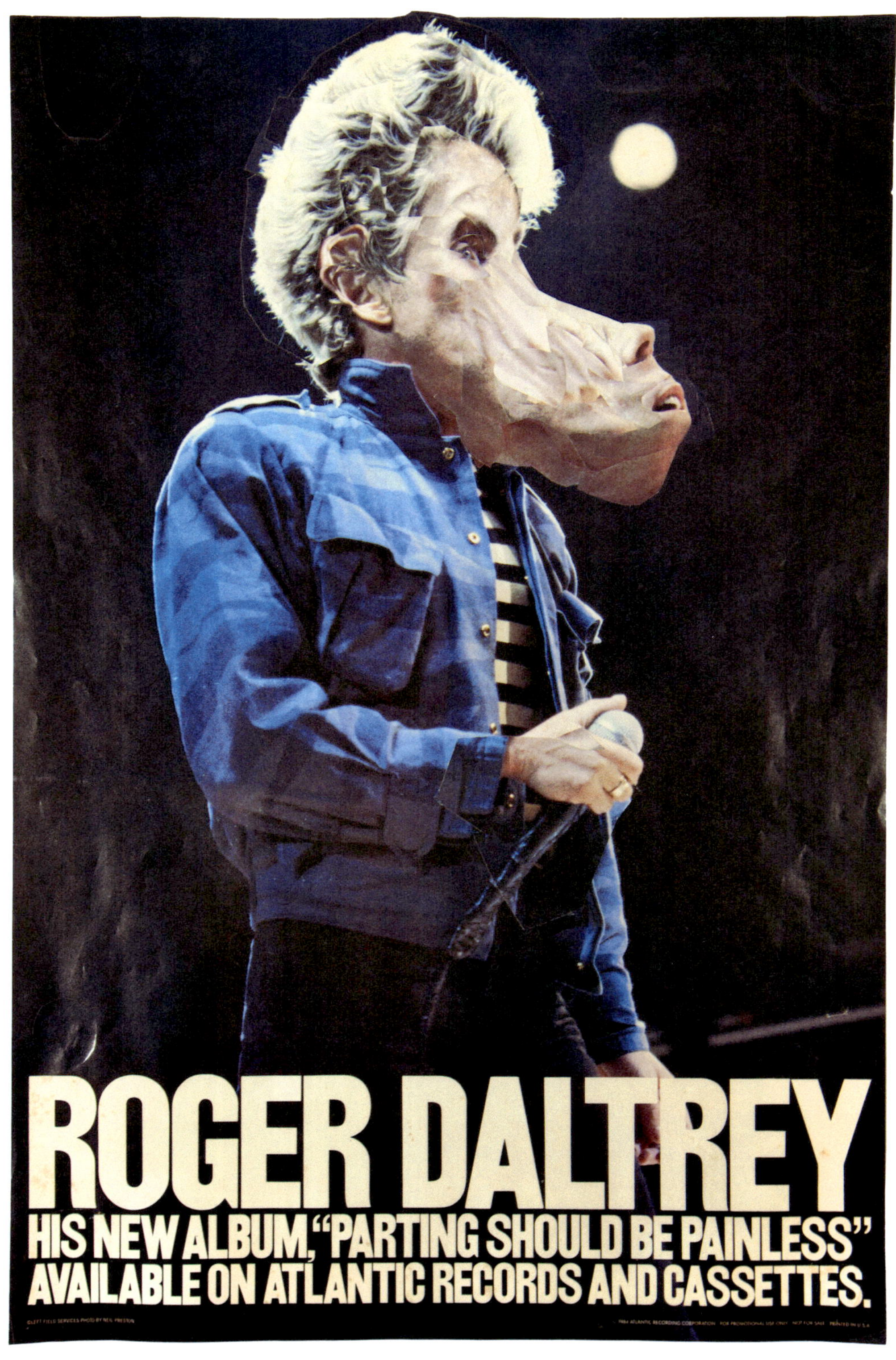

Roger Daltrey 1983 collage 27 x 18 inches

Selected Reviews cont'd

———. "Lace Value." *Dallas Morning News*, February 20, 2002.

Laster, Paul. "Mark Flood, 'The Hateful Years.'" *Time Out New York*, August 23, 2012. p. 73.

Markus, David. "Mark Flood," Artinamericamagazine.com, December 16, 2012.

"Mark Flood." *New Yorker*, June 22, 2009.

"Mark Flood." *New Yorker*, May 31, 2004.

McCormick, Carlo. "Mark Flood." *High Times*, July 1991.

Meier, Allison. "27 Questions with Irreverent Conceptual Artist Mark Flood." Blouinartinfo.com, September 24, 2012.

Miller, M. H. "The Artist Is Sort of Present." *Artnews*, October 2014.

O'Neil, Megan. "Idealizing the Imaginary: Creating the Self." Night and Day, *Detroit Metro Times*, January 11–17, 2012, pp. 38–39.

Palmerton, Elwyn. "Mark Flood." *Frieze*, October 2012.

Phelps, Paige. "Party of the Week: Marty Walker Gallery Opening." *Preston Hollow People*, March 10, 2006, p. 2A.

Plagens, Peter. "The Semi-Real, Semi-Surreal." *Wall Street Journal*, August 17, 2012.

Rosenberg, Karen. "Shred." *New York Times*, August 13, 2010, p. C24.

Rubinstein, Raphael. "Total Service Artists," Artinamericamagazine.com, October 2015.

Rush, Kate. "Marty Walker's Inner Artists." *Paper City*, March 2006.

Salsbury, Britany. "Mark Flood." Critics' Picks, Artforum.com, June 2009.

Schwendener, Martha. "The Badass and the 30-Year Hallucination." *Village Voice*, March 9, 2011, p. 29.

Sholis, Brian. "Mark Flood." Critics' Picks, Artforum.com, May 2004.

Solis, Diana. "He Avoids the Risk of Censorship." *Wall Street Journal*, August 9, 1990.

Stubbs, Phoebe. "Frieze on the Cheap: Frieze Sounds." Artslant.com, October 2014.

Tomkins, David. "Artists in Residence Summer 2007–Summer 2008: Mark Flood." *Chinatown Foundation Newsletter*, October 2008, pp. 69–72.

Vogel, Wendy. "Mark Flood Luxembourg and Dayan, New York." *Flash Art*, October 2012, p. 109.

Walleston, Aimee. "More Than Lace: Mark Flood at Luxembourg and Dayan." Artinamericamagazine.com, August 1, 2012.

Wilson, Calvin. "New Exhibitions at Contemporary Art Museum Take on Social, Political Issues." *St. Louis Post-Dispatch*, September 13, 2014.

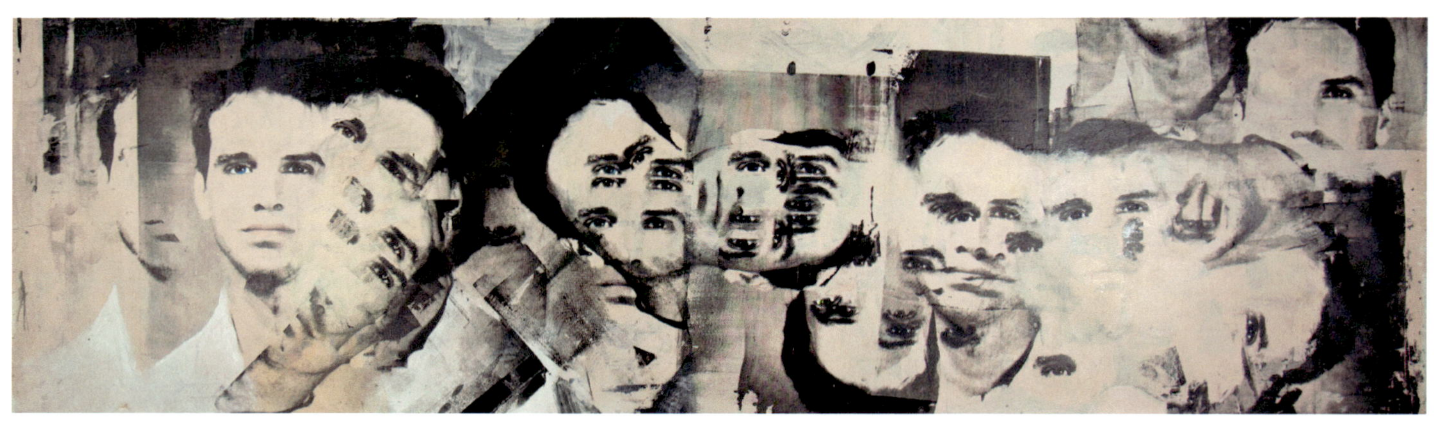

Substitute Teacher 1990 acrylic on canvas 36 x 132 inches

Works

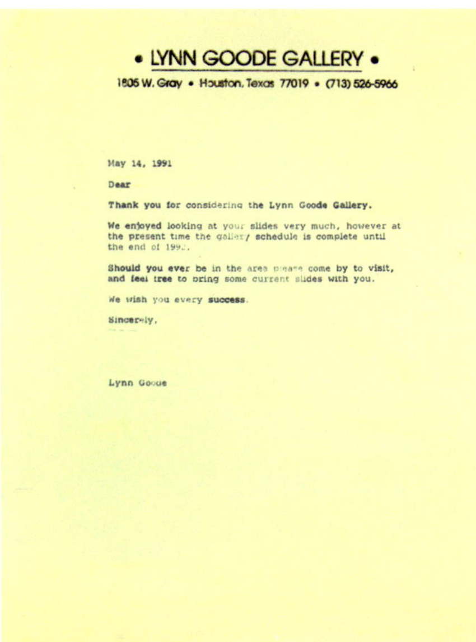

13

1 *Culturcide Memorabilia*, 1979–1997
Ephemera
Dimensions variable

2 *Exxon Man*, 1979
Oil and acrylic on canvas
20 x 16 inches

3 *Another Miracle/Consider Museums as Concentration Camps*, 1980
Vinyl record, edition of 1000
7 x 7 inches

4 *'80s Memorabilia*, 1980s
Ephemera
Dimensions variable

5 *Roger Daltrey*, 1983
Collage
27 x 18 inches

6 *Siouxsie and the Banshees*, 1983
Collage, ultraviolet ink, acrylic panel, aluminum, and florescent light bulbs
24 x 30 inches

7 *Julio Is Moving In*, 1984
Collage, ultraviolet ink, acrylic panel, aluminum, and florescent light bulbs
48 x 36 inches

8 *Tacky Souvenirs of Pre-Revolutionary America*, 1986
Vinyl record, edition of 3000
12 x 12 inches

9 *EAT HUMAN FLESH*, 1989
Spray paint and collage on billboard paper
44½ x 45¾ inches

10 *Substitute Teacher*, 1990
Acrylic on canvas
36 x 132 inches

11 *Signal with Noise B*, 1990
Acrylic on canvas
96 x 66 inches
Private collection, Houston

12 *'90s Memorabilia*, 1990s
Ephemera
Dimensions variable

13 *Lynn Goode Gallery Rejection Letter*, 1992
Acrylic on canvas
46½ x 36 inches

14 *Menil Collection Floorplan*, 1992
Acrylic on canvas
26½ x 60 inches
Private collection

15 *Bonanza*, 1995
Acrylic on canvas
40 x 80 inches

16 *Mexico City*, 1996
Acrylic on wood
15 x 15 inches

17 *OBJECTS/FEELINGS/OTHER*, 1997
Acrylic on canvas
24 x 24 inches

18 *The Deep*, 1997
Acrylic on canvas
52 x 36 inches

19 *Retrospektro*, 1998
Collage and acrylic on canvas
82 x 48 inches

20 *The Warrior*, 2006
Acrylic on canvas
168 x 84 inches

21 *MID-CAREER LOSER*, 2008
Acrylic on canvas
36 x 60 inches

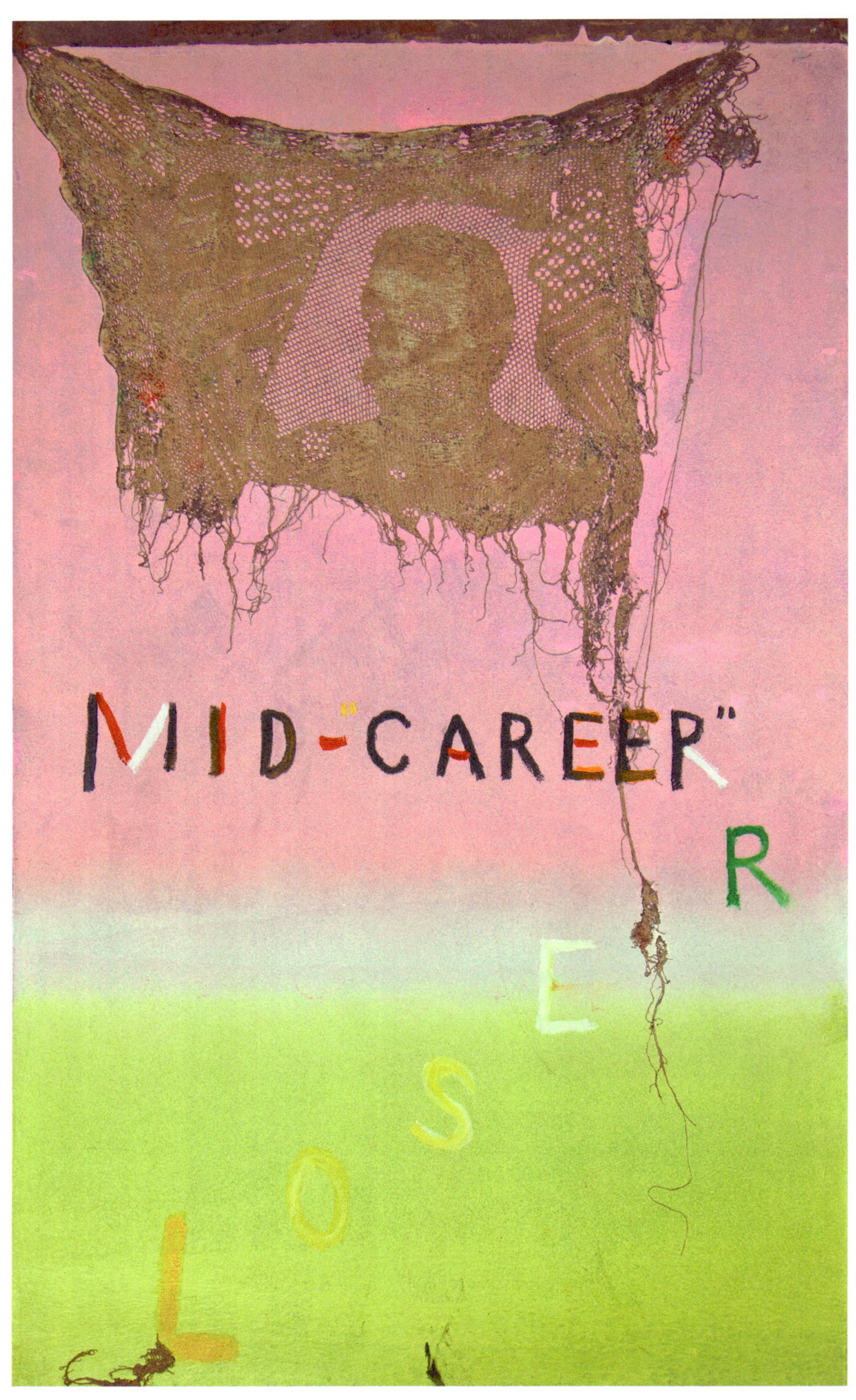

MID-CAREER LOSER 2008 acrylic on canvas 36 x 60 inches

Works *cont'd*

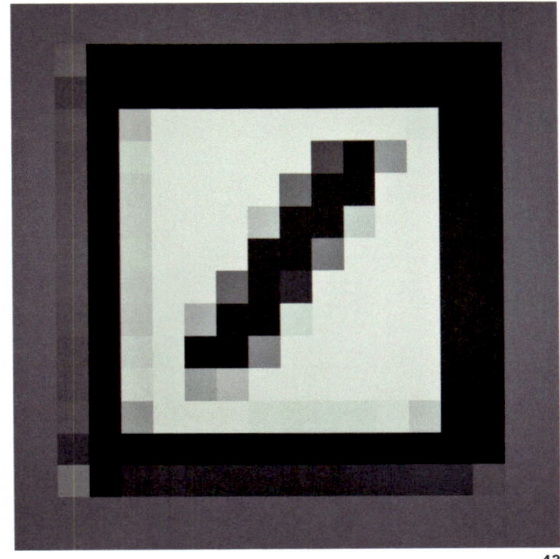

43

22 *TOTINO'S PIZZA ROLES*, 2009
Collage on Coroplast on wood
96 x 60 inches

23 *WART SCENE USA*, 2009
Spray paint, acrylic, bubble wrap, and electrical lights on wood and Coroplast panels (3 parts)
108 x 48 inches each

24 *Inscribed*, 2009
Collage on Coroplast on wood
96 x 72 inches

25 *Say Cheese*, 2009
Collage on Coroplast on wood
96 x 60 inches

26 *The Fapper*, 2010
Acrylic and collage on canvas
108 x 84 inches

27 *MURK FLUID*, 2010
Single-channel video (color, sound)
3:38 minutes

28 *ARTIST'S STATEMENT 2011*, 2011
Single-channel video (color, sound)
1:24 minutes

29 *ASK YOUR DRUG DEALER*, 2011
Acrylic on canvas
48 x 120 inches

30 *BITCH MOVES*, 2011
Single-channel video (color, sound)
3:29 minutes

31 *THE BITTERNESS OF THE RED PILL*, 2011
Single-channel video (color, sound)
3:40 minutes

32 *MAINTAIN*, 2011
Acrylic and spray paint on canvas
96 x 108 inches

33 *Monument to the Responsible Management of the Earth*, 2011
Acrylic on cardboard (3 parts)
48 x 96 inches each

34 *The Edge of Fame*, 2011
Collage
Variable dimensions

35 *ARTSTAR*, 2012
Single-channel video (color, sound)
3:42 minutes

36 *Endless Column*, 2012
Acrylic on canvas
192 x 48 inches

37 *The Hateful Years*, 2012
Single-channel video (color, sound)
4:49 minutes

38 *PEOPLE ARE STRANGLE*, 2012
Single-channel video (color, sound)
3:02 minutes

39 *Ask Officer Pepperspray chopped 'n' screwed*, 2013
Single-channel HD video (color, sound)
4:09 minutes

40 *Facebook Farm chopped 'n' screwed*, 2013
Single-channel HD video (color, sound)
6:15 minutes

41 *ATT YELLOW-RED MOON*, 2014
Archival ink on canvas
72 x 72 inches

42 *Community Standards*, 2014
Acrylic on canvas
72 x 105 inches

43 *Deutschebank 37*, 2014
Archival ink on canvas
72 x 72 inches

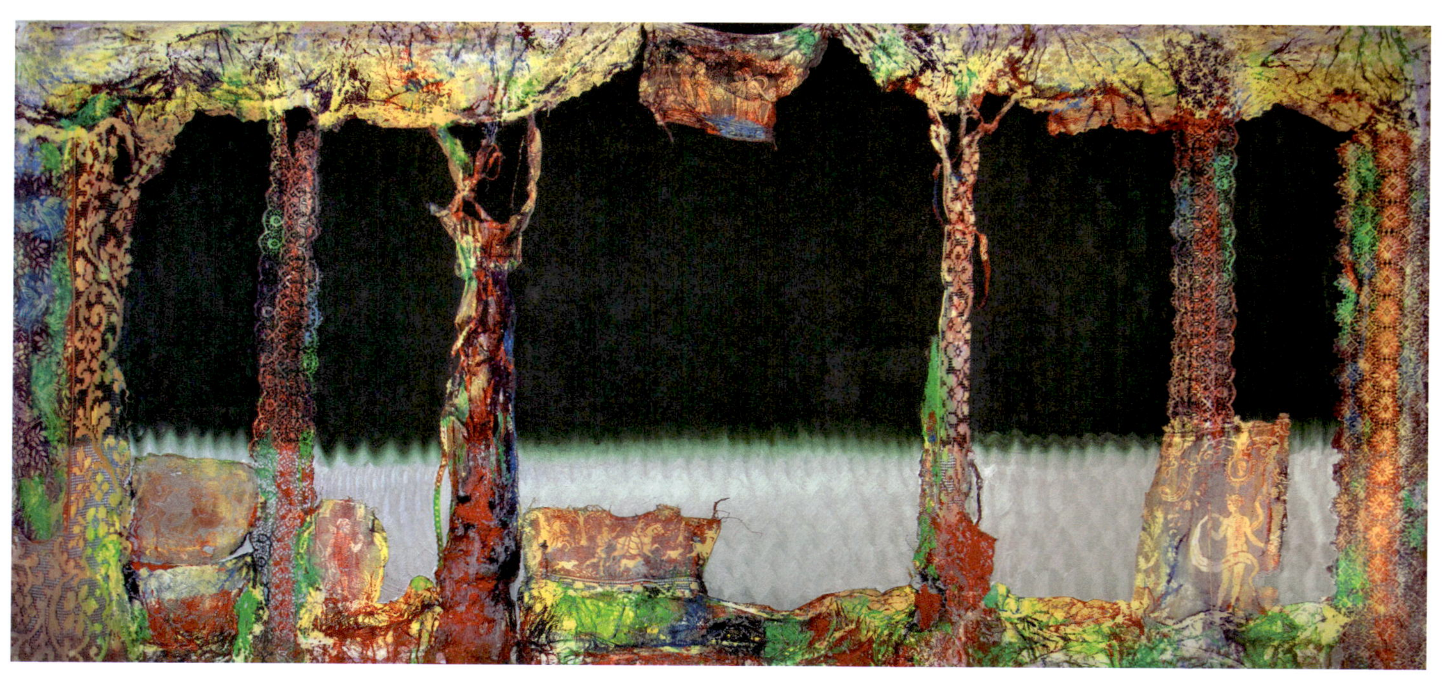

Drama in the Forest 2016 acrylic on canvas 84 x 198 inches

Works *cont'd*

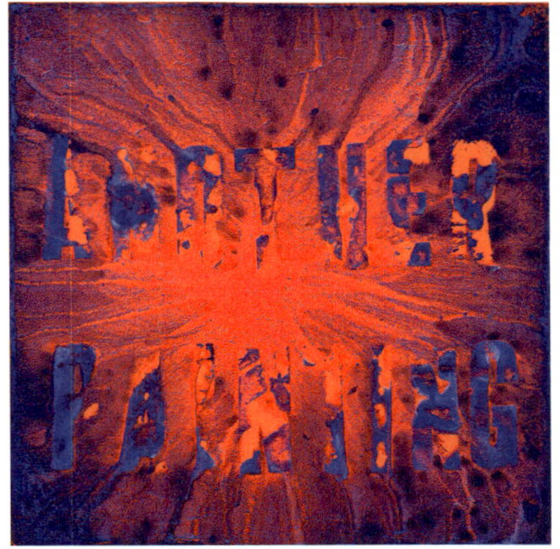

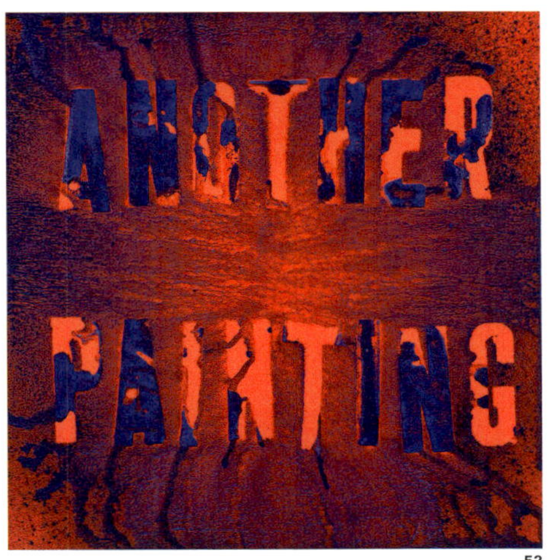

52

44 *DISGUSTING RICH PEOPLE, DISGUSTING POOR PEOPLE*, 2014
Acrylic on canvas
168 x 108 inches

45 *First Song*, 2014
Acrylic on canvas
84 x 198 inches

46 *Zombie Couple*, 2014
Archival ink on canvas
110 x 110 inches

47 *American Buffet Upgrade*, 2015
Single-channel HD video (color, sound)
2:49 minutes

48 *ASK ME*, 2015
Spray paint on printed advertisement on canvas
92 x 76 inches

49 *Heaven's Gate*, 2015
Acrylic on canvas
70 x 101 inches

50 *Indicator*, 2015
Acrylic on canvas
36 x 30 inches

51 *5000 LIKES*, 2015–16
Spray paint on canvas (5,000 parts)
12 x 16 inches each

52 *ANOTHER PAINTING (CAMH SUITE)*, 2016
Florescent and spray paint on canvas (7 parts)
40 x 40 inches each

53 *Bevilacqua's BLOOD*, 2016
Spray paint on metal sign
36 x 36 inches

54 *BLEEDING CUTTING EDGE*, 2016
Acrylic on canvas
40 x 40 inches

55 *Pink Glow*, 2016
Archival ink on canvas
54 x 108 inches

56 *David Lee Roth*, 2016
Collage, ultraviolet ink, acrylic panel, aluminum, and florescent light bulbs
24 x 48 inches

57 *The Future Is Ow*, 2016
Single-channel HD video (color, sound)
3:48 minutes

58 *Drone Collection*, 2016
Archival ink on canvas (5 parts)
164 x 50 inches each

59 *Drama in the Forest*, 2016
Acrylic on canvas
84 x 198 inches

60 *Election Painting*, 2016
Archival ink, spray paint, and collage on canvas
Dimensions variable

61 *NSA/Google Diptych*, 2016
Oil on plaster on burlap on wood panels
96 x 60 inches

62 *Tombstone*, 2016
Acrylic on canvas
16½ x 7 feet

63 *Ziggurat*, 2016
Spray paint and acrylic on canvas
101 x 60 inches

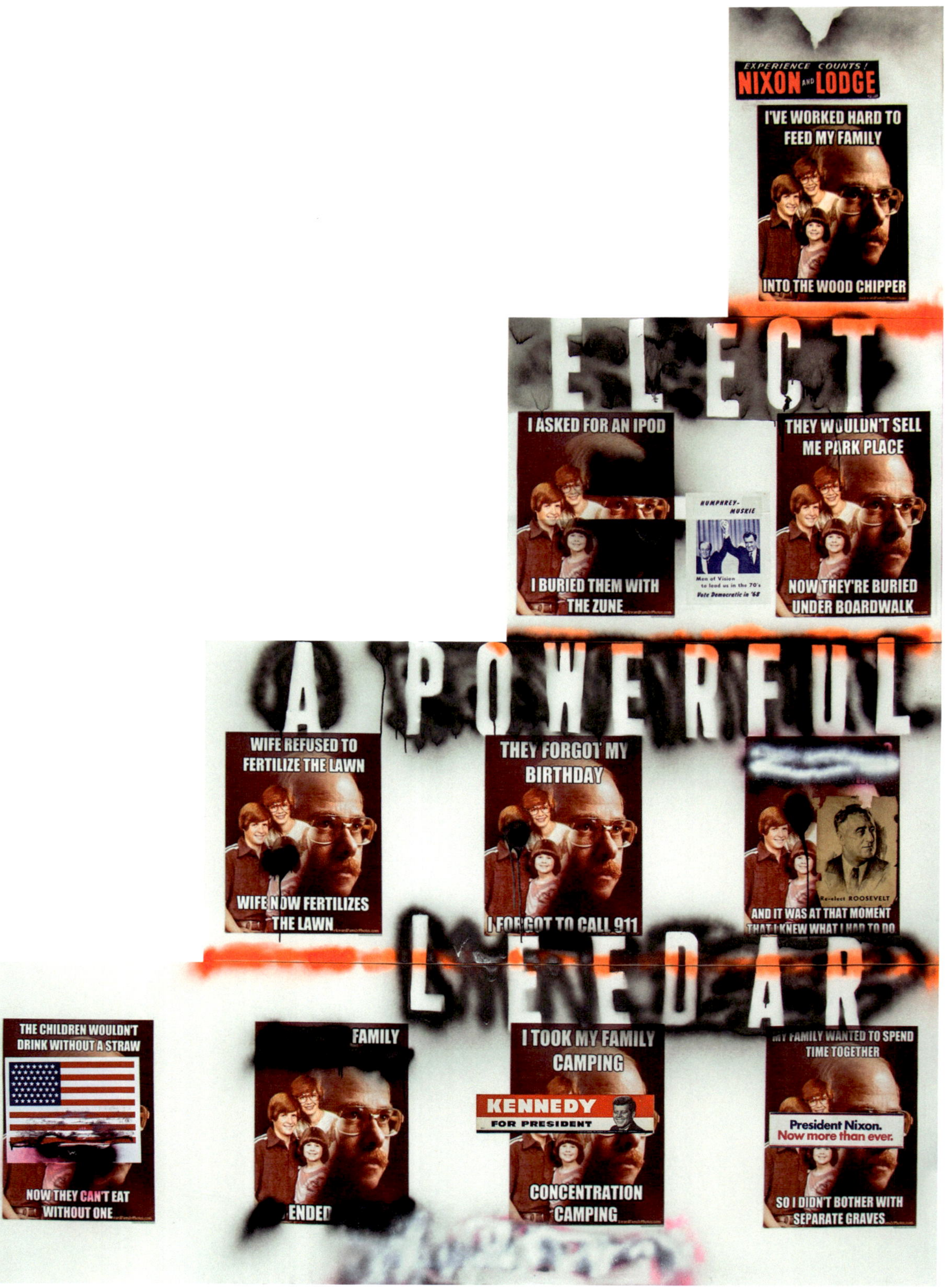

Election Painting 2016 archival ink, spray paint, and collage on canvas dimensions variable

Pink Glow 2016 archival ink on canvas 108 x 54 inches

Published on the occasion of the exhibition *Mark Flood: Gratest Hits*, organized by Bill Arning, Director of the Contemporary Arts Museum Houston

April 30–August 7, 2016

Published by
Contemporary Arts Museum Houston
5216 Montrose Boulevard
Houston, Texas 77006
CAMH.org

Distributed by
ARTBOOK | D.A.P.
155 Sixth Avenue, 2nd Floor
New York, NY 10013
ARTBOOK.com

Library of Congress
Catalog Control Number: 2016941815
ISBN: 978-1-933619-50-7

Publication coordinated by Patricia Restrepo
Edited by Betsy Stepina Zinn
Exhibition research by Sara Beck
Design by Russell Etchen
Printing in Canada by Hemlock Printers

Printed in an edition of 1350 copies

Typeset in ITC Garamond Std and Univers LT Std and printed on 100lb Cougar Opaque Text White, 100lb Topkote Gloss Text, and 130lb Topkote Gloss Cover

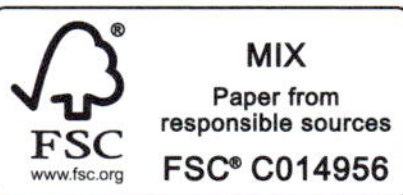

This exhibition has been made possible by the patrons, benefactors, and donors to the Museum's Friends of Steel Exhibitions:

DIRECTOR'S CIRCLE

Chinhui Juhn and Eddie Allen
Fayez Sarofim

CURATOR'S CIRCLE

Dillon Kyle Architecture, Inc.
Mr. and Mrs. I. H. Kempner III
Ms. Louisa Stude Sarofim
Robin and Andrew Schirrmeister

MAJOR EXHIBITION CIRCLE

A Fare Extraordinaire
Bergner and Johnson Design
Jereann Chaney
Sara Paschall Dodd
Marita and J.B. Fairbanks
Greg Fourticq
Barbara and Michael Gamson
Brenda and William Goldberg
Blakely and Trey Griggs
George and Mary Josephine Hamman Foundation
Leslie and Mark Hull
Jackson and Company
Anne and David Kirkland
KPMG, LLP
Beverly and Howard Robinson
Yellow Cab Houston
Michael Zilkha

Mark Flood: Gratest Hits is supported in part by Melissa and Albert J. Grobmyer IV, Susanne and William E. Pritchard III, Cynthia Toles, Margaret Vaughan, and the Union Pacific Foundation.

The catalogue accompanying the exhibition is made possible by a grant from The Brown Foundation, Inc.

Funding for the Museum's operations through the Fund for the Future is made possible by generous grants from Chinhui Juhn and Eddie Allen, Jereann Chaney, Marita and J.B. Fairbanks, Jo and Jim Furr, Barbara and Michael Gamson, Brenda and William Goldberg, Leticia Loya, Fayez Sarofim, Robin and Andrew Schirrmeister, and David and Marion Young.

The Museum's operations and programs are made possible through the generosity of the Museum's trustees, patrons, members and donors. The Contemporary Arts Museum Houston receives partial operating support from The Brown Foundation, Inc., Houston Endowment, the City of Houston through the Houston Museum District Association, the National Endowment for the Arts, the Texas Commission on the Arts, The Wortham Foundation, Inc. and artMRKT Productions.

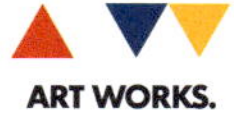

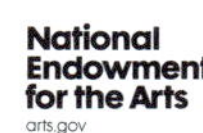

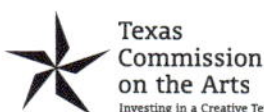

UNITED

United is the Official Airline of the Contemporary Arts Museum Houston

CAMH also thanks its artist benefactors for their support including Michael Bise, Bruce High Quality Foundation, Julia Dault, Keltie Ferris, Mark Flood, Barnaby Furnas, Theaster Gates, Jeffrey Gibson, Trenton Doyle Hancock, Jim Hodges, Joan Jonas, Jennie C. Jones, Maya Lin, Julian Lorber, Robert Mangold, Melissa Miller, Marilyn Minter, Angel Otero, McKay Otto, Enoc Perez, Rob Pruitt, Matthew Ritchie, Dario Robleto, Ed Ruscha, Cindy Sherman, Shinique Smith, John Sparagana, Al Souza, James Surls, Sam Taylor-Johnson, William Wegman, and Brenna Youngblood.

Photography Credits

Patrick Bresnan: *52, 78, 83–127*
John Champion: *144, 145, 156, 157, 160, 161, 163* (bottom)
Tom Dubrock: *Cover, Front Endpapers, 1, 2, 6, 8, 12–27, 34–37, 46–51, 62–70, 74–77, 208*
Mark Flood: *128–131, 134–143, 146–148, 154, 158, 165–167, 169–177, Back Endpapers*
Ronald Jones: *162, 163* (top), *178*
Emily Peacock: *3, 4, 9, 10, 38–40, 58, 164, 180, 182, 184, 186, 188, 190, 192, 194, 196–203, 205–207*
Susie Rosmarin: *132, 133, 150–153*

All works courtesy the artist, Peres Projects, Berlin, and Stuart Shave/Modern Art, London

Unless otherwise noted, all works appear courtesy the artist *(pp. 28, 42, 54–57, 61, 71, 79, 128–131, 134–143, 146–148, 154, 158, 165–167, 169–177, Back Endpapers)*; Peres Projects, Berlin *(pp. 72, 73)*; Stuart Shave/Modern Art, London; Feuer/Mesler, New York *(pp. 59, 80, 81)*; Blum & Poe, Los Angeles/New York/Tokyo *(pp. 29–33, 43)*; and Marlborough Chelsea *(pp. 80, 82)*

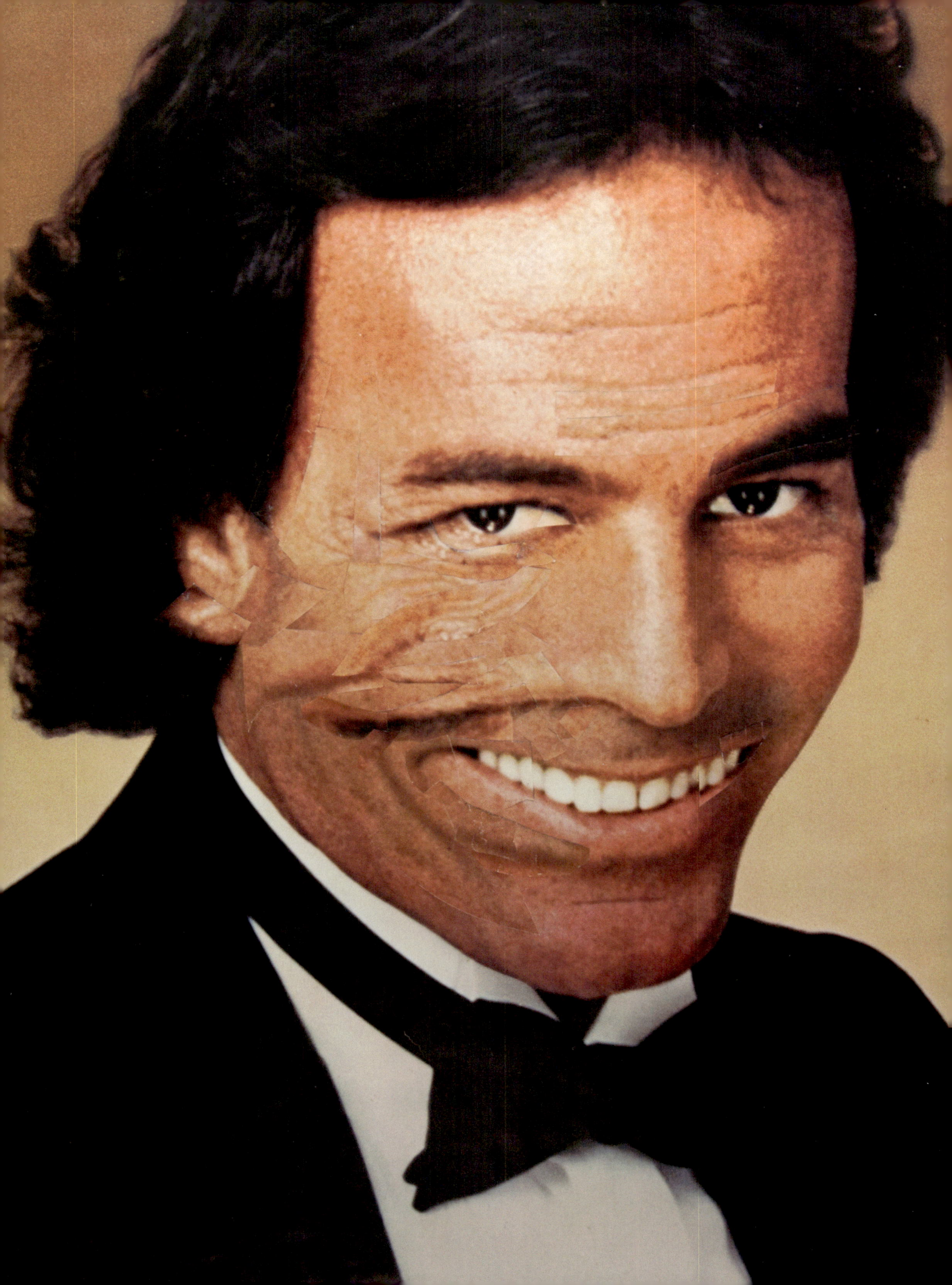

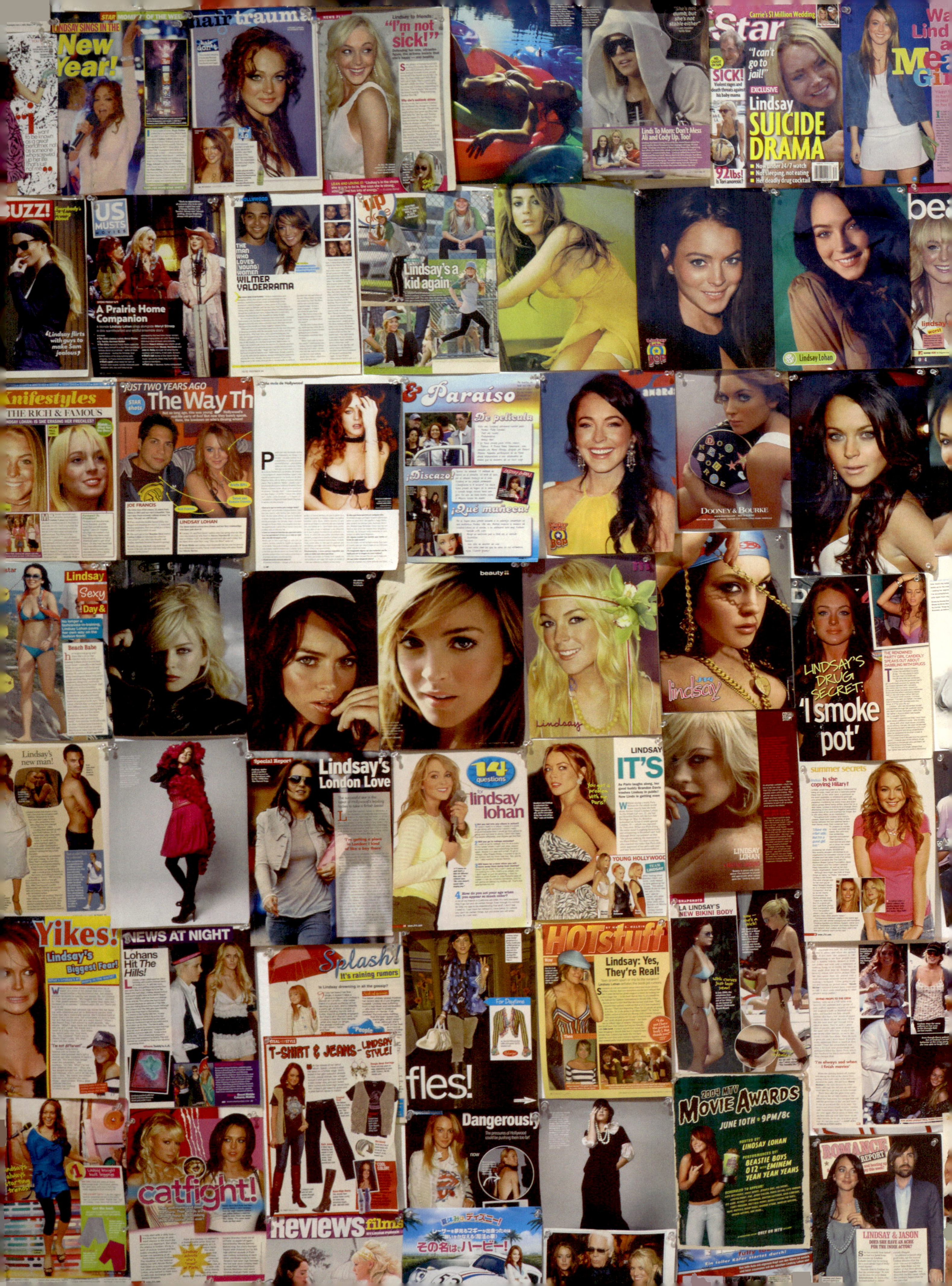

LINDSAY SINGS IN THE New Year!
hair trauma
Lindsay to friends: "I'm not sick!"
Carrie's $1 Million Wedding
Star
"I can't go to jail!"
SICK!
EXCLUSIVE
Lindsay SUICIDE DRAMA
Linds To Mom: Don't Mess Ali and Cody Up, Too!
BUZZ!
US MUSTS
A Prairie Home Companion
THE MAN WHO LOVES YOUNG WOMEN
WILMER VALDERRAMA
Lindsay's a kid again
Lindsay Lohan
Lifestyles
THE RICH & FAMOUS
JUST TWO YEARS AGO
The Way Th
JOE FRANCIS
LINDSAY LOHAN
& Paraiso
De película
¡Discazo!
¡Que muñeca!
DOONEY & BOURKE
Lindsay
Sexy Day &
Beach Babe
lindsay
LINDSAY'S DRUG SECRET: 'I smoke pot'
Lindsay's new man!
Special Report
Lindsay's London Love
14 questions
lindsay lohan
LINDSAY
IT'S
YOUNG HOLLYWOOD
summer secrets
Is she copying Hillary?
Yikes!
Lindsay's Biggest Fear!
NEWS AT NIGHT
Lohans Hit The Hills!
Splash!
It's raining rumors
T-SHIRT & JEANS–LINDSAY STYLE!
fles!
HOTstuff
Lindsay: Yes, They're Real!
LA LINDSAY'S NEW BIKINI BODY
2004 MTV MOVIE AWARDS
JUNE 10TH • 9PM/8c
HOSTED BY LINDSAY LOHAN
BEASTIE BOYS
D12 EMINEM
YEAH YEAH YEAHS
catfight!
Dangerous!
Reviews films
その名は、ハービー!
ROMANCE REPORT
LINDSAY & JASON